THE OXFORD AUTHORS

General Editor: Frank Kermode

IAN FLETCHER was educated at Dulwich College and Goldsmiths' College, University of London. After some years as a children's librarian, he became an Assistant Lecturer at the University of Reading in 1956 and was appointed a Professor in 1978. Since 1982 he has taught at Arizona State University.

Fletcher has published three volumes of poetry, has edited three volumes of critical essays, and written three monographs for the British Council on Beaumont and Fletcher, Pater, and Swinburne. He has also edited the poems of Lionel Johnson and John Gray. At present, he is at work on a study of Beardsley, a collection of essays on *fin de siècle* topics, and a bibliography of Arthur Symons. He hopes to have a 'last phase' which will be devoted to a volume of literary memoirs.

THE OXFORD AUTHORS

BRITISH POETRY
AND PROSE
1870–1905

EDITED BY

IAN FLETCHER

Oxford   New York

OXFORD UNIVERSITY PRESS

1987

Oxford University Press, Walton Street, Oxford OX2 6DP

Oxford New York Toronto
Delhi Bombay Calcutta Madras Karachi
Petaling Jaya Singapore Hong Kong Tokyo
Nairobi Dar es Salaam Cape Town
Melbourne Auckland
and associated companies in
Beirut Berlin Ibadan Nicosia

Oxford is a trade mark of Oxford University Press

British Library Cataloguing in Publication Data
British poetry and prose, 1870–1905. — (The Oxford authors)
1. English literature — 19th century
I. Fletcher, Ian, 1920–
820.8'008 PR1145
ISBN 0–19–254186–2
ISBN 0–19–281375–7 Pbk

Library of Congress Cataloging in Publication Data
British poetry and prose, 1870–1905.
(The Oxford authors)
Bibliography: p.
Includes indexes.
1. English literature — 19th century.
2. English literature — 20th century.
I. Fletcher, Ian. II. Series.
PR1145.B74 1986 820'.8' 008 86–704
ISBN 0–19–254186–2
ISBN 0–19–281375–7 (pbk.)

Set by Latimer Trend & Company Ltd, Plymouth
Printed in Great Britain by
Richard Clay Ltd.

For
Agnes and Genevra

CONTENTS

Italics indicate a poem

CONTENTS ix

INTRODUCTION

(i)

THE period covered by this anthology, extending broadly from 1870 to 1905, possesses a logical shape, although one or two of the major figures have been excluded. Historians, social, economic, and literary, have recognized the former date as marking the beginnings of a reaction against such High Victorian values and attitudes as Evangelicalism, the iron theorems of political economy, the notions of self-help, and an attitude to women that imprisoned them within stereotypes of angel and demon. The year 1905 may indeed seem a queer date with which to conclude; a more expected close might well have been the year 1900 when, as W. B. Yeats put it in his *Autobiographies*, everyone got down from their stools, when the Boer War was lumbering on, and the century turned; or 1908, which is commonly isolated as the year when the small stir of modernism can be identified with the forgotten school of pre-Imagists in poetry and the beginnings of Ezra Pound's mission to the benighted English.

The year 1905 has been chosen as a terminus partly for its political significance. The years of Conservative rule came to an end for a decade; the Cabinet was no longer fraught with peers and the tone of debate began to change from high game to new acrimony. The Imperialists by this time were split between liberal and more proconsular and harder sects. The series of European alliances which were to be the immediate cause of mobilizations for war had been established and Lord Roberts was deep in his campaign for National Service. In one sense, the famous *douceur de vivre* continued till 1914; the Edwardian period and its Georgian aftermath are a sunset, whose ominous tints were felt more than understood, in spite of such obvious threats as the rival naval programmes of England and Germany, the Agadir crisis, and the perennial Irish. The year 1906 with its technologies—telephone, wireless, and the internal-combustion engine—seems distinctly recognizable. So 1905 is a compromise date that reflects both the distant and the familiar.

As for 1870, that year marks broadly the decline of Britain as a world power. Agricultural capacity waned in the 1870s, as in the following decades did industrial competitiveness. And as Britain's industrial power faltered, so London became the international money market of the world. In 1871 George Eliot was able off-handedly to allude to 'the gorgeous plutocracy', and in that same decade the decline of the landed aristocrats and the precipitous rise of financiers dubious both as to assets and nationality, phantasms exhaled by rumour and popular newspapers, are energetically displayed by Anthony Trollope in his *The Way We Live Now* (1875). The type itself had been anticipated by George Hudson, Railway King of the 1840s, and by Dickens in his Mr Merdle of *Little Dorrit* (1857), whose name is indeed his legacy. In *After London* (1887) Richard Jefferies actually describes London after civilization has collapsed: a boiling, mephitic swamp, its largely metaphoric identity reduced to a geological image. Such changes were somewhat masked by the elaboration of overseas capitalist organizations, the cult of Imperialism, and the considerable additions to the land mass of the Empire that accrued in the years between 1870 and the Versailles Peace Conference. But such expansion was defensive: the aim of British statesmen was to conserve rather than acquire: the analogies with late Rome are plausible. And underlying the apparent national confidence, the bravura, were twinges of perception that many centrifugal forces were threatening the High Victorian synthesis. Some of these were: the notion of 'decadence'; the imbalance between urban and rural cultures; Irish Home Rule agitations; Tennyson's 'poisonous honey stolen from France' in the form of realism and naturalism in fiction; unwelcome discoveries in science; radical theologies; the emergence of the new woman allying herself with all that was anarchic in society; the new literacy brought about by the Education Acts of 1870 and 1874; the shrill new journalism and periodical literature furnished for the newly literate; a raw candour of artistic expression that intensified until the Oscar Wilde affair of 1895; a pessimism that was far from the optimism, agreeable pathos, and didacticism of an earlier period. Anti-rationalism became evident in the Celtic Twilight and in a rush of occult or 'illuminated' groups; and regional literature was stimulated by the imbalance of provincial and metropolitan culture.

The centre of the financial web was the City of London, and metropolis in those years becomes megalopolis, hinge of an empire. The constant construction and demolition of the nineteenth-century capital mirrored in its asymmetricality, its ugliness, the uncontrollable chaos first of the Industrial Revolution and then of equally powerful and abstract economic forces. Through all these changes the East End of London remained a resonant approach, a jungle and 'abyss' according to the contemporary term, especially to those on its rim, painfully hovering between skilled and unskilled labouring classes, and to those for whom poverty, vice, and pure bad luck had ensured a fall into anonymity and desperation. Only in the 1880s and 1890s in the work of Charles Booth were these three square miles of suffering and struggle surveyed with any pretence to sociological precision. On this space George Gissing provides a sour and authentic imaginative report in *The Nether World* (1889). And in a later novel, *The Whirlpool* (1897), he not only analyses a new type of woman, the *névrose*, the modern hysteric, but provides a luminous case-study of the destruction of a pretentious and ambitious heroine by the city. Acres of condensed misery, mass poverty, and prostitution, including the systematic prostitution of children—white slaves of modern Babylon—accented still further the characteristic double standards, hypocrisies, masks, and divided selves of the end of the century.

The city remained an altogether appropriate theatre for the evolutionary drama that dominated much of the thinking of the period. Religion, after all, had its own development theories: God was adapting his revelation loosely, within the parameters of the Bible and tradition, to the race as it progressed towards spiritual maturity. And Herbert Spencer's famous phrase, the survival of the fittest, was certainly adaptable to analogies between nature and civil society, and could be used to justify *laissez-faire* economics and the aggressive philistinism and flexible ethics resulting from the new financial structures. It could also be used to justify the subordinate role of women. Gissing is the novelist who most fully documents such notions. In *The Odd Women* and 'The Foolish Virgin', the distressed gentlewomen, without training for any occupation, must adapt to survive. Rosamund Jewel, for example, in 'The Foolish Virgin', must forget her gentility and take on menial household work for a hard-pressed suburban housewife. Her attempts to marry are treated cruelly by Gissing: he anticipates those twentieth-century radical feminists who regard marriage itself as 'copping out'.

George Meredith in *The Egoist* (1879) turns Darwinism to comic purposes. The aristocratic egoist Sir Willoughby Patterne proves himself and his line unfit to survive, for he is unable to marry either of the two healthy and spirited young women who have initially accepted his offers. The second indeed marries Sir Willoughby's kinsman, reluctant protégé, and secretary, and together the two represent a new strain, 'new man' and 'new woman', while Sir Willoughby must make do with the intelligent, amiable, but hardly robust Laetitia Dale. Being intelligent, she has by the end of the book no illusions about Sir Willoughby, but is unlikely to provide him with a bouncing heir, indeed with any heir at all.

Samuel Butler in *The Way of All Flesh* reverts to pre-Darwinian notions of evolution. An alternative form of evolutionary thinking was Lamarckianism. Butler, like such literary figures as Bernard Shaw and D. H. Lawrence, was attracted to the limpid teleology of the theory. Darwinism appeared to posit a purely random process of change. Lamarckian vitalism resembles that of the 'active universe' of Wordsworth and other Romantics, and this explains its later attraction for Shaw and Lawrence and, through Bergson, for T. E. Hulme. Variations in the Lamarckian sense can be induced by climatic or other environmental changes. The agent for adaptation and change in Butler's novel, largely written in the 1880s, is 'unconscious memory', another Romantic notion that is prominent also in Wordsworth, Ruskin, and Pater. Butler's hero, Ernest Pontifex, pursues an opposite path to Sir Willoughby Patterne's: the last two generations of the Pontifex family have taken a wrong turn and Ernest is able to recover the 'state of grace' of his great-grandfather John Pontifex, his earthiness, unpretentiousness, honesty, and capacity to work with his hands. John is perfectly free from the hypocrisy and cruelty of nineteenth-century Christian culture. Ernest's self-redemption will result from willing the change, the new direction, when the 'unconscious memory' is woken by a sharp stimulus, and, as his surname indicates, Ernest will build a bridge between the first and future members of his family. The passage included in this anthology shows his father Theobald tyrannizing over the young Ernest in the cruel flush of his parental and priestly authority. Butler is a supreme ironist and his biological curiosity moves into psychology. His wit is more ironic than Gilbert's and he is a darker disciple of Aristophanes.

Already in the 1870s, as we may gather from J. S. Mill's essay 'Nature', it was recognized that the ends of Nature and Culture were not merely incompatible, but actually opposed. It was, however, the great publicist of Darwinism, T. H. Huxley, who in *Evolution and Ethics*, a famous lecture of 1894, gave a savant's authority to the clash between large natural forces and culture, hitting moreover the mood of *fin de siècle*. The immediate literary fruits were the scientific fables of H. G. Wells.

Literary response to such hidden shifts was complex and various: stridently anxious in the Imperialist verse of W. E. Henley and Alfred Austin; more accomplished and ambiguous in the poems and briefer fictions of Rudyard Kipling. Naturalism was attempted by that school of fiction writers for whom, as Wilde observed, the sun rose and set in the East End of London. Few quite achieved the poetic detachment and mythic resonances of the best French writers of this school. Margaret Harkness's *A City Girl* (1887) is an early example of a pity that almost achieves detachment. The efforts of this school are represented here by Arthur Morrison's study of slum life, 'Lizerunt'. Realism is represented by the grey if powerful documentation of Hubert Crackanthorpe, a talent early extinguished by suicide.

If the imaginative response is most impressive in the prose writers, at least one poem, 'The City of Dreadful Night' (1874), deserves acclaim for its attempt to decipher the modern labyrinths both of city and of self. In the mature works of both Wordsworth (*The Prelude*, Book VII) and Dickens, the speaker searches for some transcendental order behind the centrifugal chaos of the modern metropolis. But James Thomson's city, bathed in a blank moonlight, promises no transcendence, and the alienation of the speaker is final. The poem contains two dominant symbols, Melancholia and Sphinx, much favoured later by Symbolists and Decadent writers and painters. The city is space where faith and love are purer fictions: but alienation is at least mitigated by a recognition of the 'fraternity of sorrow' and a taut stoicism.

Not until the 1880s and 1890s does contemporary London become properly accessible to lyrical poets. The idiom is nocturnal, but the note quite distinct from Thomson's: shifting colours and lights, ladies of pleasure, music halls, the Café Royal. The influence comes from Whistler and Sickert rather than from the French Impressionist painters, but the poets themselves write as if they were all eye, abstaining at their best from moral comment. Following the Decadent programme of distilling the beautiful from the ugly, Wilde in

'Symphony in Yellow' selects urban detail and concludes with a faint harmony but no overt statement: the city is merely what remains as 'given' for the artist's palette; the phallicism is an undertone:

> And at my feet the pale green Thames
> Lies like a rod of rippled jade.

Similarly Arthur Symons notes:

> A bright train flashed with all its squares
> Of warm light where the bridge lay mistily.

Another poem, following the *plage* scenes so popular with painters from Boudin to Sickert, tarnishes the effect by passing from objective record:

> The long hotel acutely white
> Withers grey green and takes the grass's tone

to a familiar mood of ennui. Objects, though, are not in these urban 'impressions' dissolved in light and colour as in Impressionist painting, but presented discretely.

> The gusty gaslight shoots a thin
> Sharp finger over cheeks and nose.

Any attempt to sense the city as a total organism or to search for some transcendental significance is now simply abandoned.

(ii)

Women's fiction of a new order is abundant in this period. For much of the nineteenth century women had supplied a large proportion of serial novels and novels for the circulating libraries, but though not without accomplishment such writers rarely strayed beyond the strictly conventional, fulfilling in general Miss Prism's definition: 'The good ended happily, the bad unhappily, that is what Fiction means,' except of course for the obligatory pathos. To this, there are obvious exceptions: Jane Austen, the Brontës, Mrs Gaskell, George Eliot. In the 1890s Ella D'Arcy, 'George Egerton', 'Sarah Grand', Muriel Dowie, and others embodied new insights, writing with an 'unladylike' frankness about sexual topics, creating 'free women' heroines, and often offering sublimated autobiography. Some brilliant brooding pages from Olive Schreiner's *The Story of an African Farm* (1883), whose topic is the growth of a young rebel, are reprinted here as representative of an interesting class of writer. The novel anticipates the stresses that woman's role as 'free' intellectual imposes. Being Imperialist, feminist, pro-Boer, and pro-native—she had a position on everything—ravaged her nerves. Her relations with men predict some of the problems that self-liberation and sexual liberation were to bring. Schreiner also gives us a small gallery of Doubles or counterparts and antagonists, through two persons, Waldo and little Em. Waldo is a woman who can survive and increase without marriage; she possesses the madness and self-sufficiency of the artist.

The advance towards any pretence of equality between the sexes was painfully slow. Mary Wollstonecraft had written her pioneering *Vindication of the Rights of Women* as far back as 1792 and J. S. Mill's tract *On The Subjection of Women* (1859) soon acquired the force of a holy book. Some attempts at formal education for girls had been attempted by that date. F. D. Maurice, the Christian Socialist, founded in 1848 Queen's College for Girls in London, while a decade later Alexandria College, Dublin, was opened; the motives here, however, were to enlarge the culture of girls from the Church of Ireland 'Ascendancy' class. The universities, though, remained closed to women. By the later part of the century women were permitted to study but not to take degrees. Mary Garrett Anderson became the first woman doctor in 1862; but her degree was foreign and it is fair to say that even in the 1980s British medical prejudice against women has barely been overcome. It was again only towards the end of the century that a married woman had any right to her own property: like her name, it was merged in that of her husband, a single legal personality. Alfred Tennyson had dealt with women's aspirations in his medley *The Princess* (1845), but, though a friend of Maurice, and not without sympathy for women's aspirations, he chose to touch the subject in a tone that blended mock heroics and sentimentality. Denied the vote and the possibility of sitting in Parliament, women were still enabled by their own efforts to take an ardent role in public affairs. Florence Nightingale proved far more formidable than the old women masquerading as General Officers in the Crimean War (1854–5), while Octavia Hill was equally formidable as a housing reformer, tied though she was to high Victorian notions, approving self-help, and distrustful of charity as by nature indiscriminate. Two of the poets here represented, Augusta Webster and Ellice Hopkins, also played an active part in social affairs: Augusta Webster acted as a member of the London School Board for many years, while Hopkins devoted herself to her 'great sad work', reclaiming prostitutes. Both were suspicious of dilettantes, who often took a rather sinister pleasure from the spectacle of condensed misery in the slums.

Besides domestic service, which was the employment of a million lower-paid females, a career lay open to women that might in rare cases lead to independence, respectability, and marriage. Prostitutes, whether full or part time, were numerous and scandalously visible. We remember Wordsworth's comment about his moral shock on first hearing a woman blaspheme. The drunken, morally hardened, and sometimes (worst of all) successful immoral woman made it difficult to sustain stereotypes about women as naturally weak, full of a delicate moral sensibility, and devoid of positive sexual appetite. A fair proportion of the 'army of the night' were barely in their teens, or even younger. Some satisfaction, however, might be gathered from the prevalence of prostitution: marriageable girls of the middle and upper-middle classes were as a consequence freed from the restless attention of their male counterparts, whose brutal energies could be successfully 'earthed' by prostitution. A more generous and eloquent case was put by W. E. Lecky, who referred to the prostitute as 'the eternal priestess of mankind', blasted for the sins of the people: and the word 'blast' here has the force of the word in Blake's lyric 'London'.

Mrs Gaskell had presented in *Ruth* (1848) a heroine who 'fell' but not irredeemably. The Pre-Raphaelite poets, William Bell Scott in 'Rosabell', D. G. Rossetti in 'Jenny', were sympathetic to fallen women as social outcasts, while 'Decadents', such as Arthur Symons, John Davidson, and Hubert Crackanthorpe in his short stories, found in them an analogue to their own isolated and alienated role in society. Nuns and prostitutes are presented dialectically and in Davidson's 'Ballad of a Nun' the nun becomes a prostitute and is redeemed by the Virgin, who takes the nun's place as portress at the convent gate and approves her self-liberation. The religious and the erotic are deliberately confused by Arthur Symons:

> Woman when in the sacrament I take
> The bread your body and the wine your kiss.

This is a double blasphemy: transubstantiation (wicked Latin Catholic superstition) is acridly spiced by Satanic degradation of the sacrament. In Kierkegaardian terms, we might say that Symons remained fixed at the religiose moment: he no longer believed in the Methodist God of his father, who was a minister, but still invested religious language with an emotional significance that was largely factitious. Still chained to Christian culture, he had no other language when he wished to move beyond the merely 'visible world', though he was to experiment rather tepidly later with the idiom of Middle Eastern mysticisms. There remained only the sacramental to express any sense of the mystery of human relationships. Symons lived through those decades that were critical in the history of God's increasing absence from nature and his evaporation from a culture becoming continuously less sacral. We may contrast Crashaw on St Teresa—'Why to show love she must shed blood'—with Symons's complacent identification of the mystically sexual sinners in 'At the Shrine at Saronno', its titillant frescos of females heads, ambiguous haloes on the one hand and on the other the two lovers exciting themselves still further by projecting their own guilt on to Luini's figures:

> Has not Luini writ in fire
> The secret of our own desire?
> Your eyelids heavy with the sense
> Of some strange passionate suspense . . .
> Yea, and my longings that would pierce
> The obscure dividing universe,
> To die into your heaven of love;
> Our passion, and the end thereof,
> Love, even to the death of love.
> You were this martyr, I the saint
> In this pretence of chastity;
> The mystic spousal that shall be
> Betwixt your Lord and you, divine
> And deathless, does but symbol mine;
> Bride of my ultimate desires,
> And equal flamelike with my fires!

Symons wishes not merely to invert the sacred and the profane, but also to make sexuality a substitute for lost numinousness. The attempt, though, is rather puerile. Symons's verse is by no means the most important of his multifarious energies. He needs no apologies as a critic, having left us one rather loosely organized but deeply influential set of essays, *The Symbolist Movement in Literature*, many evocative travel pieces, suggestive essays on aesthetics, and his autobiographical fictions, the highly distinguished *Spiritual Adventures*.

Beardsley was more deeply subversive in associating the grotesque and the erotic, while his women, high on posters with predatory glare, reminded the paterfamilias on the top of his omnibus that women like it too, even more than men. And in Swinburne, woman's sexual appetite was a force that the audience had to engage with as part of the poet's exposure of the instability of Victorian culture. The dialectic is not resolved, though temporarily perhaps deflated, by A. C. Hilton in his parody of 'Dolores': 'The Octopus'. That crustacean was really a more perfect model for the Fatal Woman, innumerable hands for beating, a horny mouth, very apt for destructive kissing and so 'bite me again'. The prevalence of the Fatal Woman image can be detected obliquely in the sudden increase in the population of androgynes, those peaceful bisexuals and hermaphrodites, unsatisfied monsters with a medical-textbook profusion of spare parts. Edward Carpenter was only one of many who became involved in notions of 'the Intermediate Sex' and the influence of Walt Whitman and 'Comradeship' was felt by John Addington Symonds, for example, with his preference for burly young proletarians. As Symonds pointed out in his *Studies in the Greek Poets* (later discreetly revised), Northern workers would not do: nothing Greek about them and too much tuberculosis.

(iii)

The story of exotic mysticisms begins with the Tennysonianly melismatic Sir Edwin Arnold's *The Light of Asia*. This can be read along with A. P. Sinnett's *Esoteric Buddhism* (1885), which synthesized illumination both Eastern and Western and influenced the young W. B. Yeats. Matthew Arnold had informed the Irish that their literary genius was characterized by a revolt against the despotism of fact, and they did their best to live up to the seductive generalization: occultism, mysticism, and illuminated politics are all characteristic of 'The Celtic Twilight', but the movement reflects also the first tremors of disquiet about the course of European civilization and the attemptedly irenic Symbolist Movement whose programme included a healing of divisions between cultures and nationalities. Another of Arnold's pronouncements that the Celt is everywhere a race, nowhere a nation, lay behind the Pan-Celtic Movement modelled on the successful romantic nationalist programme *La Jeune Belgique* of the earlier 1890s and which extended to Wales, Brittany, and Scotland, where it transformed the rather plodding William Sharp into the glamorous *anima* 'Fiona Macleod'. Only the Irish, however, were to furnish a coherent programme of blood, martyrs, sacred soil, and sacred language. The Irish movement, Young Ireland, of the 1840s can be related to notions about nationalism in the European model. To paraphrase a distinguished historian of nationalism, Hans Kohn, the idea of nation or state as a unique political unity was arrived at through Rousseau's concept of the *volonté générale*. The nation becomes the source of the General Will, which is itself the source of political action and power. It is this notion of the general will which makes possible the idea that a nation can make itself. And so we have the revolutionary transition from the nation as feeling—sentiments to the nation as will, *volonté*, according to the formulations reached by Federico Chabod in his *L'Idea di Nazione*. The logic of Easter 1916 was evolved in the 1840s.

A further body of programmatic work was furnished by the novels of Faith and Doubt so prominent in the earlier part of the century and which continued through the period after 1870. These now took the form of conflict between relative and absolute values in an attempt to accommodate to 'the higher criticism', but such works as Winwood Reade's *The Outcast* (1875) or Francis Adams's *A Child of the Age* (1894) reveal a struggle with an emergent modern consciousness. The Birmingham vitriol manufacturer J. H. Shorthouse's *John Inglesant* (1885) was a somewhat belated text in the Oxford Movement style, locating its spiritual struggles in the seventeenth century and offering memorable images of Carolean life and of Little Gidding in particular. Honest doubters hardly make forcible heroes and Mrs Humphry Ward's *Robert Elsmere* (1888) very likely belongs to the *genre ennuyeux* to which Wilde consigned it, but her somewhat gothic *Helbeck of Bannisdale* (1898) evokes vividly the closely organic world of the Old Catholic families in the north-west of England and deserves its recent reprinting.

Marius the Epicurean (1885) remains the best record of this troubled theology, though Pater was a religious Trimmer rather than an Honest

Doubter. This novel is remarkable among other things for its subtle use of a renewed typology. Typology has recently become a luminous way of entering into nineteenth-century imaginative literature: we encounter it in different forms in Dickens, Ruskin, Pater, George Eliot, Hopkins, and (polemically) in Swinburne. The word had been accepted into pre-Darwinian evolutionary theory and other disciplines. In Tennyson's *In Memoriam* (as in Hawthorne's *The Scarlet Letter*) the notions, theological and scientific, rejoin one another. Tennyson is able to reconcile evolutionary theory with his Broad Church Christianity: his dead friend Arthur Hallam is finally recognized as a Type too early born but promising (the idea that anti-typical fulfilments could in turn become types is old in biblical exegesis) the new morally evolved man, so encapsulating the Anti-type.

The fulfilment of the Types of the Old Testament—persons, events, metaphors in the New Testament—proceeds through the appearance of Anti-types. In *The Great Code* Northrop Frye remarks:

How do we know that the Gospel story is true? Because it confirms the prophecies of the Old Testament. But how do we know that the Old Testament prophecies are true? Because they are confirmed by the Gospel story . . . The two testaments form a double mirror, each reflecting the other, but neither the world outside.

Cardinal Jean Daniélou distinguishes different varieties of Type, some, for example, sacramental (baptism prefigured by the Red Sea crossing), some eschatological. The prophets promise that God will perform new wonders in the future so that with the coming of the supreme Anti-type, Christ, types are still generated. Christ providentially orders history forward to the Doom and backwards from those last days, but he indwells also within history. By the nineteenth century, the types can also be applied to a similar process of Type and Anti-type in God's other sacred book, that of Nature, which was becoming increasingly difficult to read as a consequence of the progressive absence of God from his creation and the stress of industrial pollution. All was indeed smeared and bleared with toil and the social injustices of *laissez-faire*. It is in the light of omens providentially furnished to assist 'reading' that such a prophetic work as Ruskin's *Storm Cloud of the Nineteenth Century* utilizes patiently observed natural phenomena, the appearance of new, queer cloud shapes that seemed apocalyptically accented. A similar omen appears in Hopkins's anxieties about the collapse of 'inscape'.

As there is evidence of typological usage presented already in this selection, however, it seemed more fitting to turn to Pater's much under-valued *Imaginary Portraits* rather than to take a segment of *Marius*. Two at least of the 'Portraits', those dealing with the myths of Dionysus and Apollo, fall into typological pattern, but 'A Prince of Court Painters' is nearer to orthodox fiction. Here Pater dramatizes his own celibacy and loneliness, but distances his portrait of the painter Jean-Baptiste Watteau by the use of an emotionally involved woman narrator who records the artist's life and death in her diary.

In this age of honest doubters, liberal Churchmen, and incipient modernists, distinguished hymnody was hardly possible. The torrents of good red unashamed Christian blood that light up the eighteenth century seemed now vulgar revivalism or evangelical cant. The Victorian hymn represents a low point in the history of the genre: the world is presented as a plangent arena of infant mortality and dismal probation. It is severely devoid of liturgical wit or vivid typology. The most distinguished offerings are the versions of early Christian, medieval, and Counter-Reformation texts, Neale's translations from the hymns of the Orthodox Church, or those of Adam of St Victor, full of typological ingenuity, by Archdeacon Wrangham. In general, only a few hymnodists of the later nineteenth century are worth reading: S. J. Stone, Gerald Moultrie, R. F. Littledale, the Betjemanish John Meade Falkner (the dates of his poems are difficult to establish), and the lively and versatile Sabine Baring-Gould.

The dwindling of typological interpretations of the Bible was a loss to the devotional writers as well as to those anxious to retain the 'poetry' as well as the morality of the Bible. Distrusted always by the Broad Church, by the time of Dean Farrar's famous Bampton Lectures of 1886 typology had ebbed out of the sermons and verses of both Low and High Church; but the more successful writers of religious lyrics such as Christina Rossetti, Ellice Hopkins, and Alice Meynell owed as much to the typological tradition as to their seventeenth-century metaphysical models.

(iv)

Were this a purely historical anthology, the reader might expect to find much socialist literature. If we except William Morris's *The Dream of John Ball*, Edward Carpenter's *Towards Democracy*, sentimental though it so often is, and the underrated novels of Bernard Shaw, the imaginative prose of the movement is barely distinguished. And chronologically speaking, Shaw belongs more to the twentieth than to the nineteenth century.

Morris's late romances often project a masked ideology, women's sexual liberation, for example, in the delicious Birdalone in *The Water of the Wondrous Isles*. They had been too long ignored until, like the romances of George Macdonald, they returned with the new enthusiasm for 'fantasy'. But they are not readily cannibalized and *The Twilight of the Gods* and *Zuleika Dobson* must represent what is a wide Victorian genre.

As to popular poetry, street ballads are little in evidence in this period and, although music-hall lyrics are vigorous, they demand music. The words of 'Ta-Ra-Ra-Boom-De-Aye', 'A Bird in a Gilded Cage', and even 'Under the Bamboo Tree', indeed, require not only music but a performer and the ornate smoky atmosphere of the halls themselves for their ambiance. Certainly they had a spirited effect on the poetry of the 1890s, on the ballads of Kipling, on John Davidson and even on the *Ballad of Reading Gaol*. For more information the reader is referred to the work of Jacqueline Bratton. At that time, the audience in the halls included swells, poets, and populace. T. S. Eliot's essay on Marie Lloyd may be cited as an apt elegy.

Brilliant nonsense verse was more the product of the mid-century, though W. S. Gilbert extends Lewis Carroll's mad inverse logics to operetta and ballad, both full of acrid satire of the clergy and older women. In 'The Yarn of the "Nancy Bell"' with its enigmatic refrain:

> Oh, I am a cook and a captain bold
> And the mate of the Nancy brig,
> And a bo'sun tight, and a midshipmite,
> And the crew of the captain's gig.

The narrative proves that a large number can go into a small without being dissipated in decimal points. Gilbert's enthusiasm for cannibalism is severely controlled in his stage works. Here I can give only a sampling of his Aristophanic wit and lyrical afflatus, though to term him Aristophanic is dangerous: his frivolity and fantasy tend to be of the surface not of the depth; his inversion of the social order is strictly limited in its ideological scope. Another follower of Aristophanes, though within the limits of Victorian decorum, was W. L. Courthope. In his *The Paradise of Birds* he furnished a sparkling satire on the theory of Natural Selection. Particularly funny is the grand chorus with its hieratic refrain, 'O Philoprogenitive Sponge' (another of T. S. Eliot's grand thefts). Later in the century, the bright philistines have a monopoly on humorous verse: A. C. Hilton, J. K. Stephen, and Owen Seaman whose mockery of the 'deycadongs' is penetrating and for the most part good-tempered.

The 1880s is a decade of aesthetic and moral controversy. The novel provides the focus and the novelist acquires a more self-conscious and responsible attitude to his art. The ending of *David Copperfield* (1850) might seem to furnish an index of the mid-Victorian practitioners' attitude. The novelist's is a job like any other. David ends as a complacent philistine, snug in his safe and stuffy home. However, it is possible to pursue another, deeper reading, one more in conformity with Dickens's unpredictable genius. It could rather be that David has at last come to maturity; the heart is no longer 'undisciplined'. With that passage he comes to realize that he is no novelist: once he has exorcized his past by discovering its significance in the act of writing, he has no more to say. Behind him now are his mother and Dora: he and his imagination have died with them; ahead of him there is only Agnes, death, and the silence: 'so with these lines shall close my life indeed'. Such a reading emphasizes the danger to the artist of the middle years and reveals an underlying distrust of Victorian domestic and sexual equilibrium.

A more trenchant example of authorial professionalism can be found in the posthumous publication in 1883 of Trollope's autobiography, with its self-satisfied, coldly statistical list of words written per day: 'that number sacramental and invariable'. Trollope had always been a conscientious craftsman, but here he appeared to have reduced the writing of novels to the level of the mechanical arts. The novelist questioned his roles and skills, and this involved a new relation to his public. The motivation was, however, mixed. It was in one sense socio-economic. His relationship to his public was more complex and less secure. He was also sometimes timidly, radically sometimes, protesting against the handmaid position of the novel in the mid-Victorian period as harmless diversion or dulcet tract. He was conscious also of the status (as opposed to the material rewards) of practitioners in the other fine arts. Even the actor, for long an object of suspicion or equivocal admiration, was being raised to the professional classes; Squire Bancroft and Henry Irving were both duly knighted. In 1884, Tennyson was created a baron, and, although the Royal Academy had been traditionally associated with the Court and high society and paletted knights had not been unknown—Rubens (as diplomatist, as much as painter), Kneller, Lely, Reynolds, Lawrence—it was not until 1896 that Leighton, president like Reynolds of the Academy, became the first painter to be ennobled.

The attempt to stabilize the social role of the novelist is signalized by the foundation in 1884 by Sir Walter Besant of the Society of Authors. Besant was eager that the novelist should be respected and protected; he was eager also to continue the tradition of Dickens. (Dickens had projected the rather vague Guild of Literature and Art in the early 1850s for a similar purpose.) The novel had a serious role in society: it was to probe specifically contemporary problems but to probe lightly. Besant probably sensed that by the early 1880s it was difficult for the novelist to voice the half-articulated dreams and fears of his audience as Dickens had once done. The remarkable variety of Besant's novels of the 1880s indicates not merely ambition, but unease. Besant writes a historical novel, one on contemporary literary life, one on the new woman, and two on working-class themes. Such a range exists, of course, in earlier authors, but in the same decade Moore is busy with Zolaesque documentation of provincial acting companies and the factory world of the potteries; Gissing is producing his novels of working-class London; and Henry James is sufficiently discommoded by the raw breath of the *zeitgeist* to darken his pages with anarchists and the working classes in that fascinating and unequal work, *The Princess Casamassima* (1886). Besant's own novels can be compared with the problem play. In such plays, moral problems are posed, but artificially resolved by dramatic casuistry. Mrs Tanqueray's fate is only an updated version of Peggoty's Emily or of Lady Audley's. Besant played it safe with Utopian conclusions or those, at all events, that evade the socio-economic actualities. In *All Sorts and Conditions of Men* (1882) he alludes climatically to his scheme for diverting the people of the nether world, the determinist hell of London's East End, by the creation of the People's Palace, where activities range from billiards to young maidens singing madrigals: a total art version of the Kyrle Society's aesthetic missions to the poor which encouraged them to stencil community halls and visit art galleries.

Novelists discussed their art with critics and fellow-novelists through articles in magazines, private letters, prefaces. They even wrote programmatic novels, related not to an abuse or a cause, but to principles of art—a Gallic proceeding. In 1884 Besant published in pamphlet form a lecture he had earlier given at the Royal Institution. Henry James took the opportunity of commenting on Besant's pronouncements in an important essay 'The Art of Fiction', which appeared in *Longman's Magazine* in that same year.

Besant had defended the novel as a literary form against the evangelical tradition which found it wicked *per se*, and that equally limiting tolerance which took the form for granted, admitting it only on the ground that it was make-believe, so denying it any fundamental seriousness. His plea was for a greater professionalism and he laid down prescriptions for the practitioner. These suggest that the novelist's art can be learned mechanically and above all assert that the story is everything. At a pale remove from Zola's naturalistic method, *les ébauches*, Besant also lays it down that the novelist should enter his notes in a commonplace book. To this James replies that the novelist should always be taking notes, only a fraction of which he will actually use, for the novelist's life is one of dedicated alertness, conspicuous devotion to *métier*. For James, however, prescriptions are dangerous, for 'the province of art is all life, all feeling, all observation, all vision . . . the only reason for the existence of a novel is that it attempts to represent life'; for 'humanity is immense and reality has myriad forms'. The novel, therefore, must be not merely like Mr Wopsle's version of *Hamlet*, massive and concrete; it must also be delicately shifting to catch the faintest hints that life offers. Its form should possess the richest of possibilities, for it can involve any number of individual impressions of life. James also takes issue with Besant's contention that the story is of primary importance. He was to be engaged in a similar disagreement about first principles with Stevenson, who championed the cause of romance and the story. And for too long Stevenson continued to be regarded as a story-teller for boys, though his fiction at its best (represented here in a passage from the wonderful *Weir of Hermiston*) vies with James in psychological realism.

Besant's distinction between story and theme denies the organic quality of the novel and readmits Thackeray's and Trollope's general notion of it as make-believe. Faithfulness to one's impressions involves complete freedom of expression and subject, freedom from that ideal English audience of young persons that imposed restrictions on talent. But the notion of the novelist's art as something that can be learned also appears to James to suggest that art can be separated from morality. James argues that the novelist's art is, indeed, separate from morality in so far as it is not subject to it, but that in a deeper sense art *is* morality in its power of illustration and in the quality of the authorial intelligence. This is essentially a sophisticated Realist position. 'Realism is achieved not by imitation, but by creation ... which, working with the materials of life, absolves these by the intercession of the imagination from mere factuality and translates them to a higher order,' a process James termed a 'sacrament of execution'. 'Fact and truth, the two are proposed by James ... as alternative not synonymous, and it is the liberation from a facile identification of the two that brings realism to its majority in consciousness,' as Damian Grant phrases it (*Realism* (London, 1970), pp. 15–16).

In his novels of contemporary life, Besant had at least made some attempt to handle new and controversial topics. Dickens had written, moreover, mainly from the middle-class point of view, though in Dickens's later works the point of view becomes more radical, while escaping from the tendency to tract writing we encounter in Charles Reade. The time gap narrows in the 1880s: for, as has been often observed, Dickens deals with abuses that were about to be remedied.

(vi)

The 1890s was an international decade, though the main commerce of the mind and of taste was with France. The decade divides sharply in 1895, with the trial of Wilde and subsequent suspicion of anything advanced in art. Two other emblematic dates are 1893, and 1894, the former because of the row about Degas's painting *Au Café*, erroneously thought of as a Zolaesque study of absinthe drinking, and the

latter because of the imposition of death duties and the failure of the
second bill for Home Rule in Ireland. But although the term '*fin de
siècle*' became current in England in 1890–1, the apocalyptic note
remained subdued. The decade is one of transition to the 'modern'
period, but the rejection of Victorian values is checked after 1895.

Major novels there are in the 1890s: Meredith's *One of Our
Conquerors* with its stream-of-consciousness technique; Hardy's *Tess
of the D'Urbervilles* and *Jude the Obscure*; James's virtuoso moralities,
What Maisie Knew and *The Awkward Age*. The characteristic form of
the decade, however, is the short story, often embodying a muted
stream-of-consciousness technique. H. G. Wells has described its
floriation in a famous passage:

The nineties was a good and stimulating period for a short story writer. Mr.
Kipling had made his astonishing advent with a series of little blue-grey
books, whose covers opened like windowshutters to reveal the dusty sun-glare
of the East; Mr. Barrie had demonstrated what could be done in a little space
through the panes of his *Window in Thrums*. *The National Observer* was at the
climax of its career of heroic insistence upon lyrical brevity and a vivid finish,
and Mr. Frank Harris was not only printing good short stories by other
people, but writing still better ones himself in the dignified pages of the
Fortnightly Review. *Longman's Magazine*, too, represented a clientele of
appreciative short story readers that is now scattered. Then came the generous
opportunities of the *Yellow Book*, and the *National Observer* died only to give
birth to the *New Review*. No short story of the slightest distinction went for
long unrecognised. The sixpenny popular magazines had still to deaden down
to the conception of what a short story might be to the imaginative limitation
of the common reader—and a maximum length of six thousand words. Short
stories broke out everywhere.

And Wells concludes with a litany of notables, including Conrad,
Gissing, James, Arthur Morrison, George Moore, Henry Harland.
The form proved so attractive that novelists and poets devoted
themselves to it: Moore worked over themes from his own novels in
Celibates (1895); Lionel Johnson, the Rhymers' Club poet, whose
aptitude for the short story was vestigial, produced a drably realist
tale, a Paterian 'Imaginary Portrait', and a somewhat neo-Catholic
short story which might have been a sweeping from Baron Corvo's
florid manufactory. Another poet, John Gray, has offerings of far
higher merit which could bear reprinting. Wells points to some of the
themes that were popular: the exotic, the primitive, the invalidity of
marriage in general, and tales of the East End of London recounted

with an attemptedly iron detachment. Barrie's mixture of dialect and sentiment with a spice of humour was attenuated by his followers of the Kailyard School and savagely corrected in the powerful if melodramatic fiction of George Douglas Brown.

The triumph of the short stories of the 1890s depended partly on French practice: de Maupassant with his anecdotal sharpness, his portraits of peasant greed and superstition, his wit and delicacy, his pessimism. Reaction against the Victorian novel, James's 'loose baggy monster', could hardly go further. But the decade was hospitable also to the smaller arts: the exquisitely printed and adorned volumes of slim verse; the frail effusions of dandyism in wit, dress, and art; the independent theatres with their choice audience; Conder's painted fans. The sense of instability, of identity poised between an abyss of seconds laughingly recorded in Beerbohm's phrase about the sense of being old-fashioned—'I belong to the Beardsley period'—results in an openness to the 'new', the 'intense'. Beerbohm was only twenty-two when he made his joke, and so was Beardsley. The hungry generations, indeed.

The origins of the form as practised in the 1890s are American: Poe and Hawthorne. Poe, in his review of *Twice-Told Tales*, provides the criteria for a work of art that was *sui generis*, not the detritus of a novelist's workshop or a fill-in for a magazine. Poe admired the unity of impression and the intensity of the form, what V. S. Pritchett has termed 'the power of the instantaneous'. This is close to Poe's ideal of the brief poem, though he suggests that the short story is superior to the lyric: 'a poem *too* brief may produce a vivid, but never an intense or enduring effect'.

That brevity permitted the 1890s ideal of 'finish' and intensity to be sustained. But the ideal faltered towards the end of the decade. Frederick Wedmore, who had produced one of the first volumes of *fin de siècle* short stories, *Pastorals of France* (1877), with their low-toned love themes, writing in 1898 of the short story, observed that 'the uglier forms of realism are wearing themselves out'. Wedmore's ideal for the short story resembles that of Edgar Allan Poe—'pregnant brevity'; he compares its incisiveness and economy with Whistler's use of dry-point, but his distaste for the uncompromising quality of the realist short story remains marked. De Maupassant only deviates into cheeriness when he treats 'the virtues of the *déclassés*' with ebullitions of cynicism.

Among talented writers of shorter fiction Wells and Kipling are prominent (Conrad's stories of the 1890s are beyond the scope of this discussion). This is primarily because of their mythicizing powers. Wells's finest essays in this line are nouvelles: 'The Time Traveller' and *The Island of Doctor Moreau*, but the briefer 'Country of the Blind' is here included. Like the other texts, it is a fable of evolution and touched by T. H. Huxley's views on Nature and Culture. A tribe contained by an inaccessible valley have lost the sense of sight though their sense of hearing has become correspondingly more acute: without enemies, human or feral, it is all that they require for survival. The protagonist, a guide, falls into the valley from the heights and amazingly survives. In this enclosed world, though, he discovers that the one-eyed, even the two-eyed, man, is no king but rather is at a disadvantage. After being overcome and forgiven by the tribe in his attempt to impose his will on them, he is tolerated as a half-wit with his tales of a realm of colour and light. He falls in love with a girl of the tribe but before he can marry her, the valley community determines that his eyes must be removed, for these protuberances are thought to be the cause of his fantasies and his inability to be content with the life of the tribe. Unable to endure the thought of becoming blind, he succeeds after great hardship in climbing out of the valley and we leave him still and faintly smiling somewhere on the cold heights. Perhaps he is dead, perhaps in his sleep of exhaustion he is experiencing some epiphany.

Equally ambiguous is the tenor of Kipling's 'The Man who would be King', though here it is the moral stance of the reader whch is in question. Two English loafers Daniel Dravot and his friend Peachey Carnehan found an empire among the wild tribes in a remote country beyond the Indian frontier. Dravot, the dominant figure, with the aid of the latest in small arms, is proclaimed a god but breaks the contract he and his companion have made that there should be no traffic with women. His insistence on taking a wife undoes his godhead. The tribe takes the proper view that gods should be self-sufficient and Dravot dies with dignity and courage at the hands of his former devotees, while his companion is crucified, taken down alive, and left to beg and shamble his way back over the border where he again encounters the knowing narrator who figures in so many of the earlier Kipling stories and here at least somewhat darkens our responses. Peachey in turn dies from the effects of his privations and from sprawling hatless in the torrid afternoon sun. What begins as a parody of those adventurers who come to exploit primitive places and their people gradually transforms itself into a record of splendid energies constrained by the institutionalizing of colonial rule, and the reader is left with mixed feelings.

George Moore, another dominant literary personality of the 1890s, was obsessed with technique, though the results are not altogether satisfying. More than Stevenson, even, in these decades he played the sedulous ape to disparate masters: Zola, Flaubert, Huysmans, Pater, the Irish Literary Movement, were all worshipped and for the most part betrayed. His final phase is marked by a painful limpidity, intended to be the vehicle of a musical stream-of-consciousness, where the reader is carried along a surface which hardly manifests itself as words denoting objects. But before that last phase, he became one of the talented and quarrelsome figures involved in the Irish Literary Movement with its allegiances (sometimes incompatible) to symbolism and 'The Folk'. His volume of short stories *The Untilled Field* (1903) and the nouvelle *The Lake* (1905) influenced Joyce in the detail, for example, of a more overt distaste for the priesthood. 'The Wedding Gown', reprinted here, includes some reprise of Moore's naturalist phase, but the main accent falls on a kind of natural supernaturalism associated with peasant life.

(vii)

W. H. Auden remarks of the later Victorian poets that they are often resourceful metrically, having ears classically trained, but remain depressingly conventional in their language, part of an anxiety to communicate to as wide an audience as possible. Implicit in Auden's comment is the notion that poets of the mid-twentieth century suffer from the opposite vice: their language is pungent, their control of metres uncertain or at best finite.

A candid reader must admit the force of Auden's observation. The demands of magazine editors for the tuneful, sentimental, and empty established a norm for the young poet. And by the 1870s poets had come to regard language as somehow desperately infected by science and commerce. The 'language of the tribe' had been usurped and coarsened by a dialect of popularizing scribes, the stock exchange, political institutions, popular science, the new journalism catering for the masses partially educated under the Acts of 1870 and 1874; the bourgeois next door. Loss of words of power suggested that the poet's identity had itself become infected. Responses to this crisis varied; some were distinctly more successful than others. Certain poets reverted to the grand Romantic tradition of a transcendent Nature and dealt out the double epithets and sensuous visions of Keats. This is applied, for example, in Roden Noel's 'Ganymede' as a tactic for distancing questionable erotic experience. Others, in cognate activity, developed the indirections of Tennysonian 'word painting': a poetry static, miniaturizing and blurring by periphrasis the grosser facts of the Victorian scene. Others like the Rondeliers—Gosse, Lang, Dobson—applied a dilute version of Gautier's notion that the correction of form is virtue. Others again, such as Swinburne, in his middle phase, attempted to establish modal discords between the lavish currents of rhythm and the small 'bleak' words of the surface, neither sensuous nor intellectual, but so far as possible transpicuous. Too often the power of the rhythm was such that, to quote Chapman, 'all the bottoms in the tops he steeps'. Such writers as Pater, Francis Thompson, and Lionel Johnson attempted to use words in an original latinate rectitude, an activity analogous to that of Milton in the restoration of a language that had 'fallen' with man; an attempt to stabilize a language sliding ever more rapidly into the imprecisions of the unlearned and the knowingly vulgar.

Arnold and Hopkins also attempt to redeem the language poets use. But the early Arnold's 'The Strayed Reveller', who represents a poet of direct, acute sensation as recommended by A. H. Hallam in his essay on Tennyson's poems of 1832, is already disavowed within the very poem in which Arnold gives voice to his most accomplished song. His anxiety to secure for poetry a place at the centre of culture led him to attempt the union of thought and beauty and the one poem in which this was achieved, 'Empedocles on Etna', was removed by its author from his own canon. In his later phase, Arnold's diction becomes more and more arid and, like much of Pater's prose, fatigued. Metaphor, image, die out as the poet relies on italics and a rash of 'oh's and 'O's to say nothing of 'Ah's. Only in the late lighter verse is there much vivacity of expression. Hopkins in his earlier phase is, like Arnold's 'Strayed Reveller', also Keatsian, with triple rather than double epithets and Victorian metrical ingenuity carried to extremes.

(viii)

If we except Hardy, Swinburne remains the major poet of this period. This may slant eyebrows on the cisatlantic side. There is a case to answer, for though Swinburne's poetry radiates some of the signs of genius—energy, abundance, a powerful literary identity—his range of topic, none the less, and the sensibility which informs that, seem slender. To the rapid reader the metrical effects, initially stunning, gradually dull the response. Swinburne did not sufficiently dislocate his rhythms, while his use of alliteration, confined mostly to the first letter of the word, seems brash and self-indulgent. It is an attempt to establish some dialectic between subversive mythicized depth and the opacity of a surface that is devoid of objects. Topics appear to blend into one another: the exploration of sado-masochistic psychology or the sea as mother figure; Italy as emblem of man's liberation from tyrannies political or religious; or the giving a voice towards the end of his career to the abrasive moral message of the Navy League. Moreover, he can be compared with other poets to his manifest disadvantage. With Baudelaire he has clear affinities: the quarrel with God and the inversion of *Les Litanies de Satan*; a shared distrust of overt morality as falsifying experience; a shared awareness of ennui as the human condition. But Baudelaire possessed a gift for luminous concision; his ennui is counterpointed by an energy that is by no means always frenetic. The French poet is also more aware of the tang and resonance of objects and this enables him to correlate inner and outer landscapes more memorably. This enriches in particular his interpretations of the modern city with its workmen, prostitutes, the numerous lives momentarily and momentously touching his consciousness. Baudelaire's Paris is an Inferno but, like Wordsworth's desolating image of the Blind Beggar in Book VII of *The Prelude*, it represents the irreducible human condition. A procession of seven old men moving through the fog of Paris mysteriously embodies the intimate nightmare of the outer world. To this, nothing in Swinburne corresponds. If on one occasion, at least, he invokes an industrial landscape, the human figures evade him:

> Such nights as these in England, the small town
> Chatters and scrawls its purpose out in brown
> Searing with steam the hills their naked shape:
> By juts of hurt impatience let's escape
> Quick sighs and fire from chimneyed engine works. . . .

Another possible body of work which can be compared to that of Swinburne is by the Italian poet Gabriele D'Annunzio, who was himself influenced by Swinburne, and who created a largely linguistic world. Objects, though things, in D'Annunzio's best work, possess an intense sensual presence, momentary incarnations of some panic energy in nature. We do, though, find precisely that species of energy in some of Swinburne's later poems, those, for example, devoted to the Nature God, Pan, who, uncharacteristically for the period, is presented in a sinister light. D'Annunzio can use older forms and masters marvellously, but less in the manner of the parodist, while his vocabulary is wider than Swinburne's. And Swinburne's landscapes, often describing monotonous regions, are themselves often monotonous; the eye longs for more colour than the greys and blacks and purples of moorland and littoral, but this can be viewed in the context of his polemic against Wordsworth's Nature whether transcendent or Christianized.

There are positive qualities to be set against these severe limitations: the continuously vivid typology used dialectically and exploiting all the resources of parody, invective, inversion, and on occasion wit and pun. Many of his isolated lines carry a gnomic authority: 'That these things should be thus and not otherwise'; 'Elder with younger brother / Takes mutely the cup from his hand that we all shall take'; 'a valley like an unsealed grave'. Regrettably Swinburne did not rely sufficiently on a talent for terse and sinister description. Like Hopkins he elaborates three- and four-word compound epithets, though not with the 'pied particularity' of the younger poet: 'the sea-forsaken, forlorn deep-wrinkled stretches of sound' where human no less than natural desolation is accented. Like Pater, Swinburne was fully aware of the dark doubleness of the Greek gods. The imagery of the famous chorus in *Atlanta in Calydon*, 'When the hounds of spring are on winter's traces', is dense with ambiguities, images of fruitfulness and death dependent on one another. Swinburne evades altogether the vulgar dream of moral and material progress that so conditioned the high Victorians. Nor was he a pessimist, however much he may speak of 'sleep', 'death', 'oblivion' and however languidly his rhythms may fall. For him process, not end, is all.

All Swinburne's important poems tend to be lengthy and only 'The Triumph of Time' submits itself to selection. I have reluctantly omitted that and 'Anactoria', 'Laus Veneris', and 'The Hymn to Proserpine'. These dramatic monologues with their powerful criticisms of contemporary society are generally ignored and dismissed as schoolboy naughtiness or as the expression of a narrow and exasperated sensibility. Swinburne's aim is to expose the instability of contemporary culture, more particularly its attitudes to sexuality, for it is there that the sickness of society is most evident: his cardinal insight is that sexuality *is* politics. The Victorian world in Swinburne's eyes was unable to resolve the antinomies that haunted it: the public world of bourgeois morality and repressive Christianity and what Philip Rahv has termed 'remissive culture', concessions to the thorn in the flesh—paterfamilias at the brothel on Saturday and in church on Sunday. The contradiction is only to be addressed in the closed world of pornography (to which Swinburne made his own contribution) or the counter-culture of free thinking and action.

'Anactoria' is a remarkable technical and ideological achievement. Here Sappho and the Virgin Mary become contemporaries with Venus. The dichotomy is more refined: the death-fruiting world of the Virgin, epitome of the guilt culture, and the happy, liberated world of the heterosexual Venus. Sappho finds both these ideologies inadequate. She substitutes her own religion, rejecting Venus and the Virgin for Lesbianism and song. Lesbianism expands consciousness and pain is chosen not to assuage guilt but to intensify pleasure. Venus's world remains too psychologically relaxed, too confined also within its antithetical relation to its Christian counterpart. Only by adopting a personal religion, by twice violating 'the Sacred', can Sappho sing and become, as she becomes in the allusions to her in Swinburne's later work, the song itself: a transformation of self into art as in Yeats's Byzantine poems, even though the violence of the Sacred destroys her. As a form of modal discord, 'Anactoria' is written in accomplished Popeian couplets.

In 'Laus Veneris' the speaker, Tannhaüser, is physically enslaved to a Venus now altogether demonic through the hatred and fear projected on to the goddess by the Christians. Tannhaüser's inability to reject Christianity enforces his cohabitation till the end of the world with a succubus in a Hell of sensual pleasure. Emblem of nineteenth-century man, he lives in a self-created prison of contradictory moral values.

The speaker in 'The Garden of Proserpine' has already passed beyond the dilemma posed by the coexistence of pagan and Christian, but clings still to a bankrupt paganism, associated with an animistic

Nature. We can transfer this dilemma to the nineteenth century where Christianity is now in its last phase and Nature has grown grey in the post-Romantic world. In all these problems Swinburne remains sceptical about progress, eschews the didactic: the proposed self-liberation has no goal; the process contains its own ends.

Like many elegies 'Ave Atque Vale' deals as much with the developing consciousness of the speaker as with the nominal subject: the relationship of Swinburne to Baudelaire, that of 'younger' to 'older brother'. The double alienation of Baudelaire's physical death and the rejection of his poetry has severe implications for the speaker. The theme is the redemption of Baudelaire's art and the restoration of the older poet to presence so that the younger poet may himself survive. The apocalyptic close relates the elegy to Shelley's 'Adonais' except that the iterative imagery suggests an underworld rather than some vaguely Platonized Heaven.

Among those few who admire Swinburne the late verse often proves an embarrassment. For Housman, Swinburne died as poet soon after 1870. Still, there are a number of major poems of this period, chiefly elegiac, autobiographical, on occasion in a purely lyrical vein such as 'A Nympholept' or 'A Vision of Spring in Winter'. In the autobiographical vein, most distinguished are 'On the Cliffs' and 'Thalassius'; but 'By the North Sea' represents the later Swinburne at his most accomplished. Here the speaker is challenged by a bleak landscape from which men have been driven by the inexorable rhythms of Nature. Existing as a bright opacity, Nature remains impenetrable. The dead themselves, as the sea tumbles down coffins while the cliffs erode, find no peace in a death that awaits the resurrection to bliss; yet in a sense they may be nearer to Nature than the excluded speaker. Each section represents and rejects a view of Nature: Christian, Romantic transcendental, animistic pagan in the third section that is given here, but finally the speaker hesitates to admit that there are no 'signs' in the natural world, that all meaning is projected by the mind, and that the outer world is not even hostile but indifferent. Swinburne senses but cannot express 'the ache of modernism'.

(ix)

Failed metamorphosis or, in terms that Yeats might endorse, failure to inhabit a mask that can be finally identified with self, characterizes the

Decadent poets: Lionel Johnson, Ernest Dowson, John Gray. Even the aesthetic perceptions that have been exalted as the means of vision now appear corrupt, and so corrupt the ideal objects they discover. Renunciation, abstention from possession through language, is the issue. Parsimony of language freezes into reliance on formal rhetoric in Johnson: a conscious splay of antithesis, oxymoron, anadiplosis; a vocabulary purged of metaphor varied by the sophisticated use of caesura, particularly in the French alexandrine which became quite domesticated at this phase. Dowson uses similar resources, memorable and spectral rhythms where silence is felt more than sound and a similar purged vocabulary distils itself into roses, lilies, moon, whiteness, faded romantic properties that have been emptied of all but mood and tone. As to Gray, the poems in *Silverpoints* (1893) remain frozen in a hesitation between natural and artificial, both of which appear menacing. Grace can only emerge through translation of contemporary religious verse and he typically chooses those equivocal or 'Decadent' Christians, Baudelaire and Verlaine. Gray has no language in which to speak to or about God, only versions of the language of others.

(x)

Hopkins has now displaced Swinburne as the major poet of the later nineteenth century. His spirited afterlife owes something to the drama of Bridges' publication of his poems twenty-nine years after his death. Bridges was not concerned with the need for Hopkins to get a good start in his vocation or with improving the general state of English poetry. Rather his concern was with his friend's reputation and the Hopkins family's ease of mind. In the 1890s he allowed several poems to appear: tepid poems tepidly received. He anthologized others and meditated issuing a privately printed edition. The 1918 edition of the *Poems* did not sell out for twelve years. In 1930 Michael Roberts opened his programmatic and influential *Faber Book of Modern Verse* with Hopkins, exalted now to the status of honorary modern. The affinities with the 'modern', though, are largely superficial. He remains a Victorian, his elaborations of language disconcertingly reminiscent of the mid-century's weighting of surface at the expense of structure; the clotted diction recalls the stuffy interiors of Victorian middle-class houses. His admirers have made amazing claims: 'next to

Arnold,' for example, 'the greatest Victorian critic of poetry'—all this on the basis of some scattered remarks in letters; and that he is the greatest poet of the Victorian period is widely assumed. Bridges' objection to Hopkins's work are mostly confined to single-sentence statements. He had no wish to dwell on limitations; his aim was rather to stress his dead friend's genius. Such brevity allowed those who could see little or nothing to regret in Hopkins's poetry to elaborate arguments. Of Bridges' objections, that to palpable design, to sectarianism, seems valid enough. It is also notable that a number of practising poets have protested against the overvaluation, Graves, Winters, Terence Tiller among others.

As J. Hillis Miller has noticed, Hopkins's early poetry is inhabited by violently shifting colours and shapes, signs of a 'Book of Nature' become critically centrifugal. The poems of the 1870s are full of 'minute particulars' where the manifold diction, the beadwork of epithets, reflect the structure of 'inscape' with its abrupt individuation of objects (rather than formless transitions). If not sustained by Christ's immanence, such inscape would collapse into limp, larval shapes. The poet's anxiety obtrudes in a shift from metonymy, contiguous relations, to metaphor; the relation between word and thing itself dissolves and from metaphor language collapses into tautology. It cannot grasp things (let alone God), only other words. We can follow this process from the sonnets of the 1870s with their joyful celebration of inscape to the so-called 'terrible sonnets' and some of the poems of the last phase where my God is my God and immortal diamond is immortal diamond is immortal diamond. 'Duns Scotus's Oxford' may be taken as an example of a sonnet transitional between the 1870s and the later work. Its structure is altogether typical. The octave gives us inscape and inscape betrayed, and in the sestet, like the US Cavalry or more properly perhaps the Royal Engineers, Christ or the Virgin arrives at the last moment to underpin the world. We begin by evoking the creation of the city in a timeless present which is also historic time.

> Towery city and branchy between towers;
> Cuckoo-echoing; bell-swarmèd, lark charmèd, rook-racked, river-rounded;
> The dapple-eared lily below thee; that country and town did
> Once encounter in, here coped and poisèd powers.

An ideal Arnoldian Oxford somehow still radiates its medieval dreams beyond the age of Darwin and the Higher Criticism, an age worm-eaten with Protestantism. The specious present is soon touched by a real present that actually demonstrates loss of inscape.

> Thou hast a base and brickish skirt there, sours
> That neighbour-nature thy grey beauty is grounded
> Best in; graceless growth, thou hast confounded
> Rural rural keeping—folk, flocks and flowers.

'Brickish' is an ugly word, no longer relating directly to 'thing'. The second section collapses into an amorphous present; we move rather oddly from 'here' to 'there' and the phrase 'graceless growth' implies the nightmare of a nature without significance, forever repeating itself unlike the manifold unrepeatable patternings of 'inscape'. But the sestet achieves its usual desperate triumph. It is a triumph brought about by simple naming: 'Mary'. As Duns Scotus redeemed France in the late thirteenth century, so immaculate Mary, poised outside the flux, in the nineteenth shall redeem what was once 'Mary's Dowry', England.

In the 'Terrible Sonnets' Hopkins is reduced to subjectivity, which, as the *fin de siècle* poets after him will discover, is no viable centre. And language, art even, the self, were incapable of supplying that centre. This connects Hopkins with Lionel Johnson, with whom he has sometimes been compared. 'Carrion Comfort' and 'No worst, there is none. Pitched past pitch of grief' seem rather lumpish experiments, like 'Tom's Garland', with the occasional authentic line. Hopkins is a fine poet of the second class who, besides some achieved lyrics and a handful of good sonnets, wrote one major poem, 'The Wreck of the Deutschland', a triumph he was never able to repeat. Here the sea really works on the metaphorical level while the tall Nun is indeed an ambiguous figure and the merely sectarian is muted. Among the late poems 'That Nature is a Heraclitean Fire' appears to reinstate the energy of the natural world, but a self-consuming energy. The connection between the end of time in fire and the immortal diamond seems factitious, though the carbon–diamond connection is perhaps sufficient; but the ending gutters into attemptedly dramatic tautology. Hopkins's *œuvre* rather echoes his own despairing vision of the natural; it is centrifugal, without internal logic; it differs from the work of a Keats or a Yeats. After 'The Wreck of the Deutschland' it is

Hopkins's notebooks that contain his finest poetry; they too record 'God in detail'.

Lionel Johnson is often seen as a minor Hopkins, but in terms of sensibility and sublimated homoeroticism, the conflict between the religious and the aesthetic. The affinity between the two poets, though, extends to that very quality which, critics declare, separates them: their language. Hopkins's Keatsian beginnings are hectically rich. Johnson began in the low-toned world of Arnold. But their problems with language converged: Hopkins in general ended where Johnson had begun, with tautology.

(xi)

When he was asked if he would allow his work to appear in an anthology of 1890s poets, A. E. Housman wittily distanced himself: 'to include me . . . would be just as technically correct and just as essentially inappropriate as to include Lot in a book on Sodomites'. Certainly his will-power and iron upper lip remove him from those who never, in Nietzsche's phrase, move 'more than five steps from the hospital'. Still, there remain common factors: the homoeroticism; the far more trenchant brevity; the passion for the classics and commas (publishers' pointing would be brooded over for years). The word 'lad' Housman so frequently deploys is one of the encrypted terms of the gay world and indeed occurs at once to Lord Henry Wotton on his first encounter with the twenty-year-old Dorian Gray. The marriage of sensuous and marmoreal distinguish Housman from the muted coloration of Johnson and Dowson. His atheism, like his occasional Manichaeism, is ironic and impatient: 'Whatever brute and black-guard made the world.' The inability to use occasional obscenities weakens some of Housman's lyrics, as it does those of Kipling, who is able to cheat by using homonyms. Not quite Lot in the Unjust City, Housman still 'overgoes' the nineties poets. His work has escaped kidnapping or battery by the fiercer ideologues, though it has been attacked by the Catholic swashbucklers of the Right and by one or two bad-tempered contemporary critics. Effortlessly it survives. His irony and wit are always a tonic, and as a light poet he is as formidable as he was in personality and in his grim refusal to compromise.

William Ernest Henley has been defined by some as 'Counter-

Decadent' and it is true that his *Scots* and later *National Observer*
became the focus of rowdy young fellows, virile in taste and tough in
syntax, even when, like Henry Harland, notably tubercular. However,
both Decadence and Counter-Decadence shared a common myth: the
Roman as type of the British Empire, in its later phase. And, as G. K.
Chesterton was to observe in his *Autobiography*, Imperialism readily
transformed itself into a substitute tribal religion: Kipling's use of the
Old Testament, for example. In Henley's most quoted poem—a
good–bad poem indeed, memorable and horrid—'Out of the night
which covers me' (as Yeats says of much of the Irish Nationalist
Thomas Davis's poetry, and might have said of much official British
verse) he hardly scruples to use the idiom of the jingoist popular
prints: 'black as the pit', indeed. And the poem, by contrast with most
of Housman's lyrics, is full of a swaggering and ostentatious stoicism,
which Henley certainly possessed, and is stiffened with tall nouns that
aggrandize the doers of this world, captains of arms or industry,
masters of ships and of men.

> Out of the night that covers me
> Black as the Pit from pole to pole
> I thank whatever Gods may be
> For my unconquerable soul.
>
> It matters not how straight the Gate
> How charged with punishment the scroll,
> I am the master of my Fate
> I am the captain of my Soul.

A marvellous dismissal of the whole question of God by those
arrogant personalized capitals and with one at least of the characteristics of 'Decadence': the exacerbation of the self but not in its
subjectivity.

John Davidson, a disciple though by no means a devotee of
Nietzsche, remains also a poet of the Schopenhauerian Will; his
rhythms could be related to the aggressive metronomes of Henley and
of Stevenson, in Yeats's definition, the tongue of a mechanized and
economically regulated reality. Davidson's rhythms have rather more
fluidity but answer in broad terms to the definition. He was a man of
constrictions and of contradictions: a man of family but an antinomian
(like that domesticated anarchist Verloc in Conrad's *The Secret
Agent*). He began with some remarkable versions of Stevenson's

fantasias, particularly in *The Practical Novelist*, which touches in its themes Nigel Dennis's *Cards of Identity*, circling the boundaries of fictions and actualities. The work of his middle period comprises some strong verse, melodramatic and memorable, like 'The Ballad of a Nun' with its theme of substitution derived from medieval legend but given a contemporary twist. The Virgin not only takes the Portress's place at the gate but actually approves the absentee's course when she returns from her life of sexual self-expression. Davidson, like Gissing, acutely responded to seedy suburbs, to derelict workings, East End sordors, and smokily eloquent factories whether in Glasgow or in London. But like other Scotsmen of the time, he retained his hatred and his need for an improbable deity. He is not as absolute as Nietzsche: God is not quite dead, not yet. Nietzsche hardly argues with God; he dismisses him with contempt. Davidson argues all the time, rotating in a dangerous limbo between proto-modern and modern both in diction and ideology if we discount the Miltonics of his Testaments, where he predicts a quasi-Yeatsian 'self as God'. For Yeats it was perhaps easier to 'deify' himself with a solid income and the prestige of the Fine Gael toga. Davidson had a family, debts, ill health; and his audience had left, so God became a suicide. A case of continued interest, he has been consistently underrated in the lazy canons of the present century. And then Hugh Macdiarmid wrote a noble tribute to his predecessor which has at least assured his apotheosis in the Scots literary revival. The late long poems such as those on the London railway termini and on Fleet Street are among his finest offerings but too lengthy for inclusion here.

Of the other poets of the period Wilde's first volume contains several accomplished poems, while 'The Harlot's House', with its appropriate clockwork rhythm, strikes his own individual vulgar note, the note that has preserved him as a popular classic as much as his symbolic life. 'The Ballad of Reading Gaol' is a large good–bad poem which needs to be printed virtually in its entirety, quite free of Yeats's editorial purge in his *Oxford Book of Modern Verse*, and of course to be published as a broadside. The paradox of the great aesthete producing a poem and some letters on prison life that go to the heart of an unjust society has often been remarked. But his prison experiences and his development of insights already present in, say, 'The Soul of Man Under Socialism' hardly amount to modernism. Modern enough through his middle phase, in *De Profundis* and *The*

Ballad the 'religiose' takes over. And Wagner, so beloved of Symbolist and Decadent, who kept at Bayreuth his gaudy sanctuary, dramatizes in the later phases of *The Ring* the actual instance of fissure. Wotan after controlling and assigning Siegmund to his love and death, leaves Siegfried free to pursue the contours of his own will. Wotan dies; Valhalla itself totters, the 'death of God' is visually encountered with intimations of a secularized *dies irae*. But *The Ring*'s fully modern closure is at once betrayed by the seductive religiosity of *Parsifal* so hated of Nietzsche, that first free-standing man, and so adored by the Verlaines and John Grays of this world. And here perhaps we can determine why the 1890s still seem so marginal and evasive; its figures retreat from that critical moment when we must reject a given language and a dependent self. Decadent religiosity is no more than an attempt at sublimating loneliness.

(xii)

This anthology moves through a proto-modernism that halts before the frontiers of modernism itself. The notorious formulations are rather belated—Virginia Woolf's comic pomp of certainty about human nature being irreversibly changed by the post-Impressionist showing of 1910 along with the pronunciamentos of Pound and Marinetti. But the condition, if not the formulation, is perfectly apparent thirty years before. We must return to the late-Romantic and High Victorian intimations of God hunted from Nature by man's defacement of God's Second Book and its types: the virgin mountain sanctuary, for example, where all those high-minded mid-Victorian atheists sought some substitute deity. We return to the separation of the Christian and a scientific and aggressively non-sacral culture of the 1880s if we wish to identify incipient modernism and those who were unable to accept the misery of their freedom. Some accept God's absence and his death, while others remain fixed in nostalgic aesthetic attempts to steal the clothes he has left behind him under the self-induced impressions that he is not dead but risen. Kierkegaard's Religious Man must be severely distinguished from those who fully accept the burden of God's death and of man's necessity to remake himself as God. It is not so much the bravura of Yeats's surface, his swaggering colloquialisms, but precisely the effort of re-creating the self that constitutes him as one who has transcended Romanticism, for the re-creation involves Nature as well as Culture. But Yeats's work also undermines the myth of a self-generating modernism. It responds to all the cultural shifts of a sixty-year period, ending with the bleakness of immediate Second World War insights and a dubiety about his own 'system'.

(xiii)

The five years after the turn of the century are severely devoid of considerable poetry, if we except Hardy and Charles Montague Doughty's queer epics and some later poems of John Davidson. The major works of fiction are by established masters: Conrad, Wells, and Kipling, and we must wait until the later part of the decade for the early work of Forster and the major fictions of Arnold Bennett and Ford Madox Ford. By 1905 Synge had produced three one-act plays and the Irish Dramatic Movement was moving towards almost the last of a set of radical crises. The ending of this anthology is therefore inconclusive, anticlimactic, though not altogether formless. The themes of the city; the recourse to the 'self' as the shaper of its own reality; the recognition of the role of women; the return of the irrational in the form of the new psychologies; illuminated, occult societies, illuminated politics, and the attempt to gather rather more of the 'given' into works of art (from adultery and violence to the farts and masturbation of Joyce), all furnish a unity for these years 1870 to 1905. The velocity of change and the uncertainty of direction test the response of novelists and poets and the force and variety of that response. Attempts at inclusiveness made it inevitable that there should be silences, repetitions, formal returns to more certain but faded modes.

(xiv)

Having glanced at 1905 in the present perspective, perhaps finally we might invert the process. The decade is now an idiom of culture. Each decade has its own style. But the years 1900 to 1914 are queerly transitory and mistily contoured, prolonging the Victorian synthesis and eliding into the Armageddon years. It remains one of those periods characterized by much mellow cultural introspectiveness that are generally inhospitable to considerable art.

The analogue between 1900–1905 and the 1980s, which have all too readily developed their own style, is obvious: we still tend to enjoy the Englishness of English Art, a formula projected by Nikolaus Pevsner, a naturalized German, under pressure of an international art history of the modern movement that is no longer fashionable. The return to the vernacular in architecture is the most marked consequence, but the effects can be sensed in literature also. Such proneness in the sub-culture is well enough: delightful though Betjeman was, distinguished though Larkin was, monoglot talking in one's sleep is an arid exercise. And this remains even more true of those whose celebrations are confined to the regional and local past: back to John Clare or back to Edward Thomas, back to Ivor Gurney; to some inch or other that is forever England. England is still there but all so shrunk and so different. The Empire has gone leaving a few shabbily treated islands and enclaves clinging desperately to their only cultural and economic identity. In 1905, too, the working class probably felt a very modified pride in the Empire, except perhaps at points of crises. But another empire yet remains: London is still a money centre but more pertinently a centre of culture and tourism: an up-market Disneyland. Just as manufacturing industries in Britain have severely declined as service industries have increased, so London has become less of a producer, more of a processor of culture, and the culture it processes is less and less from contemporary native English sources even if we allow some vitality to contemporary drama and the regions. No facile cyclical comparison need be intended, but we can establish a broad analogy between the later Roman Empire and the Britain of the 1980s. Martial and Augustine were raised far from metropolitan Rome. So, too, we must hope for a renewal from the old Commonwealth, from British Indians, British West Indians. Only in the tribal world of Ulster, where history runs down a violent bed, the harsh and tender poetry of the time is being written: Seamus Heaney, Paul Muldoon, Tom Paulin, Medbh McGuckian.

ACKNOWLEDGEMENTS

The author and publisher are grateful for permission to include the following copyright material:

Max Beerbohm: from *Zuleika Dobson*. Reprinted by permission of Mrs Eva Reichmann.

A. E. Housman: 'When I watch the living meet' from 'A Shropshire Lad'—Authorized Edition. Copyright 1939, 1940, © 1965 by Holt, Rinehart and Winston. Copyright © 1967, 1968 by Robert E. Symons. 'Stone, steel, dominions pass', 'Crossing alone the nighted ferry', and 'Diffugere Nives'. Copyright 1936 by Barclays Bank Ltd. Copyright © 1964 by Robert E. Symons. 'Revolution', 'Tell me not here, it needs not saying', 'The Oracles', and 'The Night is freezing fast'. Copyright 1922 by Holt, Rinehart and Winston. Copyright 1950 by Barclays Bank Ltd. 'Infant Innocence' and 'Fragment of a Greek Tragedy'. All reprinted from *The Collected Poems* of A. E. Housman by permission of the Society of Authors as the literary representative of the Estate of A. E. Housman, Jonathan Cape Ltd., and of Holt, Rinehart and Winston, Publishers.

Rudyard Kipling: 'The Way Through the Woods'. Copyright 1910 by Rudyard Kipling. Reprinted from *Rudyard Kipling's Verse: Definitive Edition* by permission of Doubleday & Company Inc., and A. P. Watt Ltd., for the National Trust for Places of Historic Interest or Natural Beauty and Macmillan, London Ltd. 'The Song of the Banjo', 'Danny Deever', and 'Mandalay' from *Rudyard Kipling's Verse: Definitive Edition* and 'The Man who would be King' are reprinted by permission of A. P. Watt Ltd., for The National Trust and Macmillan, London Ltd.

Richard le Gallienne: 'A Ballad of London' is reprinted by permission of The Society of Authors as the literary representative of the Estate of Richard le Gallienne.

Arthur Morrison: 'Lizerunt' is reprinted by permission of A. P. Watt Ltd., for the Estate of Arthur Morrison.

Henry Newbolt: 'Drake's Drum' and 'Messmates' from *Selected Poems of Henry Newbolt* (Hodder & Stoughton, 1981). Reprinted by permission of Peter Newbolt.

George William Russell ('A.E.'): 'Germinal' and 'Continuity' from *Selected Poems* (1935). Reprinted by permission of Colin Smythe Limited on behalf of Mrs Diarmuid Russell.

Algernon Charles Swinburne: 'The Ballad of Villon and Fat Madge' from *New Writings* by Swinburne, edited by Cecil Y. Lang (Syracuse University Press, NY, 1964), pp. 13–14. Reprinted by permission of the publisher.

Arthur Symons: 'Episode of a Night of May', 'Colour Studies, At Dieppe', 'Nini Patteen-l'air', and 'Faint Love' are all reprinted by permission of B. Read.

H. G. Wells: 'The Country of the Blind' is reprinted by permission of A. P. Watt Ltd.

W. B. Yeats: 'The Song of Wandering Aengus', 'The Man Who Dreamed of Faeryland', 'He Reproves the Curlew', 'He Hears the Cry of the Sedge', and 'He Thinks of Those Who Have Spoken Evil of His Beloved' from *Poems of W. B. Yeats*, edited by Richard J. Finneran (New York: Macmillan, 1983). Reprinted by permission of Macmillan, New York and of A. P. Watt Ltd., on behalf of Michael B. Yeats and Macmillan, London Ltd.

CHRONOLOGY

1870 Franco-Prussian War; death of Charles Dickens; W. J. Courthope, *The Paradise of Birds*; Arthur O'Shaughnessy, *An Epic of Women*; D. G. Rossetti, *Poems. 1870*; G. W. Stubbs, *Select Charters*

1871 French surrender to the Germans; the Paris Commune; J. Ruskin, *Fors Claveriga* (1871–84); Robert Browning, *Fifine at the Fair*; Charles Darwin, *The Descent of Man*; George Eliot, *Middlemarch*; Benjamin Jowett, translation of *The Dialogues of Plato*; A. C. Swinburne, *Songs before Sunrise*; Alfred Tennyson, *The Last Tournament*; E. B. Taylor, *Primitive Culture*.

1872 Death of F. D. Maurice; Samuel Butler, *Erewhon*; J. A. Froude, *The English in Ireland in the Eighteenth Century* (1872–4); Thomas Hardy, *Under the Greenwood Tree*; Andrew Lang, *Ballads and Lyrics of Old France*; J. Ruskin, *Munera Pulveris*; A. Tennyson, *Gareth and Lynette*.

1873 Death of J. S. Mill; Matthew Arnold, *Literature and Dogma*; Robert Bridges, *Shorter Poems*, I; Austin Dobson, *Vignettes in Rhyme and Verse de Société*; Edmund Gosse, *On Viol and Flute*; T. Hardy, *A Pair of Blue Eyes*; J. S.

Le Fanu, *In A Glass Darkly*; J. S. Mill, *Autobiography* and *Three Essays on Religion*; Walter Pater, *The Renaissance*; Winwood Reade, *The Martyrdom of Man*; J. A. Symonds, *Studies in the Greek Poets*; Anthony Trollope, *The Eustace Diamonds*.

1874 Benjamin Disraeli elected Conservative Prime Minister; G. Eliot, *Daniel Deronda* (serialized 1874–6); T. Hardy, *Far From the Madding Crowd*; A. O'Shaughnessey, *Music and Moonlight*; G. W. Stubbs, *The Constitutional History of England* (1874–8).

1875 Death of Charles Kingsley; W. S. Blunt, *Sonnets and Songs* by Proteus; Gilbert and Sullivan, *Trial by Jury*; J. A. Symonds, *History of the Renaissance in Italy* (1875–6); A. Trollope, *The Way We Live Now*.

1876 F. H. Bradley, *Ethical Studies*; C. M. Doughty, *Arabia Deserta* (1876–8); George Meredith, *Beauchamp's Career*; William Morris, *Sigurd the Volsung*; W. J. Renton, *Oils and Water Colours*.

1877 Grant Allen, *Physiological Aesthetics*; Austin Dobson, *Proverbs in Porcelain and other Verses*; W. H. Mallock,

The New Republic; G. Meredith, *Essay on Comedy.*

1878   Congress of Berlin; Gilbert and Sullivan, *H.M.S. Pinafore*; T. Hardy, *The Return of the Native*; Richard Jefferies, *The Gamekeeper at Home*; W. H. Mallock, *The New Paul and Virginia*; George Moore, *Flowers of Passion*; A. C. Swinburne, *Poems and Ballads, Second Series.*

1879   Sir Edwin Arnold, *The Light of Asia*; William Bagehot, *Literary Studies* (2 vols); R. Bridges, *Shorter Poems, II*; E. Gosse, *Studies in the Literature of Northern Europe*; Henry James, *Daisy Miller*; R. Jefferies, *Greene Fern Farm*; G. Meredith, *The Egoist.*

1880   W. E. Gladstone elected Liberal Prime Minister; death of George Eliot; First Boer War; Sabine Baring-Gould, *Mehalah*; Gilbert and Sullivan, *The Pirates of Penzance*; H. James, *Washington Square*; Andrew Lang, *Ballads in Blue China*; G. Meredith, *The Tragic Comedians.*

1881   Death of Disraeli; death of Carlyle; Battle of Majuba, Britain gives up the Transvaal; T. Carlyle, *Reminiscences*; Gilbert and Sullivan, *Patience*; H. James, *The Portrait of a Lady*; A. O'Shaughnessy, *Songs of a Worker*; Christina Rossetti, *A Pageant and other Poems*;

D. G. Rossetti, *Ballads and Sonnets*; George Bernard Shaw, *Love Among the Artists*; J. M. Shorthouse, *John Inglesant*; E. B. Tylor, *Anthropology*; Oscar Wilde, *Poems.*

1882   Death of D. G. Rossetti; death of Anthony Trollope; death of James Thomson; T. G. Anstey, *Vice-Versa*; J. A. Froude, *History of the First Forty Years of Carlyle's Life*; Gilbert and Sullivan, *Iolanthe*; R. Jefferies, *Bevis*; G. B. Shaw, *Cashel Byron's Profession*; R. L. Stevenson, *Treasure Island*; A. C. Swinburne, *Tristram of Lyonesse.*

1883   Edward Carpenter, *Towards Democracy* (expanded in later editions); E. Gosse, *Seventeenth Century Studies*; Ellice Hopkins, *Poems*; G. B. Shaw, *An Unsocial Socialist.*

1884   Morris founds The Socialist League; *The Century Guild Hobby Horse* (1884–92), *The Hobby Horse* (1893–4); J. A. Froude, *Carlyle's Life in London*; Gilbert and Sullivan, *Princess Ida*; George Gissing, *The Unclassed*; 'Vernon Lee', *Miss Brown*; G. Moore, *A Mummer's Wife*; J. Ruskin, 'The Storm-Cloud of the Nineteenth Century'.

1885   Gilbert and Sullivan, *The Mikado*; T. Hardy, *The Mayor of Casterbridge*; W. H. Hudson, *The Purple Land*; R. Jefferies, *After London*; Rudyard Kipling, *Depart-*

mental Ditties; G. Meredith, *Diana of the Crossways*; G. Moore, *Literature at Nurse*; W. Pater, *Marius the Epicurean*; J. Ruskin, *Praeterita* (1885–9).

1886   Irish Home Rule Bill fails to pass the House of Commons; J. A. Froude, *Oceana*; G. Gissing, *Demos*; Rider Haggard, *King Solomon's Mines*; H. James, *The Bostonians*; R. Jefferies, *Amaryllis at the Fair*; G. B. Shaw, *Cashel Byron's Profession*; R. L. Stevenson, *Dr Jekyll and Mr Hyde* and *Kidnapped*.

1887   Arthur Conan Doyle, *A Study in Scarlet*; J. G. Frazer, *Totemism*; Gilbert and Sullivan, *Ruddigore*; R. Haggard, *Allan Quartermain* and *She*; T. Hardy, *The Woodlanders* (serialized 1886–7); W. Pater, *Imaginary Portraits*; 'Mark Rutherford' (William Hale White), *The Revolution in Tanner's Lane*; R. L. Stevenson, *Underwoods*.

1888   Matthew Arnold, *Essays in Criticism*, Second Series; R. Bridges, *Shorter Poems*, III; Richard Garnett, *Twilight of the Gods and other tales*; Gilbert and Sullivan, *The Yeoman of the Guard*; G. Moore, *Confessions of a Young Man*; William Morris, *Signs of Change* and *The Dream of John Ball*; Mrs Humphrey Ward, *Robert Elsmere*; W. B. Yeats, *The Wanderings of Oisin and Other Poems*.

1889   Death of Robert Browning; death of Gerard Manley Hopkins; Charles Booth, *Life and Labour of the People in London* (seventeen volumes, 1889–1903); R. Browning, *Asolando*; 'Michael Field' (Katharine Bradley and Edith Cooper), *Long Ago*; Gilbert and Sullivan, *The Gondoliers*; G. Gissing, *The Nether World*; W. Pater, *Appreciations*; 'Mark Rutherford', *Catherine Furze*; R. L. Stevenson, *Master of Ballantrae*.

1890   R. Bridges, *Shorter Poems*, IV; Havelock Ellis, *The New Spirit*; J. G. Frazer, *The Golden Bough*; E. Gosse, *Northern Studies*; H. James, *The Tragic Muse*; R. Kipling, *Wee Willie Winkie and Other Stories*; 'Mark Rutherford', *Miriam's Schooling*; G. B. Shaw, *Quintessence of Ibsenism*; J. M. Whistler, *The Gentle Art of Making Enemies*.

1891   A. Conan Doyle, *The Adventures of Sherlock Holmes*; John Davidson, *In a Music Hall*; G. Gissing, *The New Grub Street*; T. Hardy, *Tess of the D'Urbervilles*; G. Moore, *Impressions and Opinions*; W. Morris, *News from Nowhere* and *Poems by the Way*; O. Wilde, *Intentions* and *The Picture of Dorian Gray*.

1892   Death of Tennyson; A. Dobson, *Eighteenth Century Vignettes* (1892, 1894, 1896); 'Michael Field', *Underneath the Bough*; 'Michael Field', *Sight and Song*; G. Gissing, *Born in Exile*; R. Haggard, *Nada the Lily*; R. Kipling, *Barrack Room Ballads*; *The Book of the Rhymers' Club*; Arthur Symons, *Silhouettes*; A. B. Walkley, *Playhouse Impressions*; William Watson, *Lachrymae Musarum*; O. Wilde, *Lady Windermere's Fan*; W. B. Yeats, *The Countess Cathleen and other Poems*.

1893 Second Home Rule Bill passed by the House of Commons rejected decisively by the Lords; Francis Adams, *A Child of the Age*; F. H. Bradley, *Appearance and Reality*; R. Bridges, *Shorter Poems, V*; Hubert Crackanthorpe, *Wreckage*; J. Davidson, *Fleet Street Eclogues*; George Gissing, *The Odd Women*; John Gray, *Silverpoints*; R. le Gallienne, *The Religion of a Literary Man*; G. Moore, *Modern Painting*; W. Pater, *Plato and Platonism*; Sir Arthur Pinero, *The Second Mrs Tanqueray*; J. A. Symonds, *In the Key of Blue*; Lord de Tabley, *Poems. Lyric and Dramatic*; Francis Thompson, *Poems*; O. Wilde, *Salome* (illustrations by Beardsley).

1894 Death of Christina Rossetti; F. Adams, *Tiberius*; Laurence Binyon, *Poems*; A. Conan Doyle, *The Memoirs of Sherlock Holmes*; Havelock Ellis, *Man and Woman: A Study of Human Secondary Sexual Characteristics*; G. Gissing, *In*

the Year of Jubilee; E. Gosse, *In Russet and Silver*; Anthony Hope, *The Dolly Dialogues*; R. Kipling, *The Jungle Book*; E. Lee-Hamilton, *Sonnets of the Wingless Hours*; Arthur Machen, *The Great God Pan*; G. Meredith, *The Amazing Marriage*; G. Moore, *Esther Waters*; Arthur Morrison, *Tales of Mean Streets*; *The Second Book of the Rhymers' Club*; A.E. (George William Russell), *Homeward Songs by the Way*; Mrs Humphrey Ward, *Marcella*; O. Wilde, *The Sphinx*; *The Yellow Book* (1894–7).

1895 Arrest, trial, and conviction of Oscar Wilde; Beardsley sacked from *The Yellow Book*; Election of Conservative Government, Lord Salisbury Prime Minister; Grant Allen, *The Woman Who Did*; Joseph Conrad, *Almayer's Folly*; Ella d'Arcy, *Monochromes*; T. Hardy, *Jude the Obscure*; Lionel Johnson, *Poems*; A. Machen, *The Three Imposters*; R. Kipling, *The Second Jungle Book*; G. B. Shaw, *The Sanity of Art* (in answer to M. Nordau's *Degeneration*); A. Symons, *London Nights*; H. G. Wells, *The Time Machine*; O. Wilde, *An Ideal Husband* and *The Importance of Being Earnest*; W. B. Yeats, *Poems*.

1896 Alfred Austin appointed Poet Laureate; *The Works of Max Beerbohm*; A. Conan Doyle, *The Exploits of Brigadier Ger-*

ard; J. Conrad, *An Outcast of the Islands*; J. Davidson, *New Ballads*; Ernest Dowson, *Verses*; T. Hardy, *Jude the Obscure*; A. E. Housman, *A Shropshire Lad*; R. Kipling, *The Seven Seas*; W. Morris, *The Well at the World's End*; A. Morrison, *A Child of the Jago*; 'Mark Rutherford', *Clara Hapgood*; *The Savoy* (January–December); F. Thompson, *New Poems*; H. G. Wells, *The Island of Doctor Moreau*.

1897   H. Ellis, *Sexual Inversion*; G. Gissing, *The Whirlpool*; H. James, *What Maisie Knew*; Henry Arthur Jones, *The Liars*; Somerset Maugham, *Liza of Lambeth*; Stephen Phillips, *Poems*; A.E. (George William Russell), *The Earth Breath and Other Poems*; R. L. Stevenson, *Weir of Hermiston*; H. G. Wells, *The Invisible Man*; W. B. Yeats, *The Secret Rose*.

1898   Ella D'Arcy, *Modern Instances*; Arnold Bennett, *A Man from the North*; J. Conrad, *Tales of Unrest*; Havelock Ellis, *Affirmations*; T. Hardy, *Wessex Poems*; H. James, *The Two Magics* (*The Turn of the Screw*); R. Kipling, *The Day's Work*; G. Moore, *Evelyn Innes*; G. B. Shaw, *Plays Pleasant and Unpleasant* and *The Perfect Wagnerite*; Mrs Humphrey Ward, *Helbeck of Bannisdale*; O. Wilde, *The Ballad of Reading Gaol*.

1899   Second Boer War; British Reverses, December; Lord Alfred Douglas, *The City of the Soul*; H. Ellis, *The Evolution of Modesty. The Phenomenon of Sexual Periodicity*; E. Gosse, *The Life and Letters of John Donne*; H. James, *The Awkward Age*; R. Kipling, *Stalky and Co.*; S. Phillips, *Paolo and Francesca*; A. Symons, *The Symbolist Movement in Literature*; H. G. Wells, *When the Sleeper Awakes*; W. B. Yeats, *The Wind Among the Reeds*.

1900   J. Conrad, *Lord Jim*; A. Symons, *Images of Good and Evil* and *Studies in Seven Arts*; W. B. Yeats, *The Shadowy Waters*.

1901   G. D. Brown, *The House with the Green Shutters*; J. Davidson, *The Testament of a Vivisector* and *The Testament of a Man Forbid*; R. Kipling, *Kim*; A. Meynell, *Later Poems*.

1902   Death of Samuel Butler; A. Bennett, *Anna of the Five Towns*; A. Conan Doyle, *The Hound of the Baskervilles*; J. Davidson, *Testament of an Empire Builder*; H. James, *The Wings of the Dove*; R. Kipling, *Just So Stories*; A. Morrison, *The Hole in the Wall*.

1903   S. Butler, *The Way of All Flesh*; H. Ellis, *Analysis of the Sexual Impulse* and *Love and Pain*; H. James, *The Am-*

bassadors; G. Moore, *The Untilled Field*; G. B. Shaw, *Man and Superman*; J. M. Synge, *In the Shadow of the Glen*.

1904 J. Conrad, *Nostromo*; J. Davidson, *Testament of a Prime Minister*; J. Galsworthy, *The Island Pharisees*;

H. James, *The Golden Bowl*; J. M. Synge, *Riders to the Sea*.

1905 H. Granville Barker, *The Voysey Inheritance*; G. Moore, *The Lake*; J. M. Synge, *The Well of the Saints*.

NOTE ON THE TEXT

The extracts here are arranged chronologically. Notes are cued by a degree sign (°); general headnotes, however, are not cued, but a degree sign is used if there is a specific headnote for the title, an epigraph, or a dedication. The text used for each poem or prose piece is listed in the notes. The Further Reading is divided into individual bibliographies, followed by a select general bibliography; the individual bibliographies are divided into a section on bibliography (if available) and works, and a section on commentary (again if, as in most cases, available). There is a biographical index, followed by an index of titles.

SIR EDWIN ARNOLD

From *The Light of Asia*

Om, amitaya! measure not with words°
    Th' Immeasurable: nor sink the string of thought
Into the Fathomless. Who asks doth err,
    Who answers, errs. Say nought!

The Books teach Darkness was, at first of all,
    And Brahm, sole meditating in that Night:°
Look not for Brahm and the Beginning there!
    Nor him, nor any light

Shall any gazer see with mortal eyes,
    Or any searcher know by mortal mind;   10
Veil after veil will lift—but there must be
    Veil upon veil behind.

Stars sweep and question not. This is enough
    That life and death and joy and woe abide;
And cause and sequence, and the course of time,
    And Being's ceaseless tide,

Which, ever-changing, runs, linked like a river
    By ripples following ripples, fast or slow—
The same yet not the same—from far-off fountain
    To where its waters flow   20

Into the seas. These, steaming to the Sun,
    Give the lost wavelets back in cloudy fleece
To trickle down the hills, and glide again;
    Having no pause or peace.

This is enough to know, the phantasms are;
    The Heavens, Earths, Worlds, and changes changing them
A mighty whirling wheel of strife and stress
    Which none can stay or stem.

Pray not! the Darkness will not brighten! Ask
    Nought from the Silence, for it cannot speak!   30
Vex not your mournful minds with pious pains!
    Ah! Brothers, Sisters! seek

Nought from the helpless gods by gift and hymn,
    Nor bribe with blood, nor feed with fruits and cakes;
Within yourselves deliverance must be sought;
    Each man his prison makes.

Each hath such lordship as the loftiest ones;
    Nay, for with Powers above, around, below,
As with all flesh and whatsoever lives,
    Act maketh joy and woe.   40

What hath been bringeth what shall be, and is,
    Worse—better—last for first and first for last;
The Angels in the Heavens of Gladness reap
    Fruits of a holy past.

The devils in the underworlds wear out
    Deeds that were wicked in an age gone by.
Nothing endures: fair virtues waste with time,
    Foul sins grow purged thereby.

Who toiled a slave may come anew a Prince
    For gentle worthiness and merit won;   50
Who ruled a King may wander earth in rags
    For things done and undone.

Higher than Indra's ye may lift your lot,
    And sink it lower than the worm or gnat;
The end of many myriad lives is this,
    The end of myriads that.

Only, while turns this wheel invisible,
    No pause, no peace, no staying-place can be;
Who mounts will fall, who falls may mount; the spokes
    Go round unceasingly!   60

If ye lay bound upon the wheel of change,
  And no way were of breaking from the chain,
The Heart of boundless Being is a curse,
  The Soul of Things fell Pain.

Ye are not bound! the Soul of Things is sweet,
  The Heart of Being is celestial rest;
Stronger than woe is will: that which was Good
  Doth pass to Better—Best.

I, Buddh, who wept with all my brothers' tears,
  Whose heart was broken by a whole world's woe,   70
Laugh and am glad, for there is Liberty!
  Ho! ye who suffer! know

Ye suffer from yourselves. None else compels,
  None other holds you that ye live and die,
And whirl upon the wheel, and hug and kiss
  Its spokes of agony,

Its tire of tears, its nave of nothingness.
  Behold, I show you Truth! Lower than hell,
Higher than Heaven, outside the utmost stars,
  Farther than Brahm doth dwell,   80

Before beginning, and without an end,
  As space eternal and as surety sure,
Is fixed a Power divine which moves to good,
  Only its laws endure.

This is its touch upon the blossomed rose,
  The fashion of its hand shaped lotus-leaves;
In dark soil and the silence of the seeds
  The robe of Spring it weaves;

That is its painting on the glorious clouds,
  And these its emeralds on the peacock's train;   90
It hath its stations in the stars; its slaves
  In lightning, wind, and rain.

Out of the dark it wrought the heart of man,
   Out of dull shells the pheasant's pencilled neck;
Ever at toil, it brings to loveliness
   All ancient wrath and wreck.

The gray eggs in the golden sun-bird's nest
   Its treasures are, the bees' six-sided cell
Its honey-pot; the ant wots of its ways,
   The white doves know them well.   100

It spreadeth forth for flight the eagle's wings
   What time she beareth home her prey; it sends
The she-wolf to her cubs: for unloved things
   It findeth and food friends.

It is not marred nor stayed in any use,
   All liketh it; the sweet white milk it brings
To mothers' breasts; it brings the white drops, too,
   Wherewith the young snake stings.

The ordered music of the marching orbs
   It makes in viewless canopy of sky;   110
In deep abyss of earth it hides up gold,
   Sards, sapphires, lazuli.

Ever and ever fetching secrets forth,
   It sitteth in the green of forest-glades
Nursing strange seedlings at the cedar's root,
   Devising leaves, blooms, blades.

It slayeth and it saveth, nowise moved
   Except unto the working out of doom;
Its threads are Love and Life; and Death and Pain
   The shuttles of its loom.   120

It maketh and unmaketh, mending all;
   What it hath wrought is better than hath been;
Slow grows the splendid pattern that it plans
   Its wistful hands between.

This is its work upon the things ye see:
　　The unseen things are more; men's hearts and minds,
The thoughts of peoples and their ways and wills,
　　Those, too, the great Law binds.

Unseen it helpeth ye with faithful hands,
　　Unheard it speaketh stronger than the storm.　　　130
Pity and Love are man's because long stress
　　Moulded blind mass to form.

It will not be contemned of any one;
　　Who thwarts it loses, and who serves it gains;
The hidden good it pays with peace and bliss,
　　The hidden ill with pains.

It seeth everywhere and marketh all;
　　Do right—it recompenseth! do one wrong—
The equal retribution must be made,
　　Though Dharma tarry long.°　　　140

It knows not wrath nor pardon; utter-true
　　Its measure mete, its faultless balance weighs;
Times are as nought, to-morrow it will judge,
　　Or after many days.

By this the slayer's knife did stab himself;
　　The unjust judge hath lost his own defender;
The false tongue dooms its lie; the creeping thief
　　And spoiler rob, to render.

Such is the Law which moves to righteousness,
　　Which none at last can turn aside or stay;　　　150
The heart of it is Love, the end of it
　　Is Peace and Consummation sweet. Obey!

The Books say well, my Brothers! each man's life
　　The outcome of his former living is;
The bygone wrongs bring forth sorrows and woes
　　The bygone right breeds bliss.

That which ye sow ye reap. See yonder fields!
 The sesamum was sesamum, the corn°
Was corn. The Silence and the Darkness knew!
 So is a man's fate born.   160

He cometh, reaper of the things he sowed,
 Sesamum, corn, so much cast in past birth;
And so much weed and poison-stuff, which mar
 Him and the aching earth.

If he shall labour rightly, rooting these,
 And planting wholesome seedlings where they grew,
Fruitful and fair and clean the ground shall be,
 And rich the harvest due.

If he who liveth, learning whence woe springs,
 Endureth patiently, striving to pay   170
His utmost debt for ancient evils done
 In Love and Truth alway;

If making none to lack, he thoroughly purge
 The lie and lust of self forth from his blood;
Suffering all meekly, rendering for offence
 Nothing but grace and good;

If he shall day by day dwell merciful,
 Holy and just and kind and true; and rend
Desire from where it clings with bleeding roots,
 Till love of life have end: 180

He—dying—leaveth as the sum of him
 A life-count closed, whose ills are dead and quit,
Whose good is quick and mighty, far and near,
 So that fruits follow it.

No need hath such to live as ye name life;
 That which began in him when he began
Is finished: he hath wrought the purpose through
 Of what did make him Man.

Never shall yearnings torture him, nor sins
   Stain him, nor ache of earthly joys and woes   190
Invade his safe eternal peace; nor deaths
   And lives recur. He goes

Unto Nirvâna. He is one with Life°
   Yet lives not. He is blest, ceasing to be.
Om, mani padme, om! the Dewdrop slips°
   Into the shining sea!

.   .   .   .

             Here endeth what I write
Who love the Master for his love of us.
A little knowing, little have I told
Touching the Teacher and the Ways of Peace.   200
Forty-five rains thereafter showed he those
In many lands and many tongues and gave
Our Asia light, that still is beautiful,
Conquering the world with spirit of strong grace:
All which is written in the holy Books,
And where he passed and what proud Emperors
Carved his sweet words upon rocks and caves:
And how—in fullness of the times—it fell
The Buddha died, the great Tathâgato,
Even as a man 'mongst men, fulfilling all: 210
And how a thousand thousand lakhs since then
Have trod the Path which leads whither he went
Unto NIRVÂNA where the Silence lives.

   Ah! Blessed Lord! Oh, High Deliverer!
Forgive this feeble script, which doth thee wrong.
Measuring with little wit thy lofty Love.
Ah! Lover! Brother! Guide! Lamp of the Law!
I take my refuge in thy name and thee!
I take my refuge in thy Law of Good;
I take my refuge in thy Order! *OM!*   220
The Dew is on the lotus!—rise, Great Sun!

And lift my leaf and mix me with the wave.
Om mani padme hum, the Sunrise comes!
The Dewdrop slips into the shining Sea!

JAMES THOMSON

A Real Vision of Sin

[At the head of the original MS is the following remark, by the author, in
pencil: 'Written in disgust at Tennyson's, which is very pretty and clever and
silly and truthless.']

Like a soaking blanket overhead
Spongy and lax the sky was spread,
Opaque as the eye of a fish long dead.

Like trees in a drawing gummed together
Some trees stood dim in the drizzling weather;
Sweating mere blood-flowers gloomed the heather.

Like a festering gash left gaping wide
That foul canal, long swooned from tide,
The marshy moorland did divide.

In a slushy hollow near its bank,   10
Where noisome weeds grew thick and dank,
And the very soil like an old corpse stank,

They cowered together, the man and crone,
Two old bags of carious bone;
They and a mangy cur alone:

Ragged, haggard, filthy, both;
Viewing each the other loath;
Growling now and then an oath.

She at length with a spasm raised
Her strong grey eyes, still strong tho' glazed;   20
And thus her meditations phrased:

'No mite left of all our treasure;
Sin itself has no more pleasure:
Drained out, drained out our full measure!'

He quavered back: 'It does seem so:
The sun 'e died out long ago;
The earth and the sky are a-rottin' slow.'

She writhed her thick brows, dirty grey:
'Then take at once my easy way
Of swamping misery from our clay.   30

'No trembling, dear red-rat-eyes! Come!
We slip together through that green scum,
And then with the world here rot on dumb.'

He sat still, nipping spiteful blows
On the snarling cur's amorphous nose;
Relishing faintly her propose.

'Well *you* look lovely, so you do,
To call *me* names: a-drowndin' you
Would go to spoil this pleasant view!

'This 'ere damned life is bad enough;   40
But, say we smother in that stuff,
Our next life's only worse, you muff!'

The woman thereto coldly sneered:
'Of course, as usual all afeared,
Old slaver-dewy stubble-beard.

'Idiot and coward! hell-flames feed
On certain fuel; but, indeed,
A used-up soul won't sate their greed.

'When Earth once gets us cold and stark
She'll keep us safely in the dark: 50
No fear of rousing with the lark!

'Full long ago in grim despair,
She growled, *How those two witch-fires flare!*
They'll get no second chance I swear!'

She laught this truth out 'gainst the man;
Who shuffling, ill at ease, began:
'You can be devilish sore, you can.

'Suppose you're right; this life's a one
That's cursèd bad, but better than none. . . .
I wish they'd light another Sun.   60

'We used to spree and we don't spree now;
A screw is loose in the world allow,
We didn't make it, anyhow.

'Say Life's hard-up, No-life's more glum:
Just think—a lashing lot of rum,
And a night with you and a cool old chum!'

She fingered a toad from its love-work sweet,
And flung to the cur with a 'mangy, eat;
They say there's poison in the meat;

'And so the next time you bite this dear   70
He'll die off mad; for else I fear
He'd fester for ever and ever here.'

Its loose fangs squashed the nectarous lump;
Then it went and crouched on a doddered stump,
With an evil eye on the Male Sin's hump.

He blinked and shuffled and swore and groaned:
Rasping the bristly beard she owned,
She thought drear thoughts until she moaned.

'I see the truth,' with a scornful laugh,
'I have starved abroad on the swine-fouled draff,   80
While sleek at home sucked the fatt'ning calf.

'Too late, too late! Yet it's good to see,
If only damnation, thoroughly;
My Life has never met with me.

'And *you*, you never loved me, *you!*
A heart that never once beat true,
How could it love? I loved for two.

'This dirty crumpled rag of a breast
Was globed with milk once; I possest
The means of being grandly blest!   90

'Did the babe of mine suck luscious sips,
Soothing the nipple with rose-soft lips
While her eyes dropped mild in a dear eclipse?

'A babe!—could I now squeeze out three drops
Between that poor cur's ulcerous chaps,
He'd die as livid as yon tree-tops.

'You know where it rests, that child-dream gone?
Come, grope in this charming water-lawn,
Through ooze and slime and filth and spawn:

'Perhaps we shall find a shudderous feel,   100
Neither of eft nor toad nor eel;
May hear a long long stifled squeal.

'Touch the rotten bones of a murdered brat
Whose flesh was daint to the water-rat,—°
If it *does* gnaw flesh it would relish that!'

He ventured, 'Curse all memory!
It's more than thirty years'—but she
Continued fierce unheedingly—

'Come, and this loathsome life out-smother,
No fear that we'll ever have another: 110
The rain may beat and the wind may wuther,

'But we shall rot with the rotting soil,
Safe in sleep from the whole sad coil;
Sleep's better than corn and wine and oil.°

'Here's a kiss; now at once!' effused the witch,
And dragged the wildered male to the ditch,
And plunged there prone by a bladdery bitch.

Drowned dead, stone dead, and still her grasp
Clawed *him*: but with a frenzied gasp
He shuddered off the scranny clasp.   120

Up the soddened bank in a fury of funk
He sprawled: 'She's awful! but she's sunk;
I daren't die except dead drunk.'

He managed at length the hollow to win;
And was gulping down with a pang-writhed grin
The black bottle's last of vitriol gin,

When his gorge was choked by a sudden blight:
The cur growled mad with venom and fright,
And its blotches of hair all bristled upright.

Its frenzy burst out in a wolfish yell;   130
It leaped at his throat like an imp of hell;
In a spasm of horror the bottle fell:

It griped up his flaccid throat with a force
That made his terrorment gurgle hoarse,
While he turned as blue as a cholera-corse.

It haled him into the festering dike;
So all sank dead in its clam alike,—
The Man, the Woman, the virtuous Tyke.

And the dense rain crooned in its sullen flow
From the sodden sky stretch drooping low   140
To the sodden earth; and to and fro

Crept a maundering wind too weak to blow;
And the dim world murmured dismal woe:
For the earth and the sky *were* a-rotting slow.

In the Room

'Ceste insigne fable et tragicque comedie.'—RABELAIS.

I

The sun was down, and twilight grey
    Filled half the air; but in the room,
Whose curtain had been drawn all day,
    The twilight was a dusky gloom:
Which seemed at first as still as death,
    And void; but was indeed all rife
With subtle thrills, the pulse and breath
    Of multitudinous lower life.

2

In their abrupt and headlong way
    Bewildered flies for light had dashed   10
Against the curtain all the day,
    And now slept wintrily abashed;
And nimble mice slept, wearied out
    With such a double night's uproar;
But solid beetles crawled about
    The chilly hearth and naked floor.

3

And so throughout the twilight hour
    That vaguely murmurous hush and rest
There brooded; and beneath its power
    Life throbbing held its throbs supprest: 20
Until the thin-voiced mirror sighed,
    I am all blurred with dust and damp,
So long ago the clear day died,
    So long has gleamed nor fire nor lamp.

4

Whereon the curtain murmured back,
　　Some change is on us, good or ill;
Behind me and before is black
　　As when those human things lie still:
But I have seen the darkness grow
　　As grows the daylight every morn;   30
Have felt out there long shine and glow,
　　In here long chilly dusk forlorn.

5

The cupboard grumbled with a groan,
　　Each new day worse starvation brings:
Since *he* came here I have not known
　　Or sweets or cates or wholesome things:
But now! a pinch of meal, a crust,
　　Throughout the week is all I get.
I am so empty; it is just
　　As when they said we were to let.   40

6

What is become, then, of our Man?
　　The petulant old glass exclaimed;
If all this time he slumber can,
　　He really ought to be ashamed.
I wish we had our Girl again,
　　So gay and busy, bright and fair:
The girls are better than these men,
　　Who only for their dull selves care.

7

It is so many hours ago—
　　The lamp and fire were both alight—   50
I saw him pacing to and fro,
　　Perturbing restlessly the night.
His face was pale to give one fear,
　　His eyes when lifted looked too bright;
He muttered; what, I could not hear:
　　Bad words though; something was not right.

8

The table said, He wrote so long
    That I grew weary of his weight;
The pen kept up a cricket song,
    It ran and ran at such a rate: 60
And in the longer pauses he
    With both his folded arms downpressed
And stared as one who does not see,
    Or sank his head upon his breast.

9

The fire-grate said, I am as cold
    As if I never had a blaze;
The few dead cinders here I hold,
    I held unburned for days and days.
Last night he made them flare; but still
    What good did all his writing do?   70
Among my ashes curl and thrill
    Thin ghosts of all those papers too.

10

The table answered, Not quite all;
    He saved and folded up one sheet,
And sealed it fast, and let it fall;
    And here it lies now white and neat.
Whereon the letter's whisper came,
    My writing is closed up too well;
Outside there's not a single name,
    And who should read me I can't tell.   80

11

The mirror sneered with scornful spite,
    (That ancient crack which spoiled her looks
Had marred her temper), Write and write!
    And read those stupid, worn-out books!
That's all he does, read, write, and read,
    And smoke that nasty pipe which stinks:
He never takes the slightest heed
    How any of us feels or thinks.

12

But Lucy fifty times a day
   Would come and smile here in my face,   90
Adjust a tress that curled astray,
   Or tie a ribbon with more grace:
She looked so young and fresh and fair,
   She blushed with such a charming bloom,
It did one good to see her there,
   And brightened all things in the room.

13

She did not sit hours stark and dumb
   As pale as moonshine by the lamp;
To lie in bed when day was come,
   And leave us curtained chill and damp.   100
She slept away the dreary dark,
   And rose to greet the pleasant morn;
And sang as gaily as a lark
   While busy as the flies sun-born.

14

And how she loved us every one;
   And dusted this and mended that,
With trills and laughs and freaks of fun,
   And tender scoldings in her chat!
And then her bird, that sang as shrill
   As she sang sweet; her darling flowers   110
That grew there in the window-sill,
   Where she would sit at work for hours.

15

It was not much she ever wrote;
   Her fingers had good work to do;
Say, once a week a pretty note;
   And very long it took her too.
And little more she read, I wis;
   Just now and then a pictured sheet,
Besides those letters she would kiss
   And croon for hours, they were so sweet.   120

16

She had her friends too, blithe young girls,
　　Who whispered, babbled, laughed, caressed,
And romped and danced with dancing curls,
　　And gave our life a joyous zest.
But with this dullard, glum and sour,
　　Not one of all his fellow-men
Has ever passed a social hour;
　　We might be in some wild beast's den.

17

This long tirade aroused the bed,
　　Who spoke in deep and ponderous bass,　　130
Befitting that calm life he led,
　　As if firm-rooted in his place:
In broad majestic bulk alone,
　　As in thrice venerable age,
He stood at once the royal throne,
　　The monarch, the experienced sage:

18

I know what is and what has been;
　　Not anything to me comes strange,
Who in so many years have seen
　　And lived through every kind of change.　　140
I know when men are good or bad,
　　When well or ill, he slowly said;
When sad or glad, when sane or mad,
　　And when they sleep alive or dead.

19

At this last word of solemn lore
　　A tremor circled through the gloom,
As if a crash upon the floor
　　Had jarred and shaken all the room:
For nearly all the listening things
　　Were old and worn, and knew what curse　　150
Of violent change death often brings,
　　From good to bad, from bad to worse;

20

They get to know each other well,
    To feel at home and settled down;
Death bursts among them like a shell,
    And strews them over all the town.
The bed went on, This man who lies
    Upon me now is stark and cold;
He will not any more arise,
    And do the things he did of old.   160

21

But we shall have short peace or rest;
    For soon up here will come a rout,
And nail him in a queer long chest,
    And carry him like luggage out.
They will be muffled all in black
    And whisper much, and sigh and weep:
But he will never more come back,
    And some one else in me must sleep.

22

Thereon a little phial shrilled,
    Here empty on the chair I lie: 170
I heard one say, as I was filled,
    With half of this a man would die.
The man there drank me with slow breath,
    And murmured, Thus ends barren strife:
O sweeter, thou cold wine of death,
    Than ever sweet warm wine of life.

23

One of my cousins long ago,
    A little thing, the mirror said,
Was carried to a couch to show,
    Whether a man was really dead.   180
Two great improvements marked the case:
    He did not blur her with his breath,
His many-wrinkled, twitching face
    Was smooth old ivory: verdict, Death.—

24

It lay, the lowest thing there, lulled
    Sweet-sleep-like in corruption's truce;
The form whose purpose was annulled,
    While all the other shapes meant use.
It lay, the *he* become now *it*,
    Unconscious of the deep disgrace,   190
Unanxious how its parts might flit
    Through what new forms in time and space.

25

It lay and preached, as dumb things do,
    More powerfully than tongues can prate;
Though life be torture through and through,
    Man is but weak to plain of fate:
The drear path crawls on drearier still
    To wounded feet and hopeless breast?
Well, he can lie down when he will,
    And straight all ends in endless rest.   200

26

And while the black night nothing saw,
    And till the cold morn came at last,
That old bed held the room in awe
    With tales of its experience vast.
It thrilled the gloom; it told such tales
    Of human sorrows and delights,
Of fever moans and infant wails,
    Of births and deaths and bridal nights.

from *The City of Dreadful Night*°

I

As I came through the desert thus it was,
As I came through the desert: All was black,
In heaven no single star, on earth no track;

A brooding hush without a stir or note,
The air so thick it clotted in my throat;
And thus for hours, then some enormous things
Swooped past with savage cries and clanking wings:
      But I strode on austere;
      No hope could have no fear.

As I came through the desert thus it was,   10
As I came through the desert: Eyes of fire
Glared at me throbbing with a starved desire;
The hoarse and heavy and carnivorous breath
Was hot upon me from deep jaws of death;
Sharp claws, swift talons, fleshless fingers cold
Plucked at me from the bushes, tried to hold:
      But I strode on austere;
      No hope could have no fear.

As I came through the desert thus it was,
As I came through the desert: Lo you, there,   20
That hillock burning with a brazen glare;
Those myriad dusky flames with points a-glow
Which writhed and hissed and darted to and fro;
A Sabbath of the Serpents, heaped pell-mell
For Devil's roll-call and some *fête* of Hell:
      Yet I strode on austere;
      No hope could have no fear.

As I came through the desert thus it was,
As I came through the desert: Meteors ran
And crossed their javelins on the black sky-span;   30
The zenith opened to a gulf of flame,
The dreadful thunderbolts jarred earth's fixed frame;
The ground all heaved in waves of fire that surged
And weltered round me sole there unsubmerged:
      Yet I strode on austere;
      No hope could have no fear.

As I came through the desert thus it was,
As I came through the desert: Air once more,
And I was close upon a wild sea-shore;

Enormous cliffs arose on either hand,   40
The deep tide thundered up a league-broad strand;
White foambelts seethed there, wan spray swept and flew;
The sky broke, moon and stars and clouds and blue:
    And I strode on austere;
    No hope could have no fear.

As I came through the desert thus it was,
As I came through the desert: On the left
The sun arose and crowned a broad crag-cleft;
There stopped and burned out black, except a rim,
A bleeding eyeless socket, red and dim;   50
Whereon the moon fell suddenly south-west
And stood above the right-hand cliffs at rest:
    Still I strode on austere;
    No hope could have no fear.

As I came through the desert thus it was,
As I came through the desert: From the right
A shape came slowly with a ruddy light;
A woman with a red lamp in her hand,°
Bareheaded and barefooted on that strand;
O desolation moving with such grace!   60
O anguish with such beauty in thy face!
    I fell as on my bier,
    Hope travailed with such fear.

As I came through the desert thus it was,
As I came through the desert: I was twain,°
Two selves distinct that cannot join again;
One stood apart and knew but could not stir,
And watched the other stark in swoon and her;
And she came on, and never turned aside,
Between such sun and moon and roaring tide: 70
    And as she came more near
    My soul grew mad with fear.

As I came through the desert thus it was,
As I came through the desert: Hell is mild
And piteous matched with that accursèd wild;

A large black sign was on her breast that bowed,
A broad blackband ran down her snow-white shroud;
That lamp she held was her own burning heart,
Whose blood-drops trickled step by step apart:
     The mystery was clear;   80
     Mad rage had swallowed fear.

As I came through the desert thus it was,
As I came through the desert: By the sea
She knelt and bent above that senseless me;
Those lamp-drops fell upon my white brow there,
She tried to cleanse them with her tears and hair;
She murmured words of pity, love, and woe,
She heeded not the level rushing flow:
     And mad with rage and fear,
     I stood stonebound so near.   90

As I came through the desert thus it was,
As I came through the desert: When the tide
Swept up to her there kneeling by my side,
She clasped that corpse-like me, and they were borne
Away, and this vile me was left forlorn;
I know the whole sea cannot quench that heart,
Or cleanse that brow, or wash those two apart:
     They love; their doom is drear,
     Yet they nor hope nor fear;
     But I, what do I here?   100

II

Anear the centre of that northern crest°
  Stands out a level upland bleak and bare,
From which the city east and south and west
  Sinks gently in long waves; and thronèd there
An Image sits, stupendous, superhuman,
The bronze colossus of a wingèd Woman,
  Upon a graded granite base foursquare.

Low-seated she leans forward massively,
  With cheek on clenched left hand, the forearm's might

Erect, its elbow on her rounded knee;   110
   Across a clasped book in her lap the right
Upholds a pair of compasses; she gazes
With full set eyes, but wandering in thick mazes
   Of sombre thought beholds no outward sight.

Words cannot picture her; but all men know
   That solemn sketch the pure sad artist wrought
Three centuries and threescore years ago,
   With phantasies of his peculiar thought:
The instruments of carpentry and science
Scattered about her feet, in strange alliance   120
   With the keen wolf-hound sleeping undistraught;

Scales, hour-glass, bell, and magic-square above;
   The grave and solid infant perched beside,
With open winglets that might bear a dove,
   Intent upon its tablets, heavy-eyed;
Her folded wings as of a mighty eagle,
But all too impotent to lift the regal
   Robustness of her earth-born strength and pride;

And with those wings, and that light wreath which seems
   To mock her grand head and the knotted frown   130
Of forehead charged with baleful thoughts and dreams,
   The household bunch of keys, the housewife's gown
Voluminous, indented, and yet rigid
As if a shell of burnished metal frigid,
   The feet thick-shod to tread all weakness down;

The comet hanging o'er the waste dark seas,
   The massy rainbow curved in front of it
Beyond the village with the masts and trees;
   The snaky imp, dog-headed, from the Pit,
Bearing upon its batlike leathern pinions   140
Her name unfolded in the sun's dominions,
   The 'MELENCOLIA' that transcends all wit.

Thus has the artist copied her, and thus
   Surrounded to expound her form sublime,
Her fate heroic and calamitous;
   Fronting the dreadful mysteries of Time,
Unvanquished in defeat and desolation,
Undaunted in the hopeless conflagration
   Of the day setting on her baffled prime.

Baffled and beaten back she works on still,   150
   Weary and sick of soul she works the more,
Sustained by her indomitable will:
   The hands shall fashion and the brain shall pore,
And all her sorrow shall be turned to labour,
Till Death the friend-foe piercing with his sabre
   That mighty heart of hearts ends bitter war.

But as if blacker night could dawn on night,
   With tenfold gloom on moonless night unstarred,
A sense more tragic than defeat and blight,
   More desperate than strife with hope debarred,   160
More fatal than the adamantine Never
Encompassing her passionate endeavour,
   Dawns glooming in her tenebrous regard:

The sense that every struggle brings defeat
   Because Fate holds no prize to crown success;
That all the oracles are dumb or cheat
   Because they have no secret to express;
That none can pierce the vast black veil uncertain
Because there is no light beyond the curtain;
   That all is vanity and nothingness.   170

Titanic from her high throne in the north,
   That City's sombre Patroness and Queen,
In bronze sublimity she gazes forth
   Over her Capital of teen and threne,
Over the river with its isles and bridges,
The marsh and moorland, to the stern rock-ridges,
   Confronting them with a coëval mien.

The moving moon and stars from east to west
   Circle before her in the sea of air;
Shadows and gleams glide round her solemn rest.   180
   Her subjects often gaze up to her there:
The strong to drink new strength of iron endurance,
The weak new terrors; all, renewed assurance
   And confirmation of the old despair.

RODEN NOEL

Ganymede

Azure the heaven with rare a feathery cloud;
Azure the sea, far-scintillating light,
Soft rich like velvet yielding to the eye;
Horizons haunted with some dream-like sails;
A temple hypaethral open to sweet air°
Nigh on the height, columned with solid flame,
Of flutings and acanthus-work instinct
With lithe green lizards and the shadows sharp
Slant barring golden floor and inner wall.

   A locust-tree condensing all the light   10
On glossy leaves, and flaky spilling some
Sparkling among cool umbrage underneath;
There magically sobered mellow soft
At unaware beholding gently laid
A youth barelimbed the loveliest in the world,
Gloatingly falling on his lily side,
Smoothing one rounded arm and dainty hand
Whereon his head conscious and conquering
All chestnut-curled rests listless and superb;
Near him and leaning on the chequered bole   20
Sits his companion gazing on him fond,
A goat-herd whose rough hand on bulky knee
Holds a rude hollow reeden pipe of Pan,
Tanned clad with goatskin rudely-moulded huge;

While yonder, browsing in the rosemary
And cytisus, you hear a bearded goat,
Hear a fly humming with a droning bee
In yon wild thyme and in the myrtles low
That breathe in every feebly-blowing air;
Whose foamy bloom fair Ganymede anon   30
Plucks with a royal motion and an aim
Toward his comrade's tolerant fond face.
Far off cicada shrills among the pine,
And one may hear low tinkling where a stream
Yonder in planes and willows, from the beam
Of day coy hiding, runs with many a pool
Where the twain bathe how often in the cool!

And so they know not of the gradual cloud
That stains the zenith with a little stain,
Then grows expansive, nearing one would say   40
The happy earth—until at last a noise
As of a rushing wind invades the ear,
Gathering volume, and the shepherd sees,
Amazed forth-peering, dusking closing all
Startled and tremulous rock-roses nigh,
Portentous shadow; and before he may
Rise to explore the open, like a bolt
From heaven a prodigy descends at hand,
Absorbing daylight; some tremendous bird,
An eagle, yet in plumage as in form   50
And stature far transcending any bird
Imperial inhabiting lone clefts
And piny crags of this Idaean range.

But lo! the supernatural dread thing,
Creating wind from cavernous vast vans,
Now slanting swoops toward them, hovering
Over the fair boy smitten dumb with awe.
A moment more, and how no mortal knows,
The bird hath seized him, if it be a bird,
And he though wildered hardly seems afraid,   60
So lightly lovingly those eagle talons
Lock the soft yielding flesh of either flank,

His back so tender, thigh and shoulder pillowed
How warmly whitely in the tawny down
Of that imperial eagle amorous!
Whose beakèd head with eyes of burning flame
Nestles along the tremulous sweet heave
Of his fair bosom budding with a blush,
So that one arm droops pensile all aglow
Over the neck immense, and hangs a hand   70
Frail like a shell, pink like an apple bloom;
While shadowy wings expansive waving wind
Jealously hide some beauty from the sun.

    Poor hind! he fancied as the pinions clanged
In their ascent, he looking open-mouthed
Distraught yet passive, that the boy's blue eye
Sought him in soaring; his own gaze be sure
Wearied not famished feeding upon all
The youth's dear charms for ever vanishing
From his poor longing, hungered for in heaven—   80
Took his last fill of delicate flushed face,
And swelling leg and rose-depending foot,
Slim ankle, dimpling body rich and full.
Behold! he fades receding evermore
From straining vision misting dim with tears,
Gleaming aloft swanwhite into the blue
Relieved upon the dusky ravisher,
Deeper and deeper glutting amorous light,
That cruel swallows him for evermore.

ALFRED AUSTIN

from *The Season*

They each require and ply their sensual sport;
The one for praise, the others hunt for port.
And all must own that neither act their best
Till the half-drunk lean over the half-dressed.

    .   .   .   .

The sentimental to the sensuous grows,
The pointless trilling into pointless toes.
Now wake the fathers who securely slept
Whilst Alfred wooed and Violetta wept,
Rub up their spectacles and strain their gaze
At bounding Zina dressed in shoes and stays:
Now love-struck boys transfer their fickle eyes
From Mary's trinkets to Morlacchi's thighs;
Whilst mothers, sisters, sweethearts, wives applaud
The tight proportions of a twirling bawd.

.   .   .   .

Here, with complacency, strict matrons see
Maids and Moss-troopers polking, knee to knee. . . .
Whirl fast! whirl long! ye gallants and ye girls!
Cling closer still; dance down these cursèd churls. . . .
Whirl faster, closer, until passion's drouth
Play in the tell-tale muscles of the mouth,
The furious Circle bid a truce to masks,
And Nature answer all that Nature asks. . . .
This scene, your anti-sensual strictures doom,
Is not an Orgy, but—an auction-room.
These panting damsels, dancing for their lives,
Are only maidens waltzing into wives.
Those smiling matrons are appraisers sly
Who regulate the dance, the squeeze, the sigh,
And each base cheapening buyer having chid,
Knock down their daughters to the noblest bid.

SAMUEL BUTLER

from *The Way of All Flesh*

FATHER AND SON

The birth of his son opened Theobald's eyes to a good deal which he
had but faintly realized hitherto. He had had no idea how great a
nuisance a baby was. Babies come into the world so suddenly at the

end, and upset everything so terribly when they do come: why cannot they steal in upon us with less of a shock to the domestic system? His wife, too, did not recover rapidly from her confinement; she remained an invalid for months; here was another nuisance, and an expensive one, which interfered with the amount which Theobald liked to put by out of his income against, as he said, a rainy day, or to make provision for his family if he should have one. Now he was getting a family, so that it became all the more necessary to put money by, and here was the baby hindering him. Theorists may say what they like about a man's children being a continuation of his own identity, but it will generally be found that those who talk in this way have no children of their own. Practical family men know better.

About twelve months after the birth of Ernest there came a second, also a boy, who was christened Joseph, and less than twelve months afterwards, a girl to whom was given the name Charlotte. A few months before this girl was born Christina paid a visit to the John Pontifexes in London, and, knowing her condition, passed a good deal of time at the Royal Academy exhibition looking at the types of female beauty portrayed by the Academicians, for she had made up her mind that the child this time was to be a girl. Alethaea warned her not to do this but she persisted, and certainly the child turned out plain, but whether the pictures caused this or no I cannot say.

Theobald had never liked children. He had always got away from them as soon as he could, and so had they from him; oh, why he was inclined to ask himself could not children be born into the world grown up? If Christina could have given birth to a few full-grown clergymen in priest's orders—of moderate views, but inclining rather to Evangelicism, with comfortable livings and in all respects facsimilies of Theobald and Christina themselves—why there might have been more sense in it; or if people could buy ready-made children of whatever age and sex they liked at a shop instead of always having to make them at home and to begin at the beginning with them—that might do better, but as it was he did not like it. He felt as he had felt when he had been required to come and be married to Christina—that he had been going on for a long time quite nicely and would much rather continue things on their present footing. In the matter of getting married he had been obliged to pretend he liked it; but times were changed, and if he did not like a thing now, he could find a hundred unexceptionable ways of making his dislike apparent.

It might have been better if Theobald in his younger days had kicked more against his father. The fact that he had not done so encouraged him to expect the most implicit obedience from his own children. He could trust himself, he said, and so did Christina, to be more lenient than perhaps his father had been to himself; his danger, he said (and so again did Christina) would be rather in the direction of being too indulgent; he must be on his guard against this, for no duty could be more paramount than that of teaching a child to obey its parents in all things.

He had read not long since of an Eastern traveller, who while exploring somewhere in the more remote parts of Arabia or Asia Minor, had come upon a remarkably hardy, sober, industrious little Christian community—all of them in the best of health—who had turned out to be the actual living descendants of Jonadab the son of Rechab; and two men in European costume indeed, but speaking English with a broken accent, and by their colour evidently oriental, had come begging to Battersby soon afterwards, and represented themselves as belonging to these people; they had said they were collecting funds to promote the conversion of their fellow tribesmen to the English branch of the Christian religion. True, they turned out to be imposters, for when he gave them a pound, and Christina five shillings from her private purse, they went and got drunk with it in the next village but one to Battersby; still this did not invalidate the story of the Eastern traveller. Then there were the Romans—whose greatness was probably due to the wholesome authority exercised by the head of a family over all its members. Some Romans had even killed their children; this was going too far, but then the Romans were not Christians, and knew no better.

The practical outcome of the foregoing was a conviction in Theobald's mind, and if in his, then in Christina's, that it was their duty to begin training up their children in the way they should go, even from their earliest infancy. The first signs of self-will must be carefully looked for, and plucked up by the roots at once before they had time to grow. Theobald picked up this numb serpent of a metaphor and cherished it in his bosom.

Before Ernest could well crawl he was taught to kneel; before he could well speak he was taught to lisp the Lord's prayer, and the general confession. How was it possible that these things could be taught too early? If his attention flagged, or his memory failed him, here was an ill weed which would grow apace, unless it were plucked out immediately, and the only way to pluck it out was to whip him, or shut him up in a cupboard, or dock him of some of the small pleasures of childhood. Before he was three years old he could read, and, after a fashion, write. Before he was four he was learning Latin, and could do rule of three sums.

As for the child himself, naturally of an even temper, he doted upon his nurse, on kittens and puppies and on all things that would do him the kindness of allowing him to be fond of them. He was fond of his mother too, but as regards his father, he has told me in later life, he could remember no feeling but fear and shrinking. Christina did not remonstrate with Theobald concerning the severity of the tasks imposed upon their boy, nor yet as to the continual whippings that were daily found necessary at lesson times. Indeed, when during any absence of Theobald's the lessons were entrusted to her, she found to her sorrow that it was the only thing to do, and she did it no less effectually than Theobald himself; nevertheless she was fond of her boy, which Theobald never was, and it was long before she could destroy all affection for herself in the mind of her first-born. But she persevered.

Strange! for she believed she doted upon him and certainly she loved him better than either of her other children. Her version of the matter was that there had never yet been two parents so self-denying and devoted to the highest welfare of their children as Theobald and herself. For Ernest, a very great future—she was certain of it—was in store. This made severity all the more necessary, so that from the first he might have been kept pure from every taint of evil. She could not allow herself the scope for castle building which, we read, was indulged in by every Jewish matron before the appearance of the Messiah, for the Messiah had now come; but there was to be a millennium shortly, certainly not later than 1866, when Ernest would be just about the right age for it, and a modern Elias would be wanted to herald its approach. Heaven would bear her witness that she had never shrunk from the idea of martyrdom for herself and Theobald, nor would she avoid it for her boy, if his life was required of her in her Redeemer's service. Oh no! If God told her to offer up her first-born as he had told Abraham, she would take him up to Pigbury Beacon and plunge the .... No—that she could not do, but it would be

unnecessary—some one else might do that. It was not for nothing that
Ernest had been baptized in water from the Jordan. It had not been
her doing, nor yet Theobald's. They had not sought it. When water
from the sacred stream was wanted for a sacred infant, the channel
had been found through which it was to flow from far Palestine over
land and sea to the door of the house where the child was lying. Why it
was a miracle! It was! It was! She saw it all now. The Jordan had left
its bed and flowed into her own house. It was idle to say that this was
not a miracle. No miracle was effected without means of some kind;
the difference between the faithful and the unbeliever consisted in the
very fact that the former could see a miracle where the latter could
not. The Jews could see no miracle even in the raising of Lazarus and
the feeding of the five thousand. The John Pontifexes would see no
miracle in this matter of the water from the Jordan. The essence of a
miracle lay not in the fact that means had been dispensed with, but in
the adoption of means to a great end that had not been available
without interference; and no one would suppose that Dr Jones would
have brought the water unless he had been directed. She would tell
this to Theobald, and get him to see it in the ... and yet perhaps it
would be better not. The insight of women upon matters of this sort
was deeper and more unerring than that of men. It was a woman and
not a man who had been filled most completely with the whole fullness
of the Deity. But why had they not treasured up the water after it was
used? It ought never, never, to have been thrown away, but it had
been. Perhaps, however, this too was for the best—they might have
been tempted to set too much store by it, and it might have become a
source of spiritual danger to them—perhaps even of spiritual pride—
the very sin of all others which she most abhorred. As for the channel
through which the Jordan had flowed to Battersby, that mattered not
more than the earth through which the river ran in Palestine itself. Dr
Jones was certainly wordly—very worldly; so, she regretted to feel had
been her father-in-law, though in a less degree; spiritual, at heart,
doubtless, and becoming more and more spiritual continually as he
grew older, still he was tainted with the world, till a very few hours,
probably, before his death, whereas she and Theobald had given up
all for Christ's sake. *They* were not worldly. At least Theobald was
not. She *had been* but she knew that that was all forgiven her now—all,
washed white in the blood of her dear, dear Redeemer. She was sure

she had grown in grace since she had left off eating things strangled and blood—this was as the washing in Jordan as against Abana and Pharpar rivers of Damascus. Her boy should never touch a strangled fowl nor a black pudding—that, at any rate, she could see to. He should have a coral from the neighbourhood of Joppa—there were coral insects on those coasts, so that the thing could easily be done with a little energy; she would write to Dr Jones about it, etc., etc. And so on for hours together day after day for years. Truly Mrs Theobald loved her child according to her lights with an exceeding great fondness, but the dreams she dreamed in sleep were sober realities in comparison with those she indulged in while awake.

When Ernest was in his second year, Theobald, as I have already said, began to teach him to read. He began to whip him two days after he had begun to teach him.

It was painful, as he said to Christina, but it was the only thing to do—and it was done. The child was puny, white and sickly, so they sent continually for the doctor who dosed him with calomel and James's powder. All was done in love, anxiety, timidity, stupidity and impatience. They were stupid in little things; and he that is stupid in little will be stupid also in much.

Presently old Mr Pontifex died, and then came the revelation of the little alteration he had made in his will simultaneously with his bequest to Ernest. It was rather hard to bear, especially as there was no way of conveying a bit of their minds to the testator now that he could no longer hurt them. As regards the boy himself anyone must see that the bequest would be an unmitigated misfortune to him. To leave him a small independence was perhaps the greatest injury which one could inflict upon a young man. It would cripple his energies, and deaden his desire for active employment. Many a youth was led into evil courses by the knowledge that on arriving at majority he would come into a few thousands. They might surely have been trusted to have their boy's interests at heart, and must be better judges of those interests than he, at twenty-one, could be expected to be: besides if Jonadab, the son of Rechab's father—or perhaps it might be simpler under the circumstances to say Rechab at once—if Rechab, then, had left handsome legacies to his grandchildren—why Jonadab might not have found those children so easy to deal with, etc. 'My dear,' said Theobald after having discussed the matter with Christina for the twentieth time, 'my dear, the only thing to guide and console us under misfortunes of this kind is to take refuge in practical work. I will go and pay a visit to Mrs Jones.'

On those days Mrs Jones would be told that her sins were all washed white, etc., a little sooner and a little more peremptorily, than on others.

I used to stay at Battersby for a day or two sometimes, while my godson and his brother and sister were children. I hardly know why I went, for Theobald and I grew yearly more and more apart, but one gets into grooves sometimes, and the supposed friendship between myself and the Pontifexes continued to exist, though it was now little more than rudimentary. My godson pleased me more than either of the other children, but he had not much of the buoyancy of childhood, and was more like a puny sallow little old man than I liked. The young people however were very ready to be friendly.

I remember Ernest and his brother hovered round me on the first day of one of these visits with their hands full of fading flowers, which they at length proffered me. On this I did what I suppose was expected, and enquired if there was a shop near where they could buy sweeties. They said there was, so I felt in my pockets, but only succeeded in finding twopence halfpenny in small money. This I gave them, and the youngsters aged four and three toddled off at once. Ere long they returned, and Ernest said, 'We can't get sweeties for all this money' (I felt rebuked, but no rebuke was intended); 'we can get sweeties for this,' and he added the halfpenny to the twopence. I suppose they had wanted a twopenny cake, or something like that. I was amused and left them to solve the difficulty their own way, being anxious to see what they would do.

Presently Ernest said, 'May we give you back this' (showing the halfpenny) 'and not give you back this and this' (showing the pence)? I assenting, they gave a sigh of relief and went on their way rejoicing. A few more presents of pence and small toys completed the conquest, and they then began to take me into their confidence.

They told me a good deal which I am afraid I ought not to have listened to. They said that if grandpapa had lived longer he would most likely have been made a lord, and that then papa would have been the honourable and reverend, but that grandpapa was now in heaven singing beautiful hymns with Grandmamma Allaby to Jesus

Christ, who was very fond of them; and that when Ernest was ill, his mamma had told him he need not be afraid of dying, for he would go straight to heaven, if only he would be sorry for having done his lessons so badly and vexed his dear papa, and if he would promise never, never to vex him any more; and that when he got to heaven Grandpapa and Grandmamma Allaby would meet him and he would be always with them, and they would be very good to him and teach him to sing ever such beautiful hymns, more beautiful by far than those which he was now so fond of, etc., etc.; but he did not wish to die, and was glad when he got better, for there were no kittens in heaven, and he did not think there were cowslips to make cowslip tea with.

Their mother was plainly disappointed in them. 'My children are none of them geniuses, Mr Overton,' she had said to me at breakfast one morning. 'They have fair abilities, and thanks to Theobald's tuition they are forward for their years, but they have nothing like genius: genius is a thing quite apart from this, is it not?'

Of course I said it was 'a thing quite apart from this,' but if my thoughts had been laid bare they would have appeared as 'Give me my coffee ma'am immediately and don't talk.' I have no idea what genius is, but so far as I can form any conception about it I should say it was a stupid word which cannot be too soon abandoned to scientific and literary *claqueurs*.

I do not know exactly what Christina expected but I should imagine it was something like this—'My children ought to be all geniuses because they are mine and Theobald's, and it is naughty of them not to be; but of course they cannot be so good and clever as Theobald and I were, and if they show signs of being so it will be naughty of them. Happily however they are not this, and yet it is very dreadful that they are not. As for genius—hoity-toity indeed, why a genius should turn intellectual somersaults as soon as it is born, and none of my children have yet been able to get into the newspapers. I will not have children of mine give themselves airs—it is enough for them that Theobald and I should do so.'

She did not know, poor woman, that the true greatness wears an invisible cloak, under cover of which it goes in and out among men without being suspected; if its cloak does not conceal it from itself always, and from others for many years, its greatness will ere long shrink to very ordinary dimensions. What, then, it may be asked is the good of being great? The answer is that you may understand greatness better in others whether alive or dead, and choose better company from these, and enjoy and understand that company better when you have chosen it—also that you may be able to give pleasure to the best people and live in the lives of those who are yet unborn. This, one would think, was substantial gain enough for greatness without its wanting to ride roughshod over us—not even when disguised as humility.

I was there on a Sunday, and observed the rigour with which the young people were taught to observe the Sabbath: they might not cut out things, nor use their paint box on a Sunday, and this they thought rather hard because their cousins the John Pontifexes might do these things. Their cousins might play with their toy train on Sunday, but though they had promised that they would run none but Sunday trains, all traffic had been prohibited. One treat only was allowed them—on Sunday evening they might choose their own hymns.

In the course of the evening they came into the drawing-room and as an especial treat were to sing some of their hymns to me instead of saying them, so that I might hear how nicely they sang. Ernest was to choose the first hymn and he chose one about some people who were to come to the sunset tree. I am no botanist, and do not know what kind of tree a sunset tree is, but the words began, 'Come, come, come; come to the sunset tree for the day is past and gone.' The tune was rather pretty and had taken Ernest's fancy, for he was unusually fond of music and had a sweet little child's voice which he liked using.

He was, however, very late in being able to sound a hard C or K, and instead of saying 'Come', he said 'tum, tum, tum'.

'Ernest,' said Theobald from the armchair in front of the fire where he was sitting with his hands folded before him, 'don't you think it would be very nice if you were to say "come" like other people, instead of "tum"?'

'I do say tum,' replied Ernest, meaning that he had said 'come'.

Theobald was always in a bad temper on Sunday evening. Whether it is that they are as much bored with the day as their neighbours, or whether they are tired, or whatever the cause may be, clergymen are seldom at their best on Sunday evening; I had already seen signs that evening that my host was cross, and was a little nervous at hearing Ernest say so promptly, 'I do say tum,' when his papa had said he did not say it as he should.

Theobald noticed the fact that he was being contradicted in a moment. He had been sitting in an armchair in front of the fire with his hands folded doing nothing, but he got up at once and went to the piano.

'No, Ernest, you don't,' he said; 'you say nothing of the kind, you say "tum" not "come". Now say "come" after me, as I do.'

'Tum,' said Ernest at once, 'is that better?' I have no doubt he thought it was, but it was not.

'Now, Ernest, you are not taking pains: you are not trying as you ought to do. It is high time you learned to say "come"; why Joey can say "come", can't you, Joey?'

'Yeth I can,' replied Joey promptly, and he said something which was not far off 'come'.

'There, Ernest, do you hear that? There's no difficulty about it nor shadow of difficulty. Now take your own time: think about it and say "come" after me.'

The boy remained silent for a few seconds and then said 'tum' again.

I laughed, but Theobald turned to me impatiently and said, 'Please do not laugh, Overton, it will make the boy think it does not matter, and it matters a great deal'; then turning to Ernest he said, 'Now, Ernest, I will give you one more chance, and if you don't say "come" I shall know that you are self-willed and naughty.'

He looked very angry and a shade came over Ernest's face, like that which comes upon the face of a puppy when it is being scolded without understanding why. The child saw well what was coming now, was frightened, and of course said 'tum' once more.

'Very well, Ernest,' said his father catching him angrily by the shoulder. 'I have done my best to save you, but if you will have it so you will,' and he lugged the little wretch out of the room crying by anticipation. A few minutes more and we could hear screams coming from the dining-room across the hall which separated the drawing-room from the dining-room, and knew that poor Ernest was being beaten.

'I have sent him up to bed,' said Theobald, as he returned to the drawing-room, 'and now, Christina, I think we will have the servants in to prayers,' and he rang the bell for them, red-handed as he was.

RICHARD GARNETT

The Demon Pope

'So you won't sell me your soul?' said the devil.

'Thank you,' replied the student, 'I had rather keep it myself, if it's all the same to you.'

'But it's not all the same to me. I want it very particularly. Come, I'll be liberal. I said twenty years. You can have thirty.'

The student shook his head.

'Forty!'

Another shake.

'Fifty!'

As before.

'Now,' said the devil, 'I know I'm going to do a foolish thing, but I cannot bear to see a clever, spirited young man throw himself away. I'll make you another kind of offer. We won't have any bargain at present, but I will push you on in the world for the next forty years. This day forty years I come back and ask you for a boon; not your soul, mind, or anything not perfectly in your power to grant. If you give it, we are quits; if not, I fly away with you. What say you to this?'

The student reflected for some minutes. 'Agreed,' he said at last.

Scarcely had the devil disappeared, which he did instantaneously, ere a messenger reined in his smoking steed at the gate of the University of Cordova (the judicious reader will already have remarked that Lucifer could never have been allowed inside a Christian seat of learning), and, inquiring for the student Gerbert, presented him with the Emperor Otho's nomination to the Abbacy of Bobbio, in consideration, said the document, of his virtue and learning, well-nigh miraculous in one so young. Such messengers were frequent visitors during Gerbert's prosperous career. Abbot, bishop, archbishop, cardinal, he was ultimately enthroned Pope on April 2, 999, and assumed the appellation of Silvester the Second.° It was then a general belief that the world would come to an end in the following year, a catastrophe which to many seemed the more imminent from the election of a chief pastor whose celebrity as a theologian, though not inconsiderable, by no means equalled his reputation as a necromancer.

The world, notwithstanding, revolved scatheless through the dreaded twelvemonth, and early in the first year of the eleventh century Gerbert was sitting peacefully in his study, perusing a book of magic. Volumes of algebra, astrology, alchemy, Aristotelian philosophy, and other such light reading filled his bookcase; and on a table stood an improved clock of his invention, next to his introduction of the Arabic numerals, his chief legacy to posterity. Suddenly a sound of wings was heard, and Lucifer stood by his side.

'It is a long time', said the fiend, 'since I have had the pleasure of seeing you. I have now called to remind you of our little contract, concluded this day forty years.'

'You remember', said Silvester, 'that you are not to ask anything exceeding my power to perform.'

'I have no such intention,' said Lucifer. 'On the contrary, I am about to solicit a favour which can be bestowed by you alone. You are Pope, I desire that you would make me a Cardinal.'

'In the expectation, I presume,' returned Gerbert, 'of becoming Pope on the next vacancy.'

'An expectation', replied Lucifer, 'which I may most reasonably entertain, considering my enormous wealth, my proficiency in intrigue, and the present condition of the Sacred College.'

'You would doubtless', said Gerbert, 'endeavour to subvert the foundations of the Faith, and, by a course of profligacy and licentiousness, render the Holy See odious and contemptible.'

'On the contrary,' said the fiend, 'I would extirpate heresy, and all learning and knowledge as inevitably tending thereunto. I would suffer no man to read but the priest, and confine his reading to his breviary. I would burn your books together with your bones on the first convenient opportunity. I would observe an austere propriety of conduct, and be especially careful not to loosen one rivet in the tremendous yoke I was forging for the minds and consciences of mankind.'

'If it be so,' said Gerbert, 'let's be off!'

'What!' exclaimed Lucifer, 'you are willing to accompany me to the infernal regions!'

'Assuredly, rather than be accessory to the burning of Plato and Aristotle, and give place to the darkness against which I have been contending all my life.'

'Gerbert,' replied the demon, 'this is arrant trifling. Know you not that no good man can enter my dominions? that, were such a thing possible, my empire would become intolerable to me, and I should be compelled to abdicate?'

'I do know it,' said Gerbert, 'and hence I have been able to receive your visit with composure.'

'Gerbert,' said the devil, with tears in his eyes, 'I put it to you—is this fair, is this honest? I undertake to promote your interests in the world; I fulfil my promise abundantly. You obtain through my instrumentality a position to which you could never otherwise have aspired. Often have I had a hand in the election of a Pope, but never before have I contributed to confer the tiara on one eminent for virtue and learning. You profit by my assistance to the full, and now take advantage of an adventitious circumstance to deprive me of my reasonable guerdon. It is my constant experience that the good people are much more slippery than the sinners, and drive much harder bargains.'

'Lucifer,' answered Gerbert, 'I have always sought to treat you as a gentleman, hoping that you would approve yourself such in return. I will not inquire whether it was entirely in harmony with this character to seek to intimidate me into compliance with your demand by threatening me with a penalty which you well knew could not be enforced. I will overlook this little irregularity, and concede even more than you have requested. You have asked to be a Cardinal. I will make you Pope——'

'Ha!' exclaimed Lucifer, and an internal glow suffused his sooty hide, as the light of a fading ember is revived by breathing upon it.

'For twelve hours,' continued Gerbert. 'At the expiration of that time we will consider the matter further; and if, as I anticipate, you are more anxious to divest yourself of the Papal dignity than you were to assume it, I promise to bestow upon you any boon you may ask within my power to grant, and not plainly inconsistent with religion or morals.'

'Done!' cried the demon. Gerbert uttered some cabalistic words, and in a moment the apartment held two Pope Silvesters, entirely indistinguishable save by their attire, and the fact that one limped slightly with the left foot.

'You will find the Pontifical apparel in this cupboard,' said Gerbert, and, taking his book of magic with him, he retreated through a masked door to a secret chamber. As the door closed behind him he chuckled, and muttered to himself, 'Poor old Lucifer! Sold again!'

If Lucifer was sold he did not seem to know it. He approached a large slab of silver which did duty as a mirror, and contemplated his personal appearance with some dissatisfaction.

'I certainly don't look half so well without my horns,' he soliloquized, 'and I am sure I shall miss my tail most grievously.'

A tiara and a train, however, made fair amends for the deficient appendages, and Lucifer now looked every inch a Pope. He was about to call the master of the ceremonies, and summon a consistory, when the door was burst open, and seven cardinals, brandishing poniards, rushed into the room.

'Down with the sorcerer!' they cried, as they seized and gagged him.

'Death to the Saracen!'

'Practises algebra, and other devilish arts!'

'Knows Greek!'

'Talks Arabic!'

'Reads Hebrew!'

'Burn him!'

'Smother him!'

'Let him be deposed by a general council,' said a young and inexperienced Cardinal.

'Heaven forbid!' said an old and wary one, *sotto voce*.

Lucifer struggled frantically, but the feeble frame he was doomed to inhabit for the next eleven hours was speedily exhausted. Bound and helpless, he swooned away.

'Brethren,' said one of the senior cardinals, 'it hath been delivered by the exorcists that a sorcerer or other individual in league with the demon doth usually bear upon his person some visible token of his infernal compact. I propose that we forthwith institute a search for this stigma, the discovery of which may contribute to justify our proceedings in the eyes of the world.'

'I heartily approve of our brother Anno's proposition,' said another, 'the rather as we cannot possibly fail to discover such a mark, if, indeed, we desire to find it.'

The search was accordingly instituted, and had not proceeded far ere a simultaneous yell from all the seven cardinals indicated that their investigation had brought more to light than they had ventured to expect.

The Holy Father had a cloven foot!

For the next five minutes the Cardinals remained utterly stunned, silent, and stupefied with amazement. As they gradually recovered their faculties it would have become manifest to a nice observer that the Pope had risen very considerably in their good opinion.

'This is an affair requiring very mature deliberation,' said one.

'I always feared that we might be proceeding too precipitately,' said another.

'It is written, "the devils believe",' said a third: 'the Holy Father, therefore, is not a heretic at any rate.'

'Brethren,' said Anno, 'this affair, as our brother Benno well remarks, doth indeed call for mature deliberation. I therefore propose that, instead of smothering his Holiness with cushions, as originally contemplated, we immure him for the present in the dungeon adjoining hereunto, and, after spending the night in meditation and prayer, resume the consideration of the business tomorrow morning.'

'Informing the officials of the palace', said Benno, 'that his Holiness has retired for his devotions, and desires on no account to be disturbed.'

'A pious fraud,' said Anno, 'which not one of the Fathers would for a moment have scrupled to commit.'

The Cardinals accordingly lifted the still insensible Lucifer, and bore him carefully, almost tenderly, to the apartment appointed for his detention. Each would fain have lingered in hopes of his recovery, but each felt that the eyes of his six brethren were upon him: and all, therefore, retired simultaneously, each taking a key of the cell.

Lucifer regained consciousness almost immediately afterwards. He had the most confused idea of the circumstances which had involved him in his present scrape, and could only say to himself that if they were the usual concomitants of the Papal dignity, these were by no means to his taste, and he wished he had been made acquainted with them sooner. The dungeon was not only perfectly dark, but horribly cold, and the poor devil in his present form had no latent store of infernal heat to draw upon. His teeth chattered, he shivered in every limb, and felt devoured with hunger and thirst. There is much probability in the assertion of some of his biographers that it was on this occasion that he invented ardent spirits; but, even if he did, the mere conception of a glass of brandy could only increase his sufferings. So the long January night wore wearily on, and Lucifer seemed likely to expire from inanition, when a key turned in the lock, and Cardinal Anno cautiously glided in, bearing a lamp, a loaf, half a cold roast kid, and a bottle of wine.

'I trust', he said, bowing courteously, 'that I may be excused any slight breach of etiquette of which I may render myself culpable from the difficulty under which I labour of determining whether, under present circumstances, "Your Holiness", or "Your Infernal Majesty" be the form of address most befitting me to employ.'

'Bub–ub–bub–boo,' went Lucifer, who still had the gag in his mouth.

'Heavens!' exclaimed the Cardinal, 'I crave your Infernal Holiness's forgiveness. What a lamentable oversight!'

And, relieving Lucifer from his gag and bonds, he set out the refection, upon which the demon fell voraciously.

'Why the devil, if I may so express myself,' pursued Anno, 'did not your Holiness inform us that you *were* the devil? Not a hand would then have been raised against you. I have myself been seeking all my life for the audience now happily vouchsafed me. Whence this mistrust of your faithful Anno, who has served you so loyally and zealously these many years?'

Lucifer pointed significantly to the gag and fetters.

'I shall never forgive myself', protested the Cardinal, 'for the part I have borne in this unfortunate transaction. Next to ministering to your Majesty's bodily necessities, there is nothing I have so much at heart as to express my penitence. But I entreat your Majesty to remember that I believed myself to be acting in your Majesty's interest by overthrowing a magician who was accustomed to send your Majesty upon errands, and who might at any time enclose you in a box, and cast you into the sea. It is deplorable that your Majesty's most devoted servants should have been thus misled.'

'Reasons of State,'° suggested Lucifer.

'I trust that they no longer operate,' said the Cardinal. 'However, the Sacred College is now fully possessed of the whole matter: it is therefore unnecessary to pursue this department of the subject further. I would now humbly crave leave to confer with your Majesty, or rather, perhaps, your Holiness, since I am about to speak of spiritual things, on the important and delicate point of your Holiness's successor. I am ignorant how long your Holiness proposes to occupy the Apostolic chair; but of course you are aware that public opinion will not suffer you to hold it for a term exceeding that of the pontificate of Peter. A vacancy, therefore, must one day occur; and I am humbly to represent that the office could not be filled by one more congenial than myself to the present incumbent, or on whom he could more fully rely to carry out in every respect his views and intentions.'

And the Cardinal proceeded to detail various circumstances of his past life, which certainly seemed to corroborate his assertion. He had not, however, proceeded far ere he was disturbed by the grating of another key in the lock, and had just time to whisper impressively, 'Beware of Benno,' ere he dived under a table.

Benno was also provided with a lamp, wine, and cold viands. Warned by the other lamp and the remains of Lucifer's repast that some colleague had been beforehand with him, and not knowing how many more might be in the field, he came briefly to the point as regarded the Papacy, and preferred his claim in much the same manner as Anno. While he was earnestly cautioning Lucifer against this Cardinal as one who could and would cheat the very Devil himself, another key turned in the lock, and Benno escaped under the table, where Anno immediately inserted his finger into his right eye. The little squeal consequent upon this occurrence Lucifer successfully smothered by a fit of coughing.

Cardinal No. 3, a Frenchman, bore a Bayonne ham, and exhibited the same disgust as Benno on seeing himself forestalled. So far as his requests transpired they were moderate, but no one knows where he would have stopped if he had not been scared by the advent of Cardinal No. 4. Up to this time he had only asked for an inexhaustible purse, power to call up the Devil *ad libitum*, and a ring of invisibility to allow him free access to his mistress, who was unfortunately a married woman.

Cardinal No. 4 chiefly wanted to be put into the way of poisoning Cardinal No. 5; and Cardinal No. 5 preferred the same petition as respected Cardinal No. 4.

Cardinal No. 6, an Englishman, demanded the reversion of the Archbishoprics of Canterbury and York, with the faculty of holding them together, and of unlimited non-residence. In the course of his harangue he made use of the phrase *non obstantibus*,° of which Lucifer immediately took a note.

What the seventh Cardinal would have solicited is not known, for he had hardly opened his mouth when the twelfth hour expired, and Lucifer, regaining his vigour with his shape, sent the Prince of the Church spinning to the other end of the room, and split the marble table with a single stroke of his tail. The six crouched and huddling Cardinals cowered revealed to one another, and at the same time enjoyed the spectacle of his Holiness darting through the stone ceiling, which yielded like a film to his passage, and closed up afterwards as if nothing had happened. After the first shock of dismay they unanimously rushed to the door, but found it bolted on the outside. There was no other exit, and no means of giving an alarm. In this emergency the demeanour of the Italian Cardinals set a bright example to their ultramontane colleagues. '*Bisogna pazienza*,'° they said, as they shrugged their shoulders. Nothing could exceed the mutual politeness of Cardinals Anno and Benno, unless that of the two who had sought to poison each other. The Frenchman was held to have gravely derogated from good manners by alluding to this circumstance, which had reached his ears while he was under the table: and the Englishman swore so outrageously at the plight in which he found himself that the Italians then and there silently registered a vow that none of his nation should ever be Pope, a maxim which, with one exception,° has been observed to this day.

Lucifer, meanwhile, had repaired to Silvester, whom he found arrayed in all the insignia of his dignity; of which, as he remarked, he thought his visitor had probably had enough.

'I should think so indeed,' replied Lucifer. 'But at the same time I feel myself fully repaid for all I have undergone by the assurance of the loyalty of my friends and admirers, and the conviction that it is needless for me to devote any considerable amount of personal attention to ecclesiastical affairs. I now claim the promised boon, which it will be in no way inconsistent with thy functions to grant, seeing that it is a work of mercy. I demand that the Cardinals be released, and that their conspiracy against thee, by which I alone suffered, be buried in oblivion.'

'I hoped you would carry them all off,' said Gerbert, with an expression of disappointment.

'Thank you,' said the Devil. 'It is more to my interest to leave them where they are.'

So the dungeon-door was unbolted, and the Cardinals came forth,

sheepish and crestfallen. If, after all, they did less mischief than
Lucifer had expected from them, the cause was their entire bewilderment by what had passed, and their utter inability to penetrate the
policy of Gerbert, who henceforth devoted himself even with osten-
tation to good works. They could never quite satisfy themselves
whether they were speaking to the Pope or to the Devil, and when
under the latter impression habitually emitted propositions which
Gerbert justly stigmatized as rash, temerarious, and scandalous. They
plagued him with allusions to certain matters mentioned in their
interviews with Lucifer, with which they naturally but erroneously
supposed him to be conversant, and worried him by continual nods
and titterings as they glanced at his nether extremities. To abolish this
nuisance, and at the same time silence sundry unpleasant rumours
which had somehow got abroad, Gerbert devised the ceremony of
kissing the Pope's feet,° which, in a grievously mutilated form,
endures to this day. The stupefaction of the Cardinals on discovering
that the Holy Father had lost his hoof surpasses all description, and
they went to their graves without having obtained the least insight into
the mystery.

LORD DE TABLEY

The Study of a Spider

From holy flower to holy flower
Thou weavest thine unhallowed bower.
The harmless dewdrops, beaded thin,
Ripple along thy ropes of sin.
Thy house a grave, a gulf thy throne
Affright the fairies every one.
Thy winding sheets are grey and fell,
Imprisoning with nets of hell
The lovely births that winnow by,
Winged sisters of the rainbow sky: 10
Elf-darlings, fluffy, bee-bright things,
And owl-white moths with mealy wings,

And tiny flies, as gauzy thin
As e'er were shut electrum in.°
These are thy death spoils, insect ghoul,
With their dear life thy fangs are foul.
Thou felon anchorite of pain
Who sittest in a world of slain.
Hermit, who tunest song unsweet
To heaving wing and writhing feet.   20

A glutton of creation's sighs,
Miser of many miseries.
Toper, whose lonely feasting chair
Sways in inhospitable air.
The board is bare, the bloated host
Drinks to himself toast after toast.
His lip requires no goblet brink,
But like a weasel must he drink.
The vintage is as old as time
And bright as sunset, pressed and prime.   30

Ah, venom mouth and shaggy thighs
And paunch grown sleek with sacrifice,
Thy dolphin back and shoulders round
Coarse-hairy, as some goblin hound
Whom a hag rides to sabbath on,
While shuddering stars in fear grow wan.
Thou palace priest of treachery,
Thou type of selfish lechery,
I break the toils around thy head
And from their gibbets take thy dead.   40

A Song of Faith Forsworn

Take back your suit.
It came when I was weary and distraught
With hunger. Could I guess the fruit you brought?
I ate in mere desire of any food,
Nibbled its edge and nowhere found it good.
Take back your suit.

Take back your love,
It is a bird poached from my neighbour's wood:
Its wings are wet with tears, its beak with blood.
'Tis a strange fowl with feathers like a crow: 10
Death's raven, it may be, for all we know.
Take back your love.

Take back your gifts.
False is the hand that gave them; and the mind
That planned them, as a hawk spread in the wind
To poise and snatch the trembling mouse below.
To ruin where it dares—and then to go.
Take back your gifts.

Take back your vows.
Elsewhere you trimmed and taught these lamps to burn;   20
You bring them stale and dim to serve my turn.
You lit those candles in another shrine,
Guttered and cold you offer them on mine.
Take back your vows.

Take back your words.
What is your love? Leaves on a woodland plain,
Where some are running and where some remain:
What is your faith? Straws on a mountain height
Dancing like demons on Walpurgis night.
Take back your words.   30

Take back your lies.
Have them again: they wore a rainbow face,
Hollow with sin and leprous with disgrace;
Their tongue was like a mellow turret bell
To toll hearts burning into wide-lipped hell.
Take back your lies.

Take back your kiss.
Shall I be meek, and lend my lips again
To let this adder daub them with his stain?
Shall I turn cheek to answer, when I hate?   40
You kiss like Judas in the garden gate!
Take back your kiss.

Take back delight,
A paper boat launched on a heaving pool
To please a child, and folded by a fool;
The wild elms roared: it sailed—a yard or more.
Out went our ship but never came to shore.
Take back delight.

Take back your wreath.
Has it done service on a fairer brow?
Fresh, was it folded round her bosom snow?
Her cast-off weed my breast will never wear:
Your word is 'love me'. My reply 'despair!'
Take back your wreath.

50

ALFRED LYALL

Studies at Delhi, 1876.
II.—Badminton.

Hardly a shot from the gate we stormed,
  Under the Moree battlement's shade;°
Close to the glacis our game was formed,°
  There had the fight been, and there we played.

Lightly the demoiselles tittered and leapt,
  Merrily capered the players all;
North, was the garden where Nicholson slept,°
  South, was the sweep of a battered wall.

Near me a Musalmán, civil and mild,
  Watched as the shuttlecocks rose and fell;
And he said, as he counted his beads and smiled,
  'God smite their souls to the depths of hell.'

10

SIR W. S. GILBERT

from *Patience*°

I

BUNTHORNE. It is a wild, weird, fleshly thing; yet very tender, very yearning, very precious. It is called, 'Oh, Hollow! Hollow! Hollow!'

PATIENCE. Is it a hunting song?

BUN. A hunting song? No, it is *not* a hunting song. It is the wail of the poet's heart on discovering that everything is commonplace. To understand it, cling passionately to one another and think of faint lilies. (*They do so, as he recites.*)

'OH, HOLLOW! HOLLOW! HOLLOW!'

What time the poet hath hymned
The writhing maid, lithe-limbed,
   Quivering on amaranthine asphodel,°
How can he paint her woes,
Knowing, as well he knows,
   That all can be set right with calomel?°

When from the poet's plinth°
The amorous colocynth°
   Yearns for the aloe, faint with rapturous thrills,°
How can he hymn their throes
Knowing, as well he knows,
   That they are only uncompounded pills?

Is it, and can it be,
Nature hath this decree,
   Nothing poetic in the world shall dwell?
Or that in all her works
Something poetic lurks,
   Even in colocynth and calomel?
           I cannot tell.

ANGELA. How purely fragrant!

SAPHIR. How earnestly precious!

DUKE. Well, it seems to me to be nonsense.
SAPH. Nonsense; yes, perhaps—but, oh, what precious nonsense!
ALL. Ah!

II
BUNTHORNE

Am I alone,
　　And unobserved? I am!
Then let me own
　　I'm an aesthetic sham!
This air severe
　　Is but a mere
　　　　Veneer
This cynic smile
　　Is but a wile
　　　　Of guile!
This costume chaste
　　Is but good taste
　　　　Misplaced!

　　Let me confess!
A languid love for lilies does *not* blight me!
Lank limbs and haggard cheeks do *not* delight me!
　　I do *not* care for dirty greens
　　　　By any means.
　　I do *not* long for all one sees
　　　　That's Japanese.
　　I am *not* fond of uttering platitudes
　　　　In stained-glass attitudes.
　　In short, my mediaevalism's affectation,
　　Born of a morbid love of admiration!

SONG

If you're anxious for to shine in the high aesthetic line as a man of
　　culture rare,
You must get up all the germs of the transcendental terms, and
　　plant them everywhere.
You must lie upon the daisies, and discourse in novel phrases of
　　your complicated state of mind,

The meaning doesn't matter if it's only idle chatter of a transcendental kind.
> And every one will say,
> As you walk your mystic way,

'If this young man expresses himself in terms too deep for *me*,
Why what a very singularly deep young man this deep young man must be!'

Be eloquent in praise of the very dull old days which have long since passed away,
And convince 'em, if you can, that the reign of good Queen Anne was Culture's palmiest day.°   10
Of course you will pooh-pooh whatever's fresh and new, and declare it's crude and mean,
 For Art stopped short in the cultivated court of the Empress Josephine.°
> And every one will say,
> As you walk your mystic way,

'If that's not good enough for him which is good enough for *me*,
Why what a very cultivated kind of youth this kind of youth must be!'

Then a sentimental passion of a vegetable fashion must excite your languid spleen,
An attachment *à la* Plato for a bashful young potato, or a not-too-French French bean!°
Though the Philistines may jostle, you will rank as an apostle in the high aesthetic band,°
If you walk down Piccadilly with a poppy or a lily in your mediaeval hand.°   20
> And every one will say,
> As you walk your flowery way,

'If he's content with a vegetable love, which would certainly not suit *me*,
Why what a most particularly pure young man this pure young man must be!'

At the end of his song PATIENCE *enters. He sees her.*

BUN. Ah! Patience, come hither. I am pleased with thee. The bitter-hearted one, who finds all else hollow, is pleased with thee. For you are not hollow. *Are* you?

PA. I beg your pardon—I interrupt you.

BUN. Life is made up of interruptions. The tortured soul, yearning for solitude, writhes under them. Oh, but my heart is a-weary! Oh, I am a cursed thing! Don't go.

PA. Really, I'm very sorry—

BUN. Tell me, girl, do you ever yearn?

PA. [*misunderstanding him*]. I earn my living.

BUN. [*impatiently*]. No, no! Do you know what it is to be heart-hungry? Do you know what it is to yearn for the Indefinable, and yet to be brought face to face, daily, with the Multiplication Table? Do you know what it is to seek oceans and to find puddles?—to long for whirlwinds and to have to do the best you can with the bellows? That's my case. Oh, I am a cursed thing!

PA. If you please, I don't understand you—you frighten me!

BUN. Don't be frightened—it's only poetry.

PA. If that's poetry, I don't like poetry.

BUN. [*eagerly*]. Don't you? [*Aside.*] Can I trust her? [*Aloud.*] Patience, you don't like poetry—well, between you and me, *I* don't like poetry. It's hollow, unsubstantial—unsatisfactory. What's the use of yearning for Elysian Fields when you know you can't get 'em, and would only let 'em out on building leases if you had 'em?

PA. Sir, I——

BUN. Don't go. Patience, I have long loved you—let me tell you a secret. I am not as bilious as I look. If you like I will cut my hair. There is more innocent fun within me than a casual spectator would imagine. You have never seen me frolicsome. Be a good girl—a very good girl—and you shall.

PA. Sir, I will speak plainly. In the matter of love I am untaught, I have never loved but my great-aunt. But I am quite certain that, under any circumstances, I couldn't possibly love *you*.

from *Iolanthe*

THE NIGHTMARE

When you're lying awake with a dismal headache, and repose is
taboo'd by anxiety,
I conceive you may use any language you choose to indulge in,
without impropriety;
For your brain is on fire—the bedclothes conspire of usual
slumber to plunder you:
First your counterpane goes, and uncovers your toes, and your
sheet slips demurely from under you;
Then the blanketing tickles—you feel like mixed pickles—so
terribly sharp is the pricking,
And you're hot, and you're cross, and you tumble and toss till
there's nothing 'twixt you and the ticking.

Then the bedclothes all creep to the ground in a heap, and you
pick 'em all up in a tangle;
Next your pillow resigns and politely declines to remain at its
usual angle!
Well, you get some repose in the form of a doze, with hot eye-
balls and head ever aching,
But your slumbering teems with such horrible dreams that you'd
very much better be waking;   10
For you dream you are crossing the Channel, and tossing about in
a steamer from Harwich—
Which is something between a large bathing machine and a very
small second-class carriage—
And you're giving a treat (penny ice and cold meat) to a party of
friends and relations—
They're a ravenous horde—and they all came on board at Sloane
Square and South Kensington Stations.
And bound on that journey you find your attorney (who started
that morning from Devon);
He's a bit undersized, and you don't feel surprised when he tells
you he's only eleven.

Well, you're driving like mad with this singular lad (by-the-bye
    the ship's now a four-wheeler),
And you're playing round games, and he calls you bad names
    when you tell him that 'ties pay the dealer';
But this you can't stand, so you throw up your hand, and you find
    you're as cold as an icicle,
In your shirt and your socks (the black silk with gold clocks),
    crossing Salisbury Plain on a bicycle: 20
And he and the crew are on bicycles too—which they've some-
    how or other invested in—
And he's telling the tars, all the particu*lars* of a company he's
    interested in—
It's a scheme of devices, to get at low prices, all goods from cough
    mixtures to cables
(Which tickled the sailors) by treating retailers, as though they
    were all vege*ta*bles—
You get a good spadesman to plant a small tradesman, (first take
    off his boots with a boot-tree),
And his legs will take root, and his fingers will shoot, and they'll
    blossom and bud like a fruit-tree—
From the greengrocer tree you get grapes and green pea,
    cauliflower, pineapple, and cranberries,
While the pastrycook plant, cherry brandy will grant, apple puffs,
    and three-corners, and banberries—
The shares are a penny, and ever so many are taken by Rothschild
    and Baring,
And just as a few are allotted to you, you awake with a shudder
    despairing—   30
You're a regular wreck, with a crick in your neck, and no wonder
    you snore, for your head's on the floor, and you've needles and
    pins from your soles to your shins, and your flesh is a-creep for
    your left leg's asleep, and you've cramp in your toes, and a fly
    on your nose, and some fluff in your lung, and a feverish
    tongue, and a thirst that's intense, and a general sense that you
    haven't been sleeping in clover;
But the darkness has passed, and it's daylight at last, and the
    night has been long—ditto ditto my song—and thank goodness
    they're both of them over!

ELLICE HOPKINS

Life in Death

I heard him in the autumn winds,
    I felt him in the cadent star,
And in the shattered mirror of the wave,
    That still in death a rapture finds,
    I caught his image faint and far;
And musing in the twilight on the grave,
    I heard his footstep stealing by,
    Where the long churchyard grasses sigh.

But never might I see his face,
    Though everywhere I found Death's hand,   10
And his large language all things living spake;
    And ever heavy with the grace
    Of bygone things through all the land
The song of birds or distant church-bells brake.
    'I will arise and seek his face,'
    I said, 'ere wrapped in his embrace.'

'For Death is king of life,' I cried,
    'Beauty is but his pomp and state;
His kiss is on the apple's crimson cheek,
    And with the grape his feet are dyed,   20
    Treading at noon the purple vat;
And flowers, more radiant hued, more quickly seek
    His face, betraying, in disguise
    Their young blooms are but autumn dyes.'

Then I arose ere dawn, and found
    A faded lily. 'Lo, 'tis He!
I will surprise him in his golden bed,
    Where, muffled close from light and sound,
    He sleeps the day up.' Noiselessly
I drew the faded curtains from his head,   30
    And, peeping, found, not Death below,
    But fairy life set all arow.

A chrysalis next I chanced upon:
  'Death in this dusty shroud has dwelt!'
But stooping saw a wingèd Thing, sun-kist,
  Crusted with jewels Life had won
  From Death's dim dust; and as I knelt,
Some passion shook the jewels into mist,
  Some ecstasy of coming flight,
  And lo, he passed in morning light.   40

And as I paced, still questioning,
  Behold, a dead bird at my feet;
The faded violets of his filmy eyes,
  And tender loosened throat, to sing
  No more to us his nocturns sweet,
Told me that death at length before me lies.
  But gazing, quick I turned in fear,
  Not Death, but teeming Life was there.

Then haply Death keeps house within?
  And with the scalpel of keen thought   50
I traced the chemic travail of the brain,
  The throb and pulse of Life's machine,
  And mystic force with force still caught
In the embrace that maketh one of twain;
  And all the beatings, swift and slow,
  Of Life's vibration to and fro.

And still I found the downward swing,
  Decay, but ere I cried 'Lo, here!'
The upward stroke rang out glad life and breath;
  And still dead winters changed with spring,   60
  And graves the new birth's cradle were;
And still I grasped the flying skirts of Death,
  And still he turned, and, beaming fair,
  The radiant face of Life was there!

Life's Cost

I could not at the first be born
But through another's bitter wailing pain;
Another's loss must be my sweetest gain,
And love, only to win that I might be,
      Must wet her couch forlorn
  With tears of blood and sweat of agony.

Since then I cannot live a week,
But some fair thing must leave the daisied dells,
The joy of pastures, bubbling springs and wells,
And grassy murmurs of its peaceful days,   10
      To bleed in pain, and reek,
  And die, for me to tread life's pleasant ways.

I cannot, sure, be warmed or lit,
But men must crouch and toil in tortuous caves
Bowed on themselves, while day and night in waves
Of blackness wash away their sunless lives;
      Or blasted and sore hit,
  Dark life to darker death the miner drives.

Naked, I cannot clothed be,
But worms must patient weave their satin shroud,   20
The sheep must shiver to the April cloud,
Yielding his one white coat to keep me warm;
      In shop and factory
  For me must weary toiling millions swarm.

With gems I deck not brow or hands,
But through the roaring dark of cruel seas
Some wretch, with shuddering breath and trembling knees,
Goes headlong, while the sea-sharks dodge his quest;
      Then at my door he stands,
  Naked, with bleeding ears and heaving chest.   30

I fall not on my knees and pray,
But God must come from heaven to fetch that sigh,
And piercèd Hands must bear it back on high;
And through His broken heart and cloven side
     Love makes an open way
  For me, who could not live but that He died.

    O awful sweetest life of mine,
That God and man both serve in blood and tears!
O prayers I breathe not but through other prayers!
O breath of life, compact of others' sighs!   40
     With this dread gift divine,
  Ah! whither go, what worthily devise?

    If on myself I dare to spend
This dreadful thing, in pleasure lapped and reared,
What am I but a hideous idol smeared
With human blood, that with its carven smile,
     Alike to foe and friend,
  Maddens the wretch who perishes the while?

    I will away and find my God,
And what I dare not keep, ask Him to take,   50
And, taking, Love's sweet sacrifice to make.
Then, like a wave, the sorrow and the pain
     High heaven with glory flood;
  For me, for them, for all, a splendid gain.

On a Dead Robin in a Church

What, dead, dear heart? thy throat, so dainty sweet,
  Limp as Long Purples of the meadow grass,
  Laid low and fading where the mowers pass;
             Thy pretty feet
Curled up, their tender trefoils shut beneath
                Chill dews of death.

Must never more against the wintry west
  Thy thin sweet song be heard beside our door,
  Piping of spring amid the branches hoar?
                Thy ruffled breast   10
Red as a russet beech-leaf in the sun,
               When day is done.

Many rude storms thou knew'st, thou tender thing,
  Many a roaring dark about thy bed,
  No stouter roof above thy harmless head
              Than thine own wing,
And God's great care for thee His little one,
            Who faileth none.

Yet here within this cool and silent place
  Thou need'st must find thy death where souls find life,   20
  And windless calms amid the tempests, strife,
             And heaven's own grace.
Our tenderest balms but bruise thy harmless head,
           And leave thee dead.

How was it, Dear? These jewelled panes o'erhead
  Didst take for the rich summer dawns divine,
  That filled those dark leaf lattices of thine
             With trembling red;
And flying upwards those strange splendours dread
           Did strike thee dead?   30

Or seemed these quaint carved figures, lying prone,
  Thine own dear babes grown old, and dead to fame,
  Grown old waiting a love that never came,
             And turned to stone?
Freezing thy life-blood in thy balmy breast
           With their cold rest.

Or didst thou recognize again the Woe,
  That erst thy pious breast did ruddy stain,
  And fling thyself against the pictured pane,
            In vain, nor know   40
But blessed beams now pierce those hands and side
           With ruby dyed?

Or broke thy heart alone for thy loved haunts,
 Thy daisies that one touch of crimson makes
 Akin with thee, thy meads, thy bosky brakes,
     And woodland chaunts?
All thy wide life of pastures, wood, and rosy sky,
     Left, here to die.

Couldst thou not stay and let us sing together?
 Thy world, that like a raindrop on a thorn   50
 No shadow casts, and our great world forlorn,
     That casteth ever
The shadow, Death, and in heaven's topmost height
     Behold, 'tis night.

Or did the golden throats that throb in thunder
 With man's great adoration and his pain,
 O'erpower thine, shatter thy simple strain,
     And break asunder
Thy glad child-hymns, and daisy-linkèd days,
     With vaster praise?   60

I know not; only that thy life was caught
 Within a vaster life that shut thee in
 With thunders and with lightnings, death and sin;
     And thou distraught
Didst dash thyself against that alien light,
     And die that night.

ALGERNON CHARLES SWINBURNE

In the Orchard°

(PROVENÇAL BURDEN)

Leave go my hands, let me catch breath and see,
Let the dew-fall drench either side of me;
 Clear apple-leaves are soft upon that moon
Seen sidelong like a blossom in the tree;
 Ah God, ah God, that day should be so soon.

The grass is thick and cool, it lets us lie.
Kissed upon either cheek and either eye,
    I turn to thee as some green afternoon
Turns toward sunset, and is loth to die;
    Ah God, ah God, that day should be so soon.   10

Lie closer, lean your face upon my side,
Feel where the dew fell that has hardly dried,
    Hear how the blood beats that went nigh to swoon;
The pleasure lives there when the sense has died;
    Ah God, ah God, that day should be so soon.

O my fair lord, I charge you leave me this:
Is it not sweeter than a foolish kiss?
    Nay take it then, my flower, my first in June,
My rose, so like a tender mouth it is:
    Ah God, ah God, that day should be so soon.   20

Love, till dawn sunder night from day with fire,
Dividing my delight and my desire,
    The crescent life and love the plenilune,°
Love me though dusk begin and dark retire;
    Ah God, ah God, that day should be so soon.

Ah, my heart fails, my blood draws back; I know,
When life runs over, life is near to go;
    And with the slain of love love's ways are strewn,°
And with their blood, if love will have it so;
    Ah God, ah God, that day should be so soon.   30

Ah, do thy will now; slay me if thou wilt;
There is no building now the walls are built,
    No quarrying now the corner-stone is hewn,
No drinking now the vine's whole blood is spilt;
    Ah God, ah God, that day should be so soon.

Nay, slay me now; nay, for I will be slain;
Pluck thy red pleasure from the teeth of pain,
    Break down thy vine ere yet grape-gatherers prune,
Slay me ere day can slay desire again;
    Ah God, ah God, that day should be so soon.   40

Yea, with thy sweet lips, with thy sweet sword; yea,
Take life and all, for I will die, I say;
  Love, I gave love, is life a better boon?
For sweet night's sake I will not live till day;
  Ah God, ah God, that day should be so soon.

Nay, I will sleep then only; nay, but go.
Ah sweet, too sweet to me, my sweet, I know
  Love, sleep, and death go to the sweet same tune;
Hold my hair fast, and kiss me through it so.
  Ah God, ah God, that day should be so soon. 50

Itylus°

Swallow, my sister, O sister swallow,
  How can thine heart be full of the spring?
    A thousand summers are over and dead.
What hast thou found in the spring to follow?
  What hast thou found in thine heart to sing?
    What wilt thou do when the summer is shed?

O swallow, sister, O fair swift swallow,
  Why wilt thou fly after spring to the south,
    The soft south whither thine heart is set?
Shall not the grief of the old time follow?   10
  Shall not the song thereof cleave to thy mouth?
    Hast thou forgotten ere I forget?

Sister, my sister, O fleet sweet swallow,
  Thy way is long to the sun and the south;
    But I, fulfilled of my heart's desire,
Shedding my song upon height, upon hollow,
  From tawny body and sweet small mouth
    Feed the heart of the night with fire.

I the nightingale all spring through,
  O swallow, sister, O changing swallow,   20
    All spring through till the spring be done,
Clothed with the light of the night on the dew,
  Sing, while the hours and the wild birds follow,
    Take flight and follow and find the sun.

Sister, my sister, O soft light swallow,
  Though all things feast in the spring's guest-chamber,
    How hast thou heart to be glad thereof yet?
For where thou fliest I shall not follow,
  Till life forget and death remember,
    Till thou remember and I forget.   30

Swallow, my sister, O singing swallow,
  I know not how thou hast heart to sing.
    Hast thou the heart? is it all past over?
Thy lord the summer is good to follow,
  And fair the feet of thy lover the spring:
    But what wilt thou say to the spring thy lover?

O swallow, sister, O fleeting swallow,
  My heart in me is a molten ember
    And over my head the waves have met.
But thou wouldst tarry or I would follow,   40
  Could I forget or thou remember,
    Couldst thou remember and I forget.

O sweet stray sister, O shifting swallow,
  The heart's division divideth us.
    Thy heart is light as a leaf of a tree;
But mine goes forth among sea-gulfs hollow
  To the place of the slaying of Itylus,
    The feast of Daulis, the Thracian sea.°

O swallow, sister, O rapid swallow,
  I pray thee sing not a little space.   50
    Are not the roofs and the lintels wet?
The woven web that was plain to follow,
  The small slain body, the flower-like face,
    Can I remember if thou forget?

O sister, sister, thy first-begotten!
  The hands that cling and the feet that follow,
    The voice of the child's blood crying yet
    Who hath remembered me? who hath forgotten?
  Thou hast forgotten, O summer swallow,
    But the world shall end when I forget.   60

A Leave-Taking

Let us go hence, my songs; she will not hear.
Let us go hence together without fear;
Keep silence now, for singing-time is over,
And over all old things and all things dear.
She loves not you nor me as we all love her.
Yea, though we sang as angels in her ear,
      She would not hear.

Let us rise up and part; she will not know.
Let us go seaward as the great winds go,
Full of blown sand and foam; what help is here?   10
There is no help, for all these things are so,
And all the world is bitter as a tear.
And how these things are, though ye strove to show,
      She would not know.

Let us go home and hence; she will not weep.
We gave love many dreams and days to keep,
Flowers without scent, and fruits that would not grow,
Saying, 'If thou wilt, thrust in thy sickle and reap.'
All is reaped now; no grass is left to mow;
And we that sowed, though all we fell on sleep,   20
      She would not weep.

Let us go hence and rest; she will not love.
She shall not hear us if we sing hereof,
Nor see love's ways, how sore they are and steep.
Come hence, let be, lie still: it is enough.
Love is a barren sea, bitter and deep;
And though she saw all heaven in flower above,
      She would not love.

Let us give up, go down; she will not care.
Though all the stars made gold of all the air,   30
And the sea moving saw before it move
One moon-flower making all the foam-flowers fair;
Though all those waves went over us, and drove
Deep down the stifling lips and drowning hair,
      She would not care.

Let us go hence, go hence; she will not see.
Sing all once more together; surely she,
She too, remembering days and words that were,
Will turn a little toward us, sighing; but we,
We are hence, we are gone, as though we had not been there.   40
Nay, and though all men seeing had pity on me,
      She would not see.

The Garden of Proserpine°

Here, where the world is quiet,
    Here, where all trouble seems
Dead winds' and spent waves' riot
    In doubtful dreams of dreams;
I watch the green field growing
For reaping folk and sowing,
For harvest-time and mowing,
    A sleepy world of streams.

I am tired of tears and laughter,
    And men that laugh and weep   10
Of what may come hereafter
    For men that sow to reap:
I am weary of days and hours,
Blown buds of barren flowers,°
Desires and dreams and powers
    And everything but sleep.

Here life has death for neighbour
    And far from eye or ear
Wan waves and wet winds labour,
    Weak ships and spirits steer;   20
They drive adrift, and whither
They wot not who make thither;°
But no such winds blow hither,
    And no such things grow here.

No growth of moor or coppice,
   No heather-flower or vine,
But bloomless buds of poppies,°
   Green grapes of Proserpine,
Pale beds of blowing rushes
Where no leaf blooms or blushes   30
Save this whereout she crushes
   For dead men deadly wine.

Pale, without name or number,
   In fruitless fields of corn,
They bow themselves and slumber
   All night till light is born;
And like a soul belated,
In hell and heaven unmated,
By cloud and mist abated
   Comes out of darkness morn.   40

Though one were strong as seven,
   He too with death shall dwell,
Nor wake with wings in heaven,
   Nor weep for pains in hell;
Though one were fair as roses,
His beauty clouds and closes;
And well though love reposes,
   In the end it is not well.

Pale, beyond porch and portal,
   Crowned with calm leaves, she stands   50
Who gathers all things mortal
   With cold immortal hands;
Her languid lips are sweeter
Than love's who fears to greet her
To men that mix and meet her
   From many times and lands.

She waits for each and other,
   She waits for all men born;
Forgets the earth her mother,

The life of fruits and corn;   60
And spring and seed and swallow
Take wing for her and follow
Where summer song rings hollow
    And flowers are put to scorn.

There go the loves that wither,
    The old loves with wearier wings:
And all dead years draw thither,
    And all disastrous things;
Dead dreams of days forsaken,
Blind buds that snows have shaken,   70
Wild leaves that winds have taken,
    Red strays of ruined springs.

We are not sure of sorrow,
    And joy was never sure;
To–day will die to–morrow;
    Time stoops to no man's lure;
And love, grown faint and fretful,
With lips but half regretful
Sighs, and with eyes forgetful
    Weeps that no loves endure.   80

From too much love of living,
    From hope and fear set free,
We thank with brief thanksgiving
    Whatever gods may be
That no life lives for ever;
That dead men rise up never;
That even the weariest river
    Winds somewhere safe to sea.

Then star nor sun shall waken,
    Nor any change of light: 90
Nor sound of waters shaken,
    Nor any sound or sight:
Nor wintry leaves nor vernal,
Nor days nor things diurnal;°
Only the sleep eternal
    In an eternal night.

from *Atalanta in Calydon*

When the hounds of spring are on winter's traces,
    The mother of months in meadow or plain°
Fills the shadows and windy places
    With lisp of leaves and ripple of rain;
And the brown bright nightingale amorous
Is half assuaged for Itylus,
For the Thracian ships and the foreign faces,
    The tongueless vigil, and all the pain.

Come with bows bent and with emptying of quivers,°
    Maiden most perfect, lady of light,   10
With a noise of winds and many rivers,
    With a clamour of waters, and with might;
Bind on thy sandals, O thou most fleet,
Over the splendour and speed of thy feet;
For the faint east quickens, the wan west shivers,
    Round the feet of the day and the feet of the night.

Where shall we find her, how shall we sing to her,
    Fold our hands round her knees, and cling?
O that man's heart were as fire and could spring to her,
    Fire, or the strength of the streams that spring!   20
For the stars and the winds are unto her
As raiment, as songs of the harp-player;
For the risen stars and the fallen cling to her,
    And the southwest-wind and the west-wind sing.

For winter's rains and ruins are over,
    And all the season of snows and sins;
The days dividing lover and lover,
    The light that loses, the night that wins;°
And time remembered is grief forgotten,
And frosts are slain and flowers begotten,   30
And in green underwood and cover
    Blossom by blossom the spring begins.

The full streams feed on flower of rushes,°
  Ripe grasses trammel a travelling foot,
The faint fresh flame of the young year flushes
  From leaf to flower and flower to fruit;
And fruit and leaf are as gold and fire,
And the oat is heard above the lyre,°
And the hoofèd heel of a satyr crushes
  The chestnut-husk at the chestnut-root.   40

And Pan by noon and Bacchus by night,
  Fleeter of foot than the fleet-foot kid,
Follows with dancing and fills with delight
  The Maenad and the Bassarid,°
And soft as lips that laugh and hide
The laughing leaves of the trees divide,
And screen from seeing and leave in sight
  The god pursuing, the maiden hid.

The ivy falls with the Bacchanal's hair°
  Over her eyebrows hiding her eyes;   50
The wild vine slipping down leaves bare
  Her bright breast shortening into sighs;
The wild vine slips with the weight of its leaves,
But the berried ivy catches and cleaves
To the limbs that glitter, the feet that scare
  The wolf that follows, the fawn that flies.

Ave Atque Vale

IN MEMORY OF CHARLES BAUDELAIRE

Nous devrions pourtant lui porter quelques fleurs;°
Les morts, les pauvres morts, ont de grandes douleurs,
Et quand Octobre souffle, émondeur des vieux arbres,
Son vent mélancolique à l'entour de leurs marbres,
Certes, ils doivent trouver les vivants bien ingrats.
                        Les Fleurs du Mal.

1

Shall I strew on thee rose or rue or laurel,°
    Brother, on this that was the veil of thee?°
    Or quiet sea-flower moulded by the sea,
Or simplest growth of meadow-sweet or sorrel,
    Such as the summer-sleepy Dryads weave,°
    Waked up by snow-soft sudden rains at eve?
Or wilt thou rather, as on earth before,
    Half-faded fiery blossoms, pale with heat
    And full of bitter summer, but more sweet
To thee than gleanings of a northern shore   10
    Trod by no tropic feet?°

2

For always thee the fervid languid glories
    Allured of heavier suns in mightier skies;
    Thine ears knew all the wandering watery sighs°
Where the sea sobs round Lesbian promontories,
    The barren kiss of piteous wave to wave
    That knows not where is that Leucadian grave
Which hides too deep the supreme head of song.
    Ah, salt and sterile as her kisses were,
    The wild sea winds her and the green gulfs bear   20
Hither and thither, and vex and work her wrong.
    Blind gods that cannot spare.

3

Thou sawest, in thine old singing season, brother,
    Secrets and sorrows unbeheld of us:
    Fierce loves, and lovely leaf-buds poisonous,
Bare to thy subtler eye, but for none other
    Blowing by night in some unbreathed-in clime;
    The hidden harvest of luxurious time,
Sin without shape, and pleasure without speech;
    And where strange dreams in a tumultuous sleep   30
    Make the shut eyes of stricken spirits weep;
And with each face thou sawest the shadow on each,
    Seeing as men sow men reap.°

4

O sleepless heart and sombre soul unsleeping,
    That were athirst for sleep and no more life
    And no more love, for peace and no more strife!
Now the dim gods of death have in their keeping
    Spirit and body and all the springs of song,
    Is it well now where love can do no wrong,
Where stingless pleasure has no foam or fang   40
    Behind the unopening closure of her lips?
    Is it not well where soul from body slips
And flesh from bone divides without a pang
    As dew from flower-bell drips?

5

It is enough; the end and the beginning
    Are one thing to thee, who art past the end.
    O hand unclasped of unbeholden friend,
For thee no fruits to pluck, no palms for winning,
    No triumph and no labour and no lust,
    Only dead yew-leaves and a little dust.   50
O quiet eyes wherein the light saith nought,
    Whereto the day is dumb, nor any night
    With obscure finger silences your sight,
Nor in your speech the sudden soul speaks thought,
    Sleep, and have sleep for light.

6

Now all strange hours and all strange loves are over,
    Dreams and desires and sombre songs and sweet,
    Hast thou found place at the great knees and feet
Of some pale Titan-woman like a lover,°
    Such as thy vision here solicited,   60
    Under the shadow of her fair vast head,
The deep division of prodigious breasts,
    The solemn slope of mighty limbs asleep,
    The weight of awful tresses that still keep
The savour and shade of old-world pine-forests
    Where the wet hill-winds weep?

7

Hast thou found any likeness for thy vision?
    O gardener of strange flowers, what bud, what bloom,
    Hast thou found sown, what gathered in the gloom?
What of despair, of rapture, of derision,   70
    What of life is there, what of ill or good?
    Are the fruits grey like dust or bright like blood?
Does the dim ground grow any seed of ours,
    The faint fields quicken any terrene root,
    In low lands where the sun and moon are mute
And all the stars keep silence? Are there flowers
    At all, or any fruit?

8

Alas, but though my flying song flies after,
    O sweet strange elder singer, thy more fleet
    Singing, and footprints of thy fleeter feet,   80
Some dim derision of mysterious laughter
    From the blind tongueless warders of the dead,°
    Some gainless glimpse of Proserpine's veiled head,°
Some little sound of unregarded tears
    Wept by effaced unprofitable eyes,
    And from pale mouths some cadence of dead sighs—
These only, these the hearkening spirit hears,
    Sees only such things rise.

9

Thou art far too far for wings of words to follow,
    Far too far off for thought or any prayer.   90
    What ails us with thee, who art wind and air?
What ails us gazing where all seen is hollow?
    Yet with some fancy, yet with some desire,
    Dreams pursue death as winds a flying fire,
Our dreams pursue our dead and do not find.
    Still, and more swift than they, the thin flame flies,
    The low light fails us in elusive skies,
Still the foiled earnest ear is deaf, and blind
    Are still the eluded eyes.

10

Not thee, O never thee, in all time's changes,   100
     Not thee, but this the sound of thy sad soul,
     The shadow of thy swift spirit, this shut scroll
I lay my hand on, and not death estranges
     My spirit from communion of thy song—
     These memories and these melodies that throng
Veiled porches of a Muse funereal—°
     These I salute, these touch, these clasp and fold
     As though a hand were in my hand to hold,
Or through mine ears a mourning musical
     Of many mourners rolled.   110

11

I among these, I also, in such station
     As when the pyre was charred, and piled the sods,
     And offering to the dead made, and their gods,
The old mourners had, standing to make libation,
     I stand, and to the gods and to the dead
     Do reverence without prayer or praise, and shed
Offering to these unknown, the gods of gloom,
     And what of honey and spice my seedlands bear,
     And what I may of fruits in this chilled air,
And lay, Orestes-like, across the tomb°   120
     A curl of severed hair.

12

But by no hand nor any treason stricken,
     Not like the low-lying head of Him, the King,°
     The flame that made of Troy a ruinous thing,
Thou liest, and on this dust no tears could quicken
     There fall no tears like theirs that all men hear
     Fall tear by sweet imperishable tear
Down the opening leaves of holy poets' pages.
     Thee not Orestes, not Electra mourns;
     But bending us-ward with memorial urns   130
The most high Muses that fulfil all ages
     Weep, and our God's heart yearns.

13

For, sparing of his sacred strength, not often
    Among us darkling here the lord of light°
    Makes manifest his music and his might
In hearts that open and in lips that soften
    With the soft flame and heat of songs that shine.
    Thy lips indeed he touched with bitter wine,
And nourished them indeed with bitter bread;
    Yet surely from his hand thy soul's food came,   140
    The fire that scarred thy spirit at his flame
Was lighted, and thine hungering heart he fed
    Who feeds our hearts with fame.

14

Therefore he too now at thy soul's sunsetting,
    God of all suns and songs, he too bends down
    To mix his laurel with thy cypress crown,°
And save thy dust from blame and from forgetting.
    Therefore he too, seeing all thou wert and art,
    Compassionate, with sad and sacred heart,
Mourns thee of many his children the last dead,   150
    And hallows with strange tears and alien sighs
    Thine unmelodious mouth and sunless eyes,
And over thine irrevocable head
    Sheds light from the under skies.

15

And one weeps with him in the ways Lethean,
    And stains with tears her changing bosom chill:
    That obscure Venus of the hollow hill,°
That thing transformed which was the Cytherean,
    With lips that lost their Grecian laugh divine
    Long since, and face no more called Erycine;°   160
A ghost, a bitter and luxurious god.
    Thee also with fair flesh and singing spell
    Did she, a sad and second prey, compel
Into the footless places once more trod,
    And shadows hot from hell.

16

And now no sacred staff shall break in blossom,°
    No choral salutation lure to light
    A spirit sick with perfume and sweet night
And love's tired eyes and hands and barren bosom.
    There is no help for these things; none to mend   170
    And none to mar; not all our songs, O friend,
Will make death clear or make life durable.
    Howbeit with rose and ivy and wild vine
    And with wild notes about this dust of thine
At least I fill the place where white dreams dwell
    And wreathe an unseen shrine.

17

Sleep; and if life was bitter to thee, pardon,
    If sweet, give thanks; thou hast no more to live;
    And to give thanks is good, and to forgive.
Out of the mystic and the mournful garden   180
    Where all day through thine hands in barren braid
    Wove the sick flowers of secrecy and shade,
Green buds of sorrow and sin, and remnants grey,
    Sweet-smelling, pale with poison, sanguine-hearted,
    Passions that sprang from sleep and thoughts that started,
Shall death not bring us all as thee one day
    Among the days departed?

18

For thee, O now a silent soul, my brother,°
    Take at my hands this garland, and farewell.
    Thin is the leaf, and chill the wintry smell,   190
And chill the solemn earth, a fatal mother,
    With sadder than the Niobean womb,
    And in the hollow of her breasts a tomb.
Content thee, howsoe'er, whose days are done;
    There lies not any troublous thing before,
    Nor sight nor sound to war against thee more,
For whom all winds are quiet as the sun,
    All waters as the shore.

A Forsaken Garden°

In a coign of the cliff between lowland and highland,°
   At the sea-down's edge between windward and lee,
Walled round with rocks as an inland island,
   The ghost of a garden fronts the sea.
A girdle of brushwood and thorn encloses
   The steep square slope of the blossomless bed
Where the weeds that grew green from the graves of its roses
      Now lie dead.

The fields fall southward, abrupt and broken,
   To the low last edge of the long lone land.   10
If a step should sound or a word be spoken,
   Would a ghost not rise at the strange guest's hand?
So long have the grey bare walks lain guestless,
   Through branches and briars if a man make way,
He shall find no life but the sea-wind's, restless
      Night and day.

The dense hard passage is blind and stifled
   That crawls by a track none turn to climb
To the strait waste place that the years have rifled
   Of all but the thorns that are touched not of time.   20
The thorns he spares when the rose is taken;
   The rocks are left when he wastes the plain.
The wind that wanders, the weeds wind-shaken,
      These remain.

Not a flower to be pressed of the foot that falls not;
   As the heart of a dead man the seed-plots are dry;
From the thicket of thorns whence the nightingale calls not,
   Could she call, there were never a rose to reply.
Over the meadows that blossom and wither
   Rings but the note of a sea-bird's song;   30
Only the sun and the rain come hither
      All year long.

The sun burns sere and the rain dishevels
   One gaunt bleak blossom of scentless breath.
Only the wind here hovers and revels
   In a round where life seems barren as death.
Here there was laughing of old, there was weeping,
   Haply, of lovers none ever will know,
Whose eyes went seaward a hundred sleeping
      Years ago.   40

Heart handfast in heart as they stood, 'Look thither,'
   Did he whisper? 'look forth from the flowers to the sea;
For the foam-flowers endure when the rose-blossoms wither,
   And men that love lightly may die—but we?'
And the same wind sang and the same waves whitened,
   And or ever the garden's last petals were shed,
In the lips that had whispered, the eyes that had lightened,
      Love was dead.

Or they loved their life through, and then went whither?
   And were one to the end—but what end who knows?   50
Love deep as the sea as a rose must wither,
   As the rose-red seaweed that mocks the rose.
Shall the dead take thought for the dead to love them?
   What love was ever as deep as a grave?
They are loveless now as the grass above them
      Or the wave.

All are at one now, roses and lovers,
   Not known of the cliffs and the fields and the sea.
Not a breath of the time that has been hovers
   In the air now soft with a summer to be.   60
Not a breath shall there sweeten the seasons hereafter
   Of the flowers or the lovers that laugh now or weep,
When as they that are free now of weeping and laughter
      We shall sleep.

Here death may deal not again for ever;
   Here change may come not till all change end.
From the graves they have made they shall rise up never,

Who have left nought living to ravage and rend.
Earth, stones, and thorns of the wild ground growing,
   While the sun and the rain live, these shall be;   70
Till a last wind's breath upon all these blowing
      Roll the sea.

Till the slow sea rise and the sheer cliff crumble,
   Till terrace and meadow the deep gulfs drink,
Till the strength of the waves of the high tides humble
   The fields that lessen, the rocks that shrink,
Here now in his triumph where all things falter,
   Stretched out on the spoils that his own hand spread,
As a god self-slain on his own strange altar,
      Death lies dead.   80

from *By the North Sea*°

1

Miles, and miles, and miles of desolation!
   Leagues on leagues on leagues without a change!
Sign or token of some eldest nation
   Here would make the strange land not so strange.
Time-forgotten, yea since time's creation,
   Seem these borders where the sea-birds range.

2

Slowly, gladly, full of peace and wonder
   Grows his heart who journeys here alone.
Earth and all its thoughts of earth sink under
   Deep as deep in water sinks a stone.   10
Hardly knows it if the rollers thunder,
   Hardly whence the lonely wind is blown.

3

Tall the plumage of the rush-flower tosses,
   Sharp and soft in many a curve and line
Gleam and glow the sea-coloured marsh-mosses

Salt and splendid from the circling brine.
Streak on streak of glimmering seashine crosses
    All the land sea-saturate as with wine.

4

Far, and far between, in divers orders,
    Clear grey steeples cleave the low grey sky;   20
Fast and firm as time-unshaken warders,
    Hearts made sure by faith, by hope made high.
These alone in all the wild sea-borders
    Fear no blast of days and nights that die.

5

All the land is like as one man's face is,
    Pale and troubled still with change of cares.
Doubt and death pervade her clouded spaces:
    Strength and length of life and peace are theirs;
Theirs alone amid these weary places,
    Seeing not how the wild world frets and fares.   30

6

Firm and fast where all is cloud that changes
    Cloud-clogged sunlight, cloud by sunlight thinned,
Stern and sweet, above the sand-hill ranges
    Watch the towers and tombs of men that sinned
Once, now calm as earth whose only change is
    Wind, and light, and wind, and cloud, and wind.

7

Out and in and out the sharp straits wander,
    In and out and in the wild way strives,
Starred and paved and lined with flowers that squander
    Gold as golden as the gold of hives,   40
Salt and moist and multiform: but yonder
    See, what sign of life or death survives?

8

Seen then only when the songs of olden
   Harps were young whose echoes yet endure,
Hymned of Homer when his years were golden,
   Known of only when the world was pure,
Here is Hades, manifest, beholden,
   Surely, surely here, if aught be sure!

9

Where the border-line was crossed, that, sundering
   Death from life, keeps weariness from rest,   50
None can tell, who fares here forward wondering;
   None may doubt but here might end his quest.
Here life's lightning joys and woes once thundering
   Sea-like round him cease like storm suppressed.

10

Here the wise wave-wandering steadfast-hearted
   Guest of many a lord of many a land
Saw the shape or shade of years departed,
   Saw the semblance risen and hard at hand,
Saw the mother long from love's reach parted,
   Anticleia, like a statue stand.°   60

11

Statue? nay, nor tissued image woven
   Fair on hangings in his father's hall;
Nay, too fast her faith of heart was proven,
   Far too firm her loveliest love of all;
Love wherethrough the loving heart was cloven,
   Love that hears not when the loud Fates call.

12

Love that lives and stands up re-created
   Then when life has ebbed and anguish fled;
Love more strong than death or all things fated,
   Child's and mother's, lit by love and led;   70
Love that found what life so long awaited
   Here, when life came down among the dead.

13

Here, where never came alive another,
  Came her son across the sundering tide
Crossed before by many a warrior brother
  Once that warred on Ilion at his side;
Here spread forth vain hands to clasp the mother
  Dead, that sorrowing for his love's sake died.

14

Parted, though by narrowest of divisions,
  Clasp he might not, only might implore,   80
Sundered yet by bitterest of derisions,
  Son, and mother from the son she bore—
Here? But all dispeopled here of visions
  Lies, forlorn of shadows even, the shore.

15

All too sweet such men's Hellenic speech is,
  All too fain they lived of light to see,
Once to see the darkness of these beaches,
  Once to sing this Hades found of me
Ghostless, all its gulfs and creeks and reaches,
  Sky, and shore, and cloud, and waste, and sea.   90

Oscar Wilde°

When Oscar came to join his God,
Not earth to earth, but sod to sod,
It was for sinners such as this
Hell was created bottomless.

The Higher Pantheism in a Nutshell°

One, who is not, we see: but one, whom we see not, is:
Surely this is not that: but that is assuredly this.

What, and wherefore, and whence? for under is over and under:
If thunder could be without lightning, lightning could be without
   thunder.

Doubt is faith in the main: but faith, on the whole, is doubt:
We cannot believe by proof: but could we believe without?

Why, and whither, and how? for barley and rye are not clover:
Neither are straight lines curves: yet over is under and over.

Two and two may be four: but four and four are not eight:
Fate and God may be twain: but God is the same thing as fate.

Ask a man what he thinks, and get from a man what he feels:
God, once caught in the fact, shows you a fair pair of heels.

Body and spirit are twins: God only knows which is which:
The soul squats down in the flesh, like a tinker drunk in a ditch.

More is the whole than a part: but half is more than the whole:
Clearly, the soul is the body: but is not the body the soul?

One and two are not one: but one and nothing is two:
Truth can hardly be false, if falsehood cannot be true.

Once the mastodon was: pterodactyls were common as cocks:
Then the mammoth was God: now is He a prize ox.

Parallels all things are: yet many of these are askew:
You are certainly I: but certainly I am not you.

Springs the rock from the plain, shoots the stream from the rock:
Cocks exist for the hen: but hens exist for the cock.

God, whom we see not, is: and God, who is not, we see:
Fiddle, we know, is diddle: and diddle, we take it, is dee.

The Ballad of Villon and Fat Madge°

'''Tis no sin for a man to labour in his vocation.' Falstaff
'The night cometh, when no man can work.'

What though the beauty I love and serve be cheap,
    Ought you to take me for a beast or fool?
All things a man could wish are in her keep;
    For her I turn swashbuckler in love's school.
    When folk drop in, I take my pot and stool
And fall to drinking with no more ado.
I fetch them bread, fruit, cheese, and water, too;
    I say all's right so long as I'm well paid;
'Look in again when your flesh troubles you.
    Inside this brothel where we drive our trade.'   10

But soon the devil's among us flesh and fell,
    When penniless to bed comes Madge my whore;
I loathe the very sight of her like hell.
    I snatch gown, girdle, surcoat, all she wore,
    And tell her, these shall stand against her score.
She grips her hips with both hands, cursing God,
Swearing by Jesus' body, bones, and blood,
    That they shall not. Then I, no whit dismayed,
Cross her cracked nose with some stray shiver of wood
    Inside this brothel where we drive our trade.   20

When all's made up she drops me a windy word,
    Bloat like a beetle puffed and poisonous:
Grins, thumps my pate, and calls me dickey-bird,
    And cuffs me with a fist that's ponderous.
    We sleep like logs, being drunken both of us;
Then when we wake her womb begins to stir;
To save her seed she gets me under her
    Wheezing and whining, flat as planks are laid:
And thus she spoils me for a whoremonger
    Inside this brothel where we drive our trade.   30

Blow, hail or freeze, I've bread here baked rent free!
Whoring's my trade, and my whore pleases me;
   Bad cat, bad rat; we're just the same if weighed.
We that love filth, filth follows us, you see;
Honour flies from us, as from her we flee
   Inside this brothel where we drive our trade.

I bequeath likewise to fat Madge
   This little song to learn and study;
By God's head she's a sweet fat fadge,
   Devout and soft of flesh and ruddy;   40
   I love her with my soul and body,
So doth she me, sweet dainty thing.
   If you fall in with such a lady,
Read it, and give it her to sing.

WALTER PATER

A Prince of Court Painters°

EXTRACTS FROM AN OLD FRENCH JOURNAL

VALENCIENNES, September 1701.

They have been renovating my father's large workroom. That delightful, tumble-down old place has lost its moss-grown tiles and the green
weather-stains we have known all our lives on the high whitewashed
wall, opposite which we sit, in the little sculptor's yard, for the
coolness, in summertime. Among old Watteau's workpeople came his
son, 'the genius', my father's godson and namesake, a dark-haired
youth, whose large, unquiet eyes seemed perpetually wandering to the
various drawings which lie exposed here. My father will have it that he
is a genius indeed, and a painter born. We have had our September
Fair in the Grande Place, a wonderful stir of sound and colour in the
wide, open space beneath our windows. And just where the crowd was
busiest young Antony was found, hoisted into one of those empty
niches of the old Hôtel de Ville, sketching the scene to the life, but
with a kind of grace—a marvellous tact of omission, as my father

pointed out to us, in dealing with the vulgar reality seen from one's own window—which has made trite old Harlequin, Clown, and Columbine, seem like people in some fairyland; or like infinitely clever tragic actors, who, for the humour of the thing, have put on motley for once, and are able to throw a world of serious innuendo into their burlesque looks, with a sort of comedy which shall be but tragedy seen from the other side. He brought his sketch to our house to-day, and I was present when my father questioned him and commended his work. But the lad seemed not greatly pleased, and left untasted the glass of old Malaga which was offered to him. His father will hear nothing of educating him as a painter. Yet he is not ill-to-do, and has lately built himself a new stone house, big and grey and cold. Their old plastered house with the black timbers, in the Rue des Cardinaux, was prettier; dating from the time of the Spaniards, and one of the oldest in Valenciennes.

October 1701.

Chiefly through the solicitations of my father, old Watteau has consented to place Antony with a teacher of painting here. I meet him betimes on the way to his lessons, as I return from Mass, for he still works with the masons, but making the most of late and early hours, of every moment of liberty. And then he has the feast-days, of which there are so many in this old-fashioned place. Ah! such gifts as his, surely, may once in a way make much industry seem worth while. He makes a wonderful progress. And yet, far from being set-up, and too easily pleased with what, after all, comes to him so easily, he has, my father thinks, too little self-approval for ultimate success. He is apt, in truth, to fall out too hastily with himself and what he produces. Yet here also there is the 'golden mean'. Yes! I could fancy myself offended by a sort of irony which sometimes crosses the half-melancholy sweetness of manner habitual with him; only that as I can see, he treats himself to the same quality.

October 1701.

Antony Watteau comes here often now. It is the instinct of a natural fineness in him, to escape when he can from that blank stone house, with so little to interest, and that homely old man and woman. The rudeness of his home has turned his feeling for even the simpler graces of life into a physical want, like hunger or thirst, which might come to greed; and methinks he perhaps overvalues these things. Still, made as he is, his hard fate in that rude place must needs touch one. And then, he profits by the experience of my father, who has much knowledge in matters of art beyond his own art of sculpture; and Antony is not unwelcome to him. In these last rainy weeks especially, when he can't sketch out of doors, when the wind only half dries the pavement before another torrent comes, and people stay at home, and the only sound from without is the creaking of a restless shutter on its hinges, or the march across the Place of those weary soldiers, coming and going so interminably, one hardly knows whether to or from battle with the English and the Austrians, from victory or defeat—Well! he has become like one of our family. 'He will go far!' my father declares. He would go far, in the literal sense, if he might—to Paris, to Rome. It must be admitted that our Valenciennes is a quiet, nay! a sleepy place; sleepier than ever since it became French, and ceased to be so near the frontier. The grass is growing deep on our old ramparts, and it is pleasant to walk there—to walk there and muse; pleasant for a tame, unambitious soul such as mine.

December 1702.

Antony Watteau left us for Paris this morning. It came upon us quite suddenly. They amuse themselves in Paris. A scene-painter we have here, well known in Flanders, has been engaged to work in one of the Parisian playhouses; and young Watteau, of whom he had some slight knowledge, has departed in his company. He doesn't know it was I who persuaded the scene-painter to take him; that he would find the lad useful. We offered him our little presents—fine thread-lace of our own making for his ruffles, and the like; for one must make a figure in Paris, and he is slim and well-formed. For myself, I presented him with a silken purse I had long ago embroidered for another. Well! we shall follow his fortunes (of which I for one feel quite sure) at a distance. Old Watteau didn't know of his departure, and has been here in great anger.

December 1703.

Twelve months to-day since Antony went to Paris! The first struggle must be a sharp one for an unknown lad in that vast, overcrowded place, even if he be as clever as young Antony Watteau. We may think, however, that he is on the way to his chosen end, for he returns not home; though, in truth, he tells those poor old people very little of himself. The apprentices of the M. Métayer for whom he works, labour all day long, each at a single part only—*coiffure*, or robe, or hand—of the cheap pictures of religion or fantasy he exposes for sale at a low price along the footways of the Pont Notre-Dame. Antony is already the most skilful of them, and seems to have been promoted of late to work on church pictures. I like the thought of that. He receives three *livres* a week for his pains, and his soup daily.

May 1705.

Antony Watteau has parted from the dealer in pictures *à bon marché*, and works now with a painter of furniture pieces (those headpieces for doors and the like, now in fashion) who is also *concierge* of the Palace of the Luxembourg. Antony is actually lodged somewhere in that grand place, which contains the king's collection of the Italian pictures he would so willingly copy. Its gardens also are magnificent, with something, as we understand from him, altogether of a novel kind in their disposition and embellishment. Ah! how I delight myself, in fancy at least, in those beautiful gardens, freer and trimmed less stiffly than those of other royal houses. Methinks I see him there, when his long summerday's work is over, enjoying the cool shade of the stately, broad-foliaged trees, each of which is a great courtier, though it has its way almost as if it belonged to that open and unbuilt country beyond, over which the sun is sinking.

His thoughts, however, in the midst of all this, are not wholly away from home, if I may judge by the subject of a picture he hopes to sell for as much as sixty *livres*— *Un Départ de Troupes*,° Soldiers Departing—one of those scenes of military life one can study so well here at Valenciennes.

June 1705.

Young Watteau has returned home—proof, with a character so independent as his, that things have gone well with him; and (it is agreed!) stays with us, instead of in the stonemason's house. The old people suppose he comes to us for the sake of my father's instruction. French people as we are become, we are still old Flemish, if not at heart, yet on the surface. Even in *French* Flanders, at Douai and Saint Omer, as I understand, in the churches and in people's houses, as may be seen from the very streets, there is noticeable a minute and scrupulous air of care-taking and neatness. Antony Watteau remarks this more than ever on returning to Valenciennes, and savours greatly, after his lodging in Paris, our Flemish cleanliness, lover as he is of distinction and elegance. Those worldly graces he seemed when a young lad almost to hunger and thirst for, as though truly the mere adornments of life were its necessaries, he already takes as if he had been always used to them. And there is something noble—shall I say?—in his half-disdainful way of serving himself with what he still, as I think, secretly values over-much. There is an air of seemly thought—*le bel sérieux*—about him, which makes me think of one of those grave old Dutch statesmen in their youth, such as that famous William the Silent.° And yet the effect of this first success of his (of more importance than its mere money value, as insuring for the future the full play of his natural powers) I can trace like the bloom of a flower upon him; and he has, now and then, the gaieties which from time to time, surely, must refresh all true artists, however hardworking and 'painful'.

July 1705.

The charm of all this—his physiognomy and manner of being—has touched even my young brother, Jean-Baptiste. He is greatly taken with Antony, clings to him almost too attentively, and will be nothing but a painter, though my father would have trained him to follow his own profession. It may do the child good. He needs the expansion of some generous sympathy or sentiment in that close little soul of his, as I have thought, watching sometimes how this small face and hands are moved in sleep. A child of ten who cares only to save and possess, to hoard his tiny savings! Yet he is not otherwise selfish, and loves us all with a warm heart. Just now it is the moments of Antony's company he counts, like a little miser. Well! that may save him perhaps from developing a certain meanness of character I have sometimes feared for him.

August 1705.

We returned home late this summer evening—Antony Watteau, my father and sisters, young Jean-Baptiste, and myself—from an excur-

sion to Saint-Amand, in celebration of Antony's last day with us.
After visiting the great abbey-church and its range of chapels, with
their costly encumbrance of carved shrines and golden reliquaries and
funeral scutcheons in the coloured glass, half seen through a rich
enclosure of marble and brasswork, we supped at the little inn in the
forest. Antony, looking well in his new-fashioned, long-skirted coat,
and taller than he really is, made us bring our cream and wild
strawberries out of doors, ranging ourselves according to his judgment
(for a hasty sketch in that big pocket-book he carries) on the soft slope
of one of those fresh spaces in the wood, where the trees unclose a
little, while Jean-Baptiste and my youngest sister danced a minuet on
the grass, to the notes of some strolling lutanist who had found us out.
He is visibly cheerful at the thought of his return to Paris, and became
for a moment freer and more animated than I have ever yet seen him,
as he discoursed to us about the paintings of Peter Paul Rubens in the
church here. His words, as he spoke of them, seemed full of a kind of
rich sunset with some moving glory within it. Yet I like far better than
any of these pictures of Rubens a work of that old Dutch master, Peter
Porbus,° which hangs, though almost out of sight indeed, in our
church at home. The patron saints, simple, and standing firmly on
either side, present two homely old people to Our Lady enthroned in
the midst, with the look and attitude of one for whom, amid her
'glories' (depicted in dim little circular pictures, set in the openings of
a chaplet of pale flowers around her) all feelings are over, except a
great pitifulness. Her robe of shadowy blue suits my eyes better far
than the hot flesh-tints of the Medicean ladies of the great Peter Paul,
in spite of that amplitude and royal ease of action under their stiff
court costumes, at which Antony Watteau declares himself in dismay.

August 1705.

I am just returned from early Mass. I lingered long after the office was
ended, watching, pondering how in the world one could help a small
bird which had flown into the church but could find no way out again.
I suspect it will remain there, fluttering round and round distractedly,
far up under the arched roof, till it dies exhausted. I seem to have
heard of a writer° who likened man's life to a bird passing just once
only, on some winter night, from window to window, across a
cheerfully-lighted hall. The bird, taken captive by the ill-luck of a

moment, re-tracing its issueless circle till it expires within the close vaulting of that great stone church—human life may be like that bird too!

Antony Watteau returned to Paris yesterday. Yes!—Certainly, great heights of achievement would seem to lie before him; access to regions whither one may find it increasingly hard to follow him even in imagination, and figure to one's self after what manner his life moves therein.

January 1709.

Antony Watteau has competed for what is called the *Prix de Rome*, desiring greatly to profit by the grand establishment founded at Rome by King Lewis the Fourteenth, for the encouragement of French artists. He obtained only the second place, but does not renounce his desire to make the journey to Italy. Could I save enough by careful economies for that purpose? It might be conveyed to him in some indirect way that would not offend.

February 1712.

We read, with much pleasure for all of us, in the *Gazette* to-day, among other events of the great world, that Antony Watteau had been elected to the Academy of Painting under the new title of *Peintre des Fêtes Galantes*, and had been named also *Peintre du Roi*. My brother, Jean-Baptiste, ran to tell the news to old Jean-Philippe and Michelle Watteau.

A new manner of painting! The old furniture of people's rooms must needs be changed throughout, it would seem, to accord with this painting; or rather, the painting is designed exclusively to suit one particular kind of apartment. A manner of painting greatly prized, as we understand, by those Parisian judges who have had the best opportunity of acquainting themselves with whatever is most enjoyable in the arts—such is the achievement of the young Watteau! He looks to receive more orders for his work than he will be able to execute. He will certainly relish—he, so elegant, so hungry for the colours of life—a free intercourse with those wealthy lovers of the arts, M. de Crozat, M. de Julienne, the Abbé de la Roque, the Count de Caylus, and M. Gersaint, the famous dealer in pictures, who are so anxious to lodge him in their fine *hôtels*, and to have him of their company at their country houses. Paris, we hear, has never been wealthier and more luxurious than now: and the great ladies outbid each other to carry his work upon their very fans. Those vast fortunes, however, seem to change hands very rapidly. And Antony's new manner? I am unable even to divine it—to conceive the trick and effect of it—at all. Only, something of lightness and coquetry I discern there, at variance, methinks, with his own singular gravity and even sadness of mien and mind, more answerable to the stately apparelling of the age of Henry the Fourth, or of Lewis the Thirteenth, in these old, sombre Spanish houses of ours.

March 1713.

We have all been very happy—Jean-Baptiste as if in a delightful dream. Antony Watteau, being consulted with regard to the lad's training as a painter, has most generously offered to receive him for his own pupil. My father, for some reason unknown to me, seemed to hesitate at the first; but Jean-Baptiste, whose enthusiasm for Antony visibly refines and beautifies his whole nature, has won the necessary permission, and this dear young brother will leave us tomorrow. Our regrets and his, at his parting from us for the first time, overtook our joy at his good fortune by surprise, at the last moment, just as we were about to bid each other goodnight. For a while there had seemed to be an uneasiness under our cheerful talk, as if each one present were concealing something with an effort; and it was Jean-Baptiste himself who gave way at last. And then we sat down again, still together, and allowed free play to what was in our hearts, almost till morning, my sisters weeping much. I know better how to control myself. In a few days that delightful new life will have begun for him: and I have made him promise to write often to us. With how small a part of my whole life shall I really be living at Valenciennes.

January 1714.

Jean-Philippe Watteau has received a letter from his son to-day. Old Michelle Watteau, whose sight is failing, though she still works (half by touch, indeed) at her pillow-lace, was glad to hear me read the letter aloud more than once. It recounts—how modestly, and almost as a matter of course!—his late successes. And yet!—does he, in writing to these old people, purposely underrate his great good fortune and seeming happiness, not to shock them too much by the contrast between the delicate enjoyments of the life he now leads among the wealthy and refined, and that bald existence of theirs in his old home? A life, agitated, exigent, unsatisfying! That is what this letter really discloses, below so attractive a surface. As his gift expands so does that incurable restlessness one supposed but the humour natural to a promising youth who had still everything to do. And now the only realized enjoyment he has of all this might seem to be the thought of the independence it has purchased him, so that he can escape from one lodging-place to another, just as it may please him. He has already deserted, somewhat incontinently, more than one of those fine houses, the liberal air of which he used so greatly to affect, and which have so readily received him. Has he failed truly to grasp the fact of his great success and the rewards that lie before him? At all events, he seems, after all, not greatly to value that dainty world he is now privileged to enter, and has certainly but little relish for his own works—those works which I for one so thirst to see.

March 1714.

We were all—Jean-Philippe, Michelle Watteau, and ourselves—half in expectation of a visit from Antony; and to-day, quite suddenly, he is with us. I was lingering after early Mass this morning in the church of Saint Vaast. It is good for me to be there. Our people lie under one of the great marble slabs before the *jubé*,° some of the memorial brass ballusters of which are engraved with their names and the dates of their decease. The settle of carved oak which runs all round the wide nave is my father's own work. The quiet spaciousness of the place is itself like a meditation, an 'act of recollection', and clears away the confusions of the heart. I suppose the heavy droning of the *carillon* had smothered the sound of his footsteps, for on my turning round, when I supposed myself alone, Antony Watteau was standing near me. Constant observer as he is of the lights and shadows of things, he visits places of this kind at odd times. He has left Jean-Baptiste at work in Paris, and will stay this time with the old people, not at our house; though he has spent the better part of to-day in my father's workroom. He hasn't yet put off, in spite of all his late intercourse with the great world, his distant and preoccupied manner—a manner, it is true, the same to every one. It is certainly not through pride in his success, as some might fancy, for he was thus always. It is rather as if, with all that success, life and its daily social routine were somewhat of a burden to him.

April 1714.

At last we shall understand something of that new style of his—the *Watteau* style—so much relished by the fine people at Paris. He has taken it into his kind head to paint and decorate our chief *salon*—the room with the three long windows, which occupies the first floor of the house.

The room was a landmark, as we used to think, an inviolable milestone and landmark, of old Valenciennes fashion—that sombre style, indulging much in contrasts of black or deep brown with white, which the Spaniards left behind them here. Doubtless their eyes had found its shadows cool and pleasant, when they shut themselves in from the cutting sunshine of their own country. But in our country, where we must needs economize not the shade but the sun, its grandiosity weighs a little on one's spirits. Well! the rough plaster we used to cover as well as might be with morsels of old figured arras-work, is replaced by dainty panelling of wood, with mimic columns, and a quite aerial scrollwork around sunken spaces of a pale-rose stuff and certain oval openings—two over the doors, opening on each side of the great couch which faces the windows, one over the chimney-piece, and one above the buffet which forms its *vis-à-vis*—four spaces in all, to be filled by and by with 'fantasies' of the Four Seasons, painted by his own hand. He will send us from Paris arm-chairs of a new pattern he has devised, suitably covered, and a painted *clavecin*. Our old silver candlesticks look well on the chimney-piece. Odd, faint-coloured flowers fill coquettishly the little empty spaces here and there, like ghosts of nosegays left by visitors long ago, which paled thus, sympathetically, at the decease of their old owners; for, in spite of its new-fashionedness, all this array is really less like a new thing than the last surviving result of all the more lightsome adornments of past times. Only, the very walls seem to cry out—No! to make delicate insinuation, for a music, a conversation, nimbler than any we have known, or are likely to find here. For himself, he converses well, but very sparingly. He assures us, indeed, that the 'new style' is in truth a thing of old days, of his own old days here in Valenciennes, when, working long hours as a mason's boy, he in fancy reclothed the walls of

this or that house he was employed in, with this fairy arrangement—
itself like a piece of 'chamber-music', methinks, part answering to
part; while no too trenchant note is allowed to break through the
delicate harmony of white and pale red and little golden touches. Yet
it is all very comfortable also, it must be confessed; with an elegant
open place for the fire, instead of the big old stove of brown tiles. The
ancient, heavy furniture of our grandparents goes up, with difficulty,
into the garrets, much against my father's inclination. To reconcile
him to the change, Antony is painting his portrait in a vast *perruque*,
and with more vigorous massing of light and shadow than he is wont
to permit himself.

June 1714.

He has completed the ovals—The Four Seasons. Oh! the summerlike
grace, the freedom and softness, of the 'Summer'—a hayfield such as
we visited to–day, but boundless, and with touches of level Italian
architecture in the hot, white, elusive distance, and wreaths of flowers,
fairy hayrakes and the like, suspended from tree to tree, with that
wonderful lightness which is one of the charms of his work. I can
understand through this, at last, what it is he enjoys, what he selects
by preference, from all that various world we pass our lives in. I am
struck by the purity of the room he has re-fashioned for us—a sort of
moral purity; yet, in the *forms* and *colours* of things. Is the actual life of
Paris, to which he will soon return, equally pure, that it relishes this
kind of thing so strongly? Only, methinks 'tis a pity to incorporate so
much of his work, of himself, with objects of use, which must perish
by use, or disappear, like our own old furniture, with mere change of
fashion.

July 1714.

On the last day of Antony Watteau's visit we made a party to Cambrai.
We entered the cathedral church: it was the hour of Vespers, and it
happened that Monseigneur le Prince de Cambrai,° the author of
Télémaque, was in his place in the choir. He appears to be of great age,
assists but rarely at the offices of religion, and is never to be seen in
Paris; and Antony had much desired to behold him. Certainly it was
worth while to have come so far only to see him and hear him give his
pontifical blessing, in a voice feeble but of infinite sweetness, and with
an inexpressibly graceful movement of the hands. A veritable *grand*

seigneur! His refined old age, the impress of genius and honours, even
his disappointments, concur with natural graces to make him seem too
distinguished (a fitter word fails me) for this world. *Omnia vanitas*! he
seems to say, yet with a profound resignation, which makes the things
we are most of us so fondly occupied with look petty enough. *Omnia
vanitas*! Is that indeed the proper comment on our lives, coming, as it
does in this case, from one who might have made his own all that life
has to bestow? Yet he was never to be seen at court, and has lived here
almost as an exile. Was our 'Great King Lewis' jealous of a true *grand
seigneur* or *grand monarque* by natural gift and the favour of heaven,
that he could not endure his presence?

July 1714.

My own portrait remains unfinished at his sudden departure. I sat for
it in a walking-dress, made under his direction—a gown of a peculiar
silken stuff, falling into an abundance of small folds, giving me 'a
certain air of piquancy' which pleases him, but is far enough from my
true self. My old Flemish *faille*,° which I shall always wear, suits me
better.

  I notice that our good-hearted but sometimes difficult friend said
little of our brother Jean-Baptiste, though he knows us so anxious on
his account—spoke only of his constant industry, cautiously, and not
altogether with satisfaction, as if the sight of it wearied him.

September 1714.

Will Antony ever accomplish that long-pondered journey to Italy? For
his own sake, I should be glad he might. Yet it seems desolately far,
across those great hills and plains. I remember how I formed a plan
for providing him with a sum sufficient for the purpose. But that he no
longer needs.

  With myself, how to get through time becomes sometimes the
question—unavoidably; though it strikes me as a thing unspeakably
sad in a life so short as ours. The sullenness of a long wet day is
yielding just now to an outburst of watery sunset, which strikes from
the far horizon of this quiet world of ours, over fields and willow-
woods, upon the shifty weathervanes and long-pointed windows of the
tower on the square—from which the *Angelus* is sounding—with a
momentary promise of a fine night. I prefer the *Salut* at Saint Vaast.

The walk thither is a longer one, and I have a fancy always that I may meet Antony Watteau there again, any time; just as, when a child, having found one day a tiny box in the shape of a silver coin, for long afterwards I used to try every piece of money that came into my hands, expecting it to open.

September 1714.

We were sitting in the *Watteau* chamber for the coolness, this sultry evening. A sudden gust of wind ruffled the lights in the sconces on the walls: the distant rumblings, which had continued all the afternoon, broke out at last; and through the driving rain, a coach, rattling across the Place, stops at our door: in a moment Jean-Baptiste is with us once again; but with bitter tears in his eyes—dismissed!

October 1714.

Jean-Baptiste! he too, rejected by Antony! It makes our friendship and fraternal sympathy closer. And still as he labours, not less sedulously than of old, and still so full of loyalty to his old master, in that *Watteau* chamber, I seem to see Antony himself, of whom Jean-Baptiste dares not yet speak—to come very near his work, and understand his great parts. So Jean-Baptiste's work, in its nearness to his, may stand, for the future, as the central interest of my life. I bury myself in that.

February 1715.

If I understand anything of these matters, Antony Watteau paints that delicate life of Paris so excellently, with so much spirit, partly because, after all, he looks down upon it or despises it. To persuade myself of that, is my womanly satisfaction for his preference—his apparent preference—for a world so different from mine. Those coquetries, those vain and perishable graces, can be rendered so perfectly, only through an intimate understanding of them. For him, to understand must be to despise them; while (I think I know why), he nevertheless undergoes their fascination. Hence that discontent with himself, which keeps pace with his fame. It would have been better for him— he would have enjoyed a purer and more real happiness—had he remained here, obscure; as it might have been better for me!

It is altogether different with Jean-Baptiste. He approaches that life, and all its pretty nothingness, from a level no higher than its own;

and beginning just where Antony Watteau leaves off in disdain,
produces a solid and veritable likeness of it and of its ways.

March 1715.

There are points in his painting (I apprehend this through his own
persistently modest observations) at which he works out his purpose
more excellently than Watteau; of whom he has trusted himself to
speak at last, with a wonderful self-effacement, pointing out in each of
his pictures, for the rest so just and true, how Antony would have
managed this or that, and, with what an easy superiority, have done
the thing better—done the impossible.

February 1716.

There are good things, attractive things, in life, meant for one and not
for another—not meant perhaps for me; as there are pretty clothes
which are not suitable for every one. I find a certain immobility of
disposition in me, to quicken or interfere with which is like physical
pain. He, so brilliant, petulant, mobile! I am better far beside Jean-
Baptiste—in contact with his quiet, even labour, and manner of being.
At first he did the work to which he had set himself, sullenly; but the
mechanical labour of it has cleared his mind and temper at last, as a
sullen day turns quite clear and fine by imperceptible change. With
the earliest dawn he enters his workroom, the *Watteau* chamber,
where he remains at work all day. The dark evenings he spends in
industrious preparation with the *crayon* for the pictures he is to finish
during the hours of daylight. His toil is also his amusement: he goes
but rarely into the society whose manners he has to re-produce. The
animals in his pictures, pet animals, are mere toys: he knows it. But he
finishes a large number of works, door-heads, *clavecin* cases, and the
like. His happiest, his most genial moments, he puts, like savings of
fine gold, into one particular picture (true *opus magnum*, as he hopes),
The Swing. He has the secret of surprising effects with a certain pearl-
grey silken stuff of his predilection; and it must be confessed that he
paints hands—which a draughtsman, of course, should understand at
least twice as well as all other people—with surpassing expression.

March 1716.

Is it the depressing result of this labour, of a too exacting labour? I know not. But at times (it is his one melancholy!) he expresses a strange apprehension of poverty, of penury and mean surroundings in old age; reminding me of that childish disposition to hoard, which I noticed in him of old. And then—inglorious Watteau, as he is!—at times that steadiness, in which he is so great a contrast to Antony, as it were accumulates, changes, into a ray of genius, a grace, an inexplicable touch of truth, in which all his heaviness leaves him for a while, and he actually goes beyond the master; as himself protests to me, yet modestly. And still, it is precisely at those moments that he feels most the difference between himself and Antony Watteau. 'In *that* country, *all* the pebbles are golden nuggets,' he says; with perfect good humour.

June 1716.

'Tis truly in a delightful abode that Antony Watteau is just now lodged—the *hôtel*, or townhouse of M. de Crozat, which is not only a comfortable dwelling-place, but also a precious museum lucky people go far to see. Jean-Baptiste, too, has seen the place, and describes it. The antiquities, beautiful curiosities of all sorts—above all, the original drawings of those old masters Antony so greatly admires—are arranged all around one there, that the influence, the genius, of those things may imperceptibly play upon and enter into one, and form what one does. The house is situated near the Rue Richelieu, but has a large garden about it. M. de Crozat gives his musical parties there, and Antony Watteau has painted the walls of one of the apartments with the Four Seasons, after the manner of ours, but doubtless improved by second thoughts. This beautiful place is now Antony's home for a while. The house has but one story, with attics in the *mansard* roofs,° like those of a farmhouse in the country. I fancy Antony fled thither for a few moments, from the visitors who weary him; breathing the freshness of that dewy garden in the very midst of Paris. As for me, I suffocate this summer afternoon in this pretty *Watteau* chamber of ours, where Jean-Baptiste is at work so contentedly.

May 1717.

In spite of all that happened, Jean-Baptiste has been looking forward to a visit to Valenciennes which Antony Watteau had proposed to make. He hopes always—has a patient hope—that Antony's former patronage of him may be revived. And now he is among us, actually at his work—restless and disquieting, meagre, like a woman with some nervous malady. Is it pity, then, pity only, one must feel for the brilliant one? He has been criticizing the work of Jean-Baptiste, who takes his judgments generously, gratefully. Can it be that, after all, he despises and is no true lover of his own art, and is but chilled by an enthusiasm for it in another, such as that of Jean-Baptiste? as if Jean-Baptiste over-valued it, or as if some ignobleness or blunder, some sign that he has really missed his aim, started into sight from his work at the sound of praise—as if such praise could hardly be altogether sincere.

June 1717.

And at last one has actual sight of his work—what it is. He has brought with him certain long-cherished designs to finish here in quiet, as he protests he has never finished before. That charming *Noblesse*—can it be really so distinguished to the minutest point, so naturally aristocratic? Half in masquerade, playing the drawing-room or garden comedy of life, these persons have upon them, not less than the landscape he composes, and among the accidents of which they group themselves with such a perfect fittingness, a certain light we should seek for in vain upon anything real. For their framework they have around them a veritable architecture—a tree-architecture—to which those moss-grown balusters, *termes*,° statues, fountains, are really but accessories. Only, as I gaze upon those windless afternoons, I find myself always saying to myself involuntarily, 'The evening will be a wet one.' The storm is always brooding through the massy splendour of the trees, above those sun-dried glades or lawns, where delicate children may be trusted thinly clad; and the secular trees themselves will hardly outlast another generation.

July 1717.

There has been an exhibition of his pictures in the Hall of the Academy of Saint Luke; and all the world has been to see.

Yes! Besides that unreal, imaginary light upon these scenes, these persons, which is pure gift of his, there was a light, a poetry, in those persons and things themselves, close at hand *we* had not seen. He has enabled us to see it: we are so much the better-off thereby, and I, for

one, the better. The world he sets before us so engagingly has its care
for purity, its cleanly preferences, in what one is to *see*—in the
outsides of things—and there is something, a sign, a memento, at the
least, of what makes life really valuable, even in that. There, is my
simple notion, wholly womanly perhaps, but which I may hold by, of
the purpose of the arts.

August 1717.

And yet! (to read my mind, my experience, in somewhat different
terms) methinks Antony Watteau reproduces that gallant world, those
patched and powdered ladies and fine cavaliers, so much to its own
satisfaction, partly because he despises it; if this be a possible
condition of excellent artistic production. People talk of a new era now
dawning upon the world, of fraternity, liberty, humanity, of a novel
sort of social freedom in which men's natural goodness of heart will
blossom at a thousand points hitherto repressed, of wars disappearing
from the world in an infinite, benevolent ease of life—yes! perhaps of
infinite littleness also. And it is the outward manner of that, which,
partly by anticipation, and through pure intellectual power, Antony
Watteau has caught, together with a flattering something of his own,
added thereto. Himself really of the old time—that serious old time
which is passing away, the impress of which he carries on his
physiognomy—he dignifies, by what in him is neither more nor less
than a profound melancholy, the essential insignificance of what he
wills to touch in all that, transforming its mere pettiness into grace. It
looks certainly very graceful, fresh, animated, 'piquant', as they love
to say—yes! and withal, I repeat, perfectly pure, and may well
congratulate itself on the loan of a fallacious grace, not its own. For in
truth Antony Watteau is still the mason's boy, and deals with that
world under a fascination, of the nature of which he is half-conscious
methinks, puzzled at 'the queer trick he possesses', to use his own
phrase. You see him growing ever more and more meagre, as he goes
through the world and its applause. Yet he reaches with wonderful
sagacity the secret of an adjustment of colours, a *coiffure*, a toilette,
setting I know not what air of real superiority on such things. He will
never overcome his early training; and these light things will possess
for him always a kind of representative or borrowed worth, as
characterizing that impossible or forbidden world which the mason's
boy saw through the closed gateways of the enchanted garden. Those

trifling and petty graces, the *insignia* to him of that nobler world of aspiration and idea, even now that he is aware, as I conceive, of their true littleness, bring back to him, by the power of association, all the old magical exhilaration of his dream—his dream of a better world than the real one. There, is the formula, as I apprehend, of his success—of his extraordinary hold on things so alien from himself. And I think there is more real hilarity in my brother's *fêtes champêtres*°—more truth to life, and therefore less distinction. Yes! the world profits by such reflection of its poor, coarse self, in one who renders all its caprices from the height of a Corneille. That is my way of making up to myself for the fact that I think *his* days, too, would have been really happier, had he remained obscure at Valenciennes.

September 1717.

My own poor likeness, begun so long ago, still remains unfinished on the easel, at his departure from Valenciennes—perhaps for ever; since the old people departed this life in the hard winter of last year, at no distant time from each other. It is pleasanter to him to sketch and plan than to paint and finish; and he is often out of humour with himself because he cannot project into a picture the life and spirit of his first thought with the *crayon*. He would fain begin where that famous master Gerard Dow left off, and snatch, as it were with a single stroke, what in him was the result of infinite patience. It is the sign of this sort of promptitude that he values solely in the work of another. To my thinking there is a kind of greed or grasping in that humour; as if things were not to last very long, and one must snatch opportunity. And often he succeeds. The old Dutch painter cherished with a kind of piety his colours and pencils. Antony Watteau, on the contrary, will hardly make any preparations for his work at all, or even clean his palette, in the dead-set he makes at improvisation. 'Tis the contrast perhaps between the staid Dutch genius and the petulant, sparkling French temper of this new era, into which he has thrown himself. Alas! it is already apparent that the result also loses something of longevity, of durability—the colours fading or changing, from the first, somewhat rapidly, as Jean-Baptiste notes. 'Tis true, a mere trifle alters or produces the expression. But then, on the other hand, in pictures the whole effect of which lies in a kind of harmony, the treachery of a single colour must needs involve the failure of the whole to outlast the fleeting grace of those social conjunctions it is meant to perpetuate. This is what has happened, in part, to that portrait on the easel. Meantime, he has commanded Jean-Baptiste to finish it; and so it must be.

October 1717.

Antony Watteau is an excellent judge of literature, and I have been reading (with infinite surprise!) in my afternoon walks in the little wood here, a new book he left behind him—a great favourite of his; as it has been a favourite with large numbers in Paris. Those pathetic shocks of fortune, those sudden alternations of pleasure and remorse, which must always lie among the very conditions of an irregular and guilty love, as in sinful games of chance—they have begun to talk of these things in Paris, to amuse themselves with the spectacle of them, set forth here, in the story of poor Manon Lescaut°—for whom fidelity is impossible, so vulgarly eager for the money which can buy pleasures such as hers—with an art like Watteau's own, for lightness and grace. Incapacity of truth, yet with such tenderness, such a gift of tears, on the one side: on the other, a faith so absolute as to give to an illicit love almost the regularity of marriage! And this is the book those fine ladies in Watteau's 'conversations', who look so exquisitely pure, lay down on the cushion when the children run up to have their laces righted. Yet the pity of it! What floods of weeping! There is a tone about it which strikes me as going well with the grace of these leafless birch-trees against the sky, the pale silver of their bark, and a certain delicate odour of decay which rises from the soil. It is all one half-light; and the heroine, nay! the hero himself also, that dainty Chevalier des Grieux, with all his fervour, have, I think, but a half-life in them truly, from the first. And I could fancy myself almost of their condition sitting here alone this evening, in which a premature touch of winter makes the world look but an inhospitable place of entertainment for one's spirit. With so little genial warmth to hold it there, one feels that the merest accident might detach that flighty guest altogether. So chilled at heart things seem to me, as I gaze on that glacial point in the motionless sky, like some mortal spot whence death begins to creep over the body!

And yet, in the midst of this, by mere force of contrast, comes back to me, very vividly, the true colour, ruddy with blossom and fruit, of the past summer, among the streets and gardens of some of our old towns we visited; when the thought of cold was a luxury, and the earth dry enough to sleep on. The summer was indeed a fine one; and the whole country seemed bewitched. A kind of infectious sentiment passed upon us, like an efflux from its flowers and flower-like architecture—flower-like to me at least, but of which I never felt the beauty before.

And as I think of that, certainly I have to confess that there is a wonderful reality about this lovers' story; an accordance between themselves and the conditions of things around them, so deep as to make it seem that the course of their lives could hardly have been other than it was. That impression comes, perhaps, wholly of the writer's skill; but, at all events, I must read the book no more.

June 1718.

And he has allowed that Mademoiselle Rosalba°—'*ce bel esprit*'—who can discourse upon the arts like a master, to paint his portrait: has painted hers in return! She holds a lapful of white roses with her two hands. *Rosa Alba*—himself has inscribed it! It will be engraved, to circulate and perpetuate it the better.

One's journal, here in one's solitude, is of service at least in this, that it affords an escape for vain regrets, angers, impatience. One puts this and that angry spasm into it, and is delivered from it so.

And then, it was at the desire of M. de Crozat that the thing was done. One must oblige one's patrons. The lady also, they tell me, is consumptive, like Antony himself, and like to die. And he, who has always lacked either the money or the spirits to make that long-pondered, much-desired journey to Italy, has found in her work the veritable accent and colour of those old Venetian masters he would so willingly have studied under the sunshine of their own land. Alas! How little peace have his great successes given him; how little of that quietude of mind, without which, methinks, one fails in true dignity of character.

November 1718.

His thirst for change of place has actually driven him to England, that veritable home of the consumptive. Ah me! I feel it may be the finishing stroke. To have run into the native country of consumption!

Strange caprice of that desire to travel, which he has really indulged so little in his life—of the restlessness which, they tell me, is itself a symptom of this terrible disease!

January 1720.

As once before, after long silence, a token has reached us, a slight token that he remembers—an etched plate, one of very few he has executed, with that old subject: *Soldiers on the March*. And the weary soldier himself is returning once more to Valenciennes, on his way from England to Paris.

February 1720.

Those sharply-arched brows, those restless eyes which seem larger than ever—something that seizes on one, and is almost terrible, in his expression—speak clearly, and irresistibly set one on the thought of a summing-up of his life. I am reminded of the day when, already with that air of seemly thought, *le bel sérieux*, he was found sketching, with so much truth to the inmost mind in them, those picturesque mountebanks at the Fair in the Grande Place; and I find, throughout his course of life, something of the essential melancholy of the comedian. He, so fastidious and cold, and who has never 'ventured the representation of passion', does but amuse the gay world; and is aware of that, though certainly unamused himself all the while. Just now, however, he is finishing a very different picture—that too, full of humour—an English family-group, with a little girl riding a wooden horse: the father, and the mother holding his tobacco-pipe, stand in the centre.

March 1720.

Tomorrow he will depart finally. And this evening the Syndics of the Academy of Saint Luke came with their scarves and banners to conduct their illustrious fellow-citizen, by torchlight, to supper in their Guildhall, where all their beautiful old corporation plate will be displayed. The *Watteau salon* was lighted up to receive them. There is something in the payment of great honours to the living which fills one with apprehension, especially when the recipient of them looks so like a dying man. God have mercy on him!

April 1721.

We were on the point of retiring to rest last evening when a messenger arrived post-haste with a letter on behalf of Antony Watteau, desiring Jean-Baptiste's presence at Paris. We did not go to bed that night; and my brother was on his way before daylight, his heart full of a strange conflict of joy and apprehension.

May 1721.

A letter at last! from Jean-Baptiste, occupied with cares of all sorts at the bedside of the sufferer. Antony fancying that the air of the country might do him good, the Abbé Haranger, one of the canons of the Church of Saint Germain l'Auxerrois, where he was in the habit of hearing Mass, has lent him a house at Nogent-sur-Marne. There he receives a few visitors. But in truth the places he once liked best, the people, nay! the very friends, have become to him nothing less than insupportable. Though he still dreams of change, and would fain try his native air once more, he is at work constantly upon his art; but solely by way of a teacher, instructing (with a kind of remorseful diligence, it would seem) Jean-Baptiste, who will be heir to his unfinished work, and take up many of his pictures where he has left them. He seems now anxious for one thing only, to give his old 'dismissed' disciple what remains of himself, and the last secrets of his genius. His property—9000 *livres* only—goes to his relations. Jean-Baptiste has found these last weeks immeasurably useful.

For the rest, bodily exhaustion perhaps, and this new interest in an old friend, have brought him tranquillity at last, a tranquillity in which he is much occupied with matters of religion. Ah! it was ever so with me. And one *lives* also most reasonably so.—With women, at least, it is thus, quite certainly. Yet I know not what there is of a pity which strikes deep, at the thought of a man, a while since so strong, turning his face to the wall from the things which most occupy men's lives. 'Tis that homely, but honest *curé* of Nogent he has caricatured so often, who attends him.

July 1721.

Our incomparable Watteau is no more! Jean-Baptiste returned unexpectedly. I heard his hasty footstep on the stairs. We turned together into that room; and he told his story there. Antony Watteau departed suddenly, in the arms of M. Gersaint, on one of the late hot days of July. At the last moment he had been at work upon a crucifix for the good *curé* of Nogent, liking little the very rude one he possessed. He died with all the sentiments of religion.

He has been a sick man all his life. He was always a seeker after something in the world that is there in no satisfying measure, or not at all.

AUGUSTA WEBSTER

Circe°

The sun drops luridly into the west;
Darkness has raised her arms to draw him down
Before the time, not waiting as of wont
Till he has come to her behind the sea;
And the smooth waves grow sullen in the gloom
And wear their threatening purple; more and more
The plain of waters sways and seems to rise
Convexly from its level of the shores;
And low dull thunder rolls along the beach:
There will be storm at last, storm, glorious storm.   10

Oh welcome, welcome, though it rend my bowers,
Scattering my blossomed roses like the dust,
Splitting the shrieking branches, tossing down
My riotous vines with their young half-tinged grapes
Like small round amethysts or beryls strung
Tumultuously in clusters, though it sate
Its ravenous spite among my goodliest pines
Standing there round and still against the sky
That makes blue lakes between their sombre tufts,
Or harry from my silvery olive slopes   20
Some hoary king whose gnarled fantastic limbs
Wear rugged armour of a thousand years;
Though it will hurl high on my flowery shores
The hostile wave that rives at the poor sward
And drags it down the slants, that swirls its foam

Over my terraces, shakes their firm blocks
Of great bright marbles into tumbled heaps,
And makes my pleached and mossy labyrinths,
Where the small odorous blossoms grow like stars
Strewn in the milky way, a briny marsh.   30
What matter? let it come and bring me change,
Breaking the sickly sweet monotony.

What fate is mine who, far apart from pains
And fears and turmoils of the cross-grained world,
Dwell like a lonely god in a charmed isle
Where I am first and only, and, like one
Who should love poisonous savours more than mead,
Long for a tempest on me and grow sick
Of rest and of divine free carelessness!
Oh me, I am a woman, not a god;   40
Yea, those who tend me, even, are more than I,
My nymphs who have the souls of flowers and birds,
Singing and blossoming immortally.

Ah me! these love a day and laugh again,
And loving, laughing, find a full content;
But I know naught of peace, and have not loved.

Where is my love? Does some one cry for me
Not knowing whom he calls? does his soul cry
For mind to grow beside it, grow in it?

Oh sunlike glory of pale glittering hairs,   50
Bright as the filmy wires my weavers take
To make me golden gauzes—oh deep eyes,
Darker and softer than the bluest dusk
Of August violets, darker and deep
Like crystal fathomless lakes in summer noons;
Oh sad sweet longing smile—oh lips that tempt
My very self to kisses—oh round cheeks
Tenderly radiant with the even flush
Of pale smoothed coral—perfect lovely face
Answering my gaze from out this fleckless pool—   60

Wonder of glossy shoulders, chiselled limbs—
Should I be so your lover as I am,
Drinking an exquisite joy to watch you thus
In all a hundred changes through the day,
But that I love you for him till he comes,
But that my beauty means his loving it?

Oh, look! a speck on this side of the sun,
Coming—yes, coming with the rising wind
That frays the darkening cloud-wrack on the verge
And in a little while will leap abroad,   70
Spattering the sky with rushing blacknesses,
Dashing the hissing mountainous waves at the stars.
'Twill drive me that black speck a shuddering hulk
Caught in the buffeting waves, dashed impotent
From ridge to ridge, will drive it in the night
With that dull jarring crash upon the beach,
And the cries for help and the cries of fear and hope.

And then to-morrow they will thoughtfully,
With grave low voices, count their perils up,
And thank the gods for having let them live,   80
And tell of wives or mothers in their homes,
And children, who would have such loss in them
That they must weep (and may be I weep too)
With fancy of the weepings had they died.
And the next morrow they will feel their ease
And sigh with sleek content, or laugh elate,
Tasting delights of rest and revelling,
Music and perfumes, joyaunce for the eyes
Of rosy faces and luxurious pomps,
The savour of the banquet and the glow   90
And fragrance of the wine-cup; and they'll talk
How good it is to house in palaces
Out of the storms and struggles, and what luck
Strewed their good ship on our accessless coast.
Then the next day the beast in them will wake,
And one will strike and bicker, and one swell
With puffed up greatness, and one gibe and strut

In apish pranks, and one will line his sleeve
With pilfered booties, and one snatch the gems
Out of the carven goblets as they pass,   100
One will grow mad with fever of the wine,
And one will sluggishly besot himself,
And one be lewd, and one be gluttonous;
And I shall sickly look, and loathe them all.

Oh my rare cup! my pure and crystal cup
With not one speck of colour to make false
The entering lights, or flaw to make them swerve!
My cup of Truth! How the lost fools will laugh
And thank me for my boon, as if I gave
Some momentary flash of the gods' joy,   110
To drink where *I* have drunk and touch the touch
Of *my* lips with their own! Aye, let them touch.

Too cruel am I? And the silly beasts,
Crowding around me when I pass their way,
Glower on me and, although they love me still,
(With their poor sorts of love such as they could)
Call wrath and vengeance to their humid eyes
To scare me into mercy, or creep near
With piteous fawnings, supplicating bleats.
Too cruel? Did I choose them what they are?   120
Or change them from themselves by poisonous charms?
But any draught, pure water, natural wine,
Out of my cup, revealed them to themselves
And to each other. Change? there was no change;
Only disguise gone from them unawares:
And had there been one true right man of them
He would have drunk the draught as I had drunk,
And stood unharmed and looked me in the eyes,
Abashing me before him. But these things—
Why, which of them has even shown the kind   130
Of some one nobler beast? Pah! yapping wolves
And pitiless stealthy wild-cats, curs and apes
And gorging swine and slinking venomous snakes,
All false and ravenous and sensual brutes
That shame the Earth that bore them, these they are.

Lo, lo! the shivering blueness darting forth
On half the heaven, and the forked thin fire
Strikes to the sea, and hark, the sudden voice
That rushes through the trees before the storm,
And shuddering of the branches. Yet the sky   140
Is blue against them still, and early stars
Sparkle above the pine-tops; and the air
Clings faint and motionless around me here.

Another burst of flame—and the black speck
Shows in the glare, lashed onwards. It were well
I bade make ready for our guests to-night.

AUSTIN DOBSON

A Virtuoso°

Be seated, pray. 'A grave appeal'?
    The sufferers by the war, of course;
Ah, what a sight for us who feel,—
    This monstrous *mélodrame* of Force!
We, Sir, we connoisseurs, should know,
    On whom its heaviest burden falls;
Collections shattered at a blow,
    Museums turned to hospitals!

'And worse,' you say; 'the wide distress!'
    Alas, 'tis true distress exists,   10
Though, let me add, our worthy Press
    Have no mean skill as colourists;
Speaking of colour, next your seat
    There hangs a sketch from Vernet's hand;°
Some Moscow fancy, incomplete,
    Yet not indifferently planned;

Note specially the gray old guard,
    Who tears his tattered coat to wrap

A closer bandage round the scarred
    And frozen comrade in his lap;—   20
But, as regards the present war,—
    Now don't you think our pride of pence
Goes—may I say it?—somewhat far
    For objects of benevolence?

You hesitate. For my part, I—
    Though ranking Paris next to Rome,
Aesthetically—still reply
    That 'Charity begins at Home.'
The words remind me. Did you catch
    My so-named 'Hunt'? The girl's a gem;°   30
And look how those lean rascals snatch
    The pile of scraps she brings to them!

'But your appeal's for home,'—you say,—
    For home, and English poor! Indeed!
I thought Philanthropy to-day
    Was blind to mere domestic need—
However sore—Yet though one grants
    That home should have the foremost claims,
At least these Continental wants
    Assume intelligible names;   40

While here with us—Ah! who could hope
    To verify the varied pleas,
Or from his private means to cope
    With all our shrill necessities!
Impossible! One might as well
    Attempt comparison of creeds;
Or fill that huge Malayan shell
    With these half-dozen Indian beads.

Moreover, add that every one
    So well exalts his pet distress,   50
'Tis—Give to all, or give to none,
    If you'd avoid invidiousness.

Your case, I feel, is sad as A.'s,
    The same applies to B.'s and C.'s;
By my selection I should raise
    An alphabet of rivalries;

And life is short,—I see you look
    At yonder dish, a priceless bit;
You'll find it etched in Jacquemart's book,
    They say that Raphael painted it;—   60
And life is short, you understand;
    So, if I only hold you out
An open though an empty hand,
    Why, you'll forgive me, I've no doubt.

Nay, do not rise. You seem amused;
    One can but be consistent, Sir!
'Twas on these grounds I just refused
    Some gushing lady-almoner,—
Believe me, on these very grounds.
    Good-bye, then. Ah, a rarity!   70
That cost me quite three hundred pounds,—
    That Dürer figure,—'Charity.'°

On a Fan that Belonged to the Marquise de Pompadour°

Chicken-skin, delicate, white,
    Painted by Carlo Vanloo,°
Loves in a riot of light,
    Roses and vaporous blue;
    Hark to the dainty *frou-frou*!°
Picture above if you can,
    Eyes that could melt as the dew,—
This was the Pompadour's fan!

See how they rise at the sight,
    Thronging the *Œil de Bœuf* through,°   10
Courtiers as butterflies bright,

Beauties that Fragonard drew,°
Talon-rouge, falbala, queue,°
Cardinal, Duke,—to a man,
Eager to sigh or to sue,—
This was the Pompadour's fan!

Ah! but things more than polite
.   Hung on this toy, *voyez vous*!
Matters of state and of might,
Things that great ministers do;   20
Things that, maybe, overthrew
Those in whose brains they began;
Here was the sign and the cue,—
This was the Pompadour's fan!

ENVOY

Where are the secrets it knew?
Weavings of plot and of plan?
—But where is the Pompadour, too?
This was the Pompadour's *Fan*!

JOHN ADDINGTON SYMONDS

In the Key of Blue°

A symphony of black and blue—
Venice asleep, vast night, and you;
The skies were blurred with vapours dank:
The long canal stretched inky-blank,
With lights on heaving water shed
From lamps that trembled overhead.
Pitch-dark! You were the one thing blue;
Four tints of pure celestial hue:
The larkspur blouse by tones degraded
Through silken sash of sapphire faded,   10
The faintly floating violet tie,
The hose of lapis-lazuli.

How blue you were amid that black,
Lighting the wave, the ebon wrack!
The ivory pallor of your face
Gleamed from those glowing azures back
Against the golden gaslight; grapes°
Of dusky curls your brows embrace,
And round you all the vast night gapes.

A symphony of blues and white—   20
You, the acacias, dewy-bright,
Transparent skies of chrysolite.°
We wind along these leafy hills;
One chord of blue the landscape thrills,
Your three blent azures merged in those
Cerulean heavens above the blouse.
The highest tones flash forth in white:
Acacia branches bowed with snow
Of scented blossom; broken light;
The ivory of your brows, the glow   30
Of those large orbs that are your eyes:
Those starry orbs of lustrous jet
In clear enamelled turquoise set,
Pale as the marge of morning skies.

A symphony of blues and brown—
We were together in the town:
A grimy tavern with blurred walls,
Where dingy lamplight floats and falls
On working men and women, clad
In sober watchet, umber sad.   40
Two viols and one 'cello scream
Waltz music through the smoke and steam:
You rise, you clasp a comrade, who
Is clothed in triple blues like you:
Sunk in some dream voluptuously
Circle those azures richly blent,
Swim through the dusk, the melody;
Languidly breathing, you and he,
Uplifting the environment;

Ivory face and swart face laid   50
Cheek unto cheek, like man, like maid.
A symphony of pink and blue,
The lamp, the little maid, and you.
Your strong man's stature in those three
Blent azures clothed, so loved by me;

Your grave face framed in felt thrown back;
Your sad sweet lips, eyes glossy black,
Now laughing, while your wan cheeks flush
Like warm white roses with a blush.
Clasped to your breast, held by your hands,   60
Smothered in blues, the baby stands:
Her frock like some carnation gleams;
Her hair, a golden torrent, streams:
Blue as forget-me-not her eyes,
Or azure-wingèd butterflies:
Her cheeks and mouth so richly red,
One would not think her city-bred.
Your beautiful pale face of pain
Leaned to the child's cheeks breathing health;
Like feathers dropped from raven's wing,   70
The curls that round your forehead rain
Merged with her tresses' yellow wealth;
Her mouth that was a rose in spring
Touched yours, her pouting nether lip
Clasped your fine upper lip, whose brink,
Wherefrom Love's self a bee might sip,
Is pencilled with faint Indian ink.
Such was the group I saw one night
Illumined by a flaring light,
In that dim tavern where we meet   80
Sometimes to smoke, and drink and eat;
Exquisite contrast, not of tone,
Or tint, or form, or face alone.

A symphony of blues and gold,
Among ravines of grey stones rolled
Adown the steep from mountains old.

Laburnum branches drop their dew
Of amber bloom on me, on you:
With cytisus and paler broom,
Electron glimmering through the gloom.   90
Around us all the field flames up,
Goldenrod, hawkweed, buttercup;
While curling through lush grass one spies
Tendrils of honeyed helichryse.
'Tis saffron, topaz, solar rays,
Dissolved in fervent chrysoprase.
Cool, yet how luminous, the blue,
Centred in triple tones by you,
Uniting all that yellow glare
With the blue circumambient air,   100
The violet shades, the hard cobalt
Of noon's inexorable vault.

A symphony of blues and green,
Swart indigo and eau-marine.
Stripped to the waist two dyers kneel
On grey steps strewn with orange peel;
The glaucous water to the brink
Welters with clouds of purplish pink:
The men wring cloth that drips and takes
Verditer hues of water-snakes,°   110
While *pali* paled by sun and seas°
Repeat the tint in verdigris.
Those brows, nude breasts, and arms of might,
The pride of youth and manhood white,
Now smirched with woad, proclaim the doom
Of labour and its life-long gloom.
Only the eyes emergent shine,
These black as coals, those opaline;
Lighten from storms of tangled hair,
Black curls and blonde curls debonnair,   120
Proving man's untamed spirit there.

A symphony of blues and red—
The broad lagoon, and overhead
Sunset, a sanguine banner, spread.

Fretty of azure and pure gules°
Are sea, sky, city, stagnant pools:
You, by my side, within the boat,
Imperially purple float,
Beneath a burning sail, straight on
Into the west's vermilion.   130
The triple azures melt and glow
Like flaunting iris-flowers arow;
One amethystine gem of three
Fused by the heaven's effulgency.
Now fails the splendour, day dies down
Beyond the hills by Padua's town;
And all along the eastern sky
Blue reassumes ascendency.
Lapped in those tints of fluor-spar,
You shine intense, an azure star,   140
With roses flushed that slowly fade
Against the vast aërial shade.
At Castelfranco, with a blouse
Venetian, blent of triple blues,
I walked all through the sleepy town,
Worshipped Madonna gazing down
From that high throne Giorgione painted
Above the knight and friar sainted,
Drank in the landscape golden-green,
The dim primeval pastoral-scene.   150
The blouse beside me thrilled no less
Than I to that mute loveliness;
Spoke little, turned aside, and dwelt
Perchance on what he dumbly felt.
There throbbed a man's heart neath the shirt,
The sash, the hose, a life alert,
Veiled by that dominating hurt.
Then swept a storm-cloud from the hills;
Eddying dust the city fills,
The thunder crashes, and the rain   160
Hisses on roof and flooded plain.
Ere midnight, when the moon sailed low,
Peering through veils of indigo,

We went abroad, and heard the wail
Of many a darkling nightingale,
Pouring as birds will only pour
Their souls forth when heaven's strife is o'er.
Those red walls, and the mighty towers,
Which lustrous ivy over-flowers,
Loomed through the murk divinely warm,   170
As palpitating after storm.
Hushed was the night for friendly talk;
Under the dark arcades we walk,
Pace the wet pavement, where light steals
And swoons amid the huge abeles:°
Then seek our chamber. All the blues
Dissolve, the symphony of hues
Fades out of sight, and leaves at length
A flawless form of simple strength,
Sleep-seeking, breathing, ivory-white,   180
Upon the couch in candle-light.

MARGARET VELEY

A Japanese Fan

Though to talk too much of Heaven
        Is not well,
Though agreeable people never
        Mention Hell,
Yet the woman who betrayed me,
        Whom I kissed,
In that bygone summer taught me
        Both exist.
I was ardent, she was always
        Wisely cool,   10

So my lady played the traitor—
        I, the fool.

Oh! your pardon! but remember
If you please,
I'm translating: this is only
Japanese.

EDWARD DOWDEN

In the Cathedral Close

In the Dean's porch a nest of clay
    With five small tenants may be seen;
Five solemn faces, each as wise
    As if its owner were a Dean;

Five downy fledglings in a row,
    Packed close, as in the antique pew
The school-girls are whose foreheads clear
    At the *Venite* shine on you.

Day after day the swallows sit
    With scarce a stir, with scarce a sound,   10
But dreaming and digesting much
    They grow thus wise and soft and round:

They watch the Canons come to dine,
    And hear, the mullion-bars across,
Over the fragrant fruit and wine
    Deep talk of rood-screen and reredos.

Her hands with field-flowers drenched, a child
    Leaps past in wind-blown dress and hair,
The swallows turn their heads askew—
    Five judges deem that she is fair.   20

Prelusive touches sound within,
    Straightway they recognise the sign,
And, blandly nodding, they approve
    The minuet of Rubinstein.

They mark the cousins' schoolboy talk,
   (Male birds flown wide from minster bell),
And blink at each broad term of art,
   Binomial or bicycle.

Ah! downy young ones, soft and warm,
   Doth such a stillness mask from sight   30
Such swiftness? can such peace conceal
   Passion and ecstasy of flight?

Yet somewhere 'mid your Eastern suns,
   Under a white Greek architrave
At morn, or when the shaft of fire
   Lies large upon the Indian wave,

A sense of something dear gone by
   Will stir, strange longings thrill the heart
For a small world embowered close,
   Of which ye sometime were a part.   40

The dew–drenched flowers, the child's glad eyes
   Your joy inhuman shall control,
And in your wings a light and wind
   Shall move from the Maestro's soul.

Beau Rivage Hotel

SATURDAY EVENING

Below there's a brumming and strumming,
   And twiddling and fiddling amain,
And sweeping of muslins and laughter,
   And pattering of luminous rain.

'Miss Lucy fatiguéed?' 'Non, Monsieur!'
   'Ach Himmel!' 'How precious a smother!'
But the happiest is brisk little Polly
   To galop with only her brother.

And up to the fourth étage landing
  Come the violins' passionate cries,   10
Where the pale femme-de-chambre is sitting
  With sleep in her beautiful eyes.

ANONYMOUS

Poem by a Perfectly Furious Academician

I takes and I paints,
Hears no complaints,
And sells before I'm dry;
Till savage Ruskin
He sticks his tusk in,
Then nobody will buy.

ROBERT BRIDGES

London Snow

When men were all asleep the snow came flying,
In large white flakes falling on the city brown,
Stealthily and perpetually settling and loosely lying,
  Hushing the latest traffic of the drowsy town;
Deadening, muffling, stifling its murmurs failing;
Lazily and incessantly floating down and down:
  Silently sifting and veiling road, roof and railing;
Hiding difference, making unevenness even,
Into angles and crevices softly drifting and sailing.
  All night it fell, and when full inches seven   10
It lay in the depth of its uncompacted lightness,
The clouds blew off from a high and frosty heaven;
  And all woke earlier for the unaccustomed brightness
Of the winter dawning, the strange unheavenly glare:
The eye marvelled—marvelled at the dazzling whiteness;
  The ear hearkened to the stillness of the solemn air;

No sound of wheel rumbling nor of foot falling,
And the busy morning cries came thin and spare.
   Then boys I heard, as they went to school, calling,
They gathered up the crystal manna to freeze   20
Their tongues with tasting, their hands with snowballing;
   Or rioted in a drift, plunging up to the knees;
Or peering up from under the white-mossed wonder,
'O look at the trees!' they cried, 'O look at the trees!'
   With lessened load a few carts creak and blunder,
Following along the white deserted way,
A country company long dispersed asunder:
   When now already the sun, in pale display
Standing by Paul's high dome, spread forth below
His sparkling beams, and awoke the stir of the day.   30

   For now doors open, and war is waged with the snow;
And trains of sombre men, past tale of number,
Tread long brown paths, as toward their toil they go:
   But even for them awhile no cares encumber
Their minds diverted; the daily word is unspoken,
The daily thoughts of labour and sorrow slumber
At the sight of the beauty that greets them, for the charm they have
   broken.

Angel Spirits

    Angel spirits of sleep,
    White-robed, with silver hair;
    In your meadows fair,
    Where the willows weep,
    And the sad moonbeam
    On the gliding stream
    Writes her scattered dream:

    Angel spirits of sleep,
    Dancing to the weir
    In the hollow roar   10
    Of its waters deep;

Know ye how men say
That ye haunt no more
Isle and grassy shore
With your moonlit play;
That ye dance not here,
White-robed spirits of sleep,
All the summer night
Threading dances light?

Nightingales

Beautiful must be the mountains whence ye come,
And bright in the fruitful valleys the streams, wherefrom
                    Ye learn your song:
Where are those starry woods? O might I wander there,
    Among the flowers, which in that heavenly air
                    Bloom the year long!

Nay, barren are those mountains and spent the streams;
Our song is the voice of desire, that haunts our dreams,
                    A throe of the heart,
Whose pining visions dim, forbidden hopes profound,   10
    No dying cadence nor long sigh can sound,
                    For all our art.

Alone, aloud in the raptured ear of men
We pour our dark nocturnal secret; and then,
                    As night is withdrawn
From these sweet-springing meads and bursting boughs of May,
    Dream, while the innumerable choir of day
                    Welcome the dawn.

Flycatchers

Sweet pretty fledgelings, perched on the rail arow,
Expectantly happy, where ye can watch below
Your parents a-hunting i' the meadow grasses
All the gay morning to feed you with flies;

Ye recall me a time sixty summers ago,
When, a young chubby chap, I sat just so
With others on a school-form rank'd in a row,
Not less eager and hungry than you, I trow,
With intelligences agape and eyes aglow,
While an authoritative old wise-acre   10
Stood over us and from a desk fed us with flies.

  Dead flies—such as litter the library south-window,
That buzzed at the panes until they fell stiff-baked on the sill,
Or are roll'd up asleep i' the blinds at sunrise,
Or wafer'd flat in a shrunken folio.

  A dry biped he was, nurtured likewise
On skins and skeletons, stale from top to toe
With all manner of rubbish and all manner of lies.

Poor Poll

I saw it all, Polly, how when you had call'd for sop
and your good friend the cook came and fill'd up your pan
you yerk'd it out deftly by beakfuls scattering it
away far as you might upon the sunny lawn
then summon'd with loud cry the little garden birds
to take their feast. Quickly came they flustering around
Ruddock and Merle and Finch squabbling among themselves
nor gave you thanks nor heed while you sat silently
watching, and I beside you in perplexity
lost in the maze of all mystery and all knowledge   10
felt how deep lieth the fount of man's benevolence
if a bird can share it and take pleasure in it.
  If you, my bird, I thought, had a philosophy
it might be a sounder scheme than what our moralists
propound: because thou, Poll, livest in the darkness
which human Reason searching from outside would pierce,
but, being of so feeble a candle-power, can only
show up to view the cloud that it illuminates.
Thus reason'd I: then marvell'd how you can adapt

your wild bird-mood to endure your tame environment   20
the domesticities of English household life
and your small brass-wire cabin, who sh'dst live on wing
harrying the tropical branch-flowering wilderness:
Yet Nature gave you a gift of easy mimicry
whereby you have come to win uncanny sympathies
and morsell'd utterance of our Germanic talk
as schoolmasters in Greek will flaunt their hackney'd tags
φωνᾶντα συνετοῖσιν and κτῆμα εἰς ἀεὶ,°
ἡ γλῶσσ' ὀμώμοχ', ἡ δὲ φρὴν ἀνώμοτος°
tho' you with a better ear copy ús more perfectly   30
nor without connotation as when you call'd for sop
all with that stumpy wooden tongue and vicious beak
that dry whistling shrieking tearing cutting pincer
now eagerly subservient to your cautious claws
exploring all varieties of attitude
in irrespressible blind groping for escape
—a very figure and image of man's soul on earth
the almighty cosmic Will fidgeting in a trap—
in your quenchless unknown desire for the unknown life
of which some homely British sailor robb'd you, alas!   40
'Tis all that doth your silly thoughts so busy keep
the while you sit moping like Patience on a perch
———Wie viele Tag' und Nächte bist du geblieben!°
La possa delle gambe posta in tregue—°
the impeccable spruceness of your grey-feather'd pôll
a model in hairdressing for the dandiest old Duke
enough to quality you for the House of Lords
or the Athenaeum Club, to poke among the nobs
great intellectual nobs and literary nobs
scientific nobs and Bishops ex officio: 50
nor lack you simulation of profoundest wisdom
such as men's features oft acquire in very old age
by mere cooling of passion and decay of muscle
by faint renunciation even of untold regrets;
who seeing themselves a picture of that wh: man should-be
learn almost what it were to be what they are-not.
But you can never have cherish'd a determined hope
consciously to renounce or lose it, you will live

your threescore years and ten idle and puzzle-headed
as any mumping monk in his unfurnish'd cell   60
in peace that, poor Polly, passeth Understanding—
merely because you lack what we men understand
by Understanding. Well! well! that's the difference
C'est la seule différence, mais c'est important.°
Ah! your pale sedentary life! but would you change?
exchange it for one crowded hour of glorious life,
one blind furious tussle with a madden'd monkey
who would throttle you and throw your crude fragments away
shreds unintelligible of an unmeaning act
dans la profonde horreur de l'éternelle nuit?°   70
Why ask? You cannot know. 'Twas by no choice of yours
that you mischanged for monkeys' man's society,
'twas that British sailor drove you from Paradise—
Εἴθ' ὤφελ' Ἀργοῦς μὴ διαπτάσθαι σκάφος!°
I'd hold embargoes on such a ghastly traffic.
    I am writing verses to you and grieve that you sh'd be
absolument incapable de les comprendre,°
Tu, Polle, nescis ista nec potes scire:—°
Alas! Iambic, scazon and alexandrine,°
spondee or choriamb, all is alike to you—   80
my well-continued fanciful experiment
wherein so many strange verses amalgamate
on the secure bedrock of Milton's prosody:
not but that when I speak you will incline an ear
in critical attention lest by chánce I míght
póssibly say sómething that was worth repeating:
I am adding (do you think?) pages to literature
that gouty excrement of human intellect
accumulating slowly and everlastingly
depositing, like guano on the Peruvian shore,   90
to be perhaps exhumed in some remotest age
(*piis secunda, vate me, detur fuga*)°
to fertilize the scanty dwarf'd intelligence
of a new race of beings the unhallow'd offspring
of them who shall have quite dismember'd and destroy'd
our temple of Christian faith and fair Hellenic art
just as that monkey would, poor Polly, have done for you.

EDWARD CARPENTER

Except the Lord Build the House

She lies, whom Money has killed, and the greed of Money,
The thrice-driven slave, whom a man has calmly tortured,
And cast away in the dust—and calls it not murder,
Because he only looked on; while his trusted lieutenants
Supply and Demand pinned the victim down—and her own
    mother Nature slew her!

The old story of the sewing machine—the treadle machine;
Ten hours a day and five shillings a week, a penny an hour
    or so—if the numbers were of importance.
Of course she fell ill. Indeed she had long been ailing, and
    the effort and the torture were slowly disorganizing her
    frame; and already the grim question had been asked:
    'Might she have rest?' (—the doctor said *must*—and for
    many a month, too).
And the answer came promptly as usual. 'Have rest?—as
    much as she wanted! It was a pity, but of course if she
    could not work she could go. They would make no
    difficulty, as Supply would fill up her place as soon as
    vacant.'
One more struggle then. And now she *must* go, for work is
    impossible, and Supply *has* filled her place, and there is
    no difficulty—or difference—except to her.   10
For her only the hospital pallet, and the low moaning of the
    distant world;
For her only the fever and the wasting pain and the
    nightmare of the loud unceasing treadles;
And the strange contrast in quiet moments of the still
    chamber and the one kindly face of the house-surgeon,
    stethoscope in hand, at her bedside;
For her only, hour after hour, the dull throbbing recollection
    of the injustice of the world,
The bleak unlovely light of averted eyes thrown backwards
    and forwards over her whole life,

And the unstaunched wound of the soul which is their bitter
    denial.
And at last the lessening of the pain, and a sense of quietude
    and space, and through the murky tormented air of the
    great city a light, a ray of still hope on her eyes peacefully
    falling;
And then in a moment the passing of the light, and a silence
    in the long high-windowed ward;
And one with an aster or two and a few chrysanthemums
    and one with a white rain-bewept rose half-timidly
    coming,
To lay on her couch, with tears.   20

And so a grave.
In the dank smoke-blackened cemetery, in the dismal rain of
    the half-awakened winter day,
A grave, for her and her only.

And yet not for her only, but for thousands—
For hundreds of thousands—to lie undone, forsaken,
Tossed impatiently back from the whirling iron—
The broken wheels, or may be merely defective—
Who cares?—
That as they spin roll off and are lost in the darkness,
Run swiftly away (as if they were alive!) into the darkness,
    and are hidden;   30
Who cares? who cares?
Since for each one that is gone Supply will provide a
    thousand.

Who cares? who cares?
O tear-laden heart!
O blown white rose heavy with rain!
O sacred heart of the people!
Rose, of innumerable petals, through the long night ever
    blossoming!
Surely by thy fragrance wafted through the still night-air,
Surely by thy spirit exhaled over the sleeping world, I know,
Out of the bruised heart of thee exhaled, I know—   40
And the vision lifts itself before my eyes:—

*Except the Lord build the house, they labour in vain who build
    it.*
In vain millions of yards of calico and miles of lacework
    turned out per annum;
In vain a people well clad in machine-made cloth and
    hosiery;
In vain a flourishing foreign trade and loose cash enough for
    a small war;
In vain universal congratulations and lectures on Political
    Economy;
In vain the steady whirr of wheels all over the land, and men
    and women serving stunted and pale before them, as
    natural as possible;
Except Love build the house, they labour in vain who build it.

from *After Long Ages*

That day—the day of deliverance—shall come to you in what
    place you know not; it shall come but you know not the time.
In the pulpit while you are preaching the sermon, behold!
    suddenly the ties and the bands—in the cradle and the
    coffin, the cerements and swathing-clothes—shall drop off.
In the prison One shall come; and the chains which are
    stronger than iron, the fetters harder than steel, shall
    dissolve—you shall go free for ever.
In the sick-room, amid life-long suffering and tears and
    weariness, there shall be a sound of wings—and you shall
    know that the end is near—
(O loved one arise! come gently with me; be not too eager—lest
    joy itself should undo you.)
In the field with the plough and chain-harrow; by the side of
    your horse in the stall;
In the brothel amid indecency and idleness and repairing your
    own and your companions' dresses;
In the midst of fashionable life, in making and receiving
    morning calls, in idleness, and arranging knicknacks in your
    drawing room—even there, who knows?—
It shall duly, at the appointed hour, come.

Ask no questions: all that you have for love's sake spend;   10
For as the lightning flashes from the East to the West, so shall
     the coming of that day be.

All tools shall serve—all trades, professions, ranks, and occu-
     pations.
The spade shall serve. It shall unearth a treasure beyond price.
The stone-hammer and the shovel, the maul-stick and palette,
     the high stool and the desk, the elsin and the clamms and the
     taching ends, the whipping-lines and swingle-tree, will do;
To make a living by translating men's worn-out coats into
     boys' jackets—that also will do.
The coronet shall not be a hindrance to its wearer; the robes of
     office shall not detain the statesman; lands, estates, posses-
     sions, shall part aside for him who knows how to use them;
     he shall emerge from the midst of them, free.
The writer shall write, the compositor shall set up, the student
     by his midnight lamp shall read, a word never seen before.
The railway porter shall open the carriage door and the long
     expected friend shall descend to meet him.
The engine-driver shall drive in faith through the night. With
     one hand on the regulator he shall lean sideways and peer
     into the darkness—and lo! a new signal not given in the
     printed instructions shall duly in course appear.
The government official shall sit in his pigeon-holed den, the
     publican shall recline on his couch in the back-parlour, the
     burglar shall plan his midnight raid, the grocer's boy shall
     take the weekly orders in the kitchen, the nail-maker shall
     put his rod back in the fire and take a heated one out in its
     place;   20
The delicate-bred girl shall walk the correct thing in her
     salmon-pink silk slashed with blue; the sempstress shall sit
     in her bare attic straining the last hour of daylight—and by
     every stitch done in loyalty of heart shall she sew for herself
     a shining garment of deliverance.
The mother shall wear herself out with domestic duties and
     attending to her children; she shall have no time to herself,
     yet before she dies her face shall shine like heaven.
The Magdalen shall run down to answer the knock at the door,
     and Jesus her lover himself shall enter in.

The Word

Underneath all now comes this Word, turning the edges of the
other words where they meet it.

Politics, art, science, commerce, religion, customs and methods
of daily life, the very outer shows and semblances of
ordinary objects—

The rose in the garden, the axe hanging behind the door in the
outhouse—

Their meanings must all now be absorbed and recast in this
word, or else fall off like dry husks before its disclosure.

Do you not see that your individual life is and can only be
secured at the cost of the continual sacrifice of other lives,

And that therefore you can only hold it on condition that you
are ready in your turn to sacrifice it for others?

The law of Indifference which must henceforth be plainly
recognized and acted upon.

Art can no longer be separated from life;

The old canons fail; her tutelage completed she becomes
equivalent to Nature, and hangs her curtains continuous
with the clouds and waterfalls;

Science empties itself out of the books; all that the books have
said only falls like the faintest gauze before the reality—
hardly concealing a single blade of grass, or damaging the
light of the tiniest star;   10

The form of man emerges in all objects, baffling the old
classifications and definitions;

(Beautiful the form of man emerges, the celestial ideal—

The feet pressing the ground, the supple strong ankles and
wrists, the cleave of the loins, the shoulders, and poised head
aureoled by the sun;)

The politician turns round upon himself—like the scientist he
acknowledges his brain baffled by the problems; he reaches
his hand for help to the hand of the People;

The commercial man turns round—the firm ground gives way
beneath his feet also; to give now seems better than to get—
and what sort of a trade-motto is that?

All the customs of society change, for all are significant; and the
    long-accepted axioms of everyday life are dislocated like a
    hill-side in a landslip;
The old structures can no longer stand—their very founda-
    tions are shifted—
And men run forth in terror from the old before they can yet
    find firm ground for the new.

In all directions gulfs and yawning abysses,
The ground of society cracking, the fire showing through,   20
The old ties giving way beneath the strain, and the great pent
    heart heaving as though it would break—
At the sound of the new word spoken—
At the sound of the word Democracy.

No volcano bursting up through peaceful pastures is a greater
    revolution than this;
No vast mountain chain thrown out from ocean depths to form
    the primitive streak of a new continent looks further down
    the future;
For this is lava springing out of the very heart of Man;
This is the upheaval of heaven-kissing summits whose streams
    shall feed the farthest generations,
This is the draft and outline of a new creature,
The forming of the wings of Man beneath the outer husk—
The outspread pinions of Equality, whereon arising he shall at
    last lift himself over the Earth and launch forth to sail
    through Heaven.   30

GERARD MANLEY HOPKINS

The Habit of Perfection

Elected Silence, sing to me
And beat upon my whorlèd ear,
Pipe me to pastures still and be
The music that I care to hear.

Shape nothing, lips; be lovely-dumb:
It is the shut, the curfew sent
From there where all surrenders come
Which only makes you eloquent.

Be shellèd, eyes, with double dark
And find the uncreated light: 10
This ruck and reel which you remark
Coils, keeps, and teases simple sight.

Palate, the hutch of tasty lust,
Desire not to be rinsed with wine:
The can must be so sweet, the crust
So fresh that come in fasts divine!

Nostrils, your careless breath that spend
Upon the stir and keep of pride,
What relish shall the censers send 20
Along the sanctuary side!

O feel-of-primrose hands, O feet
That want the yield of plushy sward,
But you shall walk the golden street
And you unhouse and house the Lord.

And, Poverty, be thou the bride
And now the marriage feast begun,
And lily-coloured clothes provide
Your spouse not laboured-at nor spun.

The Wreck
of the Deutschland

To the
happy memory of five Franciscan Nuns
exiles by the Falk Laws°
drowned between midnight and morning of
Dec. 7th, 1875

PART THE FIRST

1

Thou mastering me
  God! giver of breath and bread;
   World's strand, sway of the sea;°
    Lord of living and dead;
Thou hast bound bones and veins in me, fastened me flesh,°
And after it almost unmade, what with dread,
   Thy doing: and dost thou touch me afresh?
Over again I feel thy finger and find thee.°

2

    I did say yes°   10
  O at lightning and lashed rod;
   Thou heardst me truer than tongue confess
    Thy terror, O Christ, O God;
Thou knowest the walls, altar and hour and night:
The swoon of a heart that the sweep and the hurl of thee trod
   Hard down with a horror of height:
And the midriff astrain with leaning of, laced with fire of stress.

3

    The frown of his face
  Before me, the hurtle of hell
   Behind, where, where was a, where was a place?
    I whirled out wings that spell   20
And fled with a fling of the heart to the heart of the Host.
  My heart, but you were dovewinged, I can tell,
   Carrier-witted, I am bold to boast,°
To flash from the flame to the flame then, tower from the grace to
    the grace.°

4

I am soft sift
In an hourglass—at the wall
Fast, but mined with a motion, a drift,
And it crowds and it combs to the fall;°
I steady as a water in a well, to a poise, to a pane,
But roped with, always, all the way down from the tall°   30
Fells or flanks of the voel, a vein°
Of the gospel proffer, a pressure, a principle, Christ's gift.°

5

I kiss my hand
To the stars, lovely-asunder
Starlight, wafting him out of it; and
Glow, glory in thunder;
Kiss my hand to the dappled-with-damson west:
Since, tho' he is under the world's splendour and wonder,
His mystery must be instressed, stressed;°   39
For I greet him the days I meet him, and bless when I understand.

6

Not out of his bliss°
Springs the stress felt
Nor first from heaven (and few know this)
Swings the stroke dealt—
Stroke and a stress that stars and storms deliver,
That guilt is hushed by, hearts are flushed by and melt—
But it rides time like riding a river
(And here the faithful waver, the faithless fable and miss).

7

It dates from day
Of his going in Galilee;   50
Warm-laid grave of a womb-life grey;
Manger, maiden's knee;
The dense and the driven Passion, and frightful sweat;

Thence the discharge of it, there its swelling to be,
   Though felt before, though in high flood yet—
What none would have known of it, only the heart, being hard at
      bay.

8

   Is out with it! Oh,
      We lash with the best or worst°
   Word last! How a lush-kept plush-capped sloe
      Will, mouthed to flesh-burst,
Gush!—flush the man, the being with it, sour or sweet,   60
   Brim, in a flash, full!—Hither then, last or first,°
      To hero of Calvary, Christ's feet—
Never ask if meaning it, wanting it, warned of it—men go.

9

   Be adored among men,
      God, three-numberèd form;
   Wring thy rebel, dogged in den,°
      Man's malice, with wrecking and storm.
Beyond saying sweet, past telling of tongue,
   Thou art lightning and love, I found it, a winter and warm;   70
      Father and fondler of heart thou hast wrung:
Hast thy dark descending and most art merciful then.°

10

   With an anvil-ding
      And with fire in him forge thy will
   Or rather, rather then, stealing as Spring
      Through him, melt him but master him still:
Whether at once, as once at a crash Paul,°
   Or as Austin, a lingering-out swéet skíll,
      Make mercy in all of us, out of us all
Mastery, but be adored, but be adored King.   80

PART THE SECOND

11

'Some find me a sword; some
  The flange and the rail; flame,°
Fang, or flood' goes Death on drum,
  And storms bugle his fame.
But wé dream we are rooted in earth—Dust!°
Flesh falls within sight of us, we, though our flower the same,
  Wave with the meadow, forget that there must
The sour scythe cringe, and the blear share come.°

12

On Saturday sailed from Bremen,°
  American-outward-bound,   90
Take settler and seamen, tell men with women,
  Two hundred souls in the round—
O Father, not under thy feathers nor ever as guessing
The goal was a shoal, of a fourth the doom to be drowned;
  Yet did the dark side of the bay of thy blessing°
Not vault them, the millions of rounds of thy mercy not reeve even
    them in?°

13

Into the snows she sweeps,
  Hurling the haven behind,°
The *Deutschland*, on Sunday; and so the sky keeps,
  For the infinite air is unkind,   100
And the sea flint-flake, black-backed in the regular blow,°
Sitting Eastnortheast, in cursed quarter, the wind;
  Wiry and white-fiery and whirlwind-swivellèd snow°
Spins to the widow-making unchilding unfathering deeps.

14

She drove in the dark to leeward,
  She struck—not a reef or a rock
But the combs of a smother of sand; night drew her°
  Dead to the Kentish Knock;

And she beat the bank down with her bows and the ride of her
    keel:
The breakers rolled on her beam with ruinous shock;   110
    And canvas and compass, the whorl and the wheel°
Idle for ever to waft her or wind her with, these she endured.°

15

    Hope had grown grey hairs,
    Hope had mourning on,
  Trenched with tears, carved with cares,
    Hope was twelve hours gone;°
And frightful a nightfall folded rueful a day
Nor rescue, only rocket and lightship, shone,
  And lives at last were washing away:
To the shrouds they took,—they shook in the hurling and horrible
    airs.°   120

16

    One stirred from the rigging to save
    The wild woman-kind below,
  With a rope's end round the man, handy and brave—
    He was pitched to his death at a blow,
For all his dreadnought breast and braids of thew:
They could tell him for hours, dandled the to and fro
  Through the cobbled foam-fleece, what could he do
With the burl of the fountains of air, buck and the flood of the
    wave?°

17

    They fought with God's cold—
    And they could not and fell to the deck   130
  (Crushed them) or water (and drowned them) or rolled
    With the sea-romp over the wreck.
Night roared, with the heart-break hearing a heart-broke rabble,
The woman's wailing, the crying of child without check—
  Till a lioness arose breasting the babble,°
A prophetess towered in the tumult, a virginal tongue told.°

18

Ah, touched in your bower of bone°
    Are you! turned for an exquisite smart,
  Have you! make words break from me here all alone,
        Do you!—mother of being in me, heart.   140
  O unteachably after evil, but uttering truth,
    Why, tears! is it? tears; such a melting, a madrigal start!°
      Never-eldering revel and river of youth,
What can it be, this glee? the good you have there of your own?

19

Sister, a sister calling
    A master, her master and mine!—
  And the inboard seas run swirling and hawling;°
      The rash smart sloggering brine°
  Blinds her; but she that weather sees one thing, one;
  Has one fetch in her: she rears herself to divine°   150
      Ears, and the call of the tall nun
To the men in the tops and the tackle rode over the storm's
        brawling.

20

She was first of a five and came
    Of a coifèd sisterhood.°
  (O Deutschland, double a desperate name!°
      O world wide of its good!
  But Gertrude, lily, and Luther, are two of a town,°
  Christ's lily and beast of the waste wood:°
      From life's dawn it is drawn down,   159
Abel is Cain's brother and breasts they have sucked the same.)

21

Loathed for a love men knew in them,
    Banned by the land of their birth,
  Rhine refused them. Thames would ruin them;
      Surf, snow, river and earth
Gnashed: but thou art above, thou Orion of light;°

Thy unchancelling poising palms were weighing the worth,°
   Thou martyr-master: in thy sight
Storm flakes were scroll-leaved flowers, lily showers—sweet heaven
    was astrew in them.°

22

   Five! the finding and sake°   170
    And cipher of suffering Christ.
   Mark, the mark is of man's make°
    And the word of it Sacrificed.
But he scores it in scarlet himself on his own bespoken,
Before-time-taken, dearest prizèd and priced—
   Stigma, signal, cinquefoil token
For lettering of the lamb's fleece, ruddying of the rose-flake.

23

   Joy fall to thee, father Francis,°
    Drawn to the Life that died;
   With the gnarls of the nails in thee, niche of the lance, his
    Lovescape crucified°   180
And seal of his seraph-arrival! and these thy daughters°
And five-livèd and leavèd favour and pride,°
   Are sisterly sealed in wild waters,
To bathe in his fall-gold mercies, to breathe in his all-fire glances.

24

   Away in the loveable west,
    On a pastoral forehead of Wales,
   I was under a roof here, I was at rest,
    And they the prey of the gales;
She to the black-about air, to the breaker, the thickly
Falling flakes, to the throng that catches and quails°   190
   Was calling 'O Christ, Christ come quickly':
The cross to her she calls Christ to her, christens her wild-worst
    Best.°

25

The majesty! what did she mean?
    Breathe, arch and original Breath.°
Is it love in her of the being as her lover had been?°
    Breathe, body of lovely Death.°
They were else-minded then, altogether, the men°
Woke thee with a *we are perishing* in the weather of Gennesareth.
    Or is it that she cried for the crown then,°
The keener to come at the comfort for feeling the combating keen? 200

26

For how to the heart's cheering
    The down-dugged ground-hugged grey°
Hovers off, the jay-blue heavens appearing
    Of pied and peeled May!
Blue-beating and hoary-glow height; or night, still higher,
With belled fire and the moth-soft Milky Way,
    What by your measure is the heaven of desire,
The treasure never eyesight got, nor was ever guessed what for the
        hearing?

27

No, but it was not these.°
    The jading and jar of the cart,   210
Time's tasking, it is fathers that asking for ease
    Of the sodden-with-its-sorrowing heart,
Not danger, electrical horror; then further it finds
The appealing of the Passion is tenderer in prayer apart:
    Other, I gather, in measure her mind's°
Burden, in wind's burly and beat of endragonèd seas.

28

But how shall I . . . make me room there:
    Reach me a . . . Fancy, come faster—°
Strike you the sight of it? look at it loom there,
    Thing that she . . . there then! the Master,   220
Ipse, the only one, Christ, King, Head:°

He was to cure the extremity where he had cast her;
    Do, deal, lord it with living and dead;
Let him ride, her pride, in his triumph, despatch and have done
      with his doom there.

29

    Ah! there was a heart right
    There was single eye!°
Read the unshapeable shock night°
    And knew the who and the why;
Wording it how but by him that present and past,°
Heaven and earth are word of, worded by?—   230
    The Simon Peter of a soul! to the blast°
Tarpeian-fast, but a blown beacon of light.°

30

    Jesu, heart's light,
    Jesu, maid's son,
What was the feast followed the night°
    Thou hadst glory of this nun?—
Feast of the one woman without stain.
For so conceivèd, so to conceive thee is done;°
    But here was heart-throe, birth of a brain,°
Word, that heard and kept thee and uttered thee outright.°   240

31

    Well, she has thee for the pain, for the
    Patience; but pity of the rest of them!
Heart, go and bleed at a bitterer vein for the
    Comfortless unconfessed of them—°
No not uncomforted: lovely-felicitous Providence
Finger of a tender of, O of a feathery delicacy, the breast of the
    Maiden could obey so, be a bell to, ring of it, and
Startle the poor sheep back! is the shipwrack then a harvest, does
      tempest carry the grain for thee?

32

I admire thee, master of the tides,
    Of the Yore-flood, of the year's fall;°   250
  The recurb and the recovery of the gulf's sides,°
    The girth of it and the wharf of it and the wall;
Stanching, quenching ocean of a motionable mind;°
Ground of being, and granite of it: past all
    Grasp God, throned behind
Death with a sovereignty that heeds but hides, bodes but abides;°

33

With a mercy that outrides
    The all of water, an ark
  For the listener; for the lingerer with a love glides
    Lower than death and the dark;°   260
A vein for the visiting of the past-prayer, pent in prison,°
The-last-breath penitent spirits—the uttermost mark
    Our passion-plungèd giant risen,
The Christ of the Father compassionate, fetched in the storm of his
        strides.

34

Now burn, new born to the world,°
    Doubled-naturèd name,
  The heaven-flung, heart-fleshed, maiden-furled°
    Miracle-in-Mary-of-flame,
Mid-numbered He in three of the thunder-throne!°
Not a dooms-day dazzle in his coming nor dark as he came;°   270
    Kind, but royally reclaiming his own;
A released shower, let flash to the shire, not a lightning of fire
        hard-hurled.°

35

Dame, at our door°
    Drowned, and among our shoals,
  Remember us in the roads, the heaven-haven of the Reward:°
    Our King back, oh, upon English souls!

Let him easter in us, be a dayspring to the dimness of us, be a
     crimson-cresseted east,°
More brightening her, rare-dear Britain, as his reign rolls,
    Pride, rose, prince, hero of us, high-priest,
Our hearts' charity's hearth's fire, our thoughts' chivalry's throng's
     Lord.   280

The Starlight Night°

Look at the stars! look, look up at the skies!
  O look at all the fire-folk sitting in the air!
  The bright boroughs, the circle-citadels there!
Down in dim woods the diamond delves! the elves'-eyes!

The grey lawns cold where gold, where quickgold lies!°
  Wind-beat whitebeam! airy abeles set on a flare!°
  Flake-doves sent floating forth at a farmyard scare!—
Ah well! it is all a purchase, all is a prize.

Buy then! bid then!—What?—Prayer, patience, alms, vows.
Look, look: a May-mess, like on orchard boughs!°   10
  Look! March-bloom, like on mealed-with-yellow sallows!°
These are indeed the barn; withindoors house°
The shocks. This piece-bright paling shuts the spouse°
  Christ home, Christ and his mother and all his hallows.

Spring and Fall:°

TO A YOUNG CHILD

Márgarét, are you gríeving
Over Goldengrove unleaving?°
Leáves, líke the things of man, you
With your fresh thoughts care for, can you?
Áh! ás the heart grows older
It will come to such sights colder°

By and by, nor spare a sigh
Though worlds of wanwood leafmeal lie;°
And yet you will weep and know why.°
Now no matter, child, the name: 10
Sórrow's springs áre the same.
Nor mouth had, no nor mind, expressed
What heart heard of, ghost guessed:
It ís the blight man was born for,°
It is Margaret you mourn for.

Inversnaid

This darksome burn, horseback brown,°
His rollrock highroad roaring down,
In coop and in comb the fleece of his foam°
Flutes and low to the lake falls home.°

A windpuff-bonnet of fáwn-fróth°
Turns and twindles over the broth°
Of a pool so pitchblack, féll frówning,
It rounds and rounds Despair to drowning.

Degged with dew, dappled with dew°
Are the groins of the braes that the brook treads through,   10
Wiry heathpacks, flitches of fern,°
And the beadbonny ash that sits over the burn.°

What would the world be, once bereft
Of wet and of wildness? Let them be left,
O let them be left, wildness and wet;
Long live the weeds and the wilderness yet.

Duns Scotus's Oxford°

Towery city and branchy between towers;
Cuckoo-echoing, bell-swarmèd, lark-charmèd, rook-racked,
    river-rounded;°
The dapple-eared lily below thee; that country and town did
Once encounter in, here coped and poisèd powers;

Thou hast a base and brickish skirt there, sours°
That neighbour-nature thy grey beauty is grounded
Best in; graceless growth, thou hast confounded
Rural rural keeping—folk, flocks, and flowers.

Yet ah! this air I gather and I release
He lived on; these weeds and waters, these walls are what   10
He haunted who of all men most sways my spirits to peace;°

Of realty the rarest-veinèd unraveller; a not°
Rivalled insight, be rival Italy or Greece;°
Who fired France for Mary without spot.°

Felix Randal

Felix Randal the farrier, O he is dead then? my duty all ended,°
Who have watched his mould of man, big-boned and
    hardy-handsome
Pining, pining, till time when reason rambled in it and some
Fatal four disorders, fleshed there, all contended?

Sickness broke him. Impatient he cursed at first, but mended°
Being anointed and all; though a heavenlier heart began some
Months earlier, since I had our sweet reprieve and ransom°
Tendered to him. Ah well, God rest him all road ever he offended!°

This seeing the sick endears them to us, us too it endears.°   9
My tongue had taught thee comfort, touch had quenched thy tears,
Thy tears that touched my heart, child Felix, poor Felix Randal;

How far from then forethought of, all thy more boisterous years,
When thou at the random grim forge, powerful amidst peers,°
Didst fettle for the great grey drayhorse his bright and battering
    sandal!°

'I wake and feel the fell of dark, not day'

I wake and feel the fell of dark, not day.°
What hours, O what black hoürs we have spent
This night! what sights you, heart, saw; ways you went!
And more must, in yet longer light's delay.°
    With witness I speak this. But where I say
Hours I mean years, mean life. And my lament
Is cries countless, cries like dead letters sent
To dearest him that lives alas! away.

    I am gall, I am heartburn. God's most deep decree
Bitter would have me taste: my taste was me;   10
Bones built in me, flesh filled, blood brimmed the curse.
    Selfyeast of spirit a dull dough sours. I see°
The lost are like this, and their scourge to be
As I am mine, their sweating selves; but worse.

That Nature is a Heraclitean Fire and of the Comfort of the Resurrection°

Cloud-puffball, torn tufts, tossed pillows flaunt forth, then chevy on an air-°
built thoroughfare: heaven-roysterers, in gay-gangs they throng: they glitter in marches.
Down roughcast, down dazzling whitewash, wherever an elm arches,
Shivelights and shadowtackle in long lashes lace, lance, and pair.°
Delightfully the bright wind boisterous ropes, wrestles, beats earth bare°
Of yestertempest's creases; in pool and rut peel parches°
Squandering ooze to squeezed dough, crust, dust; stanches, starches
Squadroned masks and manmarks treadmire toil there
Footfretted in it. Million-fuelèd, nature's bonfire burns on.
But quench her bonniest, dearest to her, her clearest-selvèd spark 10

Man, how fast his firedint, his mark on mind, is gone!
Both are in an unfathomable, all is in an enormous dark
Drowned. O pity and indignation! Manshape, that shone
Sheer off, disseveral, a star, death blots black out; nor mark°
        Is any of him at all so stark
But vastness blurs and time beats level. Enough! the Resurrection,
A heart's-clarion! Away grief's gasping, joyless days, dejection.
        Across my foundering deck shone
A beacon, an eternal beam. Flesh fade, and mortal trash
Fall to the residuary worm; world's wildfire, leave but ash: 20
        In a flash, at a trumpet crash,°
I am all at once what Christ is, since he was what I am, and
This Jack, joke, poor potsherd, patch, matchwood, immortal
  diamond,°
        Is immortal diamond.

'Thou art indeed just, Lord, if I contend'

*Justus quidem tu es, Domine, si disputem tecum: verumtamen justa loquar ad te:
Quare via impiorum prosperatur? &c.*

    Thou art indeed just, Lord, if I contend
    With thee; but, sir, so what I plead is just.
    Why do sinners' ways prosper? and why must
Disappointment all I endeavour end?
    Wert thou my enemy, O thou my friend,
    How wouldst thou worse, I wonder, than thou dost
    Defeat, thwart me? Oh, the sots and thralls of lust
Do in spare hours more thrive than I that spend,
    Sir, life upon thy cause. See, banks and brakes
    Now, leavèd how thick! lacèd they are again   10
    With fretty chervil, look, and fresh wind shakes
Them; birds build—but not I build; no, but strain,
    Time's eunuch, and not breed one work that wakes.
Mine, O thou lord of life, send my roots rain.

ANDREW LANG
Brahma

If the wild bowler thinks he bowls,
    Or if the batsman thinks he's bowled,
They know not, poor misguided souls,
    They too shall perish unconsoled.
I am the batsman and the bat,
    I am the bowler and the ball,
The umpire, the pavilion cat,
    The roller, pitch, and stumps, and all.

ARTHUR O'SHAUGNESSY
Silences
To———

'Tis a world of silences. I gave a cry
    In the first sorrow my heart could not withstand;
I saw men pause, and listen, and look sad,
As though an answer in their hearts they had;
    Some turned away, some came and took my hand,
For all reply.

I stood beside a grave. Years had passed by;
    Sick with unanswered life I turned to death,
And whispered all my question to the grave,
And watched the flowers desolately wave,
    And grass stir on it with a fitful breath,
For all reply.

I raised my eyes to heaven; my prayer went high
    Into the luminous mystery of the blue;
My thought of God was purer than a flame
And God it seemed a little nearer came,
    Then passed; and greater still the silence grew,
For all reply.

10

But you! If I can speak before I die,
   I spoke to you with all my soul, and when   20
I look at you 'tis still my soul you see.
Oh, in your heart was there no word for me?
   All would have answered had you answered then
With even a sigh.

The Cypress

O Ivory bird, that shakest thy wan plumes,
   And dost forget the sweetness of thy throat
   For a most strange and melancholy note—
That wilt forsake the summer and the blooms
   And go to winter in a place remote!

The country where thou goest, Ivory bird!
   It hath no pleasant nesting-place for thee;
   There are no skies nor flowers fair to see,
Nor any shade at noon—as I have heard—
   But the black shadow of the Cypress tree.   10

The Cypress tree, it groweth on a mound;
   And sickly are the flowers it hath of May,
   Full of a false and subtle spell are they;
For whoso breathes the scent of them around,
   He shall not see the happy Summer day.

In June, it bringeth forth, O Ivory bird!
   A winter berry, bitter as the sea;
   And whoso eateth of it, woe is he—
He shall fall pale, and sleep—as I have heard—
   Long in the shadow of the Cypress tree.   20

EUGENE LEE-HAMILTON

Ipsissimus°

Thou priest that art behind the screen
  Of this confessional, give ear:
I need God's help, for I have seen
  What turns my vitals limp with fear.
O Christ, O Christ, I must have done
More mortal sin than any one
  Who says his prayers in Venice here!

And yet by stealth I only tried
  To kill my enemy, God knows;
And who on earth has yet denied   10
  A man the right to kill his foes?
He won the race of the Gondoliers;
I hate him and the skin he wears;
  I hate him and the shade he throws.

I hate him through each day and hour;
  All ills that curse me seem his fault;
He makes my daily soup taste sour,
  He makes my daily bread taste salt.
And so I hung upon his track
At dusk, to stab him in the back   20
  In some lone street or archway vault.

But oh, give heed!—As I was stealing
  Upon his heels, with knife grasped tight,
There crept across my soul a feeling
  That I myself was kept in sight.
Each time I turned, dodge as I would,
A masked and unknown watcher stood,
  Who baffled all my plans that night.

What mask is this, I thought and thought,
  Who dogs me thus, when least I care?   30

His figure is nor tall nor short,
 And yet has a familiar air.
But oh, despite this watcher's eye,
I'll reach my man yet, by-and-by,
 And snuff his life out yet, elsewhere!

And though compelled to thus defer,
 I schemed another project soon;
I armed my boat with a hidden spur,
 To run him down in the lagoon.
At dusk I saw him row one day   40
Where low and wide the waters lay,
 Reflecting scarce the dim white moon.

No boat, as far as sight could strain,
 Loomed on the solitary sea;
I saw my oar each minute gain
 Upon my death-doomed enemy. . . .
When lo, a black-masked gondolier,
Silent and spectre-like, drew near,
 And stepped between my deed and me.

He seemed to rise from out the flood,   50
 And hovered near, to mar my game;
I knew him and his cursed hood,
 His cursed mask: he was the same.
So, balked once more, enraged and cowed,
Back through the still lagoon I rowed
 In mingled wonder, wrath, and shame.

Oh, were I not to come and pray
 Thee for thy absolution here
In the confessional to-day,
 My very ribs would burst with fear.   60
Leave not, good Father, in the lurch,
An honest son of Mother Church,
 Whose faith is firm and soul sincere.

Behind St Luke's, as the dead men know,
    A pale apothecary dwells,
Who deals in death both quick and slow,
    And baleful philtres, withering spells.
He sells alike to rich and poor
Who know what knocks to give his door,
    The yellow powder that rings the knells.   70

Well then, I went and knocked the knock
    With cautious hand, as I'd been taught;
The door revolved with silent lock,
    And I went in, suspecting naught.
But oh, the self-same form stood masked
Behind the counter, and unasked
    In silence proffered what I sought.

My knees and hands like aspens shook:
    I spilt the powder on the ground;
I dared not turn, I dared not look;   80
    My palsied tongue would make no sound.
Then through the door I fled at last,
With feet that seemed more slow than fast,
    And dared not even once turn round.

And yet I am an honest man,
    Who only sought to kill his foe:
Could I sit down and see each plan
    That I took up frustrated so?
God wot, as every scheme was balked,
And in the sun my man still walked,   90
    I felt my hatred grow and grow.

I thought, 'At dusk, with stealthy tread
    I'll seek his dwelling, and I'll creep
Upstairs, and hide beneath his bed,
    And in the night I'll strike him deep.'
And so I went; but at his door
The figure, masked just as before,
    Sat on the step, as if asleep.

Bent, spite all fear, upon my task,
   I tried to pass: there was no space.   100
Then rage prevailed; I snatched the mask
   From off the baffling figure's face. . . .
And (oh, unutterable dread!)
The face was mine,—mine white and dead,—
   Stiff with some frightful death's grimace.

What sins are mine, oh, luckless wight!
   That fate should play me such a trick,
And make me see a sudden sight
   That turns both soul and body sick?
Stretch out thy hands, thou Priest unseen,   110
That sittest there behind the screen,
   And give me absolution quick!

O God, O God, his hands are dead!
   His hands are mine, oh, monstrous spell!
I feel them clammy on my head:
   Is he my own dead self as well?
Those hands are mine,—their scars, their shape:
O God, O God, there's no escape,
   And seeking Heaven, I fall on Hell!

On Two of Signorelli's Frescoes°

I. — THE RISING OF THE DEAD

I saw a vast bare plain, and, overhead,
   A half-chilled sun that shed a sickly light;
   While far and wide, till out of reach of sight,
The earth's thin crust was heaving with the dead,

Who, as they struggled from their dusty bed,
   At first mere bones, by countless years made white,
   Took gradual flesh, and stood all huddled tight
In mute, dull groups, as yet too numb to dread.

And all the while the summoning trump on high
  With rolling thunder never ceased to shake   10
The livid vault of that unclouded sky,

Calling fresh hosts of skeletons to take
  Each his identity; until well-nigh
The whole dry worn-out earth appeared to wake.

II.—THE BINDING OF THE LOST

In monstrous caverns, lit but by the glare
  From pools of molten stone, the lost are pent
  In silent herds,—dim, shadowy, vaguely blent,
Yet each alone with his own black despair;

While, through the thickness of the lurid air,
  The flying fiends, from some far unseen vent,
  Bring on their bat-wing'd backs, in swift descent,
The souls who swell the waiting myriads there.

And then begins the binding of the lost
  With snaky thongs, before they be transferred   10
To realms of utter flame or utter frost;

And, like a sudden ocean boom, is heard,
  Uprising from the dim and countless host,
Pain's first vague roar, Hell's first wild useless word.

Judith and Holofernes°

There was a gleam of jewels in the tent
  Which one dim cresset lit—a baleful gleam—
  And from his scattered armour seemed to stream
A dusky, evil light that came and went.

But from her eyes, as over him she bent,
  Watching the surface of his drunken dream,
  There shot a deadlier ray, a darker beam,
A look in which her life's one lust found vent.

There was a hissing through her tightened teeth,
  As with her scimitar she crouched above   10
  His dark, doomed head, and held her perilous breath,

While ever and anon she saw him move
  His red lascivious lips, and smile beneath
His curled and scented beard, and mutter love.

Fading Glories

In or and azure were they shrined of old,
  Where led dim aisle to glowing stained-glass rose,
  Like life's dim lane, with Heaven at its close;
Where censer swung, and organ-thunder rolled;

Where mitred, croziered, and superbly stoled,°
  Pale pontiffs gleamed, in dusky minster shows;
  Where, like a soul that trembling skyward goes,
The Easter hymn soared up on wings of gold.

And now they stand with aureoles that time dims
  Near young Greek fauns that pagan berries wreathe,   10
In crowded glaring galleries of dead art.

Their hands still fold; their lips still sing faint hymns;
  Or are they prayers that beautiful shapes breathe
For shelter in some cold eclectic heart?

WILLIAM JAMES RENTON

Clouded

Within the wood the cattle black and dun
  Are slowly straying.
Small need to hide from aught the hidden sun
  Is raying.

Else would a deeper shadow blur
   Those ruby-mantled props
   Of plumy fir,
And shake the velvet dust from out their tops.

Wych-Elms

Gray rock is brown beneath the flow
Of limpid water, splashed below
In foam and warm with flush
Of lemon in the level gush
That dartles under.
Where interlaced,
As thwarting one another in their haste
To find the calm they seek,
Or to bespeak
The careless water wonder,   10
Twin elm shoots stretch across
The streamlet, swathed in drooping moss.
Like dripping oars suspended;
With silver spaces clear, unblended,
Unlost
Amid the green,
Like the white foam embossed
On the fair fall they overlean.

Pool

Pool from sea,
   Sea-rocks slope,
   Sea-weeds grope
Into thee,
Whose the opal-lemon is
Above the blood anemones.

The Bee°

He comes, with threatening murmur known,
But none cares whence, nor how long flown
From the dear tuft he sounded last—
Birdsfoot or wild thyme—fretting past,
Fumbling and stammering the while.
But here he comes, and clears the stile,
And sways him in his devious course
To sweets his singing trump had spoken
Afar. Now he alights perforce—
The thistle cushions swerve in token.   10
But he, he bustles gaily stern
And importunes them all in turn;
Speaking aside, and muttering
With menace sunk to inuendo,
Or stifled in the last lush thing.

But now it steals a clear crescendo,
As up he swarms and will not stop,
Albeit the trial bend him double,
Till he has climbed the midmost top.
Stumbling and mumbling on he fares   20
As gingerly as hound in stubble;
Then settles to his task—a tug—
A droning lisp—and all is snug.
Like gossamer veils the wings he bears
Stream by him; and he has a mind
By fits to chafe his limbs behind.
He grumbles, rises, off he wears—
A moment heaves in sight and comes
Cruising in middle air and hums,
Then luffs and goes, his hum and he.   30
He vanishes, the buccaneer!
He follows wealth where'er he steer;
He finds him health where'er he presses:

He drinks him health—and so may we—
We drink his health: The brindled Bee!
The summer season's velveteer,
And pursuivant of fragrant wildernesses.

ALICE MEYNELL

The Rainy Summer

There's much afoot in heaven and earth this year;
   The winds hunt up the sun, hunt up the moon,
Trouble the dubious dawn, hasten the drear
   Height of a threatening noon.

No breath of boughs, no breath of leaves, of fronds
   May linger or grow warm; the trees are loud;
The forest, rooted, tosses in his bonds,
   And strains against the cloud.

No scents may pause within the garden-fold;
   The rifled flowers are cold as ocean-shells;   10
Bees, humming in the storm, carry their cold
   Wild honey to cold cells.

The Lady Poverty°

The Lady Poverty was fair:
But she has lost her looks of late,
With change of times and change of air.
Ah slattern! she neglects her hair,
Her gown, her shoes; she keeps no state
As once when her pure feet were bare.

Or—almost worse, if worse can be—
She scolds in parlours, dusts and trims,

Watches and counts. Oh, is this she
Whom Francis met, whose step was free, 10
Who with Obedience carolled hymns,
In Umbria walked with Chastity?

Where is her ladyhood? Not here,
Not among modern kinds of men;
But in the stony fields, where clear
Through the thin trees the skies appear,
In delicate spare soil and fen,
And slender landscape and austere.

The Launch

Forth, to the alien gravity,
Forth, to the laws of ocean, we
   Builders on earth by laws of land
   Entrust this creature of our hand
Upon the calculated sea.

Fast bound to shore we cling, we creep,
And make our ship ready to leap
   Light to the flood, equipped to ride
   The strange conditions of the tide—
New weight, new force, new world: the Deep. 10

Ah thus—not thus—the Dying, kissed,
Cherished, exhorted, shriven, dismissed;
   By all the eager means we hold
   We, warm, prepare him for the cold,
To keep the incalculable tryst.

Parentage

When Augustus Caesar legislated against the unmarried citizens of Rome, he
declared them to be, in some sort, slayers of the people.

Ah no, not these!
These, who were childless, are not they who gave
So many dead unto the journeying wave,
The helpless nurselings of the cradling seas;
Not they who doomed by infallible decrees
Unnumbered man to the innumerable grave.

But those who slay
Are fathers. Theirs are armies. Death is theirs;
The death of innocences and despairs;
The dying of the golden and the grey.   10
The sentence, when these speak it, has no Nay.
And she who slays is she who bears, who bears.

Unto us a Son is Given°

Given, not lent,
And not withdrawn—once sent,
This Infant of mankind, this One,
Is still the little welcome Son.

New every year,
New born and newly dear,
He comes with tidings and a song,
The ages long, the ages long;

Even as the cold
Keen winter grows not old,   10
As childhood is so fresh, foreseen,
And spring in the familiar green.

Sudden as sweet
Come the expected feet.
All joy is young, and new all art,
And He, too, Whom we have by heart.

'I am the Way'°

Thou art the Way.
Hadst Thou been nothing but the goal,
        I cannot say
If Thou hadst ever met my soul.

        I cannot see—
I, child of process—if there lies
        An end for me,
Full of repose, full of replies.

        I'll not reproach
The road that winds, my feet that err.   10
        Access, approach
Art Thou, Time, Way, and Wayfarer.

DIGBY MACKWORTH DOLBEN

A Song of the Bar

She is only an innkeeper's daughter—
    I know it, I own it with tears,
And her eyes are accustomed to slaughter
    The ranks of the Builth volunteers.°

I know in her sweet conversation
    The Hs are laboured and rare,
But her cheek is unfading carnation,
    And the sun never sets in her hair.

Can it be that those delicate fingers
    Beer, 'bacca and sperrits dispense?   10
Can it be that at evening she lingers
    To talk with some lout at the fence?

Can it be that no distant ideal
   Has ever illumined her dreams?
Can it be that her love for that real
   Young farmer is all that it seems?

Can it be that no poetical fancies
   Ever dawned in those violet eyes?
Can it be that those exquisite glances
   Are devoted to bonnets and ties?   20

O were I a knight in a story,
   And could ride with a pennon and lance,
I would will for her napkin such glory
   As would make her a Queen of Romance.

EDWIN JOHN ELLIS

Himself

I

At Golgotha I stood alone,
   And trembled in the empty night:
The shadow of a cross was shown
   And Christ thereon who died upright.°

The shadow murmured as I went,
   'I cannot see thee,—who art thou?
Art thou my friend? or art thou sent
   In hate to rail upon me now.

'I have been Christ who linger here,
   A shadow only weak and light,   10
And I go mad with tear on tear,
   A ghost of sorrow through the night.

'I wrote with finger on the ground
   One pardon, then with blood on wood.
The priests and elders waited round,
   But none could read of all that stood.

'None read, and now I linger here,
　　Only the ghost of one who died,
For God forsakes me, and the spear
　　Runs ever cold into my side.　　　　　20

'I have believed in thee when then
　　Thou wert not born, nor might I tell
Thy face among the souls of men
　　Unborn, but yet I loved thee well.

'Pity me now for this my death;
　　Love me a little for my love,
I loved and died, the story saith,
　　And telleth over and above.

'Of all my early days of want,
　　And days of work, and then the end,　　30
But telleth not how still I haunt
　　My place of death and seek a friend.

'My God who lived in me to bless
　　The earth He made has passed away;
And left me here companionless,
　　A weary spectre night and day.

'I am the Ghost of Christ the Less,
　　Jesus the man, whose ghost was bound
And banished in the wilderness
　　And trodden deep beneath the ground.　　40

'I called it "Satan," this that still
　　Was I, and mine I might not slay,
Until the rulers came to kill
　　The God in me, who fled away.

'I saw him go, and cried to him,
　　"Eli, thou hast forsaken me!"
The nails were burning through each limb:
　　He fled to find felicity.

'Ah! then I knew the foolish wrong
    That I upon myself had wrought,   50
Then floated off that Spirit strong
    That once had seemed my own heart's thought.

'He would not stay to see my grave,
    I could not hold him, and I heard
A mocker say I could not save
    Myself, when I had lost the Word.

'Of all thy will and life, and be,
    Christ come again by flesh of thine,
Thou too shalt know what came to me,
    Then when I bound my self-hood fine   60

'And called it Satan for his sake,
    And lived, and saved the world, and died
Only for him, my light, to make
    His joy, who floated from my side,

'And left me here with wound of spears,
    A cast-off ghostly shade to rave,
And haunt the place for endless years,
    Crying, "Himself he cannot save!"'

So spoke the ghost of Joseph's son
    Haunting the place where Christ was slain: 70
I pray that e'er this world be done,
    Christ may relieve his piteous pain.

II

Yet more and more we know and see,
    For Golgotha the shade retains
Of Him who died, the Form of Thee,
    Of Him who bore Thy fleshly pains.

Nor there alone, this Form shall be
    Still seen within us, Thou dost say
Until there shine on earth and sea
    Light of the unforeboded Day.   80

O Christ the Wanderer, marked as Cain,
   We know the sign upon Thy brow;
We know the trailing cross, the stain;
   The passing footstep whispers now.

It was Thy hand, we learn at last,
   That nailed Thee in that far-off year;
Thy hand as now Thou wanderest past,
   Drives deep within Thy side the spear.

While evil holds the world in grip
   And men revile the eternal powers,   90
This vision holds Thee lip to lip
   Close to our love and makes Thee ours.

RICHARD JEFFERIES

from *The Life of the Fields*

UPTILL A THORN

Save the nightingale alone;°
She, poor bird, as all forlorn,
Lean'd her breast uptill a thorn.
                    The Passionate Pilgrim

She pinned her torn dress with a thorn torn from the bushes through
which she had scrambled to the hay-field. The gap from the lane was
narrow, made more narrow by the rapid growth of summer; her rake
caught in an ashspray, and in releasing it she 'ranted' the bosom of her
print dress. So soon as she had got through she dropped her rake on
the hay, searched for a long, nail-like thorn, and thrust it through, for
the good-looking, careless hussy never had any provision of pins about
her. Then, taking a June rose which pricked her finger, she put the
flower by the 'rant', or tear, and went to join the rest of the hay-
makers. The blood welled up out of the scratch in the finger more
freely than would have been supposed from so small a place. She put
her lips to it to suck it away, as folk do in all quarters of the earth yet

discovered, being one of those instinctive things which come without teaching. A red dot of blood stained her soft white cheek, for, in brushing back her hair with her hand, she forgot the wounded finger. With red blood on her face, a thorn and a rose in her bosom, and a hurt on her hand, she reached the chorus of rakers.

The farmer and the sun are the leading actors, and the hay-makers are the chorus, who bear the burden of the play. Marching, each a step behind the other, and yet in a row, they presented a slanting front, and so crossed the field, turning the 'wallows'. At the hedge she took her place, the last in the row. There were five men and eight women; all flouted her. The men teased her for being late again at work; she said it was so far to come. The women jeered at her for tearing her dress— she couldn't get through a 'thornin'' hedge right. There was only one thing she could do, and that was to 'make a vool of zum veller' (make a fool of some fellow). Dolly did not take much notice, except that her nervous temperament showed slight excitement in the manner she used her rake, now turning the hay quickly, now missing altogether, then catching the teeth of the rake in the buttercup-runners. The women did not fail to tell her how awkward she was. By-and-by Dolly bounced forward, and, with a flush on her cheek, took the place next to the men. They teased her too, you see, but there was no spiteful malice in their tongues. There are some natures which, naturally meek, if much condemned, defy that condemnation, and willingly give it ground of justification by open guilt. The women accused her of too free a carriage with the men; she replied by seeking their company in the broad glare of the summer day. They laughed loudly, joked, but welcomed her; they chatted with her gaily; they compelled her to sip from their ale as they paused by the hedge. By noon there was a high colour on her cheeks; the sun, the exercise, the badinage had brought it up.

So fair a complexion could not brown even in summer, exposed to the utmost heat. The beams indeed did heighten the hue of her cheeks a little, but it did not shade to brown. Her chin and neck were wholly untanned, white and soft, and the blue veins roamed at their will. Lips red, a little full perhaps; teeth slightly prominent but white and gleamy as she smiled. Dark brown hair in no great abundance, always slipping out of its confinement and straggling, now on her forehead, and now on her shoulders, like wandering bines of bryony. The softest of brown eyes under long eyelashes; eyes that seemed to see everything in its gentlest aspect, that could see no harm anywhere. A ready smile on the face, and a smile in the form. Her shape yielded so easily at each movement that it seemed to smile as she walked. Her nose was the least pleasing feature—not delicate enough to fit with the complexion, and distinctly upturned, though not offensively. But it was not noticed; no one saw anything beyond the laughing lips, the laughing shape, the eyes that melted so near to tears. The torn dress, the straggling hair, the tattered shoes, the unmended stocking, the straw hat split, the mingled poverty and carelessness—perhaps rather dreaminess—disappeared when once you had met the full untroubled gaze of those beautiful eyes. Untroubled, that is, with any ulterior thought of evil or cunning; they were as open as the day, the day which you can make your own for evil or good. So, too, like the day was she ready to the making.

No stability; now fast in motion; now slow; now by fits and starts; washing her face to-day, her hands to-morrow. Never going straight, even along the road; talking with the waggoner, helping a child to pick watercress, patting the shepherd's dog, finding a flower, and late every morning at the hay-field. It was so far to come, she said; no doubt it was, if these stoppings and doublings were counted in. No character whatever, no more than the wind; she was like a well-hung gate swinging to a touch; like water yielding to let a reed sway; like a singing-flame rising and falling to a word, and even to an altered tone of voice. A word pushed her this way; a word pushed her that. Always yielding, sweet, and gentle. Is not this the most seductive of all characters in women?

Had they left her alone, would it have been any different? Those bitter, coarse feminine tongues which gave her the name of evil, and so led her to openly announce that, as she had the name, she would carry on the game. That is an old country saying, 'Bear the name, carry the game.' If you have the name of a poacher, then poach; you will be no worse off, and you will have the pleasure of the poaching. It is a serious matter, indeed, to give any one a bad name, more especially a sensitive, nervous, beautiful girl.

Under the shady oaks at luncheon the men all petted her and flattered her in their rude way, which, rude as it was, had the advantage of admitting of no mistake. Two or three more men strolled up from other fields, luncheon in hand and eating as they came, merely to chat with her. One was a mower—a powerful fellow, big boned, big everywhere, and heavy fisted; his chest had been open since four o'clock that morning to the sun, and was tanned like his face. He took her in his mighty arms and kissed her before them all; not one dared move, for the weight of that bone-smashing fist was known. Big Mat drank, as all strong men do; he fought; beyond that there was nothing against him. He worked hard, and farmers are only too glad of a man who will work. He was rather a favourite with the master, and trusted. He kissed her twice, and then went back to his work of mowing, which needs more strength than any other country labour—a mower is to a man what a dray-horse is to a horse.

They lingered long over the luncheon under the shady oaks with the great blue tile of the sky overhead, and the sweet scent of hay around them. They lingered so long, that young Mr Andrew came to start them again, and found Dolly's cheeks all a-glow. The heat and the laughter had warmed them; her cheeks burned, in contrast to her white, pure forehead—for her hat was off—and to the cool shade of the trees. She lingered yet a little longer chatting with Mr Andrew— lingered a full half-hour—and when they parted, she had given him a rose from the hedge. Young Mr Andrew was but half a farmer's son; he was destined for a merchant's office in town; he had been educated for it, and was only awaiting the promised opening. He was young, but no yokel; too knowing of town cunning and selfish hardness to entangle himself. Yet those soft brown eyes, that laughing shape; Andrew was very young and so was she, and the summer sun burned warm.

The blackbirds whistled the day away, and the swallows sought their nests under the eaves. The curved moon hung on the sky as the hunter's horn on the wall. Timid Wat—the hare—came ambling along the lane, and almost ran against two lovers in a recess of the bushes by an elm. Andrew, Andrew! these lips are too sweet for you; get you to your desk—that sailing shape, those shaded, soft brown eyes, let them alone. Be generous—do not awaken hopes you can never, never fulfil. The new-mown hay is scented yet more sweetly in the evening—of a summer's eve it is always too soon to go home.

The blackbirds whistled again, big Mat slew the grass from the rising to the going down of the sun—moondaisies, sorrel, and buttercups lay in rows of swathe as he mowed. I wonder whether the man ever thought, as he reposed at noontide on a couch of grass under the hedge? Did he think that those immense muscles, that broad, rough-hewn plank of a chest of his, those vast bones encased in sinewy limbs—being flesh in its fulness—ought to have more of this earth than mere common men, and still more than thin-faced people—mere people, not men—in black coats? Did he dimly claim the rights of strength in his mind, and arrogate to himself the prerogatives of arbitrary kings? Who knows what big processes of reasoning, dim and big, passed through his mind in the summer days? Did he conclude he had a right to take what others only asked or worked for?

The sweet scent of the new-mown hay disappeared, the hay became whiter, the ricks rose higher, and were topped and finished. Hourly the year grew drier and sultry, as the time of wheat-harvest approached. Sap of spring had dried away; dry stalk of high summer remained, browned with heat. Mr Andrew (in the country the son is always called by his Christian name, with the prefix Master or Mr) had been sent for to London to fill the promised lucrative berth. The reapers were in the corn—Dolly tying up; big Mat slashing at the yellow stalks. Why the man worked so hard no one could imagine, unless it was for pure physical pleasure of using those great muscles. Unless, indeed, a fire, as it were, was burning in his mind, and drove him to labour to smother it, as they smother fires by beating them. Dolly was happier than ever—the gayest of the gay. She sang, she laughed, her white, gleaming teeth shone in the sunshine; it was as if she had some secret which enabled her to defy the taunts and cruel, shameless words hurled at her, like clods of earth, by the other women. Gay she was, as the brilliant poppies who, having the sun as their own, cared for nothing else.

Till suddenly, just before the close of harvest, Dolly and Mat were missing from the field. Of course their absence was slanderously connected, but there was no known ground for it. Big Mat was found intoxicated at the tavern, from which he never moved for a fortnight, spending in one long drain of drink the lump of money his mighty arms had torn from the sun in the burning hours of work. Dolly was ill at home; sometimes in her room, sometimes downstairs; but ill, shaky and weak—ague they called it. There were dark circles round her eyes, her chin drooped to her breast; she wrapped herself in a shawl in all the heat. It was some time before even the necessity of working brought her forth again, and then her manner was hurried and furtive; she would begin trembling all of a minute, and her eyes filled quickly.

By degrees the autumn advanced, and the rooks followed the

ploughman. Dolly gradually recovered something of her physical buoyancy; her former lightheartedness never returned. Sometimes an incident would cause a flash of the old gaiety, only for her to sink back into subdued quietness. The change was most noticeable in her eyes; soft and tender still, brown and velvety, there was a deep sadness in them—the longer she looked at you, the more it was visible. They seemed as if her spirit had suffered some great wrong; too great for redress, and that could only be borne in silence.

How beautiful are beautiful eyes! Not from one aspect only, as a picture is, where the light falls rightly on it—the painter's point of view—they vary to every and any aspect. The orb rolls to meet the changing circumstance, and is adjusted to all. But a little enquiry into the mechanism of the eyes will indicate how wondrously they are formed. Science has dispelled many illusions, broken many dreams; but here, in the investigation of the eye, it has added to our marvelling interest. The eye is still like the work of a magician: it is physically divine. Besides the liquid flesh which delights the beholder, there is then the retina, the mysterious nerve which receives a thousand pictures on one surface and confuses none; and further, the mystery of the brain, which reproduces them at will, twenty years, yes, threescore years and ten, afterwards. Perhaps of all physical things, the eye is most beautiful, most divine.

Her eyes were still beautiful, but subdued and full of a great wrong. What that wrong was became apparent in the course of time. Dolly had to live with Mat, and, unhappily, not as his wife. Next harvest there was a child wrapped in a red shawl with her in the field, placed under the shocks while she worked. Her brother Bill talked and threatened—of what avail was it? The law gave no redress, and among men in these things, force is master still. There were none who could meet big Mat in fight.

Something seemed to burn in Mat like fire. Now he worked, and now he drank, but the drink which would have killed another did him no injury. He grew and flourished upon it, more bone, more muscle, more of the savage nature of original man. But there was something within on fire. Was he not satisfied even yet? Did he arrogate yet further prerogatives of kings?—prerogatives which even kings claim no longer. One day, while in drink, his heavy fist descended—he forgot his might; he did not check it, like Ulysses in the battle with Irus°—and Dolly fell.

When they lifted her up, one eye was gone.

It was utterly put out, organically destroyed; no skill, no money, no loving care could restore it. The soft, brown velvet, the laugh, the tear gone for ever. The divine eye was broken—battered as a stone might be. The exquisite structure which reflected the trees and flowers, and took to itself the colour of the summer sky, was shapeless.

In the second year, Mr Andrew came down, and one day met her in the village. He did not know her. The stoop, the dress which clothed, but responded to no curve, the sunken breast, and the sightless eye, how should he recognize these? This ragged, plain, this ugly, repellent creature—he did not know her. She spoke; Mr Andrew hastily fumbled in his pocket, fetched out half a crown, gave it, and passed on quickly. How fortunate that he had not entangled himself!

Meantime, Mat drank and worked harder than ever, and became more morose, so that no one dared cross him, yet as a worker he was trusted by the farmer. Whatever it was, the fire in him burned deeper, and to the very quick. The poppies came and went once more, the harvest moon rose yellow and ruddy, all the joy of the year proceeded, but Dolly was like a violet over which a waggon-wheel had rolled. The thorn had gone deep into her bosom.

SIR EDMUND GOSSE

Neurasthenia°

Curs'd from the cradle and awry they come,
   Masking their torment from a world at ease;
On eyes of dark entreaty, vague and dumb,
   They bear the stigma of their souls' disease.

Bewildered by the shadowy ban of birth,
   They learn that they are not as others are,
Till some go mad, and some sink prone to earth,
   And some push stumbling on without a star;

And some, of sterner mould, set hard their hearts,
   To act the dreadful comedy of life,   10

And wearily grow perfect in their parts;—
    But all are wretched and their years are strife.

The common cheer that animates mankind,
    The tender general comfort of the race,
To them is colour chattered to the blind,
    A book held up against a sightless face.

Like sailors drifting under cliffs of steel,
    Whose fluttering magnets leap with lying poles,
They doubt the truth of every law they feel,
    And death yawns for them if they trust their souls.   20

The loneliest creatures in the wash of air,
    They search the world for solace, but in vain;
No priest rewards their confidence with prayer,
    And no physician remedies their pain.

Ah! let us spare our wrath for these, forlorn,
    Nor chase a bubble on the intolerant wave;
Let pity quell the gathering storm of scorn,
    And God, who made them so, may soothe and save.

Opium Harvest

High up in hollow valleys where dim lakes
    In Karahissar find no watershed,°
    By many a snow-gorged roaring river-bed,
In long white fluttering waves the poppy shakes;

But spring-tide comes at last, and April wakes,
    And tears the petals from the golden head,
    Till, of its pink wings disinherited,
The opium-laden capsule bends and bakes.

Then, after sunset, the sleek farmers creep
    To slash the poppy-globes, and leave them soon   10
    Oozing green tears beneath the gibbous moon;

Tears, that in scallop-shells, when dawn shall peep,
    Patient, they'll gather; then, dismiss the boon
Round the wide world in bales of solid sleep.

Manes, the Heretic°

To J. L., De T.

Dark, dark at last! and this warm tide of scent, —
A west wind in a cedarn element, —
These cold leaves of the lily out of sight,
And the long single ray of sacred light!

'Tis night, then; I have slept, and o'er my sleep
The soul of love has hovered close and deep.

A bat moves in the porphyry capitals,
And cuts the clear-drawn radiance as it falls;
So man, intruding in his bestial way,
Shears from the lamp of God the heavenly ray.   10

Ah! to my keen and tempered senses rise
The temple-perfumes like a people's cries, —
The cinnamon, a prayer beneath the stars,
Adoring love pulsed from the nenuphars,
Sharp aloes, like a soul that strives with sin,
And myrrh, the song of one all chaste within;
In each I join, on each my spirit flies
To float, a thread of mist, along the skies.

By every way I soar to God's abode,   20
But rising perfumes pave the smoothest road.
Hail! Soul of all things, parted, yet not lost,
One sea of myriad breakers torn and tost,
One river eastward, westward, northward bent
And branching through a monstrous continent,
Yet drawn at last by every winding road
Down to that noiseless marish which is God!

Thou art the wind that like a player's hand
Strikes out harp-music where these columns stand,
Thou art the small hushed cry of crisp dry life   30
The terebinth gives beneath the carver's knife,
And the soft alabaster sighs for Thee
When the pale sculptor shreds it on his knee.

I pluck these fig-leaves, broad, and smooth as silk,
And godhead weeps from them in tears of milk;
I catch those fish of glimmering head and tail,
And godhead sparkles from each fading scale.
I draw the Indian curtain from my bed,
And Thou the lustrous arch above my head;
It falls in folds, and this one beam I see,   40
O tender heavenly Light, is trebly Thee!

Ah! Thou, invoked by many a mystic sign,
Bend hither from Thy secret crystalline;
O'er Thy twin angels' arms be seen to move;
Let Light and Perfume teach me Thou art Love.
In this dusk world of scentless, hueless man
My soul once heard Thee, and to light it ran,
Shot leaf and bud from out its watery bed,
And in adoring fragrance Thee-wards spread.
Then Thy soft ray, ineffable, divine,   50
Flushed my cold petals with ecstatic wine,
The pistils trembled, and the stamens flew
Straight to the centre, where their god they knew,
Clung quivering there, enkindled and aglow,
Sank, big with blessing, on the leaves below;
I bowed,—and deep within my soul I found
A fount of balm for dying worlds around.

And now, within the temple they have built,
I live to expiate a nation's guilt;
To me they blindly pray, I handing on   60
To Thee the essence of each orison.
I bask within one narrow'd beam all day,
And sleep all night within this single ray;

While, like the sound of many an instrument,
Floats round me ever this rich tide of scent.
So may I live till all my dreams are o'er,
Then on a shaft of radiance upward soar,
Fade as a thread of dew the sun draws up,
And, kindled high in heaven's inverted cup,
Like some aroma melt into the sense
Of Thy supine and cold omnipotence.

WILLIAM ERNEST HENLEY

Nocturn

At the barren heart of midnight,
    When the shadow shuts and opens
    As the loud flames pulse and flutter,
    I can hear a cistern leaking.

Dripping, dropping, in a rhythm,
    Rough, unequal, half-melodious,
    Like the measures aped from nature
    In the infancy of music;

Like the buzzing of an insect,
    Still, irrational, persistent . . .
    I must listen, listen, listen   10
    In a passion of attention;

Till it taps upon my heartstrings,
    And my very life goes dripping,
    Dropping, dripping, drip-drip-dropping,
    In the drip-drop of the cistern.

'Out of the night that covers me'

Out of the night that covers me,
    Black as the Pit from pole to pole,°
I thank whatever gods may be°
    For my unconquerable soul.

In the fell clutch of circumstance
   I have not winced nor cried aloud.
Under the bludgeonings of chance
   My head is bloody, but unbowed.

Beyond this place of wrath and tears
   Looms but the Horror of the shade   10
And yet the menace of the years
   Finds, and shall find, me unafraid.

It matters not how strait the gate,°
   How charged with punishments the scroll,°
I am the master of my fate:
   I am the captain of my soul.

'Madam Life's a piece in bloom'

Madam Life's a piece in bloom°
   Death goes dogging everywhere:
She's the tenant of the room,
   He's the ruffian on the stair.

You shall see her as a friend,
   You shall bilk him once and twice;
But he'll trap you in the end,
   And he'll stick you for her price.

With his kneebones at your chest,
   And his knuckles in your throat,   10
You would reason—plead—protest!
   Clutching at her petticoat;

But she's heard it all before,
   Well she knows you've had your fun,
Gingerly she gains the door,
   And your little job is done.

Villon's Straight Tip to All Cross Coves°

Tout aux tavernes et aux filles.°

Suppose you screeve? or go cheap-jack?°
  Or fake the broads? or fig a nag?°
Or thimble-rig? or knap a yack?°
  Or pitch a snide? or smash a rag?°
  Suppose you duff? or nose and lag?°
Or get the straight, and land your pot?°
  How do you melt the multy swag?°
Booze and the blowens cop the lot.°

Fiddle, or fence, or mace, or mack;°
  Or moskeneer, or flash the drag;°   10
Dead-lurk a crib, or do a crack;°
  Pad with a slang, or chuck a fag;°
  Bonnet, or tout, or mump and gag;°
Rattle the tats, or mark the spot;°
  You can not bank a single stag;°
Booze and the blowens cop the lot.

Suppose you try a different tack,
  And on the square you flash your flag?°
At penny-a-lining make your whack,°
  Or with the mummers mug and gag?°   20
  For nix, for nix the dibbs you bag!°
At any graft, no matter what,°
  Your merry goblins soon stravag:°
Booze and the blowens cop the lot.

THE MORAL

It's up the spout and Charley Wag°
With wipes and tickers and what not.°
  Until the squeezer nips your scrag,°
Booze and the blowens cop the lot.

ROBERT LOUIS STEVENSON

from *Weir of Hermiston*

CHAPTER I

LIFE AND DEATH OF MRS WEIR

The Lord Justice-Clerk was a stranger in that part of the country; but his lady wife was known there from a child, as her race had been before her. The old 'riding Rutherfords of Hermiston', of whom she was the last descendant, had been famous men of yore, ill neighbours, ill subjects, and ill husbands to their wives though not their properties. Tales of them were rife for twenty miles about; and their name was even printed in the page of our Scots histories, not always to their credit. One bit the dust at Flodden;° one was hanged at his peel door° by James the Fifth;° another fell dead in a carouse with Tom Dalzell; while a fourth (and that was Jean's own father) died presiding at a Hell-Fire Club,° of which he was the founder. There were many heads shaken in Crossmichael at that judgement; the more so as the man had a villainous reputation among high and low, and both with the godly and the worldly. At that very hour of his demise, he had ten going pleas before the session, eight of them oppressive. And the same doom extended even to his agents; his grieve,° that had been his right hand in many a left-hand business, being cast from his horse one night and drowned in a peat-hag° on the Kye-skairs;° and his very doer (although lawyers have long spoons) surviving him not long, and dying on a sudden in a bloody flux.

In all these generations, while a male Rutherford was in the saddle with his lads, or brawling in a change-house, there would be always a white-faced wife immured at home in the old peel or the later mansion-house. It seemed this succession of martyrs bided long, but took their vengeance in the end, and that was in the person of the last descendant, Jean. She bore the name of the Rutherfords, but she was the daughter of their trembling wives. At the first she was not wholly without charm. Neighbours recalled in her, as a child, a strain of elfin wilfulness, gentle little mutinies, sad little gaieties, even a morning gleam of beauty that was not to be fulfilled. She withered in the growing, and (whether it was the sins of her sires or the sorrows of her mothers) came to her maturity depressed, and, as it were, defaced; no blood of life in her, no grasp or gaiety; pious, anxious, tender, tearful, and incompetent.

It was a wonder to many that she had married—seeming so wholly of the stuff that makes old maids. But chance cast her in the path of Adam Weir, then the new Lord Advocate, a recognized, risen man, the conqueror of many obstacles, and thus late in the day beginning to think upon a wife. He was one who looked rather to obedience than beauty, yet it would seem he was struck with her at the first look. 'Wha's she?' he said, turning to his host; and, when he had been told, 'Ay,' says he, 'she looks menseful.° She minds me——'; and then, after a pause (which some have been daring enough to set down to sentimental recollections), 'Is she releegious?' he asked, and was shortly after, at his own request, presented. The acquaintance, which it seems profane to call a courtship, was pursued with Mr Weir's accustomed industry, and was long a legend, or rather a source of legends, in the Parliament House. He was described coming, rosy with much port, into the drawing-room, walking direct up to the lady, and assailing her with pleasantries, to which the embarrassed fair one responded, in what seemed a kind of agony, 'Eh, Mr Weir!' or 'O, Mr Weir!' or 'Keep me, Mr Weir!' On the very eve of their engagement it was related that one had drawn near to the tender couple, and had overheard the lady cry out, with the tones of one who talked for the sake of talking, 'Keep me, Mr Weir, and what became of him?' and the profound accents of the suitor's reply, 'Haangit, mem, haangit.' The motives upon either side were much debated. Mr Weir must have supposed his bride to be somehow suitable; perhaps he belonged to that class of men who think a weak head the ornament of women—an opinion invariably punished in this life. Her descent and her estate were beyond question. Her wayfaring ancestors and her litigious father had done well by Jean. There was ready money and there were broad acres, ready to fall wholly to the husband, to lend dignity to his descendants, and to himself a title, when he should be called upon the Bench. On the side of Jean there was perhaps some fascination of curiosity as to this unknown male animal that approached her with the roughness of a ploughman and the *aplomb* of an advocate. Being so trenchantly opposed to all she knew, loved, or understood, he may well have seemed to her the extreme, if scarcely the ideal, of his sex. And besides, he was an ill man to refuse. A little over forty at the period of his marriage, he looked already older, and to the force of manhood added the senatorial dignity of years; it was, perhaps, with an unreverend awe, but he was awful. The Bench, the Bar, and the most experienced and reluctant witness, bowed to his authority—and why not Jeannie Rutherford?

The heresy about foolish women is always punished, I have said, and Lord Hermiston began to pay the penalty at once. His house in George Square was wretchedly ill-guided; nothing answerable to the expense of maintenance but the cellar, which was his own private care. When things went wrong at dinner, as they continually did, my lord would look up the table at his wife: 'I think these broth would be better to swim in than to sup.' Or else to the butler: 'Here, M'Killop, awa' wi' this Raadical gigot°—tak' it to the French, man, and bring me some puddocks!° It seems rather a sore kind of business that I should be all day in Court haanging Raadicals, and get nawthing to my denner.' Of course this was but a manner of speaking, and he had never hanged a man for being a Radical in his life; the law, of which he was the faithful minister, directing otherwise. And of course these growls were in the nature of pleasantry, but it was of a recondite sort; and uttered as they were in his resounding voice, and commented on by that expression which they called in the Parliament House 'Hermiston's hanging face'—they struck mere dismay into the wife. She sat before him speechless and fluttering; at each dish, as at a fresh ordeal, her eye hovered toward my lord's countenance and fell again; if he but ate in silence, unspeakable relief was her portion; if there were complaint, the world was darkened. She would seek out the cook, who was always her *sister in the Lord*. 'O my dear, this is the most dreidful thing that my lord can never be contented in his own house!' she would begin; and weep and pray with the cook; and then the cook would pray with Mrs Wier; and the next day's meal would never be a penny the better—and the next cook (when she came) would be worse, if anything, but just as pious. It was often wondered that Lord Hermiston bore it as he did; indeed he was a stoical old voluptuary, contented with sound wine and plenty of it. But there were moments when he overflowed. Perhaps half a dozen times in the history of his married life—'Here! tak' it awa', and bring me a piece of bread and kebbuck!'° he had exclaimed, with an appalling explosion of his voice and rare gestures. None thought to dispute or to make excuses; the service was arrested; Mrs Weir sat at the head of the table whimpering without disguise; and his lordship opposite munched his bread and cheese in ostentatious disregard. Once only Mrs Weir had ventured to appeal. He was passing her chair on his way into the study.

'O, Edom!' she wailed, in a voice tragic with tears, and reaching out to him both hands, in one of which she held a sopping pocket-handkerchief.

He paused and looked upon her with a face of wrath, into which there stole, as he looked, a twinkle of humour.

'Noansense!' he said. 'You and your noansense! What do I want with a Christian faim'ly? I want Christian broth! Get me a lass that can plain-boil a potato, if she was a whüre off the streets.' And with these words, which echoed in her tender ears like blasphemy, he had passed on to his study and shut the door behind him.

Such was the housewifery in George Square. It was better at Hermiston, where Kirstie Elliot, the sister of a neighbouring bonnet-laird,° and an eighteenth cousin of the lady's, bore the charge of all, and kept a trim house and a good country table. Kirstie was a woman in a thousand, clean, capable, notable; once a moorland Helen, and still comely as a blood horse and healthy as the hill wind. High in flesh and voice and colour, she ran the house with her whole intemperate soul, in a bustle, not without buffets. Scarce more pious than decency in those days required, she was the cause of many an anxious thought and many a tearful prayer to Mrs Weir. Housekeeper and mistress renewed the parts of Martha and Mary; and though with a pricking conscience Mary reposed on Martha's strength as on a rock. Even Lord Hermiston held Kirstie in a particular regard. There were few with whom he unbent so gladly, few whom he favoured with so many pleasantries. 'Kirstie and me maun have our joke,' he would declare, in high good-humour, as he buttered Kirstie's scones and she waited at table. A man who had no need either of love or of popularity, a keen reader of men and of events, there was perhaps only one truth for which he was quite unprepared: he would have been quite unprepared to learn that Kirstie hated him. He thought maid and master were well matched; hard, handy, healthy, broad Scots folk, without a hair of nonsense to the pair of them. And the fact was that she made a goddess and an only child of the effete and tearful lady; and even as she waited at table her hands would sometimes itch for my lord's ears.

Thus, at least, when the family were at Hermiston, not only my lord, but Mrs Weir too, enjoyed a holiday. Free from the dreadful looking-for of the miscarried dinner, she would mind her seam, read her piety books, and take her walk (which was my lord's orders), sometimes by herself, sometimes with Archie, the only child of that scarce natural union. The child was her next bond to life. Her frosted sentiment bloomed again, she breathed deep of life, she let loose her heart, in that society. The miracle of her motherhood was ever new to her. The sight of the little man at her skirt intoxicated her with the sense of power, and froze her with the consciousness of her responsibility. She looked forward, and, seeing him in fancy grow up and play his diverse part on the world's theatre, caught in her breath and lifted up her courage with a lively effort. It was only with the child that she forgot herself and was at moments natural; yet it was only with the child that she had conceived and managed to pursue a scheme of conduct. Archie was to be a great man and a good; a minister if possible, a saint for certain. She tried to engage his mind upon her favourite books, Rutherford's 'Letters',° Scougal's 'Grace Abounding',° and the like. It was a common practice of hers (and strange to remember now) that she would carry the child to the Deil's Hags, sit with him on the Praying Weaver's stone and talk of the Covenanters till their tears ran down. Her view of history was wholly artless, a design in snow and ink; upon the one side, tender innocents with psalms upon their lips; upon the other the persecutors, booted, bloody-minded, flushed with wine; a suffering Christ, a raging Beelzebub. Persecutor was a word that knocked upon the woman's heart; it was her highest thought of wickedness, and the mark of it was on her house. Her great-great-grandfather had drawn the sword against the Lord's anointed on the field of Rullion Green, and breathed his last (tradition said) in the arms of the detestable Dalyell. Nor could she blind herself to this, that had they lived in these old days, Hermiston himself would have been numbered alongside of Bloody Mackenzie° and the politic Lauderdale° and Rothes,° in the band of God's immediate enemies. The sense of this moved her to the more fervour; she had a voice for that name of persecutor that thrilled in the child's marrow; and when one day the mob hooted and hissed them all in my lord's travelling carriage, and cried, 'Down with the persecutor! down with Hanging Hermiston!' and mamma covered her eyes and wept, and papa let down the glass and looked out upon the rabble with his droll formidable face, bitter and smiling, as they said he sometimes looked when he gave sentence, Archie was for the moment too much amazed to be alarmed, but he had scarce got his mother by herself before his shrill voice was raised demanding an explanation: Why had they called papa a persecutor?

'Keep me, my precious!' she exclaimed. 'Keep me, my dear! this is poleetical. Ye must never ask me anything poleetical, Erchie. Your faither is a great man, my dear, and it's no for me or you to be judging him. It would be telling us all, if we behaved ourselves in our several stations the way your faither does in his high office; and let me hear no more of any such disrespectful and undutiful questions! No that you meant to be undutiful, my lamb; your mother kens that—she kens it well, dearie!' and so slid off to safer topics, and left on the mind of the child an obscure but ineradicable sense of something wrong.

Mrs Weir's philosophy of life was summed in one expression—tenderness. In her view of the universe, which was all lighted up with a glow out of the doors of hell, good people must walk there in a kind of ecstasy of tenderness. The beasts and plants had no soul; they were here but for a day, and let their day pass gently! And as for the immortal men, on what black, downward path were many of them wending, and to what a horror of an immortality! 'Are not two sparrows,' 'Whosoever shall smite thee,' 'God sendeth His rain,' 'Judge not that ye be not judged'—these texts made her body of divinity; she put them on in the morning with her clothes and lay down to sleep with them at night; they haunted her like a favourite air, they clung about her like a favourite perfume. Their minister was a marrowy expounder of the law, and my lord sat under him with relish; but Mrs Weir respected him from far off; heard him (like the cannon of a beleaguered city) usefully booming outside on the dogmatic ramparts; and meanwhile, within and out of shot, dwelt in her private garden, which she watered with grateful tears. It seems strange to say of this colourless and ineffectual woman, but she was a true enthusiast, and might have made the sunshine and the glory of a cloister. Perhaps none but Archie knew she could be eloquent; perhaps none but he had seen her—her colour raised, her hands clasped or quivering—glow with gentle ardour. There is a corner of the policy° of Hermiston, where you come suddenly in view of the summit of Black Fell, sometimes like the mere grass top of a hill, sometimes (and this is her own expression) like a precious jewel in the heavens. On such days, upon the sudden view of it, her hand would tighten on the child's fingers, her voice rise like a song. 'I to the hills!' she would repeat.

'And O, Erchie, are na these like the hills of Naphtali?'° and her easy tears would flow.

Upon an impressionable child the effect of this continual and pretty accompaniment to life was deep. The woman's quietism and piety passed on to his different nature undiminished; but whereas in her it was a native sentiment, in him it was only an implanted dogma. Nature and the child's pugnacity at times revolted. A cad from the Potterrow once struck him in the mouth; he struck back, the pair fought it out in the back stable lane towards the Meadows, and Archie returned with a considerable decline in the number of his front teeth, and unregenerately boasting of the losses of the foe. It was a sore day for Mrs Weir; she wept and prayed over the infant backslider until my lord was due from Court, and she must resume that air of tremulous composure with which she always greeted him. The judge was that day in an observant mood, and remarked upon the absent teeth.

'I am afraid Erchie will have been fechting with some of they blagyard lads,' said Mrs Weir.

My lord's voice rang out as it did seldom in the privacy of his own house. 'I'll have nonn of that, sir!' he cried. 'Do you hear me?—nonn of that! No son of mine shall be speldering in the glaur° with any dirty raibble.'

The anxious mother was grateful for so much support; she had even feared the contrary. And that night when she put the child to bed— 'Now, my dear, ye see!' she said, 'I told you what your faither would think of it, if he heard ye had fallen into this dreidful sin; and let you and me pray to God that ye may be keepit from the like temptation or stren'thened to resist it!'

The womanly falsity of this was thrown away. Ice and iron cannot be welded; and the points of view of the Justice-Clerk and Mrs Weir were not less unassimilable. The character and position of his father had long been a stumbling-block to Archie, and with every year of his age the difficulty grew more instant. The man was mostly silent; when he spoke at all, it was to speak of the things of the world, always in a worldly spirit, often in language that the child had been schooled to think coarse, and sometimes with words that he knew to be sins in themselves. Tenderness was the first duty, and my lord was invariably harsh. God was love; the name of my lord (to all who knew him) was fear. In the world, as schematized for Archie by his mother, the place was marked for such a creature. There were some whom it was good to pity and well (though very likely useless) to pray for; they were named reprobates, goats, God's enemies, brands for the burning; and Archie tallied every mark of identification, and drew the inevitable private inference that the Lord Justice-Clerk was the chief of sinners.

The mother's honesty was scarce complete. There was one influence she feared for the child and still secretly combated; that was my lord's; and half consciously, half in a wilful blindness, she continued to undermine her husband with his son. As long as Archie remained silent, she did so ruthlessly, with a single eye to heaven and the child's salvation; but the day came when Archie spoke. It was 1801, and Archie was seven, and beyond his years for curiosity and logic, when he brought the case up openly. If judging were sinful and forbidden, how came papa to be a judge? to have that sin for a trade? to bear the name of it for a distinction?

'I can't see it,' said the little Rabbi, and wagged his head.

Mrs Weir abounded in commonplace replies.

'No, I canna see it,' reiterated Archie. 'And I'll tell you what, mamma, I don't think you and me's justifeed in staying with him.'

The woman awoke to remorse; she saw herself disloyal to her man, her sovereign and breadwinner, in whom (with what she had of worldliness) she took a certain subdued pride. She expatiated in reply on my lord's honour and greatness; his useful services in this world of sorrow and wrong, and the place in which he stood, far above where babes and innocents could hope to see or criticize. But she had builded too well—Archie had his answers pat: Were not babes and innocents the type of the kingdom of heaven? Were not honour and greatness the badges of the world? And at any rate, how about the mob that had once seethed about the carriage?

'It's all very fine,' he concluded, 'but in my opinion, papa has no right to be it. And it seems that's not the worst yet of it. It seems he's called "the Hanging Judge"—it seems he's crooool. I'll tell you what it is, mamma, there's a tex' borne in upon me: It were better for that man if a mile-stone were bound upon his back and him flung into the deepestmost pairts of the sea.'

'O my lamb, ye must never say the like of that!' she cried. 'Ye're to honour faither and mother, dear, that your days may be long in the land. It's Atheists that cry out against him—French Atheists, Erchie! Ye would never surely even yourself down to be saying the same thing as French Atheists? It would break my heart to think that of you. And

O, Erchie, here arena *you* setting up to *judge*? And have ye no' forgot God's plain command—the First with Promise, dear? Mind you upon the beam and the mote!'

Having thus carried the war into the enemy's camp, the terrified lady breathed again. And no doubt it is easy thus to circumvent a child with catchwords, but it may be questioned how far it is effectual. An instinct in his breast detects the quibble, and the voice condemns it. He will instantly submit, privately hold the same opinion. For even in this simple and antique relation of the mother and the child, hypocrisies are multiplied.

When the Court rose that year and the family returned to Hermiston, it was a common remark in all the country that the lady was sore failed. She seemed to lose and seize again her touch with life, now sitting inert in a sort of durable bewilderment, anon waking to feverish and weak activity. She dawdled about the lasses at their work, looking stupidly on; she fell to rummaging in old cabinets and presses, and desisted when half through; she would begin remarks with an air of animation and drop them without a struggle. Her common appearance was one who has forgotten something and is trying to remember; and when she overhauled, one after another, the worthless and touching mementoes of her youth, she might have been seeking the clue to that lost thought. During this period she gave many gifts to the neighbours and house lassies, giving them with a manner of regret that embarrassed the recipients.

The last night of all she was busy on some female work, and toiled upon it with so manifest and painful a devotion that my lord (who was not often curious) inquired as to its nature.

She blushed to the eyes. 'O, Edom, it's for you!' she said. 'It's slippers. I—I hae never made ye any.'

'Ye daft auld wife!' returned his lordship. 'A bonny figure I would be, palmering about in bauchles!'°

The next day, at the hour of her walk, Kirstie interfered. Kirstie took this decay of her mistress very hard; bore her a grudge, quarrelled with and railed upon her, the anxiety of a genuine love wearing the disguise of temper. This day of all days she insisted disrespectfully, with rustic fury, that Mrs Weir should stay at home. But, 'No, no,' she said, 'it's my lord's orders,' and set forth as usual. Archie was visible in the acre bog, engaged upon some childish enterprise, the instrument of which was mire; and she stood and looked at him a while like one about to call; then thought otherwise, sighed, and shook her head, and proceeded on her rounds alone. The house lassies were at the burnside washing, and saw her pass with her loose, weary, dowdy gait.

'She's a terrible feckless wife, the mistress!' said the one.

'Tut,' said the other, 'the wumman's seeck.'

'Weel, I canna see nae differ in her,' returned the first. 'A füshionless° quean,° a feckless carline.'°

The poor creature thus discussed rambled a while in the grounds without a purpose. Tides in her mind ebbed and flowed, and carried her to and fro like seaweed. She tried a path, paused, returned, and tried another; questing, forgetting her quest; the spirit of choice extinct in her bosom, or devoid of sequency. On a sudden, it appeared as though she had remembered, or had formed a resolution, wheeled about, returned with hurried steps, and appeared in the dining-room where Kirstie was at the cleaning, like one charged with an important errand.

'Kirstie!' she began, and paused; and then with conviction, 'Mr Weir isna speeritually minded, but he has been a good man to me.'

It was perhaps the first time since her husband's elevation that she had forgotten the handle to his name, of which the tender, inconsistent woman was not a little proud. And when Kirstie looked up at the speaker's face, she was aware of a change.

'Godsake, what's the maitter wi' ye, mem?' cried the housekeeper, starting from the rug.

'I do not ken,' answered her mistress, shaking her head. 'But he is not speeritually minded, my dear.'

'Here, sit down with ye! Godsake, what ails the wife?' cried Kirstie, and helped and forced her into my lord's own chair by the cheek of the hearth.°

'Keep me, what's this?' she gasped. 'Kirstie, what's this? I'm frich'ened.'

They were her last words.

It was the lowering nightfall when my lord returned. He had the sunset in his back, all clouds and glory; and before him, by the wayside, spied Kirstie Elliott waiting. She was dissolved in tears, and addressed him in the high, false note of barbarous mourning, such as still lingers modified among Scots heather.

'The Lord peety ye, Hermiston! the Lord prepare ye!' she keened out. 'Weary upon me, that I should have to tell it!'

He reined in his horse and looked upon her with the hanging face.

'Has the French landit?' cried he.

'Man, man,' she said, 'is that a' ye can think of? The Lord prepare ye, the Lord comfort and support ye!'

'Is onybody deid?' says his lordship. 'It's no Erchie?'

'Bethankit, no!' exclaimed the woman, startled into a more natural tone. 'Na, na, it's no sae bad as that. It's the mistress, my lord; she just fair flittit before my e'en. She just gi'ed a sab and was by wi' it. Eh, my bonny Miss Jeannie, that I mind sae weel!' And forth again upon that pouring tide of lamentation in which women of her class excel and over-abound.

Lord Hermiston sat in the saddle, beholding her. Then he seemed to recover command upon himself.

'Weel, it's something of the suddenest,' said he. 'But she was a dwaibly° body from the first.'

And he rode home at a precipitate amble with Kirstie at his horse's heels.

Dressed as she was for her last walk, they had laid the dead lady on her bed. She was never interesting in life; in death she was not impressive; and as her husband stood before her, with his hands crossed behind his powerful back, that which he looked upon was the very image of the insignificant.

'Her and me were never cut out for one another,' he remarked at last. 'It was a daft-like marriage.' And then, with a most unusual gentleness of tone, 'Puir bitch,' said he, 'puir bitch!' Then suddenly: 'Where's Erchie?'

Kirstie had decoyed him to her room and given him 'a jeely-piece'.

'Ye have some kind of gumption, too,' observed the Judge, and considered his housekeeper grimly. 'When all's said,' he added, 'I micht have done waur—I micht have been marriet upon a skirling° Jezebel like you!'

'There's naebody thinking of you, Hermiston!' cried the offended woman. 'We think of her that's out of her sorrows. And could *she* have done waur? Tell me that, Hermiston—tell me that before her clay-cauld corp!'

'Weel, there's some of them gey° an' ill to please,' observed his lordship.

GEORGE MOORE

The Wedding Gown

It was said, but with what truth I cannot say, that the Roche property had been owned by the O'Dwyers many years ago, several generations past, sometime in the eighteenth century. Only a faint legend of this ownership remained; only once had young Mr Roche heard of it, and it was from his mother he had heard it; among the country people it was forgotten. His mother had told him that his great, great grandfather, who had made large sums of money abroad, had increased his property by purchase from the O'Dwyers, who then owned, as well as farmed, the hill side on which the Big House stood. The O'Dwyers themselves had forgotten that they were once much greater people than they now were, but the master never spoke to them without remembering it, for though they only thought of themselves as small farmers, dependents on the squire, everyone of them, boys and girls alike, retained an air of high birth, which at the first glance distinguished them from the other tenants of the estate. Though they were not aware of it, some sense of their remote origin must have survived in them, and I think that in a still more obscure way some sense of it survived in the country side, for the villagers did not think worse of the O'Dwyers because they kept themselves aloof from the pleasures of the village and its squabbles. The O'Dwyers kept themselves apart from their fellows without any show of pride, without wounding anyone's feelings.

The head of the family was a man of forty, and he was the trusted servant, almost the friend, of the young master, he was his bailiff and his steward, and he lived in a pretty cottage by the edge of the lake. O'Dwyer's aunts, they were old women, of sixty-eight and seventy, lived in the Big House, the elder had been cook, and younger housemaid, and both were now past their work, and they lived full of gratitude to the young master, to whom they thought they owed a great deal. He believed the debt to be all on his side, and when he was away he often thought of them, and when he returned home he went to greet them as he might go to the members of his own family. The family of the O'Dwyer's was long-lived, and Betty and Mary had a sister far older than themselves, Margaret Kirwin, 'Granny Kirwin', as she was called, and she lived in the cottage by the lake with her nephew, Alec O'Dwyer. She was over eighty, it was said that she was nearly ninety, but her age was not known exactly. Mary O'Dwyer said that Margaret was nearly twenty years older than she, but neither Betty nor Mary remembered the exact date of their sister's birth. They did not know much about her, for though she was their sister, she was almost a stranger to them. She had married when she was sixteen, and had gone away to another part of the country, and they had hardly heard of her for thirty years. It was said that she had been a very pretty girl, and that many men had been in love with her, and it was known for certain that she had gone away with the son of the gamekeeper of the grandfather of the present Mr Roche, so you can understand what a very long while ago it was, and how little of the story of her life had come to the knowledge of those living now.

It was certainly sixty years since she had gone away with this young man; she had lived with him in Meath for some years, nobody knew exactly how many years, maybe some nine or ten years, and then he had died suddenly, and his death, it appears, had taken away from her some part of her reason. It was known for certain that she left Meath after his death, and had remained away many years. She had returned to Meath about twenty years ago, though not to the place she had lived in before. Some said she had experienced misfortunes so great that they had unsettled her mind. She herself had forgotten her story, and one day news had come to Galway—news, but it was sad news, that she was living in some very poor cottage on the edge of Navan town where her strange behaviour and her strange life had made a scandal of her. The priest had to inquire out her relations, and it took him some time to do this, for the old woman's answers were incoherent, but he at length discovered she came from Galway, and he had written to the O'Dwyers. And immediately on receiving the priest's letter, Alec sent his wife to Navan, and she had come back with the old woman.

'And it was time indeed that I went to fetch her,' she said. 'The boys in the town used to make game of her, and follow her, and throw things at her, and they nearly lost the poor thing the little reason that was left to her. The rain was coming in through the thatch, there was hardly a dry place in the cabin, and she had nothing to eat but a few scraps that the neighbours gave her. Latterly she had forgotten how to make a fire, and she ate the potatoes the neighbours gave her raw, and on her back there were only a few dirty rags. She had no care for anything except for her wedding gown. She kept that in a box covered over with paper so that no damp should get to it, and she was always folding it and seeing that the moths did not touch it, and she was talking of it when I came in at the door. She thought that I had come to steal it from her. The neighbours told me that that was the way she always was, thinking that someone had come to steal her wedding gown.'

This was all the news of Margaret Kirwin that Alec O'Dwyer's wife brought back with her. The old woman was given a room in the cottage, and though with food and warmth and kind treatment she became a little less bewildered, a little less like a wild, hunted creature, she never got back her memory sufficiently to tell them all that had happened to her after her husband's death. Nor did she seem as if she wanted to try to remember, she was garrulous only of her early days when the parish bells rang for her wedding, and the furze was in bloom. This was before the Big House on the hill had been built. The hill was then a fine pasture for sheep, and Margaret would often describe the tinkling of the sheep-bells in the valley, and the yellow furze, and the bells that were ringing for her wedding. She always spoke of the bells, though no one could understand where the bells came from. It was not customary to ring the parish bell for weddings, and there was no other bell, so that it was impossible to say how Margaret could have got the idea into her head that bells were ringing for her when she crossed the hill on her way to the church, dressed in the beautiful gown, which the grandmother of the present Mr Roche had dressed her in, for she had always been the favourite, she said, with the old mistress, a much greater favourite than even her two sisters had ever been. Betty and Mary were then little children and hardly remembered the wedding, and could say nothing about the bells.

Margaret Kirwin walked with a short stick, her head lifted hardly higher than the handle and when the family were talking round the kitchen fire she would come among them for a while and say something to them, and then go away, and they felt they had seen someone from another world. She hobbled now and then as far as the garden gate, and she frightened the peasantry, so strange did she seem among the flowers—so old and forlorn, almost cut off from this world, with only one memory to link her to it. It was the spectral look in her eyes that frightened them, for Margaret was not ugly. In spite of all her wrinkles the form of the face remained, and it was easy, especially when her little grand-niece was by, to see that sixty-five years ago she must have had a long and pleasant face, such as one sees in a fox, and red hair like Molly.

Molly was sixteen, and her grey dress reached only to her ankles. Everyone was fond of the poor old woman; but it was only Molly who had no fear of her at all, and one would often see them standing together beside the pretty paling that separated the steward's garden from the high road. Chestnut trees grew about the house, and china roses over the walls, and in the course of the summer there would be lilies in the garden, and in the autumn hollyhocks and sunflowers. There were a few fruit-trees a little further on, and, lower down, a stream. A little bridge led over the stream into the meadow, and Molly and her grandaunt used to go as far as the bridge, and everyone wondered what the child and the old woman had to say to each other. Molly was never able to give any clear account of what the old woman said to her during the time they spent by the stream. She had tried once to give Molly an account of one long winter when the lake was frozen from side to side. Then there was something running in her mind about the transport of pillars in front of the Big House—how they had been drawn across the lake by oxen, and how one of the pillars was now lying at the bottom of the lake. That was how Molly took up the story from her, but she understood little of it. Molly's solicitude for the old woman was a subject of admiration, and Molly did not like to take the credit for a kindness and pity which she did not altogether feel. She had never seen anyone dead, and her secret fear was that the old woman might die before she went away to service. Her parents had promised to allow her to go away when she was eighteen, and she lived in the hope that her aunt would live two years longer, and that she would be saved the terror of seeing a dead body. And it was in this intention that she served her aunt, that she carefully minced the old woman's food and insisted on her eating often, and that she darted from her place to fetch the old woman her stick when she rose to go. When Margaret Kirwin was not in the kitchen Molly was always laughing and talking, and her father and mother often thought it was her voice that brought the old woman out of her room. So the day Molly was grieving because she could not go to the dance the old woman remained in her room, and not seeing her at tea-time they began to be afraid, and Molly was asked to go fetch her aunt.

'Something may have happened to her, mother. I daren't go.'

And when old Margaret came into the kitchen towards evening she surprised everyone by her question:—

'Why is Molly crying?'

No one else had heard Molly sob, if she had sobbed, but everyone knew the reason of her grief; indeed, she had been reproved for it many times that day.

'I will not hear any more about it,' said Mrs O'Dwyer; 'she has been very tiresome all day. Is it my fault if I cannot give her a gown to go to the dance?' And then, forgetting that old Margaret could not understand her, she told her that the servants were having a dance at the Big House, and had asked Molly to come to it. 'But what can I do? She has got no gown to go in. Even if I had the money there would not be time to send for one now, nor to make one. And there are a number of English servants stopping at the house; there are people from all parts of the country, they have brought their servants with them, and I am not going to see my girl worse dressed than the others, so she cannot go. She has heard all this, she knows it. ... I've never seen her so tiresome before.' Mrs O'Dwyer continued to chide her daughter; but her mother's reasons for not allowing her to go to the ball, though unanswerable, did not seem to console Molly, and she sat looking very miserable. 'She has been sitting like that all day,' said Mrs O'Dwyer, 'and I wish that it were to-morrow, for she will not be better until it is all over.'

'But, mother, I am saying nothing; I will go to bed. I don't know why you are blaming me. I am saying nothing. I can't help feeling miserable.'

'No, she don't look a bit cheerful,' the old woman said, 'and I don't like her to be disappointed.' This was the first time that old Margaret had seemed to understand since she came to live with them what was passing about her, and they all looked at her, Mrs O'Dwyer and Alec and Molly. They stood waiting for her to speak again, wondering if the old woman's speech was an accident, or if she had recovered her mind. 'It is a hard thing for a child at her age not to be able to go to the dance at the Big House, now that she has been asked. No wonder Molly is unhappy. I remember the time I should have been unhappy too, and she is very like me.'

'But, Granny, what can I do? She can't go in the clothes she is wearing, and she has only got one other frock, the one she goes to Mass in. I can't allow my daughter——'

But seeing the old woman was about to speak Alec stopped his wife.
'Let us hear what she has to say,' he whispered.

'There is my wedding gown: that is surely beautiful enough for anyone to wear. It has not been worn since the day I wore it when the bells were ringing, and I went over the hill and was married; and I have taken such care of it that it is the same as it was that day. Molly will look very nice in it; she will look as I looked that day.'

No one spoke; father, mother, and daughter stood looking at the old woman. Her offer to lend her wedding gown had astonished them as much as her recovery of her senses. Everything she once had, and there were tales that she had once been rich, had melted away from her; nothing but this gown remained. How she had watched over it! Since she had come to live with the O'Dwyers she had hardly allowed them to see it. When she took it out of its box to air it and to strew it with camphor she closed her room door. Only once had they seen it, and then only for a few moments. She had brought it out to show it, as a child brings its toy, but the moment they stretched their hands to touch it she had taken it away, and they had heard her locking the box it was in. But now she was going to lend it to Molly. They did not believe she meant what she was saying. They expected her to turn away and to go to her room, forgetful of what she had said. Even if she were to let Molly put the dress on, she would not let her go out of the house with it. She would change her mind at the last minute.

'When does this dancing begin?' she asked, and when they told her she said there would be just time for her to dress Molly, and she asked the girl and her mother to come into her room. Mrs O'Dwyer feared the girl would be put to a bitter disappointment, but if Molly once had the gown on she would not oblige her to take it off.

'In my gown you will be just like what I was when the bells were ringing.'

She took the gown out of its box herself, and the petticoat and the stockings and the shoes; there was everything there.

'The old mistress gave me all these. Molly has got the hair I used to have; she will look exactly like myself. Are they not beautiful shoes?' she said. 'Look at the buckles. They will fit her very well; her feet are the same size as mine were.'

And Molly's feet went into the shoes just as if they had been made for her, and the gown fitted as well as the shoes, and Molly's hair was arranged as nearly as possible according to the old woman's fancy, as she used to wear her hair when it was thick and red like a fox's.

The girl thought that Granny would regret her gift. She expected the old woman would follow her into the kitchen and ask her to take the things off, and that she would not be able to go to the ball after all. She did not feel quite safe until she was a long way from the house, about halfway up the drive. Her mother and father had said that the dance would not be over until maybe six o'clock in the morning, and they offered her the key of the house; but Granny had said that she would sit up for her.

'I will doze a bit upon a chair. If I am tired I will lie down upon my bed. I shall hear Molly; I shall not sleep much. She will not be able to enter the house without my hearing her.'

It was extraordinary to hear her speak like this, and, a little frightened by her sudden sanity, they waited up with her until midnight. Then they tried to persuade her to go to bed, to allow them to lock up the house; but she sat looking into the fire, seeming to see the girl dancing at the ball quite clearly. She seemed so contented that they left her, and for an hour she sat dreaming, seeing Molly young and beautifully dressed in the wedding gown of more than sixty years ago.

Dream after dream went by, the fire had burned low, the sods were falling into white ashes, and the moonlight began to stream into the room. It was the chilliness that had come into the air that awoke her, and she threw several sods of turf on to the fire.

An hour passed, and old Margaret awoke for the last time.

'The bells are ringing, the bells are ringing,' she said, and she went to the kitchen door, she opened it, and stood in the garden under the rays of the moon. The night of her marriage was just such a night as this one, and she had stood in the garden amid the summer flowers, just as she did now.

'The day is beginning,' she said, mistaking the moonlight for the dawn, and, listening, it seemed to her that she heard once more the sound of bells coming across the hill. 'Yes, the bells are ringing,' she said; 'I can hear them quite clearly, and I must hurry and get dressed—I must not keep him waiting.'

And, returning to the house, she went to her box, where her gown had lain so many years; and though no gown was there it seemed to her that there was one, and one more beautiful than the gown she had cherished. It was the same gown, only grown more beautiful. It had grown into softer silk, into a more delicate colour; it had become more beautiful, and she held the dream-gown in her hands and she sat with it in the moonlight, thinking how fair he would find her in it. Once her hands went to her hair, and then she dropped them again.

'I must begin to dress myself; I must not keep him waiting.'

The moonlight lay still upon her knees, but little by little the moon moved up the sky, leaving her in the shadow.

It was at this moment, as the shadows grew denser about old Margaret, that the child who was dancing at the ball came to think of her who had given her her gown, and who was waiting for her. It was in the middle of a reel she was dancing, and she was dancing it with Mr Roche, that she felt that something had happened to her aunt.

'Mr Roche,' she said, 'you must let me go away; I cannot dance any more to-night. I am sure that something has happened to my aunt, the old woman, Margaret Kirwin, who lives with us in the Lodge. It was she who lent me this gown. This was her wedding gown, and for sixty-five years it has never been out of her possession. She has hardly allowed anyone to see it; but she said that I was like her, and she heard me crying because I had no gown to go to the ball, and so she lent me her wedding gown.'

'You look very nice, Molly, in the wedding gown, and this is only a fancy.' Seeing the girl was frightened and wanted to go, he said—'But why do you think that anything has happened to your aunt?'

'She is very old.'

'But she is not much older than she was when you left her.'

'Let me go, Mr Roche; I think I must go. I feel sure that something has happened to her. I never had such a feeling before, and I could not have that feeling if there was no reason for it.'

'Well, if you must go.'

She glanced to where the moon was shining and ran down the drive, leaving Mr Roche looking after her, wondering if after all she might have had a warning of the old woman's death. The night was one of those beautiful nights in May, when the moon soars high in the sky, and all the woods and fields are clothed in the green of spring. But the stillness of the night frightened Molly, and when she stopped to pick up her dress she heard the ducks chattering in the reeds. The world seemed divided into darkness and light. The hawthorn trees threw

black shadows that reached into the hollows, and Molly did not dare
to go by the path that led through a little wood, lest she should meet
Death there. For now it seemed to her that she was running a race
with Death, and that she must get to the cottage before him. She did
not dare to take the short cut, but she ran till her breath failed her. She
ran on again, but when she went through the wicket she knew that
Death had been before her. She knocked twice; receiving no answer
she tried the latch, and was surprised to find the door unlocked. There
was a little fire among the ashes, and after blowing the sod for some
time she managed to light the candle and holding it high she looked
about the kitchen.

'Auntie, are you asleep? Have the others gone to bed?'

She approached a few steps, and then a strange curiosity came over
her, and though she had always feared death she now looked curiously
upon death, and she thought that she saw the likeness which her aunt
had often noticed.

'Yes,' she said, 'she is like me. I shall be like that some day if I live
long enough.'

And then she knocked at the door of the room where her parents
were sleeping.

OSCAR WILDE

The Preface to the Picture of Dorian Gray

The artist is the creator of beautiful things.
To reveal art and conceal the artist is art's aim.
The critic is he who can translate into another manner or a new
     material his impression of beautiful things.
     The highest, as the lowest, form of criticism is a mode of
          autobiography.
Those who find ugly meanings in beautiful things are corrupt
     without being charming. This is a fault.
          Those who find beautiful meanings in beautiful things are
               the cultivated. For these there is hope.
     They are the elect to whom beautiful things mean only Beauty.
          There is no such thing as a moral or an immoral book. Books
          are well written, or badly written. That is all.

The nineteenth-century dislike of Realism is the rage of Caliban seeing his own face in a glass.

> The nineteenth-century dislike of Romanticism is the rage of Caliban not seeing his own face in a glass.

The moral life of man forms part of the subject-matter of the artist, but the morality of art consists in the perfect use of an imperfect medium. No artist desires to prove anything. Even things that are true can be proved.

> No artist has ethical sympathies. An ethical sympathy in an artist is an unpardonable mannerism of style.

> No artist is ever morbid. The artist can express everything.

Thought and language are to the artist instruments of an art.

> Vice and virtue are to the artist materials for an art.

From the point of view of form, the type of all the arts is the art of the musician. From the point of view of feeling, the actor's craft is the type.

> All art is at once surface and symbol.

Those who go beneath the surface do so at their peril.

> Those who read the symbol do so at their peril.

It is the spectator, and not life, that art really mirrors.

Diversity of opinion about a work of art shows that the work is new, complex, and vital.

> When critics disagree the artist is in accord with himself.

We can forgive a man for making a useful thing as long as he does not admire it. The only excuse for making a useless thing is that one admires it intensely.

> All art is quite useless.

The Ballad of Reading Gaol

I

He did not wear his scarlet coat,°
  For blood and wine are red,
And blood and wine were on his hands
  When they found him with the dead,
The poor dead woman whom he loved,
  And murdered in her bed.

He walked amongst the Trial Men°
   In a suit of shabby grey;
A cricket cap was on his head,
   And his step seemed light and gay;   10
But I never saw a man who looked
   So wistfully at the day.

I never saw a man who looked
   With such a wistful eye
Upon that little tent of blue
   Which prisoners call the sky,
And at every drifting cloud that went
   With sails of silver by.

I walked, with other souls in pain,
   Within another ring,   20
And was wondering if the man had done
   A great or little thing,
When a voice behind me whispered low,
   'That fellow's got to swing.'

Dear Christ! the very prison walls
   Suddenly seemed to reel,
And the sky above my head became
   Like a casque of scorching steel;
And, though I was a soul in pain,   30
   My pain I could not feel.

I only knew what hunted thought
   Quickened his step, and why
He looked upon the garish day
   With such a wistful eye;
The man had killed the thing he loved,
   And so he had to die.

Yet each man kills the thing he loves,
   By each let this be heard,
Some do it with a bitter look,   40
   Some with a flattering word,
The coward does it with a kiss,
   The brave man with a sword!

Some kill their love when they are young,
  And some when they are old;
Some strangle with the hands of Lust,
  Some with the hands of Gold;
The kindest use a knife, because
  The dead so soon grow cold.

Some love too little, some too long,
  Some sell, and others buy;   50
Some do the deed with many tears,
  And some without a sigh:
For each man kills the thing he loves,
  Yet each man does not die.

He does not die a death of shame
  On a day of dark disgrace,
Nor have a noose about his neck,
  Nor a cloth upon his face,
Nor drop feet foremost through the floor   60
  Into an empty space.

He does not sit with silent men
  Who watch him night and day;
Who watch him when he tries to weep,
  And when he tries to pray;
Who watch him lest himself should rob
  The prison of its prey.

He does not wake at dawn to see
  Dread figures throng his room,
The shivering Chaplain robed in white,   70
  The Sheriff stern with gloom,
And the Governor all in shiny black,
  With the yellow face of Doom.

He does not rise in piteous haste
  To put on convict-clothes,
While some course-mouthed Doctor gloats, and notes
  Each new and nerve-twitched pose,
Fingering a watch whose little ticks
  Are like horrible hammer-blows.

He does not know that sickening thirst
    That sands one's throat, before   80
The hangman with his gardener's gloves
    Slips through the padded door,
And binds one with three leathern thongs,
    That the throat may thirst no more.

He does not bend his head to hear
    The Burial Office read,
Nor, while the terror of his soul
    Tells him he is not dead,
Cross his own coffin, as he moves
    Into the hideous shed.   90

He does not stare upon the air
    Through a little roof of glass:
He does not pray with lips of clay
    For his agony to pass;
Nor feel upon his shuddering cheek
    The kiss of Caiaphas.°

II

Six weeks our guardsman walked the yard,
    In the suit of shabby grey:
His cricket cap was on his head,
    And his step seemed light and gay,   100
But I never saw a man who looked
    So wistfully at the day.

I never saw a man who looked
    With such a wistful eye
Upon that little tent of blue
    Which prisoners call the sky,
And at every wandering cloud that trailed
    Its ravelled fleeces by.

He did not wring his hands, as do
   Those witless men who dare   110
To try to rear the changeling Hope
   In the cave of black Despair:
He only looked upon the sun,
   And drank the morning air.

He did not wring his hands nor weep,
   Nor did he peek or pine,
But he drank the air as though it held
   Some healthful anodyne;
With open mouth he drank the sun
   As though it had been wine!   120

And I and all the souls in pain,
   Who tramped the other ring,
Forgot if we ourselves had done
   A great or little thing,
And watched with gaze of dull amaze
   The man who had to swing.

And strange it was to see him pass
   With a step so light and gay,
And strange it was to see him look
   So wistfully at the day,   130
And strange it was to think that he
   Had such a debt to pay.

For oak and elm have pleasant leaves
   That in the spring-time shoot:
But grim to see is the gallows-tree,
   With its adder-bitten root,
And, green or dry, a man must die
   Before it bears its fruit!

The loftiest place is that seat of grace
   For which all worldlings try: 140
But who would stand in hempen band
   Upon a scaffold high,
And through a murderer's collar take
   His last look at the sky?

It is sweet to dance to violins
    When Love and Life are fair:
To dance to flutes, to dance to lutes
    Is delicate and rare:
But it is not sweet with nimble feet
    To dance upon the air!   150

So with curious eyes and sick surmise
    We watched him day by day,
And wondered if each one of us
    Would end the self-same way,
For none can tell to what red Hell
    His sightless soul may stray.

At last the dead man walked no more
    Amongst the Trial Men,
And I knew that he was standing up
    In the black dock's dreadful pen,   160
And that never would I see his face
    In God's sweet world again.

Like two doomed ships that pass in storm
    We had crossed each other's way:
But we made no sign, we said no word,
    We had no word to say;
For we did not meet in the holy night,
    But in the shameful day.

A prison wall was round us both,
    Two outcast men we were: 170
The world had thrust us from its heart,
    And God from out His care:
And the iron gin that waits for Sin°
    Had caught us in its snare.

III

In Debtors' Yard the stones are hard,°
    And the dripping wall is high,

So it was there he took the air
  Beneath the leaden sky,
And by each side a Warder walked,
  For fear the man might die.   180

Or else he sat with those who watched
  His anguish night and day;
Who watched him when he rose to weep,
  And when he crouched to pray;
Who watched him lest himself should rob
  Their scaffold of its prey.

The Governor was strong upon°
  The Regulations Act:
The Doctor said that Death was but   190
  A scientific fact:
And twice a day the Chaplain called,
  And left a little tract.

And twice a day he smoked his pipe,
  And drank his quart of beer:
His soul was resolute, and held
  No hiding-place for fear:
He often said that he was glad
  The hangman's hands were near.

But why he said so strange a thing
  No Warder dared to ask: 200
For he to whom a watcher's doom
  Is given as his task
Must set a lock upon his lips,
  And make his face a mask.

Or else he might be moved, and try
  To comfort or console:
And what should Human Pity do
  Pent up in Murderers' Hole?
What word of grace in such a place
  Could help a brother's soul?   210

With slouch and swing around the ring
   We trod the Fools' Parade!
We did not care: we knew we were
   The Devil's Own Brigade:
And shaven head and feet of lead
   Make a merry masquerade.

We tore the tarry rope to shreds°
   With blunt and bleeding nails;
We rubbed the doors, and scrubbed the floors,
   And cleaned the shining rails: 220
And, rank by rank, we soaped the plank,
   And clattered with the pails.

We sewed the sacks, we broke the stones,
   We turned the dusty drill:
We banged the tins, and bawled the hymns,
   And sweated on the mill:
But in the heart of every man
   Terror was lying still.

So still it lay that every day
   Crawled like a weed-clogged wave.   230
And we forgot the bitter lot
   That waits for fool and knave,
Till once, as we tramped in from work,
   We passed an open grave.

With yawning mouth the yellow hole
   Gaped for a living thing;
The very mud cried out for blood
   To the thirsty asphalte ring:
And we knew that ere one dawn grew fair
   Some prisoner had to swing.   240

Right in we went, with soul intent
   On Death and Dread and Doom:
The hangman, with his little bag,
   Went shuffling through the gloom:
And each man trembled as he crept
   Into his numbered tomb.

That night the empty corridors
   Were full of forms of Fear,
And up and down the iron town
   Stole feet we could not hear,   250
And through the bars that hide the stars
   White faces seemed to peer.

He lay as one who lies and dreams
   In a pleasant meadow-land,
The watchers watched him as he slept,
   And could not understand
How one could sleep so sweet a sleep
   With a hangman close at hand.

But there is no sleep when men must weep
   Who never yet have wept: 260
So we—the fool, the fraud, the knave—
   That endless vigil kept,
And through each brain on hands of pain
   Another's terror crept.

Alas! it is a fearful thing
   To feel another's guilt!
For, right within, the sword of Sin
   Pierced to its poisoned hilt,
And as molten lead were the tears we shed
   For the blood we had not spilt.   270

The Warders with their shoes of felt
   Crept by each padlocked door,
And peeped and saw, with eyes of awe,
   Grey figures on the floor,
And wondered why men knelt to pray
   Who never prayed before.

All through the night we knelt and prayed,
   Mad mourners of a corse!
The troubled plumes of midnight were
   The plumes upon a hearse: 280
And bitter wine upon a sponge
   Was the savour of Remorse.

The grey cock crew, the red cock crew,
   But never came the day:
And crooked shapes of Terror crouched,
   In the corners where we lay:
And each evil sprite that walks by night
   Before us seemed to play.

They glided past, they glided fast,
   Like travellers through a mist: 290
They mocked the moon in a rigadoon°
   Of delicate turn and twist,
And with formal pace and loathsome grace
   The phantoms kept their tryst.

With mop and mow, we saw them go,
   Slim shadows hand in hand:
About, about, in ghostly rout
   They trod a saraband:°
And the damned grotesques made arabesques,
   Like the wind upon the sand!   300

With the pirouettes of marionettes,°
   They tripped on pointed tread:
But with flutes of Fear they filled the ear,
   As their grisly masque they led,
And loud they sang, and long they sang,
   For they sang to wake the dead.

'*Oho!*' they cried, '*The world is wide,*
   But fettered limbs go lame!
And once, or twice, to throw the dice
   Is a gentlemanly game,   310
But he does not win who plays with Sin
   In the secret House of Shame.'

The morning wind began to moan,
   But still the night went on:
Through its giant loom the web of gloom
   Crept till each thread was spun:
And, as we prayed, we grew afraid
   Of the Justice of the Sun.

The moaning wind went wandering round
   The weeping prison-wall: 320
Till like a wheel of turning steel
   We felt the minutes crawl:
O moaning wind! what had we done
   To have such a seneschal?

At last I saw the shadowed bars,
   Like a lattice wrought in lead,
Move right across the whitewashed wall
   That faced my three-planked bed,
And I knew that somewhere in the world
   God's dreadful dawn was red.   330

At six o'clock we cleaned our cells,
   At seven all was still,
But the sough and swing of a mighty wing
   The prison seemed to fill,
For, the Lord of Death with icy breath
   Had entered in to kill.

He did not pass in purple pomp,
   Nor ride a moon-white steed.
Three yards of cord and a sliding board
   Are all the gallows' need: 340
So with rope of shame the Herald came
   To do the secret deed.

We were as men who through a fen
   Of filthy darkness grope;
We did not dare to breathe a prayer,
   Or to give our anguish scope:
Something was dead in each of us,
   And what was dead was Hope.

For man's grim Justice goes its way,
   And will not swerve aside: 350
It slays the weak, it slays the strong,
   It has a deadly stride:
With iron heel it slays the strong,
   The monstrous parricide!

We waited for the stroke of eight:
   Each tongue was thick with thirst:
For the stroke of eight is the stroke of Fate
   That makes a man accursed,
And Fate will use a running noose
   For the best man and the worst.   360

We had no other thing to do,
   Save to wait for the sign to come:
So, like things of stone in a valley lone,
   Quiet we sat and dumb:
But each man's heart beat thick and quick,
   Like a madman on a drum!

With sudden shock the prison-clock
   Smote on the shivering air,
And from all the gaol rose up a wail
   Of impotent despair,   370
Like the sound that frightened marshes hear
   From some leper in his lair.

And as one sees most fearful things
   In the crystal of a dream,
We saw the greasy hempen rope
   Hooked to the blackened beam,
And heard the prayer the hangman's snare
   Strangled into a scream.

And all the woe that moved him so
   That he gave that bitter cry,   380
And the wild regrets, and the bloody sweats,
   None knew so well as I:
For he who lives more lives than one
   More deaths than one must die.

IV

There is no chapel on the day
   On which they hang a man:

The Chaplain's heart is far too sick,
    Or his face is far too wan,
Or there is that written in his eyes
    Which none should look upon.   390

So they kept us close till nigh on noon,
    And then they rang the bell,
And the Warders with their jingling keys
    Opened each listening cell,
And down the iron stair we tramped,
    Each from his separate Hell.

Out into God's sweet air we went,
    But not in wonted way,
For this man's face was white with fear,
    And that man's face was grey,   400
And I never saw sad men who looked
    So wistfully at the day.

I never saw sad men who looked
    With such a wistful eye
Upon that little tent of blue
    We prisoners called the sky,
And at every careless cloud that passed
    In happy freedom by.

But there were those amongst us all
    Who walked, with downcast head,   410
And knew that, had each got his due,
    They should have died instead:
He had but killed a thing that lived,
    Whilst they had killed the dead.

For he who sins a second time
    Wakes a dead soul to pain,
And draws it from its spotted shroud,
    And makes it bleed again,
And makes it bleed great gouts of blood,
    And makes it bleed in vain!   420

Like ape or clown, in monstrous garb
    With crooked arrows starred,°
Silently we went round and round
    The slippery asphalte yard;
Silently we went round and round,
    And no man spoke a word.

The Warders strutted up and down,
    And kept their herd of brutes,
Their uniforms were spick and span,
    And they wore their Sunday suits,   430
But we knew the work they had been at,
    By the quicklime on their boots.

For where a grave had opened wide,
    There was no grave at all:
Only a stretch of mud and sand
    By the hideous prison-wall,
And a little heap of burning lime,
    That the man should have his pall.

For he has a pall, this wretched man,
    Such as few men can claim: 440
Deep down below a prison-yard,
    Naked for greater shame,
He lies, with fetters on each foot,
    Wrapt in a sheet of flame!

And all the while the burning lime
    Eats flesh and bone away,
It eats the brittle bone by night,
    And the soft flesh by day,
It eats the flesh and bone by turns,
    But it eats the heart alway.   450

For three long years they will not sow
    Or root or seedling there:
For three long years the unblessed spot
    Will sterile be and bare,
And look upon the wondering sky
    With unreproachful stare.

They think a murderer's heart would taint
  Each simple seed they sow.
It is not true! God's kindly earth
  Is kindlier than men know,   460
And the red rose would but blow more red,
  The white rose whiter blow.

Out of his mouth a red, red rose!
  Out of his heart a white!
For who can say by what strange way,
  Christ brings His will to light,
Since the barren staff the pilgrim bore°
  Bloomed in the great Pope's sight?

But neither milk-white rose nor red
  May bloom in prison-air;   470
The shard, the pebble, and the flint,
  Are what they give us there:
For flowers have been known to heal
  A common man's despair.

So never will wine-red rose or white,
  Petal by petal, fall
On that stretch of mud and sand that lies
  By the hideous prison-wall,
To tell the men who tramp the yard
  That God's Son died for all.   480

Yet though the hideous prison-wall
  Still hems him round and round,
And a spirit may not walk by night
  That is with fetters bound,
And a spirit may but weep that lies
  In such unholy ground,

He is at peace—this wretched man—
  At Peace, or will be soon:
There is no thing to make him mad,   490
  Nor does Terror walk at noon,
For the lampless Earth in which he lies
  Has neither Sun nor Moon.

They hanged him as a beast is hanged:
   They did not even toll
A requiem that might have brought
   Rest to his startled soul,
But hurriedly they took him out.
   And hid him in a hole.

They stripped him of his canvas clothes,   500
   And gave him to the flies:
They mocked the swollen purple throat,
   And the stark and staring eyes:
And with laughter loud they heaped the shroud
   In which their convict lies.

The Chaplain would not kneel to pray
   By his dishonoured grave:
Nor mark it with that blessed Cross
   That Christ for sinners gave,
Because the man was one of those   510
   Whom Christ came down to save.

Yet all is well; he has but passed
   To Life's appointed bourne:
And alien tears will fill for him
   Pity's long-broken urn,
For his mourners will be outcast men,
   And outcasts always mourn.

V

I know not whether Laws be right,
   Or whether Laws be wrong;
All that we know who lie in gaol   520
   Is that the wall is strong;
And that each day is like a year,
   A year whose days are long.

But this I know, that every Law
   That men have made for Man,

Since first Man took his brother's life,
  And the sad world began,
But straws the wheat and saves the chaff
  With a most evil fan.

This too I know—and wise it were   530
  If each could know the same—
That every prison that men build
  Is built with bricks of shame,
And bound with bars lest Christ should see
  How men their brothers maim.

With bars they blur the gracious moon,
  And blind the goodly sun:
And they do well to hide their Hell,
  For in it things are done
That Son of God nor son of Man   540
  Ever should look upon!

The vilest deeds, like poison weeds,
  Bloom well in prison-air;
It is only what is good in Man
  That wastes and withers there:
Pale Anguish keeps the heavy gate,
  And the Warder is Despair.

For they starve the little frightened child
  Till it weeps both night and day:
And they scourge the weak, and flog the fool,   550
  And gibe the old and grey,
And some grow mad, and all grow bad,
  And none a word may say.

Each narrow cell in which we dwell
  Is a foul and dark latrine,
And the fetid breath of living Death
  Chokes up each grated screen,
And all, but Lust, is turned to dust
  In Humanity's machine.

The brackish water that we drink   560
   Creeps with a loathsome slime,
And the bitter bread they weigh in scales
   Is full of chalk and lime,
And Sleep will not lie down, but walks
   Wild-eyed, and cries to Time.

But though lean Hunger and green Thirst
   Like asp with adder fight,
We have little care of prison fare,
   For what chills and kills outright
Is that every stone one lifts by day   570
   Becomes one's heart by night.

With midnight always in one's heart,
   And twilight in one's cell,
We turn the crank, or tear the rope,
   Each in his separate Hell,
And the silence is more awful far
   Than the sound of a brazen bell.

And never a human voice comes near
   To speak a gentle word:
And the eye that watches through the door   580
   Is pitiless and hard:
And by all forgot, we rot and rot,
   With soul and body marred.

And thus we rust Life's iron chain
   Degraded and alone:
And some men curse, and some men weep,
   And some men make no moan:
But God's eternal Laws are kind
   And break the heart of stone.

And every human heart that breaks,   590
   In prison-cell or yard,
Is as that broken box that gave
   Its treasure to the Lord,
And filled the unclean leper's house
   With the scent of costliest nard.

Ah! happy they whose hearts can break
   And peace of pardon win!
How else may man make straight his plan
   And cleanse his soul from Sin?
How else but through a broken heart   600
   May Lord Christ enter in?

And he of the swollen purple throat,
   And the stark and staring eyes,
Waits for the holy hands that took
   The Thief to Paradise;°
And a broken and a contrite heart
   The Lord will not despise.

The man in red who reads the Law
   Gave him three weeks of life,
Three little weeks in which to heal   610
   His soul of his soul's strife,
And cleanse from every blot of blood
   The hand that held the knife.

And with tears of blood he cleansed the hand,
   The hand that held the steel:
For only blood can wipe out blood,
   And only tears can heal:
And the crimson stain that was of Cain
   Became Christ's snow-white seal.

VI

In Reading gaol by Reading town   620
   There is a pit of shame,
And in it lies a wretched man
   Eaten by teeth of flame,
In a burning winding-sheet he lies,°
   And his grave has got no name.

And there, till Christ call forth the dead,
   In silence let him lie:

No need to waste the foolish tear,
   Or heave the windy sigh:
The man had killed the thing he loved,   630
   And so he had to die.

And all men kill the thing they love,
   By all let this be heard,
Some do it with a bitter look,
   Some with a flattering word,
The coward does it with a kiss,
   The brave man with a sword!

OLIVE SCHREINER

from *The Story of an African Farm*

The full African moon poured down its light from the blue sky into the wide, lonely plain. The dry, sandy earth, with its coating of stunted 'karroo' bushes a few inches high, the low hills that skirted the plain, the milk-bushes with their long finger-like leaves, all were touched by a weird and an almost oppressive beauty as they lay in the white light.

In one spot only was the solemn monotony of the plain broken. Near the centre a small solitary 'kopje' rose. Alone it lay there, a heap of round ironstones piled one upon another, as over some giant's grave. Here and there a few tufts of grass or small succulent plants had sprung up among its stones, and on the very summit a clump of prickly-pears lifted their thorny arms, and reflected, as from mirrors, the moonlight on their broad fleshy leaves. At the foot of the 'kopje' lay the homestead. First, the stone-walled 'sheep kraals' and Kaffir huts; beyond them the dwelling-house—a square red-brick building with thatched roof. Even on its bare red walls, and the wooden ladder that led up to the loft, the moonlight cast a kind of dreamy beauty, and quite etherealized the low brick wall that ran before the house, and which enclosed a bare patch of sand and two straggling sunflowers. On the zinc roof of the great open waggon-house, on the roofs of the outbuildings that jutted from its side, the moonlight glinted with a quite peculiar brightness, till it seemed that every rib in the metal was of burnished silver.

Sleep ruled everywhere, and the homestead was not less quiet than the solitary plain.

In the farm-house, on her great wooden bedstead, Tant' Sannie, the Boer-woman, rolled heavily in her sleep.

She had gone to bed, as she always did, in her clothes, and the night was warm and the room close, and she dreamed bad dreams. Not of the ghosts and devils that so haunted her waking thoughts; not of her second husband, the consumptive Englishman, whose grave lay away beyond the ostrich-camps, nor of her first, the young Boer; but only of the sheep's trotters she had eaten for supper that night. She dreamed that one stuck fast in her throat, and she rolled her huge form from side to side, and snorted horribly.

In the next room, where the maid had forgotten to close the shutter, the white moonlight fell in in a flood, and made it light as day. There were two small beds against the wall. In one lay a yellow-haired child, with a low forehead and a face of freckles; but the loving moonlight hid defects here as elsewhere, and showed only the innocent face of a child in its first sweet sleep.

The figure in the companion bed belonged of right to the moonlight, for it was of quite elfin-like beauty. The child had dropped her cover on the floor, and the moonlight looked in at the naked little limbs. Presently she opened her eyes and looked at the moonlight that was bathing her.

'Em!' she called to the sleeper in the other bed; but received no answer. Then she drew the cover from the floor, turned her pillow, and pulling the sheet over her head, went to sleep again.

Only in one of the outbuildings that jutted from the waggon-house there was someone who was not asleep. The room was dark; door and shutter were closed; not a ray of light entered anywhere. The German overseer, to whom the room belonged, lay sleeping soundly on his bed in the corner, his great arms folded, and his bushy grey and black beard rising and falling on his breast. But one in the room was not asleep. Two large eyes looked about in the darkness, and two small hands were smoothing the patchwork quilt. The boy, who slept on a box under the window, had just awakened from his first sleep. He drew the quilt up to his chin, so that little peered above it but a great head of silky black curls and the two black eyes. He stared about in the darkness. Nothing was visible, not even the outline of one worm-eaten rafter, nor of the deal table, on which lay the Bible from which his father had read before they went to bed. No one could tell where the tool-box was, and where the fireplace. There was something very impressive to the child in the complete darkness.

At the head of his father's bed hung a great silver hunting watch. It ticked loudly. The boy listened to it, and began mechanically to count. Tick—tick—tick! one, two, three, four! He lost count presently, and only listened. Tick—tick—tick—tick!

It never waited; it went on inexorably; and every time it ticked *a man died*! He raised himself a little on his elbow and listened. He wished it would leave off.

How many times had it ticked since he came to lie down? A thousand times, a million times, perhaps.

He tried to count again, and sat up to listen better.

'Dying, dying, dying!' said the watch; 'dying, dying, dying!'

He heard it distinctly. Where were they going to, all those people?

He lay down quickly, and pulled the cover up over his head; but presently the silky curls reappeared.

'Dying, dying, dying!' said the watch; 'dying, dying, dying!'

He thought of the words his father had read that evening—'For wide is the gate, and broad is the way, that leadeth to destruction, and many there be which go in thereat.'°

'Many, many, many!' said the watch.

'Because strait is the gate, and narrow is the way, that leadeth unto life, and few there be that find it.'

'Few, few, few!' said the watch.

The boy lay with his eyes wide open. He saw before him a long stream of people, a great dark multitude, that moved in one direction; then they came to the dark edge of the world, and went over. He saw them passing on before him, and there was nothing that could stop them. He thought of how that stream had rolled on through all the long ages of the past—how the old Greeks and Romans had gone over; the countless millions of China and India, they were going over now. Since he had come to bed, how many had gone!

And the watch said, 'Eternity, eternity, eternity!'

'Stop them! stop them!' cried the child.

And all the while the watch kept ticking on; just like God's will, that never changes or alters, you may do what you please.

Great beads of perspiration stood on the boy's forehead. He climbed out of bed and lay with his face turned to the mud floor.

'Oh, God, God! save them!' he cried in agony. 'Only some; only a few! Only for each moment I am praying here one!' He folded his little hands upon his head. 'God! God! save them!'

He grovelled on the floor.

Oh, the long, long ages of the past, in which they had gove over! Oh, the long, long future, in which they would pass away! Oh, God! the long, long, long eternity, which has no end!

The child wept, and crept closer to the ground.

The farm by daylight was not as the farm by moonlight. The plain was a weary flat of loose red sand, sparsely covered by dry karroo bushes, that cracked beneath the tread like tinder, and showed the red earth everywhere. Here and there a milk-bush lifted its pale-coloured rods, and in every direction the ants and beetles ran about in the blazing sand. The red walls of the farmhouse, the zinc roofs of the outbuildings, the stone walls of the 'kraals', all reflected the fierce sunlight, till the eye ached and blenched. No tree or shrub was to be seen far or near. The two sunflowers that stood before the door, out-stared by the sun, drooped their brazen faces to the sand; and the little cicada-like insects cried aloud among the stones of the 'kopje'.

The Boer-woman, seen by daylight, was even less lovely than when, in bed, she rolled and dreamed. She sat on a chair in the great front room, with her feet on a wooden stove, and wiped her flat face with the corner of her apron, and drank coffee, and in Cape Dutch swore that the beloved weather was damned. Less lovely, too, by daylight was the dead Englishman's child, her little stepdaughter, upon whose freckles and low, wrinkled forehead the sunlight had no mercy.

'Lyndall,' the child said to her little orphan cousin, who sat with her on the floor threading beads, 'how is it your beads never fall off your needle?'

'I try,' said the little one gravely, moistening her tiny fingers. 'That is why.'

The overseer, seen by daylight, was a huge German, wearing a shabby suit, and with a childish habit of rubbing his hands and nodding his head prodigiously when pleased at anything. He stood out at the 'kraals' in the blazing sun, explaining to two Kaffir boys the approaching end of the world. The boys, as they cut the cakes of dung, winked at each other, and worked as slowly as they possibly could; but the German never saw it.

Away, beyond the 'kopje', Waldo his son herded the ewes and lambs—a small and dusty herd—powdered all over from head to foot with red sand, wearing a ragged coat and shoes of undressed leather, through whose holes the toes looked out. His hat was too large, and had sunk down to his eyes, concealing completely the silky black curls. It was a curious small figure. His flock gave him little trouble. It was too hot for them to move far; they gathered round every little milk-bush as though they hoped to find shade, and stood there motionless in clumps. He himself crept under a shelving rock that lay at the foot of the 'kopje', stretched himself on his stomach, and waved his dilapidated little shoes in the air.

Soon, from the blue bag where he kept his dinner, he produced a fragment of slate, an arithmetic, and a pencil. Proceeding to put down a sum with solemn and earnest demeanour, he began to add it up aloud: 'Six and two is eight—and four is twelve—and two is fourteen—and four is eighteen.' Here he paused. 'And four is eighteen—and—four—is—eighteen.' The last was very much drawled. Slowly the pencil slipped from his fingers, and the slate followed it into the sand. For a while he lay motionless, then began muttering to himself, folded his little arms, laid his head down upon them, and might have been asleep, but for a muttering sound that from time to time proceeded from him. A curious old ewe came to sniff at him; but it was long before he raised his head. When he did, he looked at the far-off hills with his heavy eyes.

'Ye shall receive—ye shall receive—*shall, shall, shall*,' he muttered.

He sat up then. Slowly the dullness and heaviness melted from his face; it became radiant. Mid-day had come now, and the sun's rays were poured down vertically; the earth throbbed before the eye.

The boy stood up quickly, and cleared a small space from the bushes which covered it. Looking carefully, he found twelve small stones of somewhat the same size; kneeling down, he arranged them carefully on the cleared space in a square pile, in shape like an altar. Then he walked to the bag where his dinner was kept; in it was a mutton chop and a large slice of brown bread. The boy took them out

and turned the bread over in his hand, deeply considering it. Finally
he threw it away and walked to the altar with the meat, and laid it
down on the stones. Close by in the red sand he knelt down. Sure,
never since the beginning of the world was there so ragged and so
small a priest. He took off his great hat and placed it solemnly on the
ground, then closed his eyes and folded his hands. He prayed aloud.

'Oh, God, my Father, I have made Thee a sacrifice. I have only
twopence, so I cannot buy a lamb. If the lambs were mine I would
give Thee one; but now I have only this meat; it is my dinner-meat.
Please, my Father, send fire down from heaven to burn it. Thou hast
said, Whosoever shall say unto this mountain, Be thou cast into the
sea, nothing doubting, it shall be done. I ask for the sake of Jesus
Christ. Amen.'

He knelt down with his face upon the ground, and he folded his
hands upon his curls. The fierce sun poured down its heat upon his
head and upon his altar. When he looked up he knew what he should
see—the glory of God! For fear his very heart stood still, his breath
came heavily; he was half suffocated. He dared not look up. Then at
last he raised himself. Above him was the quiet blue sky, about him
the red earth; there were the clumps of silent ewes and his altar—that
was all.

He looked up—nothing broke the intense stillness of the blue
overhead. He looked round in astonishment, then he bowed again, and
this time longer than before.

When he raised himself the second time all was unaltered. Only the
sun had melted the fat of the little mutton chop, and it ran down upon
the stones.

Then, the third time he bowed himself. When at last he looked up,
some ants had come to the meat on the altar. He stood up and drove
them away. Then he put his hat on his hot curls, and sat in the shade.
He clasped his hands about his knees. He sat to watch what would
come to pass. The glory of the Lord God Almighty! He knew he
should see it.

'My dear God is trying me,' he said; and he sat there through the
fierce heat of the afternoon. Still he watched and waited when the sun
began to slope; and when it neared the horizon and the sheep began to
cast long shadows across the karroo, he still sat there. He hoped when
the first rays touched the hills till the sun dipped behind them and was

gone. Then he called his ewes together, and broke down the altar, and threw the meat far, far away into the field.

He walked home behind his flock. His heart was heavy. He reasoned so: 'God cannot lie. I had faith. No fire came. I am like Cain—I am not His. He will not hear my prayer. God hates me.'

The boy's heart was heavy. When he reached the 'kraal' gate the two girls met him.

'Come,' said the yellow-haired Em, 'let us play "coop". There is still time before it gets quite dark. You, Waldo, go and hide on the "kopje"; Lyndall and I will shut eyes here, and we will not look.'

The girls hid their faces in the stone wall of the sheep-kraal, and the boy clambered half way up the 'kopje'. He crouched down between two stones and gave the call. Just then the milk-herd came walking out of the cow-kraal with two pails. He was an ill-looking Kaffir.

'Ah!' thought the boy, 'perhaps he will die to-night, and go to hell! I must pray for him, I must pray!'

Then he thought—'Where am *I* going to?' and he prayed desperately.

'Ah—this is not right at all,' little Em said, peeping between the stones, and finding him in a very curious posture. 'What *are* you doing, Waldo? It is not the play, you know. You should run out when we come to the white stone. Ah, you do not play nicely.'

'I—I will play nicely now,' said the boy, coming out and standing sheepishly before them; 'I—I only forgot; I will play now.'

'He has been to sleep,' said freckled Em.

'No,' said beautiful little Lyndall, looking curiously at him; 'he has been crying.'

She never made a mistake.

One night, two years after, the boy sat alone on the 'kopje'. He had crept softly from his father's room and come there. He often did, because when he prayed or cried aloud, his father might awake and hear him; and none knew his great sorrow, and none knew his grief, but he himself, and he buried them deep in his heart.

He turned up the brim of his great hat and looked at the moon, but most at the leaves of the prickly pear that grew just before him. They glinted, and glinted, and glinted, just like his own heart—cold, so hard, and very wicked. His physical heart had pain also; it seemed full of little bits of glass, that hurt. He had sat there for half an hour, and he dared not go back to the close house.

He felt horribly lonely. There was not one thing so wicked as he in all the world, and he knew it. He folded his arms and began to cry — not aloud; he sobbed without making any sound, and his tears left scorched marks where they fell. He could not pray; he had prayed night and day for so many months; and to-night he could not pray. When he left off crying, he held his aching head with his brown hands. If one might have gone up to him and touched him kindly; poor, ugly little thing! Perhaps his heart was almost broken.

With his swollen eyes he sat there on a flat stone at the very top of the 'kopje'; and the tree, with every one of its wicked leaves, blinked, and blinked, and blinked at him. Presently he began to cry again, and then stopped his crying to look at it. He was quiet for a long while, then he knelt up slowly and bent forward. There was a secret he had carried in his heart for a year. He had not dared to look at it; he had not whispered it to himself; but for a year he had carried it. 'I hate God!' he said. The wind took the words and ran away with them, among the stones, and through the leaves of the prickly pear. He thought it died away half down the 'kopje'. He had told it now!

'I love Jesus Christ, but I hate God.'

The wind carried away that sound as it had done the first. Then he got up and buttoned his old coat about him. He knew he was certainly lost now; he did not care. If half the world were to be lost, why not he too? He would not pray for mercy any more. Better so — better to know certainly. It was ended now. Better so.

He began scrambling down the sides of the 'kopje' to go home.

Better so! — But oh, the loneliness, the agonized pain! for that night, and for nights on nights to come! The anguish that sleeps all day on the heart like a heavy worm, and wakes up at night to feed!

There are some of us who in after years say to Fate, 'Now deal us your hardest blow, give us what you will; but let us never again suffer as we suffered when we were children.'

The barb in the arrow of childhood's suffering is this: its intense loneliness, its intense ignorance.

At last came the year of the great drought, the year of 1862. From end to end of the land the earth cried for water. Man and beast turned their eyes to the pitiless sky, that like the roof of some brazen oven arched overhead. On the farm, day after day, month after month, the water in the dams fell lower and lower; the sheep died in the fields; the cattle, scarcely able to crawl, tottered as they moved from spot to spot in search of food. Week after week, month after month, the sun looked down from the cloudless sky, till the karroo-bushes were leafless sticks, broken into the earth, and the earth itself was naked and bare; and only the milk-bushes, like old hags, pointed their shrivelled fingers heavenwards, praying for the rain that never came.

It was on an afternoon of a long day in that thirsty summer, that on the side of the 'kopje' furthest from the homestead the two girls sat. They were somewhat grown since the days when they played hide-and-seek there, but they were mere children still.

Their dress was of dark coarse stuff; their common blue pinafores reached to their ankles, and on their feet they wore home-made 'vel-schoen'.

They sat under a shelving rock, on the surface of which were still visible some old Bushman-paintings, their red and black pigments having been preserved through long years from wind and rain by the overhanging ledge: grotesque oxen, elephants, rhinoceroses, and a one-horned beast, such as no man has seen or ever shall.

The girls sat with their backs to the paintings. In their laps were a few fern and ice-plant leaves, which by dint of much searching they had gathered under the rocks.

Em took off her big brown kappje and began vigorously to fan her red face with it; but her companion bent low over the leaves in her lap, and at last took up an ice-plant leaf and fastened it on to the front of her blue pinafore with a pin.

'Diamonds must look as these drops do,' she said, carefully bending over the leaf, and crushing one crystal drop with her delicate little nail. 'When I', she said, 'am grown up, I shall wear real diamonds, exactly like these, in my hair.'

Her companion opened her eyes and wrinkled her low forehead.

'Where will you find them, Lyndall? The stones are only crystals that we picked up yesterday. Old Otto says so.'

'And you think that I am going to stay *here* always?'

The lip trembled scornfully.

'Ah, no,' said her companion. 'I suppose some day we shall go somewhere; but now we are only twelve, and we cannot marry till we are seventeen. Four years, five—that is a long time to wait. And we might not have diamonds if we did marry.'

'And you think that I am going to stay here till then?'

'Well, where *are* you going?' asked her companion.

The girl crushed an ice-plant leaf between her fingers.

'Tant' Sannie is a miserable old woman,' she said. 'Your father married her when he was dying, because he thought she would take better care of the farm, and of us, than an Englishwoman. He said we should be taught and sent to school. Now she saves every farthing for herself, buys us not even one old book. She does not ill-use us—why? Because she is afraid of your father's ghost. Only this morning she told her Hottentot that she would have beaten you for breaking the plate, but that three nights ago she heard a rustling and a grunting behind the pantry door, and knew it was your father coming to "spook" her. She is a miserable old woman,' said the girl, throwing the leaf from her; 'but I intend to go to school.'

'And if she won't let you?'

'I shall make her.'

'How?'

The child took not the slightest notice of the last question, and folded her small arms across her knees.

'But why do you want to go, Lyndall?'

'There is nothing helps in this world', said the child slowly, 'but to be very wise, and to know everything—to be clever.'

'But I should not like to go to school!' persisted the small freckled face.

'And you do not need to. When you are seventeen this Boer-woman will go; you will have this farm and everything that is upon it for your own: but I', said Lyndall, 'will have nothing. I must learn.'

'Oh, Lyndall *I* will give you some of my sheep,' said Em, with a sudden burst of pitying generosity.

'I do not want your sheep,' said the girl slowly; 'I want things of my own. When I am grown up,' she added, the flush on her delicate features deepening at every word, 'there will be nothing that I do not know. I shall be rich, very rich; and I shall wear not only for best, but every day, a pure white silk, and little rose-buds, like the lady in Tant' Sannie's bed-room, and my petticoats will be embroidered, not only at the bottom, but all through.'

The lady in Tant' Sannie's bed-room was a gorgeous creature from a fashion-sheet, which the Boer-woman somewhere obtaining, had pasted up at the foot of her bed, to be profoundly admired by the children.

'It would be very nice,' said Em; but it seemed a dream of quite too transcendent a glory ever to be realized.

At this instant there appeared at the foot of the 'kopje' two figures—the one, a dog, white and sleek, one yellow ear hanging down over his left eye; the other, his master, a lad of fourteen, and no other than the boy Waldo, grown into a heavy, slouching youth of fourteen. The dog mounted the 'kopje' quickly, his master followed slowly. He wore an aged jacket much too large for him, and rolled up at the wrists, and, as of old, a pair of dilapidated 'vel-schoens' and a felt hat. He stood before the two girls at last.

'What have you been doing to-day?' asked Lyndall, lifting her eyes to his face.

'Looking after ewes and lambs below the dam. Here!' he said, holding out his hand awkwardly, 'I brought them for you.'

There were a few green blades of tender grass.

'Where did you find them?'

'On the dam wall.'

She fastened them beside the leaf on her blue pinafore.

'They look nice there,' said the boy, awkwardly rubbing his great hands and watching her.

'Yes; but the pinafore spoils it all; it is not pretty.'

He looked at it closely.

'Yes, the squares are ugly; but it looks nice upon you—beautiful.'

He now stood silent before them, his great hands hanging loosely at either side.

'Some one has to come to-day,' he mumbled out suddenly, when the idea struck him.

'Who?' asked both girls.

'An Englishman on foot.'

'What does he look like?' asked Em.

'I did not notice; but he has a very large nose,' said the boy slowly. 'He asked the way to the house.'

'Didn't he tell you his name?'

'Yes—Bonaparte Blenkins.'

'Bonaparte!' said Em, 'why that is like the reel Hottentot Hans plays on the violin—

'Bonaparte, Bonaparte, my wife is sick;
In the middle of the week, but Sundays not,
I give her rice and beans for soup—

It is a funny name.'

'There was a living man called Bonaparte once,' said she of the great eyes.

'Ah yes, I know,' asked Em—'the poor prophet whom the lions ate. I am always so sorry for him.'

Her companion cast a quiet glance upon her.

'He was the greatest man who ever lived,' she said, 'the man I like best.'

'And what did he do?' asked Em, conscious that she had made a mistake, and that her prophet was not the man.

'He was one man, only one,' said her little companion slowly, 'yet all the people in the world feared him. He was not born great, he was common as we are; yet he was master of the world at last. Once he was only a little child, then he was a lieutenant, then he was a general, then he was an emperor. When he said a thing to himself he never forgot it. He waited, and waited, and waited, and it came at last.'

'He must have been very happy,' said Em.

'I do not know,' said Lyndall; 'but he had what he said he would have, and that is better than being happy. He was their master, and all the people were white with fear of him. They joined together to fight him. He was one and they were many, and they got him down at last. They were like the wild cats when their teeth are fast in a great dog, like cowardly wild cats,' said the child, 'they would not let him go. They were many; he was only *one*. They sent him to an island in the sea, a lonely island, and kept him there fast. He was one man, and they were many, and they were terrified at him. It was glorious!' said the child.

'And what then?' said Em.

'Then he was alone there in that island with men to watch him always,' said her companion, slowly and quietly, 'and in the long lonely nights he used to lie awake and think of the things he had done in the old days, and the things he would do if they let him go again. In the day when he walked near the shore it seemed to him that the sea all around him was a cold chain about his body pressing him to death.'

'And then?' said Em, much interested.

'He died there in that island; he never got away.'

'It is rather a nice story,' said Em; 'but the end is sad.'

'It is a terrible, hateful ending,' said the little teller of the story, leaning forward on her folded arms; 'and the worst is, it is true. I have noticed', added the child very deliberately, 'that it is only the made-up stories that end nicely; the true ones all end so.'

As she spoke the boy's dark, heavy eyes rested on her face.

'You have read it, have you not?'

He nodded. 'Yes; but the brown history tells only what he did, not what he thought.'

'It was in the brown history that I read of him,' said the girl; 'but I *know* what he thought. Books do not tell everything.'

'No,' said the boy, slowly drawing nearer to her and sitting down at her feet. 'What you want to know they never tell.'

Then the children fell into silence, till Doss, the dog, growing uneasy at its long continuance, sniffed at one and the other, and his master broke forth suddenly—

'If *they* could talk, if *they* could tell us now!' he said, moving his hand out over the surrounding objects—'then we would know something. This "kopje", if it could tell us how it came here! The "Physical Geography" says', he went on most rapidly and confusedly, 'that what are dry lands now were once lakes; and what I think is this—these low hills were once the shores of a lake; this "kopje" is some of the stones that were at the bottom, rolled together by the water. But there is this—how did the water come to make one heap here alone, in the centre of the plain?' It was a ponderous question; no one volunteered an answer. 'When I was little,' said the boy, 'I always looked at it and wondered, and I thought a great giant was buried under it. Now I know the water must have done it; but how? It is very wonderful. Did one little stone come first, and stopped the others as they rolled?' said the boy with earnestness, in a low voice, more as speaking to himself than to them.

'Oh, Waldo, God put the little "kopje" here,' said Em with solemnity.

'But how did he put it here?'

'By wanting.'

'But how did the wanting bring it here?'

'Because it did.'

The last words were uttered with the air of one who produced a clinching argument. What effect it had on the questioner was not evident, for he made no reply, and turned away from her.

Drawing closer to Lyndall's feet, he said after a while in a low voice,

'Lyndall, has it never seemed to you that the stones *were* talking with you? Sometimes,' he added in a yet lower tone, 'I lie under there with my sheep, and it seems that the stones are really speaking—speaking of the old things, of the time when the strange fishes and animals lived that are turned into stone now, and the lakes were here; and then of the time when the little Bushmen lived here, so small and so ugly, and used to sleep in the wild dog holes, and in the "sloots", and eat snakes, and shot the bucks with their poisoned arrows. It was one of them, one of these old wild Bushmen, that painted those,' said the boy, nodding towards the pictures—'one who was different from the rest. He did not know why, but he wanted to make something beautiful—he wanted to make something, so he made these. He worked hard, very hard, to find the juice to make the paint; and then he found this place where the rocks hang over, and he painted them. To us they are only strange things, that make us laugh; but to him they were very beautiful.'

The children had turned round and looked at the pictures.

'He used to kneel here naked, painting, painting, painting; and he wondered at the things he made himself,' said the boy, rising and moving his hand in deep excitement. 'Now the Boers have shot them all, so that we never see a little yellow face peeping out among the stones.' He paused, a dreamy look coming over his face. 'And the wild bucks have gone, and those days, and we are here. But we will be gone soon, and only the stones will lie on here, looking at everything like they look now. I know that it is I who am thinking,' the fellow added slowly, 'but it seems as though it were they who are talking. Has it never seemed so to you, Lyndall?'

'No, it never seems so to me,' she answered.

The sun had dipped now below the hills, and the boy, suddenly remembering the ewes and lambs, started to his feet.

'Let us also go to the house and see who has come,' said Em, as the boy shuffled away to rejoin his flock, while Doss ran at his heels, snapping at the ends of the torn trousers as they fluttered in the wind.

As the two girls rounded the side of the 'kopje', an unusual scene presented itself. A large group was gathered at the back door of the homestead.

On the door-step stood the Boer-woman, a hand on each hip, her face red and fiery, her head nodding fiercely. At her feet sat the yellow

Hottentot maid, her satellite, and around stood the black Kaffir maids, with blankets twisted round their half-naked figures. Two, who stamped mealies in a wooden block, held the great stampers in their hands, and stared stupidly at the object of attraction. It certainly was not to look at the old German overseer, who stood in the centre of the group, that they had all gathered together. His salt-and-pepper suit, grizzly black beard, and grey eyes were as familiar to every one on the farm as the red gables of the homestead itself; but beside him stood the stranger, and on him all eyes were fixed. Ever and anon the newcomer cast a glance over his pendulous red nose to the spot where the Boer-woman stood, and smiled faintly.

'I'm not a child,' cried the Boer-woman, in low Cape Dutch, 'and I wasn't born yesterday. No, by the Lord, no! You can't take *me* in! My mother didn't wean me on Monday. One wink of my eye and I see the whole thing. I'll have no tramps sleeping on my farm,' cried Tant' Sannie blowing. 'No, by the Devil, no! not though he had sixty-times-six red noses.'

WILLIAM SHARP

The White Peacock

Here where the sunlight
Floodeth the garden,
Where the pomegranate
Reareth its glory
Of gorgeous blossom;
Where the oleanders
Dream through the noontides;
And, like surf o' the sea
Round cliffs of basalt,
The thick magnolias   10
In billowy masses
Front the sombre green of the ilexes:
Here where the heat lies
Pale blue in the hollows,
Where blue are the shadows
On the fronds of the cactus,
Where pale blue the gleaming

Of fir and cypress,
With the cones upon them
Amber or glowing   20
With virgin gold;
Here where the honey-flower
Makes the heat fragrant,
As though from the gardens
Of Gulistan,
Where the bulbul singeth
Through a mist of roses
A breath were borne:
Here where the dream-flowers,
The cream-white poppies   30
Silently waver,
And where the Scirocco,
Faint in the hollows,
Foldeth his soft white wings in the sunlight,
And lieth sleeping
Deep in the heart of
A sea of white violets:
Here, as the breath, as the soul of this beauty
Moveth in silence, and dreamlike, and slowly,
White as a snow-drift in mountain-valleys   40
When softly upon it the gold light lingers:
White as the foam o' the sea that is driven
O'er billows of azure agleam with sun-yellow:
Cream-white and soft as the breasts of a girl,
Moves the White Peacock, as though through the noontide
A dream of the moonlight were real for a moment.
Dim on the beautiful fan that he spreadeth,
Foldeth and spreadeth abroad in the sunlight,
Dim on the cream-white are blue adumbrations,
Shadows so pale in their delicate blueness   50
That visions they seem as of vanishing violets,
The fragrant white violets veined with azure,
Pale, pale as the breath of blue smoke in far woodlands.
Here, as the breath, as the soul of this beauty,
White as a cloud through the heats of the noontide
Moves the White Peacock.

MARY DUCLAUX

Etruscan Tombs

I

To think the face we love shall ever die,
    And be the indifferent earth, and know us not!
To think that one of us shall live to cry
    On one long buried in a distant spot!

O wise Etruscans, faded in the night
    Yourselves, with scarce a rose-leaf on your trace;
You kept the ashes of the dead in sight,
    And shaped the vase to seem the vanished face.

But, O my Love, my life is such an urn
    That tender memories mould with constant touch,   10
Until the dust and earth of it they turn
    To your dear image that I love so much:

A sacred urn, filled with the sacred past,
That shall recall you while the clay shall last.

II

These cinerary urns with human head
    And human arms that dangle at their sides,
The earliest potters made them for their dead,
    To keep the mother's ashes or the bride's.

O rude attempt of some long-spent despair—
    With symbol and with emblem discontent—   20
To keep the dead alive and as they were,
    The actual features and the glance that went!

The anguish of your art was not in vain,
    For lo, upon these alien shelves removed
The sad immortal images remain,
    And show that once they lived and once you loved.

But oh, when I am dead may none for me
Invoke so drear an immortality!

III

Beneath the branches of the olive yard
    Are roots where cyclamen and violet grow   30
Beneath the roots the earth is deep and hard
    And there a king was buried long ago.

The peasants digging deeply in the mould
    Cast up the autumn soil about the place,
And saw a gleam of unexpected gold,
    And underneath the earth a living face.

With sleeping lids and rosy lips he lay
    Among the wreaths and gems that mark the king
One moment; then a little dust and clay
    Fell shrivelled over wreath and urn and ring.   40

A carven slab recalls his name and deeds,
Writ in a language no man living reads.

IV

Here lies the tablet graven in the past,
    Clear-charactered and firm and fresh of line.
See, not a word is gone; and yet how fast
    The secret no man living may divine!

What did he choose for witness in the grave?
    A record of his glory on the earth?
The wail of friends? The Paens of the brave?
    The sacred promise of the second birth?   50

The tombs of ancient Greeks in Sicily
    Are sown with slender discs of graven gold
Filled with the praise of Death: 'Thrice happy he
    Wrapt in the milk-soft sleep of dreams untold!'

They sleep their patient sleep in altered lands,
The golden promise in their fleshless hands.

T. W. ROLLESTON

The Dead at Clonmacnois°

FROM THE IRISH OF ENOCH O'GILLAN

In a quiet watered land, a land of roses,
   Stands Saint Kieran's city fair;°
And the warriors of Erin in their famous generations
   Slumber there.

There beneath the dewy hillside sleep the noblest
   Of the clan of Conn,
Each below his stone with name in branching Ogham°
   And the sacred knot thereon.

There they laid to rest the seven Kings of Tara,
   There the sons of Cairbrè sleep—   10
Battle-banners of the Gael, that in Kieran's plain of crosses
   Now their final hosting keep.

And in Clonmacnois they laid the men of Teffia,
   And right many a lord of Breagh;
Deep the sod above Clan Creidè and Clan Conaill,
   Kind in hall and fierce in fray.

Many and many a son of Conn the Hundred-Fighter
   In the red earth lies at rest;
Many a blue eye of Clan Colman the turf covers,
   Many a swan-white breast.   20

JOHN DAVIDSON

The Wastrel

An eyesore to the tourist on the shoulder of the knock°
   Above the green-fledged larches where the squirrel keeps its
     house,

The pale dissenting chapel, like a pharos on a rock,
   With strong, pathetic preaching that the very dead might rouse,
Was lighted for an hour and twenty minutes by the clock,
   While the cushats moaned and muttered deep among the rustling
     boughs.°

With Conybeare-and-Howson laid on thick for local hue,°
   And Meyer's and Lange's comments to elucidate the text,°
The minister exhibited a panoramic view
   Of the story of the wastrel and the father that he vext: 10
Of little but his Bible and his creed the preacher knew,
   And dogma like a razor his emotions had unsexed.

Then came the modern instance, and the congregation stirred,
   And scrutinized the pew in which the preacher's family sat.
'I knew it,' thought each member, 'at the very opening word!'
   And felt as perspicacious as a dog that smells a rat:
The preacher's wife and daughters seized their Bibles when they
     heard;
   And his son, as red as poppies, stooped and glanced at this and
     that.

'But recently,' the preacher said, 'to London town there went
   A youth from our vicinity against his father's wish;   20
To make a fortune—honestly, if possible—he meant,
   Forgetting quite how God examines both sides of the dish:
Unless a holy life exhale to Heaven a savoury scent,
   We know how very profitless the loaves are and the fish.' . . .

The wife and daughters shrivel up and shut their eyes and cry,
   As the preacher drives the lancet home and lays their
     heart-strings bare;
But the wastrel, cool and clammy, feels a wind of fate go by,
   And hears his pulses clank above monition, praise and prayer—
'Oho, for London Town again, where folk in peace can die,
   And the thunder-and-lightning devil of a train that takes me
     there!'   30

A Northern Suburb

Nature selects the longest way,
   And winds about in tortuous grooves;
A thousand years the oaks decay;
   The wrinkled glacier hardly moves.

But here the whetted fangs of change
   Daily devour the old demesne—
The busy farm, the quiet grange,
   The wayside inn, the village green.

In gaudy yellow brick and red,
   With rooting pipes, like creepers rank,   10
The shoddy terraces o'erspread
   Meadow, and garth, and daisied bank.

With shelves for rooms the houses crowd,
   Like draughty cupboards in a row—
Ice-chests when wintry winds are loud,
   Ovens when summer breezes blow.

Roused by the fee'd policeman's knock,
   And sad that day should come again,
Under the stars the workmen flock
   In haste to reach the workmen's train.   20

For here dwell those who must fulfil
   Dull tasks in uncongenial spheres,
Who toil through dread of coming ill,
   And not with hope of happier years—

The lowly folk who scarcely dare
   Conceive themselves perhaps misplaced,
Whose prize for unremitting care
   Is only not to be disgraced.

Thirty Bob a Week

I couldn't touch a stop and turn a screw,
    And set the blooming world a-work for me,
Like such as cut their teeth—I hope, like you—
    On the handle of a skeleton gold key;
I cut mine on a leek, which I eat it every week:
    I'm a clerk at thirty bob as you can see.

But I don't allow it's luck and all a toss;
    There's no such thing as being starred and crossed;
It's just the power of some to be a boss,
    And the bally power of others to be bossed;   10
I face the music, sir; you bet I ain't a cur;
    Strike me lucky if I don't believe I'm lost!

For like a mole I journey in the dark,
    A-travelling along the underground
From my Pillar'd Halls and broad Suburbean Park,
    To come the daily dull official round;
And home again at night with my pipe all alight,
    A-scheming how to count ten bob a pound.

And it's often very cold and very wet,
    And my missis stitches towels for a hunks;°   20
And the Pillar'd Halls is half of it to let—
    Three rooms about the size of travelling trunks.
And we cough, my wife and I, to dislocate a sigh,
    When the noisy little kids are in their bunks.

But you never hear her do a growl or whine,
    For she's made of flint and roses, very odd;
And I've got to cut my meaning rather fine,
    Or I'd blubber, for I'm made of greens and sod:
So p'r'aps we are in Hell for all that I can tell,
    And lost and damn'd and served up hot to God.   30

I ain't blaspheming, Mr Silver-tongue;
   I'm saying things a bit beyond your art:
Of all the rummy starts you ever sprung,
   Thirty bob a week's the rummiest start!
With your science and your books and your the'ries about spooks,
   Did you ever hear of looking in your heart?

I didn't mean your pocket, Mr, no:
   I mean that having children and a wife,
With thirty bob on which to come and go,
   Isn't dancing to the tabor and the fife: 40
When it doesn't make you drink, by Heaven! it makes you think,
   And notice curious items about life.

I step into my heart and there I meet
   A god-almighty devil singing small,
Who would like to shout and whistle in the street,
   And squelch the passers flat against the wall;
If the whole world was a cake he had the power to take,
   He would take it, ask for more, and eat them all.

And I meet a sort of simpleton beside,
   The kind that life is always giving beans;   50
With thirty bob a week to keep a bride
   He fell in love and married in his teens:
At thirty bob he stuck; but he knows it isn't luck:
   He knows the seas are deeper than tureens.

And the god-almighty devil and the fool
   That meet me in the High Street on the strike,
When I walk about my heart a-gathering wool,
   Are my good and evil angels if you like.
And both of them together in every kind of weather
   Ride me like a double-seated bike.   60

That's rough a bit and needs its meaning curled.
   But I have a high old hot un in my mind—
A most engrugious notion of the world,°
   That leaves your lightning 'rithmetic behind:
I give it at a glance when I say 'There ain't no chance,
   Nor nothing of the lucky-lottery kind.'

And it's this way that I make it out to be:
  No fathers, mothers, countries, climates—none;
No Adam was responsible for me,
  Nor society, nor systems, nary one: 70
A little sleeping seed, I woke—I did, indeed—
  A million years before the blooming sun.

I woke because I thought the time had come;
  Beyond my will there was no other cause;
And everywhere I found myself at home,
  Because I chose to be the thing I was;
And in whatever shape of mollusc or of ape
  I always went according to the laws.

I was the love that chose my mother out;
  I joined two lives and from the union burst;   80
My weakness and my strength without a doubt
  Are mine alone for ever from the first:
It's just the very same with a difference in the name
  As 'Thy will be done.' You say it if you durst!

They say it daily up and down the land
  As easy as you take a drink, it's true;
But the difficultest go to understand,
  And the difficultest job a man can do,
Is to come it brave and meek with thirty bob a week,
  And feel that that's the proper thing for you.   90

It's a naked child against a hungry wolf;
  It's playing bowls upon a splitting wreck;
It's walking on a string across a gulf
  With millstones fore-and-aft about your neck;
But the thing is daily done by many and many a one;
  And we fall, face forward, fighting, on the deck.

Epilogue—The Last Journey

I felt the world a-spinning on its nave,
  I felt it sheering blindly round the sun;
I felt the time had come to find a grave:
  I knew it in my heart my days were done.
I took my staff in hand; I took the road,
And wandered out to seek my last abode.
        Hearts of gold and hearts of lead
          Sing it yet in sun and rain,
        'Heel and toe from dawn to dusk,
          Round the world and home again.'   10

O long before the bere was steeped for malt,
  And long before the grape was crushed for wine,
The glory of the march without a halt,
  The triumph of a stride like yours and mine
Was known to folk like us, who walked about,
To be the sprightliest cordial out and out!
        Folk like us, with hearts that beat,
          Sang it too in sun and rain—
        'Heel and toe from dawn to dusk,
          Round the world and home again.'   20

My feet are heavy now, but on I go,
  My head erect beneath the tragic years.
The way is steep, but I would have it so;
  And dusty, but I lay the dust with tears,
Though none can see me weep: alone I climb
The rugged path that leads me out of time—
        Out of time and out of all,
          Singing yet in sun and rain,
        'Heel and toe from dawn to dusk,
          Round the world and home again.'   30

Farewell the hope that mocked, farewell despair
  That went before me still and made the pace.
The earth is full of graves, and mine was there
  Before my life began, my resting-place;
And I shall find it out and with the dead
Lie down for ever, all my sayings said—
    Deeds all done and songs all sung,
      While others chant in sun and rain,
    'Heel to toe from dawn to dusk,
      Round the world and home again.'   40

SIR WILLIAM WATSON

World Strangeness

Strange the world about me lies,
  Never yet familiar grown—
Still disturbs me with surprise,
  Haunts me like a face half known.

In this house with starry dome,
  Floored with gemlike plains and seas,
Shall I never feel at home,
  Never wholly be at ease?

On from room to room I stray,
  Yet my Host can ne'er espy,   10
And I know not to this day
  Whether guest or captive I.

GEORGE GISSING

The Foolish Virgin

Coming down to breakfast, as usual rather late, Miss Jewell was
surprised to find several persons still at table. Their conversation

ceased as she entered, and all eyes were directed to her with a look in which she discerned some special meaning. For several reasons she was in an irritable humour; the significant smiles, the subdued 'Good mornings', and the silence that followed, so jarred upon her nerves that, save for curiosity, she would have turned and left the room.

Mrs Banting (generally at this hour busy in other parts of the house) inquired with a sympathetic air whether she would take porridge; the others awaited her reply as if it were a matter of general interest. Miss Jewell abruptly demanded an egg. The awkward pause was broken by a high falsetto.

'I believe you know who it is all the time, Mr Drake,' said Miss Ayres, addressing the one man present.

'I assure you I don't. Upon my word, I don't. The whole thing astonishes me.'

Resolutely silent, Miss Jewell listened to a conversation the drift of which remained dark to her, until some one spoke the name 'Mr Cheeseman'; then it was with difficulty that she controlled her face and her tongue. The servant brought her an egg. She struck it clumsily with the edge of the spoon, and asked in an affected drawl: 'What are you people talking about?'

Mrs Sleath, smiling maliciously, took it upon herself to reply.

'Mr Drake has had a letter from Mr Cheeseman. He writes that he's engaged, but doesn't say who to. Delicious mystery, isn't it?'

The listener tried to swallow a piece of bread and butter, and seemed to struggle with a constriction of the throat. Then, looking round the table, she said with contemptuous pleasantry:

'Some lodging-house servant, I shouldn't wonder.'

Everyone laughed. Then Mr Drake declared he must be off, and rose from the table. The ladies also moved, and in a minute or two Miss Jewell sat at her breakfast alone.

She was a tall, slim person, with unremarkable, not ill-moulded features. Nature meant her to be graceful in form and pleasantly feminine of countenance; unwholesome habit of mind and body was responsible for the defects that now appeared in her. She had no colour, no flesh; but an agreeable smile would well have become her lips, and her eyes needed only the illumination of healthy thought to be more than commonly attractive. A few months would see the close of her twenty-ninth year; but Mrs Banting's boarders, with some excuse, judged her on the wrong side of thirty.

Her meal, a sad pretence, was soon finished. She went to the window and stood there for five minutes looking at the cabs and pedestrians in the sunny street. Then, with the languid step which had become natural to her, she ascended the stairs and turned into the drawing-room. Here, as she had expected, two ladies sat in close conversation. Without heeding them, she walked to the piano, selected a sheet of music, and sat down to play.

Presently, whilst she drummed with vigour on the keys, some one approached; she looked up and saw Mrs Banting; the other persons had left the room.

'If it's true,' murmured Mrs Banting with genuine kindliness on her flabby lips, 'all I can say is that it's shameful—shameful!'

Miss Jewell stared at her.

'What do you mean?'

'Mr Cheeseman—to go and——'

'I don't understand you. What is it to me?'

The words were thrown out almost fiercely, and a crash on the piano drowned whatever Mrs Banting meant to utter in reply. Miss Jewell now had the drawing-room to herself.

She 'practised' for half an hour, careering through many familiar pieces with frequent mechanical correction of time-honoured blunders. When at length she was going up to her room, a grinning servant handed her a letter which had just arrived. A glance at the envelope told her from whom it came, and in privacy she at once opened it. The writer's address was Glasgow.

My Dear Rosamund, [began the letter], I can't understand why you write in such a nasty way. For some time now your letters have been horrid. I don't show them to William because if I did he would get into a tantrum. What I have to say to you now is this, that we simply can't go on sending you the money. We haven't it to spare, and that's the plain truth. You think we're rolling in money, and it's no use telling you we are not. William said last night that you must find some way of supporting yourself, and I can only say the same. You are a lady and had a thorough good education, and I am sure you have only to exert yourself. William says I may promise you a five pound note twice a year, but more than that you must not expect. Now do just think over your position——

She threw the sheet of paper aside, and sat down to brood

miserably. This little back bedroom, at no time conducive to good spirits, had seen Rosamund in many a dreary or exasperated mood; to-day it beheld her on the very verge of despair. Illuminated texts of Scripture spoke to her from the walls in vain; portraits of admired clergymen smiled vainly from the mantelpiece. She was conscious only of a dirty carpet, an ill-made bed, faded curtains, and a window that looked out on nothing. One cannot expect much for a guinea a week, when it includes board and lodging; the bedroom was at least a refuge, but even that, it seemed, would henceforth be denied her. Oh, the selfishness of people! And oh, the perfidy of man!

For eight years, since the breaking up of her home, Rosamund had lived in London boarding-houses. To begin with, she could count on a sufficient income, resulting from property in which she had a legitimate share. Owing to various causes, the value of this property had steadily diminished, until at length she became dependent upon the subsidies of kinsfolk; for more than a twelvemonth now, the only person able and willing to continue such remittances had been her married sister, and Rosamund had hardly known what it was to have a shilling of pocket-money. From time to time she thought feebly and confusedly of 'doing something', but her aims were so vague, her capabilities so inadequate that she always threw aside the intention in sheer hopelessness. Whatever will she might once have possessed had evaporated in the boarding-house atmosphere. It was hard to believe that her brother-in-law would ever withhold the poor five pounds a month. And—what is the use of boarding-houses if not to renew indefinitely the hope of marriage?

She was not of the base order of women. Conscience yet lived in her, and drew support from religion; something of modesty, of self-respect, still clad her starving soul. Ignorance and ill-luck had once or twice thrown her into such society as may be found in establishments outwardly respectable; she trembled and fled. Even in such a house as this of Mrs Banting's, she had known sickness of disgust. Herself included, four single women abode here at the present time; and the scarcely disguised purpose of every one of them was to entrap a marriageable man. In the others, it seemed to her detestable, and she hated all three, even as they in their turn detested her. Rosamund flattered herself with the persuasion that she did not aim merely at marriage and a subsistence; she would not marry any one; her desire was for sympathy, true companionship. In years gone by she had used to herself a more sacred word; nowadays the homely solace seemed enough. And of late a ray of hope had glimmered upon her dusty path. Mr Cheeseman, with his plausible airs, his engaging smile, had won something more than her confidence; an acquaintance of six months, ripening at length to intimacy, justified her in regarding him with sanguine emotion. They had walked together in Kensington Gardens; they had exchanged furtive and significant glances at table and elsewhere; everyone grew aware of the mutual preference. It shook her with a painful misgiving when Mr Cheeseman went way for his holiday and spoke no word; but probably he would write. He had written—to his friend Drake; and all was over.

Her affections suffered, but that was not the worst. Her pride had never received so cruel a blow.

After a life of degradation which might well have unsexed her, Rosamund remained a woman. The practice of affectations number- less had taught her one truth, that she could never hope to charm save by reliance upon her feminine qualities. Boarding-house girls, such numbers of whom she had observed, seemed all intent upon disown- ing their womanhood; they cultivated masculine habits, wore as far as possible male attire, talked loud slang, threw scorn (among themselves at all events) upon domestic virtues; and not a few of them seemed to profit by the prevailing fashion. Rosamund had tried these tactics, always with conscious failure. At other times, and vastly to her relief, she aimed in precisely the opposite direction, encouraging herself in feminine extremes. She would talk with babbling naïveté, exaggerate the languor induced by idleness, lack of exercise, and consequent ill- health; betray timidities and pruderies, let fall a pious phrase, rise of a morning for 'early celebration' and let the fact be known. These and the like extravagances had appeared to fascinate Mr Cheeseman, who openly professed his dislike for androgynous persons. And Rosamund enjoyed the satisfaction of moderate sincerity. Thus, or very much in this way, would she be content to live. Romantic passion she felt to be beyond her scope. Long ago—ah! perhaps long ago, when she first knew Geoffrey Hunt——

The name as it crossed her mind, suggested an escape from the insufferable ennui and humiliation of the hours till evening. It must be half a year since she called upon the Hunts, her only estimable acquaintances in or near London. They lived at Teddington, and the railway fare was always a deterrent; nor did she care much for Mrs

Hunt and her daughters, who of late years had grown reserved with her, as if uneasy about her mode of life. True, they were not at all snobbish; homely, though well-to-do people; but they had such strict views, and could not understand the existence of a woman less energetic than themselves. In her present straits, which could hardly be worse, their counsel might prove of value; though she doubted her courage when it came to making confessions.

She would do without luncheon (impossible to sit at table with those 'creatures') and hope to make up for it at tea; in truth, appetite was not likely to trouble her. Then for dress. Wearily she compared this garment with that, knowing beforehand that all were out of fashion and more or less shabby. Oh, what did it matter! She had come to beggary, the result that might have been foreseen long ago. Her faded costume suited fitly enough with her fortunes—nay, with her face. For just then she caught a sight of herself in the glass, and shrank. A lump choked her: looking desperately as if for help, for pity, through gathering tears, she saw the Bible verse on the nearest wall: 'Come unto me——.' Her heart became that of a woeful child: she put her hands before her face, and prayed in the old, simple words of childhood.

As her call must not be made before half-past three, she could not set out upon the journey forthwith; but it was a relief to get away from the house. In this bright weather, Kensington Gardens, not far away, seemed a natural place for loitering, but the alleys would remind her too vividly of late companionship; she walked in another direction, sauntered for an hour by the shop windows of Westbourne Grove, and, when she felt tired, sat at the railway station until it was time to start. At Teddington, half-a-mile's walk lay before her; though she felt no hunger, long abstinence and the sun's heat taxed her strength to the point of exhaustion; on reaching her friend's door, she stood trembling with nervousness and fatigue. The door opened, and to her dismay she learnt that Mrs Hunt was away from home. Happily, the servant added that Miss Caroline was in the garden.

'I'll go round,' said Rosamund at once. 'Don't trouble——'

The pathway round the pleasant little house soon brought her within view of a young lady who sat in a garden chair, sewing. But Miss Caroline was not alone; near to her stood a man in shirt sleeves and bare-headed, vigorously sawing a plank; he seemed to be engaged in the construction of a summer-house, and Rosamund took him at first sight for a mechanic, but when he turned round, exhibiting a ruddy face all agleam with health and good humour, she recognized the young lady's brother, Geoffrey Hunt. He, as though for the moment puzzled, looked fixedly at her.

'Oh, Miss Jewell, how glad I am to see you!'

Enlightened by his sister's words, Geoffrey dropped the saw, and stepped forward with still heartier greeting. Had civility permitted, he might easily have explained his doubts. It was some six years since his last meeting with Rosamund, and she had changed not a little; he remembered her as a graceful and rather pretty girl, with life in her, even if it ran for the most part to silliness, gaily dressed, sprightly of manner; notwithstanding the account he had received of her from his relatives, it astonished him to look upon this limp, faded woman. In Rosamund's eyes, Geoffrey was his old self, perhaps a trifle more stalwart, and if anything handsomer, but with just the same light in his eyes, the same smile on his bearded face, the same cordiality of utterance. For an instant, she compared him with Mr Cheeseman, and flushed for very shame. Unable to command her voice, she stammered incoherent nothings; only when a seat supported her weary body did she lose the dizziness which had threatened downright collapse; then she closed her eyes, and forgot everything but the sense of rest.

Geoffrey drew on his coat, and spoke jestingly of his amateur workmanship. Such employment, however, seemed not inappropriate to him, for his business was that of a timber merchant. Of late years he had lived abroad, for the most part in Canada. Rosamund learnt that at present he was having a longish holiday.

'And you go back to Canada?'

This she asked when Miss Hunt had stepped into the house to call for tea. Geoffrey answered that it was doubtful; for various reasons he rather hoped to remain in England, but the choice did not altogether rest with him.

'At all events'—she gave a poor little laugh—'you haven't pined in exile.'

'Not a bit of it. I have always had plenty of hard work—the one thing needful.'

'Yes—I remember—you always used to say that. And I used to protest. You granted, I think, that it might be different with women.'

'Did I?'

He wished to add something to the point, but refrained out of compassion. It was clear to him that Miss Jewell, at all events, would have been none the worse for exacting employment. Mrs Hunt had spoken of her with the disapprobation natural in a healthy, active woman of the old school, and Geoffrey himself could not avoid a contemptuous judgement.

'You have lived in London all this time?' he asked, before she could speak.

'Yes. Where else should I live? My sister at Glasgow doesn't want me there, and—and there's nobody else, you know.' She tried to laugh. 'I have friends in London—well, that is to say—at all events I'm not quite solitary.'

The man smiled, and could not allow her to suspect how profoundly he pitied such a condition. Caroline Hunt had reappeared; she began to talk of her mother and sister, who were enjoying themselves in Wales. Her own holiday would come upon their return; Geoffrey was going to take her to Switzerland.

Tea arrived just as Rosamund was again sinking into bodily faintness and desolation of spirit. It presently restored her, but she could hardly converse. She kept hoping that Caroline would offer her some invitation—to lunch, to dine, anything; but as yet no such thought seemed to occur to the young hostess. Suddenly the aspect of things was altered by the arrival of new callers, a whole family, man, wife and three children, strangers to Rosamund. For a time it seemed as if she must go away without any kind of solace; for Geoffrey had quitted her, and she sat alone. On the spur of irrational resentment, she rose and advanced to Miss Hunt.

'Oh, but you are not going! I want you to stay and have dinner with us, if you can. Would it make you too late?'

Rosamund flushed and could scarce contain her delight. In a moment she was playing with the youngest of the children, and even laughing aloud, so that Geoffrey glanced curiously towards her. Even the opportunity of private conversation which she had not dared to count upon was granted before long; when the callers had departed Caroline excused herself, and left her brother alone with the guest for half an hour. There was no time to be lost; Rosamund broached almost immediately the subject uppermost in her mind.

'Mr Hunt, I know how dreadful it is to have people asking for advice, but if I might—if you could have patience with me——'

'I haven't much wisdom to spare,' he answered, with easy good nature.

'Oh, you are very rich in it, compared with poor me. And my

position is so difficult. I want—I am trying to find some way of being useful in the world. I am tired of living for myself. I seem to be such a useless creature. Surely even I must have some talent, which it's my duty to put to use! Where should I turn? Could you help me with a suggestion?'

Her words, now that she had overcome the difficulty of beginning, chased each other with breathless speed, and Geoffrey was all but constrained to seriousness; he took it for granted, however, that Miss Jewell frequently used this language; doubtless it was part of her foolish, futile existence to talk of her soul's welfare, especially in *tête-à-tête* with unmarried men. The truth he did not suspect, and Rosamund could not bring herself to convey it in plain words.

'I do so envy the people who have something to live for!' Thus she panted. 'I fear I have never had a purpose in life—I'm sure I don't know why. Of course I'm only a woman, but even women nowadays are doing so much. You don't despise their efforts, do you?'

'Not indiscriminately.'

'If I could feel myself a profitable member of society! I want to be lifted above my wretched self. Is there no great end to which I could devote myself?'

Her phrases grew only more magniloquent, and all the time she was longing for courage to say: 'How can I earn money?' Geoffrey, confirmed in the suspicion that she talked only for effect, indulged his natural humour.

'I'm such a groveller, Miss Jewell. I never knew these aspirations. I see the world mainly as cubic feet of timber.'

'No, no, you won't make me believe that. I know you have ideals!'

'That word reminds me of poor old Halliday. You remember Halliday, don't you?'

In vexed silence, Rosamund shook her head.

'But I think you must have met him, in the old days. A tall, fair man—no? He talked a great deal about ideals, and meant to move the world. We lost sight of each other when I first left England, and only met again a day or two ago. He is married, and has three children, and looks fifty years old, though he can't be much more than thirty. He took me to see his wife—they live at Forest Hill.'

Rosamund was not listening, and the speaker became aware of it. Having a purpose in what he was about to say, he gently claimed her attention.

'I think Mrs Halliday is the kind of woman who would interest you. If ever any one had a purpose in life she has.'

'Indeed? And what?'

'To keep house admirably, and bring up her children as well as possible, on an income which would hardly supply some women with shoe-leather.'

'Oh, that's very dreadful!'

'Very fine, it seems to me. I never saw a woman for whom I could feel more respect. Halliday and she suit each other perfectly; they would be the happiest people in England if they had any money. As he walked back with me to the station he talked about their difficulties. They can't afford to engage a good servant (if one exists nowadays), and cheap sluts have driven them frantic, so that Mrs Halliday does everything with her own hands.'

'It must be awful.'

'Pretty hard, no doubt. She is an educated woman—otherwise, of course, she couldn't, and wouldn't manage it. And, by the by'—he paused for quiet emphasis—'she has a sister, unmarried, who lives in the country and does nothing at all. It occurs to one—doesn't it?—that the idle sister might pretty easily find scope for her energies.'

Rosamund stared at the ground. She was not so dull as to lose the significance of this story, and she imagined that Geoffrey reflected upon herself in relation to her own sister. She broke the long silence by saying awkwardly:

'I'm sure I would never allow a sister of mine to lead such a life.'

'I don't think you would,' replied the other. And, though he spoke genially, Rosamund felt it a very moderate declaration of his belief in her. Overcome by strong feeling, she exclaimed:

'I would do anything to be of use in the world. You don't think I mean it, but I do, Mr Hunt. I——'

Her voice faltered; the all important word stuck in her throat. And at that moment Geoffrey rose.

'Shall we walk about? Let me show you my mother's fernery; she is very proud of it.'

That was the end of intimate dialogue. Rosamund felt aggrieved, and tried to shape sarcasms, but the man's imperturbable good humour soon made her forget everything save the pleasure of being in his company. It was a bitter-sweet evening, yet perhaps enjoyment predominated. Of course, Geoffrey would conduct her to the station;

she never lost sight of this hope. There would be another opportunity for plain speech. But her desire was frustrated; at the time of departure, Caroline said that they might as well all go together. Rosamund could have wept for chagrin.

She returned to the detested house, the hateful little bedroom, and there let her tears have way. In dread lest the hysterical sobs should be overheard, she all but stifled herself.

Then, as if by blessed inspiration, a great thought took shape in her despairing mind. At the still hour of night she suddenly sat up in the darkness, which seemed illumined by a wondrous hope. A few minutes motionless; the mental light grew dazzling; she sprang out of bed, partly dressed herself, and by the rays of a candle sat down to write a letter:

DEAR MR HUNT,

Yesterday I did not tell you the whole truth. I have nothing to live upon, and I must find employment or starve. My brother-in-law has been support-ing me for a long time—I am ashamed to tell you, but I will—and he can do so no longer. I wanted to ask you for practical advice, but I did not make my meaning clear. For all that, you did advise me, and very well indeed. I wish to offer myself as domestic help to poor Mrs Halliday. Do you think she would have me? I ask no wages—only food and lodging. I will work harder and better than any general servant—I will indeed. My health is not bad, and I am fairly strong. Don't—don't throw scorn on this! Will you recommend me to Mrs Halliday—or ask Mrs Hunt to do so? I beg that you will. Please write to me at once, and say yes. I shall be ever grateful to you.

Very sincerely yours,

ROSAMUND JEWELL.

This she posted as early as possible. The agonies she endured in waiting for a reply served to make her heedless of boarding-house spite, and by the last post that same evening came Geoffrey's letter. He wrote that her suggestion was startling. 'Your motive seems to me very praiseworthy, but whether the thing would be possible is another question. I dare not take upon myself the responsibility of counselling you to such a step. Pray, take time, and think. I am most grieved to hear of your difficulties, but is there not some better way out of them?'

Brave words, but Rosamund attached some meaning to them. The woman in her—the ever-prevailing woman—was wrought by fears and vanities, urgencies and desires, to a strange point of exaltation. Forthwith, she wrote again: 'Send me, I entreat you, Mrs Halliday's address. I will go and see her. No, I can't do anything but work with my hands. I am no good for anything else. If Mrs Halliday refuses me, I shall go as a servant into some other house. Don't mock at me; I don't deserve it. Write at once.'

Till midnight she wept and prayed.

Geoffrey sent her the address, adding a few dry words: 'If you are willing and able to carry out this project, your ambition ought to be satisfied. You will have done your part towards solving one of the gravest problems of the time.' Rosamund did not at once understand; when the writer's meaning grew clear, she kept repeating the words, as though they were a new gospel. Yes! she would be working nobly, helping to show a way out of the great servant difficulty. It would be an example to poor ladies, like herself, who were ashamed of honest work. And Geoffrey Hunt was looking on. He must needs marvel; perhaps he would admire greatly; perhaps—oh, oh!

Of course, she found a difficulty in wording her letter to the lady who had never heard of her, and of whom she knew practically nothing. But zeal surmounted obstacles. She began by saying that she was in search of domestic employment, and that, through her friends at Teddington, she had heard of Mrs Halliday as a lady who might consider her application. Then followed an account of herself, tolerably ingenuous, and an amplification of the phrases she had addressed to Geoffrey Hunt. On an afterthought she enclosed a stamped envelope.

Whilst the outcome remained dubious, Rosamund's behaviour to her fellow-boarders was a pattern of offensiveness. She no longer shunned them—seemed, indeed, to challenge their observation for the sake of meeting it with arrogant defiance. She rudely interrupted conversations, met sneers with virulent retorts, made herself the common enemy. Mrs Banting was appealed to; ladies declared that they could not live in a house where they were exposed to vulgar insult. When nearly a week had passed, Mrs Banting found it necessary to speak in private with Miss Jewell, and to make a plaintive remonstrance. Rosamund's flashing eye and contemptuous smile foretold the upshot.

'Spare yourself the trouble, Mrs Banting. I leave the house to-morrow.'

'Oh, but——'

'There is no need for another word. Of course, I shall pay the week in lieu of notice. I am busy, and have no time to waste.'

The day before, she had been to Forest Hill, had seen Mrs Halliday, and entered into an engagement. At midday on the morrow she arrived at the house which was henceforth to be her home, the scene of her labours.

Sheer stress of circumstance accounted for Mrs Halliday's decision. Geoffrey Hunt, a dispassionate observer, was not misled in forming so high an opinion of his friend's wife. Only a year or two older than Rosamund, Mrs Halliday had the mind and the temper which enable women to front life as a rational combatant, instead of vegetating as a more or less destructive parasite. Her voice declared her; it fell easily upon a soft, clear note; the kind of voice that expresses good humour and reasonableness, and many other admirable qualities; womanly, but with no suggestion of the feminine gamut; a voice that was never likely to test its compass in extremes. She had enjoyed a country breeding; something of liberal education assisted her natural intelligence; thanks to a good mother, she discharged with ability and content the prime domestic duties. But physically she was not inexhaustible, and the laborious, anxious years had taxed her health. A woman of the ignorant class may keep house, and bring up a family, with her own hands; she has to deal only with the simplest demands of life; her home is a shelter, her food is primitive, her children live or die, according to the law of natural selection. Infinitely more complex, more trying, is the task of the educated wife and mother; if to conscientiousness be added enduring poverty, it means not seldom an early death. Fatigue and self-denial had set upon Mrs Halliday's features a stamp which could never be obliterated. Her husband, her children, suffered illnesses; she, the indispensable, durst not confess even to a headache. Such servants as from time to time she had engaged merely increased her toil and anxieties; she demanded, to be sure, the diligence and efficiency which in this new day can scarce be found among the menial ranks; what she obtained was sluttish stupidity, grotesque presumption, and every form of female viciousness. Rosamund Jewell, honest in her extravagant fervour, seemed at first a mocking apparition; only after a long talk, when Rosamund's ingenuousness had forcibly impressed her, would Mrs Halliday agree to an experiment. Miss Jewell was to live as one of the family; she did not ask this, but consented to it. She was to receive ten pounds a year, for Mrs Halliday insisted that payment there must be.

'I can't cook,' Rosamund had avowed. 'I never boiled a potato in my life. If you teach me, I shall be grateful to you.'

'The cooking I can do myself, and you can learn if you like.'

'I should think I might wash and scrub by the light of nature?'

'Perhaps. Good-will and ordinary muscles will go a long way.'

'I can't sew, but I will learn.'

Mrs Halliday reflected.

'You know that you are exchanging freedom for a hard and a very dull life?'

'My life has been hard and dull enough, if you only knew. The work will seem hard at first, no doubt, but I don't think I shall be dull with you.'

Mrs Halliday held out her work-worn hand, and received a clasp of the fingers attenuated by idleness.

It was a poor little house; built—of course—with sham display of spaciousness in front, and huddling discomfort at the rear. Mrs Halliday's servants never failed to urge the smallness of the rooms as an excuse for leaving them dirty; they had invariably been accustomed to lordly abodes, where their virtues could expand. The furniture was homely and no more than sufficient, but here and there on the walls shone a glimpse of summer landscape, done in better days by the master of the house, who knew something of various arts, but could not succeed in that of money-making. Rosamund bestowed her wordly goods in a tiny chamber which Mrs Halliday did her best to make inviting and comfortable; she had less room here than at Mrs Banting's, but the cleanliness of surroundings would depend upon herself, and she was not likely to spend much time by the bedside in weary discontent. Halliday, who came home each evening at half-past six, behaved to her on their first meeting with grave, even respectful, courtesy, his tone flattered Rosamund's ear; and nothing could have been more seemly than the modest gentleness of her replies.

At the close of the first day, she wrote to Geoffrey Hunt: 'I do believe I have made a good beginning. Mrs Halliday is perfect and I quite love her. Please do not answer this; I only write because I feel that I owe it to your kindness. I shall never be able to thank you enough.'

When Geoffrey obeyed her and kept silence, she felt that he acted prudently; perhaps Mrs Halliday might see the letter, and know his hand. But none the less she was disappointed.

Rosamund soon learnt the measure of her ignorance in domestic affairs. Thoroughly practical and systematic, her friend (this was to be their relation) set down a scheme of the day's and the week's work; it made a clear apportionment between them, with no preponderance of unpleasant drudgery for the newcomer's share. With astonishment, which she did not try to conceal, Rosamund awoke to the complexity and endlessness of home duties even in so small a house as this.

'Then you have no leisure?' she exclaimed, in sympathy, not remonstrance.

'I feel at leisure when I'm sewing—and when I take the children out. And there's Sunday.'

The eldest child was about five years old, the others three and a twelvemonth, respectively. Their ailments gave a good deal of trouble, and it often happened that Mrs Halliday was awake with one of them the greater part of the night. For children Rosamund had no natural tenderness; to endure the constant sound of their voices proved, in the beginning, her hardest trial, but the resolve to school herself in every particular soon enabled her to tend the little ones with much patience, and insensibly she grew fond of them. Until she had overcome her awkwardness in every task, it cost her no little effort to get through the day; at bedtime she ached in every joint, and morning oppressed her with a sick lassitude. Conscious, however, of Mrs Halliday's forbearance, she would not spare herself, and it soon surprised her to discover that the rigid performance of what seemed an ignoble task brought its reward. Her first success in polishing a grate gave her more delight than she had known since childhood. She summoned her friend to look, to admire, to praise.

'Haven't I done it well? Could you do it better yourself?'

'Admirable!'

Rosamund waved her blacklead brush and tasted victory.

The process of acclimatization naturally affected her health. In a month's time she began to fear that she must break down; she suffered painful disorders, crept out of sight to moan and shed a tear. Always faint, she had no appetite for wholesome food. Tossing on her bed at night, she said to herself a thousand times, 'I must go on, even if I die!' Her religion took the form of asceticism, and bade her rejoice in her miseries; she prayed constantly, and at times knew the solace of an infinite self-glorification. In such a mood she once said to Mrs Halliday:

'Don't you think I deserve some praise for the step I took?'

'You certainly deserve both praise and thanks from me.'

'But I mean—it isn't everyone who could have done it? I've a right to feel myself superior to the ordinary run of girls?'

The other gave her an embarrassed look, and murmured a few satisfying words. Later in the same day she talked to Rosamund about her health, and insisted on making certain changes which allowed her to take more open-air exercise. The result of this was a marked improvement; at the end of the second month Rosamund began to feel and look better than she had done for several years. Work no longer exhausted her. And the labour in itself seemed to diminish—a natural consequence of perfect co-operation between the two women. Mrs Halliday declared that life had never been so easy for her as now; she knew the delight of rest in which there was no self-reproach. But, for sufficient reasons, she did not venture to express to Rosamund all the gratitude that was due.

About Christmas, a letter from Forest Hill arrived at Teddington; this time it did not forbid a reply. It spoke of struggles, sufferings, achievements. 'Do I not deserve a word of praise? Have I not done something, as you said, towards solving the great question? Don't you believe in me a little?' Four more weeks went by, and brought no answer. Then, one evening, in a mood of bitterness, Rosamund took a singular step; she wrote to Mr Cheeseman. She had heard nothing of him, had utterly lost sight of the world in which they met; but his place of business was known to her, and thither she addressed the note. A few lines only: 'You are a very strange person, and I really take no interest whatever in you. But I have sometimes thought you would like to ask my forgiveness. If so, write to the above address, my sister's. I am living in London, and enjoying myself, but I don't choose to let you know where.' Having an opportunity on the morrow, Sunday, she posted this in a remote district.

The next day, a letter arrived for her from Canada. Here was the explanation of Geoffrey's silence. His words could hardly have been more cordial, but there were so few of them. On nourishment such as this no illusion could support itself; for the moment Rosamund renounced every hope. Well, she was no worse off than before the renewal of their friendship. But could it be called friendship? Geoffrey's mother and sisters paid no heed to her; they doubtless considered that she had finally sunk below their horizon; and Geoffrey himself, for all his fine words, most likely thought the same at heart. Of course they would never meet again. And for the rest of her life she would be nothing more than a domestic servant in genteel disguise— happy were the disguise preserved.

However, she had provided a distraction for her gloomy thoughts. With no more delay than was due to its transmission by way of Glasgow, there came a reply from Mr Cheeseman: two sheets of notepaper. The writer prostrated himself; he had been guilty of shameful behaviour; even Miss Jewell, with all her sweet womanliness, must find it hard to think of him with charity. But let her remember what 'the poets' had written about Remorse, and apply to him the most harrowing of their descriptions. He would be frank with her; he would 'a plain unvarnished tale unfold'. Whilst away for his holiday he by chance encountered one with whom, in days gone by, he had held tender relations. She was a young widow; his foolish heart was touched; he sacrificed honour to the passing emotion. Their marriage would be delayed, for his affairs were just now anything but flourishing. 'Dear Miss Jewell, will you not be my friend, my sister? Alas, I am not a happy man; but it is too late to lament.' And so on to the squeezed signature at the bottom of the last page.

Rosamund allowed a fortnight to pass—not before writing, but before her letter was posted. She used a tone of condescension, mingled with airy banter. 'From my heart I feel for you, but, as you say, there is no help. I am afraid you are very impulsive—yet I thought that was a fault of youth. Do not give way to despair. I really don't know whether I shall feel it right to let you hear again, but, if it soothes you, I don't think there would be any harm in your letting me know the cause of your troubles.'

This odd correspondence, sometimes with intervals of three weeks, went on until late summer. Rosamund would soon have been a year with Mrs Halliday. Her enthusiasm had long since burnt itself out; she was often a prey to vapours, to cheerless lassitude, even to the spirit of revolt against things in general, but on the whole she remained a thoroughly useful member of the household; the great experiment might fairly be called successful. At the end of August it was decided that the children must have sea air; their parents would take them away for a fortnight. When the project began to be talked of, Rosamund, perceiving a domestic difficulty, removed it by asking whether she would be at liberty to visit her sister in Scotland. Thus were things arranged.

Some days before that appointed for the general departure, Halliday received a letter which supplied him with a subject of conversation at breakfast.

'Hunt is going to be married,' he remarked to his wife just as Rosamund was bringing in the children's porridge.

Mrs Halliday looked at her helper—for no more special reason than the fact of Rosamund's acquaintance with the Hunt family; she perceived a change of expression, an emotional play of feature, and at once averted her eyes.

'Where? In Canada?' she asked, off-hand.

'No, he's in England. But the lady is a Canadian. I wonder he troubles to tell me. Hunt's a queer fellow. When we meet, once in two years, he treats me like a long lost brother; but I don't think he'd care a bit if he never saw me or heard of me again.'

'It's a family characteristic,' interposed Rosamund with a dry laugh.

That day she moved about with the gait and the eyes of a somnambulist. She broke a piece of crockery, and became hysterical over it. Her afternoon leisure she spent in the bedroom, and at night she professed a headache which obliged her to retire early.

A passion of wrath inflamed her; as vehement—though so utterly unreasonable—as in the moment when she learnt the perfidy of Mr Cheeseman. She raged at her folly in having submitted to social degradation on the mere hint of a man who uttered it in a spirit purely contemptuous. The whole hateful world had conspired against her. She banned her kinsfolk and all her acquaintances, especially the Hunts; she felt bitter even against the Hallidays—unsympathetic, selfish people, utterly indifferent to her private griefs, regarding her as a mere domestic machine. She would write to Geoffrey Hunt, and let him know very plainly what she thought of his behaviour in urging her to become a servant. Would such a thought have ever occurred to a gentleman! And her poor life was wasted, oh! oh! She would soon be thirty—thirty! The glass mocked her with savage truth. And she had not even a decent dress to put on. Self-neglect had made her appearance vulgar; her manners, her speech, doubtless, had lost their note of social superiority. Oh, it was hard! She wished for death, cried for divine justice in a better world.

On the morning of release, she travelled to London Bridge, ostensibly *en route* for the north. But, on alighting, she had her luggage taken to the cloak room, and herself went by omnibus to the West End. By noon she had engaged a lodging, one room in a street where she had never yet lived. And hither before night was transferred her property.

The next day she spent about half of her ready money in the purchase of clothing—cheap, but such as the self-respect of a 'lady' imperatively demands. She bought cosmetics; she set to work at removing from her hands the traces of ignoble occupation. On the day that followed—Sunday—early in the afternoon, she repaired to a certain corner of Kensington Gardens, where she came face to face with Mr Cheeseman.

'I have come,' said Rosamund, in a voice of nervous exhilaration which tried to subdue itself. 'Please to consider that it is more than you could expect.'

'It is! A thousand times more! You are goodness itself.'

In Rosamund's eyes the man had not improved since a year ago. The growth of a beard made him look older, and he seemed in indifferent health; but his tremulous delight, his excessive homage, atoned for the defect. She, on the other hand, was so greatly changed for the better, that Cheeseman beheld her with no less wonder than admiration. Her brisk step, her upright bearing, her clear eye, and pure-toned skin constrasted remarkably with the lassitude and sallowness he remembered; at this moment, too, she had a pleasant rosiness of cheek which made her girlish, virginal. All was set off by the new drapery and millinery, which threw a shade upon Cheeseman's very respectable, but somewhat time-honoured, Sunday costume.

They spent several hours together, Cheeseman talking of his faults, his virtues, his calamities, and his hopes, like the impulsive, well-meaning, but nerveless fellow that he was. Rosamund gathered from it all, as she had vaguely learnt from his recent correspondence, that the alluring widow no longer claimed him; but he did not enter into details on this delicate subject. They had tea at a restaurant by Notting Hill Gate; Miss Jewell appearing indefatigable, they again strolled in unfrequented ways. At length was uttered the question for which Rosamund had long ago prepared her reply.

'You cannot expect me', she said sweetly, 'to answer at once.'

'Of course not! I shouldn't have dared to hope——'

He choked and swallowed; a few beads of perspiration shining on his troubled face.

'You have my address; most likely I shall spend a week or two there. Of course you may write. I shall probably go to my sister's in Scotland, for the autumn——'

'Oh! don't say that—don't! To lose you again—so soon——'

'I only said, "probably"——'

'Oh, thank you! To go so far away—and the autumn; just when I have a little freedom; the very best time—if I dared to hope such a thing——'

Rosamund graciously allowed him to bear her company as far as to the street in which she lived.

A few days later she wrote to Mrs Halliday, heading her letter with the Glasgow address. She lamented the sudden impossibility of returning to her domestic duties. Something had happened. 'In short, dear Mrs Halliday, I am going to be married. I could not give you warning of this, it has come so unexpectedly. Do forgive me! I so earnestly hope you will find some one to take my place, some one better and more of a help to you. I know I haven't been much use. Do write to me at Glasgow and say I may still regard you as a dear friend.'

This having been dispatched, she sat musing over her prospects. Mr Cheeseman had honestly confessed the smallness of his income; he could barely count upon a hundred and fifty a year; but things might improve. She did not dislike him—no, she did not dislike him. He would be a very tractable husband. Compared, of course, with——

A letter was brought up to her room. She knew the flowing commercial hand, and broke the envelope without emotion. Two sheets—three sheets—and a half. But what was all this? 'Despair . . . thoughts of self-destruction . . . ignoble publicity . . . practical ruin . . . impossible . . . despise and forget . . . Dante's hell . . . deeper than ever plummet sounded . . . forever! . . .' So again he had deceived her! He must have known that the widow was dangerous; his reticence was mere shuffling. His behaviour to that other woman had perhaps exceeded in baseness his treatment of herself; else, how could he be so sure that a jury would give her 'ruinous damages'? Or was it all a mere illustration of a man's villainy? Why should not she also sue for damages? Why not? Why not?

The three months that followed were a time of graver peril, of
darker crises, than Rosamund, with all her slip-slop experiences, had
ever known. An observer adequately supplied with facts, psychological and material, would more than once have felt that it depended on
the mere toss of a coin whether she kept or lost her social respectability. She sounded all the depths possible to such a mind and heart—
save only that from which there could have been no redemption. A
saving memory lived within her, and, at length, in the yellow gloom of
a November morning—her tarnished, draggletailed finery thrown
aside for the garb she had worn in lowliness—Rosamund betook
herself to Forest Hill. The house of the Hallidays looked just as usual.
She slunk up to the door, rang the bell, and waited in fear of a strange
face. There appeared Mrs Halliday herself. The surprised but friendly
smile at once proved her forgiveness of Rosamund's desertion. She
had written, indeed, with calm good sense, hoping only that all would
be well.

'Let me see you alone, Mrs Halliday. How glad I am to sit in this
room again! Who is helping you now?'

'No one. Help such as I want is not easy to find.'

'Oh, let me come back! I am *not* married. No, no, there is nothing to
be ashamed of. I am no worse than I ever was. I'll tell you everything,
the whole silly, wretched story.'

She told it, blurring only her existence of the past three months.

'I would have come before, but I was so bitterly ashamed. I ran
away so disgracefully. Now I'm penniless—all but suffering hunger.
Will you have me again, Mrs Halliday? I've been a horrid fool, but—I
do believe—for the last time in my life. Try me again, dear Mrs
Halliday!'

There was no need of the miserable tears, the impassioned
pleading. Her home received her as though she had been absent but
for an hour. That night she knelt again by her bedside in the little
room, and at seven o'clock next morning she was lighting fires,
sweeping floors, mute in thankfulness.

Halliday heard the story from his wife, and shook a dreamy,
compassionate head.

'For goodness sake,' urged the practical woman, 'don't let her think
she's a martyr.'

'No, no; but the poor girl should have her taste of happiness.'

'Of course I'm sorry for her, but there are plenty of people more to be pitied. Work she must, and there's only one kind of work she's fit for. It's no small thing to find your vocation—is it? Thousands of such women—all meant by nature to scrub and cook—live and die miserably because they think themselves too good for it.'

'The whole social structure is rotten!'

'It'll last our time,' rejoined Mrs Halliday, as she gave a little laugh and stretched her weary arms.

J. K. STEPHEN

On a Rhine Steamer

Republic of the West
    Enlightened, free, sublime,
Unquestionably best
    Production of our time,

The telephone is thine,
    And thine the Pullman car,
The caucus, the divine
    Intense electric star.

To thee we likewise owe
    The venerable names   10
Of Edgar Allan Poe,
    And Mr Henry James.

In short it's due to thee,
    Thou kind of Western star,
That we have come to be
    Precisely what we are.

But every now and then,
    It cannot be denied,
You breed a kind of men
    Who are not dignified,   20

Or courteous or refined,
   Benevolent or wise,
Or gifted with a mind
   Beyond the common size,

Or notable for tact,
   Agreeable to me,
Or anything, in fact,
   That people ought to be.

FRANCIS THOMPSON

from *The Hound of Heaven*°

I fled Him, down the nights and down the days;
  I fled Him, down the arches of the years;
  I fled Him, down the labyrinthine ways
  Of my own mind; and in the mist of tears
I hid from Him, and under running laughter.
      Up vistaed hopes I sped;
      And shot, precipitated,
Adown Titanic glooms of chasmed fears,
  From those strong Feet that followed, followed after.
      But with unhurrying chase,   10
      And unperturbèd pace,
  Deliberate speed, majestic instancy,
     They beat—and a Voice beat
     More instant than the Feet—°
'All things betray thee, who betrayest Me.'

     I pleaded, outlaw-wise,
By many a hearted casement, curtained red,
  Trellised with intertwining charities;
(For, though I knew His love Who followèd,
     Yet was I sore adread   20
Lest, having Him, I must have naught beside)

But, if one little casement parted wide,
 The gust of His approach would clash it to:
 Fear wist not to evade, as Love wist to pursue.°

. . . .

 I said to Dawn: Be sudden—to Eve: Be soon;
  With thy young skiey blossoms heap me over
   From this tremendous Lover—
 Float thy vague veil about me, lest He see!

. . . .

  Now of that long pursuit
  Comes on at hand the bruit;
 That Voice is round me like a bursting sea:
 'And is thy earth so marred,
 Shattered in shard on shard?
 Lo, all things fly thee, for thou fliest Me!
 Strange, piteous, futile thing!
Wherefore should any set thee love apart?
Seeing none but I makes much of naught' (He said),
'And human love needs human meriting:
 How hast thou merited—
Of all man's clotted clay the dingiest clot?
 Alack, thou knowest not
How little worthy of any love thou art!
Whom wilt thou find to love ignoble thee,
 Save Me, save only Me?
All which I took from thee I did but take,
 Not for thy harms,
But just that thou might'st seek it in My arms.
 All which thy child's mistake
Fancies as lost, I have stored for thee at home:
 Rise, clasp My hand, and come!'

 Halts by me that footfall:
 Is my gloom, after all,
Shade of His hand, outstretched caressingly?
 'Ah, fondest, blindest, weakest,
 I am He Whom thou seekest!
Thou dravest love from thee, who dravest Me.'

The Singer Saith of His Song

The touches of man's modern speech
    Perplex her unacquainted tongue;
There seems through all her songs a sound
    Of falling tears. She is not young.

Within her eyes' profound arcane
    Resides the glory of her dreams;
Behind her secret cloud of hair
    She sees the Is beyond the Seems.

Her heart sole-towered in her steep spirit,
    Somewhat sweet is she, somewhat wan;   10
And she sings the songs of Sion
    By the streams of Babylon.

Arab Love-Song

The hunchèd camels of the night°
Trouble the bright
And silver waters of the moon.
The Maiden of the Morn will soon
Through Heaven stray and sing,
Star gathering.

Now, while the dark about our loves is strewn,
Light of my dark, blood of my heart, O come!
And night will catch her breath up, and be dumb.

Leave thy father, leave thy mother   10
And thy brother;
Leave the black tents of thy tribe apart!
Am I not thy father and thy brother,
And thy mother?
And thou—what needest with thy tribe's black tents
Who hast the red pavilion of my heart?

The Kingdom of God°

In no Strange Land°

O world invisible, we view thee,
O world intangible, we touch thee,
O world unknowable, we know thee,
Inapprehensible, we clutch thee!

Does the fish soar to find the ocean,
The eagle plunge to find the air—
That we ask of the stars in motion
If they have rumour of thee there?

Not where the wheeling systems darken,
And our benumbed conceiving soars!—   10
The drift of pinions, would we hearken,
Beats at our own clay-shuttered doors.

The angels keep their ancient places;—
Turn but a stone, and start a wing!
'Tis ye, 'tis your estrangèd faces,
That miss the many-splendoured thing.

But (when so sad thou canst not sadder)
Cry;—and upon thy so sore loss
Shall shine the traffic of Jacob's ladder°
Pitched betwixt Heaven and Charing Cross.°   20

Yea, in the night, my Soul, my daughter,
Cry,—clinging Heaven by the hems;
And lo, Christ walking on the water
Not of Gennesareth, but Thames!°

A. E. HOUSMAN

'When I watch the living meet'

When I watch the living meet,
   And the moving pageant file
Warm and breathing through the street
   Where I lodge a little while,

If the heats of hate and lust
   In the house of flesh are strong,
Let me mind the house of dust
   Where my sojourn shall be long.

In the nation that is not
   Nothing stands that stood before;   10
There revenges are forgot,
   And the hater hates no more;

Lovers lying two and two
   Ask not whom they sleep beside,
And the bridegroom all night through
   Never turns him to the bride.

'The night is freezing fast'

The night is freezing fast,
   To-morrow comes December;
      And winterfalls of old
Are with me from the past;
   And chiefly I remember
      How Dick would hate the cold.

Fall, winter, fall; for he,
   Prompt hand and headpiece clever,
      Has woven a winter robe,
And made of earth and sea   10
   His overcoat for ever,
      And wears the turning globe.

Revolution

West and away the wheels of darkness roll,
  Day's beamy banner up the east is borne,
Spectres and fears, the nightmare and her foal,
  Drown in the golden deluge of the morn.

But over sea and continent from sight
  Safe to the Indies has the earth conveyed
The vast and moon-eclipsing cone of night,
  Her towering foolscap of eternal shade.

See, in mid-heaven the sun is mounted; hark,
  The belfries tingle to the noonday chime.   10
'Tis silent, and the subterranean dark
  Has crossed the nadir, and begins to climb.

'Tell me not here, it needs not saying'

Tell me not here, it needs not saying,
  What tune the enchantress plays
In aftermaths of soft September
  Or under blanching mays,
For she and I were long acquainted
  And I knew all her ways.

On russet floors, by waters idle,
  The pine lets fall its cone;
The cuckoo shouts all day at nothing
  In leafy dells alone;   10
And traveller's joy beguiles in autumn
  Hearts that have lost their own.

On acres of the seeded grasses
  The changing burnish heaves;
Or marshalled under moons of harvest
  Stand still all night the sheaves;
Or beeches strip in storms for winter
  And stain the wind with leaves.

Possess, as I possessed a season,
 The countries I resign,   20
Where over elmy plains the highway
 Would mount the hills and shine,
And full of shade the pillared forest
 Would murmur and be mine.

For nature, heartless, witless nature,
 Will neither care nor know
What stranger's feet may find the meadow
 And trespass there and go,
Nor ask amid the dews of morning
 If they are mine or no.   30

'Crossing alone the nighted ferry'°

Crossing alone the nighted ferry
 With the one coin for fee,
Whom, on the wharf of Lethe waiting,
 Count you to find? Not me.

The brisk fond lackey to fetch and carry,
 The true, sick-hearted slave,
Expect him not in the just city
 And free land of the grave.

'Stone, steel, dominions pass'

Stone, steel, dominions pass,
 Faith too, no wonder;
So leave alone the grass
 That I am under.

All knots that lovers tie
 Are tied to sever;
Here shall your sweetheart lie,
 Untrue for ever.

The Oracles

'Tis mute, the word they went to hear on high Dodona mountain°
    When winds were in the oakenshaws and all the cauldrons tolled,
And mute's the midland navel-stone beside the singing fountain,°
    And echoes list to silence now where gods told lies of old.

I took my question to the shrine that has not ceased from speaking,
    The heart within, that tells the truth and tells it twice as plain;
And from the cave of oracles I heard the priestess shrieking
    That she and I should surely die and never live again.

Oh priestess, what you cry is clear, and sound good sense I think it;
    But let the screaming echoes rest, and froth your mouth no
        more.   10
'Tis true there's better boose than brine, but he that drowns must
        drink it;
    And oh, my lass, the news is news that men have heard before.

*The King with half the East at heel is marched from lands of
        morning;°
    Their fighters drink the rivers up, their shafts benight the air.
And he that stands will die for nought, and home there's no returning.*
    The Spartans on the sea-wet rock sat down and combed their
        hair.°

Infant Innocence

The Grizzly Bear is huge and wild;
He has devoured the infant child.
The infant child is not aware
He has been eaten by the bear.

Fragment of a Greek Tragedy°

ALCMAEON, CHORUS

CHORUS. O suitably-attired-in-leather-boots
   Head of a traveller, wherefore seeking whom°
   Whence by what way how purposed art thou come
   To this well-nightingaled vicinity?°
   My object in enquiring is to know,
   But if you happen to be deaf and dumb°
   And do not understand a word I say,
   Then wave your hand, to signify as much.
ALCMAEON. I journeyed hither a Boeotian road.
CHORUS. Sailing on horseback, or with feet for oars?   10
ALCMAEON. Plying with speed my partnership of legs.
CHORUS. Beneath a shining or a rainy Zeus?
ALCMAEON. Mud's sister, not himself, adorns my shoes.
CHORUS. To learn your name would not displease me much.
ALCMAEON. Not all that men desire do they obtain.
CHORUS. Might I then hear at what your presence shoots?
ALCMAEON. A shepherd's questioned mouth informed me that—
CHORUS. What? for I know not yet what you will say—
ALCMAEON. Nor will you ever, if you interrupt.
CHORUS. Proceed, and I will hold my speechless tongue.   20
ALCMAEON. —This house was Eriphyla's, no one's else.
CHORUS. Nor did he shame his throat with hateful lies.
ALCMAEON. May I then enter, passing through the door?
CHORUS. Go, chase into the house a lucky foot,
   And, O my son, be, on the one hand, good,
   And do not, on the other hand, be bad;
   For that is very much the safest plan.
ALCMAEON. I go into the house with heels and speed.

CHORUS. In speculation   *Strophe*
   I would not willingly acquire a name   30
      For ill-digested thought;
      But after pondering much

To this conclusion I at last have come:
  Life is uncertain.
  This truth I have written deep
  In my reflective midriff
  On tablets not of wax,
Nor with a pen did I inscribe it there,
For many reasons: *Life, I say, is not
  A stranger to uncertainty.*   40
Not from the flight of omen-yelling fowls
  This fact did I discover.
Nor did the Delphic tripod bark it out,
  Nor yet Dodona.
Its native ingenuity sufficed
  My self-taught diaphragm.

  Why should I mention   *Antistrophe*
The Inachean daughter, loved of Zeus?
  Her whom of old the gods,
  More provident than kind,   50
Provided with four hoofs, two horns, one tail,
  A gift not asked for,

  And sent her forth to learn
  The unfamiliar science
  Of how to chew the cud.
She therefore, all about the Argive fields,
Went cropping pale green grass and nettle-tops,
  Nor did they disagree with her.
But yet, howe'er nutritious, such repasts
  I do not hanker after: 60
Never may Cypris for her seat select
  My dappled liver!
Why should I mention Io! Why indeed?
  I have no notion why.

  But now does my boding heart,   *Epode*
  Unhired, unaccompanied, sing
  A strain not meet for the dance.
  Yea even the palace appears

To my yoke of circular eyes
(The right, nor omit I the left)
Like a slaughterhouse, so to speak,
Garnished with woolly deaths
And many shipwrecks of cows.
I therefore in a Cissian strain lament;
        And to the rapid,
Loud, linen–tattering thumps upon my chest
        Resounds in concert
The battering of my unlucky head.

ERIPHYLA [*within*]. O, I am smitten with a hatchet's jaw;
    And that in deed and not in word alone.   80
CHORUS. I thought I heard a sound within the house
    Unlike the voice of one that jumps for joy.
ERIPHYLA. He splits my skull, not in a friendly way,
    One more: he purposes to kill me dead.
CHORUS. I would not be reputed rash, but yet
    I doubt if all be gay within the house.
ERIPHYLA. O! O! another stroke! that makes the third.
    He stabs me to the heart against my wish.
CHORUS. If that be so, thy state of health is poor;
    But thine arithmetic is quite correct.   90

Diffugere Nives°

The snows are fled away, leaves on the shaws
    And grasses in the mead renew their birth,
The river to the river-bed withdraws,
    And altered is the fashion of the earth.

The Nymphs and Graces three put off their fear
    And unapparelled in the woodland play.
The swift hour and the brief prime of the year
    Say to the soul, *Thou wast not born for aye.*

Thaw follows frost; hard on the heel of spring
    Treads summer sure to die, for hard on hers   10
Comes autumn, with his apples scattering;
    Then back to wintertide, when nothing stirs.

But oh, whate'er the sky-led seasons mar,
  Moon upon moon rebuilds it with her beams:
Come *we* where Tullus and where Ancus are,°
  And good Aeneas, we are dust and dreams.°

Torquatus, if the gods in heaven shall add°
  The morrow to the day, what tongue has told?
Feast then thy heart, for what thy heart has had
  The fingers of no heir will ever hold.   20

When thou descendest once the shades among,
  The stern assize and equal judgment o'er,
Not thy long lineage nor thy golden tongue,
  No, nor thy righteousness, shall friend thee more.

Night holds Hippolytus the pure of stain,°
  Diana steads him nothing, he must stay;
And Theseus leaves Pirithöus in the chain°
  The love of comrades cannot take away.

MARY COLERIDGE

Jealousy

'The myrtle bush grew shady
  Down by the ford.'—
'Is it even so?' said my lady.
  'Even so!' said my lord.
'The leaves are set too thick together
  For the point of a sword.'

'The arras in your room hangs close,
  No light between!
You wedded one of those
  That see unseen.'—
'Is it even so?' said the King's Majesty.   10
  'Even so!' said the Queen.

Shadow

Child of my love! though thou be bright as day,
  Though all the sons of joy laugh and adore thee,
Thou canst not throw thy shadow self away.
  Where thou dost come, the earth is darker for thee.

When thou dost pass, a flower that saw the sun
  Sees him no longer.
The hosts of darkness are, thou radiant one,
  Through thee made stronger!

Gifts

I tossed my friend a wreath of roses, wet
  With early dew, the garland of the morn.
He lifted it—and on his brow he set
    A crackling crown of thorn.

Against my foe I hurled a murderous dart.
  He caught it in his hand—I heard him laugh—
I saw the thing that should have pierced his heart
    Turn to a golden staff.

A Clever Woman

You thought I had the strength of men,
  Because with men I dared to speak,
And courted Science now and then,
  And studied Latin for a week;
But woman's woman, even when
  She reads her Ethics in the Greek.

You thought me wiser than my kind;
  You thought me 'more than common tall';
You thought because I had a mind,
  That I could have no heart at all;
But woman's woman you will find,
  Whether she be great or small.

And then you needs must die—ah, well!
   I knew you not, you loved not me.
'Twas not because that darkness fell,
   You saw not what there was to see.
But I that saw and could not tell—
   O evil Angel, set me free!

SIR HENRY NEWBOLT

Drake's Drum°

Drake he's in his hammock an' a thousand mile away,
   (Capten, art tha sleepin' there below?),
Slung atween the round shot in Nombre Dios Bay,°
   An' dreamin' arl the time o' Plymouth Hoe.°
Yarnder lumes the Island, yarnder lie the ships,
   Wi' sailor lads a dancin' heel-an'-toe,
An' the shore-lights flashin', an' the night-tide dashin',
   He sees et arl so plainly as he saw et long ago.

Drake he was a Devon man, an' ruled the Devon seas,
   (Capten, art tha sleepin' there below?),   10
Rovin' tho' his death fell, he went wi' heart at ease,
   An' dreamin' arl the time o' Plymouth Hoe.
'Take my drum to England, hang et by the shore,
   Strike et when your powder's runnin' low;
If the Dons sight Devon, I'll quit the port o' Heaven,
   An' drum them up the Channel as we drummed them long ago.'

Drake he's in his hammock till the great Armadas come,
   (Capten, art tha sleepin' there below?),
Slung atween the round shot, listenin' for the drum,
   An' dreamin' arl the time o' Plymouth Hoe.   20
Call him on the deep sea, call him up the Sound,
   Call him when ye sail to meet the foe;
Where the old trade's plyin' an' the old flag flyin'
   They shall find him ware an' wakin', as they found him long ago!

Messmates

He gave us all a good-bye cheerily
    At the first dawn of day;
We dropped him down the side full drearily
    When the light died away.
It's a dead dark watch that he's a-keeping there,
And a long, long night that lags a-creeping there,
Where the Trades and the tides roll over him
    And the great ships go by.

He's there alone with green seas rocking him
    For a thousand miles round;   10
He's there alone with dumb things mocking him,
    And we're homeward bound.
It's a long, lone watch that he's a-keeping there,
And a dead cold night that lags a-creeping there,
While the months and the years roll over him
    And the great ships go by.

I wonder if the tramps come near enough
    As they thrash to and fro,
And the battle-ships' bells ring clear enough
    To be heard down below;   20
If through all the lone watch that he's a-keeping there,
And the long, cold night that lags a-creeping there,
The voices of the sailor-men shall comfort him
    When the great ships go by.

MICHAEL FIELD

And on my Eyes Dark Sleep by Night

'Οφθαλμοῖς δὲ μέλαις νυκτὸς ἄωρος.°

Come, dark-eyed Sleep, thou child of Night,
Give me thy dreams, thy lies;
Lead through the horny portal white
The pleasure day denies.

O bring the kiss I could not take
From lips that would not give;
Bring me the heart I could not break,
The bliss for which I live.

I care not if I slumber blest
By fond delusion; nay,
Put me on Phaon's lips to rest,
And cheat the cruel day!

Gold is the Son of Zeus: neither Moth nor Worm may Gnaw It

Διὸθ παῖθ ὁ χρυσόθ°
κεῖνον ου σὴς οὐδὲ κὶς δάπτει.

Yea, gold is son of Zeus: no rust
Its timeless light can stain;
The worm that brings man's flesh to dust
Assaults its strength in vain:
More gold than gold the love I sing,
A hard, inviolable thing.

Men say the passions should grow old
With waning years; my heart
Is incorruptible as gold,
'Tis my immortal part: 10
Nor is there any god can lay
On love the finger of decay.

To the Lord Love

(At the approach of old age)

I am thy fugitive, thy votary,
Nor even thy mother tempts me from thy shrine:
Mirror, nor gold, nor ornament of mine
Appease her: thou art all my gods to me,

And I so breathless in my loyalty,
Youth hath slipped by and left no footprint sign:
Yet there are footsteps nigh. My years decline.
Decline thy years? Burns thy torch duskily?
Lord Love, to thy great altar I retire;
Time doth pursue me, age is on my brow,   10
And there are cries and shadows of the night.
Transform me, for I cannot quit thee now:
Love, thou hast weapons visionary, bright—
Keep me perpetual in grace and fire!

Aridity

O soul, canst thou not understand
Thou art not left alone,
As a dog to howl and moan
His master's absence? Thou art as a book
Left in a room that He forsook,

But returns to by and by,
A book of His dear choice,—
That quiet waiteth for His Hand,
That quiet waiteth for His Eye,
That quiet waiteth for His Voice.   10

ARTHUR MORRISON

from *Lizerunt*

I

LIZER'S WOOING

Somewhere in the register was written the name Elizabeth Hunt; but
seventeen years after the entry the spoken name was Lizerunt.
Lizerunt worked at a pickle factory, and appeared abroad in an
elaborate and shabby costume, usually supplemented by a white
apron. Withal she was something of a beauty. That is to say, her

cheeks were very red, her teeth were very large and white, her nose was small and snub, and her fringe was long and shiny; while her face, new-washed, was susceptible of a high polish. Many such girls are married at sixteen, but Lizerunt was belated, and had never a bloke at all.

Billy Chope was a year older than Lizerunt. He wore a billycock with a thin brim and a permanent dent in the crown; he had a bobtail coat, with the collar turned up at one side and down at the other, as an expression of independence; between his meals he carried his hands in his breeches pockets; and he lived with his mother, who mangled. His conversation with Lizerunt consisted long of perfunctory nods; but great things happened this especial Thursday evening, as Lizerunt, making for home, followed the fading red beyond the furthermost end of Commercial Road.° For Billy Chope, slouching in the opposite direction, lurched across the pavement as they met, and taking the nearer hand from his pocket, caught and twisted her arm, bumping her against the wall.

'Garn,' said Lizerunt, greatly pleased, 'le' go!' For she knew that this was love.

'Where yer auf to, Lizer?'

' 'Ome, o' course, cheeky. Le' go;' and she snatched—in vain—at Billy's hat.

Billy let go, and capered in front of her. She feigned to dodge by him, careful not to be too quick, because affairs were developing.

'I say, Lizer,' said Billy, stopping his dance and becoming business-like, 'goin' anywhere Monday?'

'Not along o' you, cheeky; you go 'long o' Beller Dawson, like wot you did Easter.'

'Blow Beller Dawson; *she* ain't no good. I'm goin' on the Flats. Come?'

Lizerunt, delighted but derisive, ended with a promise to 'see'. The bloke had come at last, and she walked home with the feeling of having taken her degree. She had half assured herself of it two days before, when Sam Cardew threw an orange peel at her, but went away after a little prancing on the pavement. Sam was a smarter fellow than Billy, and earned his own living; probably his attentions were serious; but one must prefer the bird in hand. As for Billy Chope, he went his way, resolved himself to take home what mangling he should find his mother had finished, and stick to the money; also, to get all he could

from her by blandishing and bullying: that the jaunt to Wanstead
Flats might be adequately done.

There is no other fair like Whit Monday's on Wanstead Flats. Here is
a square mile and more of open land where you may howl at large;
here is no danger of losing yourself as in Epping Forest; the public-
houses are always with you; shows, shies, swings, merry-go-rounds,
fried fish stalls, donkeys are packed closer than on Hampstead Heath;
the ladies' tormentors are larger, and their contents smell worse than
at any other fair. Also, you may be drunk and disorderly without being
locked up—for the stations won't hold everybody—and when all else
has palled, you may set fire to the turf. Hereinto Billy and Lizerunt
projected themselves from the doors of the Holly Tree on Whit
Monday morning. But through hours on hours of fried fish and half-
pints both were conscious of a deficiency. For the hat of Lizerunt was
brown and old; plush it was not, and its feather was a mere foot long
and of a very rusty black. Now, it is not decent for a factory girl from
Limehouse to go bank-holidaying under any but a hat of plush, very
high in the crown, of a wild blue or a wilder green, and carrying withal
an ostrich feather, pink or scarlet or what not; a feather that springs
from the fore-part, climbs the crown, and drops as far down the
shoulders as may be. Lizerunt knew this, and, had she had no bloke,
would have stayed at home. But a chance is a chance. As it was, only
another such hapless girl could measure her bitter envy of the feathers
about her, or would so joyfully have given an ear for the proper
splendour. Billy, too, had a vague impression, muddled by but not
drowned in half-pints, that some degree of plush was condign to the
occasion and to his own expenditure. Still, there was no quarrel; and
the pair walked and ran with arms about each other's necks; and
Lizerunt thumped her bloke on the back at proper intervals; so that
the affair went regularly on the whole: although, in view of Lizerunt's
shortcomings, Billy did not insist on the customary exchange of hats.

Everything, I say, went well and well enough until Billy bought a
ladies' tormentor and began to squirt it at Lizerunt. For then Lizerunt
went scampering madly, with piercing shrieks, until her bloke was left
some little way behind, and Sam Cardew, turning up at that moment
and seeing her running alone in the crowd, threw his arms about her
waist and swung her round him again and again, as he floundered

gallantly this way and that, among the shies and the hokey-pokey barrows.

''Ullo, Lizer! Where *are* y' a–comin' to? If I 'adn't laid 'old o' ye—!' But here Billy Chope arrived to demand what the 'ell Sam Cardew was doing with his gal. Now Sam was ever readier for a fight than Billy was; but the sum of Billy's half-pints was large: wherefore the fight began. On the skirt of an hilarious ring Lizerunt, after some small outcry, triumphed aloud. Four days before, she had no bloke; and here she stood with two, and those two fighting for her! Here in the public gaze, on the Flats! For almost five minutes she was Helen of Troy.

And in much less time Billy tasted repentance. The haze of half-pints was dispelled, and some teeth went with it. Presently, whimper-ing and with a bloody muzzle, he rose and made a running kick at the other. Then, being thwarted in a bolt, he flung himself down; and it was like to go hard with him at the hands of the crowd. Punch you may on Wanstead Flats, but execration and worse is your portion if you kick anybody except your wife. But, as the ring closed, the helmets of two policemen were seen to be working in over the surrounding heads, and Sam Cardew, quickly assuming his coat, turned away with such an air of blandness as is practicable with a damaged eye; while Billy went off unheeded in an opposite direction.

Lizerunt and her new bloke went the routine of half-pints and merry-go-rounds, and were soon on right thumping terms; and Lizerunt was as well satisfied with the issue as she was proud of the adventure. Billy was all very well; but Sam was better. She resolved to draw him for a feathered hat before next bank holiday. So the sun went down on her and her bloke hanging on each other's necks and straggling toward the Romford Road with shouts and choruses. The rest was tram-car, Bow Music Hall, half-pints, and darkness.

Billy took home his wounds, and his mother having moved his wrath by asking their origin, sought refuge with a neighbour. He ac-complished his revenge in two instalments. Two nights later Lizerunt was going with a jug of beer; when somebody sprang from a dark corner, landed her under the ear, knocked her sprawling; and made off to the sound of her lamentations. She did not see who it was, but she knew; and next day Sam Cardew was swearing he'd break Billy's back.

He did not, however, for that same evening a gang of seven or eight fell on him with sticks and belts. (They were Causeway chaps, while Sam was a Brady's Laner, which would have been reason enough by itself, even if Billy Chope had not been one of them.) Sam did his best for a burst through and a run, but they pulled and battered him down; and they kicked him about the head, and they kicked him about the belly; and they took to their heels when he was speechless and still.

He lay at home for near four weeks, and when he stood up again it was in many bandages. Lizerunt came often to his bedside, and twice she brought an orange. On these occasions there was much talk of vengeance. But the weeks went on. It was a month since Sam had left his bed; and Lizerunt was getting a little tired of bandages. Also, she had begun to doubt and to consider bank holiday—scarce a fortnight off. For Sam was stone broke, and a plush hat was further away than ever. And all through the later of these weeks Billy Chope was harder than ever on his mother, and she, well knowing that if he helped her by taking home he would pocket the money at the other end, had taken to finishing and delivering in his absence, and, threats failing to get at the money, Billy Chope was impelled to punch her head and gripe her by the throat.

There was a milliner's window, with a show of nothing but fashionable plush-and-feather hats, and Lizerunt was lingering hereabouts one evening; when someone took her by the waist, and someone said, 'Which d'yer like, Lizer?—The yuller un?'

Lizerunt turned and saw that it was Billy. She pulled herself away, and backed off, sullen and distrustful. 'Garn,' she said.

'Straight,' said Billy, 'I'll sport yer one—No kid, I will.'

'Garn,' said Lizerunt once more. 'Wot yer gittin' at now?'

But presently, being convinced that bashing wasn't in it, she approached less guardedly; and she went away with a paper bag and the reddest of all the plushes and the bluest of all the feathers; a hat that challenged all the Flats the next bank holiday, a hat for which no girl need have hesitated to sell her soul. As for Billy, why, he was as good as another; and you can't have everything; and Sam Cardew, with his bandages and his grunts and groans, was no great catch after all.

This was the wooing of Lizerunt: for in a few months she and Billy married under the blessing of a benignant rector, who periodically set aside a day for free weddings, and, on principle, encouraged early matrimony. And they lived with Billy's mother.

II

LIZER'S FIRST

When Billy Chope married Lizerunt there was a small rejoicing. There was no wedding-party; because it was considered that what there might be to drink would be better in the family. Lizerunt's father was not, and her mother felt no interest in the affair; not having seen her daughter for a year, and happening, at the time, to have a month's engagement in respect of a drunk and disorderly. So that there were but three of them; and Billy Chope got exceedingly tipsy early in the day; and in the evening his bride bawled a continual chorus, while his mother, influenced by that unwonted quartern of gin the occasion sanctioned, wept dismally over her boy, who was much too far gone to resent it.

His was the chief reason for rejoicing. For Lizerunt had always been able to extract ten shillings a week from the pickle factory, and it was to be presumed that as Lizer Chope her earning capacity would not diminish; and the wages would make a very respectable addition to the precarious revenue, depending on the mangle, that Billy extorted from his mother. As for Lizer, she was married. That was the considerable thing; for she was but a few months short of eighteen, and that, as you know, is a little late.

Of course there were quarrels very soon; for the new Mrs Chope, less submissive at first than her mother-in-law, took a little breaking in, and a liberal renewal of the manual treatment once applied in her courting days. But the quarrels between the women were comforting to Billy: a diversion and a source of better service.

As soon as might be Lizer took the way of womankind. This circumstance brought an unexpected half-crown from the evangelical rector who had married the couple gratis; for recognizing Billy in the street by accident, and being told of Mrs Chope's prospects, as well as that Billy was out of work (a fact undeniable), he reflected that his principles did on occasion lead to discomfort of a material sort. And Billy, to whose comprehension the half-crown opened a new field of receipt, would doubtless have long remained a client of the rector, had not that zealot hastened to discover a vacancy for a warehouse porter, the offer of presentation whereunto alienated Billy Chope for ever. But there were meetings and demonstrations of the Unemployed; and it was said that shillings had been given away; and, as being at a meeting in a street was at least as amusing as being in a street where there was no meeting, Billy often went, on the off chance. But his lot was chiefly disappointment: wherefore he became more especially careful to furnish himself ere he left home.

For certain weeks cash came less freely than ever from the two women. Lizer spoke of providing for the necessities of the expected child: a manifestly absurd procedure, as Billy pointed out, since, if they were unable to clothe or feed it, the duty would fall on its grandmother. That was law, and nobody could get over it. But even with this argument, a shilling cost him many more demands and threats than it had used, and a deal more general trouble.

At last Lizer ceased from going to the pickle factory, and could not even help Billy's mother at the mangle for long. This lasted for near a week, when Billy, rising at ten with a bad mouth, resolved to stand no nonsense, and demanded two shillings.

'Two bob? Wot for?' Lizer asked.

''Cos I want it. None o' yer lip.'

'Ain't got it, said Lizer sulkily.

'That's a bleed'n' lie.'

'Lie yerself.'

'I'll break y'in 'arves, ye blasted 'eifer!' He ran at her throat and forced her back over a chair. 'I'll pull yer face auf! If y' don't give me the money, gawblimy, I'll do for ye!'

Lizer strained and squalled. 'Le' go! You'll kill me an' the kid too!' she grunted hoarsely. Billy's mother ran in and threw her arms about him, dragging him away. 'Don't Billy,' she said, in terror. 'Don't Billy—not now! You'll get in trouble. Come away! She might go auf, an' you'd get in trouble!'

Billy Chope flung his wife over and turned to his mother. 'Take yer 'ands auf me,' he said, 'go on, or I'll gi' ye somethin' for yerself.' And he punched her in the breast by way of illustration.

'You shall 'ave what I've got, Billy, if it's money,' the mother said. 'But don't go an' git yerself in trouble, don't. Will a shillin' do?'

'No, it won't. Think I'm a bloomin kid? I mean 'avin' two bob this mornin'.'

'I was a-keepin' it for the rent, Billy, but—'

'Yus; think o' the bleed'n lan'lord 'fore me doncher?' And he pocketed the two shillings. 'I ain't settled with you yut, my gal,' he added to Lizer; 'mikin' about at 'ome an' 'idin' money. You wait a bit.'

Lizer had climbed into an erect position, and, gravid and slow, had got as far as the passage. Mistaking this for a safe distance, she replied with defiant railings. Billy made for her with a kick that laid her on the lower stairs, and, swinging his legs round his mother as she obstructed him, entreating him not to get in trouble, he attempted to kick again in a more telling spot. But a movement among the family upstairs and a tap at the door hinted of interference, and he took himself off.

Lizer lay doubled up on the stairs, howling: but her only articulate cry was—'Gawd 'elp me, it's comin'!'

Billy went to the meeting of the Unemployed, and cheered a proposal to storm the Tower of London. But he did not join the procession following a man with a handkerchief on a stick, who promised destruction to every policeman in his path: for he knew the fate of such processions. With a few others he hung about the nearest tavern for a while, on the chance of the advent of a flush sailor from St Katharine's, disposed to treat out-o'-workers. Then he went alone to a quieter beer-house and took a pint or two at his own expense. A glance down the music-hall bills hanging in the bar having given him a notion for the evening, he bethought himself of dinner, and made for home.

The front door was open, and in the first room, where the mangle stood, there were no signs of dinner. And this was at three o'clock! Billy pushed into the room behind demanding why.

'Billy,' Lizer said faintly from her bed, 'look at the baby!'

Something was moving feebly under a flannel petticoat. Billy pulled the petticoat aside, and said—'That? Well, it *is* a measly snipe.' It was a blind, hairless homunculus, short of a foot long, with a skinny face set in a great skull. There was a black bruise on one side from hip to armpit. Billy dropped the petticoat and said, 'Where's my dinner?'

'I dunno,' Lizer responded hazily. 'Wot's the time?'

'Time? Don't try to kid me. You git up; go on. I want my dinner.'

'Mother's gittin' it, I think,' said Lizer. 'Doctor had to slap 'im like anythink 'fore 'e'd cry. 'E don't cry now much. 'E—'

'Go on; out ye git. I do'want no more damn jaw. Git my dinner.'

'I'm a-gittin of it, Billy,' his mother said, at the door. She had begun when he first entered. 'It won't be a minute.'

'You come 'ere; y'aint alwis s'ready to do er' work, are ye? She ain't no call to stop there no longer, an' I owe 'er one for this mornin'. Will ye git out, or shall I kick ye?'

'She can't, Billy,' his mother said. And Lizer snivelled and said, 'You're a damn brute. Y'ought to be bleedin' well booted.'

But Billy had her by the shoulders and began to haul; and again his mother besought him to remember what he might bring upon himself. At this moment the doctor's dispenser, a fourth-year London Hospital student of many inches, who had been washing his hands in the kitchen, came in. For a moment he failed to comprehend the scene. Then he took Billy Chope by the collar, hauled him pell-mell along the passage, kicked him (hard) into the gutter, and shut the door.

When he returned to the room, Lizer, sitting up and holding on by the bed-frame, gasped hysterically: 'Ye bleedin' makeshift, I'd 'ave yer liver out if I could reach ye! You touch my 'usband, ye long pisenin' 'ound you! Ow!' And, infirm of aim, she flung a cracked teacup at his head. Billy's mother said, 'Y'ought to be ashamed of yourself, you low blaggard. If 'is father was alive 'e'd knock yer 'ead auf. Call yourself a doctor—a passel o' boys—! Git out! Go out o' my 'ouse or I'll give y'in charge!'

'But—why, hang it, he'd have killed her.' Then to Lizer—'Lie down.'

'Shan't lay down. Keep auf! if you come near me I'll corpse ye. You go while ye're safe!'

The dispenser appealed to Billy's mother. 'For God's sake make her lie down. She'll kill herself. I'll go. Perhaps the doctor had better come.' And he went: leaving the coast clear for Billy Chope to return and avenge his kicking.

III

A CHANGE OF CIRCUMSTANCES

Lizer was some months short of twenty-one when her third child was born. The pickle factory had discarded her some time before, and since that her trade had consisted in odd jobs of charing. Odd jobs of charing have a shade the better of a pickle factory in the matter of respectability, but they are precarious, and they are worse paid at that. In the East End they are sporadic and few. Moreover, it is in the household where paid help is a rarity that the bitterness of servitude is felt. Also, the uncertainty and irregularity of the returns were a trouble to Billy Chope. He was never sure of having got them all. It might be ninepence, or a shilling, or eighteenpence. Once or twice, to his knowledge, it had been half-a-crown, from a chance job at a doctor's or a parson's, and once it was three shillings. That it might be half-a-crown or three shillings again, and that some of it was being kept back, was ever the suspicion evoked by Lizer's evening homing. Plainly, with these fluctuating and uncertain revenues, more bashing than ever was needed to ensure the extraction of the last copper; empty-handedness called for bashing on its own account; so that it was often Lizer's hap to be refused a job because of a black eye.

Lizer's self was scarcely what it had been. The red of her cheeks, once bounded only by the eyes and the mouth, had shrunk to a spot in the depth of each hollow; gaps had been driven in her big white teeth; even the snub nose had run to a point and the fringe hung dry and ragged, while the bodily outline was as a sack's. At home, the children lay in her arms or tumbled at her heels, puling and foul. Whenever she was near it, there was the mangle to be turned; for lately Billy's mother had exhibited a strange weakness, sometimes collapsing with a gasp in the act of brisk or prolonged exertion, and often leaning on whatever stood hard by and grasping at her side. This ailment she treated, when she had twopence, in such terms as made her smell of gin and peppermint; and more than once this circumstance had inflamed the breast of Billy her son, who was morally angered by this boozing away of money that was really his.

Lizer's youngest, being seven or eight months old, was mostly taking care of itself, when Billy made a welcome discovery after a hard and pinching day. The night was full of blinding wet, and the rain beat on the window as on a drum. Billy sat over a small fire in the front room smoking his pipe, while his mother folded clothes for delivery. He stamped twice on the hearth, and then, drawing off his boot, he felt inside it. It was a nail. The poker-head made a good anvil, and, looking about for a hammer, Billy bethought him of a brick from the mangle. He rose, and, lifting the lid of the weight-box, groped about among the clinkers and the other ballast till he came upon a small but rather heavy paper parcel. ' 'Ere—wot's this?' he said, and pulled it out.

His mother, whose back had been turned, hastened across the room, hand to breast (it had got to be her habit). 'What is it, Billy?' she said. 'Not that: there's nothing there. I'll get anything you want, Billy.' And she made a nervous catch at the screw of paper. But Billy fended her off, and tore the package open. It was money, arranged in little columns of farthings, halfpence, and threepenny pieces, with a few sixpences, a shilling or two, and a single half-sovereign. 'O,' said Billy, 'this is the game, is it?—'idin' money in the mangle! Got any more?' And he hastily turned the brickbats.

'No, Billy, don't take that—don't!' implored his mother. 'There'll be some money for them things when they go 'ome—'ave that. I'm savin' it, Billy, for something partic'ler: s'elp me Gawd, I am, Billy.'

'Yus,' replied Billy, raking diligently among the clinkers, 'savin' it for a good ol' booze. An' now you won't 'ave one. Bleedin' nice thing, 'idin' money away from yer own son!'

'It ain't for that, Billy—s'elp me, it ain't; it's case anythink 'appens to me. On'y to put me away decent, Billy, that's all. We never know, an' you'll be glad of it t'elp bury me if I should go any time—'

'I'll be glad of it now,' answered Billy, who had it in his pocket; an' I've got it. You ain't a dyin' sort, *you* ain't; an' if you was, the parish 'ud soon tuck *you* up. P'raps you'll be straighter about money after this.'

'Let me 'ave *some*, then—you can't want it all. Give me some, 'an' then 'ave the money for the things. There's ten dozen and seven, and you can take 'em yerself if ye like.'

'Wot—in this 'ere rain? Not me! I bet I'd 'ave the money if I wanted it without that. 'Ere—change these 'ere fardens at the draper's wen you go out: there's two bob's worth an' a penn'orth; I don't want to bust my pockets wi' them.'

While they spoke Lizer had come in from the back room. But she said nothing: she rather busied herself with a child she had in her arms. When Billy's mother, despondent and tearful, had tramped out into the rain with a pile of clothes in an oilcloth wrapper, she said sulkily, without looking up, 'You might 'a' let 'er kep' that; you git all you want.'

At another time this remonstrance would have provoked active hostilities; but now, with the money about him, Billy was complacently disposed. 'You shutcher 'ead,' he said, 'I got this, any'ow. She can make it up out o' my rent if she likes.' This last remark was a joke, and he chuckled as he made it. For Billy's rent was a simple fiction, devised, on the suggestion of a smart canvasser, to give him a parliamentary vote.

That night Billy and Lizer slept, as usual, in the bed in the back room, where the two younger children also were. Billy's mother made a bedstead nightly with three chairs and an old trunk in the front room by the mangle, and the eldest child lay in a floor-bed near her. Early in the morning Lizer awoke at a sudden outcry of the little creature. He clawed at the handle till he opened the door, and came staggering and tumbling into the room with screams of terror. 'Wring 'is blasted neck,' his father grunted sleepily. 'Wot's the kid 'owlin' for?'

'I's 'f'aid o' g'anny—I's f'aid o' g'anny!' was all the child could say; and when he had said it, he fell to screaming once more.

Lizer rose and went to the next room; and straightway came a scream from her also. 'O—O—Billy! O my Gawd! Billy come 'ere!'

And Billy, fully startled, followed in Lizer's wake. He blundered in, rubbing his eyes, and saw.

Stark on her back in the huddled bed of old wrappers and shawls lay his mother. The outline of her poor face—strained in an upward stare of painful surprise—stood sharp and meagre against the black of the grate beyond. But the muddy old skin was white, and looked cleaner than its wont, and many of the wrinkles were gone.

Billy Chope, half-way across the floor, recoiled from the corpse, and glared at it pallidly from the doorway.

'Good Gawd!' he croaked faintly, 'is she dead?'

Seized by a fit of shuddering breaths, Lizer sank on the floor, and, with her head across the body, presently broke into a storm of hysterical blubbering, while Billy, white and dazed, dressed hurriedly and got out of the house.

He was at home as little as might be until the coroner's officer carried away the body two days later. When he came for his meals, he sat doubtful and querulous in the matter of the front room door's being shut. The dead once clear away, however, he resumed his faculties and clearly saw that here was a bad change for the worse. There was the mangle, but who was to work it? If Lizer did, there would be no more charing jobs—a clear loss of one-third of his income. And it was not at all certain that the people who had given their mangling to his mother would give it to Lizer. Indeed, it was pretty sure that many would not, because mangling is a thing given by

preference to widows, and many widows of the neighbourhood were
perpetually competing for it. Widows, moreover, had the first call in
most odd jobs whereunto Lizer might turn her hand: an injustice
whereon Billy meditated with bitterness.

The inquest was formal and unremarked, the medical officer having
no difficulty in certifying a natural death from heart disease. The
bright idea of a collection among the jury, which Billy communicated,
with pitiful representations, to the coroner's officer, was brutally
swept aside by that functionary, made cunning by much experience.
So the inquest brought him naught save disappointment and a sense
of injury. . . .

The mangling orders fell away as suddenly and completely as he had
feared: they were duly absorbed among the local widows. Neglect the
children as Lizer might, she could no longer leave them as she had
done. Things, then, were bad with Billy, and neither threats nor
thumps could evoke a shilling now.

It was more than Billy could bear: so that, ' 'Ere,' he said one night,
'I've 'ad enough o' this. You go and get some money; go on.'

'Go an' git it?' replied Lizer. 'O yus. That's easy, ain't it? "Go an'
git it," says you. 'Ow?'

'Any'ow—I don't care. Go on.'

'Wy,' replied Lizer, looking up with wide eyes, 'd'ye think I can go
an' pick it up in the street?'

'Course you can. Plenty others does, don't they?'

'Gawd, Billy—wot d'ye mean?'

'Wot I say; plenty others does it. Go on—you ain't so bleed'n'
innocent as all that. Go an' see Sam Cardew. Go on—'ook it.'

Lizer who had been kneeling at the child's floor-bed, rose to her
feet, pale faced and bright of eye.

'Stow kiddin', Billy,' she said. 'You don't mean that. I'll go round
to the fact'ry in the mornin': p'raps they'll take me on temp'ry.'

'Damn the fact'ry.'

He pushed her into the passage, 'Go on—you git me some money, if
ye don't want yer bleed'n' 'ead knocked auf.'

There was a scuffle in the dark passage, with certain blows, a few
broken words, and a sob. Then the door slammed, and Lizer Chope
was in the windy street.

RUDYARD KIPLING

The Man who would be King°

Brother to a Prince and fellow to a beggar if he be found worthy

The Law, as quoted, lays down a fair conduct of life, and one not easy to follow. I have been fellow to a beggar again and again under circumstances which prevented either of us finding out whether the other was worthy. I have still to be a brother to a Prince, though I once came near to kinship with what might have been a veritable King, and was promised the reversion of a Kingdom—army, law-courts, revenue, and policy all complete. But, to-day, I greatly fear that my King is dead, and if I want a crown I must go hunt it for myself.

The beginning of everything was in a railway train upon the road to Mhow from Ajmir. There had been a Deficit in the Budget, which necessitated travelling, not Second-class, which is only half as dear as First-class, but by Intermediate, which is very awful indeed. There are no cushions in the Intermediate class, and the population are either Intermediate, which is Eurasian, or native, which for a long night journey is nasty, or Loafer, which is amusing though intoxicated. Intermediates do not buy from refreshment-rooms. They carry their food in bundles and pots, and buy sweets from the native sweetmeat-sellers, and drink the road-side water. That is why in the hot weather Intermediates are taken out of the carriages dead, and in all weathers are most properly looked down upon.

My particular Intermediate happened to be empty till I reached Nasirabad, when a big blackbrowed gentleman in shirt-sleeves entered, and, following the custom of Intermediates, passed the time of day. He was a wanderer and a vagabond like myself, but with an educated taste for whisky. He told tales of things he had seen and done, of out-of-the-way corners of the Empire into which he had penetrated, and of adventures in which he risked his life for a few days' food.

'If India was filled with men like you and me, not knowing more than the crows where they'd get their next day's rations, it isn't seventy millions of revenue the land would be paying—it's seven hundred millions,' said he; and as I looked at his mouth and chin I was disposed to agree with him.

We talked politics—the politics of Loaferdom, that sees things from the underside where the lath and plaster is not smoothed off—and we talked postal arrangements because my friend wanted to send a telegram back from the next station to Ajmir, the turning-off place from the Bombay to the Mhow line as you travel westward. My friend had no money beyond eight annas, which he wanted for dinner, and I had no money at all, owing to the hitch in the Budget mentioned. Further, I was going into a wilderness where, though I should resume touch with the Treasury, there were no telegraph offices. I was, therefore, unable to help him in any way.

'We might threaten a Station-master, and make him send a wire on tick,' said my friend, 'but that'd mean inquiries for you and for me, and *I*'ve got my hands full these days. Did you say you are travelling back along this line within any days?'

'Within ten,' I said.

'Can't you make it eight?' said he. 'Mine is rather urgent business.'

'I can send your telegram within ten days if that will serve you,' I said.

'I couldn't trust the wire to fetch him now I think of it. It's this way. He leaves Delhi on the 23rd for Bombay. That means he'll be running through Ajmir about the night of the 23rd.'

'But I'm going into the Indian Desert,' I explained.

'Well *and* good,' said he. 'You'll be changing at Marwar Junction to get into Jodhpore territory—you must do that—and he'll be coming through Marwar Junction in the early morning of the 24th by the Bombay Mail. Can you be at Marwar Junction on that time? 'Twon't be inconveniencing you because I know that there's precious few pickings to be got out of these Central India States—even though you pretend to be correspondent of the *Backwoodsman*.'

'Have you ever tried that trick?' I asked.

'Again and again, but the Residents find you out, and then you get escorted to the border before you've time to get your knife into them. But about my friend here. I *must* give him a word o' mouth to tell him what's come to me or else he won't know where to go. I would take it more than kind of you if you was to come out of Central India in time to catch him at Marwar Junction, and say to him: "He has gone South for the week." He'll know what that means. He's a big man with a red beard, and a great swell he is. You'll find him sleeping like a gentleman with all his luggage round him in a Second-class compartment. But don't you be afraid. Slip down the window, and say: "He has gone South for the week," and he'll tumble. It's only cutting your time of stay in those parts by two days. I ask you as a stranger—going to the West,' he said with emphasis.

'Where have *you* come from?' said I.

'From the East,' said he, 'and I am hoping that you will give him the message on the Square—for the sake of my Mother as well as your own.'

Englishmen are not usually softened by appeals to the memory of their mothers, but for certain reasons, which will be fully apparent, I saw fit to agree.

'It's more than a little matter,' said he, 'and that's why I asked you to do it—and now I know that I can depend on you doing it. A Second-class carriage at Marwar Junction, and a red-haired man asleep in it. You'll be sure to remember. I get out at the next station, and I must hold on there till he comes or sends me what I want.'

'I'll give the message if I catch him,' I said, 'and for the sake of your Mother as well as mine I'll give you a word of advice. Don't try to run the Central India States just now as the correspondent of the *Backwoodsman*. There's a real one knocking about there, and it might lead to trouble.'

'Thank you,' said he simply, 'and when will the swine be gone? I can't starve because he's ruining my work. I wanted to get hold of the Degumber Rajah down here about his father's widow, and give him a jump.'

'What did he do to his father's widow, then?'

'Filled her up with red pepper and slippered her to death as she hung from a beam. I found that out myself, and I'm the only man that would dare going into the State to get hush-money for it. They'll try to poison me, same as they did in Chortumna when I went on the loot there. But you'll give the man at Marwar Junction my message?'

He got out at a little roadside station, and I reflected. I had heard, more than once, of men personating correspondents of newspapers and bleeding small Native States with threats of exposure, but I had never met any of the caste before. They lead a hard life, and generally die with great suddenness. The Native States have a wholesome horror of English newspapers which may throw light on their peculiar methods of government, and do their best to choke correspondents with champagne, or drive them out of their mind with four-in-hand barouches. They do not understand that nobody cares a straw for the internal administration of Native States so long as oppression and crime are kept within decent limits, and the ruler is not drugged, drunk, or diseased from one end of the year to the other. They are the dark places of the earth, full of unimaginable cruelty, touching the Railway and the Telegraph on one side, and, on the other, the days of Harun-al-Raschid. When I left the train I did business with divers Kings, and in eight days passed through many changes of life. Sometimes I wore dress-clothes and consorted with Princes and Politicals, drinking from crystal and eating from silver. Sometimes I lay out upon the ground and devoured what I could get, from a plate made of leaves, and drank the running water, and slept under the same rug as my servant. It was all in the day's work.

Then I headed for the Great Indian Desert upon the proper date, as I had promised, and the night Mail set me down at Marwar Junction, where a funny, little, happy-go-lucky, native-managed railway runs to Jodhpore. The Bombay Mail from Delhi makes a short halt at Marwar. She arrived as I got in, and I had just time to hurry to her platform and go down the carriages. There was only one Second-class on the train. I slipped the window and looked down upon a flaming red beard, half covered by a railway rug. That was my man, fast asleep, and I dug him gently in the ribs. He woke with a grunt, and I saw his face in the light of the lamps. It was a great shining face.

'Tickets again?' said he.

'No,' said I. 'I am to tell you that he has gone South for the week. He has gone South for the week!'

The train had begun to move out. The red man rubbed his eyes. 'He has gone South for the week,' he repeated. 'Now that's just like his impidence. Did he say that I was to give you anything? 'Cause I won't.'

'He didn't,' I said, and dropped away, and watched the red lights die out in the dark. It was horribly cold because the wind was blowing off the sands. I climbed into my own train—not an Intermediate Carriage this time—and went to sleep.

If the man with the beard had given me a rupee I should have kept it as a memento of a rather curious affair. But the consciousness of having done my duty was my only reward.

Later on I reflected that two gentlemen like my friends could not do any good if they forgathered and personated correspondents of newspapers, and might, if they black-mailed one of the little rat-trap states of Central India or Southern Rajputana, get themselves into serious difficulties. I therefore took some trouble to describe them as accurately as I could remember to people who would be interested in deporting them; and succeeded, so I was later informed, in having them headed back from the Degumber borders.

Then I became respectable, and returned to an Office where there were no Kings and no incidents outside the daily manufacture of a newspaper. A newspaper office seems to attract every conceivable sort of person, to the prejudice of discipline. Zenana-mission ladies° arrive, and beg that the Editor will instantly abandon all his duties to describe a Christian prize-giving in a back-slum of a perfectly inaccessible village; Colonels who have been overpassed for command sit down and sketch the outline of a series of ten, twelve, or twenty-four leading articles on Seniority *versus* Selection; Missionaries wish to know why they have not been permitted to escape from their regular vehicles of abuse and swear at a brother-missionary under special patronage of the editorial We; stranded theatrical companies troop up to explain that they cannot pay for their advertisements, but on their return from New Zealand or Tahiti will do so with interest; inventors of patent punkah-pulling machines, carriage couplings, and unbreakable swords and axle-trees, call with specifications in their pockets and hours at their disposal; tea-companies enter and elaborate their prospectuses with the office pens; secretaries of ball-committees clamour to have the glories of their last dance more fully described; strange ladies rustle in and say, 'I want a hundred lady's cards printed *at once*, please,' which is manifestly part of an Editor's duty; and every dissolute ruffian that ever tramped the Grand Trunk Road makes it his business to ask for employment as a proof-reader. And, all the time, the telephone-bell is ringing madly, and Kings are being killed on the Continent, and Empires are saying, 'You're another,' and Mister Gladstone is calling down brimstone upon the British Dominions, and the little black copy-boys are whining, '*kaa-pi chay-ha-yeh*' (copy wanted) like tired bees, and most of the paper is as blank as Modred's shield.°

But that is the amusing part of the year. There are six other months when no one ever comes to call, and the thermometer walks inch by inch up to the top of the glass, and the office is darkened to just above reading-light, and the press-machines are red-hot of touch, and nobody writes anything but accounts of amusements in the Hill-stations or obituary notices. Then the telephone becomes a tinkling terror, because it tells you of the sudden deaths of men and women that you knew intimately, and the prickly-heat covers you with a garment, and you sit down and write: 'A slight increase of sickness is reported from the Khuda Janta Khan District. The outbreak is purely sporadic in its nature, and, thanks to the energetic efforts of the District authorities, is now almost at an end. It is, however, with deep regret we record the death, etc.'

Then the sickness really breaks out, and the less recording and reporting the better for the peace of the subscribers. But the Empires and the Kings continue to divert themselves as selfishly as before, and the Foreman thinks that a daily paper really ought to come out once in twenty-four hours, and all the people at the Hill-stations in the middle of their amusements say: 'Good gracious! Why can't the paper be sparkling? I'm sure there's plenty going on up here.'

That is the dark half of the moon, and, as the advertisements say, 'must be experienced to be appreciated'.

It was in that season, and a remarkably evil season, that the paper began running the last issue of the week on Saturday night, which is to say Sunday morning, after the custom of a London paper. This was a great convenience, for immediately after the paper was put to bed, the dawn would lower the thermometer from 96° to almost 84° for half an hour, and in that chill—you have no idea how cold is 84° on the grass until you begin to pray for it—a very tired man could get off to sleep ere the heat roused him.

One Saturday night it was my pleasant duty to put the paper to bed alone. A King or a courtier or a courtesan or a Community was going to die or get a new Constitution, or do something that was important on the other side of the world, and the paper was to be held open till the latest possible minute in order to catch the telegram.

It was a pitchy black night, as stifling as a June night can be, and the *loo*, the red-hot wind from the westward, was booming among the tinder-dry trees and pretending that the rain was on its heels. Now and again a spot of almost boiling water would fall on the dust with the flop of a frog, but all our weary world knew that was only pretence. It was a shade cooler in the press-room than the office, so I sat there, while the type ticked and clicked, and the night-jars hooted at the windows, and the all but naked compositors wiped sweat from their foreheads, and called for water. The thing that was keeping us back, whatever it was, would not come off, though the *loo* dropped and the last type was set, and the whole round earth stood still in the choking heat, with its finger on its lip, to wait the event. I drowsed, and wondered whether the telegraph was a blessing, and whether this dying man, or struggling people, might be aware of the inconvenience the delay was causing. There was no special reason beyond the heat and worry to make tension, but, as the clock-hands crept up to three o'clock, and the machines spun their fly-wheels two or three times to see that all was in order before I said the word that would set them off, I could have shrieked aloud.

Then the roar and rattle of the wheels shivered the quiet into little bits. I rose to go away, but two men in white clothes stood in front of me. The first one said: 'It's him!' The second said: 'So it is!' And they both laughed almost as loudly as the machinery roared, and mopped their foreheads. 'We seed there was a light burning across the road, and we were sleeping in that ditch there for coolness, and I said to my friend here, "The office is open. Let's come along and speak to him as turned us back from the Degumber State," ' said the smaller of the two. He was the man I had met in the Mhow train, and his fellow was the red-bearded man of Marwar Junction. There was no mistaking the eyebrows of the one or the beard of the other.

I was not pleased, because I wished to go to sleep, not to squabble with loafers. 'What do you want?' I asked.

'Half an hour's talk with you, cool and comfortable, in the office,' said the red-bearded man. 'We'd *like* some drink—the Contrack doesn't begin yet, Peachey, so you needn't look—but what we really want is advice. We don't want money. We ask you as a favour, because we found out did us a bad turn about Degumber State.'

I led from the press-room to the stifling office with the maps on the walls, and the red-haired man rubbed his hands. 'That's something like,' said he. 'This was the proper shop to come to. Now, Sir, let me introduce to you Brother Peachey Carnehan, that's him, and Brother Daniel Dravot, that is *me*, and the less said about our professions the better, for we have been most things in our time. Soldier, sailor, compositor, photographer, proof-reader, street-preacher, and correspondent of the *Backwoodsman* when we thought the paper wanted one. Carnehan is sober, and so am I. Look at us first, and see that's sure. It will save you cutting into my talk. We'll take one of your cigars apiece, and you shall see us light up.'

I watched the test. The men were absolutely sober, so I gave them each a tepid whisky and soda.

'Well *and* good,' said Carnehan of the eyebrows, wiping the froth from his moustache. 'Let *me* talk now, Dan. We have been all over India, mostly on foot. We have been boiler-fitters, engine-drivers, petty contractors, and all that, and we have decided that India isn't big enough for such as us.'

They certainly were too big for the office. Dravot's beard seemed to fill half the room and Carnehan's shoulders the other half, as they sat on the big table. Carnehan continued: 'The country isn't half worked out because they that governs it won't let you touch it. They spend all their blessed time in governing it, and you can't lift a spade, nor chip a rock, nor look for oil, nor anything like that, without all the Government saying, "Leave it alone, and let us govern." Therefore, such *as* it is, we will let it alone, and go away to some other place where a man isn't crowded and can come to his own. We are not little men, and there is nothing that we are afraid of except Drink, and we have signed a Contrack on that. *Therefore*, we are going away to be Kings.'

'Kings in our own right,' muttered Dravot.

'Yes of course,' I said. 'You've been tramping in the sun, and it's a very warm night, and hadn't you better sleep over the notion? Come tomorrow.'

'Neither drunk nor sunstruck,' said Dravot. 'We have slept over the notion half a year, and require to see Books and Atlases, and we have decided that there is only one place now in the world that two strong men can Sar-a-*whack*. They call it Kafiristan. By my reckoning it's the top right-hand corner of Afghanistan, not more than three hundred miles from Peshawar. They have two-and-thirty heathen idols there, and we'll be the thirty-third and fourth. It's a mountainous country, and the women of those parts are very beautiful.'

'But that is provided against in the Contrack,' said Carnehan. 'Neither Woman nor Liquor, Daniel.'

'And that's all we know, except that no one has gone there, and they fight, and in any place where they fight, a man who knows how to drill men can always be a King. We shall go to those parts and say to any King we find—"D'you want to vanquish your foes?" and we will show him how to drill men; for that we know better than anything else. Then we will subvert that King and seize his Throne and establish a Dy-nasty.'

'You'll be cut to pieces before you're fifty miles across the Border,' I said. 'You have to travel through Afghanistan to get to that country. It's one mass of mountains and peaks and glaciers, and no Englishman has been through it. The people are utter brutes, and even if you reached them you couldn't do anything.'

'That's more like,' said Carnehan. 'If you could think us a little more mad we would be more pleased. We have come to you to know about this country, to read a book about it, and to be shown maps. We want you to tell us that we are fools and to show us your books.' He turned to the bookcases.

'Are you at all in earnest?' I said.

'A little,' said Dravot sweetly. 'As big a map as you have got, even if it's all blank where Kafiristan is, and any books you've got. We can read, though we aren't very educated.'

I uncased the big thirty-two-miles-to-the-inch map of India, and two smaller Frontier maps, hauled down volume INF-KAN of the *Encyclopædia Britannica*, and the men consulted them.

'See here!' said Dravot, his thumb on the map. 'Up to Jagdallak, Peachey and me know the road. We was there with Roberts' Army.° We'll have to turn off to the right at Jagdallak through Laghman territory. Then we get among the hills—fourteen thousand feet— fifteen thousand—it will be cold work there, but it don't look very far on the map.'

I handed him Wood on the *Sources of the Oxus*. Carnehan was deep in the *Encyclopædia*.

'They're a mixed lot,' said Dravot reflectively; 'and it won't help us to know the names of their tribes. The more tribes the more they'll fight, and the better for us. From Jagdallak to Ashang H'mm!'

'But all the information about the country is as sketchy and inaccurate as can be,' I protested. 'No one knows anything about it really. Here's the file of the *United Services' Institute*. Read what Bellew says.'

'Blow Bellew!' said Carnehan. 'Dan, they're a stinkin' lot of heathens, but this book here says they think they're related to us English.'

I smoked while the men pored over Raverty, Wood, the maps, and the *Encyclopædia*.

'There is no use your waiting,' said Dravot politely. 'It's about four o'clock now. We'll go before six oclock if you want to sleep, and we won't steal any of the papers. Don't you sit up. We're two harmless lunatics, and if you come tomorrow evening down to the Serai we'll say goodbye to you.'

'You *are* two fools,' I answered. 'You'll be turned back at the Frontier or cut up the minute you set foot in Afghanistan. Do you want any money or a recommendation down-country? I can help you to the chance of work next week.'

'Next week we shall be hard at work ourselves, thank you,' said Dravot. 'It isn't so easy being a King as it looks. When we've got our Kingdom in going order we'll let you know, and you can come up and help us to govern it.'

'Would two lunatics make a Contrack like that?' said Carnehan, with subdued pride, showing me a greasy half-sheet of notepaper on which was written the following. I copied it, then and there, as a curiosity—

> This Contract between me and you persuing witnesseth in the name of God—Amen and so forth.
>
> (One)   That me and you will settle this matter together; i.e. to be Kings of Kafiristan.
>
> (Two)   That you and me will not, while this matter is being settled, look at any Liquor, nor any Woman black, white, or brown, so as to get mixed up with one or the other harmful.
>
> (Three)   That we conduct ourselves with Dignity and Discretion, and if one of us gets into trouble the other will stay by him.
>
>   Signed by you and me this day.
>   Peachey Taliaferro Carnehan.
>   Daniel Dravot.
>   Both Gentlemen at Large.

'There was no need for the last article,' said Carnehan, blushing modestly; 'but it looks regular. Now you know the sort of men that loafers are—we *are* loafers, Dan, until we get out of India—and *do* you think that we would sign a Contrack like that unless we was in earnest? We have kept away from the two things that make life worth having.'

'You won't enjoy your lives much longer if you are going to try this idiotic adventure. Don't set the office on fire,' I said, 'and go away before nine o'clock.'

I left them still poring over the maps and making notes on the back of the 'Contrack'. 'Be sure to come down to the Serai to-morrow,' were their parting words.

The Kumharsen Serai is the great four-square sink of humanity where the strings of camels and horses from the North load and unload. All the nationalities of Central Asia may be found there, and most of the folk of India proper. Balkh and Bokhara there meet Bengal and Bombay, and try to draw eye-teeth. You can buy ponies, turquoises, Persian pussy-cats, saddle-bags, fat-tailed sheep and musk in the Kumharsen Serai, and get many strange things for nothing. In the afternoon I went down to see whether my friends intended to keep their word or were lying there drunk.

A priest attired in fragments of ribbons and rags stalked up to me, gravely twisting a child's paper whirligig. Behind him was his servant bending under the load of a crate of mud toys. The two were loading up two camels, and the inhabitants of the Serai watched them with shrieks of laughter.

'The priest is mad,' said a horse-dealer to me. 'He is going up to Kabul to sell toys to the Amir. He will either be raised to honour or have his head cut off. He came in here this morning and has been behaving madly ever since.'

'The witless are under the protection of God,' stammered a flat-cheeked Uzbeg in broken Hindi. 'They foretell future events.'

'Would they could have foretold that my caravan would have been cut up by the Shinwaris almost within shadow of the Pass!' grunted the Yusufzai agent of a Rajputana trading-house whose goods had been diverted into the hands of other robbers just across the Border, and whose misfortunes were the laughing-stock of the bazar. 'Ohé, priest, whence come you and whither do you go?'

'From Roum have I come,' shouted the priest, waving his whirligig; 'from Roum, blown by the breath of a hundred devils across the sea! O thieves, robbers, liars, the blessing of Pir Khan on pigs, dogs, and perjurers! Who will take the Protected of God to the North to sell charms that are never still to the Amir? The camels shall not gall, the sons shall not fall sick, and the wives shall remain faithful while they are away, of the men who give me place in their caravan. Who will assist me to slipper the King of the Roos with a golden slipper with a silver heel? The protection of Pir Khan be upon his labours!' He spread out the skirts of his gaberdine and pirouetted between the lines of tethered horses.

'There starts a caravan from Peshawar to Kabul in twenty days,

Huzrut,' said the Yusufzai trader. 'My camels go therewith. Do thou also go and bring us good luck.'

'I will go even now!' shouted the priest. 'I will depart upon my winged camels, and be at Peshawar in a day! Ho! Hazar Mir Khan,' he yelled to his servant, 'drive out the camels, but let me first mount my own.'

He leaped on the back of his beast as it knelt, and, turning round to me, cried: 'Come thou also, Sahib, a little along the road, and I will sell thee a charm—an amulet that shall make thee King of Kafiristan.'

Then the light broke upon me, and I followed the two camels out of the Serai till we reached open road and the priest halted.

'What d'you think o' that?' said he in English. 'Carnehan can't talk their patter, so I've made him my servant. He makes a handsome servant. 'Tisn't for nothing that I've been knocking about the country for fourteen years. Didn't I do that talk neat? We'll hitch on to a caravan at Peshawar till we get to Jagdallak, and then we'll see if we can get donkeys for our camels, and strike into Kafiristan. Whirligigs for the Amir, O Lor! Put your hand under the camel-bags and tell me what you feel.'

I felt the butt of a Martini, and another and another.

'Twenty of 'em,' said Dravot placidly. 'Twenty of 'em and ammunition to correspond, under the whirligigs and the mud dolls.'

'Heaven help you if you are caught with those things!' I said. 'A Martini is worth her weight in silver among the Pathans.'

'Fifteen hundred rupees of capital—every rupee we could beg, borrow, or steal—are invested on these two camels,' said Dravot. 'We won't get caught. We're going through the Khyber with a regular caravan. Who'd touch a poor mad priest?'

'Have you got everything you want?' I asked, overcome with astonishment.

'Not yet, but we shall soon. Give us a memento of your kindness, *Brother*. You did me a service, yesterday, and that time in Marwar. Half my Kingdom shall you have, as the saying is.' I slipped a small charm compass from my watchchain and handed it up to the priest.

'Good-bye,' said Dravot, giving me hand cautiously. 'It's the last time we'll shake hands with an Englishman these many days. Shake hands with him, Carnehan,' he cried, as the second camel passed me.

Carnehan leaned down and shook hands. Then the camels passed away along the dusty road, and I was left alone to wonder. My eye could detect no failure in the disguises. The scene in the Serai proved that they were complete to the native mind. There was just the chance, therefore, that Carnehan and Dravot would be able to wander through Afghanistan without detection. But, beyond, they would find death—certain and awful death.

Ten days later a native correspondent, giving me the news of Peshawar, wound up his letter with: 'There has been much laughter here on account of a certain mad priest who is going in his estimation to sell petty gauds and insignificant trinkets which he ascribes as great charms to H.H. the Amir of Bokhara. He passed through Peshawar and associated himself to the Second Summer caravan that goes to Kabul. The merchants are pleased because through superstition they imagine that such mad fellows bring good fortune.'

The two, then, were beyond the Border. I would have prayed for them, but, that night, a real King died in Europe, and demanded an obituary notice.

The wheel of the world swings through the same phases again and again. Summer passed and winter thereafter, and came and passed again. The daily paper continued and I with it, and upon the third summer there fell a hot night, a night-issue, and a strained waiting for something to be telegraphed from the other side of the world, exactly as had happened before. A few great men had died in the past two years, the machines worked with more clatter, and some of the trees in the office garden were a few feet taller. But that was all the difference.

I passed over to the press-room, and went through just such a scene as I have already described. The nervous tension was stronger than it had been two years before, and I felt the heat more acutely. At three o'clock I cried, 'Print off,' and turned to go, when there crept to my chair what was left of a man. He was bent into a circle, his head was sunk between his shoulders, and he moved his feet one over the other like a bear. I could hardly see whether he walked or crawled—this rag-wrapped, whining cripple who addressed me by name, crying that he was come back. 'Can you give me a drink?' he whimpered. 'For the Lord's sake give me a drink!'

I went back to my office, the man following with groans of pain, and I turned up the lamp.

'Don't you know me?' he gasped, dropping into a chair, and he turned his drawn face, surmounted by a shock of gray hair, to the light.

I looked at him intently. Once before had I seen eyebrows that met over the nose in an inch-broad black band, but for the life of me I could not tell where.

'I don't know you,' I said, handing him the whisky. 'What can I do for you?'

He took a gulp of the spirit raw, and shivered in spite of the suffocating heat.

'I've come back,' he repeated; 'and I was the King of Kafiristan— me and Dravot—crowned Kings we was! In this office we settled it— you setting there and giving us the books. I am Peachey—Peachey Taliaferro Carnehan, and you've been setting here ever since—O Lord!'

I was more than a little astonished, and expressed my feelings accordingly.

'It's true,' said Carnehan, with a dry cackle, nursing his feet, which were wrapped in rags. 'True as gospel. Kings we were, with crowns upon our heads—me and Dravot—poor Dan—oh, poor, poor Dan, that would never take advice, not though I begged of him!'

'Take the whisky,' I said, 'and take your own time. Tell me all you can recollect of everything from beginning to end. You got across the Border on your camels, Dravot dressed as a mad priest and you his servant. Do you remember that?'

'I ain't mad—yet, but I shall be that way soon. Of course I remember. Keep looking at me, or maybe my words will go all to pieces. Keep looking at me in my eyes and don't say anything.'

I leaned forward and looked into his face as steadily as I could. He dropped one hand upon the table and I grasped it by the wrist. It was twisted like a bird's claw, and upon the back was a ragged red diamond-shaped scar.

'No, don't look there. Look at *me*,' said Carnehan. 'That comes afterwards, but for the Lord's sake don't distract me. We left with that caravan, me and Dravot playing all sorts of antics to amuse the people we were with. Dravot used to make us laugh in the evenings when all the people were cooking their dinners—cooking their dinners, and . . . what did they do then? They lit little fires with sparks that went into Dravot's beard, and we all laughed—fit to die. Little red fires they was, going into Dravot's big red beard—so funny.' His eyes left mine and he smiled foolishly.

'You went as far as Jagdallak with that caravan,' I said at a venture, 'after you had lit those fires. To Jagdallak, where you turned off to try to get into Kafiristan.'

'No, we didn't neither. What are you talking about? We turned off before Jagdallak, because we heard the roads was good. But they wasn't good enough for our two camels—mine and Dravot's. When we left the caravan, Dravot took off all his clothes and mine too, and said we would be heathen, because the Kafirs didn't allow Mohammedans to talk to them. So we dressed betwixt and between, and such a sight as Daniel Dravot I never saw nor expect to see again. He burned half his beard, and slung a sheep-skin over his shoulder, and shaved his head into patterns. He shaved mine too, and made me wear outrageous things to look like a heathen. That was in a most mountainous country, and our camels couldn't go along any more because of the mountains. They were tall and black, and coming home I saw them fight like wild goats—there are lots of goats in Kafiristan. And these mountains, they never keep still, no more than the goats. Always fighting they are, and don't let you sleep at night.'

'Take some more whisky,' I said very slowly. 'What did you and Daniel Dravot do when the camels could go no further because of the rough roads that led into Kafiristan?'

'What did which do? There was a party called Peachey Taliaferro Carnehan that was with Dravot. Shall I tell you about him? He died out there in the cold. Slap from the bridge fell old Peachey, turning and twisting in the air like a penny whirligig that you can sell to the Amir.—No; they was two for three-ha'pence, those whirligigs, or I am much mistaken and woeful sore. . . . And then these camels were no use, and Peachey said to Dravot—"For the Lord's sake let's get out of this before our heads are chopped off," and with that they killed the camels all among the mountains, not having anything in particular to eat, but first they took off the boxes with the guns and the ammunition, till two men came along driving four mules. Dravot up and dances in front of them, singing—"Sell me four mules." Says the first man—"If you are rich enough to buy, you are rich enough to rob;" but before ever he could put his hand to his knife, Dravot breaks his neck over his knee, and the other party runs away. So Carnehan loaded the mules with the rifles that was taken off the camels, and

together we starts forward into those bitter cold mountainous parts,
and never a road broader than the back of your hand.'

He paused for a moment, while I asked him if he could remember
the nature of the country through which he had journeyed.

'I am telling you as straight as I can, but my head isn't as good as it
might be. They drove nails through it to make me hear better how
Dravot died. The country was mountainous and the mules were most
contrary, and the inhabitants was dispersed and solitary. They went
up and up, and down and down, and that other party, Carnehan, was
imploring of Dravot not to sing and whistle so loud, for fear of
bringing down the tremenjus avalanches. But Dravot says that if a
King couldn't sing it wasn't worth being King, and whacked the
mules over the rump, and never took no heed for ten cold days. We
came to a big level valley all among the mountains, and the mules were
near dead, so we killed them, not having anything special for them or
us to eat. We sat upon the boxes and played odd and even with the
cartridges that was jolted out.

'Then ten men with bows and arrows ran down the valley, chasing
twenty men with bows and arrows, and the row was tremenjus. They
was fair men—fairer than you or me—with yellow hair and remarkable well built. Says Dravot, unpacking the guns—"This is the
beginning of the business. We'll fight for the ten men," and with that
he fires two rifles at the twenty men, and drops one of them at two
hundred yards from the rock where he was sitting. The other men
began to run, but Carnehan and Dravot sits on the boxes picking them
off at all ranges, up and down the valley. Then we goes up to the ten
men that had run across the snow too, and they fires a footy little
arrow at us. Dravot he shoots above their heads and they all falls down
flat. Then he walks over them and kicks them, and then lifts them up
and shakes hands all round to make them friendly like. He calls them
and gives them the boxes to carry, and waves his hand for all the world
as though he was King already. They takes the boxes and him across
the valley and up the hill into a pine wood on the top, where there was
half-a-dozen big stone idols. Dravot he goes to the biggest—a fellow
they call Imbra—and lays a rifle and a cartridge at his feet, rubbing his
nose respectful with his own nose, patting him on the head, and
saluting in front of it. He turns round to the men and nods his head,
and says—"That's all right. I'm in the know too, and all these old jim-
jams are my friends." Then he opens his mouth and points down it,

and when the first man brings him food, he says—"No"; and when the second man brings food he says—"No"; but when one of the old priests and the boss of the village brings him food, he says—"Yes," very haughty, and eats it slow. That was how we came to our first village, without any trouble, just as though we had tumbled from the skies. But we tumbled from one of those damned rope-bridges, you see, and—you couldn't expect a man to laugh much after that?'

'Take some more whisky and go on,' I said. 'That was the first village you came into. How did you get to be King?'

'I wasn't King,' said Carnehan. 'Dravot he was the King, and a handsome man he looked with the gold crown on his head and all. Him and the other party stayed in that village, and every morning Dravot sat by the side of old Imbra, and the people came and worshipped. That was Dravot's order. Then a lot of men came into the valley, and Carnehan and Dravot picks them off with the rifles before they knew where they was, and runs down into the valley and up again the other side and finds another village, same as the first one, and the people all falls down flat on their faces, and Dravot says—"Now what is the trouble between you two villages?" and the people points to a woman, as fair as you or me, that was carried off, and Dravot takes her back to the first village and counts up the dead— eight there was. For each dead man Dravot pours a little milk on the ground and waves his arms like a whirligig, and "That's all right," says he. Then he and Carnehan takes the big boss of each village by the arm and walks them down into the valley, and shows them how to scratch a line with a spear right down the valley, and gives each a sod of turf from both sides of the line. Then all the people comes down and shouts like the devil and all, and Dravot says—"Go and dig the land, and be fruitful and multiply," which they did, though they didn't understand. Then we asks the names of things in their lingo— bread and water and fire and idols and such, and Dravot leads the priest of each village up to the idol, and says he must sit there and judge the people, and if anything goes wrong he is to be shot.

'Next week they was all turning up the land in the valley as quiet as bees and much prettier, and the priests heard all the complaints and told Dravot in dumb show what it was about. "That's just the beginning," says Dravot. "They think we're Gods." He and Carne- han picks out twenty good men and shows them how to click off a rifle, and form fours, and advance in line, and they was very pleased to do so, and clever to see the hang of it. Then he takes out his pipe and his baccy-pouch and leaves one at one village, and one at the other, and off we two goes to see what was to be done in the next valley. That was all rock, and there was a little village there, and Carnehan says— "Send 'em to the old valley to plant," and takes 'em there, and gives 'em some land that wasn't took before. They were a poor lot, and we blooded 'em with a kid before letting 'em into the new Kingdom. That was to impress the people, and then they settled down quiet, and Carnehan went back to Dravot, who had got into another valley, all snow and ice and most mountainous. There was no people there and the Army got afraid, so Dravot shoots one of them, and goes on till he finds some people in a village, and the Army explains that unless the people wants to be killed they had better not shoot their little matchlocks; for they had matchlocks. We makes friends with the priest, and I stays there alone with two of the Army, teaching the men how to drill, and a thundering big Chief comes across the snow with kettle-drums and horns twanging, because he heard there was a new God kicking about. Carnehan sights for the brown of the men half a mile across the snow and wings one of them. Then he sends a message to the Chief that, unless he wished to be killed, he must come and shake hands with me and leave his arms behind. The Chief comes alone first, and Carnehan shakes hands with him and whirls his arms about, same as Dravot used, and very much surprised that Chief was, and strokes my eyebrows. Then Carnehan goes alone to the Chief, and asks him in dumb show if he had an enemy he hated. "I have," says the Chief. So Carnehan weeds out the pick of his men, and sets the two of the Army to show them drill, and at the end of two weeks the men can manœuvre about as well as Volunteers. So he marches with the Chief to a great big plain on the top of a mountain, and the Chief's men rushes into a village and takes it; we three Martinis firing into the brown of the enemy. So we took that village too, and I gives the Chief a rag from my coat and says, "Occupy till I come"; which was scriptural. By way of a reminder, when me and the Army was eighteen hundred yards away, I drops a bullet near him standing on the snow, and all the people falls flat on their faces. Then I sends a letter to Dravot wherever he be by land or by sea.'

At the risk of throwing the creature out of train I interrupted— 'How could you write a letter up yonder?'

'The letter?—Oh!—The letter! Keep looking at me between the

eyes, please. It was a string-talk letter, that we'd learned the way of it from a blind beggar in the Punjab.'

I remembered that there had once come to the office a blind man with a knotted twig and a piece of string which he wound round the twig according to some cipher of his own. He could, after the lapse of days or weeks, repeat the sentence which he had reeled up. He had reduced the alphabet to eleven primitive sounds, and tried to teach me his method, but I could not understand.

'I sent that letter to Dravot,' said Carnehan; 'and told him to come back because this Kingdom was growing too big for me to handle, and then I struck for the first valley, to see how the priests were working. They called the village we took along with the Chief, Bashkai, and the first village we took, Er-Heb. The priests at Er-Heb was doing all right, but they had a lot of pending cases about land to show me, and some men from another village had been firing arrows at night. I went out and looked for that village, and fired four rounds at it from a thousand yards. That used all the cartridges I cared to spend, and I waited for Dravot, who had been away two or three months, and I kept my people quiet.

'One morning I heard the devil's own noise of drums and horns, and Dan Dravot marches down the hill with his Army and a tail of hundreds of men, and, which was the most amazing, a great gold crown on his head. "My Gord, Carnehan," says Daniel, "this is a tremenjus business, and we've got the whole country as far as it's worth having. I am the son of Alexander by Queen Semiramis, and you're my younger brother and a God too! It's the biggest thing we've ever seen. I've been marching and fighting for six weeks with the Army, and every footy little village for fifty miles has come in rejoiceful; and more than that, I've got the key of the whole show, as you'll see, and I've got a crown for you! I told 'em to make two of 'em at a place called Shu, where the gold lies in the rock like suet in mutton. Gold I've seen, and turquoise I've kicked out of the cliffs, and there's garnets in the sands of the river, and here's a chunk of amber that a man brought me. Call up all the priests and, here, take your crown."

'One of the men opens a black hair bag, and I slips the crown on. It was too small and too heavy, but I wore it for the glory. Hammered gold it was—five pound weight, like a hoop of a barrel.

' "Peachey," says Dravot, "we don't want to fight no more. The

Craft's the trick, so help me!" and he brings forward that same Chief that I left at Bashkai—Billy Fish we called him afterwards, because he was so like Billy Fish that drove the big tank-engine at Mach on the Bolan in the old days. "Shake hands with him," says Dravot, and I shook hands and nearly dropped, for Billy Fish gave me the Grip. I said nothing, but tried him with the Fellow Craft Grip. He answers all right, and I tried the Master's Grip, but that was a slip. "A Fellow Craft he is!" I says to Dan. "Does he know the Word?"—"He does," says Dan, "and all the priests know. It's a miracle! The Chiefs and the priests can work a Fellow Craft Lodge in a way that's very like ours, and they've cut the marks on the rocks, but they don't know the Third Degree, and they've come to find out. It's Gord's Truth. I've known these long years that the Afghans knew up to the Fellow Craft Degree, but this is a miracle. A God and a Grand-Master of the Craft am I, and a Lodge in the Third Degree I will open, and we'll raise the head priests and the Chiefs of the villages."

' "It's against all the law," I says, "holding a Lodge without warrant from any one; and you know we never held office in any Lodge."

' "It's a master-stroke o' policy," says Dravot. "It means running the country as easy as a four-wheeled bogie on a down grade. We can't stop to inquire now, or they'll turn against us. I've forty Chiefs at my heel, and passed and raised according to their merit they shall be. Billet these men on the villages, and see that we run up a Lodge of some kind. The temple of Imbra will do for the Lodge-room. The women must make aprons as you show them. I'll hold a levée of Chiefs to-night and Lodge to-morrow."

'I was fair run off my legs, but I wasn't such a fool as not to see what a pull this Craft business gave us. I showed the priests' families how to make aprons of the degrees, but for Dravot's apron the blue border and marks was made up of turquoise lumps on white hide, not cloth. We took a great square stone in the temple for the Master's chair, and little stones for the officers' chairs, and painted the black pavement with white squares, and did what we could to make things regular.

'At the levée which was held that night on the hillside with big bonfires, Dravot gives out that him and me were Gods and sons of Alexander, and Past Grand-Masters in the Craft, and was come to make Kafiristan a country where every man should eat in peace and drink in quiet, and specially obey us. Then the Chiefs come round to

shake hands, and they were so hairy and white and fair it was just
shaking hands with old friends. We gave them names according as
they was like men we had known in India—Billy Fish, Holly
Dilworth, Pikky Kergan, that was Bazar-master when I was at Mhow,
and so on, and so on.

  '*The* most amazing miracles was at Lodge next night. One of the old
priests was watching us continuous, and I felt uneasy, for I knew we'd
have to fudge the Ritual, and I didn't know what the men knew. The
old priest was a stranger come in from beyond the village of Bashkai.
The minute Dravot puts on the Master's apron that the girls had
made for him, the priest fetches a whoop and a howl, and tries to
overturn the stone that Dravot was sitting on. "It's all up now," I
says. "That comes of meddling with the Craft without warrant!"
Dravot never winked an eye, not when ten priests took and tilted over
the Grand-Master's chair—which was to say the stone of Imbra. The
priest begins rubbing the bottom end of it to clear away the black dirt,
and presently he shows all the other priests the Master's Mark, same
as was on Dravot's apron, cut into the stone. Not even the priests of
the temple of Imbra knew it was there. The old chap falls flat on his
face at Dravot's feet and kisses 'em. "Luck again," says Dravot, across
the Lodge to me; "they say it's the missing Mark that no one could
understand the why of. We're more than safe now." Then he bangs
the butt of his gun for a gavel and says: "By virtue of the authority
vested in me by my own right hand and the help of Peachey, I declare
myself Grand-Master of all Freemasonry in Kafiristan in this the
Mother Lodge o' the country, and King of Kafiristan equally with
Peachey!" At that he puts on his crown and I puts on mine—I was
doing Senior Warden—and we opens the Lodge in most ample form.
It was a amazing miracle! The priests moved in Lodge through the
first two degrees almost without telling, as if the memory was coming
back to them. After that, Peachey and Dravot raised such as was
worthy—high priests and Chiefs of far-off villages. Billy Fish was the
first, and I can tell you we scared the soul out of him. It was not in any
way according to Ritual, but it served our turn. We didn't raise more
than ten of the biggest men, because we didn't want to make the
Degree common. And they was clamouring to be raised.

  ' "In another six months," says Dravot, "we'll hold another
Communication, and see how you are working." Then he asks them
about their villages, and learns that they were fighting one against the

other, and was sick and tired of it. And when they wasn't doing that they was fighting with the Mohammedans. "You can fight those when they come into our country," says Dravot. "Tell off every tenth man of your tribes for a Frontier guard, and send two hundred at a time to this valley to be drilled. Nobody is going to be shot or speared any more so long as he does well, and I know that you won't cheat me, because you're white people—sons of Alexander—and not like common, black Mohammedans. You are *my* people, and by God," says he, running off into English at the end—"I'll make a damned fine Nation of you, or I'll die in the making!"

'I can't tell all we did for the next six months, because Dravot did a lot I couldn't see the hang of, and he learned their lingo in a way I never could. My work was to help the people plough, and now and again go out with some of the Army and see what the other villages were doing, and make 'em throw rope-bridges across the ravines which cut up the country horrid. Dravot was very kind to me, but when he walked up and down in the pine wood pulling that bloody red beard of his with both fists I knew he was thinking plans I could not advise about, and I just waited for orders.

'But Dravot never showed me disrespect before the people. They were afraid of me and the Army, but they loved Dan. He was the best of friends with the priests and the Chiefs; but any one could come across the hills with a complaint, and Dravot would hear him out fair, and call four priests together and say what was to be done. He used to call in Billy Fish from Bashkai, and Pikky Kergan from Shu, and an old Chief we called Kafuzelum— it was like enough to his real name—and hold councils with 'em when there was any fighting to be done in small villages. That was his Council of War, and the four priests of Bashkai, Shu, Khawak, and Madora was his Privy Council. Between the lot of 'em they sent me, with forty men and twenty rifles and sixty men carrying turquoises, into the Ghorband country to buy those hand-made Martini rifles, that come out of the Amir's workshops at Kabul, from one of the Amir Herati regiments that would have sold the very teeth out of their mouths for turquoises.

'I stayed in Ghorband a month, and gave the Governor there the pick of my baskets for hush-money, and bribed the Colonel of the regiment some more, and, between the two and the tribespeople, we got more than a hundred hand-made Martinis, a hundred good Kohat jezails that'll throw to six hundred yards, and forty man-loads of very bad ammunition for the rifles. I came back with what I had, and distributed 'em among the men that the Chiefs sent in to me to drill. Dravot was too busy to attend to those things, but the old Army that we first made helped me and we turned out five hundred men that could drill, and two hundred that knew how to hold arms pretty straight. Even those cork-screwed, hand-made guns was a miracle to them. Dravot talked big about powder-shops and factories, walking up and down in the pine wood when the winter was coming on.

'"I won't make a Nation," says he. "I'll make an Empire! These men aren't niggers; they're English! Look at their eyes—look at their mouths. Look at the way they stand up. They sit on chairs in their own houses. They're the Lost Tribes, or something like it, and they've grown to be English. I'll take a census in the spring if the priests don't get frightened. There must be a fair two million of 'em in these hills. The villages are full o' little children. Two million people—two hundred and fifty thousand fighting men—and all English! They only want the rifles and a little drilling. Two hundred and fifty thousand men, ready to cut in on Russia's right flank when she tries for India! Peachey, man," he says chewing his beard in great hunks, "we shall be Emperors—Emperors of the Earth! Rajah Brooke will be a suckling to us. I'll treat with the Viceroy on equal terms. I'll ask him to send me twelve picked English—twelve that I know of—to help us govern a bit. There's Mackray, Sergeant-pensioner at Segowli—many's the good dinner he's given me, and his wife a pair of trousers. There's Donkin, the Warder of Tounghoo Jail; there's hundreds that I could lay my hand on if I was in India. The Viceroy shall do it for me. I'll send a man through in the spring for those men, and I'll write for a dispensation from the Grand Lodge for what I've done as Grand-Master. That—and all the Sniders that'll be thrown out when the native troops in India take up the Martini. They'll be worn smooth, but they'll do for fighting in these hills. Twelve English, a hundred thousand Sniders run through the Amir's country in driblets—I'd be content with twenty thousand in one year—and we'd be an Empire. When everything was shipshape, I'd hand over the crown—this crown I'm wearing now—to Queen Victoria on my knees, and she'd say: 'Rise up, Sir Daniel Dravot.' Oh, it's big! It's big, I tell you! But there's so much to be done in every place— Bashkai, Khawak, Shu, and everywhere else."

'"What is it?" I says. "There are no more men coming in to be drilled this autumn. Look at those fat, black clouds. They're bringing the snow."

' "It isn't that," says Daniel, putting his hand very hard on my shoulder; "and I don't wish to say anything that's against you, for no other living man would have followed me and made me what I am as you have done. You're a first-class Commander-in-Chief, and the people know you; but—it's a big country, and somehow you can't help me, Peachey, in the way I want to be helped."

' "Go to your blasted priests, then!" I said, and I was sorry when I made that remark, but it did hurt me sore to find Daniel talking so superior when I'd drilled all the men, and done all he told me.

' "Don't let's quarrel, Peachey," says Daniel without cursing. "You're a King too, and the half of this Kingdom is yours; but can't you see, Peachey, we want cleverer men than us now—three or four of 'em, that we can scatter about for our Deputies. It's a hugeous great State, and I can't always tell the right thing to do, and I haven't time for all I want to do, and here's the winter coming on and all." He put half his beard into his mouth, all red like the gold of his crown.

' "I'm sorry, Daniel," says I. "I've done all I could. I've drilled the men and shown the people how to stack their oats better; and I've brought in those tinware rifles from Ghorband—but I know what you're driving at. I take it Kings always feel oppressed that way."

' "There's another thing too," says Dravot, walking up and down. "The winter's coming and these people won't be giving much trouble, and if they do we can't move about. I want a wife."

' "For Gord's sake leave the women alone!" I says. "We've both got all the work we can, though I *am* a fool. Remember the Contrack, and keep clear o' women."

' "The Contrack only lasted till such time as we was Kings; and Kings we have been these months past," says Dravot, weighing his crown in his hand. "You go get a wife too, Peachey—a nice, strappin', plump girl that'll keep you warm in the winter. They're prettier than English girls, and we can take the pick of 'em. Boil 'em once or twice in hot water and they'll come out like chicken and ham."

' "Don't tempt me!" I says. "I will not have any dealings with a woman not till we are a dam' sight more settled than we are now. I've been doing the work o' two men, and you've been doing the work o' three. Let's lie off a bit, and see if we can get some better tobacco from Afghan country and run in some good liquor; but no women."

' "Who's talking o' *women*?" says Dravot. "I said *wife*—a Queen to breed a King's son for the King. A Queen out of the strongest tribe, that'll make them your blood-brothers, and that'll lie by your side and tell you all the people thinks about you and their own affairs. That's what I want."

' "Do you remember that Bengali woman I kept at Mogul Serai when I was a plate-layer?" says I. "A fat lot o' good she was to me. She taught me the lingo and one or two other things; but what happened? She ran away with the Station-master's servant and half my month's pay. Then she turned up at Dadur Junction in tow of a half-caste, and had the impidence to say I was her husband—all among the drivers in the running-shed too!"

' "We've done with that," says Dravot; "these women are whiter than you or me, and a Queen I will have for the winter months."

' "For the last time o' asking, Dan, do *not*," I says. "It'll only bring us harm. The Bible says that Kings ain't to waste their strength on women, 'specially when they've got a new raw Kingdom to work over."

' "For the last time of answering I will," said Dravot, and he went away through the pine-trees looking like a big red devil, the sun being on his crown and beard and all.

'But getting a wife was not as easy as Dan thought. He put it before the Council and there was no answer till Billy Fish said that he'd better ask the girls. Dravot damned them all round. "What's wrong with me?" he shouts, standing by the idol of Imbra. "Am I a dog or am I not enough of a man for your wenches? Haven't I put the shadow of my hand over this country? Who stopped the last Afghan raid?" It was me really, but Dravot was too angry to remember. "Who bought your guns? Who repaired the bridges? Who's the Grand-Master of the sign cut in the stone?" says he, and he thumped his hand on the block that he used to sit on in Lodge, and at Council, which opened like Lodge always. Billy Fish said nothing and no more did the others. "Keep your hair on, Dan," said I; "and ask the girls. That's how it's done at Home, and these people are quite English."

' "The marriage of the King is a matter of State," says Dan, in a white-hot rage, for he could feel, I hope, that he was going against his better mind. He walked out of the Council-room, and the others sat still, looking at the ground.

' "Billy Fish," says I to the Chief of Bashkai, "what's the difficulty here? A straight answer to a true friend."

' "You know," says Billy Fish. "How should a man tell you who knows everything? How can daughters of men marry Gods or Devils? It's not proper."

'I remembered something like that in the Bible; but if, after seeing us as long as they had, they still believed we were Gods, it wasn't for me to undeceive them.

' "A God can do anything," says I. "If the King is fond of a girl he'll not let her die." — "She'll have to," said Billy Fish. "There are all sorts of Gods and Devils in these mountains, and now and again a girl marries one of them and isn't seen any more. Besides, you two know the Mark cut in the stone. Only the Gods know that. We thought you were men till you showed the sign of the Master."

'I wished then that we had explained about the loss of the genuine secrets of a Master-Mason at the first go-off; but I said nothing. All that night there was a blowing of horns in a little dark temple half-way down the hill, and I heard a girl crying fit to die. One of the priests told us that she was being prepared to marry the King.

' "I'll have no nonsense of that kind," says Dan. "I don't want to interfere with your customs, but I'll take my own wife." — "The girl's a little bit afraid," says the priest. "She thinks she's going to die, and they are a-heartening of her up down in the temple."

' "Hearten her very tender, then," says Dravot, "or I'll hearten you with the butt of a gun so you'll never want to be heartened again." He licked his lips, did Dan, and stayed up walking about more than half the night, thinking of the wife that he was going to get in the morning. I wasn't any means comfortable, for I knew that dealings with a woman in foreign parts, though you was a crowned King twenty times over, could not but be risky. I got up very early in the morning while Dravot was asleep, and I saw the priests talking together in whispers, and the Chiefs talking together too, and they looked at me out of the corners of their eyes.

' "What is up, Fish?" I says to the Bashkai man, who was wrapped up in his furs and looking splendid to behold.

' "I can't rightly say," says he; "but if you can make the King drop all this nonsense about marriage, you'll be doing him and me and yourself a great service."

' "That I do believe," says I. "But sure, you know, Billy, as well as me, having fought against and for us, that the King and me are nothing more than two of the finest men that God Almighty ever made. Nothing more, I do assure you."

' "That may be," says Billy Fish, "and yet I should be sorry if it was." He sinks his head upon his great fur cloak for a minute and thinks. "King," says he, "be you man or God or Devil, I'll stick by you to-day. I have twenty of my men with me, and they will follow me. We'll go to Bashkai until the storm blows over."

'A little snow had fallen in the night, and everything was white except the greasy fat clouds that blew down and down from the north. Dravot came out with his crown on his head, swinging his arms and stamping his feet, and looking more pleased than Punch.

' "For the last time, drop it, Dan," says I in a whisper. "Billy Fish here says that there will be a row."

' "A row among my people!" says Dravot. "Not much. Peachey, you're a fool not to get a wife too. Where's the girl?" says he with a voice as loud as the braying of a jackass. "Call up all the Chiefs and priests, and let the Emperor see if his wife suits him."

'There was no need to call any one. They were all there leaning on their guns and spears round the clearing in the centre of the pine wood. A lot of priests went down to the little temple to bring up the girl, and the horns blew fit to wake the dead. Billy Fish saunters round and gets as close to Daniel as he could, and behind him stood his twenty men with matchlocks. Not a man of them under six feet. I was next to Dravot, and behind me was twenty men of the regular Army. Up comes the girl, and a strapping wench she was, covered with silver and turquoises, but white as death, and looking back every minute at the priests.

' "She'll do," said Dan, looking her over. "What's to be afraid of, lass? Come and kiss me." He puts his arm around her. She shuts her eyes, gives a bit of a squeak, and down goes her face in the side of Dan's flaming red beard.

' "The slut's bitten me!" says he, clapping his hand to his neck, and sure enough, his hand was red with blood. Billy Fish and two of his matchlock-men catches hold of Dan by the shoulders and drags him into the Bashkai lot, while the priests howls in their lingo—"Neither God nor Devil but a man!" I was taken aback, for a priest cut at me in front, and the Army behind began firing into the Bashkai men.

' "God A'mighty!" says Dan. "What is the meaning o' this?"

' "Come back! Come away!" says Billy Fish. "Ruin and Mutiny is the matter. We'll break for Bashkai if we can."

'I tried to give some sort of orders to my men—the men o' the regular Army—but it was no use, so I fired into the brown of 'em with an English Martini and drilled three beggars in a line. The valley was full of shouting, howling creatures, and every soul was shrieking, "Not a God nor a Devil but only a man!" The Bashkai troops stuck to Billy Fish all they were worth, but their matchlocks wasn't half as good as the Kabul breechloaders, and four of them dropped. Dan was bellowing like a bull, for he was very wrathy; and Billy Fish had a hard job to prevent him running out at the crowd.

' "We can't stand," says Billy Fish. "Make a run for it down the valley! The whole place is against us." The matchlock-men ran, and we went down the valley in spite of Dravot. He was swearing horrible and crying out he was a King. The priests rolled great stones on us, and the regular Army fired hard, and there wasn't more than six men, not counting Dan, Billy Fish, and me, that came down to the bottom of the valley alive.

'Then they stopped firing and the horns in the temple blew again. "Come away—for God's sake come away!" says Billy Fish. "They'll send runners out to all the villages before ever we get to Bashkai. I can protect you there, but I can't do anything now."

'My own notion is that Dan began to go mad in his head from that hour. He stared up and down like a stuck pig. Then he was all for walking back alone and killing the priests with his bare hands; which he could have done. "An Emperor am I," says Daniel, "and next year I shall be a Knight of the Queen."

' "All right, Dan," says I; "but come along now while there's time."

' "It's your fault," says he, "for not looking after your Army better. There was mutiny in the midst, and you didn't know—you damned engine-driving, plate-laying, missionary's-pass-hunting hound!" He sat upon a rock and called me every foul name he could lay tongue to. I was too heart-sick to care, though it was all his foolishness that brought the smash.

' "I'm sorry, Dan," says I, "but there's no accounting for natives. This business is our Fifty-Seven. Maybe we'll make something out of it yet, when we've got to Bashkai."

' "Let's get to Bashkai, then," says Dan, "and by God, when I come back here again I'll sweep the valley so there isn't a bug in a blanket left!"

'We walked all that day, and all that night Dan was stumping up and down on the snow, chewing his beard and muttering to himself.

' "There's no hope o' getting clear," said Billy Fish. "The priests will have sent runners to the villages to say that you are only men. Why didn't you stick on as Gods till things was more settled? I'm a dead man," says Billy Fish, and he throws himself down on the snow and begins to pray to his Gods.

'Next morning we was in a cruel bad country—all up and down, no level ground at all, and no food either. The six Bashkai men looked at Billy Fish hungry-ways as if they wanted to ask something, but they said never a word. At noon we came to the top of a flat mountain all covered with snow, and when we climbed up into it, behold, there was an Army in position waiting in the middle!

' "The runners have been very quick," says Billy Fish, with a little bit of a laugh. "They are waiting for us."

'Three or four men began to fire from the enemy's side, and a chance shot took Daniel in the calf of the leg. That brought him to his senses. He looks across the snow at the Army, and sees the rifles that we had brought into the country.

'We're done for," says he. "They are Englishmen, these people— and it's my blasted nonsense that has brought you to this. Get back, Billy Fish, and take your men away; you've done what you could, and now cut for it. Carnehan," says he, "shake hands with me and go along with Billy. Maybe they won't kill you. I'll go and meet 'em alone. It's me that did it. Me, the King!"

' "Go!" says I. "Go to Hell, Dan! I'm with you here. Billy Fish, you clear out, and we two will meet those folk."

' "I'm a Chief," says Billy Fish, quite quiet. "I stay with you. My men can go."

'The Bashkai fellows didn't wait for a second word, but ran off, and Dan and me and Billy Fish walked across to where the drums were drumming and the horns were horning. It was cold—awful cold. I've got that cold in the back of my head now. There's a lump of it there.'

The punkah-coolies had gone to sleep. Two kerosene lamps were blazing in the office, and the perspiration poured down my face and splashed on the blotter as I leaned forward. Carnehan was shivering, and I feared that his mind might go. I wiped my face, took a fresh grip of the piteously mangled hands, and said: 'What happened after that?'

The momentary shift of my eyes had broken the clear current.

'What was you pleased to say?' whined Carnehan. 'They took them without any sound. Not a little whisper all along the snow, not though the King knocked down the first man that set hand on him—not though old Peachey fired his last cartridge into the brown of 'em. Not a single solitary sound did those swines make. They just closed up tight, and I tell you their furs stunk. There was a man called Billy Fish, a good friend of us all, and they cut his throat, Sir, then and there, like a pig; and the King kicks up the bloody snow and says: "We've had a dashed fine run for our money. What's coming next?" But Peachey, Peachey Taliaferro, I tell you, Sir, in confidence as betwixt two friends, he lost his head, Sir. No, he didn't neither. The King lost his head, so he did, all along o' one of those cunning rope-bridges. Kindly let me have the paper-cutter, Sir. It tilted this way. They marched him a mile across that snow to a rope-bridge over a ravine with a river at the bottom. You may have seen such. They prodded him behind like an ox. "Damn your eyes!" says the King. "D'you suppose I can't die like a gentleman?" He turns to Peachey— Peachey that was crying like a child. "I've brought you to this, Peachey," says he. "Brought you out of your happy life to be killed in Kafiristan, where you was late Commander-in-Chief of the Emperor's forces. Say you forgive me, Peachey."—"I do," says Peachey. "Fully and freely do I forgive you, Dan."—"Shake hands, Peachey," says he. "I'm going now." Out he goes, looking neither right nor left, and when he was plumb in the middle of those dizzy dancing ropes— "Cut, you beggars," he shouts; and they cut, and old Dan fell, turning round and round and round, twenty thousand miles, for he took half an hour to fall till he struck the water, and I could see his body caught on a rock with the gold crown close beside.

'But do you know what they did to Peachey between two pine-trees? They crucified him, Sir, as Peachey's hands will show. They used wooden pegs for his hands and his feet; and he didn't die. He hung there and screamed, and they took him down next day, and said it was a miracle that he wasn't dead. They took him down—poor old Peachey that hadn't done them any harm—that hadn't done them any——'

He rocked to and fro and wept bitterly, wiping his eyes with the back of his scarred hands and moaning like a child for some ten minutes.

'They was cruel enough to feed him up in the temple, because they said he was more of a God than old Daniel that was a man. Then they turned him out on the snow, and told him to go home, and Peachey came home in about a year, begging along the roads quite safe; for Daniel Dravot he walked before and said: "Come along, Peachey. It's a big thing we're doing." The mountains they danced at night, and the mountains they tried to fall on Peachey's head, but Dan he held up his hand, and Peachey came along bent double. He never let go of Dan's hand, and he never let go of Dan's head. They gave it to him as a present in the temple, to remind him not to come again, and though the crown was pure gold, and Peachey was starving, never would Peachey sell the same. You knew Dravot, Sir! You knew Right Worshipful Brother Dravot! Look at him now!'

He fumbled in the mass of rags round his bent waist; brought out a black horsehair bag embroidered with silver thread, and shook therefrom on to my table—the dried, withered head of Daniel Dravot! The morning sun that had long been paling the lamps struck the red beard and blind sunken eyes; struck, too, a heavy circlet of gold studded with raw turquoises, that Carnehan placed tenderly on the battered temples.

'You behold now,' said Carnehan, 'the Emperor in his habit as he lived°—the King of Kafiristan with his crown upon his head. Poor old Daniel that was a monarch once!'

I shuddered, for, in spite of defacements manifold, I recognized the head of the man of Marwar Junction. Carnehan rose to go. I attempted to stop him. He was not fit to walk abroad. 'Let me take away the whisky, and give me a little money,' he gasped. 'I was a King once. I'll go to the Deputy Commissioner and ask to set in the Poorhouse till I get my health. No, thank you, I can't wait till you get a carriage for me. I've urgent private affairs—in the south—at Marwar.'

He shambled out of the office and departed in the direction of the Deputy Commissioner's house. That day at noon I had occasion to go down the blinding hot Mall, and I saw a crooked man crawling along the white dust of the roadside, his hat in his hand, quavering dolorously after the fashion of street-singers at Home. There was not a soul in sight, and he was out of all possible earshot of the houses. And he sang through his nose, turning his head from right to left:

> The Son of God goes forth to war,°
> A kingly crown to gain;
> His blood-red banner streams afar!
> Who follows in his train?

I waited to hear no more, but put the poor wretch into my carriage and drove him off to the nearest missionary for eventual transfer to the Asylum. He repeated the hymn twice while he was with me, whom he did not in the least recognize, and I left him singing it to the missionary.

Two days later I inquired after his welfare of the Superintendent of the Asylum.

'He was admitted suffering from sunstroke. He died early yesterday morning,' said the Superintendent. 'Is it true that he was half an hour bareheaded in the sun at mid-day?'

'Yes,' said I, 'but do you happen to know if he had anything upon him by any chance when he died?'

'Not to my knowledge,' said the Superintendent.

And there the matter rests.

Danny Deever

'What are the bugles blowin' for?' said Files-on-Parade.°
'To turn you out, to turn you out,' the Colour-Sergeant said.°
'What makes you look so white, so white?' said Files-on-Parade.
'I'm dreadin' what I've got to watch,' the Colour-Sergeant said.
    For they're hangin' Danny Deever, you can hear the Dead March play,
    The regiment's in 'ollow square—they're hangin' him to-day;°
    They've taken of his buttons off an' cut his stripes away,
    An' they're hangin' Danny Deever in the mornin'.

'What makes the rear-rank breathe so 'ard?' said Files-on-Parade.
'It's bitter cold, it's bitter cold,' the Colour-Sergeant said.   10
'What makes that front-rank man fall down?' said Files-on-Parade.
'A touch o' sun, a touch o' sun,' the Colour-Sergeant said.
    They are hangin' Danny Deever, they are marchin' of 'im round,
    They 'ave 'alted Danny Deever by 'is coffin on the ground;
    An' 'e'll swing in 'arf a minute for a sneakin' shootin' hound—
    O they're hangin' Danny Deever in the mornin'!

' 'Is cot was right-'and cot to mine,' said Files-on-Parade.
' 'E's sleepin' out an' far to-night,' the Colour-Sergeant said.

'I've drunk 'is beer a score o' times,' said Files-on-Parade.
' 'E's drinkin' bitter beer alone,' the Colour-Sergeant said.   20
  They are hangin' Danny Deever, you must mark 'im to 'is place,
  For 'e shot a comrade sleepin'—you must look 'im in the face;
  Nine 'undred of 'is county an' the Regiment's disgrace,°
  While they're hangin' Danny Deever in the mornin'.

'What's that so black agin the sun?' said Files-on-Parade.
'It's Danny fightin' 'ard for life,' the Colour-Sergeant said.
'What's that that whimpers over'ead?' said Files-on-Parade.
'It's Danny's soul that's passin' now,' the Colour-Sergeant said.
  For they're done with Danny Deever, you can 'ear the quickstep
    play,
  The Regiment's in column, an' they're marchin' us away;   30
  Ho! the young recruits are shakin', an' they'll want their beer to-
    day,
  After hangin' Danny Deever in the mornin'!

Mandalay°

By the old Moulmein Pagoda, lookin' eastward to the sea,
There's a Burma girl a-settin', and I know she thinks o' me;
For the wind is in the palm-trees, and the temple-bells they say:
'Come you back, you British soldier; come you back to Mandalay!'
    Come you back to Mandalay,
    Where the old Flotilla lay:°
    Can't you 'ear their paddles chunkin' from Rangoon to
      Mandalay?°
    On the road to Mandalay,
    Where the flyin'-fishes play,
    An' the dawn comes up like thunder outer China 'crost the
      Bay!   10

'Er petticoat was yaller an' 'er little cap was green,
An' 'er name was Supi-yaw-lat—jes' the same as Theebaw's Queen,°
An' I seed her first a-smokin' of a whackin' white cheroot,
An' a-wastin' Christian kisses on an 'eathen idol's foot:

Bloomin idol made o' mud—
Wot they called the Great Gawd Budd—°
Plucky lot she cared for idols when I kissed 'er where she stud!
On the road to Mandalay . . .

When the mist was on the rice-fields an' the sun was droppin' slow,
She'd git 'er little banjo an' she'd sing 'Kulla-lo-lo!'   20
With 'er arm upon my shoulder an' 'er cheek agin my cheek
We useter watch the steamers an' the *hathis* pilin' teak.°
    Elephints a-pilin' teak
    In the sludgy, squdgy creek,
    Where the silence 'ung that 'eavy you was 'arf afraid to speak!
    On the road to Mandalay . . .

But that's all shove be'ind me—long ago an' fur away,
An' there ain't no 'busses runnin' from the Bank to Mandalay;
An' I'm learnin' 'ere in London what the ten-year soldier tells:
'If you've 'eard the East a-callin', you won't never 'eed naught
    else.'   30
    No! you won't 'eed nothin' else
    But them spicy garlic smells,
    An' the sunshine an' the palm-trees an' the tinkly temple-
      bells;
    On the road to Mandalay . . .

I am sick o' wastin' leather on these gritty pavin'-stones,
An' the blasted Henglish drizzle wakes the fever in my bones;
Tho' I walks with fifty 'ousemaids outer Chelsea to the Strand,°
An' they talks a lot o' lovin', but wot do they understand?
    Beefy face an' grubby 'and—
    Law! wot do they understand?   40
    I've a neater, sweeter maiden in a cleaner, greener land!
    On the road to Mandalay . . .

Ship me somewheres east of Suez, where the best is like the worst,
Where there aren't no Ten Commandments an' a man can raise a
    thirst;
For the temple-bells are callin', an' it's there that I would be—
By the old Moulmein Pagoda, looking lazy at the sea;

On the road to Mandalay,
Where the old Flotilla lay,
With our sick beneath the awnings when we went to Manda-
    lay!
O the road to Mandalay,
Where the flyin'-fishes play,   50
An' the dawn comes up like thunder outer China 'crost the
    Bay!

The Song of the Banjo

You could n't pack a Broadwood half a mile—°
    You must n't leave a fiddle in the damp—
You could n't raft an organ up the Nile,
    And play it in an Equatorial swamp.
I travel with the cooking pots and pails—
    *I'*m sandwiched 'tween the coffee and the pork—
And when the dusty column checks and tails,°
    You should hear me spur the rearguard to a walk!

        With my '*Pilly-willy-winky-winky-popp!*'
            (Oh, it's any tune that comes into my head!)   10
        So I keep 'em moving forward till they drop;
            So I play 'em up to water and to bed.

In the silence of the camp before the fight,
    When it's good to make your will and say your prayer,
You can hear my *strumpty-tumpty* overnight,
    Explaining ten to one was always fair.
I'm the Prophet of the Utterly Absurd,
    Of the Patently Impossible and Vain—
And when the Thing that Could n't has occurred,
    Give me time to change my leg and go again.   20

        With my '*Tumpa-tumpa-tumpa-tum-pa tump!*'
            In the desert where the dung-fed camp-smoke curled.
        There was never voice before us till I led our lonely chorus,
            I—the war drum of the White Man round the world!

By the bitter road the Younger Son must tread,
  Ere he win to hearth and saddle of his own—
'Mid the riot of the shearers at the shed.
  In the silence of the herder's hut alone—
In the twilight, on a bucket upside down,
  Hear me babble what the weakest won't confess—   30
I am Memory and Torment—I am Town!
  I am all that ever went with evening dress!

    With my '*Tunka-tunka-tunka-tunka-tunk!*'
      (So the lights—the London Lights—grow near and plain!)
    So I rowel 'em afresh towards the Devil and the Flesh,°
      Till I bring my broken rankers home again.

In desire of many marvels over sea,
  Where the new-raised tropic city sweats and roars,
I have sailed with Young Ulysses from the quay
  Till the anchor rumbled down on stranger shores.   40
He is blooded to the open and the sky,°
  He is taken in a snare that shall not fail,
He shall hear me singing strongly, till he die,
  Like the shouting of a backstay in a gale.°

    With my '*Hya! Heeya! Heeya! Hullah! Haul!*'°
      (Oh the green that thunders aft along the deck!)
    Are you sick o' towns and men? You must sign and sail again,
      For it's 'Johnny Bowlegs, pack your kit and trek!'°

Through the gorge that gives the stars at noon-day clear—
  Up the pass that packs the scud beneath our wheel—   50
Round the bluff that sinks her thousand fathoms sheer—
  Down the valley with our guttering brakes asqueal:
Where the trestle groans and quivers in the snow,
  Where the many-shedded levels loop and twine,°
Hear me lead my reckless children from below
  Till we sing the Song of Roland to the pine.°

    With my '*Tinka-tinka-tinka-tinka-tink!*'
      (Oh the axe has cleared the mountain, croup and crest!)°
    And we ride the iron stallions down to drink,   60
      Through the cañons to the waters of the West!

And the tunes that means so much to you alone—
   Common tunes that make you choke and blow your nose,
Vulgar tunes that bring the laugh that brings the groan—
   I can rip your very heartstrings out with those;
With the feasting, and the folly, and the fun—
   And the lying, and the lusting, and the drink,
And the merry play that drops you, when you're done,
   To the thoughts that burn like irons if you think.

      With my *'Plunka-lunka-lunka-lunka-lunk!'*   70
        Here's a trifle on account of pleasure past,
        Ere the wit that made you win gives you eyes to see your sin
        And—the heavier repentance at the last!

Let the organ moan her sorrow to the roof—
   I have told the naked stars the Grief of Man!
Let the trumpets snare the foeman to the proof—
   I have known Defeat, and mocked it as we ran!
My bray ye may not alter nor mistake
   When I stand to jeer the fatted Soul of Things,
But the Song of Lost Endeavour that I make,   80
   Is it hidden in the twanging of the strings?

      With my *'Ta-ra-rara-rara-ra-ra-rrrp!'*
        (Is it naught to you that hear and pass me by?)
        But the word—the word is mine, when the order moves the line
        And the lean, locked ranks go roaring down to die!

The grandam of my grandam was the Lyre—
   (O the blue below the little fisher-huts!)
That the Stealer stooping beachward filled with fire,°
   Till she bore my iron head and ringing guts!
By the wisdom of the centuries I speak—   90
   To the tune of yestermorn I set the truth—
I, the joy of life unquestioned—I, the Greek—
   I, the everlasting Wonder Song of Youth!

      With my *'Tinka-tinka-tinka-tinka-tink!'*
        (What d'ye lack, my noble masters? What d'ye lack?)°
        So I draw the world together link by link:
        Yea, from Delos up to Limerick and back!°

The Way Through the Woods

They shut the road through the woods
Seventy years ago.
Weather and rain have undone it again,
And now you would never know
There was once a road through the woods
Before they planted the trees.
It is underneath the coppice and heath,
And the thin anemones.
Only the keeper sees
That, where the ring-dove broods,   10
And the badgers roll at ease,
There was once a road through the woods.

Yet, if you enter the woods
Of a summer evening late,
When the night-air cools on the trout-ringed pools
Where the otter whistles his mate,
(They fear not men in the woods,
Because they see so few.)
You will hear the beat of a horse's feet,
And the swish of a skirt in the dew,   20
Steadily cantering through
The misty solitudes,
As though they perfectly knew
The old lost road through the woods. . . .
But there is no road through the woods!

ARTHUR SYMONS

Episode of a Night of May°

The coloured lanterns lit the trees, the grass,
The little tables underneath the trees,
And the rays dappled like a delicate breeze
     Each wine-illumined glass.

The pink light flickered, and a shadow ran
Along the ground as couples came and went;
The waltzing fiddles sounded from the tent,
    And *Giroflée* began.°

They sauntered arm in arm, these two; the smiles
Grew chilly, as the best spring evenings do.   10
The words were warmer, but the words came few,
    And pauses fell at whiles.

But she yawned prettily. 'Come then,' said he.
He found a chair, Veuve Clicquot, some cigars.
They emptied glasses and admired the stars,
    The lanterns, night, the sea,

Nature, the newest opera, the dog
(So clever) who could shoulder arms and dance;
He mentioned Alphonse Daudet's last romance,
    Last Sunday's river-fog,   20

Love, Immortality; the talk ran down
To these mere lees: they wearied each of each,
And tortured ennui into hollow speech,
    And yawned, to hide a frown.

She jarred his nerves; he bored her—and so soon.
Both were polite, and neither cared to say
The word that mars a perfect night of May.
    They watched the waning moon.

Colour Studies
At Dieppe

TO WALTER SICKERT°

The grey-green stretch of sandy grass,
Indefinitely desolate;
A sea of lead, a sky of slate;
Already autumn in the air, alas!

One stark monotony of stone,
The long hotel, acutely white,
Against the after-sunset light
Withers grey-green, and takes the grass's tone.

Listless and endless it outlies,
And means, to you and me, no more   10
Than any pebble on the shore,
Or this indifferent moment as it dies.

Nini Patte-en-l'air°

(CASINO DE PARIS)

The gold Casino's Spring parterre
Flowers with the Spring, this golden week;
Glady, Toloche, Valtesse, are there;
But all eyes turn as one to seek
The drawers of Nini Patte-en-l'air.°

Surprising, sunset-coloured lace,
In billowy clouds of gold and red,
They whirl and flash before one's face;
The little heel above her head
Points an ironical grimace   10

And mark the experimental eyes,
The naughty eloquence of feet,
The appeal of subtly quivering thighs,
The insinuations indiscreet
Of pirouetting draperies.

What exquisite indecency,
Select, supreme, severe, an art!
The art of knowing how to be
Part lewd, aesthetical in part,
And *fin-de-siècle* essentially.   20

The Mænad of the Decadence,
Collectedly extravagant,
Her learned fury wakes the sense
That, fainting, needs for excitant
This science of concupiscence.

Faint Love

(FOR A FAN BY CHARLES CONDER)°

Beauty I love, yet more than this I love
Beautiful things; and, more than love, delight;
Colours that faint; dim echo far above
The crystal sound, and shadow beyond sight.

For I am tired with youth and happiness
As other men are tired with age and grief;
This is to me a longer weariness:
Sadly I ask of each sad mask's relief.

For gardens where I know not if I find
Autumn or spring about the shadowy fruit,   10
And if it is the sighing of the wind
Or if it is the sighing of the lute.

W. B. YEATS

The Man who Dreamed of Faeryland

He stood among a crowd at Dromahair;°
His heart hung all upon a silken dress,
And he had known at last some tenderness,
Before the earth took him to her stony care;
But when a man poured fish into a pile,
It seemed they raised their little silver heads,
And sang what gold morning or evening sheds
Upon a woven world-forgotten isle

Where people love beside the ravelled seas;
That Time can never mar a lover's vows   10
Under that woven changeless roof of boughs:
The singing shook him out of his new ease.

He wandered by the sands of Lissadell;°
His mind ran all on money cares and fears,
And he had known at last some prudent years
Before they heaped his grave under the hill;
But while he passed before a plashy place,
A lug-worm with its grey and muddy mouth
Sang that somewhere to north or west or south
There dwelt a gay, exulting, gentle race   20
Under the golden or the silver skies;°
That if a dancer stayed his hungry foot°
It seemed the sun and moon were in the fruit:
And at that singing he was no more wise.

He mused beside the well of Scanavin,°
He mused upon his mockers: without fail
His sudden vengeance were a country tale,
When earthy night had drunk his body in;
But one small knot-grass growing by the pool
Sang where—unnecessary cruel voice—   30
Old silence bids its chosen race rejoice,
Whatever ravelled waters rise and fall
Or stormy silver fret the gold of day,
And midnight there enfold them like a fleece
And lover there by lover be at peace.
The tale drove his fine angry mood away.

He slept under the hill of Lugnagall;°
And might have known at last unhaunted sleep
Under that cold and vapour-turbaned steep,
Now that the earth had taken man and all:
Did not the worms that spired about his bones   40

Proclaim with that unwearied, reedy cry
That God has laid His fingers on the sky,
That from those fingers glittering summer runs
Upon the dancer by the dreamless wave.
Why should those lovers that no lovers miss
Dream, until God burn Nature with a kiss?
The man has found no comfort in the grave.

The Song of Wandering Aengus°

I went out to the hazel wood,
Because a fire was in my head,
And cut and peeled a hazel wand,
And hooked a berry to a thread;
And when white moths were on the wing,
And moth-like stars were flickering out,
I dropped the berry in a stream
And caught a little silver trout.

When I had laid it on the floor
I went to blow the fire aflame,   10
But something rustled on the floor,
And some one called me by my name:
It had become a glimmering girl
With apple blossom in her hair
Who called me by my name and ran
And faded through the brightening air.

Though I am old with wandering
Through hollow lands and hilly lands,
I will find out where she has gone,
And kiss her lips and take her hands;   20
And walk among long dappled grass,
And pluck till time and times are done
The silver apples of the moon,
The golden apples of the sun.

He Reproves the Curlew

O curlew, cry no more in the air,
Or only to the water in the West;°
Because your crying brings to my mind
Passion–dimmed eyes and long heavy hair
That was shaken out over my breast:
There is enough evil in the crying of wind.°

He Hears the Cry of the Sedge

I wander by the edge
Of this desolate lake
Where wind cries in the sedge:
Until the axle break°
That keeps the stars in their round,
And hands hurl in the deep
The banners of East and West,°
And the girdle of light is unbound,
Your breast will not lie by the breast
Of your beloved in sleep.   10

He Thinks of Those Who Have Spoken Evil of His Beloved

Half close your eyelids, loosen your hair,
And dream about the great and their pride;
They have spoken against you everywhere,
But weigh this song with the great and their pride;
I made it out of a mouthful of air,°
Their children's children shall say they have lied.

JOHN GRAY

Song of the Stars

Many the children of men;
Swollen women I love.
Bite, white teeth of the frost;
Toil of the husbandmen lost;
Perish the children of men.
Praise of ease and a quiet lot;
Praise of anise and bergamot;
Praise of the note of the dove;
Many the children of men.

Pale let the warm hands wring,   10
Worn with labour and prayer;
The harvesters' heap is aflare.
I sing the corpse lying naked and robbed
On the plain's torn bosom; I sing
The cell grown cold where the faint heart throbbed.
Bursting life and the song of the thrush;
Joy of gathering; apples blush;
Air serene of the standing corn.
Women are swollen; men are born.

Bind me about in death   20
With a garland of twisted wheat.

Charleville°

IMITATED FROM THE FRENCH OF ARTHUR RIMBAUD

The square, with gravel paths and shabby lawns.
Correct, the trees and flowers repress their yawns.
The tradesman brings his favourite conceit,
To air it, while he stifles with the heat.

In the kiosk, the military band.
The shakos nod the time of the quadrilles.
The flaunting dandy strolls about the stand.
The notary, half unconscious of his seals.

On the green seats, small groups of grocermen,
Absorbed, their sticks scooping a little hole   10
Upon the path, talk market prices; then
Take up a cue: I think, upon the whole. . . .

The loutish roughs are larking on the grass.
The sentimental trooper, with a rose
Between his teeth, seeing a baby, grows
More tender, with an eye upon the nurse.

Unbuttoned, like a student, I follow
A couple of girls along the chestnut row.
They know I am following, for they turn and laugh,
Half impudent, half shy, inviting chaff.   20

I do not say a word. I only stare
At their round, fluffy necks. I follow where
The shoulders drop; I struggle to define
The subtle torso's hesitating line.

Only my rustling tread, deliberate, slow;
The rippled silence from the still leaves drips.
They think I am an idiot, they speak low;
—I feel faint kisses creeping on my lips.

Parsifal°

IMITATED FROM THE FRENCH OF PAUL VERLAINE

Conquered the flower-maidens, and the wide embrace
Of their round proffered arms, that tempt the virgin boy;
Conquered the trickling of their babbling tongues; the coy
Back glances, and the mobile breasts of subtle grace;

Conquered the Woman Beautiful, the fatal charm
Of her hot breast, the music of her babbling tongue;
Conquered the gate of Hell, into the gate the young
Man passes, with the heavy trophy at his arm,

The holy Javelin that pierced the Heart of God.
He heals the dying king, he sits upon the throne,   10
King, and high priest of that great gift, the living Blood.

In robe of gold the youth adores the glorious Sign
Of the green goblet, worships the mysterious Wine.
And oh! the chime of children's voices in the dome.

The Flying Fish°

I

Myself am Hang the buccaneer,
whom children love and brave men fear,
master of courage, come what come,
master of craft, and called Sea-scum;

student of wisdom and waterways,
course of moons and the birth of days;
to him in whose heart all things be
I bring my story of the sea.

The same am I as that sleek Hang
whose pattens along the stone quay clang   10
in sailing time, whose pile is high
on the beach when merchants come to buy.

Am he who cumbers his lowly hulk
with refuse bundles of feeble bulk;
turns sailor's eyes to the weather skies;
bows low to the Master of Merchandise;

who hoists his sails with the broken slats;
whose lean crew are scarcely food for his rats;
am he who creeps from tower-top ken
and utmost vision of all men: 20

ah then, am he who changeth line,
and which man knoweth that course of mine?
Am he, sir Sage, who sails to the sea
where an island and other wonders be.

After six days we sight the coast,
and my palace top, should a sailor boast;
sails rattle down; and then we ride,
mean junk and proud, by my palace side.

For there lives a junk in that ancient sea
where the gardens of Hang and his palace be,   30
o my fair junk! which once aboard
the pirate owns no living lord.

Its walls are painted water–green
like the green sea's self, both shade and sheen,
lest any mark it. The pirate's trade
is to hover swiftly and make afraid.

Its sails are fashioned of lithe bamboo,
all painted blue as the sky is blue,
so it be not seen till the prey be nigh.
Hang loves not that the same should fly.   40

In midst of the first a painted sun
gleams gold like the celestial yon;
in midst of the second a tender moon,
that a lover might kiss his flute and swoon;

or maid touch lute at sight of the third,
pictured with all the crystal herd;
so the silly ships are mazed at sight
of night by day and day by night.

For wind and water a goodlier junk
than any that ever sailed or sunk;   50
which junk was theirs; none fiercer than
my fathers since the fall of man.

So cotton rags lays Hang aside:
lays bare the sailor's gristly hide;
and wraps his body in vests of silk;
ilk is as beautiful as ilk.

Then Hang puts on his ancient mail,
silver and black, and scale on scale
like dragons', which his grandsire bore
before him, and his grandsire before.   60

He binds his legs with buskins grim,
tawny and gold for the pride of him;
his feet are bare like his who quelled
the dragon, his feet are feet of eld.

His head is brave with a lacquered casque,
the donning which is a heavy task;
its flaps are feathered like Yuen Yin;
'tis strapped with straps of tiger-skin.

The passions of his fathers whelm
the heart of Hang when he wears their helm.   70
Then Hang grows wrinkled betwixt his eyes;
he frowns like a devil, devil-wise;

his eyeballs start; his mask is red
like his who at last shall judge the dead;
his nostrils gape; his mouth is the mouth
of the fish that swims in the torrid south;

his beard the pirate Hang lets flow;
he lays his hand on his father's bow,
wherewith a cunning man of strength
might shoot an arrow the vessel's length.   80

I have another of sun-red lac,
of a great man's height, so the string be slack;
the charge departs with a fiery clang;
'tis drawn with the foot, the foot of Hang.

Such house and harness become me, when
I wait upon laden merchantmen;
'Twixt tears and the sea, 'twixt brine and brine,
they shudder at sight of me and mine.

II

Of the birds that fly in the farthest sea
six are stranger than others be:
under its tumble, among the fish,
six are a marvel passing wish.

First is a hawk, exceeding great;
he dwelleth alone; he hath no mate;
his neck is wound with a yellow ring;
on his breast is the crest of a former king.

The second bird is exceeding pale,
from little head to scanty tail;
she is striped with black on either wing,
which is rose-lined, like a princely thing.

Though small the bulk of the brilliant third,
of all blue birds 'tis the bluest bird;
they fly in bands; and, seen by day,
by the side of them the sky is grey.

I mind the fifth, I forget the fourth,
unless that it comes from the east by north.
The fifth is an orange white-billed duck;
he diveth for fish, like the god of Luck;

he hath never a foot on which to stand;
for water yields and he loves not land.
This is the end of many words
save one, concerning marvellous birds.

The great-faced dolphin is first of fish;
he is devil-eyed and devilish;
of all the fishes is he most brave,
he walks the sea like an angry wave.

The second the fishes call their lord;
himself a bow, his face is a sword;
his sword is armed with a hundred teeth,
fifty above and fifty beneath.   120

The third hath a scarlet suit of mail;
the fourth is naught but a feeble tail;
the fifth is a whip with a hundred strands,
and every arm hath a hundred hands.

The last strange fish is the last strange bird;
of him no sage hath ever heard;
he roams the sea in a gleaming horde
in fear of the dolphin and him of the sword.

He leaps from the sea with a silken swish;
he beats the air does the flying fish.   130
His eyes are round with excess of fright,
bright as the drops of his pinions' flight.

In sea and sky he hath no peace;
for the five strange fish are his enemies;
and the five strange fowls keep watch for him;
they know him well by his crystal gleam.

Oftwhiles, sir Sage, on my junk's white deck
have I seen this fish–bird come to wreck,
oftwhiles (fair deck) 'twixt bow and poop
have I seen this piteous sky-fish stoop.   140

Scaled bird, how his snout and gills dilate,
all quivering and roseate:
he pants in crystal and mother–of–pearl
while his body shrinks and his pinions furl.

His beauty passes like bubbles blown;
the white bright bird is a fish of stone;
the bird so fair, for its putrid sake,
is flung to the dogs in the junk's white wake.

III

Have thought, son Pirate, some such must be
as the beast thou namest in yonder sea;   150
else, bring me a symbol from nature's gear
of aspiration born of fear.

Hast been, my son, to the doctor's booth
some day when Hang had a qualm to soothe?
Hast noted the visible various sign
Of each flask's virtue, son of mine?

Rude picture of insect seldom found,
of plant that thrives in marshy ground,
goblin of east wind, fog or draught,
sign of the phial's potent craft?   160

'Tis even thus where the drug is sense,
where wisdom is more than frankincense,
wit's grain than a pound of pounded bones,
where knowledge is redder than ruby stones.

Hast thou marked how poppies are sign of sin?
how bravery's mantle is tiger-skin?
how earth is heavy and dumb with care?
how song is the speech of all the air?

A tree is the sign most whole and sure
of aspiration plain and pure;   170
of the variation one must wend
in search of the sign to the sea's wild end.

Thy fish is the fairest of all that be
in the throbbing depths of yonder sea.
He says in his iridescent heart:
I am gorgeous-eyed and a fish apart;

my back hath the secret of every shell,
the Hang of fishes knoweth well;
scales of my breast are softer still,
the ugly fishes devise my ill.   180

He prays the Maker of water-things
not for a sword, but cricket's wings,
not to be one of the sons of air,
to be rid of the water is all his prayer;

all his hope is a fear-whipped whim;
all directions are one to him.
There are seekers of wisdom no less absurd,
son Hang, than thy fish that would be a bird.

RICHARD LE GALLIENNE

A Ballad of London

Ah, London! London! our delight,
Great flower that opens but at night,
Great City of the midnight sun,
Whose day begins when day is done.

Lamp after lamp against the sky
Opens a sudden beaming eye,
Leaping alight on either hand,
The iron lilies of the Strand.

Like dragonflies, the hansoms hover,
With jewelled eyes, to catch the lover,   10
The streets are full of lights and loves,
Soft gowns, and flutter of soiled doves.°

Upon thy petals butterflies,
But at thy root, some say, there lies
A world of weeping trodden things,
Poor worms that have not eyes or wings.

From out corruption of their woe
Springs this bright flower that charms us so,
Men die and rot deep out of sight
To keep this jungle-flower bright.   20

Paris and London, World-Flowers twain
Wherewith the World-Tree blooms again,°
Since Time hath gathered Babylon
And withered Rome still withers on.

Sidon and Tyre were such as ye,
How bright they shone upon the tree!
But Time hath gathered, both are gone,
And no man sails to Babylon.

Ah, London! London! our delight,
For thee, too, the eternal night,   30
And Circe Paris hath no charm
To stay Time's unrelenting arm

Time and his moths shall eat up all.
Your chiming towers proud and tall,
He shall most utterly abase,
And set a desert in their place.

H. G. WELLS

The Country of the Blind

Three hundred miles and more from Chimborazo, one hundred from
the snows of Cotopaxi, in the wildest wastes of Ecuador's Andes, there
lies that mysterious mountain valley, cut off from the world of men,
the Country of the Blind. Long years ago that valley lay so far open to
the world that men might come at last through fruitful gorges and
over an icy pass into its equable meadows; and thither indeed men
came, a family or so of Peruvian half-breeds fleeing from the lust and
tyranny of an evil Spanish ruler. Then came the stupendous outbreak
of Mindobamba, when it was night in Quito for seventeen days, and
the water was boiling at Yaguachi and all the fish floating dying even
as far as Guayaquil; everywhere along the Pacific slopes there were
landslips and swift thawings and sudden floods, and one whole side of
the old Arauca crest slipped and came down in thunder, and cut off

the Country of the Blind for ever from the exploring feet of men. But one of these early settlers had chanced to be on the hither side of the gorges when the world had so terribly shaken itself, and he perforce had to forget his wife and child and all the friends and possessions he had left up there, and start life over again in the lower world. He started it again but ill, blindness overtook him, and he died of punishment in the mines; but the story he told begot a legend that lingers along the length of the Cordilleras of the Andes to this day.

He told of his reason for venturing back from that fastness, into which he had first been carried lashed to a llama, beside a vast bale of gear, when he was a child. The valley, he said, had in it all that the heart of man could desire—sweet water, pasture, and even climate, slopes of rich brown soil with tangles of a shrub that bore an excellent fruit, and on one side great hanging forests of pine that held the avalanches high. Far overhead, on three sides, vast cliffs of grey-green rock were capped by cliffs of ice; but the glacier stream came not to them but flowed away by the farther slopes, and only now and then huge ice masses fell on the valley side. In this valley it neither rained nor snowed, but the abundant springs gave a rich green pasture, that irrigation would spread over all the valley space. The settlers did well indeed there. Their beasts did well and multiplied, and but one thing marred their happiness. Yet it was enough to mar it greatly. A strange disease had come upon them, and had made all the children born to them there—and indeed, several older children also—blind. It was to seek some charm or antidote against this plague of blindness that he had with fatigue and danger and difficulty returned down the gorge. In those days, in such cases, men did not think of germs and infections but of sins; and it seemed to him that the reason of this affliction must lie in the negligence of these priestless immigrants to set up a shrine so soon as they entered the valley. He wanted a shrine—a handsome, cheap, effectual shrine—to be erected in the valley; he wanted relics and suchlike potent things of faith, blessed objects and mysterious medals and prayers. In his wallet he had a bar of native silver for which he would not account; he insisted there was none in the valley with something of the insistence of an inexpert liar. They had all clubbed their money and ornaments together, having little need for such treasure up there, he said, to buy them holy help against their ill. I figure this dim-eyed young mountaineer, sunburned, gaunt, and anxious, hat-brim clutched feverishly, a man all unused to the ways of the lower world, telling this story to some keen-eyed, attentive priest before the great convulsion; I can picture him presently seeking to return with pious and infallible remedies against that trouble, and the infinite dismay with which he must have faced the tumbled vastness where the gorge had once come out. But the rest of his story of mischances is lost to me, save that I know of his evil death after several years. Poor stray from that remoteness! The stream that had once made the gorge now bursts from the mouth of a rocky cave, and the legend his poor, ill-told story set going developed into the legend of a race of blind men somewhere 'over there' one may still hear to-day.

And amidst the little population of that now isolated and forgotten valley the disease ran its course. The old became groping and purblind, the young saw but dimly, and the children that were born to them saw never at all. But life was very easy in that snowrimmed basin, lost to all the world, with neither thorns nor briars, with no evil insects nor any beasts save the gentle breed of llamas they had lugged and thrust and followed up the beds of the shrunken rivers in the gorges up which they had come. The seeing had become purblind so gradually that they scarcely noted their loss. They guided the sightless youngsters hither and thither until they knew the whole valley marvellously, and when at last sight died out among them the race lived on. They had even time to adapt themselves to the blind control of fire, which they made carefully in stoves of stone. They were a simple strain of people at the first, unlettered, only slightly touched with the Spanish civilization, but with something of a tradition of the arts of the old Peru and of its lost philosophy. Generation followed generation. They forgot many things; they devised many things. Their tradition of the greater world they came from became mythical in colour and uncertain. In all things save sight they were strong and able; and presently the chance of birth and heredity sent one who had an original mind and who could talk and persuade among them, and then afterwards another. These two passed, leaving their effects, and the little community grew in numbers and in understanding, and met and settled social and economic problems that arose. Generation followed generation. Generation followed generation. There came a time when a child was born who was fifteen generations from that ancestor who went out of the valley with a bar of silver to seek God's aid, and who never returned. Thereabouts it chanced that a man came into this community from the outer world. And this is the story of that man.

He was a mountaineer from the country near Quito, a man who had been down to the sea and had seen the world, a reader of books in an original way, an acute and enterprising man, and he was taken on by a party of Englishmen who had come out to Ecuador to climb mountains to replace one of their three Swiss guides who had fallen ill. He climbed here and he climbed there, and then came the attempt on Parascotopetl, the Matterhorn of the Andes, in which he was lost to the outer world. The story of the accident has been written a dozen times. Pointer's narrative is the best. He tells how the party worked their difficult and almost vertical way up to the very foot of the last and greatest precipice, and how they built a night shelter amidst the snow upon a little shelf of rock, and, with a touch of real dramatic power, how presently they found Nunez had gone from them. They shouted, and there was no reply; shouted and whistled, and for the rest of that night they slept no more.

As the morning broke they saw the traces of his fall. It seems impossible he could have uttered a sound. He had slipped eastward towards the unknown side of the mountain; far below he had struck a steep slope of snow, and ploughed his way down it in the midst of a snow avalanche. His track went straight to the edge of a frightful precipice, and beyond that everything was hidden. Far, far below, and hazy with distance, they could see trees rising out of a narrow, shut-in valley—the lost Country of the Blind. But they did not know it was the lost Country of the Blind, nor distinguish it in any way from any other narrow streak of upland valley. Unnerved by this disaster, they abandoned their attempt in the afternoon, and Pointer was called away to the war before he could make another attack. To this day Parascotopetl lifts an unconquered crest, and Pointer's shelter crumbles unvisited amidst the snows.

And the man who fell survived.

At the end of the slope he fell a thousand feet, and came down in the midst of a cloud of snow upon a snow slope even steeper than the one above. Down this he was whirled, stunned and insensible, but without a bone broken in his body; and then at last came to gentler slopes, and at last rolled out and lay still, buried amidst a softening heap of the white masses that had accompanied and saved him. He came to

himself with a dim fancy that he was ill in bed; then realized his
position with a mountaineer's intelligence, and worked himself loose
and, after a rest or so, out until he saw the stars. He rested flat upon
his chest for a space wondering where he was and what had happened
to him. He explored his limbs, and discovered that several of his
buttons were gone and his coat turned over his head. His knife had
gone from his pocket and his hat was lost, though he had tied it under
his chin. He recalled that he had been looking for loose stones to raise
his piece of the shelter wall. His ice-axe had disappeared.

He decided he must have fallen, and looked up to see, exaggerated
by the ghastly light of the rising moon, the tremendous flight he had
taken. For a while he lay, gazing blankly at the vast pale cliff towering
above, rising moment by moment out of a subsiding tide of darkness.
Its phantasmal, mysterious beauty held him for a space, and then he
was seized with a paroxysm of sobbing laughter. . . .

After a great interval of time he became aware that he was near the
lower edge of the snow. Below, down what was now a moonlit and
practicable slope, he saw the dark and broken appearance of rock-
strewn turf. He struggled to his feet, aching in every joint and limb,
got down painfully from the heaped loose snow about him, went
downward until he was on the turf, and there dropped rather than lay
beside a boulder, drank deep from the flask in his inner pocket, and
instantly fell asleep. . . .

He was awakened by the singing of birds in the trees far below.

He sat up and perceived he was on a little alp at the foot of a vast
precipice, that was grooved by the gully down which he and his
snow had come. Over against him another wall of rock reared itself
against the sky. The gorge between these precipices ran east and west
and was full of the morning sunlight, which lit to the westward the
mass of fallen mountain that closed the descending gorge. Below him
it seemed there was a precipice equally steep, but behind the snow in
the gully he found a sort of chimney-cleft dripping with snow-water
down which a desperate man might venture. He found it easier than it
seemed, and came at last to another desolate alp, and then after a rock
climb of no particular difficulty to a steep slope of trees. He took his
bearings and turned his face up the gorge, for he saw it opened out
above upon green meadows, among which he now glimpsed quite
distinctly a cluster of stone huts of unfamiliar fashion. At times his
progress was like clambering along the face of a wall, and after a time

the rising sun ceased to strike along the gorge, the voices of the singing birds died away, and the air grew cold and dark about him. But the distant valley with its houses was all the brighter for that. He came presently to talus, and among the rocks he noted—for he was an observant man—an unfamiliar fern that seemed to clutch out of the crevices with intense green hands. He picked a frond or so and gnawed its stalk and found it helpful.

About midday he came at last out of the throat of the gorge into the plain and the sunlight. He was stiff and weary; he sat down in the shadow of a rock, filled up his flask with water from a spring and drank it down, and remained for a time resting before he went on to the houses.

They were very strange to his eyes, and indeed the whole aspect of that valley became, as he regarded it, queerer and more unfamiliar. The greater part of its surface was lush green meadow, starred with many beautiful flowers, irrigated with extraordinary care, and bearing evidence of systematic cropping piece by piece. High up and ringing the valley about was a wall, and what appeared to be a circumferential water-channel, from which the little trickles of water that fed the meadow plants came, and on the higher slopes above this flocks of llamas cropped the scanty herbage. Sheds, apparently shelters or feeding-places for the llamas, stood against the boundary wall here and there. The irrigation streams ran together into a main channel down the centre of the valley, and this was enclosed on either side by a wall breast high. This gives a singularly urban quality to this secluded place, a quality that was greatly enhanced by the fact that a number of paths paved with black and white stones, and each with a curious little kerb at the side, ran hither and thither in an orderly manner. The houses of the central village were quite unlike the casual and higgledy-piggledy agglomeration of the mountain villages he knew; they stood in a continuous row on either side of a central street of astonishing cleanness; here and there their parti-coloured façade was pierced by a door, and not a solitary window broke their even frontage. They were parti-coloured with extraordinary irregularity, smeared with a sort of plaster that was sometimes grey, sometimes drab, sometimes slate-coloured or dark brown; and it was the sight of this wild plastering first brought the word 'blind' into the thoughts of the explorer. 'The good man who did that', he thought, 'must have been as blind as a bat.'

He descended a steep place, and so came to the wall and channel that ran about the valley, near where the latter spouted out its surplus contents into the deeps of the gorge in a thin and wavering thread of cascade. He could now see a number of men and women resting on piled heaps of grass, as if taking a siesta, in the remoter part of the meadow, and nearer the village a number of recumbent children, and then nearer at hand three men carrying pails on yokes along a little path that ran from the encircling wall towards the houses. These latter were clad in garments of llama cloth and boots and belts of leather, and they wore caps of cloth with back and ear flaps. They followed one another in single file, walking slowly and yawning as they walked, like men who have been up all night. There was something so reassuringly prosperous and respectable in their bearing that after a moment's hesitation Nunez stood forward as conspicuously as possible upon his rock, and gave vent to a mighty shout that echoed round the valley.

The three men stopped, and moved their heads as though they were looking about them. They turned their faces this way and that, and Nunez gesticulated with freedom. But they did not appear to see him for all his gestures, and after a time, directing themselves towards the mountains far away to the right, they shouted as if in answer. Nunez bawled again, and then once more, and as he gestured ineffectually the word 'blind' came up to the top of his thoughts. 'The fools must be blind,' he said.

When at last, after much shouting and wrath, Nunez crossed the stream by a little bridge, came through a gate in the wall, and approached them, he was sure that they were blind. He was sure that this was the Country of the Blind of which the legends told. Conviction had sprung upon him, and a sense of great and rather enviable adventure. The three stood side by side, not looking at him but with their ears directed towards him, judging him by his unfamiliar steps. They stood close together like men a little afraid, and he could see their eyelids closed and sunken, as though the very balls beneath had shrunk away. There was an expression near awe on their faces.

'A man,' one said, in hardly recognizable Spanish—'a man it is—a man or a spirit—coming down from the rocks.'

But Nunez advanced with the confident steps of a youth who enters upon life. All the old stories of the lost valley and the Country of the

Blind had come back to his mind, and through his thoughts ran this old proverb, as if it were a refrain — —

'In the Country of the Blind the One-eyed Man is King.'

'In the Country of the Blind the One-eyed Man is King.'

And very civilly he gave them greeting. He talked to them and used his eyes.

'Where does he come from, brother Pedro?' asked one.

'Down out of the rocks.'

He found it taxed his nerve and patience more than he had anticipated, that first encounter with the population of the Country of the Blind. The place seemed larger as he drew near to it, and the smeared plasterings queerer, and a crowd of children and men and women (the women and girls, he was pleased to note, had some of them quite sweet faces, for all that their eyes were shut and sunken) came about him, holding on to him, touching him with soft, sensitive hands, smelling at him, and listening at every word he spoke. Some of the maidens and children, however, kept aloof as if afraid, and indeed his voice seemed coarse and rude beside their softer notes. They mobbed him. His three guides kept close to him with an effect of proprietorship, and said again and again, 'A wild man out of the rocks.'

'Over the mountains I come,' said Nunez, 'out of the country beyond there—where men can see. From near Bogota, where there are a hundred thousands of people, and where the city passes out of sight.'

'Sight?' muttered Pedro. 'Sight?'

'He comes', said the second blind man, 'out of the rocks.'

The cloth of their coats Nunez saw was curiously fashioned, each with a different sort of stitching.

They startled him by a simultaneous movement towards him, each with a hand outstretched. He stepped back from the advance of those spread fingers.

'Come hither,' said the third blind man, following his motion and clutching him neatly.

And they held Nunez and felt him over, saying no word further until they had done so.

'Carefully,' he cried, with a finger in his eye, and found they thought that organ, with its fluttering lids, a queer thing in him. They went over it again.

'A strange creature, Correa,' said the one called Pedro. 'Feel the coarseness of his hair. Like a llama's hair.'

'Rough he is as the rocks that begot him,' said Correa investigating Nunez's unshaven chin with a soft and slightly moist hand. 'Perhaps he will grow finer.' Nunez struggled a little under their examination, but they gripped him firm.

'Carefully,' he said again.

'He speaks,' said the third man. 'Certainly he is a man.'

'Ugh!' said Pedro, at the roughness of his coat.

'And you have come into the world?' asked Pedro.

'*Out* of the world. Over mountains and glaciers; right over above there, half-way to the sun. Out of the great big world that goes down, twelve days' journey to the sea.'

They scarcely seemed to heed him. 'Our fathers have told us men may be made by the forces of Nature,' said Correa. 'It is the warmth of things and moisture, and rottenness—rottenness.'

'Let us lead him to the elders,' said Pedro.

'Shout first,' said Correa, 'lest the children be afraid. This is a marvellous occasion.'

So they shouted, and Pedro went first and took Nunez by the hand to lead him to the houses.

He drew his hand away. 'I can see,' he said.

'See?' said Correa.

'Yes, see,' said Nunez turning towards him, and stumbled against Pedro's pail.

'His senses are still imperfect,' said the third blind man. 'He stumbles, and talks unmeaning words. Lead him by the hand.'

'As you will,' said Nunez, and was led along, laughing.

It seemed they knew nothing of sight.

Well, all in good time he would teach them.

He heard people shouting, and saw a number of figures gathering together in the middle roadway of the village.

'Bogota,' he said. 'Bogota. Over the mountain crests.'

'A wild man—using wild words,' said Pedro. 'Did you hear that— *Bogota*? His mind is hardly formed yet. He has only the beginnings of speech.'

A little boy nipped his hand. 'Bogota!' he said mockingly.

'Ay! A city to your village. I come from the great world—where men have eyes and see.'

'His name's Bogota,' they said.

'He stumbled,' said Correa, 'stumbled twice as we came hither.'

'Bring him to the elders.'

And they thrust him suddenly through a doorway into a room as black as pitch, save at the end there faintly glowed a fire. The crowd closed in behind him and shut out all but the faintest glimmer of day, and before he could arrest himself he had fallen headlong over the feet of a seated man. His arm, outflung, struck the face of someone else as he went down; he felt the soft impact of features and heard a cry of anger, and for a moment he struggled against a number of hands that clutched him. It was a one-sided fight. An inkling of the situation came to him, and he lay quiet.

'I fell down,' he said; 'I couldn't see in this pitchy darkness.'

There was a pause as if the unseen persons about him tried to understand his words. Then the voice of Correa said: 'He is but newly formed. He stumbles as he walks and mingles words that mean nothing with his speech.'

Others also said things about him that he heard or understood imperfectly.

'May I sit up?' he asked, in a pause. 'I will not struggle against you again.'

They consulted and let him rise.

The voice of an older man began to question him, and Nunez found himself trying to explain the great world out of which he had fallen, and the sky and mountains and sight and suchlike marvels, to these elders who sat in darkness in the Country of the Blind. And they would believe and understand nothing whatever he told them, a thing quite outside his expectation. They would not even understand many of his words. For fourteen generations these people had been blind and cut off from all the seeing world; the names for all the things of sight had faded and changed; the story of the outer world was faded and changed to a child's story; and they had ceased to concern themselves with anything beyond the rocky slopes above their circling wall. Blind men of genius had arisen among them and questioned the shreds of belief and tradition they had brought with them from their seeing days, and had dismissed all these things as idle fancies, and replaced them with new and saner explanations. Much of their imagination had shrivelled with their eyes, and they had made for themselves new imaginations with their ever more sensitive ears and finger-tips. Slowly Nunez realized this; that his expectation of wonder and reverence at his origin and his gifts was not to be borne out; and after his poor attempt to explain sight to them he had been set aside as the confused version of a new-made being describing the marvels of his incoherent sensations, he subsided, a little dashed, into listening to their instruction. And the eldest of the blind men explained to him life and philosophy and religion, how that the world (meaning their valley) had been first an empty hollow in the rocks, and then had come, first, inanimate things without the gift of touch, and llamas and a few other creatures that had little sense, and then men, and at last angels, whom one could hear singing and making fluttering sounds, but whom no one could touch at all, which puzzled Nunez greatly until he thought of the birds.

He went on to tell Nunez how this time had been divided into the warm and the cold, which are the blind equivalents of day and night, and how it was good to sleep in the warm and work during the cold, so that now, but for his advent, the whole town of the blind would have been asleep. He said Nunez must have been specially created to learn and serve the wisdom they had acquired, and for that all his mental incoherency and stumbling behaviour he must have courage, and do his best to learn, and at that all the people in the doorway murmured encouragingly. He said the night—for the blind call their day night— was now far gone, and it behoved every one to go back to sleep. He asked Nunez if he knew how to sleep, and Nunez said he did, but that before sleep he wanted food.

They brought him food—llama's milk in a bowl, and rough salted bread—and led him into a lonely place to eat out of their hearing, and afterwards to slumber until the chill of the mountain evening roused them to begin their day again. But Nunez slumbered not at all.

Instead, he sat up in the place where they had left him, resting his limbs and turning the unanticipated circumstances of his arrival over and over in his mind.

Every now and then he laughed, sometimes with amusement, and sometimes with indignation.

'Unformed mind!' he said. 'Got no senses yet! They little know they've been insulting their heaven-sent king and master. I see I must bring them to reason. Let me think—let me think.'

He was still thinking when the sun set.

Nunez had an eye for all beautiful things, and it seemed to him that the glow upon the snowfields and glaciers that rose about the valley on every side was the most beautiful he had ever seen. His eyes went from that inaccessible glory to the village and irrigated fields, fast sinking into the twilight, and suddenly a wave of emotion took him, and he thanked God from the bottom of his heart that the power of sight had been given him.

He heard a voice calling to him from out of the village.

'Ya ho there, Bogota! Come hither!'

At that he stood up smiling. He would show these people once and for all what sight would do for man. They would seek him, but not find him.

'You move not, Bogota,' said the voice.

He laughed noiselessly, and made two stealthy steps aside from the path.

'Trample not on the grass, Bogota; that is not allowed.'

Nunez had scarcely heard the sound he made himself. He stopped amazed.

The owner of the voice came running up the piebald path towards him.

He stepped back into the pathway. 'Here I am,' he said.

'Why did you not come when I called you?' said the blind man. 'Must you be led like a child? Cannot you hear the path as you walk?'

Nunez laughed. 'I can see it,' he said.

'There is no such word as *see*,' said the blind man, after a pause. 'Cease this folly, and follow the sound of my feet.'

Nunez followed, a little annoyed.

'My time will come,' he said.

'You'll learn,' the blind man answered. 'There is much to learn in the world.'

'Has no one told you, "In the Country of the Blind the One-eyed Man is King"?'

'What is blind?' asked the blind man carelessly over his shoulder.

Four days passed, and the fifth found the King of the Blind still incognito, as a clumsy and useless stranger among his subjects.

It was, he found, much more difficult to proclaim himself than he had supposed, and in the meantime, while he meditated his *coup d'état*, he did what he was told and learned the manners and customs of the Country of the Blind. He found working and going about at night a particularly irksome thing, and he decided that that should be the first thing he would change.

They led a simple, laborious life, these people, with all the elements of virtue and happiness, as these things can be understood by men. They toiled, but not oppressively; they had food and clothing sufficient for their needs; they had days and seasons of rest; they made much of music and singing, and there was love among them, and little children.

It was marvellous with what confidence and precision they went about their ordered world. Everything, you see, had been made to fit their needs; each of the radiating paths of the valley area had a constant angle to the others, and was distinguished by a special notch upon its kerbing; all obstacles and irregularities of path or meadow had long since been cleared away; all their methods and procedure arose naturally from their special needs. Their senses had become marvellously acute; they could hear and judge the slightest gesture of a man a dozen paces away—could hear the very beating of his heart. Intonation had long replaced expression with them, and touches gesture, and their work with hoe and spade and fork was free and confident as garden work can be. Their sense of smell was extraordinarily fine; they could distinguish individual differences as readily as a dog can, and they went about the tending of the llamas, who lived among the rocks above and came to the wall for food and shelter, with ease and confidence. It was only when at last Nunez sought to assert himself that he found how easy and confident their movements could be.

He rebelled only after he had tried persuasion.

He tried at first on several occasions to tell them of sight. 'Look you here, you people,' he said. 'There are things you do not understand in me.'

Once or twice one or two of them attended to him; they sat with faces downcast and ears turned intelligently towards him, and he did his best to tell them what it was to see. Among his hearers was a girl, with eyelids less red and sunken than the others, so that one could almost fancy she was hiding eyes, whom especially he hoped to persuade. He spoke of the beauties of sight, of watching the mountains, of the sky and the sunrise, and they heard him with amused incredulity that presently became condemnatory. They told him there were indeed no mountains at all, but that the end of the rocks where the llamas grazed was indeed the end of the world; thence sprang a cavernous roof of the universe, from which the dew and the avalanches fell; and when he maintained stoutly the world had neither end nor roof such as they supposed, they said his thoughts were wicked. So far as he could describe sky and clouds and stars to them it seemed to them a hideous void, a terrible blankness in the place of the smooth roof to things in which they believed—it was an article of faith with them that the cavern roof was exquisitely smooth to the touch. He saw that in some manner he shocked them, and gave up that aspect of the matter altogether, and tried to show them the practical value of sight. One morning he saw Pedro in the path called Seventeen and coming towards the central houses, but still too far off for hearing or scent, and he told them as much. 'In a little while,' he prophesied, 'Pedro will be here.' An old man remarked that Pedro had no business on path Seventeen, and then, as if in confirmation, that individual as he drew near turned and went transversely into path Ten, and so back with nimble paces towards the outer wall. They mocked Nunez when Pedro did not arrive, and afterwards, when he asked Pedro questions to clear his character, Pedro denied and outfaced him, and was afterwards hostile to him.

Then he induced them to let them go a long way up the sloping meadows towards the wall with one complacent individual, and to him he promised to describe all that happened among the houses. He noted certain goings and comings, but the things that really seemed to signify to these people happened inside of or behind the windowless houses—the only things they took note of to test him by—and of these he could see or tell nothing; and it was after the failure of this attempt, and the ridicule they could not repress, that he resorted to force. He thought of seizing a spade and suddenly smiting one or two of them to earth, and so in fair combat showing the advantage of eyes. He went so far with that resolution as to seize his spade, and then he discovered a new thing about himself, and that was that it was impossible for him to hit a blind man in cold blood.

He hesitated, and found them all aware that he had snatched up the spade. They stood alert, with their heads on one side, and bent ears towards him for what he would do next.

'Put that spade down,' said one, and he felt a sort of helpless horror. He came near obedience.

Then he thrust one backwards against a house wall, and fled past him and out of the village.

He went athwart one of their meadows, leaving a track of trampled grass behind his feet, and presently sat down by the side of one of their ways. He felt something of the buoyancy that comes to all men in the beginning of a fight, but more perplexity. He began to realize that you cannot even fight happily with creatures who stand upon a different mental basis to yourself. Far away he saw a number of men carrying spades and sticks come out of the street of houses, and advance in a spreading line along the several paths towards him. They advanced slowly, speaking frequently to one another, and ever and again the whole cordon would halt and sniff the air and listen.

The first time they did this Nunez laughed. But afterwards he did not laugh.

One struck his trail in the meadow grass, and came stooping and feeling his way along it.

For five minutes he watched the slow extension of the cordon, and then his vague disposition to do something forthwith became frantic. He stood up, went a pace or so towards the circumferential wall, turned, and went back a little way. There they all stood in a crescent, still and listening.

He also stood still, gripping his spade very tightly in both hands. Should he charge them?

The pulse in his ears ran into the rhythm of 'In the Country of the Blind the One-eyed Man is King!'

Should he charge them?

He looked back at the high and unclimbable wall behind—unclimbable because of its smooth plastering, but withal pierced with many little doors, and at the approaching line of seekers. Behind these, others were now coming out of the street of houses.

Should he charge them?

'Bogota!' called one. 'Bogota! where are you?'

He gripped his spade still tighter, and advanced down the meadows towards the place of habitations, and directly he moved they converged upon him. 'I'll hit them if they touch me,' he swore; 'by Heaven, I will. I'll hit.' He called aloud, 'Look here, I'm going to do what I like in this valley. Do you hear? I'm going to do what I like and go where I like!'

They were moving in upon him quickly, groping, yet moving

rapidly. It was like playing blind man's buff, with everyone blind-folded except one. 'Get hold of him!' cried one. He found himself in the arc of a loose curve of pursuers. He felt suddenly he must be active and resolute.

'You don't understand,' he cried in a voice that was meant to be great and resolute, and which broke. 'You are blind, and I can see. Leave me alone!'

'Bogota! Put down that spade, and come off the grass!'

The last order, grotesque in its urban familiarity, produced a gust of anger.

'I'll hurt you,' he said, sobbing with emotion. 'By Heaven, I'll hurt you. Leave me alone!'

He began to run, not knowing clearly where to run. He ran from the nearest blind man, because it was a horror to hit him. He stopped, and then made a dash to escape from their closing ranks. He made for where a gap was wide, and the men on either side, with a quick perception of the approach of his paces, rushed in on one another. He sprang forward, and then saw he must be caught, and *swish!* the spade had struck. He felt the soft thud of hand and arm, and the man was down with a yell of pain, and he was through.

Through! And then he was close to the street of houses again, and blind men, whirling spades and stakes, were running with a sort of reasoned swiftness hither and thither.

He heard steps behind him just in time, and found a tall man rushing forward and swiping at the sound of him. He lost his nerve, hurled his spade a yard wide at his antagonist, and whirled about and fled, fairly yelling as he dodged another.

He was panic-stricken. He ran furiously to and fro, dodging when there was no need to dodge, and in his anxiety to see on every side of him at once, stumbling. For a moment he was down and they heard his fall. Far away in the circumferential wall a little doorway looked like heaven, and he set off in a wild rush for it. He did not even look round at his pursuers until it was gained, and he had stumbled across the bridge, clambered a little way among the rocks, to the surprise and dismay of a young llama, who went leaping out of sight, and lay down sobbing for breath.

And so his *coup d'état* came to an end.

He stayed outside the wall of the valley of the Blind for two nights and days without food or shelter, and meditated upon the unexpected.

During these meditations he repeated very frequently and always with a profounder note of derision the exploded proverb: 'In the Country of the Blind the One-eyed Man is King.' He thought chiefly of ways of fighting and conquering these people, and it grew clear that for him no practicable way was possible. He had no weapons, and now it would be hard to get one.

The canker of civilization had got to him even in Bogota, and he could not find it in himself to go down and assassinate a blind man. Of course, if he did that, he might then dictate terms on the threat of assassinating them all. But—sooner or later he must sleep! ...

He tried also to find food among the pine trees, to be comfortable under pine boughs while the frost fell at night, and—with less confidence—to catch a llama by artifice in order to try to kill it— perhaps by hammering it with a stone—and so finally, perhaps, to eat some of it. But the llamas had a doubt of him and regarded him with distrustful brown eyes, and spat when he drew near. Fear came on him the second day and fits of shivering. Finally he crawled down to the wall of the Country of the Blind and tried to make terms. He crawled along by the stream, shouting, until two blind men came out to the gate and talked to him.

'I was mad,' he said. 'But I was only newly made.'

They said that was better.

He told them he was wiser now, and repented of all he had done.

Then he wept without intention, for he was very weak and ill now, and they took that as a favourable sign.

They asked him if he still thought he could '*see*'.

'No,' he said. 'That was folly. The word means nothing—less than nothing!'

They asked him what was overhead.

'About ten times ten the height of a man there is a roof above the world—of rock—and very, very smooth.' ... He burst again into hysterical tears. 'Before you ask me any more, give me some food or I shall die.'

He expected dire punishments, but these blind people were capable of toleration. They regarded his rebellion as but one more proof of his general idiocy and inferiority; and after they had whipped him they appointed him to do the simplest and heaviest work they had for anyone to do, and he, seeing no other way of living, did submissively what he was told.

He was ill for some days, and they nursed him kindly. That refined his submission. But they insisted on his lying in the dark, and that was a great misery. And blind philosophers came and talked to him of the wicked levity of his mind, and reproved him so impressively for his doubts about the lid of rock that covered their cosmic casserole that he almost doubted whether indeed he was not the victim of hallucination in not seeing it overhead.

So Nunez became a citizen of the Country of the Blind, and these people ceased to be a generalized people and became individualities and familiar to him, while the world beyond the mountains became more and more remote and unreal. There was Yacob, his master, a kindly man when not annoyed; there was Pedro, Yacob's nephew; and there was Medina-saroté, who was the youngest daughter of Yacob. She was little esteemed in the world of the blind, because she had a clear-cut face, and lacked that satisfying, glossy smoothness that is the blind man's ideal of feminine beauty; but Nunez thought her beautiful at first, and presently the most beautiful thing in the whole creation. Her closed eyelids were not sunken and red after the common way of the valley, but lay as though they might open again at any moment; and she had long eyelashes, which were considered a grave disfigurement. And her voice was strong, and did not satisfy the acute hearing of the valley swains. So that she had no lover.

There came a time when Nunez thought that, could he win her, he would be resigned to live in the valley for all the rest of his days.

He watched her; he sought opportunities of doing her little services, and presently he found that she observed him. Once at a rest-day gathering they sat side by side in the dim starlight, and the music was sweet. His hand came upon hers and he dared to clasp it. Then very tenderly she returned his pressure. And one day, as they were at their meal in the darkness, he felt her hand very softly seeking him, and as it chanced the fire leaped then and he saw the tenderness of her face.

He sought to speak to her.

He went to her one day when she was sitting in the summer moonlight spinning. The light made her a thing of silver and mystery. He sat down at her feet and told her he loved her, and told her how beautiful she seemed to him. He had a lover's voice, he spoke with a tender reverence that came near to awe, and she had never before been touched by adoration. She made him no definite answer, but it was clear his words pleased her.

After that he talked to her whenever he could take an opportunity. The valley became the world for him, and the world beyond the mountains where men lived in sunlight seemed no more than a fairy tale he would some day pour into her ears. Very tentatively and timidly he spoke to her of sight.

Sight seemed to her the most poetical of fancies, and she listened to his description of the stars and the mountains and her own sweet white-lit beauty as though it was a guilty indulgence. She did not believe, she could only half understand, but she was mysteriously delighted, and it seemed to him that she completely understood.

His love lost its awe and took courage. Presently he was for demanding her of Yacob and the elders in marriage, but she became fearful and delayed. And it was one of her elder sisters who first told Yacob that Medina-saroté and Nunez were in love.

There was from the first very great opposition to the marriage of Nunez and Medina-saroté; not so much because they valued her as because they held him as being apart, an idiot, incompetent thing below the permissible level of a man. Her sisters opposed it bitterly as bringing discredit on them all; and old Yacob, though he had formed a sort of liking for his clumsy, obedient serf, shook his head and said the thing could not be. The young men were all angry at the idea of corrupting the race, and one went so far as to revile and strike Nunez. He struck back. Then for the first time he found an advantage in seeing, even by twilight, and after that fight was over no one was disposed to raise a hand against him. But they still found his marriage impossible.

Old Yacob had a tenderness for his last little daughter, and was grieved to have her weep upon his shoulder.

'You see, my dear, he's an idiot. He has delusions; he can't do anything right.'

'I know,' wept Medina-saroté. 'But he's better than he was. He's getting better. And he's strong, dear father, and kind—stronger and kinder than any other man in the world. And he loves me—and, father I love him.'

Old Yacob was greatly distressed to find her inconsolable, and besides—what made it more distressing—he liked Nunez for many things. So he went and sat in the windowless council-chamber with the other elders and watched the trend of the talk, and said at the proper time, 'He's better than he was. Very likely, some day, we shall find him as sane as ourselves.'

Then afterwards one of the elders, who thought deeply, had an idea. He was the great doctor among these people, their medicine-man, and he had a very philosophical and inventive mind, and the idea of curing Nunez of his peculiarities appealed to him. One day when Yacob was present he returned to the topic of Nunez.

'I have examined Bogota,' he said, 'and the case is clearer to me. I think very probably he might be cured.

'That is what I have always hoped,' said old Yacob.

'His brain is affected,' said the blind doctor.

The elders murmured assent.

'Now, *what* affects it?'

'Ah!' said old Yacob.

'*This*,' said the doctor, answering his own question. 'Those queer things that are called the eyes, and which exist to make an agreeable soft depression in the face, are diseased, in the case of Bogota, in such a way as to affect his brain. They are greatly distended, he has eyelashes, and his eyelids move, and consequently his brain is in a state of constant irritation and distraction.'

'Yes?' said old Yacob. 'Yes?'

'And I think I may say with reasonable certainty that, in order to cure him completely, all that we need do is a simple and easy surgical operation—namely to remove these irritant bodies.'

'And then he will be sane?'

'Then he will be perfectly sane, and a quite admirable citizen.'

'Thank Heaven for science!' said old Yacob, and went forth at once to tell Nunez of his happy hopes.

But Nunez's manner of receiving the good news struck him as being cold and disappointing.

'One might think,' he said, 'from the tone you take, that you did not care for my daughter.'

It was Medina-saroté who persuaded Nunez to face the blind surgeons.

'*You* do not want me', he said, 'to lose my gift of sight?'

She shook her head.

'My world is sight.'

Her head drooped lower.

'There are the beautiful things, the beautiful little things—the flowers, the lichens among the rocks, the lightness and softness on a piece of fur, the far sky with its drifting down of clouds, the sunsets and the stars. And there is *you*. For you alone it is good to have sight, to see your sweet, serene face, your kindly lips, your dear, beautiful hands folded together. . . . It is these eyes of mine you won, these eyes that hold me to you, that these idiots seek. Instead, I must touch you, hear you, and never see you again. I must come under that roof of rock and stone and darkness, that horrible roof under which your imagination stoops . . . No; you would not have me do that?'

A disagreeable doubt had arisen in him. He stopped, and left the thing a question.

'I wish', she said, 'sometimes—' She paused.

'Yes,' said he, a little apprehensively.

'I wish sometimes—you would not talk like that.'

'Like what?'

'I know it's pretty—it's your imagination. I love it, but *now*—'

He felt cold. '*Now?*' he said faintly.

She sat quite still.

'You mean—you think—I should be better, better perhaps—'

He was realizing things very swiftly. He felt anger, indeed, anger at the dull course of fate, but also sympathy for her lack of understanding—a sympathy near akin to pity.

'*Dear*,' he said, and he could see by her whiteness how intensely her spirit pressed against the things she could not say. He put his arms about her, he kissed her ear, and they sat for a time in silence.

'If I were to consent to this?' he said at last, in a voice that was very gentle.

She flung her arms about him, weeping wildly. 'Oh, if you would,' she sobbed, 'if only you would!'

For a week before the operation that was to raise him from his servitude and inferiority to the level of a blind citizen, Nunez knew nothing of sleep, and all through the warm sunlit hours, while the others slumbered happily, he sat brooding or wandered aimlessly, trying to bring his mind to bear on his dilemma. He had given his answer, he had given his consent, and still he was not sure. And at last work-time was over, the sun rose in splendour over the golden crests, and his last day of vision began for him. He had a few minutes with Medina-sarote before she went apart to sleep.

'To-morrow,' he said, 'I shall see no more.'

'Dear heart!' she answered, and pressed his hands with all her strength.

'They will hurt you but little,' she said; 'and you are going through this pain—you are going through it, dear lover, for *me*. . . . Dear, if a woman's heart and life can do it, I will repay you. My dearest one, my dearest with the tender voice, I will repay.'

He was drenched in pity for himself and her.

He held her in his arms, and pressed his lips to hers, and looked on her sweet face for the last time.

'Good-bye!' he whispered at that dear sight, 'good-bye!'

And then in silence he turned away from her.

She could hear his slow retreating footsteps, and something in the rhythm of them threw her into a passion of weeping.

He had fully meant to go to a lonely place where the meadows were beautiful with white narcissus, and there remain until the hour of his sacrifice should come, but as he went he lifted up his eyes and saw the morning, the morning like an angel in golden armour, marching down the steeps. . . .

It seemed to him that before this splendour he, and this blind world in the valley, and his love, and all, were no more than a pit of sin.

He did not turn aside as he had meant to do, but went on, and passed through the wall of the circumference and out upon the rocks, and his eyes were always upon the sunlit ice and snow.

He saw their infinite beauty, and his imagination soared over them to the things beyond he was now to resign for ever.

He thought of that great free world he was parted from, the world that was his own, and he had a vision of those further slopes, distance beyond distance, with Bogota, a place of multitudinous stirring beauty, a glory by day, a luminous mystery by night, a place of palaces and fountains and statues and white houses, lying beautifully in the middle distance. He thought how for a day or so one might come down through passes, drawing ever nearer and nearer to its busy streets and ways. He thought of the river journey, day by day, from great Bogota to the still vaster world beyond, through towns and villages, forest and desert places, the rushing river day by day, until its banks receded and the big steamers came splashing by, and one had reached the sea—the limitless sea, with its thousand islands, its thousands of islands, and its ships seen dimly far away in their incessant journeyings round and about that greater world. And there, unpent by mountains, one saw the sky—the sky, not such a disc as one saw it here, but an arch of immeasurable blue, a deep of deeps in which the circling stars were floating. . . .

His eyes scrutinized the great curtain of the mountains with a keener inquiry.

For example, if one went so, up that gully and to that chimney there, then one might come out high among those stunted pines that ran round in a sort of shelf and rose still higher and higher as it passed above the gorge. And then? That talus might be managed. Thence perhaps a climb might be found to take him up to the precipice that came below the snow; and if that chimney failed, then another farther to the east might serve his purpose better. And then? Then one would be out upon the amber-lit snow there, and half-way up to the crest of those beautiful desolations.

He glanced back at the village, then turned right round and regarded it steadfastly.

He thought of Medina-saroté, and she had become small and remote.

He turned again towards the mountain wall, down which the day had come to him.

Then circumspectly he began to climb.

When sunset came he was no longer climbing, but he was far and high. He had been higher, but he was still very high. His clothes were torn, his limbs were blood-stained, he was bruised in many places, but he lay as if he were at his ease, and there was a smile on his face.

From where he rested the valley seemed as if it were in a pit and nearly a mile below. Already it was dim with haze and shadow, though the mountain summits around him were things of light and fire. The mountain summits around him were things of light and fire, and the little details of the rocks near at hand were drenched with subtle beauty—a vein of green mineral piercing the grey, the flash of crystal faces here and there, a minute, minutely beautiful orange lichen close beside his face. There were deep mysterious shadows in the gorge, blue deepening into purple, and purple into a luminous darkness, and overhead was the illimitable vastness of the sky. But he heeded these things no longer, but lay quite inactive there, smiling as if he were satisfied merely to have escaped from the valley of the Blind in which he had thought to be King.

The glow of the sunset passed, and the night came, and still he lay peacefully contented under the cold stars.

LIONEL JOHNSON

Mystic and Cavalier

Go from me: I am one of those, who fall.
What! hath no cold wind swept your heart at all,
In my sad company? Before the end,
    Go from me, dear my friend!

Yours are the victories of light: your feet
Rest from good toil, where rest is brave and sweet.
But after warfare in a mourning gloom,
    I rest in clouds of doom.

Have you not read so, looking in these eyes?
Is it the common light of the pure skies,   10
Lights up their shadowy depths? The end is set:
    Though the end be not yet.

When gracious music stirs, and all is bright,
And beauty triumphs through a courtly night;
When I too joy, a man like other men:
    Yet, am I like them, then?

And in the battle, when the horsemen sweep
Against a thousand deaths, and fall on sleep:
Who ever sought that sudden calm, if I
    Sought not? Yet, could not die.   20

Seek with thine eyes to pierce this crystal sphere:
Canst read a fate there, prosperous and clear?
Only the mists, only the weeping clouds:
　　Dimness, and airy shrouds.

Beneath, what angels are at work? What powers
Prepare the secret of the fatal hours?
See! the mists tremble, and the clouds are stirred:
　　When comes the calling word?

The clouds are breaking from the crystal ball,
Breaking and clearing: and I look to fall.   30
When the cold winds and airs of portent sweep,
　　My spirit may have sleep.

O rich and sounding voices of the air!
Interpreters and prophets of despair:
Priests of a fearful sacrament! I come,
　　To make with you mine home.

The Dark Angel

Dark Angel, with thine aching lust
To rid the world of penitence:
Malicious Angel, who still dost
My soul such subtile violence!

Because of thee, no thought, no thing
Abides for me undesecrate:
Dark Angel, ever on the wing,
Who never reachest me too late!

When music sounds, then changest thou
Its silvery to a sultry fire: 10
Nor will thine envious heart allow
Delight untortured by desire.

Through thee, the gracious Muses turn
To Furies, O mine Enemy!°
And all the things of beauty burn
With flames of evil ecstasy.

Because of thee, the land of dreams
Becomes a gathering place of fears:
Until tormented slumber seems
One vehemence of useless tears.   20

When sunlight glows upon the flowers,
Or ripples down the dancing sea:
Thou, with thy troop of passionate powers,
Beleaguerest, bewilderest, me.

Within the breath of autumn woods,
Within the winter silences:
Thy venomous spirit stirs and broods,
O Master of impieties!

The ardour of red flame is thine,
And thine the steely soul of ice: 30
Thou poisonest the fair design
Of nature, with unfair device.

Apples of ashes, golden bright;°
Waters of bitterness, how sweet!
O banquet of a foul delight,
Prepared by thee, dark Paraclete!°

Thou art the whisper in the gloom,
The hinting tone, the haunting laugh:
Thou art the adorner of my tomb,
The minstrel of mine epitaph.   40

I fight thee, in the Holy Name!
Yet, what thou dost, is what God saith:
Tempter! should I escape thy flame,
Thou wilt have helped my soul from Death:

The second Death, that never dies,°
That cannot die, when time is dead:
Live Death, wherein the lost soul cries,
Eternally uncomforted.

Dark Angel, with thine aching lust!
Of two defeats, of two despairs: 50
Less dread, a change to drifting dust,
Than thine eternity of cares.

Do what thou wilt, thou shalt not so,
Dark Angel! triumph over me:
Lonely, unto the Lone I go;°
Divine, to the Divinity.

By the Statue of King Charles at Charing Cross°

Sombre and rich, the skies;
Great glooms, and starry plains.
Gently the night wind sighs;
Else a vast silence reigns.

The splendid silence clings
Around me: and around
The saddest of all kings
Crowned and again discrowned.

Comely and calm, he rides
Hard by his own Whitehall:°   10
Only the night wind glides:
No crowds, nor rebels, brawl.

Gone, too, his Court: and yet,
The stars his courtiers are:
Stars in their stations set;
And every wandering star.

Alone he rides, alone,
The fair and fatal king:
Dark night is all his own,
That strange and solemn thing.   20

Which are more full of fate:
The stars; or those sad eyes?
Which are more still and great:
Those brows; or the dark skies?

Although his whole heart yearn
In passionate tragedy:
Never was face so stern
With sweet austerity.

Vanquished in life, his death
By beauty made amends: 30
The passing of his breath°
Won his defeated ends.

Brief life, and hapless? Nay:
Through death, life grew sublime.
Speak after sentence? Yea:°
And to the end of time.

Armoured he rides, his head
Bare to the stars of doom:
He triumphs now, the dead,
Beholding London's gloom.   40

Our wearier spirit faints,
Vexed in the world's employ:
His soul was of the saints;
And art to him was joy.°

King, tried in fires of woe!
Men hunger for thy grace:
And through the night I go,
Loving thy mournful face.

Yet, when the city sleeps;
When all the cries are still:
The stars and heavenly deeps
Work out a perfect will.

'*Ah! fair face gone from sight*'

Ah! fair face gone from sight,
    With all its light
Of eyes, that pierced the deep
    Of human night!
Ah! fair face calm in sleep.

Ah! fair lips hushed in death!
    Now their glad breath
Breathes not upon our air
    Music, that saith
Love only, and things fair.

Ah! lost brother! Ah! sweet
    Still hands and feet!
May those feet haste to reach,
    Those hands to greet,
Us, where love needs no speech.

A Decadent's Lyric°

Sometimes, in very joy of shame,
Our flesh becomes one living flame:
And she and I
Are no more separate, but the same.

Ardour and agony unite;
Desire, delirium, delight:
And I and she
Faint in the fierce and fevered night.

Her body music is: and ah,
The accords of lute and viola,   10
When she and I
Play on live limbs love's opera!

ERNEST DOWSON

Non Sum Qualis Eram Bonae Sub Regno Cynarae°

Last night, ah, yesternight, betwixt her lips and mine
There fell thy shadow, Cynara! thy breath was shed
Upon my soul between the kisses and the wine;
And I was desolate and sick of an old passion,
    Yea, I was desolate and bowed my head:
I have been faithful to thee, Cynara! in my fashion.

All night upon mine heart I felt her warm heart beat,
Night-long within mine arms in love and sleep she lay;
Surely the kisses of her bought red mouth were sweet;
But I was desolate and sick of an old passion,   10
    When I awoke and found the dawn was gray:
I have been faithful to thee, Cynara! in my fashion.

I have forgot much, Cynara! gone with the wind,
Flung roses, roses riotously with the throng,
Dancing, to put thy pale, lost lilies out of mind;
But I was desolate and sick of an old passion,
    Yea, all the time, because the dance was long:
I have been faithful to thee, Cynara! in my fashion.

I cried for madder music and for stronger wine,
But when the feast is finished and the lamps expire,   20
Then falls thy shadow, Cynara! the night is thine;
And I am desolate and sick of an old passion,
    Yea, hungry for the lips of my desire:
I have been faithful to thee, Cynara! in my fashion.

Nuns of the Perpetual Adoration°

Calm, sad, secure; behind high convent walls,
    These watch the sacred lamp, these watch and pray:
And it is one with them when evening falls,
    And one with them the cold return of day.

These heed not time; their nights and days they make
    Into a long, returning rosary,
Whereon their lives are threaded for Christ's sake:
    Meekness and vigilance and chastity.

A vowed patrol, in silent companies,
    Life-long they keep before the living Christ: 10
In the dim church, their prayers and penances
    Are fragrant incense to the Sacrificed.

Outside, the world is wild and passionate;
    Man's weary laughter and his sick despair
Entreat at their impenetrable gate:
    They heed no voices in their dream of prayer.

They saw the glory of the world displayed;
    They saw the bitter of it, and the sweet;
They knew the roses of the world should fade,
    And be trod under by the hurrying feet.   20

Therefore they rather put away desire,
    And crossed their hands and came to sanctuary;
And veiled their heads and put on coarse attire:
    Because their comeliness was vanity.

And there they rest; they have serene insight
    Of the illuminating dawn to be:
Mary's sweet Star dispels for them the night,
    The proper darkness of humanity.°

Calm, sad, secure; with faces worn and mild:
    Surely their choice of vigil is the best?   30
Yea! for our roses fade, the world is wild;
    But there, beside the altar, there, is rest.

Extreme Unction°

Upon the eyes, the lips, the feet,
  On all the passages of sense,
The atoning oil is spread with sweet
  Renewal of lost innocence.

The feet, that lately ran so fast
  To meet desire, are soothly sealed;
The eyes, that were so often cast
  On vanity, are touched and healed.

From troublous sights and sounds set free;
  In such a twilight hour of breath   10
Shall one retrace his life, or see,
  Through shadows, the true face of death?

Vials of mercy! Sacring oils!
  I know not where nor when I come,
Nor through what wanderings and toils,
  To crave of you Viaticum.°

Yet, when the walls of flesh grow weak,
  In such an hour, it well may be,
Through mist and darkness, light will break,
  And each anointed sense will see.   20

To One in Bedlam°

With delicate, mad hands, behind his sordid bars,
Surely he hath his posies, which they tear and twine;
Those scentless wisps of straw, that miserably line
His strait, caged universe, whereat the dull world stares,

Pedant and pitiful. O, how his rapt gaze wars
With their stupidity! Know they what dreams divine
Lift his long, laughing reveries like enchaunted wine,
And make his melancholy germane to the stars'?

O lamentable brother! if those pity thee,
Am I not fain of all thy lone eyes promise me;   10
Half a fool's kingdom, far from men who sow and reap,
All their days, vanity? Better than mortal flowers,
Thy moon-kissed roses seem: better than love or sleep,
The star-crowned solitude of thine oblivious hours!

Flos Lunae°

I would not alter thy cold eyes,
Nor trouble the calm fount of speech
With aught of passion or surprise.
The heart of thee I cannot reach:
I would not alter thy cold eyes!

I would not alter thy cold eyes;
Nor have thee smile, nor make thee weep:
Though all my life droops down and dies,
Desiring thee, desiring sleep,
I would not alter thy cold eyes.   10

I would not alter thy cold eyes;
I would not change thee if I might,
To whom my prayers for incense rise,
Daughter of dreams! my moon of night!
I would not alter thy cold eyes.

I would not alter thy cold eyes,
With trouble of the human heart:
Within their glance my spirit lies,
A frozen thing, alone, apart;
I would not alter thy cold eyes.   20

Epigram

Because I am idolatrous and have besought,
With grievous supplication and consuming prayer,
The admirable image that my dreams have wrought°
Out of her swan's neck and her dark, abundant hair:
The jealous gods, who brook no worship save their own,
Turned my live idol marble and her heart to stone.

GEORGE WILLIAM RUSSELL — 'A. E.'

Continuity

No sign is made while empires pass.
The flowers and stars are still His care,
The constellations hid in grass,
The golden miracles in air.

Life in an instant will be rent
Where death is glittering blind and wild —
The Heavenly Brooding is intent
To that last instant on Its child.

It breathes the glow in brain and heart,
Life is made magical. Until   10
Body and spirit are apart
The Everlasting works Its will.

In that wild orchid that your feet
In their next falling shall destroy,
Minute and passionate and sweet
The Mighty Master holds His joy.

Though the crushed jewels droop and fade
The Artist's labours will not cease,
And of the ruins shall be made
Some yet more lovely masterpiece.   20

Germinal°

Call not thy wanderer home as yet
   Though it be late.
Now is his first assailing of
   The invisible gate.
Be still through that light knocking. The hour
   Is thronged with fate.

To that first tapping at the invisible door
   Fate answereth.
What shining image or voice, what sigh
   Or honied breath,   10
Comes forth, shall be the master of life
   Even to death.

Satyrs may follow after. Seraphs
   On crystal wing
May blaze. But the delicate first comer
   It shall be King.
They shall obey, even the mightiest,
   That gentle thing.

All the strong powers of Dante were bowed
   To a child's mild eyes,   20
That wrought within him that travail
   From depths up to skies,
Inferno, Purgatorio
   And Paradise.

Amid the soul's grave councillors
   A petulant boy
Laughs under the laurels and purples, the elf
   Who snatched at his joy,
Ordering Cæsar's legions to bring him
   The world for his toy.   30

In ancient shadows and twilights
   Where childhood had strayed,
The world's great sorrows were born
   And its heroes were made.
In the lost boyhood of Judas
   Christ was betrayed.

Let thy young wanderer dream on:
   Call him not home.
A door opens, a breath, a voice
   From the ancient room,   40
Speaks to him now. Be it dark or bright
   He is knit with his doom.

CHARLOTTE MEW

The Changeling

Toll no bell for me, dear Father, dear Mother,
   Waste no sighs;
There are my sisters, there is my little brother
   Who plays in the place called Paradise,
Your children all, your children for ever;
   But I, so wild,
Your disgrace, with the queer brown face, was never,
   Never, I know, but half your child!

In the garden at play, all day, last summer,
   Far and away I heard   10
The sweet 'tweet-tweet' of a strange new-comer,
   The dearest, clearest call of a bird.
It lived down there in the deep green hollow,
   My own old home, and the fairies say
The word of a bird is a thing to follow,
   So I was away a night and a day.

One evening, too, by the nursery fire,
  We snuggled close and sat round so still,
When suddenly as the wind blew higher,
  Something scratched on the window-sill.   20
A pinched brown face peered in—I shivered;
  No one listened or seemed to see;
The arms of it waved and the wings of it quivered,
  Whoo—I knew it had come for me;
  Some are as bad as bad can be!
All night long they danced in the rain,
Round and round in a dripping chain,
Threw their caps at the window-pane,
  Tried to make me scream and shout
  And fling the bedclothes all about: 30
I meant to stay in bed that night,
And if only you had left a light
  They would never have got me out.

  Sometimes I wouldn't speak, you see,
  Or answer when you spoke to me,
Because in the long, still dusks of Spring
You can hear the whole world whispering:
  The shy green grasses making love,
  The feathers grow on the dear, grey dove,
  The tiny heart of the redstart beat,   40
  The patter of the squirrel's feet,
The pebbles pushing in the silver streams,
The rushes talking in their dreams,
  The swish-swish of the bat's black wings,
  The wild-wood bluebell's sweet ting-tings,
  Humming and hammering at your ear,
    Everything there is to hear
In the heart of hidden things,
  But not in the midst of the nursery riot,
  That's why I wanted to be quiet,   50
    Couldn't do my sums, or sing,
    Or settle down to anything.
  And when, for that, I was sent upstairs
  I *did* kneel down to say my prayers;

But the King who sits on your high church steeple
Has nothing to do with us fairy people!

'Times I pleased you, dear Father, dear Mother,
    Learned all my lessons and liked to play,
And dearly I loved the little pale brother
    Whom some other bird must have called away.   60
Why did They bring me here to make me
    Not quite bad and not quite good,
Why, unless They're wicked, do They want, in spite, to take me
    Back to their wet, wild wood?
Now, every night I shall see the windows shining,
    The gold lamp's glow, and the fire's red gleam,
While the best of us are twining twigs and the rest of us are whining
      In the hollow by the stream.
Black and chill are Their nights on the wold;
    And They live so long and They feel no pain: 70
I shall grow up, but never grow old,
I shall always, always be very cold,
    I shall never come back again!

In Nunhead Cemetery°

It is the clay that makes the earth stick to his spade;
    He fills in holes like this year after year;
The others have gone; they were tired, and half afraid,
    But I would rather be standing here;

There is nowhere else to go. I have seen this place
    From the windows of the train that's going past
Against the sky. This rain on my face—
    It was raining here when I saw it last.

There is something horrible about a flower;
    This, broken in my hand, is one of those   10
He threw in just now: it will not live another hour;
    There are thousands more: you do not miss a rose.

One of the children hanging about
  Pointed at the whole dreadful heap and smiled
This morning, after THAT was carried out;
  There is something terrible about a child.

We were like children, last week, in the Strand;
  That was the day you laughed at me
Because I tried to make you understand
  The cheap, stale chap I used to be   20
  Before I saw the things you made me see.

This is not a real place; perhaps by-and-by
  I shall wake—I am getting drenched with all this rain:
To-morrow I will tell you about the eyes of the Crystal Palace train
  Looking down on us, and you will laugh and I shall see what you
  see again.

  Not here, not now. We said 'Not yet
  Across our low stone parapet
Will the quick shadows of the sparrows fall'.

A. C. MIALL

The Boudoir

FROM THE FRENCH OF PAUL VERLAINE°

The piano that a slender hand has kissed
Shines rose and grey in the grey evening mist;
While, with light murmurs as of wings that beat,
An ancient tender melody and sweet
Treads hushed, an almost timid wanderer,
Through the boudoir long odorous of Her.

Ah, what is this that as a cradle now
Lulls my poor heart?—how tenderly and slow!
What would you with me, dainty song? and, ah!
What would you, hesitating sweet refrain,   10
So quickly by the window dead again,
The window on the garden just ajar?

The Shepherd's Hour

FROM THE FRENCH OF PAUL VERLAINE°

Low lies the moon red in the smoky sky,
And in a dancing mist the meadow-land
Lies asleep, veiled; a frog croaks near at hand,
'Mid green reeds where a shiver rustles by.

The water-lilies close their crowns in sleep;
Far distant poplars, straight and closely bound,
Profile uncertain shadows; on the ground
Towards the thickets now the glow-worms creep.

The screech-owls wake and pass in silent flight,
With heavy soft wings fanning the dark air;   10
The zenith fills with glimmerings, faintly clear.
Venus emerges, pale, and it is Night.

HUBERT CRACKANTHORPE

The Struggle for Life

It was a chilly October night in a notorious 'den' beyond the water—
since closed by the police.

Half a dozen gross gas-jets lit up the long, low room, making a
procession of queer-shaped shadows dance restlessly about the walls:
here and there, dotted about, crudely coloured chromos of the Queen,
the Prince of Wales, and one or two half-naked prize-fighters.

It was a Saturday night, so the place was quite full—bargemen with
grimy furrows across their bronzed faces; plenty of typical river
casuals sucking stumpy clay-pipes; in a corner a group of pasty-faced
youths quarrelling over their greasy cards; and scattered about the
room some riverside prostitutes, their cheap finery all bedraggled with
mud. A veritable Babel rose from these dregs of a population—hoarse
laughter, snatches of songs and oaths.

It was hot, a foul, unhealthy heat; the very walls were sweating, and
a bluish haze was filling the room up to the blackened ceiling.

I was vainly looking about me for a seat, when a mason, whose corduroys were still white with lime, pulled my arm and motioned me to a place next him, at the same time lifting the woman who was occupying it on to his knees.

Then he began again to beat the table, with an empty pewter-pot, to the refrain of a popular song. At intervals he would stop, grin across at me, and hug his companion.

She, too, was young: perhaps she had been striking-looking once; at least her eyes were still fine, but the lips were shapeless, the voice was hoarse and overpitched, and the complexion was muddy-coloured. I was watching this typical couple, when suddenly I heard a plaintive voice behind me.

A girl stood there, death-white, with dark rings round her eyes. The corners of her bloodless lips were quivering, as though she were in great pain.

'Jack,' murmured the plaintive voice, 'ain't yer comin' back?'

The mason looked across at her with drunken solemnity, shrugged his shoulders, and put his arms round the woman on his knees.

In one flash the eyes of the two women met; of a sudden the whole expression of the young girl's face changed. Like wild beasts, they glared at each other: the one, with all the exasperated fury of interrupted appetite; the other, with the instinctive desperate hatred of a mother defending her young.

She clutched at a pewter-pot as if to fling it in her rival's face, but the impulse passed away, and letting it fall listlessly, she turned again to the mason and said in the same plaintive voice:

'Jack, come along, do.'

' 'Ee knows when 'ee's well off, my dear,' said the prostitute, pursing up her heavy lips and offering them to her companion.

'At least give us some money,' went on the other, 'the kids ain't touched a bit since morning, and I've nothing.'

The mason, by this time exasperated, burst out, bringing his fist down on the table:

'Go to hell!'

'But baby'll die, if she don't get something,' persisted the girl.

A hoarse laugh from the prostitute was all the reply.

This little scene was beginning to attract the attention of the occupants of the surrounding tables—the gambling group in the corner threw down their cards at the prospect of a fight; two women opposite began to jeer.

Whiter than ever, the girl stood there, braving them all; then dropping her head, she ran out of the room like a hunted animal. I had already left my seat and was watching the scene from the doorway. When the girl passed out, I followed her, curious to see the end of it.

She hurried along, through the ill-lit streets till she came to the river.

It was a starless night, but the full moon had just risen from behind the thin, headless necks of a cluster of chimneys which stood out black against the lurid glow reflected by the lights of the city; across the river lay a ragged pathway of quivering, silver light.

There was an uncanny stillness about the spot. The water flowed sluggishly, stealthily by; not a sign of life on board the black hulks moored to the banks, only from the distance came the feverish rumble of the great city.

A cab was crawling up, its yellow lamps gleaming like the round eyes of some great night beetle; nearer, at the street corner, a policeman and a woman stood talking. The girl, crossing the road, made straight for the river; and the policeman turned to follow her. She stopped when she came to the edge, for she saw the policeman was close behind her; leaning against the parapet she stared down at the water, her head between her hands.

I passed close by her. The moonlight made her pinched face seem whiter than ever, the tears were dripping on to the pavement. I sat down on a bench a few yards off and waited.

Presently, the small, black figure of a man came slinking along under the wall. When he saw the girl leaning over the parapet, he stopped and went slowly up to her.

He passed behind her, turned, and passed again. She had not stirred. He was now standing by her side, examining her from head to foot, cynically, as a horse-dealer examines a horse. Presently he put his hand on her arm and spoke to her.

I could not hear what they were saying; but I saw the girl shake her head several times, while the other seemed to be speaking very fast.

After a while, they moved away together, and as they passed in front of the bench where I was sitting I heard her saying in a broken voice:

'Half a crown then, and I can go home in an hour.'

Dissolving View

In a low, roomy armchair, puffing gently at a long-stemmed pipe, Vivian Marston was listening to the wail of the wind as it swept fitfully down the street, complacently pitying the wretches who, cut by its blast, were shivering outside, this bleak November evening. Slowly his eyes travelled round the luxuriously furnished room, every detail of which reminded him of his own cosiness, and he became conscious of a vague glow of internal satisfaction. Resting his feet on the fender-bar, he began to think of himself.

Leisurely he recapitulated all that conduced to his self-satisfaction. His silky hair, which one woman had liked to stroke; his large, grey eyes, 'expressive', another had called them; his money, it pleased him to remember that he was rich, richer even than most rich people; next, how his new hunter, thanks to the excellent line he had taken, had shown the whole field the way on Saturday, and how, last week, he had crumpled up pheasant after pheasant in a tearing wind, when the others couldn't touch them; last, of Gwynnie, the biggest triumph of all, Gwynnie, his Gwynnie, whom he was going to marry in the spring. And before him defiled, in a grotesque procession, all the men who wanted to marry her; each one, as he passed, looking up in jealous admiration.

From Gwynnie, his thoughts wandered to the others to whom he had made love before her. And a gentle, sentimental melancholy, which was delicious, stole over him. The images of most of them were blurred, half-effaced by time; one alone remained clear-cut. Many weeks it was since he had thought of her, for there was nothing in his life now to remind him of her. She was only a little chorus-girl, yellow-eyed and freckled, with a cracked voice that grated on the ear. He wondered, looking back over it all, what had been the link between them. Perhaps her splendid masses of hair, dark chestnut shot with gold; perhaps her quaint, clinging winsomeness. Towards the end she had grown capricious and fretful, and he had tired considerably of her; but that he did not remember. Only he heard once again the small imperfect voice raised in anger, as they stood together the last evening in the narrow, theatre corridor, with the single gas jet flaring behind. The next day she was gone, with a Frenchman who played third fiddle in the orchestra, so they said. And Vivian, the first moment of pique

over, forgot her. With curious ease she dropped out of his life. At the
end of a week the gap she had left was scarce perceptible. All that
happened ten months ago.

He unlocked a drawer in the writing-table, and took from it a packet
of letters—ten or perhaps a dozen in all, and three of them much
longer than the rest. These last she had written in the autumn when he
was away in the Mediterranean yachting. One after the other he read
them, and, as he did so, a curious uncomfortable feeling crept over
him. The vision of the thick, rich hair, encircling the yellow eyes, and
little freckled face, seemed to change, charged with new meaning.
Between the lines he began to read all that the mis-spelt scrawlings on
these cheap, shiny half-sheets of note-paper had meant for her. He
remembered how their illegibility had used to amuse him, and he was
puzzled that he had not understood them then as he did now. There
was one, worse written than the others, full of reproaches, that she had
not seen him for three days. After that he read no more, but
impatiently threw the packet into the blazing grate.

He lit another pipe, and for some little time more sat on exasperated, trying to force his thoughts into another channel.

96 Paxton Street, W.C.
Sunday

Dear Viv,
i am very ill the Dr says i shall get better but it is not true. i have got
a little boy he was born last tusday you are his farther so you will see to him
when i am ded will you not dear Viv. Louis is gone to Parris he was mad
because of the child. Viv dear for the sake of old times com and see me gest
once it is not a grand place were i am but I do long to see your dear face again.
Plese Viv forgiv me for going of with Louis but i thought you did not care for
me anny more and it made me mad i am sending this to the old adress i hope
you will get it alright.
Your loving
Kit.

Motionless, he was staring at the sheet of paper in his hand. He could
not think; stunned, his brain refused to function. Thus a whole
minute passed. At last, mechanically, he picked up the envelope which
was lying on the breakfast-table. He turned it over, absently at first,
but, with returning consciousness, he noticed that there were two

addresses on it; it must have been forwarded from his old lodgings, and, looking closer, he saw that one of the postmarks was nearly a month old. Once more he read the letter through, then again, and then a third time. Gradually a dizzy faintness and a sickening feeling in his stomach came over him. The air seemed close and stifling, but he had not the strength to cross the room to open the window. He sat down feebly by the fire, and, as he did so, he became aware that his hands were clammy with perspiration.

A moment or two and it passed. His thoughts were liberated; he was able to think again.

Kit was dying; by this time perhaps dead. Kit dead—stiff and cold between white sheets, lying flat all but her feet, which, upright, projected at the foot of the bed, her face expressionless, the freckles yellower than ever against the death-pale skin. And the child? He felt a thrill of exasperation against the useless, unwanted child. But it was his child—then it was he who— —

Suddenly the door opened. He started, every nerve in his body tingling. It was the servant bringing in his breakfast. The man set down the shining covers and steaming coffee-urn, while Vivian, half-dazed, watched him curiously, for there seemed something strangely unreal about his unconcernedness.

At last he moved towards the door.

'Get me a cab,' said Vivian, huskily. Then perceiving the astonished look on the man's face he added hurriedly:

'I have to go out—at once—important business.'

As the hansom rolled along, Vivian's thoughts rushed back over the past. Incident after incident crowded up in his memory, and this hideous sequel to his love for Kit gave to each a new, ugly significance. It was the culmination towards which all the rest pointed. The cab shot past an omnibus lumbering city-ward, and he found himself marvelling at the difference between the people seated inside it and him. Surely they had never had things like this in their lives. And his thoughts writhed under the increasing pain—then, a quick twinge of hunger, reminding him that he had had no breakfast. Back came the object of his journey. He was going to see Kit. It was as if he and she had never had anything in common, as if he only knew of her by hearsay—but somehow, she and her child had spoilt everything for him. And he understood how he hated going, how he shrunk from bringing her back into his life. But for the irresistible force inside him, urging him forward, he would have turned homeward again. Gwynnie, how could he marry her after this? Strange that he felt no anger against Kit, for having come between them, only he wondered vaguely if it would be easy to get rid of her. But perhaps she was dead—oh! to know for certain that it was so; and the sense of relief, which he knew to be a delusion, was so keen that it hurt him. But the child?—the child—that would live on. They always did. Gloomily, incoherently, he brooded over what was to be done with it.

The cab turned into a side-street, scattering some squalid children from off the narrow, asphalted road. There was an untidiness about the neighbourhood, an untidiness that was almost indecent, the untidiness of a bed that has been slept in. Here and there, in the doorways, lounged slatternly women in dirty, colourless petticoats. As the cab passed they looked up, and under their gaze, Vivian winced. All the repulsive features of the neighbourhood stared him brutally in the face. Surely it must be close now? Here? The hansom pulled up before a dingy Italian restaurant: the driver was asking the way of some men smoking cigarettes before the door. They were foreigners, and answered him, all speaking at once, with gestures. A spasm of impotent rage passed over Vivian: he could almost have struck them. The cab moved slowly along: then stopped again at the end of the street. Vivian got out.

He knocked, and, before the narrow seedy-looking door, stood waiting. His excitement made his teeth chatter as with cold. This annoyed him, and, in the struggle to divert his thoughts, he forced himself to take stock of the house. There was nothing peculiar about it; its sordidness was neither greater nor less than that of those next to it or opposite to it. Only across the ground-floor window there stretched a card bearing the words 'Apartments'.

Kit was inside this house: perhaps in the very room into which he could almost see from the doorstep. He imagined himself arguing with her, persuading her, reminding her of the old days, giving her money—a large sum of money, the loss of which he would not feel—enough to make her and the child comfortable for life—doing anything and everything to get her to go away at once, to some spot where he would never even hear of her again. Surely she would agree to that. It would be for her own benefit, quite as much as for his. Yes, after all, he would be doing the handsome thing by her, and for an instant, he deluded himself into a glimmer of self-satisfaction.

The sound of a voice, breaking the train of his thoughts—in the area below a grimy woman, her sleeves rolled back over her red arms.

'Well, what d'yer want?' she asked, defiantly.

'I want to see Miss Gilston.'

'Thur ain't no Miss Gilston livin' 'ere,' she called back fiercely, evidently angry at having been disturbed for nothing. She prepared to re-enter the house.

'But,' Vivian went on, 'didn't she—about a month ago.'

'No, I tell yer, I ain't 'ad no Miss Gilston 'ere. Thur was a Mrs Marston'—at the sound of his own name shouted up through the area railings, Vivian's hands clenched and instinctively he glanced up the street to see if any one was within ear-shot—'a few weeks back, but she was took ill with a baby, and she died, poor soul.'

Mrs Marston—his name—she had taken it then,—and his head began to swim a little—but she was dead—dead—gone—dead!

'What's become of the child?' he heard himself asking. The sound of his own voice startled him, for he did not recognize it.

'The baby died along with 'er,' shouted the woman. 'She didn't leave a blessed sixpence behind 'er. Two week and a arf rent she owed me, besides 'er food, all sorts of delictasses I used to git for 'er.' Then with a change of tone, perhaps desirous of a gossip, perhaps struck by Vivian's prosperous appearance, 'Jest wait a minute. I'll come up and tell yer all about it.'

He was leaning against the area railings, scarcely hearing what she was saying, conscious only of the immense relief that was creeping over him. The child dead too. Both of them gone for ever. He became aware that the high-pitched voice had ceased; the woman had left the area. And he looked feebly around for her, the monotonous squalor of the close-packed, brown-brick houses hurt him more than before— oh! to get out of it, away from it, quickly, at once. Kit—it was as if she had never existed. It was like an episode in another man's life.

With a sudden, imperious impulse, he left the doorstep and walked rapidly away down the street.

Twenty minutes later he was seated before his breakfast-table, eating voraciously; for the morning excursion had given him a splendid appetite.

A month afterwards, Gwynnie and he were married. It was a smart wedding. There was a fashionable crowd, and the couple started to spend their honeymoon in Italy.

AUBREY BEARDSLEY

Catullus°

CARMEN CI

By ways remote and distant waters sped,
Brother, to thy sad grave-side am I come,
That I may give the last gifts to the dead,
And vainly parley with thine ashes dumb:
Since she who now bestows and now denies
Hath ta'en thee, hapless brother, from mine eyes.

But lo! these gifts, the heirlooms of past years,
Are made sad things to grace thy coffin shell,
Take them, all drenchèd with a brother's tears,
And, brother, for all time, hail and farewell!   10

SIR MAX BEERBOHM

from *Zuleika Dobson*

I

That old bell, presage of a train, had just sounded through Oxford station; and the undergraduates who were waiting there, gay figures in tweed or flannel, moved to the margin of the platform and gazed idly up the line. Young and careless, in the glow of the afternoon sunshine, they struck a sharp note of incongruity with the worn boards they stood on, with the fading signals and grey eternal walls of that antique station, which, familiar to them and insignificant, does yet whisper to the tourists the last enchantments of the Middle Age.

At the door of the first-class waiting-room, aloof and venerable, stood the Warden of Judas. An ebon pillar of tradition seemed he, in his garb of old-fashioned cleric. Aloft, between the wide brim of his silk hat and the white extent of his shirt front, appeared those eyes which hawks, that nose which eagles, had often envied. He supported his years on an ebon stick. He alone was worthy of the background.

Came a whistle from the distance. The breast of an engine was descried, and a long train curving after it, under a flight of smoke. It grew and grew. Louder and louder, its noise foreran it. It became a furious, enormous monster, and, with an instinct for safety, all men receded from the platform's margin. (Yet came there with it, unknown to them, a danger far more terrible than itself.) Into the station it came blustering, with cloud and clangour. Ere it had yet stopped, the door of one carriage flew open, and from it, in a white travelling-dress, in a toque a-twinkle with fine diamonds, a lithe and radiant creature slipped nimbly down to the platform.

A cynosure indeed! A hundred eyes were fixed on her, and half as many hearts lost to her. The Warden of Judas himself had mounted on his nose a pair of black-rimmed glasses. Him espying, the nymph darted in his direction. The throng made way for her. She was at his side.

'Grandpapa!' she cried, and kissed the old man on either cheek. (Not a youth there but would have bartered fifty years of his future for that salute.)

'My dear Zuleika,' he said, 'welcome to Oxford! Have you no luggage?'

'Heaps!' she answered. 'And a maid who will find it.'

'Then,' said the Warden, 'let us drive straight to College.' He offered her his arm, and they proceeded slowly to the entrance. She chatted gaily, blushing not in the long avenue of eyes she passed through. All the youths, under her spell, were now quite oblivious of the relatives they had come to meet. Parents, sisters, cousins, ran unclaimed about the platform. Undutiful, all the youths were forming a serried suite to their enchantress. In silence they followed her. They saw her leap into the Warden's landau, they saw the Warden seat himself upon her left. Nor was it until the landau was lost to sight that they turned—how slowly, and with how bad a grace!—to look for their relatives.

Through those slums which connect Oxford with the world, the landau rolled on towards Judas. Not many youths occurred, for nearly all—it was the Monday of Eights Week—were down by the river,

cheering the crews. There did, however, come spurring by, on a polo-
pony, a very splendid youth. His straw hat was encircled with a riband
of blue and white, and he raised it to the Warden.

'That', said the Warden, 'is the Duke of Dorset, a member of my
College. He dines at my table to-night.'

Zuleika turning to regard his Grace, saw that he had not reined in
and was not even glancing back at her over his shoulder. She gave a
little start of dismay, but scarcely had her lips pouted ere they curved
to a smile—a smile with no malice in its corners.

As the landau rolled into 'the Corn',° another youth—a pedestrian,
and very different—saluted the Warden. He wore a black jacket, rusty
and amorphous. His trousers were too short, and he himself was too
short: almost a dwarf. His face was as plain as his gait was undistinguished. He squinted behind spectacles.

'And who is that?' asked Zuleika.

A deep flush overspread the cheek of the Warden. 'That', he said,
'is also a member of Judas. His name, I believe, is Noaks.'

'Is he dining with us to-night?' asked Zuleika.

'Certainly not,' said the Warden. 'Most decidedly not.'

Noaks, unlike the Duke, had stopped for an ardent retrospect. He
gazed till the landau was out of his short sight; then, sighing, resumed
his solitary walk.

The landau was rolling into 'the Broad', over that ground which
had once blackened under the fagots lit for Latimer and Ridley. It
rolled past the portals of Balliol and of Trinity, past the Ashmolean.
From those pedestals which intersperse the railing of the Sheldonian,
the high grim busts of the Roman Emperors stared down at the fair
stranger in the equipage. Zuleika returned their stare with but a casual
glance. The inanimate had little charm for her.

A moment later, a certain old don emerged from Blackwell's,°
where he had been buying books. Looking across the road, he saw, to
his amazement, great beads of perspiration glistening on the brows of
those Emperors. He trembled, and hurried away. That evening, in
Common Room, he told what he had seen; and no amount of polite
scepticism would convince him that it was but the hallucination of one
who had been reading too much Mommsen.° He persisted that he had
seen what he described. It was not until two days had elapsed that
some credence was accorded him.

Yes, as the landau rolled by, sweat started from the brows of the

Emperors. They, at least, foresaw the peril that was overhanging
Oxford, and they gave such warning as they could. Let that be
remembered to their credit. Let that incline us to think more gently of
them. In their lives we know, they were infamous, some of them—
'nihil non commiserunt stupri, saevitiae, impietatis.' But are they too
little punished, after all? Here in Oxford, exposed eternally and
inexorably to heat and frost, to the four winds that lash them and the
rains that wear them away, they are expiating, in effigy, the abomina-
tions of their pride and cruelty and lust. Who were lechers, they are
without bodies; who were tyrants, they are crowned never but with
crowns of snow; who made themselves even with the gods, they are by
American visitors frequently mistaken for the Twelve Apostles. It is
but a little way down the road that the two Bishops perished for their
faith, and even now we do never pass the spot without a tear for them.
Yet how quickly they died in the flames! To these Emperors, for
whom none weeps, time will give no surcease. Surely, it is sign of
some grace in them that they rejoiced not, this bright afternoon, in the
evil that was to befall the city of their penance.

II

The sun streamed through the bay-window of a 'best' bedroom in the
Warden's house, and glorified the pale crayon-portraits on the wall,
the dimity curtains, the old fresh chintz. He invaded the many trunks
which—all painted Z. D.—gaped, in various stages of excavation,
around the room. The doors of the huge wardrobe stood, like the
doors of Janus' temple in time of war, majestically open; and the sun
seized this opportunity of exploring the mahogany recesses. But the
carpet, which had faded under his immemorial visitations, was now
almost *entirely* hidden from him, hidden under layers of fair fine linen,
layers of silk, brocade, satin, chiffon, muslin. All the colours of the
rainbow, materialized by modistes, were there. Stacked on chairs were
I know not what of sachets, glove-cases, fan-cases. There were
innumerable packages in silver-paper and pink ribands. There was a
pyramid of band-boxes. There was a virgin forest of boot-trees. And
rustling quickly hither and thither, in and out of this profusion, with
armfuls of finery, was an obviously French maid. Alert, unerring, like
a swallow she dipped and darted. Nothing escaped her, and she never
rested. She had the air of the born unpacker—swift and firm, yet
withal tender. Scarce had her arms been laden but their loads were

lying lightly between shelves or tightly in drawers. To calculate, catch, distribute, seemed in her but a single process. She was one of those who are born to make chaos cosmic.

Insomuch that ere the loud chapel-clock tolled another hour all the trunks had been sent empty away. The carpet was unflecked by any scrap of silver-paper. From the mantelpiece, photographs of Zuleika surveyed the room with a possessive air. Zuleika's pincushion, a-bristle with new pins, lay on the dimity-flounced toilet-table, and round it stood a multitude of multiform glass vessels, domed, all of them, with dull gold, on which Z. D., in zianites and diamonds, was encrusted. On a small table stood a great casket of malachite, initialled in like fashion. On another small table stood Zuleika's library. Both books were in covers of dull gold. On the back of one cover *Bradshaw*, in beryls, was encrusted; on the back of the other, *A.B.C. Guide*, in amethysts, beryls, chrysoprases, and garnets. And Zuleika's great cheval-glass stood ready to reflect her. Always it travelled with her, in a great case specially made for it. It was framed in ivory, and of fluted ivory were the slim columns it swung between. Of gold were its twin sconces, and four tall tapers in each of them.

The door opened and the Warden, with hospitable words, left his grand-daughter at the threshold.

Zuleika wandered to her mirror. 'Undress me, Mélisande,' she said. Like all who are wont to appear by night before the public, she had the habit of resting towards sunset.

Presently Mélisande withdrew. Her mistress, in a white peignoir tied with a blue sash, lay in a great chintz chair gazing out of the bay-window. The quadrangle below was very beautiful, with its walls of rugged grey, its cloisters, its grass carpet. But to her it was of no more interest than if it had been the rattling court-yard to one of those hotels in which she spent her life. She saw it, but heeded it not. She seemed to be thinking of herself, or of something she desired, or of someone she had never met. There was ennui, and there was wistfulness, in her gaze. Yet one would have guessed these things to be transient—to be no more than the little shadows that sometimes pass between a bright mirror and the brightness it reflects.

Zuleika was not strictly beautiful. Her eyes were a trifle large, and their lashes longer than they need have been. An anarchy of small curls was her chevelure, a dark upland of misrule, every hair asserting its rights over a not discreditable brow. For the rest, her features were

not at all original. They seemed to have been derived rather from a
gallimaufry of familiar models. From Madame la Marquise de Saint-
Ouen came the shapely tilt of the nose. The mouth was a mere replica
of Cupid's bow, lacquered scarlet and strung with the littlest pearls.
No apple-tree, no wall of peaches, had not been robbed, nor any
Tyrian rose-garden, for the glory of Miss Dobson's cheeks. Her neck
was imitation-marble. Her hands and feet were of very mean proportions. She had no waist to speak of.

Yet, though a Greek would have railed at her asymmetry, and an
Elizabethan have called her 'gipsy', Miss Dobson now, in the midst of
the Edwardian Era, was the toast of two hemispheres. Late in her
'teens she had become an orphan and a governess. Her grandfather
had refused her appeal for a home or an allowance, on the ground that
he would not be burdened with the upshot of a marriage which he had
once forbidden and not yet forgiven. Lately, however, prompted by
curiosity or by remorse, he had asked her to spend a week or so of his
declining years with him. And she, 'resting' between two engagements—one at Hammerstein's Victoria, N.Y.C., the other at the
Folies Bergères, Paris—and having never been in Oxford, had so far
let bygones be bygones as to come and gratify the old man's whim.

It may be that she still resented his indifference to those early
struggles which, even now, she shuddered to recall. For a governess's
life she had been, indeed, notably unfit. Hard she had thought it, that
penury should force her back into the school-room she was scarce out
of, there to champion the sums and maps and conjugations she had
never tried to master. Hating her work, she had failed signally to pick
up any learning from her little pupils, and had been driven from house
to house, a sullen and most ineffectual maiden. The sequence of her
situations was the swifter by reason of her pretty face. Was there a
grown-up son, always he fell in love with her, and she would let his
eyes trifle boldly with hers across the dinner-table. When he offered
her his hand, she would refuse it—not because she 'knew her place',
but because she did not love him. Even had she been a good teacher,
her presence could not have been tolerated thereafter. Her corded
trunk, heavier by another packet of billets-doux and a month's salary
in advance, was soon carried up the stairs of some other house.

It chanced that she came, at length, to be governess in a large family
that had Gibbs for its name and Notting Hill for its background.
Edward, the eldest son, was a clerk in the city, who spent his evenings

in the practice of amateur conjuring. He was a freckled youth, with hair that bristled in places where it should have lain smooth, and he fell in love with Zuleika duly, at first sight, during high-tea. In the course of the evening, he sought to win her admiration by a display of all his tricks. These were familiar to this household, and the children had been sent to bed, the mother was dozing, long before the séance was at an end. But Miss Dobson, unaccustomed to any gaieties, sat fascinated by the young man's sleight of hand, marvelling that a top-hat could hold so many gold-fish, and a handkerchief turn so swiftly into a silver florin. All that night, she lay wide awake, haunted by the miracles he had wrought. Next evening, when she asked him to repeat them, 'Nay,' he whispered, 'I cannot bear to deceive the girl I love. Permit me to explain the tricks.' So he explained them. His eyes sought hers across the bowl of gold-fish, his fingers trembled as he taught her to manipulate the magic canister. One by one, she mastered the paltry secrets. Her respect for him waned with every revelation. He complimented her on her skill. 'I could not do it more neatly myself!' he said. 'Oh, dear Miss Dobson, will you but accept my hand, all these things shall be yours—the cards, the canister, the gold-fish, the demon egg-cup—all yours!' Zuleika, with ravishing coyness, answered that if he would give her them now, she would 'think it over'. The swain consented, and at bed-time she retired with the gift under her arm. In the light of her bedroom candle Marguerite hung not in greater ecstasy over the jewel-casket than hung Zuleika over the box of tricks. She clasped her hands over the tremendous possibilities it held for her—manumission from her bondage, wealth, fame, power. Stealthily, so soon as the house slumbered, she packed her small outfit, embedding therein the precious gift. Noiselessly, she shut the lid of her trunk, corded it, shouldered it, stole down the stairs with it. Outside—how that chain had grated! and her shoulder, how it was aching—she soon found a cab. She took a night's sanctuary in some railway-hotel. Next day, she moved into a small room in a lodging-house off the Edgware Road, and there for a whole week she was sedulous in the practice of her tricks. Then she inscribed her name on the books of a 'Juvenile Party Entertainments Agency'.

The Christmas holidays were at hand, and before long she got an engagement. It was a great evening for her. Her repertory was, it must be confessed, old and obvious; but the children, in deference to their hostess, pretended not to know how the tricks were done, and assumed their prettiest airs of wonder and delight. One of them even pretended to be frightened, and was led howling from the room. In fact, the whole thing went off splendidly. The hostess was charmed, and told Zuleika that a glass of lemonade would be served to her in the hall. Other engagements soon followed. Zuleika was very, very happy. I cannot claim for her that she had a genuine passion for her art. The true conjurer finds his guerdon in the consciousness of work done perfectly and for its own sake. Lucre and applause are not necessary to him. If he were set down, with the materials of his art, on a desert island, he would yet be quite happy. He would not cease to produce the barber's pole from his mouth. To the indifferent winds he would still speak his patter, and even in the last throes of starvation would not eat his live rabbit or his gold-fish. Zuleika, on a desert island, would have spent most of her time in looking for a man's foot-print. She was, indeed, far too human a creature to care much for art. I do not say that she took her work lightly. She thought she had genius, and she liked to be told that this was so. But mainly she loved her work as a means of mere self-display. The frank admiration which, into whatsoever house she entered, the grown-up sons flashed on her; their eagerness to see her to the door; their impressive way of putting her into her omnibus—these were the things she revelled in. She was a nymph to whom men's admiration was the greater part of life. By day, whenever she went into the streets, she was conscious that no man passed her without a stare; and this consciousness gave a sharp zest to her outings. Sometimes she was followed to her door—crude flattery which she was too innocent to fear. Even when she went into the haberdasher's to make some little purchase of tape or riband, or into the grocer's—for she was an epicure in her humble way—to buy a tin of potted meat for her supper, the homage of the young men behind the counter did flatter and exhilarate her. As the homage of men became for her, more and more, a matter of course, the more subtly necessary was it to her happiness. The more she won of it, the more she treasured it. She was alone in the world, and it saved her from any moment of regret that she had neither home nor friends. For her the streets that lay around her had no squalor, since she paced them always in the gold nimbus of her fascinations. Her bedroom seemed not mean nor lonely to her, since the little square of glass, nailed above the washstand, was ever there to reflect her face. Thereinto, indeed, she was ever peering. She would droop her head from side to side, she would bend it forward and see herself from beneath her eyelashes, then tilt it back and watch herself over her supercilious chin. And she would smile, frown, pout, languish—let all the emotions hover upon her face; and always she seemed to herself lovelier than she had ever been.

Yet was there nothing Narcissine in her spirit. Her love for her own image was not cold æstheticism. She valued that image not for its own sake, but for sake of the glory it always won for her. In the little remote music-hall, where she was soon appearing nightly as an 'early turn', she reaped glory in a nightly harvest. She could feel that all the gallery-boys, because of her, were scornful of the sweethearts wedged between them, and she knew that she had but to say 'Will any gentleman in the audience be so good as to lend me his hat?' for the stalls to rise as one man and rush towards the platform. But greater things were in store for her. She was engaged at two halls in the West End. Her horizon was fast receding and expanding. Homage became nightly tangible in bouquets, rings, brooches—things acceptable and (luckier than their donors) accepted. Even Sunday was not barren for Zuleika: modish hostesses gave her postprandially to their guests. Came that Sunday night, *notanda candidissimo calculo!* when she received certain guttural compliments which made absolute her vogue and enabled her to command, thenceforth, whatever terms she asked for.

Already, indeed, she was rich. She was living at the most exorbitant hotel in all Mayfair. She had innumerable gowns and no necessity to buy jewels; and she also had, which pleased her most, the fine cheval-glass I have described. At the close of the Season, Paris claimed her for a month's engagement. Paris saw her and was prostrate. Boldini did a portrait of her. Jules Bloch wrote a song about her; and this, for a whole month, was howled up and down the cobbled alleys of Montmartre. And all the little dandies were mad for 'la Zuleika'. The jewellers of the Rue de la Paix soon had nothing left to put in their windows—everything had been bought for 'la Zuleika'. For a whole month, baccarat was not played at the Jockey Club—every member had succumbed to a nobler passion. For a whole month, the whole demi-monde was forgotten for one English virgin. Never, even in Paris, had a woman triumphed so. When the day came for her departure, the city wore such an air of sullen mourning as it had not worn since the Prussians marched to its Elysée. Zuleika, quite untouched, would not linger in the conquered city. Agents had come to her from every capital in Europe, and, for a year, she ranged, in triumphal nomady, from one capital to another. In Berlin, every night, the students escorted her home with torches. Prince Vierfünf-sechs-Siebenachtneun offered her his hand, and was condemned by the Kaiser to six months' confinement in his little castle. In Yildiz Kiosk, the tyrant who still throve there conferred on her the Order of Chastity, and offered her the central couch in his seraglio. She gave her performance in the Quirinal, and from the Vatican, the Pope launched against her a Bull which fell utterly flat. In Petersburg, the Grand Duke Salamander Salamandrovitch fell enamoured of her. Of every article in the apparatus of her conjuring-tricks he caused a replica to be made in finest gold. These treasures he presented to her in that great malachite casket which now stood on the little table in her room; and thenceforth it was with these that she performed her wonders. They did not mark the limit of the Grand Duke's generosity. He was for bestowing on Zuleika the half of his immensurable estates. The Grand Duchess appealed to the Tzar. Zuleika was conducted across the frontier, by an escort of love-sick Cossacks. On the Sunday before she left Madrid, a great bull-fight was held in her honour. Fifteen bulls received the *coup de grâce*, and Alvarez, the matador of matadors, died in the arena with her name on his lips. He had tried to kill the last bull without taking his eyes off *la divina señorita*. A prettier compliment had never been paid her, and she was immensely pleased with it. For that matter, she was immensely pleased with everything. She moved proudly to the incessant music of a pæan, aye! of a pæan that was always *crescendo*.

Its echoes followed her when she crossed the Atlantic, till they were lost in the louder, deeper, more blatant pæan that rose for her from the shores beyond. All the stops of that 'mighty organ, many-piped', the New York press, were pulled out simultaneously, as far as they could be pulled, in Zuleika's honour. She delighted in the din. She read every line that was printed about her, tasting her triumph as she had never tasted it before. And how she revelled in the Brobdingnagian drawings of her, which, printed in nineteen colours, towered between the columns or sprawled across them! There she was, measuring herself back to back with the Statue of Liberty; scudding through the firmament on a comet, whilst a crowd of tiny men in evening-dress stared up at her from the terrestrial globe; peering through a microscope held by Cupid over a diminutive Uncle Sam; teaching the American Eagle to stand on its head; and doing a hundred-and-one other things—whatever suggested itself to the fancy of native art. And through all this iridescent maze of symbolism were scattered many little slabs of realism. At home, on the street, Zuleika was the smiling target of all snap-shooters, and all the snap-shots were snapped up by the press and reproduced with annotations: Zuleika Dobson walking on Broadway in the sables gifted her by Grand Duke Salamander—she says 'You can bounce blizzards in them'; Zuleika Dobson yawning over a love-letter from millionaire Edelweiss; relishing a cup of clam-broth—she says 'They don't use clams out there'; ordering her maid to fix her a warm bath; finding a split in the gloves she has just drawn on before starting for the musicale given in her honour by Mrs Suetonius X. Meistersinger, the most exclusive woman in New York; chatting at the telephone to Miss Camille Van Spook, the best-born girl in New York; laughing over the recollection of a compliment made her by George Abimelech Post, the best-groomed man in New York; meditating a new trick; admonishing a waiter who has upset a cocktail over her skirt; having herself manicured; drinking tea in bed. Thus was Zuleika enabled daily to be, as one might say, a spectator of her own wonderful life. On her departure from New York, the papers spoke no more than the truth when they said she had had 'a lovely time'. The further she went West—millionaire Edelweiss had loaned her his private car—the lovelier her time was. Chicago drowned the echoes of New York; final Frisco dwarfed the headlines of Chicago. Like one of its own prairie-fires, she swept the country from end to end. Then she swept back, and sailed for England. She was to return for a second season in the coming Fall. At present, she was, as I have said, 'resting'.

As she sat here in the bay-window of her room, she was not reviewing the splendid pageant of her past. She was a young person whose reveries never were in retrospect. For her the past was no treasury of distinct memories, all hoarded and classified, some brighter than others and more highly valued. All memories were for her but as the motes in one fused radiance that followed her and made more luminous the pathway of her future. She was always looking forward. She was looking forward now—that shade of ennui had passed from her face—to the week she was to spend in Oxford. A new city was a new toy to her, and—for it was youth's homage that she loved best—this city of youths was a toy after her own heart.

Aye, and it was youths who gave homage to her most freely. She was of that high-stepping and flamboyant type that captivates youth most surely. Old men and men of middle age admired her, but she had not that flower-like quality of shyness and helplessness, that look of innocence, so dear to men who carry life's secrets in their heads. Yet Zuleika *was* very innocent, really. She was as pure as that young shepherdess Marcella, who, all unguarded, roved the mountains and was by all the shepherds adored. Like Marcella, she had given her heart to no man, had preferred none. Youths were reputed to have died for love of her, as Chrysostom died for love of the shepherdess; and she, like the shepherdess, had shed no tear. When Chrysosom was lying on his bier in the valley, and Marcella looked down from the high rock, Ambrosio, the dead man's comrade, cried out on her, upbraiding her with bitter words—'Oh basilisk of our mountains!' Nor do I think Ambrosio spoke too strongly. Marcella cared nothing for men's admiration, and yet, instead of retiring to one of those nunneries which are founded for her kind, she chose to rove the mountains, causing despair to all the shepherds. Zuleika, with her peculiar temperament, would have gone mad in a nunnery. 'But', you may argue, 'ought not she to have taken the veil, even at the cost of her reason, rather than cause so much despair in the world? If Marcella was a basilisk, as you seem to think, how about Miss Dobson?' Ah, but Marcella knew quite well, boasted even, that she never would or could love any man. Zuleika, on the other hand, was a woman of really passionate fibre. She may not have had that conscious, separate, and quite explicit desire to be a mother with which modern playwrights credit every unmated member of her sex. But she did know that she could love. And, surely, no woman who knows that of herself can be rightly censured for not recluding herself from the world: it is only women without the power to love who have no right to provoke men's love.

Though Zuleika had never given her heart, strong in her were the desire and the need that it should be given. Whithersoever she had fared, she had seen nothing but youths fatuously prostrate to her—not one upright figure which she could respect. There were the middle-aged men, the old men, who did not bow down to her; but from middle-age, as from eld, she had a sanguine aversion. She could love none but a youth. Nor—though she herself, womanly, would utterly abase herself before her ideal—could she love one who fell prone before her. And before her all youths always did fall prone. She was an empress, and all youths were her slaves. Their bondage delighted her, as I have said. But no empress who has any pride can adore one of her slaves. Whom, then, could proud Zuleika adore? It was a question which sometimes troubled her. There were even moments when, looking into her cheval-glass, she cried out against that arrangement in comely lines and tints which got for her the dulia she delighted in. To be able to love once—would not that be better than all the homage in the world? But would she ever meet whom, looking up to him, she could love—she, the omnisubjugant? Would she ever, ever meet him?

It was when she wondered thus, that the wistfulness came into her eyes. Even now, as she sat by the window, that shadow returned to them. She was wondering, shyly, had she met him at length? That young equestrian who had not turned to look at her; whom she was to meet at dinner tonight ... was it he? The ends of her blue sash lay across her lap, and she was lazily unravelling their fringes. 'Blue and white!' she remembered. 'They were the colours he wore round his hat.' And she gave a little laugh of coquetry. She laughed, and, long after, her lips were still parted in a smile.

So did she sit, smiling, wondering, with the fringes of her sash between her fingers, while the sun sank behind the opposite wall of the quadrangle, and the shadows crept out across the grass, thirsty for the dew.

NOTES

SIR EDWIN ARNOLD

Text: *The Light of Asia* (1879).

1   From *The Light of Asia*. l. i. *Om, amitaya!*: invocation of Amitabha or Amitayus, the Buddha of measureless light and immortality.

l. 6. *Brahm*: or Brahma: one of the supreme gods of Hinduism. In the Hindu trinity, the creator. In Vedanta, Brahma or Brahman is the final reality, the Self by which the world has come into being.

5   l. 140. *Dharma*: more commonly known as Karma. One's state in life is the result of physical and mental action in previous lives; one's present actions can determine one's destiny in future lives. A natural, impersonal law of cause and effect. Only those who have attained Nirvâna or liberation from rebirth, the wheel of life, can transcend Karma.

6   l. 158. *sesamum*: or sesame. A sacred plant. Its oil is widely used in India for cooking, food, medicine, lights, and religious ceremonies. Its seeds are used in bakery and confectionery.

7   l. 193. *Nirvâna*: a state after death to be striven after by all, but which is likely to be attained by few. There are two possible meanings. Extinction of all passions and desires, for these qualities cause rebirth; or the 'windless state' where the dead cannot be touched by any impression or disturbance from the material world, just as a light in total calm neither flickers nor is moved by any gesture of the wind. The first interpretation is the more usual.

l. 195. *Om, mani padme, om*. This phrase, which used to be continuously uttered in Tibet, revolved in countless prayer wheels and engraved on rocks, may be a precise formula or a mere ritual noise; authorities do not appear to agree. The first and last words may be mystic syllables such as frequently occur in magic formulae. *Mani padme* has been interpreted as 'Jewel of the Lotus' in Sanskrit, though it has also been suggested that it alludes to one of the many names of Avolokitesvara, god of mercy, the son of Amitabha and in the cosmic process responsible for creation. A possible reading is 'Om praise to the golden Lotus Saint'.

JAMES THOMSON

Text: *Poems and Some Letters of James Thomson*, ed. Anne Ridler (1963).

8   *A Real Vision of Sin*. The model is actually Tennyson's 'The Two Voices' which first appeared in *Poems* (1832), was republished in

Poems (1842), and which is written in triplets. Thomson dates his poem 'Friday, March 4, 1859'.

11 l. 104. *daint*: Middle English *deinte*, perhaps.

12 l. 114. *corn and wine and oil*: a conflation of two frequent Biblical phrases 'corn and wine' and 'wine and oil'. The connotations are healing and refreshment. cf. Luke 10: 34, the parable of the Good Samaritan.

19 From *The City of Dreadful Night*. Victorian exploration provides a prolonged metaphor for a subjective journey, with overtones of apocalypse. The City is that stony stepmother London, the labyrinthine Victorian city, projected in many works of fiction: Charles Dickens's *Our Mutual Friend*, Arthur Morrison's *Child of the Jago*, George Gissing's *The Whirlpool*, etc.

21 l. 58. The woman may be Thomson's fiancée who died young. The red lamp suggests healing (a Doctor's surgery), Florence Nightingale, the Lady with the Lamp, but with the ambivalence of so many nineteenth-century images of women, prostitution; and this is reinforced by the Magdalen imagery of line 86. The lamp is a general symbol, largely Christian, of guidance, knowledge, enlightenment, and immortality: 'Thy word is a lamp to my feet and a light to my path', Psalm 19, 105. The red lamp is kept burning by the altar in Latin Catholic churches as a sign of the reservation of the Sacrament. The dominant meaning suggests succour and faith.

l. 65. *I was twain*: an allusion to the double, or *doppelgänger* (double) which often appears as a sign of the divided consciousness in nineteenth-century novelists and poets. But the poet also glances at and inverts the Pauline imagery of the old man and the new.

22 ll. 101–42. An *ekphrasis* or precise description of the detail of a building or work of art; in this instance Albrecht Dürer's famous engraving of Melancholia (I). Mrs Mary M. Heaton's *The Life of Albrecht Dürer with a Translation of His Letters and Journals and an Account of His Works* (London 1869), would have been available to Thomson. 'It has usually been thought that Dürer means . . . to typify the insufficiency of human knowledge to attain wisdom, or to penetrate the secrets of nature. The old craving for the forbidden fruit is stirring in her breast.' Thomson naturalizes the details of keys and purse, which Dürer had intended to imply power and wealth respectively. Nor does Thomson comment on Melancholia's wreath of watercress and ranunculus.

RODEN NOEL

Text: *Collected Poems of Roden Noel* (1902).

25 *Ganymede*. Classical distance allows the poet to indulge his homoerotic

lingerings. We may compare the exotic machines of the Victorian painters of scenes from Olympus, or of ideal nudes in the bath or odalisques in the *hareem*, painters such as Sir Lawrence Alma-Tadema, Sir Edward Poynter, etc. Noel was probably remembering Renaissance versions of the legend. A curious feature of the style is the truncation of adverbs to adjectives, serving to slow down the poem's action and enacting the speaker's regret.

l. 5. *hypaethral*: open to the sky. Vitruvius, *De Architectura*, I, ii, remarks of hypaethral temples that they are built in honour of Jupiter Lightning, and in II, iii, observes that there are some in Greece but none in Rome. Noel implies that such temples contrast agreeably with the furtive darkness of Christian churches; each type of building is emblematic of the culture that produces it.

ALFRED AUSTIN

Text: *The Season* (1861).

SAMUEL BUTLER

Text: *The Way of All Flesh* (1903).

RICHARD GARNETT

Text: *The Twilight of the Gods* (1903).

38   *The Demon Pope. Silvester the Second*: Sylvester II was born in Auvergne, France, is reputed to have introduced Arabic numerals into Europe and credited also with the invention of the pendulum clock; quite sufficient to have roused the suspicion of his contemporaries.

43   *Reasons of State*: a perversion of the principle enounced by Cicero (*Laws*, III, iii, 8) that 'the welfare of the people is the supreme law'. Reasons of state is used by Satan in *Paradise Lost* (IV, 389–90) to justify his actions; the phrase is traditionally associated with Machiavellian justification of the means by the end.

44   *non obstantibus*: notwithstanding. A juridical formula found also in Papal contexts. Lucifer has an eye to playing both ends against the middle.

45   *Bisogna pazienza*: patience is needed.

      with one exception. Nicolas Breakspear was Pope under the title of Adrian or Hadrian the Fourth from 1154 to 1159.

46   *ceremony of kissing the Pope's feet*. The custom precedes Sylvester's pontificate (as Garnett well knew) and was accorded to secular monarchs and the Byzantine emperors.

LORD DE TABLEY

Text: *Poems Dramatic and Lyrical* (1893).

47   *The Study of a Spider*. l. 14. *electrum*: an alloy of varying proportions of silver and gold.

SIR ALFRED LYALL

Text: *Verses Written in India* (1889).

49   *Studies at Delhi, 1876. II.—Badminton*. l. 2. *Moree*. The actual word is probably More, Morah, or Mudi, a large measure of land, consisting broadly of 45 *guntas*, each 33 feet square or about 1 13/100th of an acre. It can also mean a water course, a drain or a pipe under the surface to convey water.

    l. 3. *glacis*. 'The parapet of the covered way extended in a long slope to meet the natural surface of the ground, so that every part of it shall be swept by the fire of the ramparts.' OED.

    l. 7. *Nicholson*. Brigadier-General John Nicholson (1821–57) fought vigorously in the Indian Mutiny and was killed at the assault on Delhi.

SIR W. S. GILBERT

Text: *Original Plays by W. S. Gilbert*, Third Series (1895).

50   From *Patience*. *Patience* (1882), with music by Sir Arthur Sullivan, was an operetta mildly satirizing contemporary Aestheticism, a movement that aspired to a cultivated taste in art or nature. There is no general agreement as to whom the two poets Bunthorne and Grosvenor represent. Bunthorne was popularly taken as, but was probably not intended to be identified with, Oscar Wilde, though dressed on stage in Wilde's manner. Probably the figure was a composite of Wilde, Swinburne, and others.

    '*Oh, Hollow! Hollow! Hollow!*' l. 3. *amaranthine asphodel*: purplish lily.

    l. 6. *calomel*: a purgative drug.

    l. 7. *plinth*: the block on which a statue or other architectural unit rests.

    l. 8. *colocynth*: a plant of the gourd family; it secretes a strong purgative. Its connexion with calomel suggests the link between open bowels and rigid morals.

    l. 9. *aloe*: a plant of the lily family.

52   *Bunthorne's Song*. l. 10. *Queen Anne*. A taste for the architecture and to some extent the literature of Queen Anne's reign (1702–14) was particularly marked in the 1870s, especially in aesthetic circles.

l. 12. *Empress Josephine*: first wife of Napoleon the First, Empress of the French from 1804 to 1809. The allusion is to the French Empire style in furniture and decoration.

l. 18. *à la Plato*: ostensibly a spiritualized passion. It is just possible that Gilbert is hinting at the Greek version of Platonic (i.e. homosexual) love.

l. 19. *Philistines*. The term is used by Matthew Arnold in *Culture and Anarchy* (1867) to describe those members of the middle classes who are devoid of liberal education and refinement of culture.

l. 20. *mediaeval*. The middle ages were looked back to as a time of unified culture by, among others, Carlyle, Ruskin, and the Pre-Raphaelites.

ELLICE HOPKINS

Text: *Autumn Swallows* (1882).

ALGERNON CHARLES SWINBURNE

Text: *The Collected Poetical Works of Algernon Charles Swinburne*, Volume 1, 3rd printing (1909).

61   *In the Orchard*. The burden is the refrain and the piece is in the form of an aubade or dawn song favoured by the Provençal poets of the thirteenth century.

62   l. 23. *plenilune*: the time of the full moon.

        ll. 28–9. The characteristic note of Swinburne's sado–masochism.

63   *Itylus*. Tereus, King of Thrace, married Prokne, daughter of Pandion, who bore him a son, Itys. Tereus seduced Prokne's younger sister Philomela and cut out her tongue so that she could not tell her story. Philomela sent a message to Prokne in the weaving of a dress whose imagery expressed what had happened. Prokne murdered her own son and served him up to Tereus at dinner; she and her sister then fled but Tereus pursued them with an axe. The lamenting Prokne was turned into a swallow, tongueless Philomela into a nightingale and Tereus into a hoopoe. The myth has several variants; it formed the substance of Sophocles' lost tragedy *Tereus* and is also recounted by Penelope in Odyssey XIX, Virgil and Ovid. Itylus is a diminutive of Itys. The poem is a dramatic monologue in lyric form spoken by Philomela to Prokne. Swinburne transposes the personages of the myth.

64   l. 48. *feast of Daulis*: the feast in the city of Daulis in Phocis, Greece, at which Tereus ate the flesh of his son.

66   *The Garden of Proserpine*: dramatic lyric spoken by a pagan. Languid rhythms embody the death-wish frequent in Swinburne's earlier work.

Proserpine is the goddess both of death and of fertility and gardens. The mood expressed is one of exhausted resignation to the cycle of death and birth. According to the myth, Proserpine, while gathering flowers in Sicily, was carried off by Pluto, King of the Underworld, to his kingdom of darkness and death. She was allowed to return to the world for six months out of every year, so symbolizing the change of the seasons.

l. 14. Blossoming flowers that will produce no fruit, used as emblems of unfulfilled desires and dreams.

l. 22. *wot*: know.

67   l. 27. *poppies*: flowers of oblivion, sacred to Proserpine who is often represented as crowned with them.

68   l. 94. *diurnal*: belonging to daylight.

Text: *The Collected Poetical Works of Algernon Charles Swinburne*, Volume IV, 3rd printing (1909).

69   *Chorus* from *Atalanta in Calydon*: a closet drama; the Chorus is spoken by the maidens of Aetolia. McGann (p. 104) observes that the 'dialectic' and 'cyclic contraries' are very much alive in this Chorus; that spring is an equivocal blessing and it represents Artemis with her hounds hunting Death.

l. 2. *The mother of months*: Artemis (as Selene), the moon goddess who presides over the monthly cycle.

ll. 9–13. *bows bent ... most fleet*: Artemis as huntress and as swiftest of the Gods.

l. 28. *light ... wins*: the shorter days and longer nights of winter.

70   ll. 33–40. 'The words "feed", "trammel" and "crushes" are merely the most obvious signs of impending disaster and a sustained equivocalness. The wolf, the fawn, vary the imagery of the hounds of spring ... on winter's traces, just as all culminate in the symbol of the hunting of the boar ... signs of man's tragic fate ... and death rising up even while "in green underwood and cover/Blossom by blossom the spring begins" ' (McGann, p. 105). It should be stressed that McGann's book on Swinburne is in dialogue form and itself represents several points of view.

l. 38. *oat*: shepherd's pipe made of oat straws.

l. 44. *Maenad ... Bassarid*: female followers of the wine and vegetation god Dionysus (Bacchus). Intoxicated by wine and dancing and possessed by the gods, they celebrated him in wild places by orgy and by tearing to pieces and sacrificing animals.

l. 49. *Bacchanal:* an alternative name for Maenad.

Text: *The Collected Poetical Works of Algernon Charles Swinburne*, Volume v, 3rd Printing (1909).

Ave Atque Vale. The epigraph is from Charles Baudelaire's *Fleurs du Mal*, 'Tableaux Parisiens', CXXIV, 3–7: 'Yet we should bear to him some flowers; the dead, the pitiful dead, have great sorrows, and when October, pruner of ancient trees, blows its melancholy winds about their mounds, assuredly, they will find the living ungrateful.'

71   l. 1. *rose*: symbol of love, *rue*: herb of grace, of pity and remembrance. *laurel*: garlands of laurel, sacred to poetry, used to honour the dead.

l. 2. *the veil of thee*: the body of Baudelaire.

l. 5. *Dryads*: wood nymphs.

l. 11. Alludes to Baudelaire's visit to India in 1841–2 and to his passionate and morbid verse.

ll. 14–18. Allude to the legend that Sappho, the Lesbian poetess, unhappily in love with a young man Phaon, threw herself into the sea from the cliffs of Leucas, one of the Ionian islands.

l. 33. 'Whatsoever a man soweth, that shall he also reap,' Galatians 6: 7.

72   l. 59. *pale Titan-woman*: a reference to Baudelaire's poem 'La Géante'. Titans were giants in Greek mythology who rebelled against Zeus.

73   ll. 82–3. cf. 'Garden of Proserpine'. The veil, as emblem of death, mourning, and return, relates to Prosperpine's journey from Death's Kingdom to that of light and blossom. When Hercules presents Alcestis who has given herself to death in place of her husband Admetus (Euripides' *Admetus*), she is perfectly veiled, though the hero (Hercules') intention is to evoke a rectitude of response in Alcestis' husband. Proserpine, returning as Queen, wife of Dis, so the marriage veil, representing pudor and perhaps virgin mystery, is relevant. In Alcestis' case, the sacrifice is itself a type of submitting to a 'bridal of death'.

l. 83. *Proserpine's veiled head*: wife of Pluto (Dis), Queen of the Lower World.

74   l. 106. *a Muse funereal*: Melpomene, the Muse of Tragedy.

ll. 120–1. In the opening scene of Aeschylus' *Choephori*, Orestes and his sister visit the tomb of their father Agamemnon, murdered by his wife Clytemnestra, and Orestes offers as a sacrifice to the dead a lock of his hair, an emblem of mourning.

l. 123. The reference is to Agamemnon.

75   l. 134. *lord of light*: Apollo, the sun god, god too of music and poetry.

l. 146. *cypress*: an emblem of mourning, frequent in graveyards.

ll. 157–8. The medieval Venus, a succubus, so 'a thing', lived in the hollow world under the Horsel Mount in Germany. Her beauty tempted Christian Knights and pilgrims to their damnation.

l. 160. *Erycine*: a further name for Venus, from Mount Eryx in Sicily, where there was a temple devoted to the goddess's Uranian or heavenly aspect.

76   l. 166. The blossoming staff alludes to the miracle of the Pope's staff which blossomed as a sign of God's grace having been extended to Tannhauser, the lover of Venus. The episode clearly looks back to Aaron's rod as a type. Genesis 7: 10.

ll. 188–9. A return to the title phrase which is a quotation from Catullus' memorial poem on his brother.

77   *A Forsaken Garden*. The garden on which this poem was based was at East Dene on the Isle of Wight off the coast of Southern England, where, as a child, the poet played with the cousin with whom he was to fall in love, Mary Gordon. The garden becomes emblematically that of his own childhood and his later, ruined emotional life.

l. 1. *coign*: corner, projection.

79   from *By the North Sea*: section three of a longer poem. Desolate landscapes of the East Anglian seaboard are conflated with the pagan underworld. The poem refers repeatedly to the Bible and the Nicene Creed in particular as part of a desire to spell out alternative principles (McGann, p. 145). This section arrives at a climax with recollections of Odysseus' descent into the underworld (*Odyssey* XI) where the hero meets but is unable to embrace his mother, Anticleia (ll. 59–60). This is analogous to Swinburne's own relationship to the land and the seascape (McGann, p. 144). And a further analogy is drawn between the phantasmal quality of Hades and the Christian churches crumbling into the sea.

82   *Oscar Wilde*. Oscar Wilde, convicted in 1895 of homosexual acts, had died in 1900.

The Higher Pantheism in a Nutshell: a parody of Tennyson's 'The Higher Pantheism', published in 1869.

Text: *New Writings by Swinburne or Miscellanea Nova et Curiosa* being a Medley of Poems, Critical Essays, Hoaxes and Burlesques, edited by Cecil V. Lang (Syracuse, 1964).

84   *The Ballad of Villon and Fat Madge*: Translated from *Ballade de Villon et de la Grosse Margot* with its refrain: 'En ce bordeau ou tenons nostre estat'. Villon was a hero for the late nineteenth–century English poets:

his poetry had all the positive qualities required: it was medieval, confessional. Vagabond and thief, he seemed a Verlaine of the fifteenth century, while his moods like Verlaine's alternated between piety and moral defiance in a manner that appealed to the poets of the *fin de siècle*. He was translated by such Pre-Raphaelite poets as Dante Gabriel Rossetti and John Payne.

WALTER PATER

Text: *Imaginary Portraits*, 2nd edition (1890).

85   *A Prince of Court Painters*. Antoine Watteau (1684–1721), a French painter who died early of tuberculosis and whose most achieved paintings are elegant and melancholy, plays the principal role. He is glimpsed through the diary of a young girl who is in love with him, though she does not disclose her feelings even in the pages of her diary. Her brother Jean-Baptiste Pater (1695–1736) is Watteau's disciple and a painter of talent. Pater was asked whether he was a descendant of Jean-Baptiste and replied 'I think so; I believe so; I always say so.' The diarist lives in Valenciennes, North France, an artists' centre with an important Guild of Saint Luke.

88   *Un Départ de Troupes*: the first painting in Watteau's second and more personal manner, dating from about 1708 and influenced by the technique of the famous Peter Paul Rubens.

89   *William the Silent*. William (1533–84) was Stadtholder of Holland, who united his country and ruled from 1573 till his death by assassination. Though himself remaining a Latin Catholic, his sympathies lay with the Protestants. His war with Spain was largely successful but not concluded at his death.

90   *Peter Porbus*. There were three generations of Flemish painters belonging to the Porbus family. Peter (1513–84), founder of the dynasty, was the most distinguished.

I seem to have heard of a writer: the Venerable Bede (*c*. 673–735); the episode occurs in *Historia Ecclesiastica Gentis Anglorum* (The Ecclesiastical History of the English People), Bk II, Ch. XIII.

93   *jubé*: rood-screen.

95   *Monseigneur le Prince de Cambrai*: François de Salignac de la Mothe-Fénelon (1651–1715), generally known by his last name. A French ecclesiastic of great piety and a writer with poetic elegance of style. He was much influenced by the quietism of Madame Guyon and his views were condemned by the Pope and the French King Louis XIV, who exiled him from the court to his diocese of Cambrai.

96   *faille*: material with a high rib.

99   *mansard roofs*: a roof with a double slope, the lower being both larger and steeper than the upper.

100 *termes*: garden statuary, generally consisting of head and torso.

102 *fêtes champêtres*: picnics, a genre of painting.

103 *Manon Lescaut*. The Abbé Antoine François Prevost D'Exile's *Manon Lescaut* was published in 1733 and proscribed in France.

104 *Mademoiselle Rosalba*: a Venetian miniaturist and crayon portraitist, Rosalba Carriera. She made a triumphant visit to Paris in 1720 and there met Watteau, at that time in the last year of his life.

AUGUSTA WEBSTER

Text: *Selections from the Verse of Augusta Webster* (1893).

107 *Circe*. A lightly abridged version of a dramatic monologue in which Mrs Webster gives the old allegory of Circe and the animals (reason subdued by the passions) a feminist slant. The choice of Circe rather than Ulysses as protagonist is an 'Alexandrian' habit: a late and sophisticated era tends to use an unfamiliar version or portion of a myth or to recount the story from an unusual point of view. We may compare Alfred Tennyson's *Œnone*. The source of the story is Homer, *Odyssey*, XIV.

AUSTIN DOBSON

Text: *Collected Poems* (1923).

111 *A Virtuoso*. The allusions in the first four stanzas are to the suffering caused by the Prussian occupation of Northern France after the Franco-Prussian War of 1870–1.

l. 14. *Vernet*. There are three French painters of this name. Dobson is probably alluding to Émile Jean Horace (1789–1865) known for his brilliant sketches and anecdotal skill; the latter quality would probably have a special appeal for a Victorian connoisseur.

112 l. 30. *Hunt*: William Henry Hunt (1790–1867), English painter, much admired by Ruskin, particularly noted for his technique of hatching and stippling applied in detailed paintings of natural scenes.

113 l. 72. *Dürer*: Albrecht Dürer (1471–1528), famous German painter and engraver.

On a Fan that Belonged to the Marquise de Pompadour. Jeanne Antoinette Poisson Le Normant d'Étioles, Marquise de Pompadour (1721–64), mistress of the French King Louis XV, had strong cultural and intellectual influence at court, though rather less political influence than has been commonly supposed.

l. 2. *Carlo Vanloo*: French painter (1705–65) of elegant eighteenth-century manners.

l. 5. *frou-frou*: the rustling of silk.

l. 10. *Œil de Bœuf*: a round or oval window in the upper part or wall of a building. One was placed in the second antechamber of the King's palace at Versailles built by Pierre Lepautre in 1701.

114　l. 12. *Fragonard*: Jean-Honoré Fragonard (1732–1806), graceful French painter of enormous talent, full of rococo eroticism.

l. 13. *Talon-rouge, falbala, queue*: red heels worn by the aristocracy in eighteenth-century France, plaited flounces, and pigtails.

JOHN ADDINGTON SYMONDS

Text: *In the Key of Blue* (1893).

In the Key of Blue. The title furnishes an example of the fusion of different senses and arts, prevalent among symbolists, aesthetes, and decadents; 'blue' also has overtones of the melancholic and the forbidden. The homoerotic poet addresses his favourite gondolier, imaged as a moving painting, expressing admiration for the strong harmoniously-formed bodies of working men. The discreet use of scientific imagery is also of interest.

115　l. 17. *golden gaslight*: cf. Le Gallienne's 'iron lilies' in *A Ballad of London* (p. 347); faintly self-conscious use of urban imagery.

l. 22. *chrysolite*: a name now given to the precious olivine, a silicate of magnesia and iron found in lava. In colour, it varies from pale yellowish green (the precious stone) to dark bottle green.

117　l. 110. *Verditer*: a kind of pigment of green-bluish-green, or more frequently light blue colour.

l. 111. *pali*: Middle High Indian, employed in the Buddhist Scriptures of Northern India.

118　l. 125. *azure . . . gules*: heraldic colours: Nature transformed into art.

119　l. 175. *abeles*: white poplars.

MARGARET VELEY

Text: *A Marriage of Shadows and other Poems* (1888).

EDWARD DOWDEN

Text: *Poems*, ed. E. Dowden (1914).

ANONYMOUS

122　*Poem by a Perfectly Furious Academician*. First published in *Punch* and generally attributed to Tom Taylor. Ruskin's *Notes on Pictures at the Royal Academy* were widely read.

ROBERT BRIDGES

Text: *Poetical Works of Robert Bridges*, Volume II (1899).

London Snow

123 *Angel Spirits*

124 *Nightingales*

Text: *October and Other Poems* (1917).

Flycatchers.

Text: *New Poems* (1925).

125 *Poor Poll*. The metre is classical iambic trimeter (u-u-u-u-u-u) used here with a good deal of resolution, that is a long syllable replaced by two shorts. Since its most general use is in Greek comedy, the device is appropriate to the tone and subject of this poem.

126 l. 28. 'Words to the wise', Pindar, *Olympian* 2, 85. *Phonanta synctoisin*: 'verbal shafts that speak to those with understanding'. *Ktema eis aei*: 'A possession for all time', Thucidydes, *History*, 1. 22, of his own book.

l. 29. Hippolytus, in Euripides' *Hippolytus*, l. 612: 'My tongue swore, my mind is unsworn', a sophism spoken angrily to the nurse after she had sworn him to secrecy before confiding to him his stepmother Phaedra's incestuous passion for him.

l. 43. 'How many days and nights have you been beloved!'

l. 44. 'The power of my legs placed in truce', literally 'inoperative'. Dante, *Purgatorio*, 17, 75.

127 l. 64. 'It is the only difference, but it is an important one.'

l. 70. Possibly an allusion to the famous line in Racine, *Athalie*, II, v: 'C'était pendant l'horreur d'une profonde nuit.'

l. 74. 'Would that the Argo had never flown through the Symplegades,' the famous first line of Euripides' *Medea*.

l. 77. 'Absolutely incapable of understanding them.'

l. 78. 'You, Polly, you don't know that, nor can you know.'

l. 79. *scazon*: metrical term from the Greek, meaning 'limping' or 'halting', a modification of the iambic trimeter, in which a spondee or a trochee is substituted for the final iambus. The line, however, instead of being as one might perhaps expect in a scazon, seems to scan iambically.

l. 92. 'Let a happy escape be granted to the pious, because of my poetry.' Horace, Epode 16, l. 66.

EDWARD CARPENTER

Text: *Towards Democracy* (1903).

GERARD MANLEY HOPKINS

Text: *The Poems of Gerard Manley Hopkins*, 4th edition, ed. W. H. Gardner and N. H. Mackenzie (1967).

135 *The Wreck of the Deutschland*. In the first part of the poem, the stressed syllables run to the line as 2-3-4-3-5-5-4-6; in the second part of the poem the stresses in the first line change to 3. The metre is sprung so that there is freedom in the number of unstressed syllables in any line.

the Falk Laws. German anti-clerical laws passed as part of the Kulturkampf by Bismarck's government in 1873 and 1874.

l. 3. *strand*: a pun: a thread, rope, filament, no less than a shore, or country.

l. 5. Echoes of Job 10: 8–11. 'Thy hands have made me and fashioned me wholly round about and dost thou then cast me down headlong on a sudden? Thou hast clothed me with skin and flesh; thou hast put me together with bones and sinews.' See also Psalm 139. This occurs also in the Office for the Dead in the Roman Breviary.

l. 8. *find*: finding what has been lost and discovering what may be fearful.

ll. 9–12. The rod both punishes sinners and rules the just and the speaker has experienced both. cf. Psalm 2: 9 and Psalm 23: 4.

l. 23. The allusions to the Biblical dove are prolonged by the reference to the carrier pigeon, with its homing instinct.

l. 24. Two types of flame, that of Hell and that of divine love; two types of grace, 'the fear of the Lord' and the final and perfect love of God (1 John 4: 18).

136 l. 28. *combs*: probably an intransitive verb, the action of the sea-crest just before it falls or rolls over.

ll. 30–2. The streams fall in small cascades, and by analogy the gospel is the vehicle of the precious blood.

l. 31. *voel*: Welsh word meaning generally 'the bald hill'.

l. 32. The gift of the gospel is proffered freely, but God presses for an answer.

l. 39. *instressed, stressed*. God is immanent as well as transcendent, but his presence in the world is only fully realized when acknowledged in praise.

ll. 41–2. The other stress comes neither from beauty nor from terror of nature; it is involved obscurely and deeply in history and in the human condition. Time too has its stress, which holds it together as nature is held together by instress.

137   l. 58. The best or worst words are 'yes' and 'no' and determine the future.

l. 62. *flash*: looks back to l. 24.

ll. 67–8. God's anger is his 'wringing,' directed to man's malice of sin.

l. 72. *dark descending*: suggests Christ's harrowing of Hell.

ll. 77–80. Two types of conversion: immediate as with Paul; gradual as with Augustine.

138   ll. 82–3. *flange*: the projecting rim of a train's wheel which connects with the rail, suggesting death through a railway accident where a man is run over. Other forms of death are briefly catalogued and the personification with its military briskness recalls the Dance of Death tradition of Hans Holbein and others.

l. 85. A dramatic line with the final word 'Dust!' shattering the security of the image that precedes it. The allusion, picked up ironically in l. 87, is to Isaiah 11: 6–8. 'All flesh is grass, and all the glory thereof as the flower of the field. The grass is withered and the flower is fallen.' Other texts may have suggested this passage, such as Job 14: 1–2.

l. 88. *cringe*: cause to cringe. *come*: the final word resounds like an echo of Death's drum introducing the description of the *Deutschland* as she leaves harbour for her appointment with Death.

l. 89. The tone changes here and the speaker follows the reports of the shipwreck, which appeared in *The Times* from 8 December 1875 onwards.

l. 95. *bay*: like the 'vault' of l. 96, an architectural term—a recess between pillars and buttresses—but the word also puns on the natural sense.

l. 96. *rounds*: a rope coiled in millions of rounds. *reeve*: a nautical term for passing a rope through a ring or dialectally what brings together the 'gathers' or folds of a dress. But its sound suggests 'reef', 'retrieve', 'relieve', etc.

l. 98. *haven*: a homonym with 'heaven' and, as the name of the ship suggests, the nation which has left the haven of the Catholic Church.

l. 101. The spray is like solid chips of flint.

l. 103. 'The snow is sharp as wire and, in its extreme of cold, it has the same effect as the extreme of heat' (Milward, 76).

l. 107. *smother*: cloud of dust, spray, smoke, or the obscurity caused by the cloud. Hopkins seems not unusually to be using the verb as a noun.

139 l. 111. *whorl*: the spiral-shaped screw or propeller fitted to the ship's stern.

l. 116. *twelve hours gone*: the ship struck at 5 in the morning and all day there seemed a reasonable chance of rescue as ships passed fairly near, but when the day passed the situation became hopeless. Milward suggests that 'after', rather than 'for', twelve hours should be understood (82).

l. 120. *shrouds*. The newspaper report uses the word 'rigging' but Hopkins prefers 'shrouds' for its obvious double meaning: the ropes supporting the mast of a sailing ship but also the winding sheet for a corpse.

l. 128. *burl*: used as a noun, a twisted knot in wood or wool; as a verb, to bubble up like a spring, with a glance perhaps at the epithet 'burly'; full, spinning tumult.

l. 135. *a lioness arose*. The newspaper report of 11 December states: 'two German nuns, whose bodies are now in the dead house here, clasped hands and were drowned together, the chief sister, a gaunt woman six feet high, calling out loudly and often: "O Christ, come quickly!" till the end came.' And on 13 December: 'One, noted for the extreme tallness, is the lady who at mid-night on Monday, by standing on a table in the saloon, was able to thrust her body through the skylight, and kept exclaiming in a voice heard by those in the rigging above the roar of the storm, "My God, my God, make haste, make haste." ' The lioness image relates to the chief sister's courage and is suggested also by the words 'night roared' of l. 133.

l. 136. *A prophetess*: not for prophesying but for proclaiming the divine word which gives meaning to the chaos of the human scene (Milward, 93), *towered*: prolongs the architectural metaphors and suggests a connection between the chief nun, the poet himself, and Mary as Tower of David and Tower of Ivory; while the Church is often compared to a tower. *virginal*: this refers to the nun who vowed her virginity to Christ. Her tongue is musical because 'virginal' meant a species of spinet in the sixteenth and seventeenth centuries. *told*: suggests 'tolled', which in turn looks back to 'tower', and tolls for the attention of all those about to die on the ship (Milward, 94).

140 l. 137. From this stanza the speaker turns from narration to reflection, addressing his own heart.

l. 142. The syntax breaks to indicate the speaker's surprise at his own tears. *madrigal*: prolongs the musical image of l. 136 and puns on 'madre', mother, as in l. 144, 'glee'.

l. 147 *hawling*: associates 'hauling' with 'brawling'.

l. 148. 'Rash' puns on 'reckless' and rash on the skin; smart, stinging; 'sloggering' combines 'slog', 'slobber', and 'slubbering', running at the mouth and idiot pounding (Milward, 107).

l. 150. *fetch*: resource or expedient.

l. 154. *coifèd*: coif or headdress of the sister's order.

l. 155. *double a desperate name*: of the ship, and of the country that had persecuted the nuns.

l. 157. Good and evil coexist in Germany as represented by the thirteenth-century nun and mystic, St Gertrude, who lived in a convent near Eisleben, where Martin Luther was born.

l. 158. *lily*: the emblem of chastity. *beast*. Luther is a 'beast' both because of his role as one of the principal leaders of the Reformation, and because he attacked the ideal of virginity and broke his vows to marry a nun. As a Jesuit, Hopkins vowed to reverse the effects of the Reformation.

l. 165. God as Orion, the hunter of souls. *light*: alludes to the constellation and to Jesus as 'the light of the world' (John 8: 12).

141   l. 166. *unchancelling*. The chancel is the part of a church where the altar stands and which is associated with sanctuary, which the nuns have lost.

l. 168. *scroll-leaved flowers*. Snow turns to blossom, in the sight of God, so the nuns' suffering becomes a matter for joy.

l. 169. *Five*. The number of nuns suggests the number of wounds in hands, feet, and side, suffered by Christ.

ll. 171–6. 'Mark' refers to the wounds on the human person of Christ made by men, but in l. 172 he also marks the same wounds on his followers according to his foreknowledge. Mark may also suggest not only sign but number. The lamb is an emblem of sacrifice and the rose of love and martyrdom.

l. 177. *father Francis*: St Francis of Assisi, who founded the order to which the nuns belonged and who himself carried the stigmata, the wounds in the palms.

l. 180. *Lovescape*: the pattern of the crucifixion.

l. 181. *seal of his seraph-arrival*. St Francis had a vision of Christ in the form of a flaming seraph and the saint's own wounds were the 'seal' or proof of the vision.

l. 182. A further allusion to the cinquefoil.

l. 190. *the throng that catches*. Obscure: it has been suggested that both catching breath and clutching at something for safety are intended (Walford Davies, 113).

l. 192. *The cross to her*: either holding the cross to her or accepting *her* cross as sharing a part of the sufferings of Christ on Calvary. *christens her wild-worst Best*: sacramentalizes the elements that are destroying her by recognizing Christ's presence and purpose within them (Milward, 118).

142   l. 194. *Breath*: capitalized: the Holy Spirit brooding over the waters (Genesis 1: 2) and imparting the breath of life to Adam (Genesis 2: 7).

l. 195. Does she actually wish to undergo death as Christ had done?

l. 196. Both Christ and the nun reveal the loveliness of death when suffered in unison with the will of the Father (Milward, 120). There is a deliberate contrast between the two invocations 'Breath' and 'Death'.

ll. 197–8. The disciples thought differently when they feared drowning in the lake of Galilee (Matthew 14: 26).

l. 199. Did the nun see her death as martyrdom and long for its reward (the crown)?

l. 202. *down-dugged*: a grey mist or fog compared to a sow with dugs let down to give milk.

l. 209. Neither the desire for death nor for martyrdom. See Stanza 25 (Walford Davies, 112).

ll. 215–16. I would say that she had another motive for her cry . . .

ll. 218 ff. The syntax runs brokenly, enacting the poet's joy and wonder; the insight into the nun's inner life; and, at the crucial point, the frantic efforts of the dying.

l. 221. *Ipse:* He (Christ) himself.

143   l. 226. *a single eye*: the only person who saw, understood, and acted.

l. 227. *unshapeable shock night*. The horror was without shape or meaning except for the way in which the nun responded to it.

ll. 229–30. By calling 'Christ, come quickly' the nun 'interprets' the event. Christ created the world so all things 'speak' of him, are given significance by him; and Milward suggests (134) that, following Augustine, the nun adds *words* to the elements and so gives them sacramental significance.

l. 231. *Simon Peter of a soul*: see Matthew 16: 18: 'Thou art the Christ, the Son of the living God.'

l. 232. *Tarpeian-fast*. The Tarpeian was a rock cliff on the Capitoline Hill at Rome and associated here with Peter, Rock of the Church.

l. 235. The day following the tragedy, 8 December, was the Feast of the Immaculate Conception of Mary.

l. 238. As Mary herself was immaculately conceived, that is she was conceived without the stain of original sin, so too she was able to conceive Christ without loss of virginity.

l. 239. The nun's experience of Christ at the point of death also gives birth to Christ, utters the Word of God.

l. 240. *Word*: refers back to l. 233 where Christ is directly addressed.

ll. 244 ff. The dead on the ship may die unconfessed, but God's providence through the nun 'startles' them.

144   l. 250, *Yore-flood*. This can suggest both Noah's Flood (Genesis 7) and the waters of Creation (Genesis 1: 2).

l. 251. *The recurb and the recovery*. Milward (145) suggests Job 38: 8–11: 'Who shut up the sea with doors, when it broke forth as issuing out of the womb? . . . I set my bounds around it, and made bars and doors, and I said: Hitherto thou shalt come and shalt go no further.'

l. 253. *ocean of a motionable mind*. Like the sea, man's mind, as the poet has suggested before, is governed by God.

l. 256. *heeds but hides, bodes but abides*. God's concern is not obviously revealed. 'He foresees but does not forestall', perhaps, or foresees and awaits his time to intervene.

l. 260. 1 Peter 3: 19 as condensed in the Creed: 'He descended into Hell.'

l. 261. *A vein*: a channel, to the souls in Purgatory.

l. 265. *burn*: not at the last day in judgment, but now, with the fiery grace of Baptism; not material but spiritual fire: love, not punishment (Matthew 3: 11 and Acts 1: 5).

ll. 267–8. Christ was divine, physical and nourished in Mary's womb while 'of-flame' alludes to the divine flame of the Spirit of Love. The compacted words suggest the organic connections.

l. 269. The second person of the Trinity.

l. 270. Christ is revealed not in the dazzling power of judgment; nor in the dark of his natural birth.

l. 272. *flash to the shire*: an English administrative area visited by the brilliant rain, brilliant with revelation. This leads on to the stress on the reconversion of England at the conclusion of the poem.

l. 273. *Dame*: the nun, formally addressed, as now in Heaven.

l. 275. *roads*: stretch of water near the shore where ships can ride at anchor. *reward*: will be the accomplishment of the work of Hopkins and his fellow members of the Society of Jesus for the recovery of England to the Catholic faith.

145   l. 277. *easter*: used as a verb. Let him 'rise again in us'. Fr Peter, SJ suggests that Easter, 'also nautically the East, alludes to Christ as the dayspring from on high'.

The Starlight Night. The first and ninth lines are in sprung rhythm. The theme of the sonnet is that the beauty of the night can, and must, be paid for by prayer, patience, alms, and vows, for its outward splendour is conditioned by the power and beauty of Christ.

l. 5. *quickgold*: a coined word, analogous to 'quicksilver'.

l. 6. *whitebeam ... abeles*: chess apple and white poplar. The white undersides of their leaves are exposed when fluttered by the wind.

l. 10. *May-mess*: stars like clusters of blossom on the May (hawthorn) tree. Mary-mass—festival for Mary—may be suggested.

l. 11. *mealed-with-yellow sallows*. Sallows are pussy willows and meal suggests the powdery coating of their yellow flowers. ll. 10–11 continue an equivalence between the stars and the rural scene.

l. 12. *the barn*. The suggestion that the visible beauty of night and the stars store the real wealth within the barn also evokes Christ's birth in the broken–down stable at Bethlehem.

l. 13. *This piece-bright paling*: paling is the sky's fence, bright with the stars which look like pieces of eight. Paling could also be a present participle, paling as dawn comes (so relating back to l. 5) and in comparison with the real glories behind: Christ, Mary, and the saints or hallows.

Spring and Fall. The rhythm is sprung with four stresses to a line, with a stressed first syllable at the beginning of a line following one with a falling rhythm.

l. 2. *Goldengrove*: not unknown as a proper name, though Hopkins possibly invented this description of autumn woods with their fallen leaves.

l. 6. *colder*: both 'it will come to such sights less emotionally' and 'it will also come to colder sights than this'. Both meanings stress the theme that it is not nature's death that we really mourn.

146   l. 8. *wanwood*: the pale or sick wood. *leafmeal*: like 'piecemeal'—leaves shed in scatterings.

ll. 9–16. The child in future years will know that what she mourns is human mortality, 'yet' qualifying the 'nor' of line 7. But it remains pointless to name the real source of grief. Such intimations of human mortality come at present from below the levels of understanding, from the 'heart', the emotion, the instinctive feelings, and from the 'ghost', the soul.

ll. 14. *blight*. Man was born for death, particularly as brought into the world by sin; the 'Fall' of the title also covertly refers to the Fall of man.

146 *Inversnaid*. l. 1. *burn*: a stream in Scots.

l. 3. The convex and concave 'rib' effects of water running over stones.

l. 4. *Flutes*: as of a column, 'makes grooves in'.

l. 5. The light vapour caused by the descent of a waterfall into a pool.

l. 6. *twindles*: compacts 'twists' and 'dwindles'.

l. 9. *Degged*: a Lancashire dialectal word, 'sprinkled'.

l. 11. *heathpacks*: heather clumps. *flitches*: tufts.

l. 12. *beadbonny*. Walford Davies suggests that this might allude to the purplish, almost knobbly clusters of the ordinary ash tree flowers or the bright scarlet berries of the Mountain Ash.

Duns Scotus's Oxford. The metre is sprung rhythm with 'outriding' feet. John Duns Scotus (1265/75–1308), Franciscan Scholastic philosopher, taught at Oxford. Hopkins read his works while studying at Stonyhurst; Scotus's stress on the individuality, 'haecceitas', the 'thisness' of things, mirrored Hopkins's own developing philosophy of art. Oxford has changed, in particular the clear balance between old city and country, but the speaker can walk the same city, breathe the same air, for he now has the same insight into the nature of reality.

l. 2. Onomatopaeic rendering of the raucous rook among the civil, natural noises of the city.

147 l. 5. *brickish skirt*: the suburban brick buildings that muffle the direct encounter (l. 4) between grey-walled city and the country surrounding it. The word 'which' must be understood before 'sours'.

l. 11. Hopkins pays tribute to Duns Scotus's justification of the role of the senses in the experiencing of the real.

l. 12. *realty*: reality.

l. 13. *Italy*: an allusion to St Thomas Aquinas, the thirteenth-century philosopher, one of the four Doctors of the Church and Scotus's rival. *Greece:* the source of much Western philosophy, e.g. Plato and Aristotle.

l. 14. *fired France for Mary without spot*. Lecturing in Paris, Scotus demanded the acceptance of the doctrine of the Immaculate Conception of Christ's mother and in this sense also he is a rival of Aquinas.

Felix Randal. l. 1. *farrier*: blacksmith.

l. 5. *broke him*: a suggestion of 'breaking' an animal.

l. 7. *reprieve and ransom*: Holy Communion.

l. 8. An appropriate dialectal expression: 'all road ever' is a Lancashire expression for 'in whatever way'.

l. 9. *us too*: we as priests.

l. 13. *random*: a richly expressive epithet, applying at once to rough stone and the clutter of the forge, and perhaps suggesting random sparks from the fire. *peers*: either other brawny smiths or the horses themselves.

l. 14. *fettle*: dialectal for conditioning and trimming. *sandal*: horseshoe.

148   '*I wake and feel the fell of dark, not day.*' l. 1. *fell*: a noun. The hairy skin of an animal, but the word has the force of the epithet 'fierce' or 'terrible' and suggests 'fall' in its preterite form, 'fell'.

l. 4. *And more must*: more horror till the daylight, literal or spiritual, dawns.

l. 12. 'The spirit should leaven or transform the *dull dough* of physical existence; but, being embroiled in a total selfness, it only *sours*.' (Walford Davies, p. 145.)

That Nature is a Heraclitean Fire and of the Comfort of the Resurrection. A sonnet with three codas or 'tails' modelled after Milton's one-tailed or 'caudated' sonnet. The metre is sprung rhythm. For discussion of this poem see Paul Mariana's *A Commentary on the Complete Poems of Gerard Manley Hopkins* (Ithaca and London, 1970), pp. 280–90. For this commentator all Hopkins' geese are swans.

Title: Heraclitus was a Greek philosopher (*c.* 535–*c.* 475 BC), who taught that the principle of flux is the only permanent reality. The elements are in a continuous state of conflict but fire remains the underlying substance of the universe; the other elements are merely transformations of it.

l. 1. *chevy*: scamper or chase.

l. 4. *Shivelights*: strips of light.

ll. 5–9. These describe how all signs of the human are lost as a consequence of the action of rain, wind, and sun. Nature's beauty depends on destruction and recreation.

l. 6. *rut peel*: possibly a compound word.

149   l. 14. *disseveral*: a coined word, uniting the separate and aloof: both distinct and severed (Walford Davies, 112).

l. 21. Echoes of biblical texts: 2 Peter 3: 10; 1 Corinthians 15: 52–4, and Matthew 24: 29–32.

l. 23. *Jack*: a common fellow or one without defined identity; *patch:* fool, a scrap of material used for mending.

ANDREW LANG

Text: *The Poetical Works of Andrew Lang*, Volume II, ed. Mrs Lang (1923).

ARTHUR O'SHAUGHNESSY

Text: *Poems of Arthur O'Shaughnessy*, selected and edited by William Alexander Percy (1923).

EUGENE LEE-HAMILTON

Text: *Apollo and Marsyas and other Poems* (1884).

152 *Ipsissimus.* The Latin title means the very same (man). The theme is that of the *Doppelgänger*, a dark double. The notion of the divided self of simultaneous duality and unity is not uncommon in Victorian poetry, particularly later in the century. Here the speaker's good angel or better self is treated with broad irony, almost a caricature.

Text: *Sonnets of the Wingless Hours* (1894).

155 *On Two of Signorelli's Frescoes.* These powerful frescoes are in the Cathedral of Orvieto. Of the first, a French critic remarks that Signorelli has done away with the usual Gothic or Renaissance tombs that act as a springboard for the resurrected bodies in the traditional iconography to obtain 'un effet oblique de profondeur': the dead awake from their long dream vigorous and joyful.

156 *Judith and Holofernes.* An episode taken from the apocryphal book of *Judith*, particularly 10: 10 and 13: 10, and popular with Renaissance and Baroque artists. Judith, like Salome, is a type of the Fatal Woman who beheads (castrates) the male.

157 *Fading Glories.* l. 5. *mitred, croziered, and superbly stoled*: a comment on the passing of the absolute truths of the Christian faith.

WILLIAM JAMES RENTON

Text: *Oils and Water Colours* (1876).

159 *The Bee.* Renton appears to respond to R. W. Emerson's poem, 'The Humble Bee', though there are no direct verbal reminiscences.

ALICE MEYNELL

Text: *Alice Meynell. Prose and Poetry*, Centenary Volume ed. F. G., V. M., O. S., and F. M. (1947).

160 *The Lady Poverty.* The legend of Saint Francis tells us that he had three visions of the Lady Poverty. In the first, she appeared to him

richly apparelled; by the third, she was dressed in rags but more beautiful than ever, and the saint took her in mystical marriage.

162   *Unto us a Son is Given.* The title is from Isaiah 9: 6.

163   '*I am the Way.*' The title is from John 14: 6.

DIGBY MACKWORTH DOLBEN

Text: *The Uncollected Poems of Digby Mackworth Dolben*, ed. M. Cohen (Reading, 1973).

> *A Song of the Bar.* l. 4. *Builth*: Builth Wells, a small town in Central Wales. A curious anticipation of John Betjeman's mode.

EDWIN JOHN ELLIS

Text: *Fate in Arcadia* (1892).

164   *Himself.* l. 4. *upright*: a range of meanings that includes just, bravely suffering, and the actual posture of the crucifixion.

RICHARD JEFFERIES

Text: *The Life of the Fields* (1884).

167   from *The Life of the Fields*. The epigraph appeared in the Elizabethan anthology *The Passionate Pilgrim*, ll. 8–10 from a lyric beginning 'As it fell upon a day/In the merry month of May' by Richard Barnfield (1574–1627).

172   *Ulysses in the battle with Irus.* In Homer's *Odyssey*, XVIII, Irus the Beggar is insolent to the disguised Odysseus. Odysseus meditates whether to kill Irus or to maim him severely, and decides on the latter.

SIR EDMUND GOSSE

Text: *The Collected Poems of Edmund Gosse* (1911).

173   *Neurasthenia.* The word 'neurasthenia' is first recorded in 1856 (*Oxford English Dictionary*) as indicating functional weakness of the nervous system, not unconnected with the pace and complexity of urban life in the nineteenth century.

174   *Opium Harvest.* l. 2. *Karahissar*: an area in Northern Assam, India.

175   *Manes, the Heretic.* Manes (or Mani) (*c.* 216–76) was a Persian, influenced by Gnosticism, and the dualist traditions of his own country. He saw himself as the last of a line of prophets that included the Buddha, the Hebrew prophets, and Jesus, who had been sent to assist man in his struggle to release the particles of light in men's souls,

particles which had been stolen by Satan, the adversary, from a higher world and imprisoned in men's brains. The mode of release was through stringent asceticism, including vegetarianism. The sect spread into Europe and influenced the medieval dualists. Manes met much opposition and was flayed alive.

WILLIAM ERNEST HENLEY

Text *Poems*, Vol. 1 (1908).

177 *Nocturn.*

ooo '*Out of the night that covers me*'. l. 2. *the Pit*: a not uncommon metaphor in the Authorized Version.

l. 3. A fine contempt for nice distinctions between one god and another; a swashbuckling Agnosticism. Compare Swinburne's 'The Garden of Proserpine', l. 84, 'Whatever gods may be'.

178 l. 13. *strait the gate*: cf. Matthew 7: 13 and Luke 13: 24.

l. 14. *scroll*: of the recording angel. It has apocalyptic resonances. Cf. also the *Dies Irae*; and also Isaiah 34: 4 and Revelation 6: 4.

'*Madam Life's a piece in bloom*'. l. 1. *piece*: a sexually experienced woman; here, perhaps, not so much the Madame of the brothel as a prostitute whose pimp is death.

Text: *Poems*, Vol. II (1908).

179 *Villon's Straight Tip to All Cross Coves.* A version in thieves' slang of François Villon's 'Ballade de Bonne Doctrine' (ll. 1692–1719 of *Le Testament*). The epigraph reproduces the refrain of the original. The title is Villon's good advice to all crooks.

Henley was the joint author of a dictionary of slang and argot and this has been used to gloss the vocabulary of the translation, see *Slang and its Analogues. A Dictionary Historical and Comparative of the Heterodox Speech of all Classes of Society for More than Three Hundred Years. With Synonyms in English, French, German, Italian, etc.*, compiled and edited by John S. Farmer and W. E. Henley, 3 vols. (1890–1912). It should be noted that a fair number of the words refer also to the female pudenda, one of the principal objects of Henley's research. There are only one or two argot words in Villon's original.

l. 1. *screeve*: write a begging letter. *cheap-jack*: minting and issuing counterfeit coins.

l. 2. *fake the broads*: rig playing cards. *fig a nag*: ginger up, disguise a horse for purposes of deception.

l. 3. *thimble-rig*: perform a card-sharping trick. *knap a yack*: steal a watch.

l. 4. *pitch a snide*: do business with a counterfeit coin. *smash a rag*: pass forged bank notes.

l. 5. *duff*: sell flashy, pretended well-made, stolen or fraudulently obtained goods: palm off false jewellery as real. *nose and lag*: inform the police for pay so that a criminal is convicted or a returned transport (to Australia) captured.

l. 6. *get the straight . . . land your pot*: by honest means gain a large sum.

l. 7. *melt*: blow, spend. *multy*: an intensive expletive.

l. 8. *Booze . . . blowens*: drink . . . prostitutes, or fine-built handsome girls.

l. 9. *Fiddle*: cheat, gamble. *fence*: dispose of stolen goods. *mace*: defraud. *mack*: procure, pander.

l. 10. *flash the drag*: to wear women's clothing for immoral or criminal purposes.

l. 11. *Dead-lurk*: to enter dwelling houses during church services. *crib*: house. *crack*: burgle.

l. 12. *Pad with a slang*: cheat with a false weight. *chuck a fag*: beat up.

l. 13. *Bonnet*: cheat. *tout*: a boy thief who enters by windows or acts as lookout or begs. *mump*: beg. *gag*: inform on.

l. 14. *Rattle the tats*: rapidly move the dice. *mark the spot*: pick out a victim.

l. 15. *stag*: shilling.

l. 18. *flash your flag*: sport a badge of office when off duty, be absolutely dependable.

l. 19. *penny-a-lining*: working as a literary hack.

l. 20. *mummers*: small-time actors. *mum and gag*: grimace and joke. The repetition of the word 'gag', but in a sense different from that used in l. 13, constitutes *rime riche*, a device often used in French poetry and adopted by some poets in England during the 1890s. It is not present in the Villon text.

l. 21. *nix*: nothing. *dibbs*: money.

l. 22. *graft*: work.

l. 23. *goblins*: sovereigns. *stravag*: abscond, disappear.

l. 25. *up the spout*: pawned. *Charley Wag*: disappear.

l. 26. *wipes*: handkerchiefs. *tickers*: watches.

l. 27. *squeezer*: hangman's noose. *nips*: pinches. *scrag*: neck.

ROBERT LOUIS STEVENSON

Text: *Weir of Hermiston* (1896). A posthumously published, fairly substantial fragment of a novel.

180   *Life and Death of Mrs Weir. Flodden*: an English victory over the Scots, fought 9 September 1513 near Branxton, Northumberland, on the Border. King James IV of Scotland led his troops and the Earl of Surrey was the English commander. James lost the battle and was himself killed as a consequence of an excess of chivalry.

peel door. A peel is a general word used to describe the small tower or fortified house built by both English and Scots on their borders in the sixteenth century.

James the Fifth. James V (1512–42) began his reign in 1513. He died young, of shock and depression induced by the defeat of his troops by the English at the battle of Solway Moss.

Hell-Fire Club: an aristocratic club which practised amateur Satanism in the eighteenth century and gave its name to other similar institutions.

grieve: an overseer, under-bailiff, or resident agent.

peat-hag: a projecting mass of peat forming an escarpment on a peat moor as a consequence of digging.

Kye-skairs: bare land where cows were pastured.

181   *menseful*: proper, discreet, tidy.

182   *gigot*: haunch of sheep or leg of mutton.

puddocks: frogs.

kebbuck: cheese.

183   *bonnet-laird*: a petty proprietor in Scotland, who wore a bonnet like the humbler classes.

184   *Rutherford's 'Letters'*. Samuel Rutherford (1600–61) was a Scots Presbyterian divine, who was prominent on the Parliamentary side at the time of the English Civil War and the interregnum. His letters of spiritual counsel were reprinted a number of times under the title of *Spiritual Letters or Joshua Redivivus*. They are notable for religious unction, a vigorous use of lowland Scots dialect, and a devotion, sensuous and mystical, to the human person of Jesus.

Scougal's 'Grace Abounding'. This reference is presumably to Henry Scougal (1650–78), a disciple of Archbishop Robert Leighton's mildly episcopalian Arminianism. There is no work of Scougal's with the Pauline title (cf. Bunyan's work of that title). The reference may be to his popular work, *The Life of God in the Soul of Man* (1677).

Bloody Mackenzie. Sir George Mackenzie (1636–91) acquired his nickname from his severe treatment of the Covenanters. He was King's Advocate in Scotland.

Lauderdale. John Maitland, second Earl of Lauderdale (1616–82), was Secretary for Scottish Affairs (1660–80); he aimed at making the crown absolute in that country both in church and state and persecuted religious dissenters. Created a Duke in 1672.

Rothes. John Leslie, seventh Earl and first Duke of Rothes (1630–81), became Lord Chancellor in 1667.

185   *policy*: the pleasure garden of a country house.

186   *Naphtali.* It is difficult to determine whether this is an instance of Mrs Weir's vagueness. A Mount Naphtali is mentioned in Joshua 20: 7. The name is supposed to mean 'eminence' but also describes a hilly territory west and north of Galilee.

     speldering in the glaur: fooling about in the mud.

188   *palmering about in bauchles*: wandering idly about in slippers.

189   *füshionless*: without pith or substance.

     quean: a woman, generally young, though not in this instance.

     feckless carline: incompetent old woman.

     cheek of the hearth: side of the hearth.

190   *dwaibly*: feeble or more figuratively low-spirited, devoid of nervous strength.

     skirling: screeching or screaming.

     gey: very.

GEORGE MOORE

Text: *The Untilled Field and The Lake: The Collected Works of George Moore,* Carra Edition, VIII (New York, 1923).

OSCAR WILDE

Text: *The Picture of Dorian Gray* (1891).

199   *The Preface to the Picture of Dorian Gray.*

Text: *The Ballad of Reading Gaol* (1898).

200   *The Ballad of Reading Gaol.* l. 1. *He*: Charles T. Woolridge, a former trooper in the Royal Horse Guards who had murdered his wife.

201   l. 7. *Trial Men*: prisoners whom the court has sentenced and who may have the chance of an appeal.

203   l. 96. *Caiaphas*: a high priest of the Jews who presided at the trial of Jesus. Judas bargained with him for thirty pieces of silver to be paid over when he kissed Christ, so identifying him as the enemy of the Pharisees.

205   l. 173. *gin*: trap.

     l. 175. *Debtors' Yard*: a portion of the exercise ground in the prison formerly set apart for those imprisoned for debt.

206 ll. 188–9. The Governor took a strong line which tended to mute the provisions of the act requiring humane treatment for the prisoners. Wilde was probably remembering Major Isaacson, who was Governor of Reading Gaol at the time when the poet was transferred there.

207 l. 217. *tore the tarry rope*: to make oakum for calking ships.

209 l. 291. *rigadoon*: a lively dance.

l. 298. *saraband*: a slow Spanish dance.

l. 301. *pirouettes of marionettes*: spinning on the points of the toes like dancing puppets.

213 l. 422. *crooked arrows*: the mark used to indicate convict wear.

214 ll. 466–7. *the barren staff ... sight*: see note to p. 76, l. 166 of Swinburne's *Ave Atque Vale*.

218 l. 604. See Luke 23: 39–43.

ll. 623–4. See Psalm 51: 17.

OLIVE SCHREINER

Text: *The Story of an African Farm* (1883).

221 from *The Story of an African Farm*. 'For wide is the gate ... thereat': Matthew 7: 13–14, Authorized Version.

WILLIAM SHARP

Text: *Selected Writings of William Sharp*, arranged by Mrs William Sharp, Volume I (1912).

MARY DUCLAUX

Text: *The Collected Poems, Lyrical and Narrative, of A. Mary F. Robinson* (1902).

T. W. ROLLESTON

Text: *Sea Spray* (1909).

237 *The Dead at Clonmacnois*. Clonmacnois on the bank of the Shannon, south of Athlone, was the burial place of the ancient Kings of Ireland, a sacred spot.

l. 2. *Saint Kieran's city*. Saint Kieran is now better known as Ciaran; he founded the monastery at Clonmacnois in the sixth century.

l. 7. *Ogham*: an old Irish alphabet in use from about the fifth to the tenth centuries. It had twenty characters and was based on Latin though schematized into a system of strokes and dots.

JOHN DAVIDSON

Text: *The Poems of John Davidson*, ed. Andrew Turnbull, Volume 1 (1973).

The Wastrel. l. 1. *knock*: a small hill (Scots).

238   l. 6. *cushats*: wood pigeons or ring-doves, a Scots form.

l. 7. *Conybeare-and-Howson*: *The Life and Epistles of St Paul* published in two volumes in 1852 by John Conybeare and John Howson, Dean of Chester.

l. 8. *Meyer's and Lange's comments*. The Evangelical Heinrich A. W. Meyer's critical and exegetical commentary on the New Testament was translated into English and published at Edinburgh in twenty volumes between 1873 and 1885. Johann Peter Lange was the Evangelical Professor of Theology at Bonn and his commentaries on the Gospels and the Book of Revelation were translated into English between 1839 and 1872.

240   *Thirty Bob a Week.* l. 20. *hunks*: miser.

241   l. 63. *engrugious*: egregious, extraordinary.

SIR WILLIAM WATSON

Text: *The Collected Poems of William Watson*, 1 (1898).

GEORGE GISSING

Text: *A Victim of Circumstances and Other Stories* (1927).

J. K. STEPHEN

Text: *Lapsus Calami and Other Poems*, ed. Herbert Stephen (1896).

FRANCIS THOMPSON

Text: *Francis Thompson's Poetical Works*, ed. Wilfred Meynell (1937).

266   from *The Hound of Heaven*. 'Hound' was an honorific term in Celtic Mythology and was not unknown in the African Church where one of the faithful is described as 'the hound of the divinity'. Connolly (p. 351) cites Augustine, *Confessions*, IV. iv: 'And lo, You at the heels of those who are fleeing from You, God of Vengeance and yet Fountain of Pity . . .' Compare also (Connolly, p. 356) Psalm 138: 7–12.

l. 14. *instant*: in the sense of the Latin *instans*, pressing upon, urgent.

267   l. 24. *Wist.* knew.

NOTES

437

268   *Arab Love-Song*. l. 1. Thompson's note: 'Cloud shapes observed by travellers in the East.'

269   *The Kingdom of God*. The title is taken from Luke 17: 21; the sub-title from Psalm 137: 4; Exodus 2: 22: 'I have been a stranger in a strange land.'

l. 19. *Jacob's ladder*: Genesis 28: 12. The ladder on which Jacob saw angels going up and down between heaven and earth.

l. 20. *Charing Cross*: the site of one of the crosses erected in 1290 to mark the spots where the coffin of Edward I's wife Eleaner rested on its final journey to Westminster. The nineteenth-century version of the cross is in the forecourt of the railway terminus of the same name. The site is near to Trafalgar Square, perhaps the central focus of London.

l. 24. *Gennesareth*: the sea of Galilee (Matthew 14: 25–33).

A. E. HOUSMAN

Text: *The Collected Poems of A. E. Housman* (New York, 1939).

272   '*Crossing Alone the Nighted Ferry*'. Written to a contemporary at Oxford, Moses Jackson, an athlete with whom Housman was in love and who had told the poet to 'Throw the thought away'.

273   *The Oracles*. l. 1. *Dodona*: in Thessaly, Northern Greece, sacred to Zeus and presided over by Dove Priestesses who read the omens from the oak leaves.

l. 3. *midland navel-stone*: the omphalos at Apollo's shrine, a sacred place, the navel of the world.

l. 13. *The King with half the East at heel*: Xerxes the Persian Emperor.

l. 16. *The Spartans*. Xerxes, the Persian invader, sent scouts to observe the Spartans. It was reported that they were doing exercises and combing their hair. A Greek with Xerxes' army pointed out that this was a Spartan custom when going to fight for their lives. The episode is retailed in Herodotus, Book 7, Chapters 208 and 209.

274   *Fragment of a Greek Tragedy*. A parody of woodenly literal translations of Greek tragic poetry, with some mild amusements at the stage conventions of the dramatists, e.g. the incapacity of the Chorus for action and their sententiousness.

l. 2. *Head of a traveller*: an honorific way of addressing a person, as in the first line of the *Antigone*.

l. 4. *well-nightingaled vicinity*: recalls Sophocles' *Oedipus at Colonus*, l. 18.

ll. 6–8. cf. Aeschylus' *Agamemnon*, ll. 1059–60, Clytemnestra to Cassandra: 'If you do not understand me, signify it with your outlandish hand.'

276   *Diffugere Nives*. A translation of Horace, *Odes* IV, 7.

277   l. 15. *Tullus ... Ancus*: Tullus Hostilius and Ancus Martius, early Roman kings.

l. 16. *Aeneas*: the founder of Rome and hero of Virgil's epic the *Aeneid*.

l. 17. *Torquatus*: name of an early Roman patrician family.

l. 25. *Hippolytus*: the beautiful young man devoted to chastity and the hunt, who denied Aphrodite worship and fell under the goddess's curse. His stepmother Phaedra, at Aphrodite's instigation, fell in love with him; an oath he had sworn prevented Hippolytus from telling his father what had occurred; Phaedra committed suicide to protect her children and left a note accusing Hippolytus of rape although the young man had rejected her advances. His father launched the last of three prayers which he had the power to inflict. He came to discover Hippolytus's innocence but the young man had already been mortally injured as a consequence of the curse, and Hippolytus's patroness, the goddess Artemis, was unable to save him.

l. 27. *Theseus ... Pirithöus*. These two heroes provided a signal example of noble friendship. After sharing some enterprises together, they resolved to carry off a daughter of the gods. Theseus, assisted by his friend, carried off Helen from Sparta, but Pirithous decided to take Persephone, Queen of the Dead. Although aware of the virtual impossibility of the task, Theseus out of friendship accompanied Pirithous into the underworld. Both were seized by Pluto, King of the Dead, and chained to a rock. Theseus, as the less guilty of the two, was rescued by Hercules on his visit to Hades to bring back Alcestis; but Pirithous remained in eternal torment.

MARY COLERIDGE

Text: *The Collected Poems of Mary Coleridge*, ed. Theresa Whistler (1954).

SIR HENRY NEWBOLT

Text: *Selected Poems of Henry Newbolt*, ed. Patric Dickinson (1981).

279   *Drake's Drum*. Sir Francis Drake (1540–96), was an English admiral who circumnavigated the globe (1577–80). He harried Spanish ships and settlements and acted as an admiral with the fleet that defeated the Spanish Armada in 1588. Defeated by the Spanish in the West Indies, he died at sea. As a national hero much 'after-belief' has gathered round his name, including the legend that, if his drum is beaten at a

time of national danger, he will, like the Emperor Charlemagne or King Arthur, return to save his people.

l. 3. *Nombre Dios Bay*: a major Spanish port in the West Indies, scene of several of Drake's more remarkable exploits and of his death.

l. 4. *Plymouth Hoe*: the land on the northern edge of Plymouth Sound, near Drake's home port on the south-west coast of England.

'MICHAEL FIELD'

Text: *Long Ago* (1889).

280 *And on my Eyes Dark Sleep by Night*. The epigraph is from Sappho, Fragment 34. Eds Lobel and D. Page, *Poetarum Lesbiorum Fragmenta*, Carminum Sapphicorum fragmenta incerti (Oxford, 1955): 'On my eyes the dark sleep of night.'

281 *Gold is the Son of Zeus: neither Moth nor Worm may Gnaw it*. The epigraph is from Sappho, Fragment 87, in Lobel and Page. The editors refer to a quotation in a scholion on Pindar: 'gold is the child of Zeus, neither moth nor worm devours it.'

ARTHUR MORRISON

Text: *Tales of Mean Streets* (1894).

283 from *Lizerunt. Commercial Road*: an important artery slanting from west to east in the East End of London, just north of the docklands.

RUDYARD KIPLING

Text: *The Collected Works of Rudyard Kipling*, Volume 3 (New York, 1941).

295 *The Man who would be King*. The opening scene of the story takes place in the state of Rajastan, north of Bombay and just east of the great desert and the present India–Pakistan border.

299 *Zenana-mission ladies*: women who carried on mission work among Hindu and Muslim women secluded in Purdah.

Modred's shield: Modred was the cunning and cowardly nephew of King Arthur.

303 *Roberts' Army*. General Sir Frederick (later Field-Marshal Earl) Robert (1832–1914) led a victorious small force into Afghanistan in 1878–9 and again in 1880 when he made his famous march from Kabul to Kandahar.

325 *The Emperor in his habit as he lived*: cf. *Hamlet*, III. iv. 135.

The Son of God goes forth to war: a hymn by Reginald Heber (1783–1827) who became Bishop of Calcutta.

Text: *Rudyard Kipling's Verse*: Definitive Edition (1940).

326 *Danny Deever*. l. 1. *Files-on-Parade*: a private soldier.

l. 2. *Colour-Sergeant*: the ranking non-commissioned officer.

l. 6. *'ollow square*: hollow square, a formation used for ceremonial occasions.

327 l. 23. *county*. Regiments were often recruited from and named after specific English counties.

327 *Mandalay*. Mandalay is a city in Burma along the Irriwaddy. Burma was a British protectorate from 1886 to 1947 and was garrisoned by units of the Indian Army.

l. 1. *Moulmein Pagoda*: a Buddhist temple at Moulmein, across the Gulf of Martaban from Rangoon.

l. 6. *the old Flotilla*: the boats of the Irriwaddy Flotilla Company, plying between Rangoon and Mandalay.

l. 7. *Rangoon*: a city, the centre of British administration, situated near the mouth of the Irriwaddy about 375 miles below Mandalay.

l. 12. *Supi-yaw-lat:* Supaiyah Lat, wife of Thebaw, King of Burma from 1876 to 1885.

328 l. 16. *Budd*: Buddha.

l. 22. *hathis*: elephants trained to pile up logs of teak, a hard wood used in ship construction.

l. 37. *Chelsea*: a suburb to the west of London on the north bank of the Thames, of much historical interest and associated with artists. *Strand*: a London street that runs along the left bank of the Thames between Westminster and Fleet Street, the centre of the theatre district in the 1890s.

329 *The Song of the Banjo*. l. 1. *Broadwood*: a piano.

l. 7. *tails*: straggles.

330 l. 35. *rowel*: spur.

l. 41. *blooded*: initiated.

l. 44. *backstay:* a wire rope that supports the mast of a ship; in a high wind it vibrates.

l. 45. *Hya! Heeya! . . . Haul*: a sailor chant to ensure that all heave together.

l. 48. *Johnny Bowlegs . . . trek*: alludes to a South African song: 'Pack up your kit and trek, Johnny with the limping leg.'

l. 54. *many-shedded levels*: stretches of railroad track protected from snow and avalanches by being enclosed in sheds.

l. 56. *Song of Roland*: ninth- or tenth-century French epic poem. Roland was the principal knight of the Emperor Charlemagne.

l. 58. *croup*: rump.

l. 87. *Stealer*: Hermes, god of theft and protector of thieves. After stealing some of Apollo's cattle, he made reparation by giving Apollo the lyre which he had contrived out of a sea shell.

l. 94. *What d'ye lack*: traditional appeal of London peddlars and shopkeepers to passers-by.

l. 96. *Delos*: an island in the Aegean Sea, birthplace of Apollo, God of poetry and music. *Limerick*: an Irish town in the province of Munster, that has given its name to a species of nonsense poem of five lines. The allusions stress that the banjo covers all classes of song.

ARTHUR SYMONS

Text: *Poems*, Volume One (1924).

332 *Episode of a Night of May*. Written on 21 May 1888.

333 l. 8. *Giroflée*: a dance in the form of a folding and unfolding flower.

Colour Studies: At Dieppe. The poem is dedicated to Walter Richard Sickert (1860–1942), English painter, disciple of Whistler and also influenced by the French Impressionists.

Text: *Poems*, Volume Three (1924).

334 *Nini Patte-en-l'air*. Written on 14 May 1892, at Paris.

l. 5. *Nini Patte-en-l'air*. Symons's essay on 'Dancers and Dancing' of 1897 has a section on Nini, where she is described as 'the directress of the sole *école du chuhut* at present existing in the world'. Elsewhere he describes the *chuhut* as 'the successor, one might almost say the renaissance, of the *cancan*'. The essay is reprinted in *Colour Studies in Paris* (1918).

335 *Faint Love*. Charles Conder (1868–1909) was a painter, particularly of fans.

W. B. YEATS

Text: W. B. Yeats, *The Poems. A New Edition*, ed. by Richard J. Finneran (New York, 1983).

The Man who Dreamed of Faeryland. l. 1. *Dromahair*: a village in County Leitrim, Ireland.

336 l. 13. *Lissadell*: a barony just north of the town of Sligo, Ireland, where the Gore-Booth family is seated; the first great house to which Yeats was invited as poet.

l. 21. *golden or the silver skies*: principles of the sun and moon, which when fused become an alchemical emblem of perfection.

l. 22. *a dancer*: an early appearance in Yeats's work of one of his major symbols, representing unity of body and spirit, mind and body.

l. 25. *Scanavin*: a site in County Sligo.

l. 37. *hill of Lugnagall*: a steep cliff near to Ben Bulben, a great limestone mass in County Sligo. It is also glossed as 'the hollow of the foreigners', presumably referring to the ground below the cliff.

337   *The Song of Wandering Aengus*. Aengus, the Master of Love, was the Irish god of youth, beauty, and poetry, who reigned in Tir-na-nogue, the country of the Young, here conflated with a poet, one of his devotees, rather in the manner of the Dionysus of Euripides' *Bacchae*.

338   *He Reproves the Curlew*. l. 2. *the West*: in Yeats's early poetry, the region of 'fading and dreaming things'.

l. 6. *wind*: a symbol of vague desires and hopes.

He Hears the Cry of the Sedge. l. 4. *the axle break*: the world tree, associated by Yeats with the hazel.

l. 7. An allusion to the initiation ceremony of the Rosicrucian Order of the Golden Dawn, which Yeats joined in 1890 and of which he became, after several schisms, virtual dictator.

He Thinks of Those Who Have Spoken Evil of His Beloved. l. 5. *a mouthful of air*: a phrase Yeats uses to describe the fairies: 'nations of gay creatures, having no souls, nothing in their bright bodies, but a handful of sweet air.'

JOHN GRAY

Text: *John Gray: Five Fugitive Poems*, ed. I. Fletcher (Edinburgh, 1983).

339   *Song of the Stars*.

Text: *Silverpoints* (1893).

Charleville. The original poem by Rimbaud is 'A La Musique'. Gray tends to dilute the concrete and brutal into the rococo. l.4, for example, is elegantly vague for Rimbaud: 'portent ... leurs bêtises jalouses', while the 'trooper with a rose between his teeth' is a figure out of *Opéra Bouffe*: Rimbaud's trooper is smoking 'des roses', a brand of tobacco. The mistranslation was probably deliberate; this is clear from an additional stanza from the Princeton MS of the poem, which is entitled 'Charleroi'. It occurs after l. 12.

Flattening on the seat his rotund haunch
A bourgeois with bright buttons Flemish paunch
Fondles his overstuffed tobacco pouch
Probably contraband one cannot vouch.

ll. 29–32 in the MS are also of interest:

Only my rustling tread, deliberate, slow;
The rippled silence from the still leaves drips:
I have stripped off the boots the stockings now
Naked they stand my eyes embrace their hips.

340 *Parsifal.* Verlaine's poem was first published in *La Revue Wagnerienne*, 8 January 1886, and collected in *Amour* (1888). The original has the same title. Wagner was a culture hero in the 1890s and there are many references to him, and particularly to 'Parsifal', with its mixture of religion and sexuality, in both the English and French literature of the time.

Text: *The Long Road* (1926).

341 *The Flying Fish.* C. V. Cevasco in his *John Gray* (1983) suggests that this poem reads like 'a distanced image of the aspirations of the poet' and quotes a passage from the essay 'Parallels' by Gray's friend Marc André Raffalovich. This suggests an autobiographical application for the marvellous birds enumerated in the poem—they represent 'pychics, spiritualists, and clairvoyants', among others Ailsa Cassilis, a Miss Yorke, and 'Cheiro', a medium. Raffalovich is trying to explain a section of the poem which is vigorous but obscure.

RICHARD LE GALLIENNE

Text: *Robert Louis Stevenson, An Elegy and Other Poems* (1895).

347 *A Ballad of London.* l. 12. *soiled doves*: prostitutes.

348 l. 22. *World-Tree*: allusively, Ygdrasil. In Scandinavian mythology, the great tree whose roots and branches extend through the universe.

H. G. WELLS

Text: *The Country of the Blind* (1911).

LIONEL JOHNSON

Text: *The Collected Poems of Lionel Johnson*, ed. I. Fletcher (New York, 1982).

373   *The Dark Angel.* l. 14. *Furies*: three avenging female deities, attendant on Proserpina, the Queen of Hades.

ll. 33–4. *Apples of ashes . . . Waters of bitterness*: apples of Sodom, that appear as if they are fit to be eaten, but when plucked dissolve into smoke and ashes. They were supposed to grow near the Dead Sea nearby the site of the drowned Cities of the Plain.

l. 36. *Paraclete*: advocate. Applied by St John to the Holy Spirit, but here applied to Satan, who, like the Holy Spirit, dwells within man.

374   l. 45. 'The first death forces her (the soul) from the body against her will and the second holds her in the body against her will, i.e. in eternal punishment'. Augustine, *The City of God*, VII. xxi. iii.

ll. 55–6. According to Plotinus, the third–century Neo–Platonic philosopher, in the late eighteenth-century translation of Thomas Taylor: 'the life of the Gods and of divine and happy men is a life unaccompanied with human pleasures and a flight of the alone to the alone', *Enneads*, vi. 9.

By the Statue of King Charles at Charing Cross. Charing Cross, close to Trafalgar Square in the centre of London, is the site of a contemporary statue of Charles (1600–49).

l. 10. *Whitehall*: the royal palace near Charing Cross. Only the banquet hall survives above ground. Charles was executed in front of the hall by the Parliamentary Party at the close of the Civil Wars.

375   ll. 31–2. Charles died well, with a dignity and patience that helped to ensure the restoration of his son to the English throne.

l. 35. Charles was not permitted to speak by the President of the court that tried him, for the King had refused to recognize its right of trial.

l. 44. *art . . . joy*: in his palaces at Richmond and Whitehall, Charles assembled the finest collection of works of art in Europe. It was largely dispersed by the puritan Cromwell.

A Decadent's Lyric. A parody of a minor decadent lyric of the 1890s. Arthur Symons is probably the target.

ERNEST DOWSON

Text: *The Poetical Works of Ernest Christopher Dowson*, ed. D. Flower (1954).

377   *Non Sum Qualis Eram Bonae Sub Regno Cynarae.* The title is from Horace, *Odes*, IV. i. 3–4. 'I am not what once I was under kind/Cynara's reign.'

378   *Nuns of the Perpetual Adoration.* Nuns in enclosed Orders established a

continuity of prayer, stemming the wrath of God with the world by their intercession.

l. 28. *proper*: darkness of intellect brought about by Original Sin is the distinctive characteristic of the human race beyond the closed ambit of the nuns. There may well be a glance at the technical meaning of the word, the psalm or rite appropriate to the time of the ritual year or occasion.

379   *Extreme Unction.* The sacrament administered to the dying in the rites of the Latin Catholic Church in which each of the five senses is anointed.

l. 16. *Viaticum*: Communion Host given to the sick or dying, but involving the sense also of a rite of passage.

To One in Bedlam. Bedlam is the name of a hospital (full title Bethlehem Hospital) for the insane which has existed in one form or another in London since the fourteenth century.

380   *Flos Lunae*: Moon Flower.

381   *Epigram.* ll. 3–4. Yeatsian in epithet and afflatus, though in the Augustan mode.

GEORGE WILLIAM RUSSELL — 'A.E.'

Text: *Collected Poems of A.E.* (1926).

Continuity.

Text: *Vale and Other Poems* (New York, 1931).

382   *Germinal.* Germinal is the seed month, running from 21 March to 19 April, the fourth month in the French Revolutionary calendar. In the poem, it appears to allude to the initial stages of man's development and to his divine origin. Russell suggests that infancy is destiny.

CHARLOTTE MEW

Text: *Charlotte Mew, Collected Poems and Prose*, ed. with an introduction by Val Warner (1981).

385   *In Nunhead Cemetery.* A large cemetery in South London, consecrated in 1840 and closed in 1969. I have abridged the poem.

A. C. MIALL

Text: *Nocturnes and Pastorals* (1896).

386   *The Boudoir.* Verlaine's original in *Romances Sans Paroles* (1874) is untitled and the first line runs: 'Le piano que baise une main frêle'.

387 *The Shepherd's Hour.* 'L'Heure du Berger' is from *Poèmes Saturniens* (1866). The first line runs: 'La lune est rouge au brumeux horizon'.

HUBERT CRACKANTHORPE

Text: *Wreckage* (1893).

AUBREY BEARDSLEY

Text: *Under the Hill and Other Essays in Prose and Verse* (1904).

395 *Catullus.* Catullus' memorial poem begins: 'Multas per gentes et multa per aequora vectus'.

SIR MAX BEERBOHM

Text: *Zuleika Dobson* (1911).

397 from *Zuleika Dobson.* '*the Corn*': the Cornmarket, a street in Oxford.

Blackwell's: well-known first- and second-hand bookshop in Broad Street.

Mommsen: Theodor Mommsen, highly distinguished German historian (1817–1903), known chiefly for *History of Rome* (1854–85), based on the study of coins, inscriptions and literature.

FURTHER READING

INDIVIDUAL BIBLIOGRAPHIES

SIR EDWARD ARNOLD

Works

Poetical Works (Boston, 1888).
The Light of Asia, with full and complete expository notes by Mrs I. L. Hauser (New York, 1890).
Poems National and Non-oriental (With Some New Pieces) Selected from the Works of Sir Edwin Arnold (London, 1906).

Commentary

C. Clausen, 'Sir Edwin Arnold's *The Light of Asia* and its Reception', *Blackwood's Magazine* (March 1954).
B. Wright, *Interpreter of Buddhism to the West: Sir Edwin Arnold* (New York, 1957).

ALFRED AUSTIN

Works

There is no collection of his work. For the shorter poems see *Lyrical Poems* (London, 1887).

Commentary

N. W. Crowell, *Alfred Austin: Victorian* (London, 1955).

AUBREY BEARDSLEY

Works

The Letters of Aubrey Beardsley, eds. H. Maas, J. L. Duncan, and W. B. Good (London, 1970).
Under the Hill and Other Essays in Prose and Verse (1904).

Commentary

M. Benkovitz, *Aubrey Beardsley* (London, 1981).
B. Brophy, *Black and White. A Portrait of Aubrey Beardsley* (London, 1968).
——, *Aubrey Beardsley and His World* (London, 1976).
A. Lavers, 'Aubrey Beardsley: Man of Letters', in *Romantic Mythologies*, ed. I. Fletcher (London, 1967).
B. Reade, *Aubrey Beardsley* (London, 1961).
R. Ross, *Aubrey Beardsley* (London, 1909).
A. Symons, *Under the Hill and Other Essays in Prose and Verse* (London, 1904).
S. Weintraub, *Beardsley* (London, 1976); a lively biography.
S. Wilson, *Beardsley*, revised and enlarged edn. (Oxford, 1983).

SIR MAX BEERBOHM

Works

R. Hart-Davis, *A Catalogue of the Caricatures of Max Beerbohm* (Cambridge, Mass., 1972).
Letters to Reggie Turner, ed. R. Hart-Davis (London, 1964).
Max In Verse, ed. J. G. Riewald (Brattleboro., 1963).
English Literature in Transition, 27, 4 (1984), is devoted to Beerbohm.
The Mirror of the Past, ed. L. Danson (Princeton, 1983).

Commentary

Lord D. Cecil, *Max. A Biography* (London, 1964); a hagiographic exercise.
J. Felstiner, *The Lies of Art. Max Beerbohm's Parody and Caricature* (New York, 1972).
—— 'Changing Faces in Max Beerbohm's Caricature', *Princeton Library Chronicle*, 33 (Winter, 1972).
I. Grushow, *The Imaginary Reminiscences of Sir Max Beerbohm* (Athens, Georgia, 1985).
J. G. Riewald, *Beerbohm, Man and Writer: A Critical Analysis with a Brief Life and Biography* (The Hague, 1953).

ROBERT BRIDGES

Works

Collected Poems (London, 1955).
Selected Letters, ed. D. E. Stanford (2 vols., Newark and London, 1984).

Commentary

A. Guerard, Jr., *Robert Bridges. A Study of Traditionalism in Poetry* (New York, 1942).
D. E. Stanford, *In the Classic Mode* (Newark and London, 1978).

SAMUEL BUTLER

Bibliography

There is a selected annotated bibliography by B. Quint in *English in Transition*, 16, 1 (1973); 17, 1 (1974); 18, 1 (1975).

Commentary

J. K. Crane, 'The Pontifex Genealogy: Evolution and Determinism', *College Literature*, 6 (1979).
P. Henderson, *Samuel Butler: The Incarnate Bachelor* (London, 1967).
L. E. Holt, *Samuel Butler* (Boston, 1964).

T. L. Jeffers, *Samuel Butler Revalued* (University Park, Pa. and London, 1981).

P. V. Pawly, 'Samuel Butler and His Darwinian Critics', *Victorian Studies*, 25, 2 (1982).

J. K. Wisenthal, 'Samuel Butler's Epistle to the Victorians', *Mosaic*, 13 (1979).

EDWARD CARPENTER

Bibliography and Works

Bibliography of Edward Carpenter (Sheffield City Library, Sheffield, 1940).
My Days and Dreams. Being Autobiographical Notes (London, 1916).

Commentary

E. Delavenay, *D. H. Lawrence: The Man and His Work* (London, 1972); interesting on the connections between Carpenter and Lawrence.

C. Tsuzuki, *Edward Carpenter: Prophet of Human Fellowship* (Cambridge, 1980).

MARY COLERIDGE

Works

The Collected Poems of Mary Coleridge, ed. with an introduction by Theresa Whistler (London, 1954); virtually complete.
Gathered Leaves from the Prose of Mary Coleridge, with a memoir by Edith Sichel (London, 1910).

HUBERT CRACKANTHORPE

Bibliography and Works

There is a selected annotated bibliography by W. V. Harris in *English Literature in Transition*, 16, 1 (1973).

Vignettes; these were selected by Bruno Frank for *Bruno's Chapbooks* from the pages of the *National Observer* and published in 1915; the remainder had already appeared in 1896.

Commentary

P. Coustillas, 'Gissing and Crackanthorpe: A Note on their Relationship', *Notes and Queries*, 28, 226 (1981).

D. Crackanthorpe, *Hubert Crackanthorpe and English Realism in the 1890s* (New York, 1977).

JOHN DAVIDSON

Bibliography and Works

J. A. Lester, 'John Davidson: A Grub Street Bibliography', *Bibliographical*

Society of the University of Virginia, Secretary Sheet, no. 40 (October 1958).

M. O'Connor, 'John Davidson. A Bibliography of Writings about Him', *English Literature in Transition*, 20, 5 (1977).

Collected Poems, ed. A. Turnbull (2 vols., London and Edinburgh, 1973).

Commentary

J. A. Lester, 'Prose–Poetry Transformation in the Poetry of John Davidson', Modern Philology, 56 (1958).

C. V. Peterson, *John Davidson* (Boston, 1972).

J. B. Townsend, *Davidson: Poet of Armageddon* (New Haven, 1961).

P. Turner, 'Davidson: The Novels of a Poet', *Cambridge Journal*, 5 (1952).

AUSTIN DOBSON

Bibliography and Works

A Bibliography of the First Editions and Privately Printed Books and Pamphlets by Austin Dobson, compiled by Alban Dobson, with a Preface by Sir Edmund Gosse (New York, 1925).

A Bookman's Budget (Oxford, 1917).

Collected Poems, ed. A. T. A. Dobson (London, 1923).

An Austin Dobson Letter Book, compiled by Alban Dobson (Cleveland, Ohio, 1935).

Commentary

Austin Dobson: Some Notes by Alban Dobson, with chapters by Sir Edmund Gosse and George Saintsbury (London, 1928).

H. C. Lipscomb, 'Horace and the Poetry of Austin Dobson', *American Journal of Philology*, 50 (1929).

DIGBY MACKWORTH DOLBEN

Works

Poems, ed. R. Bridges (Oxford, 1915); includes a memoir.

Uncollected Poems, ed. M. Cohen (Reading, 1973).

The Poems and Letters of Digby Mackworth Dolben, ed. M. Cohen (Amersham, 1981).

Commentary

R. Bridges, *Three Friends: Memoirs of Digby Mackworth Dolben, Richard Watson Dixon, Henry Bradley*, ed. M. M. Bridges (Oxford, 1933).

EDWARD DOWDEN

Works

Poems (2 vols., London, 1914).

Letters of Edward Dowden and His Correspondents, ed. Elizabeth Dowden (London, 1914).
Fragments from Old Letters. ED to EDW. 1869–1892 (London and New York, 1914).
A Woman's Reliquary. Poems (London, 1914).

Commentary
L. Marshall, *The Letters and Poems of Dowden* (London, 1914).
H. M. O. White, *Dowden* (Dublin, 1943).

ERNEST DOWSON

Bibliography and Works

There is a selected annotated bibliography by Jon Ramsey in *English Literature in Transition*, 18, 1 (1975).
The Poetical Works of Ernest Dowson, ed. D. Flower (London); the first edition of 1934 contains Dowson's contributions to a reprint of W. H. Ireland's translation of Voltaire's *La Pucelle*. These are omitted in later editions.
The Letters of Ernest Dowson, eds. D. Flower and H. Maas (London, 1967).
New Letters from Ernest Dowson, ed. D. Flower (Andoversford, 1984).
Stories of Ernest Dowson, ed. M. Longaker (London, 1949).

Commentary

M. Longaker, *Ernest Dowson* (Philadelphia, 1944).
M. Plarr, *Cynara* (London, 1933).
C. Snodgrass, 'Ernest Dowson's Aesthetics of Contamination', *English Literature in Transition*, 26, 8 (1982).
T. B. Swann, *Ernest Dowson* (Boston, 1964).

MARY DUCLAUX

Bibliography and Works

There is a checklist and annotated bibliography by R. M. Holmes in *English Literature in Transition*, 16, 1 (1973) and 18, 1 (1975).
Collected Poems, Lyrical and Narrative, with a Preface (London, 1902).
The Return to Nature. Songs and Symbols (London, 1904).
Images and Meditations. Poems (London, 1923).

Commentary

S. Maradon, 'Qui fût Mary Robinson?', *Les Langues modernes*, 54 (1960).

EDWIN ELLIS

Works

There are no collections or editions.

Commentary

I. Fletcher, 'The Yeats–Ellis–Blake Manuscript Cluster', *The Book Collector*, 21, 2 (1972).
W. B. Yeats, *Autobiographies* (London, 1926).

'MICHAEL FIELD'

Works

There is no collected edition.
A Selection from the Poems of Michael Field (London, 1923).
Some Letters from Charles Ricketts and Charles Shannon to Michael Field (Edinburgh, 1980).
Works and Days: Extracts from the Journals of Michael Field, eds. T. and D. C. Sturge Moore (London, 1933).

Commentary

K. Ireland, '*Sight and Song*: A Study of the Interrelations between Painting and Poetry', *Victorian Poetry*, 15, 1 (1977).
H. Locard, 'The Dionysiac Dance and the "danse macabre" in the poetry of Michael Field', *Confluents*, 5 (1979).
——, '*Works and Days*: The Journals of Michael Field', *Journal of the Eighteen Nineties Society*, 10 (1979).
M. Spurgeon, *Michael Field* (London, 1922).

RICHARD GARNETT

Works

There are no editions.

Commentary

C. Heilbron, *The Garnett Family* (London, 1961).

SIR WILLIAM SCHWENK GILBERT

Works

Plays by W. S. Gilbert, ed. with an introduction and notes by G. Rowell (Cambridge, 1982).
The Bab Ballads by W. S. Gilbert, ed. J. Fallon (Cambridge, Mass., 1970); contains almost all of Gilbert's verse; with illustrations and annotations.

Commentary

R. Allen, *W. S. Gilbert. An Anniversary Survey and Exhibition Checklist with Thirty-Five Illustrations* (Charlottesville, 1963); a comprehensive history of the dramatic works.
L. Baily, *Gilbert and Sullivan and Their World* (London, 1973).

S. Dark and R. Gray, *W. S. Gilbert. His Life and Letters* (London, 1922; repr. New York, 1972).

R. W. Garson, 'The English Aristophanes', *Revue de Littérature comparée*, 46 (1972).

J. B. Jones, 'W. S. Gilbert's Contributions to *Fun* 1865–1874', *Bulletin of the New York Public Library*, 73 (April, 1969).

—— (ed.), *W. S. Gilbert. A Century of Scholarship and Commentary* (New York, 1970).

G. W. Knight, *The Golden Labyrinth* (London, 1962).

H. Pearson, *Gilbert: His Life and Strife* ([London], 1957).

T. Searle, *Sir William Schwenk Gilbert. A Topsy Turvy Adventure*, introduction by R. E. Swartout (London, 1931).

J. Stedman (ed.), *Gilbert Before Sullivan* (Chicago, 1967); full historical introduction and annotations.

M. K. Sutton, *W. S. Gilbert* (Boston, 1975).

GEORGE GISSING

Bibliography and Works

M. Collie, *George Gissing: A Bibliography* (London, 1975).

A number of the novels have been edited with bibliographical data, introductions, and notes by the Harvester Press.

The Letters of George Gissing to Edouard Bertz 1887–1903, ed. P. Coustillas (London, 1973).

The Letters of George Gissing to Edward Clodd, ed. P. Coustillas (London, 1973).

The Letters of George Gissing to Gabrielle Fleury, ed. P. Coustillas (New York, 1964).

George Gissing and H. G. Wells: Their Friendship and Correspondence, ed. with an introduction by Royal A. Gettman (London, 1961).

London and the Life of Literature in Late Victorian England. The Diary of George Gissing, Novelist, ed. P. Coustillas (Lewisburg, 1978).

Commentary

J. Goode, *George Gissing: Ideology and Fiction* (London, 1978).

J. Halperin, *Gissing: A Life in Books* (Oxford, 1982).

J. Korg, *George Gissing: A Critical Biography* (Seattle, 1963).

J. P. Michaux (ed.), *George Gissing: Critical Essays* (London, 1981).

A. Poole, *Gissing in Context* (London and Basingstoke, 1975).

M. Roberts, *The Private Life of Henry Maitland. A Portrait of George Gissing*, ed. with an introduction by M. Bishop (London, 1958).

R. L. Selig, *George Gissing* (Boston, 1983).

G. Tindall, *The Born Exile: George Gissing* (London, 1974).

SIR EDMUND GOSSE

Works

Collected Poems (London, 1911).

Father and Son (London, 1907); ed. with an introduction by R. Hepburn (London, 1974); a comic account of his earlier years.

Commentary

Sir E. Charteris, *The Life and Letters of Sir Edmund Gosse* (London, 1931).

P. Dodd, 'The Nature of Edmund Gosse, *Father and Son*', *English Literature in Transition*, 22 (1979).

W. J. Gracie, 'Truth of Form in Edmund Gosse's *Father and Son*', *Journal of Narrative Technique*, 4 (1974).

R. T. Porter, 'Edmund Gosse's *Father and Son* Between Form and Flexibility', *Journal of Narrative Technique*, 5 (1975).

A. Thwaite, *Edmund Gosse: A Literary Landscape. 1849–1928* (Chicago, 1984).

J. D. Woolf, *Edmund Gosse* (Boston, 1972).

JOHN GRAY

Bibliography and Works

G. A. Cevasco, 'John Gray (1866–1934): A Primary and an Annotated Bibliography of Writings About Him', *English Literature in Transition*, 19 (1978).

I. Fletcher, 'Amendments and Additions to a Bibliography of John Gray', *English Literature in Transition*, 20 (1979).

John Gray's Collected Poems are in the process of being edited by I. Fletcher. A collection of the shorter prose, mostly fugitive, is much needed.

Five Fugitive Poems, ed. I. Fletcher (privately printed [London], 1982).

The Kiss. A Translation of Théodore de Banville's 'Le Baiser', ed. I. Fletcher (Edinburgh, 1983).

Park: A Fantastic Story (London, 1932; reprinted 1966).

Park, ed. T. Healy (London, 1932; Manchester, 1984).

Commentary

G. A. Cevasco, *John Gray* (Boston, 1982).

L. Dowling, 'Nature and Decadence in John Gray's *Silverpoints*', *Victorian Poetry*, 15 (1977).

J. McCormack, 'The Disciple: John Gray/Dorian Gray', *Journal of the Eighteen Nineties Society*, 5 & 6 (1975–6).

J. G. Nelson, *The Early Nineties: A View from The Bodley Head* (Cambridge, Mass., 1969); excellent criticism.

B. Sewell, *Footnote to the Nineties. A Memoir of John Gray and André Raffalovich* (London, 1968).

——, *In the Dorian Mode: A Life of John Gray, 1866–1934* (Padstow, 1983).
——, (ed.), *Two Friends: Gray and Raffalovich* (Aylesford, 1963).

WILLIAM ERNEST HENLEY

Works

A number of uncollected poems and early drafts have been published.
E. H. Cohen, 'An Early Sonnet Sequence by W. E. Henley', *Victorian Poetry*, 14 (1976).
'Uncollected Early Poems by William Ernest Henley', *Publications of the New York Public Library* (1976).

Commentary

J. H. Buckley, *William Ernest Henley. A Study in the Counter-Decadence of the Nineties* (Princeton, NJ, 1945).
'John Connell', *Henley* (London, 1949); entertainingly biographical.
A. Guillaume, *William Ernest Henley et son groupe: neo-romanticisme et impérialisme, la fin du XIXe siècle* (Paris, 1973).
E. San Juan, 'The Question of Values in Victorian Activism', *The Personalist*, 45 (1964).

GERARD MANLEY HOPKINS

Bibliography and Works

T. Dunne, *Gerard Manley Hopkins. A Comprehensive Bibliography* (Oxford, 1976).
The Poems of Gerard Manley Hopkins, eds. W. H. Gardner and N. H. Mackenzie, 4th edn. (Oxford, 1970).
The Letters of Gerard Manley Hopkins to Robert Bridges, ed. with notes and introduction by C. C. Abbott (Oxford, 2nd revised impression, 1955).
The Correspondence of Gerard Manley Hopkins and Richard Watson Dixon, ed. with notes and an introduction by C. C. Abbott (Oxford, 2nd revised impression, 1955).
Further Letters of Gerard Manley Hopkins, including his correspondence with Coventry Patmore, ed. with notes and an introduction by C. C. Abbott (Oxford, 2nd revised and enlarged edition, 1956).
Selected Prose, ed. G. Roberts (Oxford, 1980).
The Journal and Papers of Gerard Manley Hopkins, eds. H. House and G. Storey (Oxford, 1959).
The Sermons and Devotional Writings of Gerard Manley Hopkins, ed. C. Devlin (Oxford, 1959).
Gerard Manley Hopkins. The Major Poems, ed. with an introduction and notes by Walford Davies (London, 1979).

Commentary

N. H. MacKenzie, *A Reader's Guide to Gerard Manley Hopkins* (London, 1981).

P. Milward, *A Commentary on G. M. Hopkins'* 'The Wreck of the Deutsch-land', Tokyo, 1968.
J. Robinson, *In Extremity. A Study of Gerard Manley Hopkins* (Cambridge, 1978); an excellent and temperate book.
W. Schneider, *The Dragon at the Gate: Studies in the Poetry of Gerard Manley Hopkins* (Berkeley and Los Angeles, 1968).
R. K. R. Thornton, *Gerard Manley Hopkins: The Poems* (London, 1973).
I. Winters, 'The Poetry of Gerard Manley Hopkins', in *The Function of Criticism* (Denver, 1957).

A. E. HOUSMAN

Works

The Letters of A. E. Housman, ed. Henry Maas (Cambridge, Mass. 1971).
A.E.H. Some Poems, Some Letters and a Personal Memoir by His Brother Laurence Housman (London, 1937).

Commentary

R. P. Graves, *A. E. Housman: The Scholar Poet* (London and Henley, 1979).
J. Leggett, *The Poetic Art of A. E. Housman* (Lincoln, Nebraska and London, 1978).
N. Marlow, *A. E. Housman, Scholar and Poet* (London, 1956).
C. Ricks (ed.), *A. E. Housman. A Collection of Critical Essays* (Englewood Cliffs, NJ, 1968).
G. L. Watson, *A. E. Housman. A Divided Life* (London, 1957).

RICHARD JEFFERIES

Works

Much of Jefferies, particularly the fiction, remains out of print.

Commentary

J. W. Blench, 'The Novels of Jefferies', *Cambridge Journal* (1954).
W. J. Hyde, 'Jefferies and the Naturalistic Peasant', *Nineteenth-Century Fiction*, 11, 3 (1956).
W. J. Keith, *Richard Jefferies: A Critical Study* (Toronto, 1965).
E. Thomas, *Richard Jefferies: His Life and Work* (London, 1909).

LIONEL JOHNSON

Works

Collected Poems, ed. I. Fletcher (New York, 1982).

Post Liminium. Essays and Critical Papers, ed. Thomas Whittemore [and Louise Imogen Guiney] (London, 1911).
Reviews and Critical Papers, ed. with introduction by R. Shafer (London, 1921).
Some Winchester Letters [ed. Earl Russell] (London, 1919).

Commentary

A. W. Patrick, *Lionel Johnson poète et critique (1867–1902)* (Paris, 1939).
D. Scott, *Men of Letters* (London, 1916); on Johnson's critical prose.

RUDYARD KIPLING

Bibliography and Works

J. McG. Stewart, *Rudyard Kipling: A Bibliographical Catalogue* (London, 1959).
The Writings in Prose and Verse of Rudyard Kipling (38 vols., London, 1938).
The Sussex Editions of the Complete Works in Verse and Prose of Rudyard Kipling (35 vols., London, 1937–9).

Commentary

K. Amis, *Rudyard Kipling's World* (London, 1975).
Earl of Birkenhead, *Rudyard Kipling* (London, 1978); the biography suppressed by Kipling's daughter.
C. E. Carrington, *Kipling: His Life and Work* (London, 1955).
R. L. Green, *Kipling: The Critical Heritage* (London, 1971).
A. Rutherford (ed.), *Kipling's Mind and Art* (Edinburgh and London, 1965).
J. M. S. Tompkins, *The Art of Rudyard Kipling* (rev. edn., London, 1965).
A. Wilson, *The Strange Ride of Rudyard Kipling* (London, 1976).

ANDREW LANG

Works

Collected Poems (4 vols., London, 1922).

Commentary

R. L. Green, *Andrew Lang, A Critical Biography* (Leicester, 1946).
G. Hurry, *Lang the Poet* (Oxford, 1948).
E. S. Longstaff, *Andrew Lang* (Boston, 1978).
A. B. Welsher, *Concerning Lang: Being the Lang Lectures Delivered Before the University of St Andrews, 1907–1939* (Oxford, 1949).

EUGENE LEE-HAMILTON

Works

There are no editions.

Commentary

G. Macbeth, 'Lee-Hamilton and the Romantic Agony', *Critical Quarterly*, 4 (1962).

J. T. Mather, Jr., 'The Poetry of Lee-Hamilton', *The Nation* (5 November 1908).

S. Pantazzi, 'Lee-Hamilton', *Publications of the Bibliographical Society of America*, 57 (1963).

W. Sharp, 'Eugene Lee-Hamilton', *Papers Critical and Reminiscent* (London, 1912).

E. Wharton, 'The Sonnets of Lee-Hamilton', *The Bookman* (November 1907).

RICHARD LE GALLIENNE

Works

There is no collected or selected edition.
The Romantic Nineties (London, 1926); memoirs.

Commentary

R. Whittington-Egan and G. Smerdon, *The Quest of the Golden Boy. The Life and Letters of R. Le Gallienne* (London, 1960).

SIR ALFRED LYALL

Works

Poems (London, 1907).

Commentary

H. M. Durand, *The Life of Lyall* (Edinburgh, 1913).

C. P. Ubert, 'Lyall', *Proceedings of the British Academy*, 5 (1912).

CHARLOTTE MEW

Works

Collected Poems and Stories, ed. with an introduction and notes by V. Warner (London, 1981).

Commentary

P. Fitzgerald, *Charlotte Mew and Her Friends* (London, 1981).

J. Grant, *Harold Monro and the Poetry Bookshop* (London, 1967).

ALICE MEYNELL

Works

Alice Meynell. Prose and Poetry. Centenary Volume, eds. F. Page, V. Meynell, O. Sowerby, and F. Meynell (London, 1947).

Commentary

J. Badeni, *The Slender Tree* (Padstow, 1981).
V. Meynell, *Alice Meynell. A Memoir* (London, 1929).

GEORGE MOORE

Works

Letters to Lady Cunard, 1895–1933, ed. with an introduction and notes by R. Hart-Davis (London, 1957).

Commentary

M. J. Brown, *Moore: A Reconsideration* (Seattle, 1955).
R. A. Cave, *A Study of the Novels of George Moore* (New York, 1978).
N. Cunard, *G. M. Memoirs of George Moore* (London, 1956).
J. M. Hone, *The Life of Moore* (London, 1936).
G. Hough, 'Moore and the Nineties', in R. Ellmann (ed.), *Edwardians and late Victorians* (New York, 1960), repeated in *Image and Experience*, (London, 1960).
J. C. Noel, *George Moore: l'homme et l'œuvre, 1852–1933* (2 vols., Paris, 1966).
G. Owens, *George Moore: His Mind and Art* (Edinburgh, 1968).
W. B. Yeats, *Dramatis Personae* (London, 1936).

ARTHUR MORRISON

Bibliography

R. Calder, 'Arthur Morrison: An Annotated Bibliography of Writings About Him', *English Literature in Transition*, 28, 3 (1985).

Commentary

J. Bell, 'A Study of Morrison', *Essays and Studies*, 5 (1952).
V. Brome, *Four Realist Novelists* (London, 1955).
P. J. Keating (ed.), *A Child of the Jago* (London, 1969); with an excellent biographical and critical study.
V. S. Pritchett, in *The Living Novel* (London, 1946).

SIR HENRY NEWBOLT

Works

A Perpetual Memory and Other Poems (London, 1939).
Selected Poems, ed. with an introduction by J. Betjeman (London, 1940).

My World in My Time (London, 1932); autobiography.
The Later Life and Letters of Sir Henry Newbolt, ed. M. Newbolt (London, 1946).

RODEN NOEL

Works

There are no editions.
Collected Poems (London, 1901), has a brief biographical notice by Lady Victoria Buxton and a critical essay by John Addington Symonds.

Commentary

W. A. Brown, *The Metaphysical Society, 1869–1880* (New York, 1947); discusses Noel as talented amateur philosopher.
S. M. Ellis, *Mainly Victorian* (London, 1926).
P. Grosskurth, *John Addington Symonds* (1964); has information about Noel's homoerotic practices.

ARTHUR O'SHAUGHNESSY

Works

There is no collected edition of O'Shaughnessy's verse or prose.
Selected Poems, ed. W. A. Alexander (New Haven, 1923).
A Pathetic Love Episode in a Poet's Life being Letters [from Helen Snee] to Arthur W. E. O'Shaughnessy. Also a letter from him containing a dissertation on love [edited by Clement Shorter] (London, 1916).

Commentary

Anon., *Contemporary Review*, CXXVI (July, 1924).
O. Broenner, *Das Leben O'Shaughnessys* (Heidelberg, 1933).

WALTER PATER

Works

Imaginary Portraits, ed. E. E. Brzenk (New York, 1964); an excellent edition that includes not only the additional Portraits from *Miscellaneous Studies*, but 'An English Poet'.

Commentary

English Literature in Transition, 27, 1 and 2 (1984), is devoted to Pater and to *Marius the Epicurean* in particular.
G. d'Hangest, *Walter Pater: l'homme et l'œuvre* (2 vols., Paris, 1961).
I. Fletcher, *Walter Pater* (London, 1959; rev. edn., 1971).
J. S. Harrison, 'Pater, Heine and the Old Gods of Greece', *Publications of the Modern Language Association*, 39 (1924).

U. C. Knoeplflmacher, *Religious Humanism in the Victorian Novel* (Princeton, NJ, 1965); deals with *Marius the Epicurean.*
M. Levey, *The Case of Walter Pater* (London, 1978); feeble critically, but useful biographically.
G. Monsman, *Pater's Portraits* (Baltimore, 1967).
——, *Walter Pater* (Boston, 1977).
R. Seiler, *Walter Pater. The Critical Heritage* (London, 1981).
A. Ward, *Walter Pater and the Idea of Nature* (London, 1966); Pater and Hegel.

WILLIAM RENTON

Commentary

Notes on the Family of William Renton of Edinburgh (Edinburgh [1900]).

T. W. ROLLESTON

Works

There are no editions.

Commentary

C. H. Rolleston, *Portrait of an Irishman* (Dublin, 1939).

GEORGE WILLIAM RUSSELL — 'AE'

Bibliography and Works

A. Denison, *Printed Writings of George William Russell (AE) A Bibliography* (Evanston, 1961).
Collected Poems (London, 1930).
The Valley of the Bells and other Poems (Oxford, 1933).
AE. Letters to Minanlabain (New York, 1937); the introduction is useful for an account of Russell's later years.
The Candle of Vision (London, 1918); a spiritual autobiography.
The Living Torch. A.E., ed. M. Gibbon (London, 1937); selections from the prose.

Commentary

E. A. Boyd, *Ireland's Literary Renaissance* (New York, 1916).
R. B. Davis, *George William Russell* (Boston, 1977).
R. Loftus, *Nationalism in Modern Anglo-Irish Poetry* (Madison, 1964).
H. Summerfield, *That Myriad Minded Man* (Gerrard's Cross, 1975).
W. B. Yeats, *Autobiographies* (London, 1926).

OLIVE SCHREINER

Works

There is no collected edition.

The Story of An African Farm, with an introduction by Dan Jacobson (Harmondsworth, 1971).
The Story of An African Farm, with an introduction by Doris Lessing (New York, 1976).
The Letters of Olive Schreiner, ed. S. C. Cronwright-Schreiner (London, 1924).

Commentary

E. Carpenter, *My Days and Dreams* (London, 1916).
S. C. Cronwright-Schreiner, *The Life of Olive Schreiner* (London, 1924).
H. H. Ellis, *My Life* (London, 1940).
R. First and A. Scott, *Olive Schreiner* (New York, 1980).
E. Showalter, *A Literature of their Own: British Women Novelists from Brontë to Lessing* (London, 1978).

WILLIAM SHARP — 'FIONA MACLEOD'
Works

Writings (7 vols., London, 1909–10); arranged by Mrs William Sharp; omits Sharp's novels.

Commentary

F. Amaya, *William Sharp: Fiona Macleod* (Cambridge, Mass., 1970).
W. Halloran, *William Sharp and Fiona Macleod: The Development of a Literary Personality* (University Microfilms, Ann Arbor, 1965).
E. A. Sharp, *William Sharp (Fiona Macleod): A Memoir Compiled by His Wife* (2 vols., London, 1910 and 1912).

J. K. STEPHEN
Works

Lapsus Calami and Other Verses (Cambridge, 1896); this has an introduction by H. Stephen.

Commentary

A. C. Benson, *Leaves of the Trees: Studies in Biography* (London, 1911).

ROBERT LOUIS STEVENSON
Works

Collected Poems, ed. Janet Adam Smith (London, 1950).
Robert Louis Stevenson: The Critical Heritage, ed. P. Maixner (London, Boston and Henley, 1981).

Commentary

J. Calder (ed.), *Stevenson and Victorian Scotland* (Edinburgh, 1981).
G. K. Chesterton, *Robert Louis Stevenson* (London, 1928).

D. Daiches, *Robert Louis Stevenson: A Revaluation* (Norfolk, Connectitut, 1947).

E. M. Eigner, *Stevenson and the Romantic Tradition* (Princeton, NJ, 1966).

J. C. Furnas, *Voyage to Windward: The Life of Stevenson* (New York, 1951); useful biographically; of no critical value.

R. Kiely, *Stevenson and the Fiction of Adventure* (Cambridge, Mass, 1964).

A. Noble (ed.), *Robert Louis Stevenson* (London, 1983); modern essays by various hands.

M. Zabel, *Stevenson: The Two Major Novels* (New York, 1960).

ALGERNON CHARLES SWINBURNE

Works

There is no authoritative edition of the poems.

Lesbia Brandon, ed. R. Hughes (London, 1952), with an extensive commentary.

A Year's Letters, ed. F. J. Sypher (London and New York, 1976).

The Swinburne Letters, ed. C. Y. Lang (New Haven, 1959–62).

New Writings by Swinburne or Miscellanea Nova et Curiosa, being a medley of poems, critical essays, hoaxes and burlesques, ed. C. Y. Lang (Syracuse, 1964).

Swinburne Replies, ed. C. K. Hyde (Syracuse, 1966).

Commentary

S. Chew, *Swinburne* (Boston, 1929).

'The Proserpine Figure in Swinburne's *Poems and Ballads*', in G. S. Doran and D. C. Tricke (eds.), *Essays in Literature in Honour of Maurice Browning Cromer* (Bowling Green, 1975).

I. Fletcher, *Swinburne* (rev. edn., New York, 1982).

H. Harmon, 'The Swinburnian Woman', *Philological Quarterly*, 58 (1979).

J. G. Jordan, 'The Sweet Face of Mothers: Psychic Pattern in *Atalanta in Calydon*, *Victorian Poetry*, 11 (1972).

S. E. Lorsch, 'Evening on the Broads, Visionary Landscape and the Landscape of Negation', *Victorian Poetry*, 18 (1980).

J. J. McGann, *Swinburne: An Experiment in Criticism* (Chicago, 1972).

T. E. Morgan, 'Swinburne's Dramatic Monologues: Sex and Ideology', *Victorian Poetry*, 22, 2 (Summer 1984).

——, 'Tintern Abbey in Ruins: Swinburne, Arnold and Wordsworth', *Victorian Poetry*, 24, 4 (1986).

David G. Riede, *Swinburne: A Study of Romantic Mythmaking* (Charlottesville, 1978).

J. Rosenberg, 'Swinburne', *Victorian Studies*, 11 (1967), 131–52.

Victorian Poetry, 9 (1970–1). The issue is devoted to the work of Swinburne.

JOHN ADDINGTON SYMONDS

Bibliography and Works

P. L. Babington, *A Bibliography of the Works of John Addington Symonds* (London, 1925; repr. New York, 1968).

The Letters of John Addington Symonds, ed. H. M. Schueller and R. M. Peters (3 vols., Detroit, 1967).

The Memoirs of John Addington Symonds, ed. and introduced by P. Grosskurth (London, 1984).

Commentary

P. Grosskurth, *John Addington Symonds: A Biography* (London, 1964).

ARTHUR SYMONS

Works

Works (9 vols., London, 1924); prose and verse; incomplete.

Memoirs of Arthur Symons: Impressions of Life and Art in the 1890s, ed. K. Beckson (University Park, Pennsylvania, 1977); a rather more miscellaneous volume than the title might suggest.

' "The Life and Adventures of Lucy Newcomb": Preface and Text', ed. with an introduction by A. P. Johnson, *English Literature in Transition*, 28, 4 (1985).

Commentary

A. P. Johnson, 'Arthur Symons' Novel à la Goncourt', *Journal of Modern Literature* (1981–2); the projected novel is reconstructed; the heroine Lucy Newcomb, based on Muriel Broadbent, appeared in two 1890s short stories which would have afforded material for the completed work.

E. Baugh, 'Symons. A Centenary Tribute', *Review of English Literature*, 6 (1965).

T. Gibbons, 'The Shape of Things to Come: Arthur Symons and the Futurists', *Journal of Modern Literature*, 5 (1976).

R. Lhombreaud, *Arthur Symons. A Critical Biography* (London, 1963); the standard life, but not altogether accurate, and light on sources.

J. Monro, *Arthur Symons* (Boston, 1969).

A. L. Peters, 'The Salome of Symons and Beardsley', *Criticism*, 2 (1960).

K. Powell, 'Arthur Symons' Spiritual Adventures and the Art of Illusion', *Studies in the Humanities*, 5, 11 (1976).

W. B. Yeats, *Autobiographies* (London, 1926).

LORD DE TABLEY

Works

Collected Poems (London, 1903).

Commentary

R. Bridges, 'Lord de Tabley's Poems' in *Collected Essays*, vol. 7 (Oxford, 1931).

G. Pitts, 'Lord de Tabley: Poet of Frustration', *West Virginia University Philological Papers*, 14 (1963).

G. Taplin, 'The Life, Works and Literary Reputation of Lord de Tabley' (Cambridge, Mass., 1946); dissertation.

FRANCIS THOMPSON

Works

There is no satisfactory edition of the poems.

Works, ed. W. Meynell (Westminster, 1947).

Poems of Francis Thompson, ed. with biographical and critical notes by Rev. T. L. Connolly, SJ (1941; repr. Westport, 1979); forty poems are omitted; contains a bibliography of primary and secondary works up to 1940; the notes are useful for their citation of possible biblical source material.

Uncollected Verses, privately printed by C. Shorter (London, 1917).

T. L. Connolly, *An Account of the Books and Manuscripts of Francis Thompson at Boston College*, privately printed (Boston, n.d.).

Commentary

P. Danchin, *Francis Thompson* (Paris, 1939).

V. Meynell, *Francis Thompson and Wilfred Meynell* (London, 1952).

J. C. Reid, *Francis Thompson: Man and Poet* (London, 1954).

J. E. Walsh, *Strange Harp, Strange Symphony. The Life of Francis Thompson* (New York, 1967).

JAMES THOMSON

Works

Poems and Some Letters of James Thomson, ed. with a biographical and critical introduction and textual notes by A. Ridler (London, 1963). Includes the better poems.

Commentary

K. H. Byron, *The Pessimism of James Thomson* (The Hague, 1965).

F. M. Hyde, 'The Poetry of the City', in M. Bradbury and J. Macfarlane (eds.), *Modernism, 1890–1930* (Hassocks, 1978).

W. D. Lutz, 'The Death of James Thomson', *Notes and Queries*, 24 (1977).

C. N. S. Peter, 'Dreadful Mysteries of Time. Dürer's "Melancholia" in *The City of Dreadful Night*', *Victorian Poetry*, 121 (1974).

W. D. Schaeffer, *James Thomson (BV) Beyond The City* (Berkeley and Los Angeles, 1965).

—— (ed.), *The Speedy Extinction of Evil and Misery. Selected Prose of James Thomson (BV)* (Berkeley and Los Angeles, 1967).

C. Vachot, *James Thomson, 1834–1882* (Paris, 1964).

SIR WILLIAM WATSON

Works

The Poems of Sir William Watson, 1878–1935 (London, 1936).

I was an English Poet, Poems selected by Lady Watson (Ashville, 1941).

Commentary

J. G. Nelson, *William Watson* (New York, 1966).
J. M. Wilson, *I was an English Poet. A Biography of Sir William Watson* (London, 1982).

AUGUSTA WEBSTER

Works

Selection from the Poems of Augusta Webster (London, 1892).
Some of Webster's poems with a biographical notice will be found in A. Miles, *The Poets and the Poetry of the Century, Joanna Baillie to Mathilde Blind, 1905–1907* (London, 1905).

Commentary

The Dictionary of National Biography, ed. L. Stephen, vol. 20 (1922).

H. G. WELLS

Works

Experiment in Autobiography: Discoveries and Conclusions of a Very Ordinary Brain since 1866 (2 vols., 1934; 3 vols., London, 1984).
H. G. Wells's Literary Criticism, eds. P. Parrinder and R. M. Philimus (New York, 1980).

Commentary

B. Bergonzi, *The Early H. G. Wells* (Manchester, 1961).
D. Gavin and R. M. Philimus, *H. G. Wells and Modern Fiction* (Brighton, 1977).
R. D. Haynes, *H. G. Wells. Discoverer of the Future: The Influence of Science on his Thought* (New York, 1980).
P. Parrinder, *H. G. Wells* (Edinburgh, 1970).
—— (ed.), *H. G. Wells: The Critical Heritage* (London, 1972).
A. West, *H. G. Wells: A Sketch for a Portrait* (London, 1930); with a Preface by H. G. Wells.
——, 'H. G. Wells', *Encounter*, 8, 41 (1953).
——, *H. G. Wells: Aspects of a Life* (London, 1984).

OSCAR WILDE

Bibliography and Works

A select annotated bibliography by I. Fletcher and J. Stokes will be found in R. Finneran (ed.), *A Bibliography of Anglo-Irish Literature* (New York, 1976) and Supplement (New York, 1981).
There is no complete annotated edition of the works.

'Oscar Wilde: Five Fugitive Pieces', ed. Bobby Fong, *English Literature in Transition*, 22, 1 (1979).
Letters of Oscar Wilde, ed. R. Hart-Davis (London, 1962).

Commentary

R. Ellmann (ed.), *Wilde: A Collection of Critical Essays* (Englewood Cliffs, NJ, 1969).
V. Holland, *Son of Oscar Wilde* (London, 1954).
M. Hyde, *Oscar Wilde: A Biography* (London, 1975).
P. Jullian, *Oscar Wilde* (London, 1965); good on the French connection, but not always reliable.
J. McCormack, 'Masks without Faces: The Personalities of Oscar Wilde', *English Literature in Transition*, 22, 4 (1979).
A. Ojala, *Aestheticism and Oscar Wilde* (2 vols., Helsinki, 1954).
H. Pearson, *Oscar Wilde* (London, 1946).
R. Shewan, *Oscar Wilde: Art and Egotism* (London, 1977).
J. Stokes, *Oscar Wilde*, British Writers and their Work series (London, 1981).
G. Woodcock, *The Paradox of Oscar Wilde* (London, 1949).
K. Worth, *Oscar Wilde* (London, 1983).

W. B. YEATS

Bibliography and Works

There is a bibliography of secondary material up to 1976 by K. P. S. Jochum (Urbana, Chicago and London, 1977).
The best edition is that edited by R. Finneran (London, 1983), which includes uncollected material from all phases of Yeats's career and sorts out the muddle of *The Last Poems* by placing them in an order which more nearly represents Yeats's intentions.

Commentary

H. Bloom, *Yeats* (New York, 1970).
T. L. Byrd, *The Early Poetry of W. B. Yeats* (Port Washington, 1978).
D. Eddins, *Yeats: The Nineteenth-Century Matrix* (University, Alabama, 1971).
R. Fallis, 'Yeats and the Reinterpretation of Victorian Poetry', *Victorian Poetry*, 14, 2 (1976).
A. R. Grossman, *Poetic Knowledge in the Early Yeats* (Charlottesville, 1970).
B. Levine, *The Dissolving Image. The Spiritual and Aesthetic Development of W. B. Yeats* (Detroit, 1970).
P. Marcus, *Yeats and the Beginnings of the Irish Renaissance* (Ithaca, 1970).
C. Meir, *The Ballads and Songs of W. B. Yeats: The Anglo-Irish Heritage in Subject and Style* (London, 1974).
H. Murphy, *Yeats's Early Poetry. The Quest for Reconciliation* (Baton Rouge, 1975).

T. F. Parkinson, *W. B. Yeats: Self-Critic: A Study of the Early Verse and the Later Poetry*, 2 vols. (Berkeley, 1971).

R. Welch, *Irish Poetry from Moore to Yeats* (Chalfont St Giles, 1980).

SELECT GENERAL BIBLIOGRAPHY

E. B. Adams, *Bernard Shaw and the Aesthetes* (Columbus, 1971).

T. d'Arch Smith, *Love in Earnest. Some Notes on the Lives and Writings of English Uranian Poets, 1889–1930* (London, 1970).

E. Aslin, *The Aesthetic Movement: Prelude to Art Nouveau* (London, 1965).

W. E. Baker, *Syntax in English Poetry, 1870–1930* (Berkeley, 1967).

G. J. Becker, *Documents of Modern Literary Realism* (Princeton, 1963).

K. Beckson, *Aesthetes and Decadents of the 1890s. An Anthology of British Poetry and Prose* (New York, 1966).

C. F. Behrman, *Victorian Myths of the Sea* (Athens, Ohio, 1977).

J. Bratton, *The Victorian Popular Ballad* (London, 1965).

J. H. Buckley, *The Victorian Temper: A Study of Literary Culture* (New York, 1951).

——, *The Triumph of Time* (Cambridge, Mass., 1966).

C. Campos, *The View of France from Arnold to Bloomsbury* (London, 1965).

M. L. Cazamain, *Le Roman et les idées en Angleterre: l'influence de la science, 1860–1890* (Paris, 1923).

——, *Le Roman et les idées en Angleterre: l'antiintellectuelisme et l'esthéticisme, 1880–1900* (Paris, 1935).

J. E. Chamberlin, *Ripe was the Drowsy Hour: The Age of Oscar Wilde* (New York, 1977).

B. Charlesworth, *Dark Passages: The Decadent Consciousness in English Literature* (Madison and Milwaukee, 1965).

C. R. Decker, *The Victorian Conscience* (New York, 1952).

L. Dowling, *Aestheticism and Decadence. A Selected Annotated Bibliography* (New York and London, 1977).

——, 'The Aesthetes and the English Eighteenth Century', *Victorian Studies*, 20 (1977).

J. Duncan, *The Revival of Metaphysical Poetry. The History of a Style: 1800 to the Present* (Minneapolis, 1959).

F. Dyos and M. Wolff, *The Victorian City: Images and Realities* (2nd edn., London, 1973).

R. Ellmann (ed.), *Edwardians and Late Victorians* (New York, 1949).

R. C. K. Ensor, *England, 1870–1914* (Oxford, 1936).

I. Fletcher (ed.), *Romantic Mythologies* (London, 1967).

——, *Selections from British Fiction, 1880–1900* (London, 1970).

——, *Decadence and the 1890s* (London, 1979).

W. Frierson, *The English Novel in Transition* (Norman, 1942).

W. T. Gang, *Scanty Plot of Ground: Studies in the Victorian Sonnet* (The Hague, 1976).

H. Gerber, *The English Short Story in Transition, 1880–1920* (New York, 1967).

T. Gibbons, *Rooms at the Darwin Hotel* (Perth, Western Australia, 1974).

F. W. J. Hemmings, *The Age of Realism* (Harmondsworth, 1974).

D. Howard, J. Lucas, and J. Goode, *Tradition and Tolerance in Nineteenth, Century Fiction* (London, 1966).

S. Hynes, *The Edwardian Turn of Mind* (Princeton, 1968).

H. Jackson, *The Eighteen Nineties* (London, 1913).

P. J. Keating, *The Working Classes in Victorian Fiction* (London, 1971).

F. Kermode, *Romantic Image* (London, 1957).

Paul J. Korshin, *Typologies in England 1650–1820* (Princeton, 1982).

George P. Landow, *Victorian Types, Victorian Shadows, Biblical Typology, in Victorian Literature, Art and Thought* (London, 1980).

M. Larkin, *Man and Society in Nineteenth-Century Realism* (London, 1977).

J. A. Lester, *Journey Through Despair* (Princeton, 1968).

H. M. Lind, *The Eighteen Eighties* (London and New York, 1945).

Susan E. Lorsch, *Where Nature Ends: Literary Responses to the Designification of Landscape* (London and Toronto, 1983).

S. Marcus, *The Other Victorians* (New York, 1960).

W. de la Mare (ed.), *The Eighteen Eighties. Essays by Fellows of the Royal Society of Literature* (Cambridge, 1930).

P. Merivale, *Pan the Goat God and his Myth in Modern Times* (Cambridge, Mass., 1969).

J. G. Nelson, 'The Nature of the Aesthetic Experience in the Poetry of the Nineties: Ernest Dowson, Lionel Johnson, and John Gray', *English Literature in Transition*, 17, 4 (1974).

L. Nochlin, *Realism* (London, 1971).

M. Peckham, *Beyond the Tragic Vision* (New York, 1962).

R. Poggioli, *The Theory of the Avant Garde* (Cambridge, Mass., 1968).

M. Praz, *The Romantic Agony* (London, 1951).

B. Reade, *Sexual Heretics. Male Homosexuality in English Literature from 1850 to 1900. An Anthology* (New York, 1971).

J. K. Robinson, 'A Neglected Phase of the Aesthetic Movement', *Publications of the Modern Language Movement*, 68 (1953), 733–54.

A. Sandison, *The Wheel of Empire* (London, 1967).

R. Sharron, *The Crisis of British Imperialism* (London, 1976).

D. Stanford, *Short Stories of the Nineties. A Biographical Anthology* (London, 1968).

C. K. Stead, *The New Poetic* (New York, 1966).

D. D. Stone, *Novelists in a Changing World* (Cambridge, 1972).

R. Z. Temple, *The Critic's Alchemy. A Study of the Introduction of French Symbolism into England* (New York, 1953).

D. Thatcher, *Neitzsche in England. The Growth of a Reputation* (Toronto, 1970).

E. P. P. Thompson, *William Morris, Romantic to Revolutionary* (2nd rev. edn., London, 1955).

F. M. L. Thompson, *English Landed Society in the Nineteenth Century* (London, 1963).

R. K. R. Thornton, *The Decadent Dilemma* (London, 1983).

H. Williams, *Modern English Writers. Being A Study of Imaginative Literature, 1890–1914* (London, 1918).

BIOGRAPHICAL INDEX

ARNOLD, Sir Edwin (1832–1904), was educated at King's School, Rochester, King's College, London, and University College, Oxford, where he won the Newdigate Prize for his poem 'Belshazzar's Feast'. After schoolmastering in India he returned to Britain and became a leader writer on the *Daily Telegraph*. In the 1850s Arnold had published two volumes of competent verse and after a long silence there appeared his most popular work *The Light of Asia* (1879), modelled in its form on Tennyson's *Idylls of the King*. It is a set of episodes loosely culled from the life and legends of the Buddha. In 1888 he was appointed a Knight Commander of the Indian Empire. He was interested in all aspects of Far Eastern social and literary culture; he wrote, for example, an evocative account of witnessing a Japanese Noh Play (his third wife was Japanese). In his later years, he published much verse including an ambitious poem on the life of Jesus; like most sequels *The Light of the World* (1891) was a resounding failure. Arnold's verse in *The Light of Asia* is idly sensuous, spiced with exotic digression, though on occasion he could be vivid and terse. He often uses words transliterated direct from Sanskrit and other oriental languages, a habit effectively mocked by Owen Seaman in his *Battle of the Bays* (1896), parodies inspired by the hopes of a number of poets to be Tennyson's successor.

AUSTIN, Alfred (1835–1912), was the son of a Latin Catholic Yorkshire woolstapler and magistrate. Educated at Stonyhurst and Oscott, he graduated at London University. Called to the Bar in 1857, after a few years he turned to literature and journalism for a living. In 1896 he was appointed Poet Laureate in succession to Tennyson, for services to the Tory Party and because he was so anxious to obtain the post that it seemed cruel to disappoint him. Austin's later work has much in praise of rural England along with jingoistic doggerel that reads rather oddly now. He also published some mildly agreeable prose based on life at his Kentish manor house and a two-volume autobiography, devoid of humour, that only faintly reflects his self-satisfaction with himself and his world. Austin has been treated somewhat unfairly as the archetypal poetaster, but, in spite of some masterpieces of unconscious humour, much of his verse is competent, if hardly inspired.

BEARDSLEY, Aubrey (1872–98), was educated at Brighton Grammar School and from early on exhibited talent in music and letters. It was as a draughtsman that he won notoriety at home and fame abroad. His life was passed in the shadow of tuberculosis. He was a master of line block, a new technique of reproduction, and most of his work is illustrative, mediating, often mordantly, between spectator and text. As an artist, he changed his style every summer, transcending influences through parody and caricature. His finest work lies in the illustrations to the English version of *Salome* (1893) with its mixture of Japanese and *art nouveau* elements; the *Lysistrata; Mademoiselle de Maupin*; and a few drawings illustrative of Juvenal's sixth satire. Beardsley also had literary ambitions, though his work in this field is fragmentary, if not without distinction, whether in lyric or in the two versions of his Wagnerian travesty which were entitled respectively 'Under the Hill' and 'Venus and Tannhauser'. Beardsley was dismissed as art editor of *The Yellow Book* as a consequence of the Wilde trial, and became editor of the *Savoy*. He was supported in his last years by the generosity of his publisher Leonard Smithers and by André Raffalovich. Religious by temperament, he was converted a short time before his death to the Latin Church.

BEERBOHM, Sir Max (1872–1956), was the son of a grain merchant and stepbrother to the famous actor–manager Sir Herbert Beerbohm Tree. He was educated at Charterhouse and Merton College, Oxford, going down without a degree. By the early 1890s he was a London dandy, a caricaturist of brilliance and the author of witty, mannered essays. He succeeded Bernard Shaw as dramatic critic for the *Saturday Review* in 1898, a post he held for several years before retiring to Rapallo, Italy, where he lived quietly, interrupted only by the First and Second World Wars. In later years, he found a wider audience as a broadcaster.

BRIDGES, Robert (1844–1930), was educated at Eton and Corpus Christi College, Oxford, taking a First in Greats. After travel in Europe and the Middle East, he took a degree in medicine but retired from practice in 1882. He matured slowly as a poet; it was in the 1890s that he first became known to a wider public, though his work was never popular. In 1913 he was appointed Poet Laureate and his long philosophical poem *The Testament of Beauty* appeared in 1929. Bridges' work is chaste in diction, learned, and metrically sensitive.

BUTLER, Samuel (1835–1902), was born into a clerical family; his grandfather became Bishop of Lichfield; his father, a canon of Lincoln Cathedral. He was educated at Shrewsbury and St John's College, Cambridge. Intended for Holy Orders in the Anglican Church, he developed religious doubts and his father decided that he should emigrate to New Zealand, where he took up sheep farming. In 1864 he sold out and was able to subsist frugally, when he returned to England, on his invested capital. He had ambitions as a painter, studied for some years, but his achievement in this line was modest. He was one of the first admirers of Charles Darwin's *Origin of Species*. In 1872 he published his scientific fantasy *Erewhon*. His next work was *The Fair Haven*, an ironic and satirical study of the Resurrection accompanied by a memoir of the pseudonymous author, a clergyman gravely struggling with the difficulties posed by the dogma. Butler's autobiographical novel, *The Way of All Flesh*, written in the 1870s and 1880s, was published only after his death. By the late 1870s he had come to dispute Charles Darwin's notion of evolution, preferring the purposive view of older writers such as Lamarck and Charles's grandfather, Erasmus Darwin. The results of this shift can be detected in his novel, in *Life and Habit* (1877) and in *Luck or Cunning as the Main Means of Organic Manifestation* (1886). His versatility and independence emerge in such works as *Alps and Sanctuaries of Piedmont and the Canton Ticino*; in the composition of Handelian secular oratorios; and in his theory that the *Odyssey* was written by a Sicilian woman: *The Authoress of the Odyssey* (1897). As a reaction against Lang, Leaf, and Myers's florid translation of the Homeric epics, he produced his own, which, in spite of being intended as a down-to-earth version, now seems to have more than a touch of Victorian medievalism. His *Notebooks*, typically pungent and eccentric, were posthumously published.

CARPENTER, Edward (1844–1925), was the son of an Anglican clergyman and was educated at Brighton College, Heidelberg, and Trinity Hall, Cambridge. In 1868 he was tenth Wrangler, acquiring a Fellowship and Holy Orders in the following year. In 1870 he became curate to the famous Broad Churchman, F. D. Maurice. His first volume of verse, *Narcissus* (1873), by its subject, gives some indication of the development of his homoerotic temperament: Narcissus was to become a cult figure among the late nineteenth-century Uranian decadents. In 1874, he resigned both his Fellowship and his Orders, becoming a lecturer on popular science. He went to the United States twice, on both occasions visiting Walt Whitman, whose loose rhythms and notion of the liberated self, as well as his ideal of 'comradeship', had much appeal for Carpenter. Carpenter's own self-liberation resulted in emotional and sustained friendships with working-class men. By this time, he was largely vegetarian and a teetotaller. In 1883 there appeared the first series of his Whitmanesque *Towards Democracy*. These were added to over the ensuing twenty years. *Chants of Labour* (1888) reflected his unideological interest in Socialism. Friendship and the relation of the sexes was the topic of the prose *Love's Coming of Age* (1896). Although he had no wish to be a 'prophet' in the line of Carlyle and Ruskin, Carpenter could hardly deny to others the liberation he had himself achieved, and he had a distant influence on a number of late nineteenth-century and early twentieth-century authors, D. H. Lawrence among them.

COLERIDGE, Mary (1861–1907), was great grand-niece of S. T. Coleridge, and the daughter of a Clerk of the Assizes on the Midland Circuit. She was tutored by William Johnson Cory, and led a comfortable retired life. She wrote five novels, a fragment of a sixth, and essays, while some two hundred of her brief lyrics have been published.

CRACKANTHORPE, Hubert (1870–96), was the son of a distinguished lawyer and landowner in Westmoreland. Hubert was coached for Cambridge but decided to pursue a literary career in London. He jointly edited a magazine for younger writers, *The Albemarle*, in 1892 and published two volumes of short stories in a dark, realist vein, a series of prose poems on urban themes, *Vignettes*. He married Leila Macdonald, a not particularly talented writer, to whom he was devoted, and committed suicide when she ran off with another man. A last volume of stories was posthumously published in 1897 with a typically opaque preface by Henry James.

DAVIDSON, John (1857–1909), came of Scottish farming stock; his father was a minister of one of the small, strict sects that had seceded from the established Presbyterian Church of Scotland. John was educated at the Highlander's Academy, Greenock, and at Edinburgh University, but left after only one term. For eleven years he worked as a schoolmaster at Perth, Glasgow, Paisley, Crieff, and Greenock. In 1892 he arrived in London to earn his living by literature and was soon contributing to the *Speaker* and the *Star*; he became a member of the Rhymers' Club and wrote a number of novels. His lyric vein was exhausted by the later 1890s and he turned to the theatre, achieving one success in translating (and truncating) a French verse costume drama. His later dramatic attempts failed. The Edwardian years were characterized by a series of egotistical blank verse *Testaments* of occasional power and there are some notable successes among the less ambitious later poems. He retired from London to Penzance in Cornwall to economize; was granted a Civil List pension of £100 a year in 1906. Depressed and in ill-health, he drowned himself in the sea in April 1909.

DOBSON, Austin (1840–1921), was educated partly in England and partly abroad. In 1856 he was appointed to a clerkship in the Board of Trade where he became one of the group of happy 'Rondeliers' and together with Edmund Gosse and Andrew Lang revived the elaborate forms of Middle French poetry; rondeau, ballade, double ballade, sestina, and the rest. The ideal of this group was formalistic and rather remotely derived from Théophile Gautier. Dobson's work is deft, graceful, and on occasion witty, its welcome urbanity gathered from his eighteenth–century English and French models. He was a consistent and knowledgeable admirer of Augustan literature. His poetry, though, is not infrequently marred by Victorian sentimentality.

DOLBEN, Digby Mackworth (1848–67), came of a Northamptonshire county family and was educated at Eton where he became a close friend of Robert Bridges. While preparing for Oxford, he was drowned in the River Welland. Bridges wrote a memoir and collected his poems. Dolben had a religious temperament and his verse is of a High Church devotional cast with some indications of homosexual feeling.

DOWDEN, Edward (1843–1913), was born at Cork, educated at Trinity College, Dublin, and appointed its Professor of English Literature at the age of twenty-five. In 1875 he published *Shakespeare, his Mind and Art*, which made him famous and remained of value for several generations. This was succeeded by a life of Shelley, that inspired Arnold's comment 'what a set!' Dowden published several volumes of carefully crafted poetry and makes an unsympathetic appearance in W. B. Yeats's *Autobiographies*, mainly for his sceptical attitude to the new Irish Nationalist Literature.

DOWSON, Ernest (1867–1902), came from an artistic family and inherited frailty of physique and mental instability. He was privately educated, mainly abroad and at Queen's College, Oxford, but went down after four terms without taking a degree. A member of the Rhymers' Club, he spent much of his life drifting between England and France. His view of life was already low-toned before a hopeless love affair with the twelve-year-old daughter of a Polish restaurant keeper. In spite of his low vitality, he accomplished a volume of delicate short stories and numerous elegant translations. He also collaborated in three novels (only two of which were published) and produced two volumes of poetry. His talent was essentially lyrical; a delicate metrist, his themes were strictly limited, his vocabulary purged, his substance tenuous, a very minor Verlaine. His themes include remorse, a world-weary species of devotional verse, elegies over the passage of innocent girl children towards the knowingness of adolescence.

Duclaux, Mary (née Agnes Mary Francis Robinson) (1857–1944), the sister of the novelist Mabel Robinson, and daughter of an ecclesiastical architect, spent much of her childhood in Warwickshire and Lincolnshire. Her education was pursued in Belgium and Italy, being completed with literary and classical studies at University College, London. In 1888 she married James Darmester, Professor of Persian at the Collège de France. For fifty years and more she presided over a salon in Paris and published occasional reminiscences of her literary life. Her second marriage was to another Frenchman, Henri Duclaux.

Ellis, Edwin John (1848–1916), a friend of W. B. Yeats's father, collaborated with the son in a massive edition, with commentary, on the works of William Blake (1893). Ellis was a man of multifarious talent, but of limited achievement: a tepid painter in the style of Lord Leighton, an illustrator, novelist, and poet. His *Seen in Three Days* (1893), a long poem, is set out in his own calligraphy with illustrations that attempt to unify the page in the manner of Blake. His most distinguished volume of verse is *Fate in Arcadia* (1892). Ellis was a member of the Rhymers' Club and contributed to its anthologies.

'Field, Michael'. The two ladies who published under this pseudonym were aunt and niece: Katharine Bradley (1846–1914) and Edith Emma Cooper (1862–1913). Of independent means, they were united by an intense emotional bond, and devoted themselves exclusively to reading, collaboration, and visiting galleries. In the earlier part of their career, they produced a number of poetic dramas, set generally in exotic eras and locations, which, though containing much competent verse, were not altogether suited to either the stage or the closet. With plays in prose they were somewhat more successful. *A Question of Memory* (1893) was staged by J. T. Grein's Independent Theatre; another interesting piece of this kind, *Quits*, remains in manuscript. Soon, however, they returned to writing costume plays. In the later 1880s, they resorted to lyrical poetry, producing such volumes as *Long Ago* (1889)—expansions of fragments from Sappho—and *Underneath the Bough* (1893), while in the previous year they had published a set of short poems in the 'Gallery' tradition: *Sight and Song*. The most enduring work of the 'double-headed nightingale' as they were termed by their contemporaries are the journals they kept over many years, where they record with insight and some malice their meetings with many of the poets and artists of the day. A brief selection from these was posthumously published. For some years they were on close terms with Bernard Berenson, who thought highly of the niece, but considered her remarkable gifts to be stifled by her over-possessive aunt. In later years both ladies were converted to Latin Catholicism.

GARNETT, Richard (1835–1906), the son of the Assistant Keeper of Printed Books at the British Museum, was himself to devote nearly fifty years of his life to the great library. He was mostly self-educated, having at the age of sixteen refused an offer from relatives to be prepared for either Oxford or Cambridge. He rose to become Keeper of Printed Books and a legend in his lifetime for his knowledge of works in many languages. His poetry is somewhat tepid; his translations competent; his neat Voltairian tales, *The Twilight of the Gods*, constitute his finest work. His book of aphorisms, *De Flagello Myrteo* (1905), is also worth looking at. He founded a literary dynasty: his son Edward was novelist, man of letters and publisher's reader; his grandson, David, a distinguished novelist.

GISSING, George (1857–1903), was born at Wakefield, Yorkshire. His origins were lower-middle-class; his father was a chemist and his position in society enabled him to understand and to fear the classes of society beneath him. He was educated at Lindow Grove School, Alderley Edge, Cheshire, and at Owens College, Manchester, from which he was sent down for theft of money used to redeem a young prostitute Nell Harrison whom he was to marry. Gissing was sent to the United States to make a new life and he stayed for a year, practising journalism. In 1879 he returned to England, marrying Nell in London. His first novel, *Workers in the Dawn*, was published in 1880. In 1881 he separated from his wife who was now an alcoholic, setting her up in Hastings. In 1886 Nell died and in 1891 he married a lower-middle-class woman, Edith Underwood. Gissing's natural inclination was towards cultivated women of a higher class, but he was convinced that his comparative poverty and social origins made it possible for him only to marry down. Sexual frustration and loneliness drove him into this second unsatisfactory marriage, which ended in separation in 1897. In 1898 he met Gabrielle Fleury, a cultured young Frenchwoman, and lived with her until his death. Gissing's main work is *The New Grub Street* (1891) but later distinguished novels include *In the Year of Jubilee* (1895) and *The Whirlpool* (1897).

GILBERT, Sir William Schwenk (1836–1911), was educated at King's College, London, and after a period in the Civil Service was called to the Bar. His work consists of light verses, the libretti of various operettas, the best being those written in collaboration with Sir Arthur Sullivan, and plays which have been somewhat undervalued. Gilbert was knighted in 1907 and died of a heart attack while trying to rescue a friend's daughter from drowning. His work has most of the characteristics of Victorian humour, fertility of metrical invention and of rhyming, punning, and parody. His wit and his anti-feminism are his own.

GOSSE, Sir Edmund (1849–67), was the son of Philip Henry Gosse, Fellow of the Royal Society, a pious and distinguished naturalist, whose response to geological remains was that God had hidden them in the rocks to tempt man's faith. His son vividly memorialized him in *Father and Son* (1907). In 1867 Gosse was appointed an assistant librarian at the British Museum and in 1875, like several poets of his generation, found employment in the Board of Trade. A pioneer in modern Scandinavian studies, he became Clark Lecturer at Cambridge in 1885 and finally Librarian to the House of Lords. Gosse was an inaccurate scholar but his essays have charm and facility. They have overshadowed his poetry. In the last two decades of his life, he could fairly be described as a literary dictator.

GRAY, John (1866–1934), was born of working-class parents; after a year at grammar school, he became a metal turner at Woolwich Arsenal. Native wit and private study enabled him to pass an examination into the Civil Service. By 1890 he had become a librarian at the Foreign Office, an exquisite, a translator from contemporary French poetry, and author of 'black' poems. A man of striking physical beauty, Gray was probably one of the models for Dorian Gray (though he threatened a libel action against one newspaper that dared to suggest so). In 1893 he published *Silverpoints*, designed by Charles Ricketts, one of the most delicate productions of the decade. By this time Gray had passed from the protection of Wilde into the hands of André Raffalovich, a very minor poet and dramatist and author of two studies of homosexual love. In 1898 Gray went to the Scots' College at Rome and was ordained, having been converted to Latin Catholicism some years earlier. He became a formidable priest, working at first in a slum district of Edinburgh and later building his own church at Morningside, an Edinburgh suburb. In 1896 he had published a companion volume to *Silverpoints* consisting of translations from a variety of religious poems and some original devotional lyrics. His later poetry exhibits a discreet modernism and he also wrote a remarkable science fiction novel, *Park*. In 1930 he became a Canon of Edinburgh Cathedral.

HENLEY, William Ernest (1849–1903), was educated at the Crypt School, Gloucester. As a boy and a young man he suffered from tuberculosis in both legs and one leg had to be amputated. His experiences in Edinburgh, where he was in the care of Sir Joseph Lister, led to a remarkable series of hospital poems, prosaic but vivid, full of a painful minuteness of detail. It was while in hospital that he met Robert Louis Stevenson, a meeting that resulted in the most intense friendship of his life, later to be ruptured by Stevenson's marriage. Henley was a distinguished editor: *London* (1877–8); *The Scots* (later *National*) *Observer* (1888–93); and *The New Review* (1893–8). He was also art critic and dramatist. A strong Imperialist and a noisy opponent of literary and artistic 'decadence', Henley in his verse notably uses urban imagery, free verse, and, occasionally and brilliantly, the colloquial.

HOPKINS, Ellice Jane (1836–1904), was the daughter of a distinguished geologist, who was also a brilliant private tutor in mathematics at Cambridge. For much of her life she was involved in bettering the condition of vulnerable girls, her 'great, sad work'. Miss Hopkins had much to do with the passage of the Industrial Schools Act of 1880. Her publications include novels, social pamphlets, and two volumes of poetry: *English Idylls and other Poems* (1865) and *Autumn Swallows* (1882), from which such influences as George Herbert and Christina Rossetti can be inferred.

HOPKINS, Gerard Manley (1844–89), was educated at the Cholmondeley School, Highgate, and Balliol College, Oxford. He was tutored for a while by Walter Pater and took a First in Greats. While still an undergraduate, he had been converted to the Latin Catholic Church and in 1868 became a Jesuit, burning the poetry he had written to that date. He returned to composition with his elegy *The Wreck of the Deutschland*. His superiors saw fit to place him in an Irish slum parish in Liverpool. His career in the church was mediocre and unhappy. In 1884 he was appointed Professor of Greek at the Catholic University in Dublin, a post he barely relished, and after some melancholy years he died of fever. It can be said that he was one of the victims of the unimaginative post-Tridentine Catholicism that prevailed in the nineteenth century. The accident of his poems appearing almost thirty years after his death has tended to mask the fact that he is in most respects a typically Victorian poet. His work only became popular in the 1930s; his executor Robert Bridges' estimate of the appropriate time to publish his poems as a collection seems to have been accurate.

HOUSMAN, Alfred Edward (1859–1936), the son of a lawyer, was educated at Edward VI School at Bromsgrove and at St John's College, Oxford, where, as a consequence of reading widely but ignoring some of the set books, he failed his final examinations in Greats. His emotional involvement, not physically reciprocated, with an athletic engineering contemporary, Moses Jackson, may also have had its effect. For ten years Housman worked in the Patent Offices, publishing masterful articles on Greek and Latin literature, and was elected in 1892 to the Chair of Latin at University College, London. In 1896 he published *A Shropshire Lad* and in 1903 there appeared the first volume of his edition of the *Astronomica* of Manilius, a poet of the third class with a snarled text. This labour confirmed his growing reputation as one of the most distinguished classical scholars of his time. In 1905 he produced an edition of Juvenal, subtitled 'for the use of editors'. In 1910 he was appointed to the Kennedy Professorship of Latin at Cambridge and to a Fellowship of Trinity College. Manilius was completed, and an edition of Lucan appeared in 1926. In 1933 Housman delivered the Leslie Stephen Lecture at Cambridge on 'The Name and Nature of Poetry', of which Dr F. R. Leavis is reported to have declared: 'It will take twenty years to undo the harm [it] has done,' with its stress on the transmission not of thought but of emotion as the aim of poetry. A formidable figure, though with a powerful charm when he cared to exercise it, Housman was a wit, a connoisseur of wine, and a felicitous writer of light verse.

JEFFERIES, Richard (1848–87), was the son of a small Wiltshire farmer. After a formal education that concluded at the age of seventeen, he became a journalist on a local paper, wrote a number of unsuccessful 'sensation' novels, and in 1878 published the first of his popular books on natural history, *The Gamekeeper at Home*. He wrote two agreeable books for young people, *Bevis* and *Wood Magic*. *After London* (1885) is a powerful account of an England sunk into barbarism with London a poisonous swamp. It has a startling 'open ending'. Other major novels are the lyrical *The Dewy Morn* (1884), *Greene Fern Farm* (1880), and *Amaryllis at the Fair* (1887). The pantheistic sentimentality of *The Story of My Heart* (1883) reads rather less well.

JOHNSON, Lionel (1867–1902), came from an upper-middle-class family; his grandfather had been created a baronet for service to the crown in the Irish rebellion of 1798. Lionel was educated at Winchester and New College, Oxford, where he took a First in Greats. He came to London in 1890 and augmented his small private income with literary journalism. In the late 1880s he had become acquainted with Herbert Horne and the Century Guild circle and in 1891 became a member of the Rhymers' Club. He was converted to the Latin Catholic Church in that same year. Insomnia and ill health led him into excessive drinking and he died without altogether fulfilling his gifts. A deeply read and judicious critic—his *Art of Thomas Hardy* (1894) is still consulted—his poetry reflects a temperament learned and correct; parsimonious in imagery, it is flushed occasionally by preoccupations that are not far short of obsessions: guilt; remorse; respect for institutions; a muted homosexual note; a somewhat sectarian religious tone, and a love for his adopted country Ireland. He collaborated closely with Yeats in the programme of the cultural revival. He has a neat satiric touch in both prose and verse.

KIPLING, Rudyard (1865–1936). Kipling's father, a book illustrator, was appointed Professor of Architectural Sculpture at Bombay. His mother was one of the Macdonald sisters, the others becoming the wives of Burne Jones, Edward Poynter, later President of the Royal Academy, and Alfred Baldwin, industrialist and father of the future Prime Minister, Stanley Baldwin. Rudyard's earliest years were spent in India; his parents took him back to England and left him with foster parents at Southsea. Here he suffered the canings and inquisitions of a religious tyrant, Mrs Holloway, before going to Westward Ho School, whose headmaster Cormell Price had been an associate of the Pre-Raphaelites. The school forms the basis for the stories of *Stalky and Co* (1899). In 1882 Kipling took up a post on the Lahore *Military and Civil Gazette* and his experiences at this time confirmed his Imperialism and his admiration for technical special skills. He also learned his mastery of the short story. In 1889 he returned to Britain with a reputation already made by his vivid evocations of post-Mutiny India. He became the unofficial Laureate of Empire, though there are often undertones of pessimism and doubt in his writings. In 1907 Kipling was awarded the Nobel Prize for Literature. For many years there was a reaction against him, largely on account of his politics, but his reputation is now secure as a great writer of short fiction and a distinguished poet.

LANG, Andrew (1844–1912), a Scot, was educated at St Andrew's University and Balliol College, Oxford. A versatile man of letters, he was also an anthropologist, and gave the Gifford Lectures on Natural Religion at St Andrews in 1888. Lang translated with taste and felicity the *Odyssey*, Theocritus, and the tale of *Aucassin and Nicolette*, besides producing a life of the Earl of Iddesleigh and works of popular history. His retelling of fairy stories for children, *The Blue Fairy Book*, *The Violet Fairy Book*, etc., have probably lasted better than any of his more elaborate works. As a poet, Lang's work tends to the tepid and empty.

LEE-HAMILTON, Eugene (1845–1907), was half-brother to Violet Paget 'Vernon Lee', critic, aesthetician, novelist. He was educated privately abroad and at Oriel College, Oxford, going down without a degree. His career lay in the Diplomatic Service, but the outer world was not altogether to his liking and he contracted a severe psycho-somatic illness of a cerebro-spinal kind which confined him to his bed for over twenty years. He finally recovered soon after his mother died, married and had a child, who died young. Lee-Hamilton's verse has affinities with the Parnassians, with its jewelled surface and stress on form; while its subject matter allies him with the poets of the 'Decadence'. It has recently received renewed attention.

LE GALLIENNE, Richard (1866–1947), born Richard Gallienne, of a middle-class family, was educated at Liverpool College and for some years worked as an accountant. In 1891 he settled in London and wrote prolifically, fiction, essays, criticism, and verse. Graceful, sentimental, faintly vulgar in tone, his work was soon popular. In 1903 he emigrated to the United States. His last years were spent in France, where he was well treated by the Germans but refused any form of co-operation. As a poet, he has the alertness of the journalist to topics of immediate interest.

LYALL, Sir Alfred (1835–1911), was educated at Eton and entered the Indian Civil Service, where he had a markedly successful career. He was appointed Home Secretary in 1873 and Foreign Secretary in 1878; he was Lieutenant-Governor of the North Western Provinces in 1882 and in 1888 became a member of the Council of India. His KCB was gazetted in 1881. He may be said to have inaugurated a school of Anglo-Indian poetry, of which Kipling is the best-known representative.

MEW, Charlotte (1869–1928), was the daughter of an architect, and spent most of her life in London. She was educated at Lucy Harrison's School for

Girls in Gower Street and attended lectures nearby at University College, London, reading widely in French and English. She contributed a short story to *The Yellow Book* and attended the Saturday evening gatherings of the editor, Henry Harland. Charlotte passed for an 'advanced' woman, moving about unchaperoned, smoking and swearing. She published from about 1900 onwards poems, short stories, and articles in various magazines. For two years she was a close friend of May Sinclair, the novelist, and it has been suggested that the friendship was broken off abruptly as a consequence of Charlotte's sapphic advances. There was a good deal of mental instability in Charlotte's family and soon after the death of her sister Anne, to whom she was deeply attached, she committed suicide. Her poetry records her attraction to and repulsion from Latin Catholicism, and her main themes are death and mental illness.

MEYNELL, Alice (1847–1922), born Alice Thompson, fell in love with a priest and was received into the Latin Catholic Church. In 1877 she married Wilfrid Meynell, editor and critic. Her shaped and chastened poetry is superior to her criticism with its conventional judgements. In the 1890s she became the centre of a circle of Catholic authors and at her house in Palace Court, London, ran something of a salon. She and her husband were among those who precipitated Beardsley's dismissal from *The Yellow Book*.

MIALL, Arthur Bernard, published two volumes of verse, *Nocturnes and Pastorals* (1896) influenced by Arthur Symons's impressionism and urban lyrics, along with the less accomplished *Poems* (1899). He turned to translation and quarried works in French, Danish, Italian, German, and Spanish.

MOORE, George (1852–1933), was born into an upper-middle-class Anglo-Irish Latin Catholic family in the West of Ireland. Educated at St Mary's, Oscott, he left school early, studying to be a painter and completing his training in Paris. In the late 1870s he abandoned painting for poetry and produced two volumes of bad Baudelairian verse, *Flowers of Passion* (1878) and *Pagan Poems* (1881). His next enthusiasm was for Zola, and under that master's influence he produced two of his better novels, *A Mummer's Wife* (1885) and *Esther Waters* (1894), in which, like the Goncourt brothers, he made a maidservant the central figure. Always open to new influences, or as Yeats put it 'conducting his education in public', he passed under the influence of Pater, then of Yeats, the Irish Literary Movement, and Symbolism. *The Untilled Field* (1903) and *The Lake* (1905) are the fruits of this phase. The last part of his career is characterized by a limpid, musical prose in which both narrator and narrative are refracted and distanced, as in *The Brook Kerith* (1916) and *Heloise and Abelard* (1921). His disillusionment with Ireland and Catholicism led him into his most fruitful genre: comic autobiographical fantasy. *Confessions of a Young Man* (1888) had been an audacious forerunner. In *Hail and Farewell* (1911–14) he presents himself as a Siegfried who fails to redeem his country and treats friends and acquaintances, with the exception of George William

Russell, with off-hand mockery. Moore's status as a writer still remains faintly equivocal; he is an instance of severe dedication and openness transforming a writer of moderate talent into a formidable artist. In any case, he deserves respect as a courageous man of letters and as one of those who helped in overcoming the insularity of English culture in the later nineteenth century.

MORRISON, Arthur (1863–1945), was entirely reserved about his early life, but it seems he was born in East London, the son of a steamfitter. He assisted for some time at the People's Palace, Mile End, from which he derived first-hand experience of the East End of London, though he had been brought up within its boundaries. In the 1890s he contributed short stories to W. E. Henley's *National Observer* and won an immediate reputation with a volume of short stories, *Tales of Mean Streets* (1894). Later works of distinction are *A Child of the Jago* (1896) and a brilliant children's book *The Hole in the Wall* (1902). Although he continued to write short stories and plays, his best work was now done. In later years he became a collector of Orientalia and at his death his collections were given to the British Museum.

NEWBOLT, Sir Henry (1862–1938), was the son of an Anglican clergyman. He was educated at Clifton College and at Corpus Christi College, Oxford. Called to the Bar, he practised for a dozen years before turning wholly to literature. Between 1900 and 1904 he edited *The Monthly Review*, served on numerous government commissions and was responsible for Volumes iv and v of the official *History of the Great War: Naval Operations*. In 1915 he was knighted, and awarded the CH in 1922. His naval and patriotic verses form only a part of his *œuvre*. He also wrote novels and a fantastic allegory *Aladore* (1914). He has been described as a 'Kipling of the upper classes' but this is not altogether accurate. He was a Liberal Imperialist; if there is less of the dark side of Kipling, there is distinctly less of the genius.

NOEL, The Honourable Roden Berkeley Wriothesley (1834–94), the son of the First Earl of Gainsborough by a fourth marriage, was educated at Harrow and Cambridge. He travelled in the Near East and married Alice de Broe, daughter of a banker in Beirut. Noel was happily bisexual, promiscuous without guilt, and wrote a number of poems celebrating male beauty. In later years he became sympathetic to socialism. He was also a mildly talented amateur philosopher.

O'SHAUGHNESSY, Arthur (1844–81). It was suggested by the Irish journalist Clement Shorter that O'Shaughnessy was the illegitimate child of Edward Bulwer, first Lord Lytton, who procured for him at the age of seventeen a post as a zoologist at the British Museum, though the evidence is not strong. O'Shaughnessy was later transferred to the Natural History Museum, though without training. By diligent study, he made himself an expert in the reptile field. His poetry has an Irish fluency and melody along with Pre-Raphaelite and Parnassian qualities.

PATER, Walter Horatio (1839–94), son of a doctor, was born at Shadwell in the East End of London. Educated at King's School, Canterbury, and at Queen's College, Oxford, he secured a Fellowship at Brasenose College in 1864. With the exception of the years from 1886 to 1893, which were spent in London, Oxford remained his home for the rest of his life, though he travelled frequently on the Continent. From the middle 1860s he had published striking, but anonymous essays, mainly in the radical *Westminster Review*. When these were revised and collected as *Studies in the History of the Renaissance* under his own name with a Preface and a provocative Conclusion, the book caused something of a scandal, owing to its recommendations of 'life as the end of life', of prolonging our moments as they pass by burning with 'a pure gem like flame' and by the love of art for its own sake. To some extent, Pater muted and augmented this philosophy in his philosophical romance *Marius the Epicurean* (1885), a work which reveals a more sympathetic attitude to Christianity. His literary criticism was gathered in *Appreciations* (1889): the essays on Wordsworth and Coleridge are particularly notable. His finest book is *Imaginary Portraits* (1887) (there are several uncollected examples of the *genre*), four brief narrative studies set in different European cultural phases. Pater's first fame was as stylist; then as appreciative critic; more recently his work as an art critic has attracted attention and he is now also seen as a significant precursor of 'modernism'.

RENTON, William James (born *c*.1845), was an Extension Lecturer for the Scottish Universities. Besides a novel *Bishopspool* (1883) and two works of luminously vulgarizing philosophy, he published two volumes of verse: *Oils and Water Colours* (1876) from which the poems here are taken, and the inferior *Songs* of 1893. The later volume has 'William Renton' on the title page and may be by another author.

ROLLESTON, Thomas William Hazen (1857–1920), came from a middle-class 'Ascendancy' family. He was educated at St Columba's College, Dublin, Rathfarnham and Trinity College, Dublin, and his first published poems appeared in the University magazine *Kottabos*. For some years Rolleston lived in Germany, perfecting his knowledge of that language and translating a wide variety of texts. He was a man of impressive personality and culture but as a whole his career was fragmented and disappointing. Between 1885 and 1886 he edited the *Dublin University Review* in which a number of the early poems of W. B. Yeats were published. In 1892 he was invited to be Taylorian lecturer at Oxford and his contribution was later published in *Studies in European Literature* (1900). He acted as first secretary to the Irish Literary Society in London from 1892 to 1893. In 1891 he became a member of the Rhymers' Club and contributed to its two anthologies of 1892 and 1894. From 1894 to 1897 he was the Managing Director and Secretary of the Irish Industries Association, and between 1893 and 1900 worked as a leader writer for the *Dublin Daily Express* and as Dublin correspondent to the London *Daily Chronicle*. In 1900 he edited with Stopford Brooke a *Treasury of Irish Poetry*. Between 1900 and 1905 he

arranged lectures for the Irish Department of Agricultural and Technical
Instruction and in that capacity organized the Irish Historical Loan
Collection for the Saint Louis Exhibition of 1904. From 1906 to 1908 he
acted as Honorary Secretary to the Irish Arts and Crafts Society. Rolleston
also wrote popular accounts of Irish myths and heroic stories that have gone
through a number of editions. His last writings reflect gloom at the
worsening situation in Ireland. As a poet he was costive without being
lapidary, producing a single volume *Sea Spray* (1909), selected from a
somewhat larger output. Too multifarious, too 'West British', for real
influence or public success, Rolleston accomplished much good and quiet
work and, if he succeeded far less than George William Russell in
influencing the current of affairs for good, he has, none the less, been rather
undeservedly forgotten.

RUSSELL, George William ('A.E.') (1867–1935), was the son of a book-keeper
and at the age of thirteen enrolled in a Dublin art school, continuing
attendance to the age of eighteen. It was here in all probability that he met
W. B. Yeats. In 1888 or 1889 he joined the Theosophical Society of Dublin.
For a few years he worked as a draper's clerk. In 1895 he joined the Irish
Literary Society and two years later Count Plunkett appointed Russell to
his staff on the Irish Agricultural Society as a Banks Organizer. In the
following year he was appointed Assistant Secretary to the Organization.
He had published in 1894 the first of his volumes of mystical verses
Homeward Songs by the Way, and *The Earth Breath* appeared in 1897. In
1902 he was appointed Vice-President of the Irish National Theatre; his
play *Deirdre* was given in that same year. The first public exhibition of his
paintings took place in Dublin in 1904. From 1904 till 1933 Russell was a
member of the re-established Dublin Theosophical Society, which seceded
from the Society in 1909, of which he became President. In 1905 he had
been appointed editor of the *Irish Homestead* and he continued his
supervision of co-operative banks. He took a constructive part in trying to
limit the activities of William Martin Murphy and his associates who
countered the Dublin general strike of 1913 by a lock-out, and spoke at the
Royal Albert Hall meeting in November 1913 in favour of the strikers.
Russell was one of the members of the Home Rule Convention in 1917, but
soon resigned. He took a temperate anti-Republican stand in the Irish Civil
War of 1922–3. The *Irish Homestead* merged with the *Irish Statesman* in
1923 and he continued as editor. Trinity College, Dublin, awarded him an
Honorary D. Litt. in 1924. From 1933 to the time of his death he lived
generally in England, with occasional trips to the United States on fund-
raising activities. Russell was an attractive figure, touching Irish life at
many points; his natural goodness resisted even the malice of George
Moore. Indeed, Moore presents him in *Hail and Farewell* as a kind of saint,
a standard by which his prominent contemporaries are judged. His poetry,
like his painting, is somewhat vaporous and monotonous, but retains some
vitality through the genuine mysticism that underlies it.

SCHREINER, Olive (1855–1920), was born at the Witteburg Mission Station in South Africa. She herself rejected Christianity, though not the Bible, at an early age. After an education, largely autodidactic, she worked as a governess for several years before coming to England in 1881. Here she met Havelock Ellis, Edward Carpenter, and Karl Pearson and became a close friend also of Eleanor Marx. Her novel *The Story of an African Farm* (1883), largely autobiographical, eloquently evokes the bare and intense landscapes of the veldt and the religious problems of the period. For years she worked at a longer novel about prostitution, *Man to Man*, but this was never concluded and published only after her death. In 1889 she returned to South Africa and, as in England, became involved in liberal causes. She found a new form, the allegory. In this vein *Trooper Peter Halkett of Mashonaland* (1897) is her most achieved work. A woman of strong imaginative powers, she was unable to find a suitable vehicle for her insights. She visited England for six months and lived there from 1914 till her death. She opposed the Boer War, later adopted the cause of the Blacks in South Africa, was a strong feminist and pacifist. Altogether a remarkable example of 'the new woman', whose literary gifts were nobly dissipated in the service of her many causes.

SHARP, William (1855–1905), was born at Paisley, Scotland, of substantial middle-class stock, and after a brief period at Edinburgh University was placed by his parents in a lawyer's office. After a trip to Australia in 1876–7, he returned and worked briefly in a London bank. In 1879 he was introduced into the circle (by then much restricted) of Dante Gabriel Rossetti, whose life he was rather rapidly and carelessly to write. Indeed he became something of a higher journalistic hack in the 1880s. In 1882 he published his first volume of verse, *The Human Inheritance*. After some years of incessant writing—novels, biography, verse—in 1890 Sharp left London. Influenced by the Belgian Literary Movement, and by the Celtic Revival in general, which he sought to extend to the Scottish Highlands, he elaborated a second self, a so-called cousin 'Fiona Macleod', and produced much verse and fiction under that name. For much of his life Sharp had suffered from a rheumatic heart and hypertension; this was aggravated by continuous overwork and the strain of maintaining two literary careers, for he continued to write prolifically under his real name. His novels retain some mild interest, largely for their themes, while his free verse poems are of literary–historical importance.

STEPHEN, James Kenneth (1859–92), was the second son of the distinguished Judge and essayist, Sir James Fitzjames Stephen, who was a half-brother of Sir Leslie Stephen, Virginia Woolf's father. Educated at Eton and King's College, Cambridge, J. K. Stephen took a First in the Historical Tripos and a Third Class in the Law Tripos. At King's, he was a member of the Apostles, an essay and conversation club established earlier in the century, to which Tennyson had belonged and which survives to the present. In 1885 Stephen became a Fellow of King's and for a while was Tutor to King

Edward VII's elder son, later Duke of Clarence. Both Stephen and Clarence have been suggested as possible suspects for the 'Jack the Ripper' murders, Clarence because he was a degenerate (though actually an amiable one) and Stephen because of temporary insanity as a consequence of a severe blow on the head he suffered in 1886 and which finally resulted in his death. At Cambridge he was already known as an essayist, an accomplished writer of light verse, a typical Victorian genre and one especially practised at the universities. He died suddenly at an early age, leaving two volumes of verse, *Lapsus Calami* and *Quia, Musa, Tendis*, both published in 1891. In 1896 the two volumes, with some additions, were edited by his brother Herbert Stephen.

STEVENSON, Robert Louis (1850–94), was born in Edinburgh, son of a distinguished engineer. He was intended by his father to follow the same profession, but at Edinburgh University turned to literature. Much of his life was spent travelling in search of health. His works embrace essays, travel books, novels, short stories, criticism, and poetry. The unfinished *Weir of Hermiston* (1896) is his masterpiece, but other works of fiction, such as *Dr Jekyll and Mr Hyde*, *Markheim*, and *Treasure Island*, are equally achieved. His poetry is neat, but a little mechanical in its rhythms: 'the rhythms of the will' in W. B. Yeats's phrase. There is a scatter of memorable lyrics, which are omitted here for reasons of space.

SWINBURNE, Algernon Charles (1837–1909), was the son of Admiral C. H. Swinburne and Lady Jane Henrietta Ashburnham, daughter of the third Earl of Ashburnham. The poet's paternal grandfather was a baronet. Swinburne therefore is one of the few aristocratic poets that the English tradition has produced. He was educated at Eton and Balliol College, Oxford, where he earned the friendship and respect of the famous Master, Benjamin Jowett, for his knowledge of the classics. Indeed, there are stories of Swinburne correcting Jowett's translations of Plato with the cheery comment: 'Another howler, Master!' He went down, however, without taking a degree. His first success was with *Atalanta in Calydon* (1865), a drama modelled somewhat loosely on Greek tragic poetry, the choruses being particularly admired. His first notoriety came with the publication of *Poems and Ballads* (1866), written earlier than *Atalanta*, where his fascination with the more peripheral aspects of love became evident. This volume touches on hermaphroditism, sado-masochism, the death-wish, sapphism, enthusiasm for pagan morality, and polemic against Christianity, topics that the mid-Victorian writers tended to avoid. 'The libidinous laureate of a pack of satyrs' was a typical comment by one of the contemporary reviewers. Swinburne was deeply attracted by his cousin Mary Gordon and on her marriage to a much older man his emotional life became chaotic. He paid regular visits to a flagellation brothel and was frequently drunk in the later 1860s and 1870s, though as much with nervous excitement as with alcohol. In 1879, by arrangement with his parents, he was taken into care by the critic and poet Theodore Watts-Dunton and the quality of his poetry declined gradually over the next thirty years of staid domesticity, though remarkable items are still to be found among his later work. A distinguished critic, a skilled metrist, a brilliant parodist, Swinburne was adept at composition in several languages.

SYMONDS, John Addington (1840–93), was the son of a doctor of intellectual tastes. He was educated at Harrow and Balliol College, Oxford, where he took the Newdigate Prize and a First in Greats. His health was weak. He contracted tuberculosis and was compelled to spend much of his life abroad, particularly in Switzerland, which was favoured by those suffering from pulmonary diseases. Symonds's major work is his six-volume *Renaissance in Italy* which became indispensable to the later nineteenth-century tourist, supplementing the works of Ruskin with their exclusive devotion to the Gothic. This book can still be read with profit, though the volume on the Counter-Reformation is, as one might expect at the date at which it was written, notably unsympathetic and weak. Symonds also wrote a volume on the Greek poets which in its first edition had a remarkably frank Preface (suppressed in the second edition) extolling the Mediterranean and Paganism at the expense of Puritanism and the climate of Northern Europe, and making no secret of the author's admiration for male beauty. Symonds was an able translator and an engaging travel writer, but his poetry is disappointing. His *A Problem in Greek Ethics* (1893), like *A Problem in Modern Ethics* (1891), reflects on his own homoerotic temperament; both are pioneering works.

SYMONS, Arthur (1865–1945). Symons's father, a yeoman of Cornish origin, became a Methodist minister. Arthur was educated at different establishments as his father stayed at most three years in one place on circuit. His literary career began early with editions of Shakespeare, and with reviews, though his main energies were given to poetry. In 1889 he published his first volume *Days and Nights*, which was admired by Pater, who, however advised Symons to turn to prose. In that same year he paid the first of many visits to Paris. During the 1890s he became known as a graceful and alert journalist, submitted in turn to 'Decadent' and 'Symbolist' influences, and edited the most memorable of the 'little' magazines of the decade, the *Savoy* in 1896. He was an important mediator between English and French culture. Alive to the poetry of the city, he was learned in the music hall. The poems collected as *Silhouettes* (1892) and *London Nights* (1895) show the influence of impressionism, and both volumes provoked the moralists. Symons was a member of the Rhymers' Club and between 1895 and 1900 in particular became closely associated with W. B. Yeats. Their dialogue issued in Yeats's *Ideas of Good and Evil* and in Symons's most influential critical work *The Symbolist Movement in Literature* (1899). His finest prose belongs to the first decade of the present century, such collections as *Plays, Acting and Music* (1903) and *Studies in Seven Arts* (1905). He aimed at a total aesthetic, but his impressionist method derived from Pater hardly permitted its establishment. In 1906 *Spiritual Adventures*—brilliant brief 'imaginary portraits'—made its appearance and in the following year an uncharacteristically well-documented study of Blake that remains required reading. Signs of hypomania resulting from overwork and the need to support a wife had been evident for several years and in 1908 he suffered a severe breakdown from which, after some years, he made a partial recovery. Most of his later works were collections of essays written before his breakdown or poems that repeated rather tepidly old themes. The only noteworthy new work was his account of his mental illness, *Confessions* (1931), which is best read in the shorter version published in the periodical *Life and Letters*.

TABLEY, Lord de (1835-95). The Hon. John Byrne Leicester Warren, later Lord de Tabley, was educated at Eton and Christ Church, Oxford, and called to the Bar in 1860. His versatility extended to botany and numismatics. He was equally versatile in poetry, his range involving dramatic monologue, classical drama such as *Philoctetes* and *Orestes*, and lyric. His later work is, if anything, more achieved than his earlier.

THOMPSON, Francis (1859-1907), was born at Preston, Lancashire, son of a Latin Catholic doctor. His parents tended to over-indulgence; he was educated at home by a governess and private tutors and then sent to the Catholic College of Saint Cuthbert at Ushaw, where he developed ambitions to become a priest, ambitions that were sensibly discouraged. Already his natural indolence of character and his incapacity to distinguish between fact and fantasy were marked and by his twentieth year he had become addicted to the laudanum that resolved the disparity between what should be and what actually was. In 1878 his father sent him to Owen's College (later Manchester University) with a view to training as a doctor. Here Francis made an elaborate pretence of study, but spent most of his time dreaming and watching cricket. In 1885 his father's patience was exhausted and, unable to face failure, Thompson disappeared to London where he starved, bought much laudanum (which was cheaper than food), and underwent experiences that suspiciously duplicated those of one of his heroes, Thomas De Quincey, author of *Confessions of an English Opium Eater*. The story of his discovery in 1887 by Wilfred Meynell, editor of the Catholic periodical *Merrie England*, which published several of his early, rather undistinguished poems, has often been told. Wilfred and his wife, the distinguished poet, Alice Meynell, took him under their protection and had him sent to a monastery for cure and rehabilitation. The phase of withdrawal from laudanum seems to have been fruitful for his poetry and he rapidly began to produce work of a far higher merit. His first volume, published in 1893, was received enthusiastically, but the later *Sister Songs* (1895) and *New Poems* (1897) were reviewed with some savagery, partly from the sense that Thompson had been unduly 'puffed' by his co-religionists, partly by the plain pretentiousness of some of his work. After

1897 his inspiration largely faded and his better work was accomplished in criticism. He died in 1907 of the tuberculosis from which he had long suffered. Among his papers was found the splendid 'In No Strange Land' which, with 'The Hound of Heaven' and a handful of less florid verses, ensures his survival. It was erroneously thought in the 1890s that he was a latter day Metaphysical (the school was enjoying some popularity at this time), but Thompson has a distinctly moderate sense of the macrocosmic--microcosmic analogies, the typological wit, and the intellectual severity of his models. It is only fair to state that his reputation is now unduly shaded by the exalted after-life of Hopkins.

THOMSON, James (1834–82), born of Scots parents at Port-Glasgow, was trained as an army schoolmaster. He became a friend of Charles Bradlaugh, the free-thought agitator whose influence confirmed Thomson in his secularist beliefs. Thomson lost his mother early, then his fiancée, and in 1862 his job, probably as a consequence of the recurrent bouts of uncontrolled drinking which had begun in his middle twenties. He was already melancholic and insomniac, though at times happy and witty. It was in Bradlaugh's weekly paper the *National Reformer* that Thomson published his most famous poem, *The City of Dreadful Night* (1874). He quarrelled with Bradlaugh and the later part of his life was largely spent in seedy lodgings.

VELEY, Margaret (1843–87), was the daughter of an ecclesiastical solicitor and received her education at home, becoming well versed in French. In her later years she suffered much from depression, brought about by the deaths of her two married sisters. She contributed short stories to the *Cornhill* magazine and published several novels of which the most popular was *For Percival* (1872). Her poems were collected posthumously as *A Marriage of Shadows and Other Poems* (1888) with a preface and biographical introduction by Leslie Stephen.

WATSON, Sir William (1858–1935), the son of a Yorkshire businessman, was brought up in Liverpool and Southport. Ill health reduced his formal education, though he read widely and came to have some acquaintance with modern languages and the classics. He published his first volume of poems in 1880, and its failure brought out a latent paranoia, resulting in the first of several breakdowns. The years of his greatest popularity were the 1890s. The more conventional aspects of the literary establishment saw in him a counterweight to French Decadence, Naturalism, Impressionism, and other heresies of art. In 1892, during another breakdown, he stopped a carriage in which Prince Alfred, Duke of Edinburgh and his family were travelling, probably with the notion of protesting against the indifference of the public to his work. He was immured for some time in an asylum. By the end of the decade, his popularity had begun to wane, partly as a consequence of his manifest agnosticism and his radical positions in politics. However, he recovered some reputation for a short while with the production of his elaborate *Ode on the Coronation of King Edward the*

Seventh (1902). He had hopes, though his instability and the extremity of his opinions must have made the appointment unlikely, of becoming Poet Laureate. In 1917 he was knighted, but faded gradually into obscurity, having come to seem the personification of Victorian earnestness. His poetry occasionally strikes an eloquent attitude and his championship of such causes as Boer and Irish independence deserves remembrance.

WEBSTER, Augusta (1840–94), daughter of Vice-Admiral George Davies, married a Fellow of Trinity College, Cambridge, and, moving to London with her husband, was soon deeply involved in social causes. For some years she was a member of the London School Board. Her *Dramatic Studies* of 1866 reveal her 'intense and passionate study of women's position and destiny' and to her contemporaries appeared to show bias against men. As this title and her *Portraits* of 1870 indicate, her work owes something to Browning, and like Browning she wrote a number of plays in verse without marked success, along with translations of Greek tragic poetry. She published several volumes of verse also under the pseudonym of 'Cecil Home'.

WELLS, Herbert George (1866–1947), the son of a gardener turned unsuccessful storekeeper, was educated at a faintly dubious private academy in Bromley, Kent up to the age of fourteen. He was then apprenticed to a draper, became a pupil teacher, and at the age of eighteen won a scholarship to the Normal School of Science in South Kensington. He attended Huxley's lectures for the first year and was to be influenced by the notions outlined in *Evolution and Ethics* (1894). For emotional reasons, Wells idled during his last two years at South Kensington and failed his examination. After illnesses and more teaching jobs, his first article appeared in Frank Harris's *Fortnightly Review* in 1892, attracting the attention of Oscar Wilde. He became a member of the gradualist Fabian Society and was soon writing articles for the many magazines catering for the new literate public created by the Education Acts of the 1870s. In the mid-1890s he rapidly produced a number of brilliant science fiction novels, novellas, and short stories such as *The Island of Doctor Moreau*, *The Time Traveller*, *The Invisible Man*, *The Wonderful Visit*, and *The War of the Worlds*. In the 1900s his novels became more autobiographical, but after 1910 will tended to replace imagination and the novelist began to be superseded by the prophet. Most things by Wells are worth reading, but the later part of his career is something of an anti-climax.

WILDE, Oscar O'Flahertie Fingal Wills (1854–1900), was the younger son of Sir William Wilde, antiquarian and surgeon–oculist to Queen Victoria, and Maria Francesca Elgee, who under the *nom de plume* of 'Speranza' wrote uninhibited Irish National verses and translated from the German, French, and Italian. Lady Wilde also wrote agreeably on Celtic myth and legend. Oscar was educated at Portora Royal School, Enniskillen, Trinity College, Dublin, and Magdalen College, Oxford, going down with a First in Greats, after winning the Newdigate Prize with his poem *Ravenna*. His first volume of poems appeared in 1881. Although distinguished as a clever lecturer and a brilliant conversationalist, it was only after recognizing and submitting to his homosexuality that he produced his major work: the witty and sometimes profound criticism of *Intentions* (1891); the short story 'Lord Arthur Savile's Crime'; the essay 'The Soul of Man under Socialism'; the novel *The Picture of Dorian Gray*; and the symbolist one-act drama *Salome* of 1892. By this last year he had begun his disastrous love affair with Lord Alfred Douglas and his work over the next three years until his arrest and conviction for homosexual acts was less voluminous though equally brilliant: three comedies and one sparkling farce, *The Importance of Being Earnest* (1895). In that same year Wilde was convicted of performing homosexual acts and given the savage sentence of two years with hard labour. He was condemned as much for his writings, personality, and opinions as for his conduct. He emerged from prison broken in spirit and health, and, with the exception of some letters and *The Ballad of Reading Gaol*, his career was over. During his time in prison Wilde wrote a long letter to Alfred Douglas, analysing himself and his friend, and discussing their relationship in its aesthetic and financial dimensions. Douglas he saw as being largely responsible for his downfall both as man and artist, and history has partly endorsed the judgement. The letter was first published in abridged form, with the large sections relating to Douglas omitted, under the title *De Profundis*. That portion of the work records one of the last of Wilde's many masks, 'Oscar as Christ'. The full text appeared in 1950 as *Epistola in Carcere et Vinculis* (*A Letter in Prison and in Chains*). Wilde's prison experience also resulted in *The Ballad of Reading Gaol* (1898), a memorable if uneven work, in which realism jostles somewhat uneasily with the usual purple of Wilde's verse. He also wrote several letters on prison which were a notable contribution to penal reform. In his own words, Wilde had put his genius into his life and his talent into his writing; but this is only a half-truth. For years the British literary establishment derided him, but his reputation was always secure with the average reader and abroad. His works have been constantly reprinted and translated. He is a classic by popular acclaim, even though some of his reputation derives from the drama of his life and his role as 'the homintern Messiah'.

YEATS, William Butler (1865–1939), came of professional Anglo-Irish stock. His father, John Butler Yeats, was a distinguished portrait painter, admirable letter writer, and brilliant conversationalist. The son inherited both the Anglo-Irish and English literary traditions. Patriotic, but not narrowly nationalist, he took the Fenian oath under the influence of the woman who was to be the object of his 'barren passion', Maude Gonne, an agitator of remarkable appearance to whom he wrote most of his finest love poems. Another woman friend, who also inspired fine poetry and his most eloquent letters, was Olivia Shakespear. Yeats was in many ways a typical poet of the *fin de siècle*: in ill health for many years, poverty stricken, unhappily in love, with a religious devotion to art and beauty, given to falling rhythms and a tone that was pessimistic. A member of the Rhymers' Club group of poets, Yeats was also prominent in the movement that attempted to promote cultural unity in Ireland when the political movement faltered after the defeat and death of Charles Stewart Parnell in 1891. His earlier poetry was generally held in higher esteem, until the proponents of the 'modern movement' suggested that there had been a creative fracture in his work as a consequence of his practical experience of writing plays for the Abbey theatre and the schoolmasterly role of Ezra Pound. The earlier work has once again risen in esteem, though *The Tower* (1928) remains his major volume. Yeats was the only poet of his 'tragic' generation who was able to 'remake' himself largely through the range of his commitments and of his dissatisfactions. The mysticism which runs through all his works, in tension with the attractions of the visible world, is now also taken more seriously than it was thirty years ago. Dramatist, poet, man of letters, politician, theatre manager, senator of the Irish Free State, and Nobel Prize winner, Yeats led a various but remarkably unified life.

INDEX OF TITLES

Italics indicate a poem